Impacts of Digital Technologies Across Generations

Muhammad Anshari
Universiti Brunei Darussalam, Brunei

Mohammad Nabil Almunawar
Universiti Brunei Darussalam, Brunei

Patricia Ordóñez de Pablos
University of Oviedo, Spain

IGI Global
Scientific Publishing
Publishing Tomorrow's Research Today

Vice President of Editorial	Melissa Wagner
Managing Editor of Acquisitions	Mikaela Felty
Managing Editor of Book Development	Jocelynn Hessler
Production Manager	Mike Brehm
Cover Design	Phillip Shickler

Published in the United States of America by
IGI Global Scientific Publishing
701 East Chocolate Avenue
Hershey, PA, 17033, USA
Tel: 717-533-8845
Fax: 717-533-8661
Website: https://www.igi-global.com E-mail: cust@igi-global.com

Library of Congress Cataloging-in-Publication Data

Names: Anshari, Muhammad, 1977- editor. | Almunawar, Mohammad Nabil, 1960- editor. | Ordóñez de Pablos, Patricia, 1975- editor.
Title: Impacts of digital technologies across generations / edited by Muhammad Anshari, Mohammad Nabil Almunawar, Patricia Ordóñez de Pablos.
Description: Hershey, PA : IGI Global, [2025] | Includes bibliographical references and index. | Summary: "The objective of this book is to provide a comprehensive understanding of how digital technologies have influenced and shaped the lives of individuals from different generational cohorts"-- Provided by publisher.
Identifiers: LCCN 2024051846 (print) | LCCN 2024051847 (ebook) | ISBN 9798369363669 (hardcover) | ISBN 9798369363676 (paperback) | ISBN 9798369363683 (ebook)
Subjects: LCSH: Technological innovations--Case studies. | Industry 5.0--Case studies. | Conflict of generations--Case studies.
Classification: LCC T173.8 .I455 2025 (print) | LCC T173.8 (ebook) | DDC 303.48/3--dc23/eng/20250108
LC record available at https://lccn.loc.gov/2024051846
LC ebook record available at https://lccn.loc.gov/2024051847
British Cataloguing in Publication Data
A Cataloguing in Publication record for this book is available from the British Library.

Editorial Advisory Board

Editorial Advisory Board

List of Reviewers

Ranjit Singha, *Christ University, India*
Hamza Yusuf, *RMIT University, Australia*

Table of Contents

Detailed Table of Contents

This chapter looks at the broad impact of advanced innovations across different parts of society, zeroing in on generational elements and the more extensive ramifications of computerized change. The chapter gives a top to bottom examination of how advanced advances, including man-made consciousness (computer-based intelligence) and the web of things (IoT), influence different age gatherings, from their effect on individual prosperity to changes in authoritative designs and cultural standards. It investigates the effects of developing digital literacy and skills, adopting new technologies, and their implications for cognitive processes and interactions between humans and computers. Also, the chapter tends to advanced prosperity concerns, including web dependence and systems for upgrading computerized health. It features the advancing job of computerized advancements in training, business, and public strategy, accentuating the requirement for comprehensive practices and moral contemplations.

The integration of robotics and artificial intelligence (AI) is transforming industries, enhancing efficiency, safety, and productivity. This chapter explores the impact of autonomous systems across various sectors, including manufacturing, healthcare, transportation, and agriculture. The convergence of robotics and AI enables adaptive systems to perform complex tasks independently, driving innovation and reshaping business operations. Machine learning, computer vision, and sensor fusion empower robots to learn from data, recognize patterns, and interact with humans. Successful applications include self-driving cars, robotic-assisted surgery, precision farming, and smart home devices. However, challenges persist, such as reliability, safety, ethics, data privacy, and complexity of implementation. As autonomous systems continue to evolve, they will drive sustainable practices, optimize resource use, and encourage interdisciplinary collaboration. Future research should focus on developing robust algorithms, enhancing safety protocols, and establishing ethical guidelines.

In 2020, the COVID-19 pandemic came out to be a massive destruction for human-being, in terms of life and economy. Lockdown in most of the countries invoked the teleworking as a solution to boost economy and social distancing for combating the highly transmissible virus, but teleworking can't be a full replacement. Traditional methods and working conditions are slowly replaced by digitization and by automating the processes of work. Moreover, work from home conditions have facilitated the houses as offices for the individuals in the world ultimately leading to digital transformation acceleration, replacing traditional work cultures. Information and communication technologies facilitated the digitization process. This chapter explores the journey of working conditions before pandemic, during pandemic, and possible scenario post pandemic after incorporating digitization has been done, involving also about mental/physical health effects on employees/students during pandemic and how the people and organizations collectively paced up the digitization for fulfilling the work assignments/projects.

In the wake of the pandemic, workplace dynamics have changed significantly, particularly the integration of digital technologies. The new workplace is also experiencing changes in its demographics as this is the first time in history that five generations are working together, causing generational disparities leading to misperceptions, stereotypes, and intergenerational biases when adapting to and utilizing digital tools. The lack of systematic literature reviews analyzing digital technologies and artificial intelligence (AI) among multigenerational employees in the fourth industrial revolution context demands further investigation.

Preface

The rapid evolution of digital technologies has left an indelible mark on societies, economies, and cultures worldwide, influencing how generations adapt, innovate, and interact. This edited volume, Impacts of Digital Technologies Across Generations, developed by Muhammad Anshari, Mohammad Nabil Almunawar, and Patricia Ordóñez de Pablos, compiles the transformative potential of digital tools and systems, addressing their multifaceted impact across diverse spheres of life.

This collection brings together fourteen compelling studies from international scholars, each offering unique insights into the complex relationship between technological advancement and generational dynamics:

1. **Bridging Generations: Digital Transformation and Its Multifaceted Impact Across Societal Sectors***Muhammad Usman Tariq* (Abu Dhabi University, UAE) Examines the comprehensive implications of digital transformation across different societal domains.
2. **Digital Transformation Across Generations - Robotics and AI in Action***Shalom Akhai, Prabhleen Kaur, Tavleen Kaur* (MMEC-MM(DU), CCE-CGC Jhanjeri, India) Investigates the practical applications and generational perceptions of robotics and artificial intelligence.
3. **Digital Technologies in Education: AI, Robotics, and Generational Challenges or Opportunities***Bitan Roy, Sanchita Ghosh, Piyal Roy, Saptarshi Kumar Sarkar, Nobhonil Roy Choudhury* (Brainware University, India) Explores the transformative potential of digital technologies in educational settings.
4. **From Fear to Fascination: A Generational Analysis of Attitudes Towards Robotics***Andi Asrifan, L. Santhosh Kumar, Sheik Mohamed S H, Azizah Amal* (Universitas Negeri Makassar, Kristu Jayanti College, St. Thomas College, Indonesia/India) Analyzes the evolving perceptions of robotics across different generational groups.
5. **Exploring AI Attitude, Perception, and AI Anxiety Among Indian Students***Souvik Rajbanshi, Madalaimuthu Anthony, Ganesh Kumar J* (Christ University, India) Investigates the psychological dimensions of artificial intelligence adoption among students.
6. **Digital Divide and Technological Determinism: Factors Influencing the Digital Divide***Gulay Ekren* (Sinop University, Turkiye) Critically examines the structural factors perpetuating technological disparities.
7. **Socio-demographic Influences on Digital Wallet Adoption Behavior***Muhammad Azmi Sait, Muhammad Anshari, Mohammad Nabil Almunawar, Masairol Masri, Nazatul Haziqah Junit* (Universiti Brunei Darussalam, Brunei Darussalam) Provides a detailed analysis of technological adoption patterns.
8. **iGenius: Exploring Gen Z's Reliance on AI Tools in Education***Koppala Venugopal* (Aditya Institute of Technology and Management, India) Focuses on the unique technological engagement of the youngest generation.

9. **Digital Well-Being and Internet Addiction Across the Lifespan***Ranjit Singha, Surjit Singha* (Christ University, Kristu Jayanti College, India) Explores the psychological implications of digital technologies across different life stages.
10. **Health Impacts of Smartphone and Internet Addictions Across Age Groups***Vettriselvan R* (Academy of Maritime Education and Training, India) Examines the physical and mental health consequences of digital technology use.
11. **Evolution of Digital Colonization: Penetrating the Malaysian Business Landscape***Faerozh Bin Madli, Yuzainy Janin, Shaierah Gulabdin, Wong Sing Yun, Kelvin Yong, Diana Nabila Chau Abdullah* (Universiti Malaysia Sabah, Malaysia) Investigates the broader economic and cultural impacts of digital transformation.
12. **Navigating Remote Work Evolution: Generational Perspectives on Digital Transformation** *Vineeta Singh, Ankur Prakash, Shivam Swarup, Sumit Babu, Mohd. Shah Alam, Shesh Mani Tiwari, Alok Kumar, Deepak Kumar Verma, Vandana Dixit Kaushik, Nahed Tawfik, Shilpa Mehta* (Multiple Institutions from India, Egypt, and New Zealand) Analyzes the changing landscape of work in the digital age.
13. **Digital Technologies' Impact on the Multigenerational Workforce in the Post-Covid Environment***Melina Doargajudhur, Shabanaz Baboo* (Edinburgh Napier University, UK; Curtin University, Mauritius) Explores workforce dynamics in the context of digital transformation.
14. **Agricultural Digital Technologies' Impact on Youth Generations for Food Security and Rural Development***Muhamad Rusliyadi, Yu Hua Chen* (Polytechnic of Agricultural Development Yogyakarta, Indonesia; National Taiwan University, Taiwan) Examines technological innovations in agricultural contexts.

This volume represents a critical intervention in understanding the complex, multifaceted impacts of digital technologies across generational boundaries. By bringing together diverse perspectives from multiple disciplines and geographical contexts, the book offers a nuanced, comprehensive exploration of how technological innovations are fundamentally reshaping human experiences. The chapters collectively challenge simplistic narratives about technological adoption, instead presenting a sophisticated, contextually rich understanding of digital transformation's profound societal implications.

We believe this book will serve as an essential resource for researchers, practitioners, and policymakers seeking to understand and navigate the complex interplay between digital technologies and generational dynamics. We extend our deepest gratitude to the contributing authors and reviewers who made this collaborative endeavour possible.

Introduction

The digital revolution brought about a significant change that affected every aspect of our lives. Digital technologies have become an essential component of our daily routines, changing the way we communicate, work, access information, and make decisions. This edited volume, *Impacts of Digital Technologies Across Generations* examined the many ways in which this digital revolution has affected people, businesses, communities, and governments. In an effort to pave the way for a future where the advantages of digitisation were fairly distributed among generations, the book sought to offer a thorough understanding of the difficulties and possibilities that resulted from this unparalleled technological revolution.

In our connected world, where digital natives and digital immigrants lived together, it was important to look at the differences in digital knowledge, skills, and adoption between age groups. This book scrutinises the impact of digital technologies on individuals, elucidating how our engagement with these tools shapes our cognition, attention, and human-computer interaction. Furthermore, it examined the complex relationship between digital well-being and internet addiction throughout the lifespan, providing insights into the possible repercussions of excessive technology usage on mental and physical health.The book examined the revolutionary impacts of digital technology on business models, workforce changes, and the future of work at the organisational level. It analysed the intergenerational dynamics in the digital workplace, emphasising the problems and opportunities stemming from the integration of various age groups in a progressively digitised work setting. The book examines the influence of organisational change, innovation, and digital leadership on managing the intricacies of digital business transformation.The book examines the societal implications of developing technologies, including artificial intelligence and the internet of things, beyond individual and organisational viewpoints. It examined the digital divisions and disparities that emerged between generations, along with the privacy, ethical, and cybersecurity issues associated with the extensive usage of digital technologies. Moreover, the book analyses the impacts of these technologies on education and lifelong learning, highlighting their capacity to improve knowledge acquisition and promote equal access to educational opportunities.

The book assesses the policy implications of digital transformation, examining the need for digital governance frameworks and regulations to foster innovation and effectively address the challenges posed by rapidly evolving technologies. The study examined the significance of digital identity management and citizen services, along with the need for a resilient digital infrastructure and strategic investment goals. Furthermore, the book examines the notion of smart urban and community design across generations, emphasizing the capacity of digital technologies to improve urban living and foster sustainable development.

This edited volume is a significant resource for scholars, researchers, and practitioners aiming to comprehend and negotiate the complexity of the digital age through a thorough examination of the consequences of digital technology across generations.

Chapter 1
Bridging Generations: Digital Transformation and Its Multifaceted Impact Across Societal Sectors

Muhammad Usman Tariq
https://orcid.org/0000-0002-7605-3040
Abu Dhabi University, UAE & University College Cork, Ireland

ABSTRACT

This chapter looks at the broad impact of advanced innovations across different parts of society, zeroing in on generational elements and the more extensive ramifications of computerized change. The chapter gives a top to bottom examination of how advanced advances, including man-made consciousness (computer-based intelligence) and the web of things (IoT), influence different age gatherings, from their effect on individual prosperity to changes in authoritative designs and cultural standards. It investigates the effects of developing digital literacy and skills, adopting new technologies, and their implications for cognitive processes and interactions between humans and computers. Also, the chapter tends to advanced prosperity concerns, including web dependence and systems for upgrading computerized health. It features the advancing job of computerized advancements in training, business, and public strategy, accentuating the requirement for comprehensive practices and moral contemplations.

INTRODUCTION

The digital revolution, which is characterized by the rapid development of innovative technologies, is an outstanding phenomenon in postmodern culture, dovetailing with various spheres of human activity. The result of this transformation is not simply a technological change, but a complete alteration of the social, economic, and cultural fabric. With the advancement of technology, people's ways of interacting, performing tasks, and gaining knowledge are affected, imprinting society's systemic framework. Digital tools, including mobile devices, AI, and IoT, have become part of people's lives, and knowledge transfer and decisions are quicker and supported by data and digital interfaces, which has become more challenging (Dwivedi et al., 2024). The Digital Revolution: Society is a very complex and large system; transforming it mainly refers to the alteration of its properties or mode of functioning, which has been discussed previously. The process of shifting from the analogue to the digital paradigm which started in the second half of the twentieth century proceeded in the twenty-first century, even faster, changing the

DOI: 10.4018/979-8-3693-6366-9.ch001

nature of society. This revolution is defined by the increased use of technologies accepted in almost all industries, economies, and people's daily practices. The technological change that took place and signified a move from analogue to digital has allowed easier access to information, eased communication, and brought about a global village. For example, the Internet began as a system of communication between colleges and universities and governmental institutions, and has emerged as one of the central platforms of today's society used for shopping, communication, etc. With the emergence of new platforms, such as Google, Facebook, and Amazon, business models as well as consumers' and the general population's behaviours and expectations (George, 2024).

In the business domain, digitalisation has acted as a catalyst that has helped introduce numerous changes and improvements. Fortune 500 companies utilise big data, cloud computing, and artificial intelligence to improve efficiency, tweak customer experience, and generate more sales and revenue. For instance, with the help of AI in customer care involving chatbots and other options, businesses have managed to develop new ways of serving customers, which are prompt and as unique as possible (Brenner, 2018). Technology has also affected industries, such as finance and healthcare departments, through the modern advancement of technology. In finance, blockchain technology is bringing changes in the areas of transactions and records; in health care, telemedicine and digital health records are major changes in the healthcare industry. The educational sector has also come a long way to go, engaging in digital technologies to define new ways of delivering and experiencing learning. Distance education, digital classrooms, and the use of artificial intelligence in the educational process have brought about a revolution in the field of education. For example, current online learning platforms, including Coursera and Khan Academy, can enhance learning throughout a person's lifetime and assist a person in developing different skills at his or her convenience. In addition, AI-based tools, such as intelligent tutor systems, provide feedback and learning suggestions according to the learner's requirements, as they identify each learner's strengths and weaknesses (Aithal & Maiya, 2023). However, this is not without its drawbacks, as illustrated by the following facts. While people of the current civilisation age are gradually becoming engrossed in the various uses of digital technologies, this has also led to an increase in social vices, including digital inequality, privacy breaches, and the emergence of the digital divide. The gap that exists between people who have or do not have access to digital technologies, also known as the digital divide, could also be felt, especially in the developing world. This divide results in social and economic injustice in education, health, employment, and accessibility to basic needs, thus perpetuating inequality. Further, there are cases of privacy and cyber security that are major issues because of the growing use of Internet services to store and process special and even personal information.

Primarily post-WWII, known as the baby boom generation, who were born between 1946 and 1964, came of age during TV, personal computers, and the Internet. Currently, many people from this generation, when starting to use digital technology, use it more as an auxiliary to everything, and the primary focus was on other activities. Nevertheless, with the growing prominence and integrated roles of technology in nearly all sectors of life, the Baby Boomers' generational cohort has been forced to incorporate digitally oriented tools for diverse contexts, meaning that they may consider new technologies as important to sustaining relationships with family, make purchases online, or monitor health through digital health solutions. Despite being the most active in their use of digital platforms, this generation is usually conservative in their interaction with the technology, with most voicing their fears about privacy and data protection (George, 2024). Generation X, which is commonly defined as being born between 1965 and 1980, is described as the generation between the traditional and the new media. This generation was born in the middle of the analogue and digital worlds, and thus witnessed the world both at its pre-Internet and pre-personal computing stages. Therefore, in many aspects, Generation X tends to be technologically literate, appreciating technology that enhances work training, interaction, and leisure. This generation is also adaptive, as they have experienced drastic changes in technology during their early working years and even during their college years (Marzo, 2024). Still, in the same vein, like Baby Boomers, Generation X may fear technological advancement, especially in relation to the world of work and overall social norms.

BACKGROUND

Generation Y, commonly known as millennials, are individuals who were born between 1981 and 1996 and unlike generation X they are the so-called 'digital natives". This generation is highly digitally oriented and effectively applies digital technologies to communication, purchases, education, and employment. To date, millennials have not only taken advantage of computing systems in their communication, business, and entertainment; hence, they are the most involved group in the use of social networks, e-commerce, and video streaming. Employment expectations shaped by technology comfort include flexibility, innovation, and learning in the workplace, as pointed out by Bera 2023. Although digital technology integration among this group of people has equally raised worrying features such as digital dependency and mental health among other vices that attribute the decline of face-to-face communication. Gen Z, also known as Digital Natives, GEN Includes those who have been born from 1997 and onwards, and are those who know smartphone, social media and, Artificial Intelligence based world right from their childhood. This generation is digital, seeing digital technologies as an inherent part of oneself, or at least the many adults of this generation. The generation has great skills in working with several digital platforms at once, applying them for learning, fun, protesting, and sharing their voices. These traits make them perfect for embracing new technologies and creating new solutions in the market that past generations cannot fathom (Aithal & Maiya, 2023). More importantly, they worried about the negative effects of digital life on teenagers' and youths' mental health, privacy, and social skills. It is also essential to note that Generation Z is a tech-savvy generation; thus, they are conscientious of digital injustice and privacy (Czerniewicz, 2022; Vassilakopoulou & Hustad, 2023; Wu and Yang, 2024).

Digital transformation has emerged as a key subject in many industries, changing the way businesses run, provide services, and communicate with stakeholders (Younus & Zaenuri, 2024; George, 2024). While new engagement and efficiency paradigms have been cultivated by the development of digital technology, the effects have not been evenly distributed. The unique features of industries including business, healthcare, and education draw attention to the subtleties of the digital transition. Digital transformation has its roots in the 1960s and 1970s, when computers were first introduced, and their primary functions were process automation and increased operational efficiency. The advent of social media, mobile technology, and the internet throughout the years has sparked a more thorough integration of digital tools, which has given rise to the modern concept of the "digital economy." Digital revolution in education has moved the focus from information availability to immersive learning environments that encourage teamwork and critical thinking. This change is demonstrated by the widespread use of digital assessment tools, virtual classrooms, and online learning platforms. Because of pedagogical traditions and opposition to change, education has historically frequently trailed behind technical progress (Tariq, 2025). On the other hand, the COVID-19 epidemic acted as a spur, quickening the adoption of digital technologies and emphasizing the need for digital literacy in both teachers and pupils. Recent case studies in this area show how educational institutions have used technology to improve engagement through individualized and interactive learning experiences, in addition to preserving continuity amid interruptions (Aithal & Maiya, 2023).

Digital technology has also significantly changed the healthcare industry, with telemedicine, electronic health records, and data analytics all contributing to better patient outcomes. Healthcare technology has developed in a similar way to communication and computer technologies, historically concentrating on enhancing patient care and operational effectiveness. The implementation of telehealth services within the pandemic presents a noteworthy example of how healthcare providers may promptly adapt to changing demands. According to data from previous research, patients who used telehealth services expressed more satisfaction and had easier access to care. There are still issues, though, mainly with data security and the requirement for healthcare workers to become more digitally literate to make good use of these tools (Sołtysik et al., 2024). The demand for operational resilience and competitive advantage drives digital transformation in the business sector. Businesses have used technology in the past to increase customer satisfaction, expedite procedures, and support data-driven decision-making. The emergence of customer relationship management (CRM) systems, data analytics tools, and e-commerce is indicative of how firms have adapted to changing client needs. Current empirical research emphasizes how crucial it is to match organizational culture and strategy with technology to fully reap the rewards of digital transformation. Effective case studies demonstrate how integrating digital technology may result in increased customer loyalty and better performance. Examples of these case studies include those from businesses that have adopted digital-first strategies (Aithal & Maiya, 2023; Tariq, 2024).

The way that technology is adopted by different generations has a significant impact on how the digital transformation landscape is shaped. The degree of familiarity and expertise that different generations have with digital technologies influences how businesses use and adjust to technological changes. Research suggests that younger generations—often referred to as "digital natives"are better at using technology to facilitate communication and learning. On the other hand, because they are unfamiliar with digital technologies, older generations could encounter difficulties. Building an inclusive workplace culture and implementing focused training programs are crucial to bridging the age gaps in firms (Sołtysik et al., 2024). As the digital transformation process progresses, scholars must integrate a range of studies that focus on industry-specific technology innovations. Scholars may offer significant insights into the distinct potential and problems posed by digital transformation in various contexts by scrutinizing case studies from the domains of education, healthcare, and business. The knowledge of how digital technologies are transforming sectors will be enhanced by empirical data and historical trends, which will also influence the best practices for future deployments. The increasing amount of scholarly literature on digital literacy, generational differences, and industry-specific innovations will provide a basis for businesses seeking to effectively manage the challenges posed by digital transformation. This all-encompassing strategy will help the conversation around digital transformation to more accurately represent the complex nature of technological development and its effects on different industries (George, 2024).

Individual Impacts of Digital Technologies

Digital technologies have impacted different aspects of people's lives by modifying the process through which they learn, engage in their occupations, and go around. As these technologies are in the process of development, they have different effects on various generations of the population, thus playing a role in forming digital competencies, skills, and cognitive abilities. This section discusses these impacts by analysing differences in digital literacy and skills by age, generations' attitudes toward and use of digital technologies, and distinctions in cognition and human-computer interaction due to technological advances. Information literacy, described as the capacity to locate, organise, analyse, evaluate, and create information using digital technology, is highly desirable in today's world. The general digital literacy outline also differs across generations due to the timing and circumstances of exposure to digital technology (Tariq, 2024). For older generations, digital literacy can be about conquering barriers when it comes to embracing technologies and improving the ways in which given technologies augment people's lives. For instance, individuals born in the Baby Boom generation, who did not grow up using digital technologies, faced difficulties in acquiring new digital competencies. This generation has been forced to shift from the use of basic means of communication and information gathering and processing, such as phones, newspapers, and magazines, to the use of computers and the Internet to conduct business and personal activities, such as sending emails, banking, and using social networks. Such dismal literacy levels have been achieved through efforts such as digital literacy clinics in senior community centres and online training (George, 2024). Such programs assist elderly people in trusting the use of technologies to effectively manage finances, maintain and establish relationships, and seek medical assistance (Marzo, 2024).

Regarding this, the author stated that while members of Generation X are more used to the transition from analogue to digital than baby boomers, the latter are slightly more comfortable with the use of technology than the former. This generation can trace the advancement of computing from fundamental computing to the latest applications such as cloud computing and social networks. Thus, Generation X has a pragmatic perception of the digital technologies which they use mainly at work and to bring work and personal life into harmony. However, they can still experience difficulties in maintaining the rate of implementing technological advancements in their work and adjusting new tools into work practice (Vial, 2021). Thus, the representatives of the Millennials subpopulation are digital natives since they grew up with the internet, smartphones, and social media. Based on the concentric circles the given generation is greatly known for their skills in handling on one hand with the new technologies that are in the market in one way or the other either as a tool for learning, a tool for career enhancement or even as a tool for developing social networks. Social media, messages, entertainment, and work-related tasks are conducted through multiple devices by millennials. They have a good mastery in the use of technology in their daily lives which is best illustrated by their ability to browse complex digital spaces and use different platforms to communicate and share resources (Bera, 2023; Tariq, 2024).

The first representatives of Generation Z are also considered to be the first digitally active generation that has been using digital technologies since childhood. This generation is fluent in the use of a broad array of online applications and sites that they incorporate into their existence fluidly. The way Generation Z consumes information can also be observed in their active use of creating content and sharing materials on social networks, using artificial intelligence to develop applications and programs, and interacting with virtual reality. On a positive note, constant exposure to digital media has also elicited worry about its effect on children's cognitive and social-emotional competence (Aithal & Maiya, 2023). Analysis of the use of digital technologies and their readiness differs depending on the age of the population. The attitude toward technology in each generational group depends on the historical period and opportunities to use digital technologies in the youth (George, 2024; Hoodbhoy, 2023).

Societal and Policy-Level Impacts

The trends in emerging technologies such as AI and IoT are increasing at a faster pace and are radically changing social systems and formulating policies across platforms. In terms of various generations, these technologies are very significant and have several vital issues, such as digital gaps, privacy, ethical issues, and cyber security concerns, and it is essential to rethink digital governance and smart infrastructure for smart communities (Tariq, 2024). New technologies such as Artificial Intelligence and the Internet of Things, which are currently prominent, bring about changes in the social structure and affect various generations in diverse manners. Smart city technologies provide an enrichment for young generations who can develop connections with each other to receive services and find solutions. For instance, artificial intelligence checkpoints, such as personalized learning systems, apply data analytics to develop educational content relevant to students' learning styles, which, if implemented, may enhance the results for those in the education sector (Marzo, 2024). Likewise, IoT goods, for instance, home technologies and health-related wearables owned by youngsters and post-sibilants give them full control and information pertaining to their physical surroundings and health conditions. Hence, older generations who may be unfamiliar with such technologies are likely to experience different challenges. The constant emergence and evolution of new technologies has resulted in challenges in implementing these technologies in everyday life. For instance, it might be difficult for older people to operate smart gadgets or comprehend AI-facilitated solutions, which will lead to the enhancement of existing inequalities in terms of digital inclusion and exclusion and barriers when it comes to access to services (Younus & Zaenuri, 2024). Mitigating these generational divides is key to ensuring that future innovative technologies are available.

Social inequality between and within nations has expanded owing to the advancement of digital technologies. The term 'digital divide' was used to represent the difference between people who possess exposure to digital technologies and those who cannot or are incompetent in their use. This gap is felt based on income, education, and geographical region, resulting in variations in technology and internet use. For instance, studies conducted by Czerniewicz (2022, p. 1614) show that people in less-developed areas or in developing nations may not have a proper Internet connection and updated technologies which widen the gap in the digital divide. Other issues related to privacy and ethical aspects have also been observed with the development of AI and the IoT. It is these technologies that view downloading and analysing a tremendous volume of personal data that questions pertaining to data protection, consent, and moral usage of information emerge. For example, AI systems will have mischievous onsets of existing enhanced bias in training data, making applications such as hiring algorithms or credit scoring discriminatory (Zelenev, 2022). These are among the reasons why privacy and ethical standards must be forged to reduce these risks and build confidence in these technologies.

Another aspect that forms the foundation of digital governance is identity management, especially when it comes to smart community design. Since digital identities are integrated into the use of various services and engagement in online activities, reliable and secure identity management systems are crucial. These systems must avoid cases of identity theft and fraud while allowing users to access services online in a very efficient and secure manner (Marzo, 2024). It is vital to note the presence of digital infrastructure in smart communities. Smart communities adopt ICT to improve people's quality of life in cities, improve the use of resources, and promote sustainable growth. For instance, smart grid systems, ITS, and connected civic services are recommended to improve the efficiency and enhance the responses of cities. Accompanying these activities, there is a need to improve investment in the strong base of digital infrastructure for smarter communities, which can provide equal and appropriate opportunities for every inhabitant of the residential area, as pointed out by Das (2024).

Well-being and Health Implications

Digital technologies have become ubiquitous and have massive consequences for the physical and mental well-being of people and families of any given age. With the current trends in the integration of digital devices and social media in society, one must embrace both opportunities and dangers in this ever-evolving field. It assists in creating proper behavioural patterns and treatments concerning the use of digital technology to improve health and avoid adverse consequences. In the current study, four direct mediating effects of digital technology use on physical health are proposed. At the same time, it is vital to acknowledge the advantages of using digital technologies in healthcare, including telemedicine services that provide people with the opportunity to address a healthcare professional or purchase wearable devices to monitor the condition of their bodies and physical activity (Marzo, 2024). For example, Fitbit for exercising and smartwatches assists in tracking people's exercise, and promoting a healthier lifestyle may enhance physical health (Vassilakopoulou & Hustad, 2023). However, effects such as increased screen time and sedentary behaviour related to the use of digital devices have repercussions on physical health. Various studies suggest that a significant number of hours spent on screen are associated with adversities such as obesity, posture, and eye strain, as determined by Das in 2024. For example, musculoskeletal disorders deleteriously include back and neck issues that result from improper working postures while using computers and smartphones for prolonged periods (Sołtysik et al., 2024). Knowledge about the correct operation of the equipment as well as adherence to ergonomic basics helps neutralise harm. The impact of technology on mental health is equally devastating in the following ways. This is because digital tools can enhance social connectivity and extend resources for mental health problems while contributing to the causes of anxiety, depression, and digital dependency. For instance, engaging with social media platforms can significantly harm customers' mental health because of social comparison, cyberbullying, and the need to create an impressive online persona (Shehadeh, 2024). Studies have suggested that social media addiction intensifies loneliness and anxiety, and these effects are largely felt by teenagers and young people (Czerniewicz, 2022). It should be noted that the information provided concerns effective DW and intervention approaches, based on the conception of individuals as active users of technology.

Some practices and interventions should be put in place to avoid the negative effects of using digital technology and enhance digital well-being, and it is important to follow healthy uses of digital devices to enhance the health of the physical and the mental kind. For instance, following the 20-20-20 rule as a suggestion that implies one should look at something that is 20 feet away, for 20 seconds after work for 20 minutes can be of significant help in the prevention of eye strain and manifestation of symptoms related to digital eye fatigue, as predicted by Younus and Zaenuri in 2024. Reducing the risks of physical discomfort that often come with extensive use of the screen can also be achieved by engaging in regular physical activity and integrating ergonomic practices into people's daily activities (Marzo, 2024). Mental health can be improved by engaging technology in a suitable manner. It is possible to limit the time spent using electronic devices; for example, devices can be excluded during meals or before going to bed (Vassilakopoulou & Hustad, 2023). Further, it is possible to encourage specialised digital detoxification, where people do not use digital devices for some time, as such treatments positively affect mental health and make for less stressed people (Das, 2024). Organisations and educational institutions can also help maintain people's digital well-being. For example, integrating digital wellness educational modules into school curricula and organizational wellness promotion programs will assist people in establishing safe digital behaviour and, at the same time, recognise related dangers (Sołtysik et al., 2024). It may also be possible for employees to reduce their digital stress and improve their mental health through policy options such as flexible working hours and/or working from home (Shehadeh, 2024).

CHALLENGES AND KEY ISSUES

The use of technology across generations is becoming more and more pronounced as various age groups use digital tools in different ways and with diverse preferences. Younger generations, also known as "digital natives," have grown up surrounded by technology, which has made them more accustomed to using it instinctively and casually. They frequently share personal information without fully understanding the ramifications for data privacy as they tend to adopt new platforms and applications quickly. Gen Z, for example, uses social media and internet services often, yet they might not realize the hazards of data breaches and privacy intrusions. On the other hand, older generations—Baby Boomers and Gen X, for example, tend to be more cautious while using technology. Their experiences, which are frequently influenced by notable data privacy scandals and cyber threats, raise people's awareness of the hazards associated with using digital platforms. Although being cautious might result in better practices for managing personal data, it can also make people reluctant to accept new technology, which could lead to a gap in digital literacy. For instance, older persons may be reluctant to utilize online banking services because they are concerned about possible fraud, which may prevent them from having access to easy financial solutions (Vassilakopoulou & Hustad, 2023).

The conversation is made more difficult because generational differences overlap with important topics like cybersecurity and AI ethics. As artificial intelligence (AI) technology permeates everyday life, moral questions about justice and prejudice surface. Younger users could challenge ethical standards and push for openness in AI systems, whereas older users might not be aware of these difficulties since they haven't been exposed to as many AI talks. Another urgent issue is cybersecurity, as younger people can be less aware of security precautions and hence more susceptible to cyberattacks (Vassilakopoulou & Hustad, 2023). This gap emphasizes how important it is to launch focused educational programs that cater to the requirements and worries of every generation. To ensure that people of all ages can safely and successfully traverse the intricacies of the digital world, society may strive toward a more inclusive approach to technology use by encouraging intergenerational discourse and collaboration. Generation X is considered the intermediary generation that came between the pre-digital age and the new era, and therefore, has a more balanced way of functioning when it comes to technology integration. This generation in one way or the other applies various technologies in their working life, buying products and services online, social networking among others. Based on the results of this study, Generation X's use of digital tools is pragmatic and can be explained by the necessity and aim to improve work productivity. For instance, the availability and utilisation of emails and productivity software in Generation X depict how they included digital platforms in their working and personal lives (Marzo, 2024).

Millennials have been cited as a group that embraces new tools and products because they are willing to connect and are also interested in new products. This generation employs digital technologies for various operations at work, such as social relations, purchasing products and services, and consuming content. Another important tendency, which might be traced with the help of the material, is the availability of applications typical for millennials, who use them to adopt digital tools into different spheres of their lives, from health tracking to the accounting of their money expenditures. Self-generated users also agree with the fact that due to their high level of digital use, they have high expectations of digital experience, such as smooth end-user interactions and customised content (Bera, 2023). Generation Z is known to be completely embedded in the digital environment from childhood; thus, they can be referred to as highly digitally savvy. This generation's use of digital technology involves the use of superior gadgets and applications, such as social networking, games, and virtual environments. Generation Z's digital behaviours involve content production and consumption, community engagement, infotainment, learning, and hobbies. This high level of digitisation is apparent for their comfort in dealing with the shortcomings and ability to manage complicated digital environments (Zelenev, 2022).

The inescapable utilisation of advanced innovations fundamentally affects mental cycles, capacities to focus, and human-PC collaboration. As people communicate with advanced apparatuses, these impacts manifest in different ways, affecting how individuals process data, keep up with the centre, and draw in with innovation. Advanced innovations have been shown to influence mental cycles including data handling and memory. Consistent openness to advanced content and performing multiple task requests can influence how people process and hold data. Research proposes that the incessant utilisation of computerised apparatuses may lead to diminished capacities to focus and challenges with supported centres. For instance, the fast utilisation of data through web-based entertainment and news channels can add to the mental overburden and diminished capacity to focus on undertakings for broadened periods (Czerniewicz, 2022). Specifically, the ability to focus is impacted by the quick-moving nature of computerised associations.

The consistent inundation of warnings, messages, and updates can be considered to thwart the capacity to connect profoundly with assignments. Studies have demonstrated that people who often use computerised innovations might encounter more limited capacities to focus and a propensity to switch between undertakings. According to Imran (2023), this phenomenon, also known as "digital distraction," can affect productivity and cognitive performance. Human-PC communication (HCI) is likewise affected by the planning and utilisation of computerised advances. Experience and contentment are shaped by how people interact with digital interfaces such as websites, apps, and virtual environments. Modern HCI research has focused on making digital interfaces more usable, accessible, and enjoyable for users. For instance, the improvement of instinctive UIs and versatile advance plans to upgrade communication and lessen mental burden, and developments such as voice-controlled connection points and motion-based communications are instances of how HCI is advancing to oblige different client needs and inclinations (Das, 2024). Additionally, advanced innovations have presented new types of human-PC communication, such as computer-generated simulation (VR) and increased reality (AR), which offer vivid and intelligent encounters. These innovations offer suggestions for different spaces including training, amusement, and medical services. For example, VR-based learning conditions provide drawing in and intelligent encounters that can improve learning results and mental commitment. In addition, AR applications in medical services offer creative ways of imagining and connecting with clinical information, further developing the analysis and therapy processes (Marzo, 2024).

Digital Well-Being Across the Lifespan

Computer prosperity is a developing concern, as innovation continues to saturate each part of life. It focuses on maintaining mental, emotional, and physical health while increasing digital engagement, and strikes a balance between the benefits and drawbacks of technology use. The difficulty of navigating a digital world is reflected in strategies for enhancing digital wellness and the prevalence of Internet addiction across generations. These aspects were examined in this section, highlighting the effects of Internet addiction and presenting digital wellness strategies. Analyses of the prevalence of Internet addiction and digital well-being across generations. The predominance of web dependence shifts across ages, affected by the various ways in which each age group draws in with computerised advancements. Web fixation, portrayed by the unreasonable or impulsive utilisation of online assets to the disadvantage of genuine obligations and connections, has emerged as a huge issue. Its effect is felt to be diversely based on generational setting and the idea of computerised connections. Gen X-ers, who encountered the ascent of the Web sometime down the road, for the most part have lower paces of Web enslavement contrasted with more youthful ages. They frequently use digital technologies for more deliberate and useful purposes, such as managing their finances, staying up-to-date, and communicating with family. Although some children in postwar America might encounter difficulties with exorbitant use, particularly as advanced innovations become more coordinated into day-to-day exercises, the pervasiveness of extreme web fixation will, in general, be lower in this gathering. To increase productivity and connectivity, Baby Boomers frequently emphasise enhancing digital literacy and managing online activities (George, 2024). Between the pre-digital and digital eras, Generation X was in the transitional phase. This age has taken on computerised advances to upgrade work and individual life; however, they are additionally defenceless to web enslavement. The ascent of web-based entertainment and online amusement has presented new open doors for extremely computerised commitments. Age X might battle by adjusting their Internet-based presence with disconnected liabilities, possibly prompting issues such as diminished efficiency and social communication challenges (Hoodbhoy, 2023). Systems to address these concerns incorporate advanced solid innovation propensities and defining limits for computerised use. Twenty to thirty-year-olds are known for their elevated degrees of advanced commitment, and in that capacity, they are at a more serious gamble of web fixation. This age's consistent coordination of advanced innovations into each part of life — mingling, work, instruction, and amusement — can prompt enthusiastic utilisation of designs.

The constant connectivity provided by mobile apps, streaming services, social media platforms, and streaming services frequently results in fewer in-person interactions and can affect mental health. According to Marzo (2024), millennials may experience elevated levels of anxiety, depression, and sleep disturbances because of excessive technological use. Age Z, the most carefully drenched age, faced extraordinary difficulties with respect to web compulsion. Growing up with cell phones, virtual entertainment, and a steady Internet-based network, Age Z is exceptionally defenceless to urgent innovation use. Their well-being can be significantly impacted by the pressure to maintain an online presence and the pervasive nature of digital distractions. This age-dependence on computerised stages frequently appears in challenges with focus, rest aggravations, and adverse consequences on emotional wellness. Research features the requirement for designated mediations to resolve these issues, including advancing computerised detoxes and empowering adjusted innovation use (Zelenev, 2022). Computerised prosperity requires a multi-layered approach, integrating methodologies to improve computerised well-being and moderate the adverse consequences of innovation use. These systems are fundamental for maintaining a good balance between the advantages of computerised innovations and the potential dangers related to their unnecessary use. Advancing computerised proficiency across all age groups is the primary method for improving computerised health. Education programs that teach people how to use digital tools safely and effectively can help reduce the dangers of using technology. For example, studios and online courses directed toward instructing clients about protected and solid innovation propensities can enable people to deal with their computerised lives more successfully (Bera, 2023). Drives, for example, computerised wellbeing training in schools and public venues, can provide important assets for creating solid innovation rehearses from early on. To prevent internet addiction and promote digital well-being, it is essential to establish boundaries for digital use.

Utilising apps to track and limit screen time, establishing technology-free zones at home, and establishing specific times for online activities can assist individuals in better managing their digital engagement. According to Sołysik et al. (2024), limiting screen time before bed or scheduling specific times to check social media can improve sleep quality and lower the risk of digital addiction. Advancing disconnected exercises and empowering close and personal cooperation can assist in offsetting the impact of extreme computerised use. Taking part in leisure activities, actual activities, and get-togethers gives amazing open doors to people to associate with others and appreciate encounters past the computerised domain. For example, partaking in local areas, chasing imaginative interests, or investing energy outside can upgrade general prosperity and lessen dependence on computerised advancements for amusement and socialisation (Das, 2024).

Another effective way to reduce the negative effects is to design digital technologies with user well-being. Features like customisable notifications, usage reminders, and settings that encourage breaks can be incorporated by developers and designers. Providing options for digital detox periods or incorporating built-in tools that enable users to monitor and manage their screen time can assist individuals in maintaining a healthier balance with technology (Dwivedi et al., 2024). Bringing issues to light about the effect of innovation on psychological well-being is fundamental for encouraging computerized health. Giving assets and backing to people encountering pessimistic impacts connected with computerised use, such as nervousness or wretchedness, can assist them in seeking proper assistance and settling on informed conclusions about their innovative propensities. Mental health campaigns, counselling services, and digital well-being-focused support groups can be helpful in addressing psychological issues caused by excessive technology use (Kickbusch et al., 2021). Empowering practices, such as advanced detoxification and care, can help people reconnect with themselves and their environmental elements. Digital detox is a brief absence from digital devices that concentrate on offline activities and personal health. Care rehearsals, such as contemplation and unwinding strategies, can assist people in overseeing pressure and foster a better relationship with innovation. It is possible to improve mental health and overall well-being by implementing regular digital detox periods and incorporating mindfulness into daily routines (Marzo, 2024).

The advent of digital transformation has had a profound impact on many facets of life, including wellbeing and mental health. Although the research now in publication frequently discusses the negative effects of technology on both physical and mental health, a more thorough examination of the generational disparities in terms of digital reliance, social media use, and digital burnout is necessary. Different age groups engage with digital technology in different ways, which has different effects on mental health (Vial, 2021).As an example, younger generations—often referred to as "digital natives "generally have more ease using digital communication tools and social media platforms. Nevertheless, the strain of upholding an online persona and interacting with the well-curated lives of their peers may also cause them to feel more anxious, depressed, and lonely (Younus & Zaenuri, 2024). On the other hand, older generations can find it difficult to keep up with the quick speed of technological advancement, which could cause them to feel inadequate and frustrated and worsen mental health problems (Vial, 2021). The issue of digital reliance is becoming more and more important, particularly as more people depend on technology for their everyday tasks, social connections, and employment. Significant mental health issues, such as digital burnout, which is typified by intense feelings of exhaustion and detachment from reality, can arise from this habit. Different generations of people may react to digital burnout in different ways. For instance, younger users could utilize likes and shares to get approval from others, while elderly users who find it difficult to interact with new platforms may feel separated and alienated. It is essential to comprehend these generational disparities to create focused mental health interventions and support networks. On the other hand, older generations can find it difficult to keep up with the quick speed of technological advancement, which could cause them to feel inadequate and frustrated and worsen mental health problems (Zelenev, 2022).

In addition, case studies that demonstrate effective cross-generational cooperation with digital technologies should be included in this chapter. Insights into how technology might close gaps rather than widen them can be gained from examples of projects where different generations have collaborated well. Initiatives like these might involve mentorship programs, in which more experienced workers assist less experienced staff members in using digital technologies, improving their job satisfaction and digital literacy. Community initiatives that promote intergenerational cooperation in addressing local concerns using digital platforms can also be effective examples of how technology promotes intergenerational relationships (Mundhe, 2024). The influence of policy and government reactions to the digital revolution is another important factor that must be taken into consideration. The digital gap and the necessity to regulate developing technologies are becoming more and more apparent to policymakers, as they have a substantial influence on people's mental health and general wellbeing. Governments across the globe have begun to create frameworks to guarantee fair access to technology, encourage digital literacy, and protect users from offensive information. The digital gap, for example, can be lessened by programs that increase internet access in disadvantaged regions, enabling people from different backgrounds to use digital tools. Regulations pertaining to mental health services and data protection can also enable consumers to interact with technology in a safer and more responsible manner (Tohit & Haque, 2024).

The world is becoming more and more interconnected with digital technology, and this has significant ramifications for mental health. A comprehensive strategy that considers the various experiences of various generations with relation to social media use, digital dependence, and digital burnout is desperately needed. The chapter can offer a thorough grasp of the many effects of digital transformation by delving further into these topics and looking at successful cross-generational collaboration and efficient government policies. This knowledge is essential for creating policies that support mental health in a world going digital. It is important to involve a diverse range of stakeholders, including educators, mental health experts, legislators, and technology developers, to foster an inclusive and progressive dialogue on digital transformation that effectively addresses the concerns and difficulties faced by all age groups.

STRATEGIES AND SOLUTIONS

Organizational Transformation

Digital advancements drive organizational transformation, which fundamentally alters the business landscape. This change envelops the coordination of new advancements, the rise of imaginative plans of action, and the development of the labour force. Analysing how digital advancements affect modern workplace leadership styles, workforce dynamics, and business operations is necessary to comprehend these shifts. Bits of knowledge into Computerized Business Change and Arising Plans of action

Computerized business change is a complete cycle that includes the reception and reconciliation of computerized innovations to upgrade business tasks, make new incentives, and drive upper hand. This change goes past simple innovative overhauls; it generally changes how organisations work and convey value to clients. One critical part of computerised business change is the development of new action plans affected by advanced headways. For example, platform-based business models show how digital technologies can make it possible for new ways to create and capture value. To demonstrate the need for intergenerational cooperation in tackling the problems brought about by digital transformation, several case studies and actual instances from various industries show how different age groups may cooperate. Furthermore, incorporating current studies on ethical frameworks, regulatory actions, and digital policies offers a thorough understanding of the continuous attempts to reduce the hazards connected to developing technology (Wu & Yang, 2024).

The field of education offers a noteworthy illustration of cross-generational cooperation. Initiatives to close the digital gap have been put into place in a number of school districts throughout the country by matching younger, tech-savvy students with older persons, especially senior citizens, in order to improve digital literacy. High school students are given the opportunity to help elders use cellphones, social media, and internet platforms through programs like "Tech Tutors" at community centers. This program demonstrates the benefits of cross-generational learning by helping younger generations acquire empathy and communication skills while simultaneously fostering critical abilities in elderly persons. These kinds of partnerships may greatly improve digital literacy and encourage a culture of lifelong learning in local communities (Tohit & Haque, 2024). The emergence of telehealth services amid the COVID-19 epidemic is a prime example of successful intergenerational cooperation in the healthcare industry. It was acknowledged by healthcare professionals that all patients, regardless of age, ought to have access to telehealth resources. Younger medical practitioners assisted older patients who might have been reluctant to use digital health technologies in the beginning by guiding them through these platforms. Working together allowed us to address people's worries about technology while still providing vital services throughout the epidemic. According to recent study, telehealth services have helped older persons' health outcomes, which emphasizes the significance of inclusive digital practices that serve a range of age groups (Wu & Yang, 2024).

In the commercial world, where intergenerational teams are widely acknowledged for their capacity to spur creativity, there is another noteworthy case study. Organizations such as IBM have launched programs to promote cooperation between entry-level workers and more experienced staff members. These programs make use of the advantages of both generations: younger workers frequently provide new ideas and a familiarity with technology, while elderly workers provide priceless experience and industry expertise. For example, IBM's "MentorPlace" initiative matches more junior people with more senior mentors to promote knowledge exchange and assist in career advancement. These kinds of projects show how varied teams may support a more creative and adaptable workplace (Das, 2024). Recent study emphasizes the significance of regulatory measures in guaranteeing ethical behaviors across many industries about digital policies and ethical frameworks. One important example of a comprehensive framework created to safeguard individual privacy rights and provide responsibility for data management is the General Data Protection Regulation (GDPR) in Europe. The General Data Protection Regulation (GDPR) addresses ethical concerns about data privacy and encourages enterprises to embrace more responsible data management practices by imposing tight limits for data collection, storage, and sharing. This regulatory strategy facilitates a more ethical digital ecosystem by protecting customers and building confidence between firms and their users (Bera, 2023; Das, 2024).

Thus, case studies of intergenerational cooperation in a variety of fields, including business, healthcare, and education, offer insightful information on the advantages of including a range of viewpoints when tackling the difficulties associated with digital transformation. We can improve the conversation on digital policy, ethical frameworks, and regulatory measures by showcasing fresh research. To address the intricacies of our quickly changing technology world and create a more inclusive and ethical digital landscape, it will be imperative to foster intergenerational collaboration and embrace comprehensive regulatory methods (Tohit & Haque, 2024). Organisations such as Uber and Airbnb influence advanced stages to associate clients with administrations in imaginative ways, disturbing customary businesses and setting out new market open doors (Dwivedi et al., 2024). These stages work with distributed exchanges, enhance asset use, and provide versatile arrangements that are unrealistic with customary plans of action. Another example of digital business model innovation is the subscription-based model. Organisations such as Netflix and Spotify have changed the media and media outlets by offering membership benefits that give admittance to an immense library of content for repetitive charges. This model creates consistent income streams and upgrades client commitment by proposing customised content proposals and adaptable access (Brenner, 2018). The impact of digital transformation on business operations has also been highlighted by the rise in data-driven business models. Data analytics and artificial intelligence (AI) are increasingly used by businesses to gain insight into customer behaviour, improve supply chains, and make well-informed strategic decisions. For instance, organisations such as Amazon use information examination to customise shopping encounters, figure interest, and effectively oversee stock.

According to Vassiliakopoulou and Hustad (2023), this data-driven strategy enables businesses to maintain their competitiveness and swiftly respond to shifts in the market. Advanced innovations are changing plans of action as well as reshaping the labour force and the fate of work. Computerisation, artificial intelligence, and far-off-coordinated effort apparatuses are driving significant changes in how work is performed and made. Computerisation and artificial intelligence have prompted the robotisation of routine undertakings and expansion of human capacities. Automation technologies streamline operations, decrease errors, and increase efficiency in the financial services and manufacturing sectors. For example, mechanical cycle computerisation (RPA) is utilised to mechanise dreary errands, such as information passage and receipt handling, permitting representatives to zero in more key and worth added exercises (George, 2024). Manmade intelligence-controlled instruments are likewise upgrading dynamic cycles by providing high-level information examination and prescient bits of knowledge, empowering associations to proactively answer business challenges. The ascent of remote work and virtual joint efforts is one of the most massive changes achieved by advanced innovations. The Coronavirus pandemic sped up the reception of remote work instruments, such as Zoom, Microsoft Groups, and Slack, which have become vital to present-day workplaces. These apparatuses work with continuous correspondence, project the board, coordinate efforts, and empower groups to work in various areas. Flexible work arrangements have also emerged because of the shift toward remote work, enabling employees to manage their personal and professional lives better (Shehadeh, 2024). Ability advancement and reskilling are vital parts of labour force change. As innovation continues to develop, interest in new abilities and capabilities is also developing. Associations are putting resources into reskilling and upskilling projects to assist representatives by adjusting to mechanical changes and remain pertinent in the advanced economy. According to Sotysik et al. (2024), businesses are offering training programs in data analytics, digital marketing, and cybersecurity to provide workers with the skills they will need in the workplace in the future. Maintaining a competitive edge and encouraging innovation requires a focus on ongoing learning and development. The computerised change in working environments is critical between generational elements that influence how different age bunches draw in with innovation and adjust to hierarchical change. The leadership and management of organizational change require an understanding of these dynamics.

Generational contrasts in innovation reception impact how representatives associate with computerised apparatuses and adjust to better approaches for working. Children of post-war America and Age X, who have encountered a steady mix of computerised advances, may move toward new apparatuses with fluctuating levels of incredulity and transformation challenges, in contrast to recent college graders and Age Z, who are advanced locals. For instance, while people born after WW2 might favor eye-to-eye correspondence and conventional work strategies, more youthful ages are more OK with computerised cooperation instruments and remote work game plans (George, 2024). Understanding these generational differences and implementing strategies to bridge the gap between diverse technological preferences and work styles is necessary for effective leadership in digital workplaces. Leadership and change management play crucial roles in successfully navigating the complexities of digital transformation. Pioneers should exhibit deftness, flexibility, and groundbreaking mentality to direct associations through the difficulties of computerised change. This includes cultivating a culture of development, empowering trial and error, and supporting representatives to adjust to new advances and cycles. For example, pioneers can establish conditions that embrace consistent improvement and learning, give assets to ability advancement, and elevate open correspondence to address concerns connected with computerised change (Vassilakopoulou and Hustad, 2023).

Digital Technologies in Education and Lifelong Learning

Digital technologies are dramatically changing the forms of education and creating lifelong learning processes within generations. Currently, AI and robotics are also utilised in classrooms, and digital tools have become ubiquitous, both for individuals' self-improvement and in the professional sphere, affecting how education is provided and received. Overall, the advancement of digital technologies has brought profound changes by providing fresh ideas and methods in educational processes and continuous education. For instance, AI-related applications are utilised to develop customer-tailored learning arrangements. These systems use the performance data of the students to recommend instructional content that best fits the student and then provide feedback on performance. Such an approach not only enhances students' interest but also enhances their efficiency in meeting learning deficits (Marzo, 2024). Robotics is another technology that has a tremendous influence in the field of education. Robots used in teaching, especially in STEM programs, are useful in providing students with practical lessons to improve comprehension. For instance, LEGO Mindstorms and VEX Robotics are programmable, making students have better engineering, coding, and problem-solving skills because they design, build, and program the robots they want (George, 2024). These are all types of interactions and important components of teaching environments where students can gain a better understanding of what is being learned.

Case Studies on Implementation

An interesting application of AI is the application of adaptive learning models. Sites such as Dream Box and Khan Academy incorporate AI, which changes the level of difficulty in exercises according to students' responses. For instance, in Dream Box, educators use real-time data to offer new lessons concerning mathematics, which changes instruction, difficulty level, and rate correspondingly in accordance with the student's ability level (Dwivedi et al., 2024). This type has been said to benefit students, since it enriches the concept of differential teaching planned to help different students more than the general approach to learning. We owe the following improvements across the fields of robotics to the integration of robotic coding programs in schools; for instance, the Robotics Academy program in several U.S. schools has brought into force new trends of increased student attendance and better problem-solving skills. Students engage in activities, such as the construction and control of robots. In addition to improving students' technical skills, it fosters teamwork and an innovative spirit among students (Zelenev, 2022).

Technology is also a critical determinant of lifelong learning, because it offers convenient and portable learning solutions for adults. Massive open online courses provided by Coursera, edX, Udacity, and other online platforms allow learners to develop new competencies and expand their knowledge in various fields relying on the concept of flexibility. These platforms are usually filled with courses created in cooperation with well-known universities and industry specialists, thus guaranteeing the highest quality of education and information (Sołtysik et al., 2024). For instance, the 'Professional Certificate in AI' program provided on edX prepares individuals for the modern world of work by extending knowledge in the increasingly popular AI, ML, and data analysis. Moreover, technology-supported teachers' training and development through Continuing Professional Development has been brought to the fore by the COVID-19 pandemic. Technological advances, such as the use of virtual classes and video conferencing, have made it possible for teachers and students to proceed with their learning activities, even if they are physically apart. It has pointed to the possibility of using technology-enhanced learning and being able to change one's learning plan and approach as the circumstances require (Hoodbhoy, 2023).

EMERGING TOPICS AND FUTURE DIRECTIONS

The action fields relating to artificial intelligence, technology, and human-robot interactions, as well as digital citizenship, show a fast pace of development and indicate that both the benefits and risks offered by these technologies must be discussed. Digital technologies are the main components of all technologies that deal with the interconnection of networks to allow the sharing of information, as follows: generational attitudes towards these digital technologies. Older people currently have a negative perception of different digital technologies, such as AI or human-robot interfaces, while the younger generation has a positive perception towards such technologies. As for the third aspect, it is worth mentioning that the current youth, who always had access to computers and the Internet, demonstrated more willingness to interact with AI and robotics. They are equally disposed to adopt these technologies as applications for efficiency, flexibility, and creativity. For instance, the increased use of artificial intelligence virtual helpers such as Siri and Alexa represent the new generation that seeks to involve AI in their lives Vol.

Older generations are seen to be less accepting of these technologies owing to issues with privacy, automation of jobs, and concerns regarding the use and creation of AI. For example, studies have found that people above the age of 60 are sceptical about AI's ability to make decisions without prejudice and would like to have some level of control over the decision-making process (George, 2024). Robots used in service occupations such as robotic health care attendants and customer service robots or cobots that interact with people also provoke questions regarding the importance of people's coping skills and the feasibility of the utmost automation of employment (Hoodbhoy, 2023). Ethical considerations and what it means to be a good digital citizen are important.

Trade-offs are inevitable in the AI age; every deployment of technology creates questions on ethical matters such as privacy, fairness, and accountability. With the increasing applications of AI in different spheres of life, including decision-making procedures in the sphere of healthcare, finance, and criminal justice, it is appropriate to pay special attention to the prognostic transparency and absence of system biases. For instance, the incorporation of AI in autotching tools which are used for predicting crimes, has been said to reinstate the bias of remand and arrest by police and courts, bringing out the need for regulation of ethical behaviours in AI (Marzo, 2024). Fostering digital citizenship and connectedness is about creating for itself, which enhances the appropriate usage of the available technology instruments and closing the digital divide. Efforts which are targeted to reduce the digital divide, for example, offering access to and training in digital skills to disadvantaged populations, must be seen as critical in promoting digital citizenship. Moreover, it may be possible to approach the issue of responsible AI based on the principles developed at the international level, create corresponding frameworks to regulate AI's development and application of AI, and identify the risks that need to be minimised (Shehadeh, 2024).

Computerised technologies afford the prospects of developing an organism's intergenerational interactions. Sites such as social networks, Web-Conferencing, and other online collaboration tools facilitate users from different generations to engage, exchange ideas, and solve problems of working together on common projects. For instance, communication through technology, such as video conferencing instead of physical work, has enabled cross-pollination in skills between young and elderly employees (Das, 2024). Other improvements in intergenerational communication can also be achieved through educational and community applications utilising digital media. Through such activities as a digital storytelling task, in which the elderly narrate their life experiences to the next generation through multimedia technology, this can enhance cross-generation understanding (Vassilakopoulou & Hustad, 2023). Likewise, mentoring programs in which experienced workers are connected to new persons with the help of digital media resources can help in career advancement and knowledge sharing (Sołtysik et al., 2024). Future digital transformation will be greatly influenced by new technologies like 5G connection, quantum computing, and artificial intelligence (AI). All these advances promise to both introduce new paradigms for productivity and engagement across different industries and improve the capabilities that already exist. But as we investigate these patterns, we must critically assess their consequences, difficulties, and possible inequalities (George, 2024).

Artificial Intelligence (AI) is at the vanguard of digital transformation, enabling enhanced data analytics, automation, and customization. Organizations can make better decisions more quickly because of their real-time analysis of large data volumes. But as AI develops quickly, ethical questions like data privacy, algorithmic prejudice, and job displacement become more pressing. Strong legal frameworks are urgently needed to handle these moral conundrums and guarantee that AI technologies be applied ethically and openly as organizations depend more and more on AI-driven operations (Ahmed, 2024). Another game changer is 5G technology, which can completely transform industry by providing faster and more dependable internet connections. The Internet of Things (IoT) will be empowered by the improved connection, enabling immediate data sharing and seamless device communication. This raise worries about security flaws and the possibility of more surveillance, even though it can result in major breakthroughs in industries like healthcare by enabling real-time patient monitoring and remote diagnostics (Czerniewicz, 2022; Dwivedi et al., 2024).

With the ability to address challenging issues that are now unsolvable for conventional computers, quantum computing promises a dramatic leap in processing capacity. Quantum algorithms have great potential to improve optimization and simulation activities in several industries, including banking, medicines, and logistics. However, the technology is still in its early stages, and there are several substantial obstacles to be addressed, such as the high cost of implementing quantum solutions into current infrastructures and the requirement for specialized skills (Hoodbhoy, 2023).

Furthermore, because quantum computing may overcome existing encryption methods, it poses a risk to sensitive data, which has significant consequences for cybersecurity. Thus, although exciting developments in digital transformation are heralded by AI, 5G, and quantum computing, a rigorous examination uncovers a complicated environment of potential and problems. Consideration must be given to the ethical ramifications of AI, the unequal deployment of 5G, and the emerging field of quantum computing (Kamel, 2021). In addition to innovation, organizations need to prioritize ethical responsibility, fair access, and proactive policymaking to fully realize the promise of modern technologies. Through a holistic strategy to digital transformation that incorporates these important studies, firms may maximize the advantages of emerging technologies, minimize possible hazards, and better navigate the future environment (George, 2024).

CONCLUSION

The various effects on the physical and mental health of various age groups were highlighted by the investigation of the individual impacts of digital technologies. Digital tools have many advantages, such as easier access to information and improved communication; however, they also carry risks for mental and physical health issues. Advanced education and the improvement of sound innovation propensities are fundamental to relieving these dangers and cultivating positive results across age groups (Das, 2024; Shehadeh, 2024). Digital transformation alters workforce dynamics and business models at the organizational level. The combination of simulated intelligence, robotisation, and computerised instruments into the working environment can possibly upgrade efficiency and productivity, but it also brings up issues about work removal and generational joint effort (Hoodbhoy, 2023; Sołtysik et al., 2024). Viable administration of these progressions requires an emphasis on comprehensive practices and methodologies that address the necessity of a different labour force. On a cultural and strategic level, the rise of innovations such as simulated intelligence and IoT presents two potential open doors and moral difficulties. Issues related to computerised partitions, security, and network safety require insightful administration and strategies that advance advanced considerations and safeguard individual privileges (Vassilakopoulou and Hustad, 2023). The job of an advanced foundation in a shrewd local area configuration further features the requirement for thorough wanting to guarantee impartial access and commitment. Future bearings point towards the rising significance of intergenerational cooperation with computerised devices. It is possible to improve communication and knowledge transfer between different age groups, which is a significant possibility (Younus & Zaenuri, 2024); however, this can only happen if ongoing efforts are made to reduce generational gaps and increase digital literacy among all demographics. Proposals for Policymakers, Instructors, and Business Pioneers Several suggestions can be made for effectively utilising digital transformation for inclusive social benefits:

Policymakers: Come up with and implement policies that close the digital divide and ensure that everyone has equal access to technology. This remembers effective money management for computerised frameworks, giving preparation projects to advanced proficiency and guaranteeing that security and online protection measures are strong and straightforward (Marzo, 2024; Shehadeh, 2024). To avoid bias and ensure fair outcomes, policymakers should also consider ethical guidelines for AI and emerging technologies.

Instructors: Integrate advanced proficiency and health training into educational plans to prepare understudies for the computerised age. To give students the skills they need to successfully navigate digital environments, the development of critical thinking and responsible technology use should be emphasised (Vassilakopoulou & Hustad, 2023). Encourage opportunities for intergenerational learning that make use of digital tools to close knowledge gaps and improve comprehension.

Business Pioneers: Embrace computerised change with an emphasis on inclusivity and worker prosperity. Create opportunities for intergenerational collaboration within the workforce, implement flexible work arrangements, and invest in digital tools that boost productivity (Sotysik et al., 2024). Create strategies to control how AI and automation affect jobs, such as retraining programs and employee support. In conclusion, a multifaceted strategy that addresses individual well-being, organizational dynamics, societal challenges, and future trends is necessary to bridge generational gaps using digital technology. By implementing smart strategies, instructive drives, and strategic policies, partners can tackle the advantages of computerised change to create a more comprehensive and impartial society. The ongoing development of digital technology presents exciting possibilities, but it also requires constant attention to ensure that these advancements benefit all generations.

REFERENCES

Ahmed, F. (2024). From bricks and mortar to bits and bytes: The transformation of engineering in the digital age. *Kashf Journal of Multidisciplinary Research*, 1(1), 28–36.

Aithal, P. S., & Maiya, A. K. (2023). Innovations in higher education industry–Shaping the future. *International Journal of Case Studies in Business, IT, and Education*, 7(4), 283–311. DOI: 10.47992/IJCSBE.2581.6942.0321

Bera, S. D. (2023). Digital transformation in family firms: Exploring the interplay of tradition and innovation.

Brenner, B. (2018). Transformative sustainable business models in the light of the digital imperative—A global business economics perspective. *Sustainability (Basel)*, 10(12), 4428. DOI: 10.3390/su10124428

Czerniewicz, L. (2022). Multi-layered digital inequalities in HEIs: The paradox of the post-digital society. In *New visions for higher education towards 2030-Part 2: Transitions: Key topics, key voices.*

Das, D. K. (2024). Exploring the symbiotic relationship between digital transformation, infrastructure, service delivery, and governance for smart sustainable cities. *Smart Cities*, 7(2), 806–835. DOI: 10.3390/smartcities7020034

Doukidis, G. I., Mylonopoulos, N., & Pouloudi, N. (Eds.). (2004). *Social and economic transformation in the digital era.* IGI Global. DOI: 10.4018/978-1-59140-158-2

Dwivedi, Y. K., Jeyaraj, A., Hughes, L., Davies, G. H., Ahuja, M., Albashrawi, M. A., Al-Busaidi, A. S., Al-Sharhan, S., Al-Sulaiti, K. I., Altinay, L., Amalaya, S., Archak, S., Ballestar, M. T., Bhagwat, S. A., Bharadwaj, A., Bhushan, A., Bose, I., Budhwar, P., Bunker, D., & Walton, P. (2024). "Real impact": Challenges and opportunities in bridging the gap between research and practice–Making a difference in industry, policy, and society. *International Journal of Information Management*, 102750, 102750. Advance online publication. DOI: 10.1016/j.ijinfomgt.2023.102750

Gaikwad, S. S. (2024). *Modern trends in multi-disciplinary research* (Vol-1).

George, A. S. (2024). Bridging the digital divide: Understanding the human impacts of digital transformation.

Georgescu, R. I., & Bodislav, D. A. (2024). The generational divide-A debate on technology and the decision-making process. *Theoretical & Applied Economics, 31*(2).

Hoodbhoy, P. (2023). Sustainable infrastructures: Bridging the gap between technological advancements and societal needs. *Liberal Journal of Language and Literature Review*, 1(01), 12–21.

Imran, A. (2023). Why addressing digital inequality should be a priority. *The Electronic Journal on Information Systems in Developing Countries*, 89(3), e12255. DOI: 10.1002/isd2.12255

Kamel, S. (2021, September). The potential impact of digital transformation on Egypt. Giza, Egypt: Economic Research Forum (ERF).

Kickbusch, I., Piselli, D., Agrawal, A., Balicer, R., Banner, O., Adelhardt, M., . . . Wong, B. L. H. (2021). The Lancet and Financial Times Commission on governing health futures 2030: Growing up in a digital world. *The Lancet, 398*(10312), 1727-1776. DOI: 10.1016/S0140-6736(21)02113-0

King, B., Devare, M., Overduin, M., Wong, K., Kropff, W., Perez, S., ... Jarvis, A. (2021). Toward a digital One CGIAR: Strategic research on digital transformation in food, land, and water systems in a climate crisis.

Martínez-Peláez, R., Ochoa-Brust, A., Rivera, S., Félix, V. G., Ostos, R., Brito, H., Félix, R. A., & Mena, L. J. (2023). Role of digital transformation for achieving sustainability: Mediated role of stakeholders, key capabilities, and technology. *Sustainability (Basel)*, 15(14), 11221. DOI: 10.3390/su151411221

Marzo, R. R. (2024). Bridging the gap: Understanding and fostering intergenerational communication in the digital age. In *Intergenerational relations-contemporary theories, studies and policies*. IntechOpen. DOI: 10.5772/intechopen.1003205

Mundhe, D. E. (2024). *Rethink revolution: Transformative waves across disciplines.*

Shehadeh, M. (2024). Digital transformation: A catalyst for sustainable business practices. In *Technological innovations for business, education and sustainability* (pp. 29–45). Emerald Publishing Limited. DOI: 10.1108/978-1-83753-106-620241003

Shrivastava, P., Smith, M. S., O'Brien, K., & Zsolnai, L. (2020). Transforming sustainability science to generate positive social and environmental change globally. *One Earth*, 2(4), 329–340. DOI: 10.1016/j.oneear.2020.04.010 PMID: 33501419

Sołtysik, M., Wojnarowska, M., Urbaniec, M., Zabkar, V., Ćwiklicki, M., & Varese, E. (2024). *Sustainable business in the era of digital transformation: Strategic and entrepreneurial perspectives*. Taylor & Francis. DOI: 10.4324/9781032697895

Tariq, M. U. (2024). Harnessing Persuasive Technologies for Enhanced Learner Engagement and Motivation. In M. Sanmugam, D. Lim, N. Mohd Barkhaya, W. Wan Yahaya, & Z. Khlaif (Eds.), *Power of Persuasive Educational Technologies in Enhancing Learning* (pp. 30-62). IGI Global. DOI: 10.4018/979-8-3693-6397-3.ch002

Tariq, M. U. (2024). Leveraging AI for Entrepreneurial Innovation in Healthcare. In Özsungur, F. (Ed.), *Generating Entrepreneurial Ideas With AI* (pp. 192–216). IGI Global. DOI: 10.4018/979-8-3693-3498-0.ch009

Tariq, M. U. (2024). The role of AI in skilling, upskilling, and reskilling the workforce. In Doshi, R., Dadhich, M., Poddar, S., & Hiran, K. (Eds.), *Integrating generative AI in education to achieve sustainable development goals* (pp. 421–433). IGI Global. DOI: 10.4018/979-8-3693-2440-0.ch023

Tariq, M. U. (2025). *AI-Driven Learning and Engagement in Higher Education*. IGI Global. DOI: 10.4018/979-8-3693-4074-5

Tariq, M. U. (2025). Navigating Bias and Fairness in Digital AI Systems. In Bhattacharya, P., Hassan, A., Liu, H., & Bhushan, B. (Eds.), *Ethical Dimensions of AI Development* (pp. 127–156). IGI Global. DOI: 10.4018/979-8-3693-4147-6.ch006

Tariq, M. U. (2025). Strategic Integration of Technological Advances in Modern Business Practices. In Sedky, A. (Ed.), *Building Business Knowledge for Complex Modern Business Environments* (pp. 95–120). IGI Global. DOI: 10.4018/979-8-3693-6447-5.ch004

Tariq, M. U. (2025). Leveraging Open Innovation for Sustainable Growth in the Digital Era. In Taherdoost, H. (Ed.), *Mastering Innovation in Business* (pp. 157–192). IGI Global. DOI: 10.4018/979-8-3693-3759-2.ch007

Tohit, N. F. M., & Haque, M. (2024). Preparing the younger generation for an aging society: Strategies, challenges, and opportunities. *Cureus*, 16(7). Advance online publication. DOI: 10.7759/cureus.12145 PMID: 38983672

Vassilakopoulou, P., & Hustad, E. (2023). Bridging digital divides: A literature review and research agenda for information systems research. *Information Systems Frontiers*, 25(3), 955–969. DOI: 10.1007/s10796-020-10096-3 PMID: 33424421

Vial, G. (2021). Understanding digital transformation: A review and a research agenda. In *Managing digital transformation* (pp. 13-66).

Wu, W., & Yang, W. (2024). Methodology for digital transformation in TVET. In *Digital transformation in global TVET: Methodology and practices*. UNESCO Chair on Digitalization in TVET.

Younus, M., & Zaenuri, M. (2024). Public-private collaboration to overcome the digital divide in digital transformation of government. *Digital Zone: Jurnal Teknologi Informasi dan Komunikasi, 15*(1), 28-41.

Yu, P. K. (2002). Bridging the digital divide: Equality in the information age. *SSRN*, 20(1), 1–46. DOI: 10.2139/ssrn.309841

Zelenev, S. (2022). Promoting digital inclusion. In *Digital transformation and social well-being: Promoting an inclusive society* (pp. 3–22). Routledge. DOI: 10.4324/9781003312208-2

KEY TERMS AND DEFINITIONS

Digital Literacy: The ability to effectively and critically navigate, understand, and engage with digital technologies and online platforms.

Digital Transformation: The integration of digital technologies into various sectors, leading to changes in societal structures, organisational models, and individual lifestyles.

Digital Well-Being: The optimal balance of technology use that promotes mental, emotional, and physical health across all ages.

Emerging Technologies: Innovative technologies like AI, IoT, and robotics that are reshaping societal, economic, and cultural practices.

Intergenerational Dynamics: The interactions and relationships between different age groups, especially concerning the adoption and use of digital technologies.

Chapter 2
Digital Transformation Across Generations:
Robotics and AI in Action

Shalom Akhai
https://orcid.org/0000-0002-7533-457X
Maharishi Markandeshwar University, Mullana, India

Mahapara Abbass
https://orcid.org/0000-0002-0838-2598
Maharishi Markandeshwar University, Mullana, India

Prabhleen Kaur
Chandigarh College of Engineering, Chandigarh Group of Colleges, Jhanjeri, India

Tavleen Kaur
Chandigarh College of Engineering, Chandigarh Group of Colleges, Jhanjeri, India

ABSTRACT

The integration of robotics and artificial intelligence (AI) is transforming industries, enhancing efficiency, safety, and productivity. This chapter explores the impact of autonomous systems across various sectors, including manufacturing, healthcare, transportation, and agriculture. The convergence of robotics and AI enables adaptive systems to perform complex tasks independently, driving innovation and reshaping business operations. Machine learning, computer vision, and sensor fusion empower robots to learn from data, recognize patterns, and interact with humans. Successful applications include self-driving cars, robotic-assisted surgery, precision farming, and smart home devices. However, challenges persist, such as reliability, safety, ethics, data privacy, and complexity of implementation. As autonomous systems continue to evolve, they will drive sustainable practices, optimize resource use, and encourage inter-disciplinary collaboration. Future research should focus on developing robust algorithms, enhancing safety protocols, and establishing ethical guidelines.

DOI: 10.4018/979-8-3693-6366-9.ch002

1. INTRODUCTION

Automation has revolutionized various industries, including manufacturing, healthcare, scientific discovery, and transportation (Ashimaet al., 2021). The fusion of robotics and artificial intelligence (AI) has led to the creation of intelligent robots capable of performing tasks independently and efficiently (Murphy 2019). Robotics serves as the physical conduit through which AI algorithms engage with the surrounding environment, enabling them to gather data from their surroundings and execute tasks (Alamouti et al., 2024). AI empowers these robots to process collected data, make informed decisions, and dynamically adapt to shifting circumstances (Aldoseri et al., 2024). The use of advanced algorithms, sensor fusion, and human-machine interfaces is being explored to enhance the dependability of autonomous systems (Singh & Akhai 2024). Safety assurance is crucial for the public's approval and responsible implementation of autonomous systems (Akhai & Balu 2022). Measures include rigorous testing, functional safety standards, redundancy, fail-safes, human supervision, transparency, and comprehensibility (Arif & Akhai 2024; Abbass et al., 2025).Autonomous systems, consisting of intelligent robots capable of performing tasks without human intervention, are at the forefront of this transformation. They improve performance and adaptability by acquiring knowledge from people through various learning mechanisms. Machine learning is at the core of integrating AI into robotics, enabling robots to learn from data, identify intricate patterns, and enhance their performance over time without the need for explicit programming (Wadhwa et al., 2024).The incorporation of computer vision emerges as a pivotal element, enabling robots to decipher and comprehend visual information from their environment. Empowered by AI-driven computer vision, robots can proficiently recognize objects, navigate complex terrains, and engage with humans in a more intuitive and effective manner. Effective collaboration, reinforcement, and impersonation are essential for decision-making processes (Akhai 2024). The adoption and acceptance of healthcare autonomous systems require adherence to regulations, trust establishment, data privacy and security assurance, and interaction with existing legacy systems (Akhai 2023; Akhai 2024; Mala et al., 2025). Interoperability and effective communication are essential for autonomous systems to communicate and exchange data across different platforms (Akhai et al., 2024; Akhai & Wadhwa 2024).The convergence of robotics and AI heralds a new era of autonomous systems that exhibit unparalleled precision and autonomy in executing multifaceted tasks. This synergistic integration unlocks a myriad of possibilities across diverse sectors, highlighting the transformative potential of intelligent robots in enhancing productivity, safety, and operational efficiency on a global scale (Singh& Khan 2024).

2. BACKGROUND

The 18th century saw the emergence of automation technologies, which later led to the development of robotics and artificial intelligence (Reese 2018; Acemoglu & Restrepo 2018). Advancements in computing power, sensor technology, and machine learning have significantly accelerated progress in autonomous systems, such as autonomous vehicles, unmanned aerial vehicles, robotic medical equipment, and industrial robots (Sharma & Akhai, 2019; Khang & Akhai, 2024; Akhai, 2024; Motia et al., 2024). Early robotic systems were limited to industrial applications, but AI has enabled them to learn from data, recognize patterns, and make decisions (Akhai & Khang, 2024; Ahmed et al., 2022; Arents & Greitans, 2022; Jagatheesaperumal et al., 2021). Achieving more autonomy requires standardized automation procedures, communication and cost advantages, and economies of scale(Bathla et al., 2022). Sensor technology advancements have greatly enhanced autonomous systems, including LiDAR, sensor fusion, smart sensors, and wireless communication. Machine learning (ML) is used to acquire knowledge from data and adjust to novel situations, while computer vision is used for tasks like obstacle detection, facial recognition, quality control, and environmental mapping. Natural language processing (NLP) enhances human-robot interaction, context understanding, and information retrieval (Adawy et al., 2024; Akhai 2023, Akhai 2024). Current developments in robotic surgical assistants, including enhanced precision and control, integration of augmented reality, AI-powered decision support, and teleoperated surgery, are revolutionizing robotic surgery by improving patient outcomes and surgical team capabilities. Integrated sensor fusion enhances the precision of autonomous systems by combining data from several sensor types to get a deeper understanding of the environment (Rajamani et al., 2024; Das, 2024; Lin et al., 2024). Autonomous vehicle sensors and fusion algorithms have established the feasibility of safe and reliable self-driving automobiles. This field raises important questions about ethics, safety, and the future of human-robot collaboration, making it a dynamic area of research and development with far-reaching implications (Yeong et al., 2021; Bhavana et al., 2025; Allawadi et al., 2024).

3. ROBOTICS AND AI: A SYNERGISTIC RELATIONSHIP

Robotics and AI have evolved independently, but now work together to create intelligent robots capable of performing physical tasks, thinking, learning, and adapting. Robotics focuses on designing machines for specific tasks, while AI focuses on developing algorithms and systems that mimic human intelligence. When integrating robotics and AI, the result is intelligent robots that can perceive, learn, and make decisions independently. Robotics provides the physical platform for AI algorithms to interact with the environment, while AI empowers robots to process data, make decisions, and adapt to changing conditions. The intersection of these fields is where autonomous systems thrive. One key aspect of integrating AI into robotics is machine learning, which allows robots to learn from data, recognize patterns, and improve their performance without explicit programming. This enhances their efficiency and adaptability in various tasks. AI adds a layer of cognitive capabilities that enables robots to learn, adapt, and make decisions based on data. This synergistic relationship is foundational for the development of autonomous systems, allowing them to perform complex tasks, adapt to their environments, and interact meaningfully with humans and other systems (Bautista, 2024; Bibri et al., 2024; Artyukhov et al., 2024; Afrin et al., 2024).AI and robots enhance performance in complex environments and learning in dynamic settings through intelligent perception, autonomous decision-making, and adaptation, as illustrated in Figure 1.

Figure 1. Adaptive Learning and Decision-Making in AI-Robot Systems

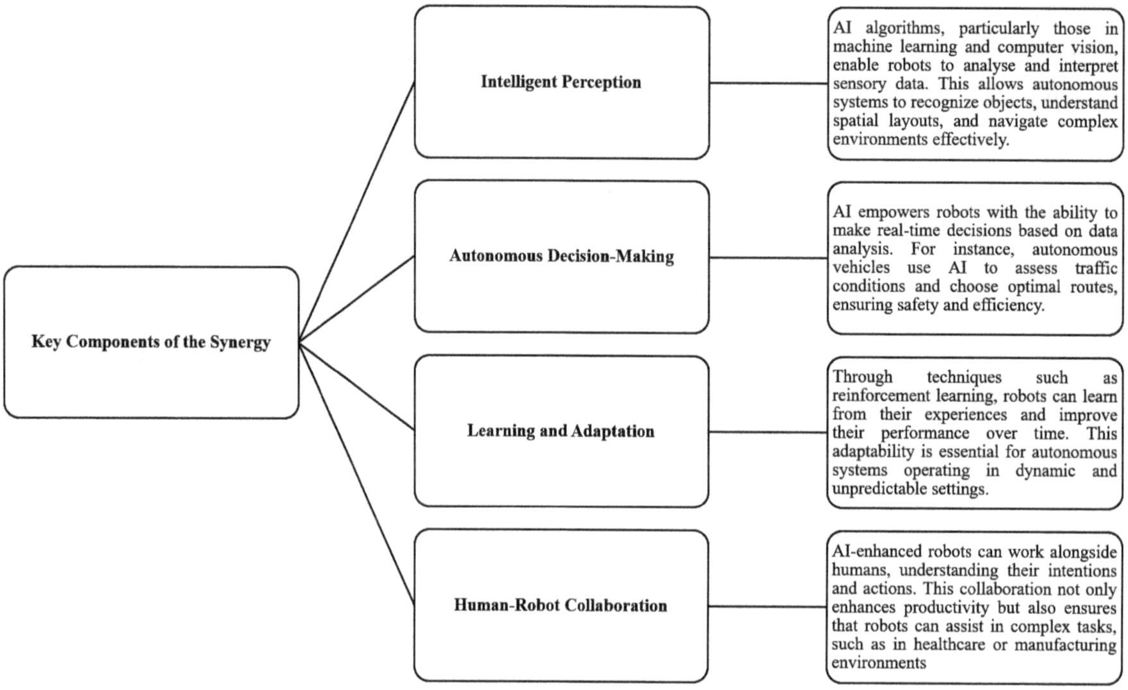

4. BENEFITS AND CHALLENGES OF INTEGRATING ROBOTICS AND AI

The integration of robotics and artificial intelligence (AI) offers numerous benefits, including increased operational efficiency, improved accuracy, and the ability to perform hazardous tasks in hazardous environments. This integration enhances safety by reducing human error in critical operations. The synergy between robotics and AI allows machines to adapt and learn from their experiences, leading to continuous improvement in performance. This is crucial in dynamic environments where real-time decision-making is essential, such as autonomous vehicles navigating complex road conditions. Robots can perform repetitive tasks faster and with greater precision than humans, streamlining production processes and reducing costs. AI algorithms enhance decision-making capabilities, particularly in quality control applications. However, integrating robotics and AI poses challenges, including ethical implications, job displacement, and the need for regulatory frameworks. Ensuring transparency and accountability in the decision-making process of AI-powered robots is crucial to maintain trust and ethical standards. The complexity of integrating robotics and AI requires a skilled workforce capable of developing, maintaining, and troubleshooting these systems. AI integration enables robots to learn from their experiences, making them more adaptable and effective in monitoring their surroundings.

In conclusion, while the integration of robotics and AI presents significant opportunities, it also raises ethical concerns, safety, and the need for regulatory frameworks. Continued research and interdisciplinary collaboration are vital for refining autonomous systems, with the future holding immense potential for innovations that enhance efficiency, safety, and human-robot interaction, ultimately reshaping various industries.

5. CHALLENGES OF INTEGRATING ROBOTICS AND AI

The integration of robotics and artificial intelligence (AI) into autonomous systems presents numerous challenges, including reliability, safety, ethical considerations, data privacy, and complexity of implementation. Reliability is crucial for autonomous systems to function reliably in all scenarios, requiring robust training and testing. Safety concerns arise, especially in environments where humans and robots interact, necessitating the development of fail-safes and emergency protocols. Ethical considerations include job displacement implications and the need for regulations governing autonomous system use. Data privacy and security are critical, as autonomous systems often rely on large amounts of data for training and operation.Computer vision is another crucial element, enabling robots to perceive and understand visual information from their surroundings. With AI-powered computer vision, robots can recognize objects, navigate environments, and interact with humans more effectively. This synergy opens up possibilities for applications in various fields such as manufacturing, healthcare, agriculture, and more, where intelligent robots can enhance productivity, safety, and efficiency. Implementation can be complex and resource-intensive, requiring organizations to invest in infrastructure, training, and maintenance.Key challenges include safety and reliability, ethical and social concerns, data privacy and security, regulatory and legal frameworks, integration and interoperability, human-robot interaction, cost and resource constraints, and user trust. Technical failures, lack of standards, compliance challenges, system compatibility, and user trust are some of the key challenges.In conclusion, while the integration of robotics and AI into autonomous systems offers transformative benefits, addressing these challenges is crucial for their successful implementation. Ongoing research, collaboration among stakeholders, and proactive regulatory measures will be essential in navigating these hurdles and unlocking the full potential of this synergistic relationship (Gabsi, 2024; Priyadharshini, 2024; Obaigbena et al., 2024; Licardo et al., 2024; Akhai, 2023).

6. APPLICATIONS OF AI-ROBOT INTEGRATION

The integration of robotics and artificial intelligence (AI) into autonomous systems presents numerous challenges, including reliability, safety, ethical considerations, data privacy, and complexity of implementation (Akpuokwe et al., 2024). Reliability is crucial for autonomous systems to function reliably in all scenarios, requiring robust training and testing. Safety concerns arise, especially in environments where humans and robots interact, necessitating the development of fail-safes and emergency protocols. Ethical considerations include job displacement implications and the need for regulations governing autonomous system use (Andreoni et al., 2024). Data privacy and security are critical, as autonomous systems often rely on large amounts of data for training and operation (Amiri et al., 2024). Computer vision is another crucial element, enabling robots to perceive and understand visual information from their surroundings(Rojas et al., 2024). With AI-powered computer vision, robots can recognize objects, navigate environments, and interact with humans more effectively (Soori et al., 2023). This synergy opens up possibilities for applications in various fields such as manufacturing, healthcare, agriculture, and more, where intelligent robots can enhance productivity, safety, and efficiency. Implementation can be complex and resource-intensive, requiring organizations to invest in infrastructure, training, and maintenance. Key challenges include safety and reliability, ethical and social concerns, data privacy and security, regulatory and legal frameworks, integration and interoperability, human-robot interaction, cost and resource constraints, and user trust. Technical failures, lack of standards, compliance challenges, system compatibility, and user trust are some of the key challenges (Javaid et al., 2023; Rashid & Kausik, 2024; Ahmad et al., 2024; Nagaty, 2023; Akhai & Pandita, 2013). Table 1 discusses challenges, solutions, and applications in integrating robotics and AI in autonomous systems, navigating complexities and overcoming barriers.

Table 1. Key Considerations for Implementing Autonomous Systems: Challenges, Solutions, and Applications

Category	Key Challenges	Details	Solutions/Recommendations	Potential Applications
Reliability	Ensuring systems function reliably in all scenarios	Requires robust training, testing, and fail-safe mechanisms to prevent unexpected failures	Implement extensive testing, simulations, and real-world trials; design fail-safes and redundancy systems	Autonomous vehicles, industrial automation, defense systems
Safety	Human-robot interaction and safety protocols	Development of emergency protocols and fail-safes is necessary in human-robot environments	Establish clear safety standards, real-time monitoring, and emergency protocols for robot shutdowns	Healthcare, manufacturing, service robots
Ethical Considerations	Job displacement, societal impact, and regulation of autonomous systems	Need for addressing the implications on employment and establishing guidelines for responsible AI usage	Develop ethical frameworks, retrain displaced workers for new roles, and create fair usage policies	Autonomous driving, retail automation, warehousing
Data Privacy & Security	Protection of sensitive data used for AI training and operation	Autonomous systems require vast amounts of data, raising concerns over data breaches and privacy	Implement strong encryption, data anonymization, secure data storage, and access controls	Smart cities, autonomous drones, personal assistants
Complexity of Implementation	Infrastructure, training, and maintenance challenges	Implementation is resource-intensive and requires significant investment in infrastructure, training, and upkeep	Create modular systems, train employees, and allocate resources for infrastructure upgrades	Advanced manufacturing, agriculture, logistics
Computer Vision	Visual perception and interpretation for navigation and interaction	AI-powered vision helps robots recognize objects and navigate environments but adds to implementation complexity	Invest in advanced AI algorithms and vision sensors; continuous improvement in real-time processing	Surveillance, autonomous driving, robotics in surgery
Regulatory & Legal Frameworks	Compliance with standards and creation of new laws	Legal guidelines and standards for safety, liability, and ethical use of autonomous systems need development	Collaborate with governments to create new regulations; establish safety and liability standards	Healthcare, autonomous delivery systems, law enforcement

continued on following page

Table 1. Continued

Category	Key Challenges	Details	Solutions/Recommendations	Potential Applications
Integration & Interoperability	System compatibility and smooth integration into existing workflows	Lack of standardized protocols can hinder integration with other systems and limit interoperability	Develop industry standards, open-source protocols, and collaborative platforms	Smart factories, supply chain automation, connected homes
Human-Robot Interaction	Designing intuitive and safe interaction between robots and humans	Effective communication, safety, and user interface design are crucial for smooth human-robot collaboration	Design user-friendly interfaces, safety mechanisms, and create effective communication channels	Home care, assistive robots, hospitality
Cost & Resource Constraints	High costs of development, deployment, and maintenance	Large upfront investment in hardware, software, and ongoing system maintenance is a significant barrier	Seek funding, reduce costs through economies of scale, focus on affordable solutions for SMEs	Agriculture, logistics, and SME automation
User Trust	Gaining trust from users and society regarding autonomous system usage	Transparency, reliability, and ethical considerations are necessary to build trust in autonomous technologies	Increase transparency through explainable AI, clear user guidelines, and continuous support	Public transportation, autonomous taxis, medical assistance
Technical Failures	Unforeseen malfunctions or system breakdowns	Requires strong diagnostics, real-time monitoring, and responsive troubleshooting to mitigate risks	Implement predictive maintenance, develop robust monitoring systems, and contingency plans	Robotics in production lines, critical healthcare systems
Lack of Standards	Absence of universally accepted protocols and guidelines	Standardization is needed for both safety and interoperability between different systems	Collaborate on global standard-setting initiatives and participate in industry alliances	Cross-industry systems, global supply chain management

In conclusion, while the integration of robotics and AI into autonomous systems offers transformative benefits, addressing these challenges is crucial for their successful implementation. Ongoing research, collaboration among stakeholders, and proactive regulatory measures will be essential in navigating these hurdles and unlocking the full potential of this synergistic relationship.

7. CASE STUDIES OF AUTONOMOUS SYSTEMS IN ACTION

Case studies highlight the effectiveness of autonomous systems, such as the deployment of autonomous delivery drones in urban areas and the use of robotic systems in hospitals for patient care. Amazon utilizes AI-driven robots in warehouses to enhance supply chain efficiency. Waymo's self-driving cars navigate real-world conditions, demonstrating the cutting edge of autonomous driving. The Da Vinci Surgical System uses AI-powered robotic arms for precision in minimally invasive surgeries. Amazon Robotics has revolutionized warehouse operations by integrating autonomous robots to assist in order fulfilment. These robots automate the movement of goods, significantly improving efficiency. In Boston Dynamics – Robotic Assistance in Disaster Response Boston Dynamics – Robotic Assistance in Disaster Response. DJI – Aerial Surveillance and Delivery drones are used for infrastructure inspections, agricultural monitoring, and even delivering medical supplies in remote areas, showcasing versatility in application. These case studies illustrate the diverse applications and significant benefits of autonomous systems across industries. From improving safety and efficiency to enabling innovative solutions in challenging environments, the successful integration of robotics and AI is paving the way for a future where autonomy plays a central role in everyday operations and decision-making. Table 2 showcases real-world applications of robotics and AI, including pioneering and successful cases across various industries, highlighting their innovative use and industry benefits.

Table 2. Real-World Applications of Robotics and AI

Case Study	Industry/ Application	Description	Key Benefits	Impact on Industry
Amazon Robotics - Warehouse Automation(Bancarzewski, 2024; Teng et al., 2023)	Supply Chain, Warehousing	Integration of AI-driven robots to automate movement of goods and assist in order fulfillment.	Enhanced efficiency, reduced labor costs, faster operations	Revolutionized warehouse operations by optimizing supply chain logistics, leading to quicker deliveries and cost savings.
Waymo - Autonomous Driving(Singh & Saini 2021)	Autonomous Driving, Transportation	Self-driving cars navigating real-world urban conditions, demonstrating advanced autonomous driving capabilities.	Increased safety, reduced human error, convenience	Pioneered self-driving technologies, pushing forward regulatory discussions and advancing the future of autonomous transportation systems.
Da Vinci Surgical System - Precision Surgery(Ngu et al., 2017; Najarian et al., 2011; Johansson et al., 2021)	Healthcare, Medical Robotics	AI-powered robotic arms used for minimally invasive surgeries with high precision and control.	Improved precision, reduced recovery time, less invasive	Transformed surgery, allowing surgeons to perform complex procedures with enhanced precision and patient outcomes.
Boston Dynamics - Disaster Response(Nawrat & Krawczyk, 2023; Zhao et al., 2024)	Disaster Response, Robotics	Robotic systems providing assistance in search and rescue operations in hazardous and inaccessible environments.	Improved safety, reduced human risk, efficiency in rescue	Set a benchmark for how robotics can be deployed in disaster situations, minimizing human exposure and speeding up rescue and recovery efforts.

continued on following page

Table 2. Continued

Case Study	Industry/ Application	Description	Key Benefits	Impact on Industry
DJI - Aerial Surveillance and Delivery Drones(Poljak & Šterbenc, 2020; Dilshad et al., 2020)	Agriculture, Infrastructure, Healthcare	Drones used for surveillance, infrastructure inspections, agricultural monitoring, and delivering medical supplies.	Versatility, access to remote areas, real-time data	Showcased how drones can revolutionize remote monitoring, healthcare delivery, and agriculture by providing innovative solutions to traditionally slow processes.
Amazon - AI-Driven Robotics in Warehouses(Bancarzewski, 2024; Teng et al., 2023)	Supply Chain, Logistics	Use of autonomous robots to streamline logistics and order processing in Amazon warehouses.	Boosted productivity, optimized resource use, improved safety	Set new standards for automated warehouse operations, pushing forward the concept of smart factories and AI-driven logistics.

8. KEY TECHNOLOGIES AND COMPONENTS

Autonomous systems use sensors, perception systems, control and navigation systems, machine learning and AI algorithms, and communication protocols to perform complex tasks. Advanced sensors like LiDAR, radar, and cameras gather real-time data for navigation and obstacle detection. Machine learning algorithms improve performance over time. Communication protocols ensure seamless data exchange and coordination among systems. The integration of these technologies is crucial for developing sophisticated autonomous applications. Table 3 outlines essential technologies driving autonomous systems, including sensors, AI, and networking, and their components and roles in building blocks and the anatomy of autonomous systems.

Table 3. Essential Technologies Powering Autonomous Systems.

Technology/Component	Description	Role in Autonomous Systems	Examples	Key Benefits
Sensors and Perception Systems (Shit 2020)	Sensors such as LiDAR, cameras, radar, and ultrasonic devices provide real-time data for environmental mapping, obstacle detection, and navigation.	Enable autonomous systems to perceive their environment for safe navigation and operation.	LiDAR, cameras, radar, ultrasonic sensors	Enhanced perception, safety, and obstacle avoidance
Control and Navigation Systems(Bijjahalli et al., 2020)	Control systems manage movement and operation, with advanced algorithms for real-time adjustments based on environmental changes.	Ensure precise navigation, stability, and operation under varying conditions.	GPS, inertial measurement units, motion sensors	Adaptive navigation, precise movement, stability in operations
Machine Learning and AI Algorithms(Facchinetti et al., 2024; Kumar et al., 2024)	AI-driven algorithms like deep learning and reinforcement learning allow autonomous systems to interpret data and improve performance over time.	Enable decision-making, self-learning, and real-time data interpretation to enhance autonomy.	Neural networks, reinforcement learning models	Improved decision-making, self-optimization, and learning
Communication and Networking Protocols(Hakak et al., 2023)	Communication systems and networking protocols, including 5G, enable data exchange between autonomous systems and external infrastructure.	Facilitate data sharing, coordination, and collaboration among multiple autonomous systems.	5G networks, Wi-Fi, V2X communication	Seamless coordination, enhanced real-time collaboration
Artificial Intelligence Integration (Akhai 2023; Akhai 2024)	AI integration is at the core, combining data from sensors and enhancing control systems through real-time processing and predictive capabilities.	AI augments sensor data processing, enabling better decision-making and adaptability in unpredictable environments.	AI-driven predictive models	Faster decision-making, continuous learning, enhanced autonomy
Networking and Data Exchange (Akhai & Khang 2024)	Autonomous systems rely on robust networking for real-time updates, data sharing, and communication with other systems.	Ensures efficient operation in interconnected environments such as smart cities or autonomous vehicle fleets.	Cloud computing, edge networks, IoT frameworks	Real-time connectivity, collaborative intelligence

9. CHALLENGES, FUTURE TRENDS, AND OPPORTUNITIES

The integration of robotics and AI into autonomous systems presents technical, data-dependent, safety, and ethical challenges. Technical challenges include reliability and scalability, while ethical concerns include job displacement and potential biases. Regulatory and legal issues also pose challenges. Public acceptance and trust are crucial for the success of autonomous systems. Future research should focus on developing robust algorithms, enhancing safety protocols, and establishing ethical guidelines for their deployment. Ultimately, the goal is to create more adaptive systems that can operate reliably in complex environments. The integration of robotics and AI is expected to revolutionize industries like healthcare, transportation, and agriculture. Emerging technologies like edge AI and 5G will reduce latency and improve communication. Autonomous vehicles, human-robot collaboration, and AI-powered robots in healthcare settings will enhance efficiency and patient outcomes. The integration of robotics and artificial intelligence (AI) is expected to revolutionize various industries, including logistics, agriculture, and healthcare. The growth of autonomous delivery solutions, cobots, and collaborative robots will enhance productivity and safety in various sectors. Healthcare will see the rise of robotic surgery and personalized medicine, while agriculture will benefit from AI-powered precision farming. Smart cities will integrate autonomous systems for efficient urban planning and infrastructure maintenance. The advancement of machine learning algorithms and sensor technology will make autonomous systems more intelligent and adaptable, opening up opportunities in sectors like smart homes, environmental monitoring, and disaster response. However, regulatory and ethical frameworks will need to evolve to ensure safety and accountability. The future of autonomous systems will be bright, with continuous innovations paving the way for unprecedented advancements. The integration of robotics and AI will significantly impact industries like logistics, agriculture, and healthcare, enhancing efficiency, safety, and user interaction (Akhai 2023; Akhai 2024).

10. CONCLUSION

- Autonomous systems are expected to revolutionize various industries, including transportation, healthcare, agriculture, manufacturing, construction, retail, energy, security, hospitality, and education. These technologies can improve routing efficiency, reduce transportation congestion, and enhance safety. Surgical robots can improve accuracy and reduce recovery periods, while AI-driven surveillance systems monitor areas for security breaches. Service robots can improve check-in procedures, and education can benefit from tailored learning experiences and virtual classrooms. As technology advances, it will expand its influence, creating new opportunities and threats.
- Autonomous systems enhance decision-making, stimulate creativity, promote efficiency, and alter worker dynamics. They automate processes, enhance resource efficiency, and promote sustainable behaviors. They mitigate human error, improve monitoring, and promote environmental sustainability. They also establish regulatory and ethical frameworks, focusing on privacy, security, and ethical AI.
- However, challenges remain regarding dependability, scalability, and ethics. Stakeholders must participate in discourse to address technological complexity, data privacy issues, safety hazards, and ethical implications. Advancements in AI, machine learning, and communication technologies may help overcome these challenges.
- Despite the positive prospects for autonomous systems, ethical issues like employment displacement, data privacy, and algorithmic prejudice require careful examination. Collaboration among academics, practitioners, and policymakers is crucial to harness the potential of autonomous systems for social advantage.

REFERENCES

Abbass, M., Abbas, U., Jafri, R., Arif, S. M., & Akhai, S. (2025). AI and Machine Learning Applications in Sustainable Smart Cities. In *Sustainable Smart Cities and the Future of Urban Development* (pp. 1–32). IGI Global Scientific Publishing.

Acemoglu, D., & Restrepo, P. (2018). Artificial intelligence, automation, and work. In *The economics of artificial intelligence: An agenda* (pp. 197–236). University of Chicago Press.

Adawy, M., Abualese, H., El-Omari, N. K. T., & Alawadhi, A. (2024). Human-Robot Interaction (HRI) using Machine Learning (ML): A survey and taxonomy. *International Journal of Advanced Soft Computing Applications*, 16(3), 183–213. DOI: 10.15849/IJASCA.241130.11

Afrin, S., Roksana, S., & Akram, R. (2024). AI-Enhanced Robotic Process Automation: A Review of Intelligent Automation Innovations. *IEEE Access : Practical Innovations, Open Solutions.*

Ahmad, A., Liew, A. X., Venturini, F., Kalogeras, A., Candiani, A., Di Benedetto, G., Ajibola, S., Cartujo, P., Romero, P., Lykoudi, A., De Grandis, M. M., Xouris, C., Lo Bianco, R., Doddy, I., Elegbede, I., D'Urso Labate, G. F., García del Moral, L. F., & Martos, V. (2024). AI can empower agriculture for global food security: Challenges and prospects in developing nations. *Frontiers in Artificial Intelligence*, 7, 1328530. DOI: 10.3389/frai.2024.1328530 PMID: 38726306

Ahmed, I., Jeon, G., & Piccialli, F. (2022). From artificial intelligence to explainable artificial intelligence in industry 4.0: A survey on what, how, and where. *IEEE Transactions on Industrial Informatics*, 18(8), 5031–5042. DOI: 10.1109/TII.2022.3146552

Akhai, S. (2023). From Black Boxes to Transparent Machines: The Quest for Explainable AI. *Available at: Social Science Research Network, doi: http://dx.doi.org/*DOI: 10.2139/ssrn.4390887

Akhai, S. (2023). Healthcare record management for healthcare 4.0 via blockchain: a review of current applications, opportunities, challenges, and future potential. In *Blockchain for Healthcare 4.0* (Vol. 1, pp. 211–223). CRC Press. DOI: 10.1201/9781003408246-11

Akhai, S. (2023). Navigating the Potential Applications and Challenges of Intelligent and Sustainable Manufacturing for a Greener Future. *Evergreen*, 10(4), 2237–2243. DOI: 10.5109/7160899

Akhai, S. (2024). Innovating Healthcare Delivery: Harnessing Drones for Medical Services. In *Modelling of Virtual Worlds Using the Internet of Things* (Vol. 1, pp. 232-250). CRC Press.

Akhai, S. (2024). Smart Home Environment for Society: An Overview of IoT-Enabled Air Conditioners. In *Modelling of Virtual Worlds Using the Internet of Things* (Vol. 1, pp. 74-87). CRC Press.

Akhai, S. (2024). The Impact of Artificial Intelligence on Healthcare: Opportunities and Challenges. *Journal of Advanced Research in Medical Science & Technology (ISSN: 2394-6539), 11*(1&2), 1-6.

Akhai, S. (2024). Towards Trustworthy and Reliable AI The Next Frontier. In *Explainable Artificial Intelligence (XAI) in Healthcare* (Vol. 1, pp. 119-129). CRC Press, Taylor & Francis Group.

Akhai, S. (2024). Trends and Environmental Impact of Paper Consumption: A Prognostic Scenario for the Indian Market by 2030-A Case Study. In *International Conference on Interdisciplinary Approaches in Civil Engineering for Sustainable Development* (Vol. 464, pp. 11-18). Springer Nature Singapore. DOI: 10.1007/978-981-97-0910-6_2

Akhai, S., & Abbass, M. (2025). Toward Resilient Futures: The Role of AI-Driven Strategies in Climate Adaptation. In *Nexus of AI, Climatology, and Urbanism for Smart Cities* (pp. 325-340). IGI Global Scientific Publishing.

Akhai, S., & Balu, V. (2022, December). Code Injection Assault & Mitigation Model to Prevent Attacks. In *2022 11th International Conference on System Modeling & Advancement in Research Trends (SMART)* (pp. 1324-1328). IEEE. DOI: 10.1109/SMART55829.2022.10046835

Akhai, S., & Khang, A. (2024). Efficient Hospital Waste Treatment and Management Through IoT and Bioelectronics. In *Revolutionizing Automated Waste Treatment Systems: IoT and Bioelectronics* (pp. 126-140). IGI Global. DOI: 10.4018/979-8-3693-6016-3.ch009

Akhai, S., & Khang, A. (2024). Energy Efficiency and Human Comfort: AI and IoT Integration in Hospital HVAC Systems. *Medical Robotics and AI-Assisted Diagnostics for a High-Tech Healthcare Industry*, 93-108.

Akhai, S., & Khang, A. (2024). Innovations in Medical Manufacturing: A Review of 3D Printing, Robotics, and Internet of Things (IoT). In *The Quantum Evolution* (Vol. 1, pp. 226-241). CRC Press.

Akhai, S., & Kumar, V. (2024). Quantum Resilience and Distributed Trust: The Promise of Blockchain and Quantum Computing in Defense. In *Sustainable Security Practices Using Blockchain, Quantum and Post-Quantum Technologies for Real Time Applications* (pp. 125-153). Springer Nature Singapore.

Akhai, S., & Pandita, P. (2013). Design Optimization of Failure Mode for Improving Quality Control on the Engine Assembly Line. *International Journal of Emerging Technology and Advanced Engineering*, 3(12), 201–204.

Akhai, S., Singh, S., Kaur, S., & Kaur, K. (2024). Advancing Aerospace Inspection With Terahertz Technology. In *New Innovations in AI, Aviation, and Air Traffic Technology* (pp. 195-211). IGI Global. DOI: 10.4018/979-8-3693-1954-3.ch010

Akhai, S., & Wadhwa, A. S. (2024). Wireless networking solutions for climate control and comfort in modern air conditioning systems. In *Intelligent Networks* (pp. 165–181). CRC Press. DOI: 10.1201/9781003541363-11

Akpuokwe, C. U., Adeniyi, A. O., & Bakare, S. S. (2024). Legal challenges of artificial intelligence and robotics: A comprehensive review. *Computer Science & IT Research Journal*, 5(3), 544–561. DOI: 10.51594/csitrj.v5i3.860

Alamouti, S., Arjomandi, F., Burger, M., & Altakrouri, B. (2024). Building Blocks to Empower Cognitive Internet with Hybrid Edge Cloud. *arXiv preprint arXiv:2402.00876.*

Aldoseri, A., Al-Khalifa, K. N., & Hamouda, A. M. (2024). AI-Powered Innovation in Digital Transformation: Key Pillars and Industry Impact. *Sustainability (Basel)*, 16(5), 1790. DOI: 10.3390/su16051790

Allawadi, K., Panwar, S., & Chugh, M. (2024). Advancing Autonomous Driving Through Federated Learning: A Collaborative Approach. In *Sustainable Innovation for Industry 6.0* (pp. 1-30). IGI Global. DOI: 10.4018/979-8-3693-3140-8.ch001

Amiri, Z., Heidari, A., Jafari, N., & Hosseinzadeh, M. (2024). Deep study on autonomous learning techniques for complex pattern recognition in interconnected information systems. *Computer Science Review*, 54, 100666. DOI: 10.1016/j.cosrev.2024.100666

Andreoni, M., Lunardi, W. T., Lawton, G., & Thakkar, S. (2024). Enhancing autonomous system security and resilience with generative AI: A comprehensive survey. *IEEE Access : Practical Innovations, Open Solutions*, 12, 109470–109493. DOI: 10.1109/ACCESS.2024.3439363

Arents, J., & Greitans, M. (2022). Smart industrial robot control trends, challenges and opportunities within manufacturing. *Applied Sciences (Basel, Switzerland)*, 12(2), 937. DOI: 10.3390/app12020937

Arif, S. M., & Akhai, S. (2024). Fostering a Sustainable and Disaster-Resilient Transportation Infrastructure. In *Challenges, Strategies, and Resiliency in Disaster and Risk Management* (pp. 205-219). IGI Global. DOI: 10.4018/979-8-3693-2721-0.ch009

Artyukhov, A., Wołowiec, T., Artyukhova, N., Bogacki, S., & Vasylieva, T. (2024). SDG 4, Academic Integrity and Artificial Intelligence: Clash or Win-Win Cooperation? *Sustainability (Basel)*, 16(19), 8483. DOI: 10.3390/su16198483

Ashima, R., Haleem, A., Bahl, S., Javaid, M., Mahla, S. K., & Singh, S. (2021). Automation and manufacturing of smart materials in Additive Manufacturing technologies using Internet of Things towards the adoption of Industry 4.0. *Materials Today: Proceedings*, 45, 5081–5088. DOI: 10.1016/j.matpr.2021.01.583

Bancarzewski, M. (2024). Fulfilling orders: automation, control and resistance at Amazon: A review of The Warehouse: Workers and Robots at Amazon, Alessandro Delfanti (Pluto, 2021). *International Socialism journal (ISJ), 182*(Spring), 157.

Bathla, G., Bhadane, K., Singh, R. K., Kumar, R., Aluvalu, R., Krishnamurthi, R., Kumar, A., Thakur, R. N., & Basheer, S. (2022). Autonomous vehicles and intelligent automation: Applications, challenges, and opportunities. *Mobile Information Systems*, 2022(1), 7632892. DOI: 10.1155/2022/7632892

Bautista, A. (2024). Big Data and Artificial Intelligence in Robotics: An Examination of their Role, Impact, and Future Directions. *Journal of Sustainable Technologies and Infrastructure Planning*, 8(3), 1–12.

Bhavana, S., Kolachala, R., Kotamarti, S., & Rao, T. V. N. (2025). AI Advancements in Self-Driving Vehicle Technology. In *Real-World Applications of AI Innovation* (pp. 149–174). IGI Global Scientific Publishing.

Bibri, S. E., Huang, J., Jagatheesaperumal, S. K., & Krogstie, J. (2024). The synergistic interplay of artificial intelligence and digital twin in environmentally planning sustainable smart cities: A comprehensive systematic review. *Environmental Science and Ecotechnology*, 20, 100433. DOI: 10.1016/j.ese.2024.100433 PMID: 38831974

Bijjahalli, S., Sabatini, R., & Gardi, A. (2020). Advances in intelligent and autonomous navigation systems for small UAS. *Progress in Aerospace Sciences*, 115, 100617. DOI: 10.1016/j.paerosci.2020.100617

Das, H. S. (2024). Current and Future Research Directions. *Applied AI and Humanoid Robotics for the Ultra-Smart Cyberspace*, 200-231.

Dilshad, N., Hwang, J., Song, J., & Sung, N. (2020, October). Applications and challenges in video surveillance via drone: A brief survey. In *2020 International Conference on Information and Communication Technology Convergence (ICTC)* (pp. 728-732). IEEE. DOI: 10.1109/ICTC49870.2020.9289536

Facchinetti, T., Li, H., Nocera, A., Peters, D., Routhu, T., Scanzio, S., & Wisniewski, L. (2024, September). Applying AI in the Area of Automation Systems: Overview and Challenges. In *2024 IEEE 29th International Conference on Emerging Technologies and Factory Automation (ETFA)* (pp. 1-8). IEEE.

Gabsi, A. E. H. (2024). Integrating artificial intelligence in industry 4.0: Insights, challenges, and future prospects–a literature review. *Annals of Operations Research*, 1–28. DOI: 10.1007/s10479-024-06012-6

Hakak, S., Gadekallu, T. R., Maddikunta, P. K. R., Ramu, S. P., Parimala, M., De Alwis, C., & Liyanage, M. (2023). Autonomous Vehicles in 5G and beyond: A Survey. *Vehicular Communications*, 39, 100551. DOI: 10.1016/j.vehcom.2022.100551

Jagatheesaperumal, S. K., Rahouti, M., Ahmad, K., Al-Fuqaha, A., & Guizani, M. (2021). The duo of artificial intelligence and big data for industry 4.0: Applications, techniques, challenges, and future research directions. *IEEE Internet of Things Journal*, 9(15), 12861–12885. DOI: 10.1109/JIOT.2021.3139827

Javaid, M., Haleem, A., Khan, I. H., & Suman, R. (2023). Understanding the potential applications of Artificial Intelligence in Agriculture Sector. *Advanced Agrochem*, 2(1), 15–30. DOI: 10.1016/j.aac.2022.10.001

Johansson, B., Eriksson, E., Berglund, N., & Lindgren, I. (2021). Robotic surgery: Review on minimally invasive techniques. *Fusion of Multidisciplinary Research. International Journal (Toronto, Ont.)*, 2(2), 201–210.

Khang, A., & Akhai, S. (2024). Green Intelligent and Sustainable Manufacturing: Key Advancements, Benefits, Challenges, and Applications for Transforming Industry. *Machine Vision and Industrial Robotics in Manufacturing*, 405-417.

Khang, A., & Akhai, S. (2025). E-Waste and Lithium-ion Battery Recycling Insights for Sustainable Transportation. In Khang, A. (Ed.), *Driving Green Transportation System Through Artificial Intelligence and Automation. Lecture Notes in Intelligent Transportation and Infrastructure*. Springer. DOI: 10.1007/978-3-031-72617-0_11

Kumar, H., Wadhwa, A. S., Akhai, S., & Kaushik, A. (2024). Parametric analysis, modeling and optimization of the process parameters in electric discharge machining of aluminium metal matrix composite. *Engineering Research Express*, 6(2), 025542. DOI: 10.1088/2631-8695/ad4ba9

Kumar, H., Wadhwa, A. S., Akhai, S., & Kaushik, A. (2024). Parametric optimization of the machining performance of Al-SiCp composite using combination of response surface methodology and desirability function. *Engineering Research Express*, 6(2), 025505. DOI: 10.1088/2631-8695/ad38ff

Kurian, S., Faiz, M., Zubair, M., & Ahamed, S. (2024, March). Advancing Safety and Efficiency in Human-Robot Interaction. In *2024 International Conference on Distributed Computing and Optimization Techniques (ICDCOT)* (pp. 1-8). IEEE. DOI: 10.1109/ICDCOT61034.2024.10515531

Licardo, J. T., Domjan, M., & Orehovački, T. (2024). Intelligent robotics—A systematic review of emerging technologies and trends. *Electronics (Basel)*, 13(3), 542. DOI: 10.3390/electronics13030542

Lin, N., Paul, R., Guerra, S., Liu, Y., Doulgeris, J., Shi, M., & Vrionis, F. D. (2024, November). The Frontiers of Smart Healthcare Systems. *Health Care*, 12(23), 2330. PMID: 39684952

Mala, S., Deep, U., Mala, E., & Akhai, S. (2025). Digital Health Technologies for Preventive Cardiology. In *Impact of Digital Solutions for Improved Healthcare Delivery* (pp. 379–400). IGI Global.

Motia, K., Kumar, R., & Akhai, S. (2024). AI and Smart Manufacturing: Building Industry 4.0. In *Modern Management Science Practices in the Age of AI* (pp. 1-28). IGI Global.

Murphy, R. R. (2019). *Introduction to AI robotics*. MIT press.

Nagaty, K. A. (2023). Iot commercial and industrial applications and AI-powered IoT. In *Frontiers of Quality Electronic Design (QED) AI, IoT and Hardware Security* (pp. 465–500). Springer International Publishing. DOI: 10.1007/978-3-031-16344-9_12

Najarian, S., Fallahnezhad, M., & Afshari, E. (2011). Advances in medical robotic systems with specific applications in surgery—A review. *Journal of Medical Engineering & Technology*, 35(1), 19–33. DOI: 10.3109/03091902.2010.535593 PMID: 21142589

Nawrat, Z., & Krawczyk, D. (2023). Robot-Based Medicine. Robots in medicine: mobile robots versus mobile decision, necessity versus possibility and future challenges. *Mobile Robot: Motion Control and Path Planning*, 127-162.

Ngu, J. C. Y., Tsang, C. B. S., & Koh, D. C. S. (2017). The da Vinci Xi: a review of its capabilities, versatility, and potential role in robotic colorectal surgery. *Robotic Surgery: Research and Reviews*, 77-85.

Obaigbena, A., Lottu, O. A., Ugwuanyi, E. D., Jacks, B. S., Sodiya, E. O., & Daraojimba, O. D. (2024). AI and human-robot interaction: A review of recent advances and challenges. *GSC Advanced Research and Reviews*, 18(2), 321–330. DOI: 10.30574/gscarr.2024.18.2.0070

Poljak, M., & Šterbenc, A. J. C. M. (2020). Use of drones in clinical microbiology and infectious diseases: Current status, challenges and barriers. *Clinical Microbiology and Infection*, 26(4), 425–430. DOI: 10.1016/j.cmi.2019.09.014 PMID: 31574337

Priyadharshini, S. (2024). Prospects and Challenges of AI in Robotics and Automation. *International Journal of Advanced Scientific Multidisciplinary Research*, 1(2), 46–49.

Rajamani, S. K., Iyer, R. S., & Ahmed, I. (2024). Current State of Robotic Surgery and Telesurgery: A Review of Current Developments and Future Insights. *Technologies for Sustainable Healthcare Development*, 194-216.

Rashid, A. B., & Kausik, A. K. (2024). AI revolutionizing industries worldwide: A comprehensive overview of its diverse applications. *Hybrid Advances*, 100277.

Reese, B. (2018). *The fourth age: Smart robots, conscious computers, and the future of humanity*. Simon and Schuster.

Rojas, S. (2024). Harnessing Computer Vision and Mechanical Design for Intelligent Robotic Systems. *Innovative Computer Sciences Journal, 10*(1).

Sharma, V., & Akhai, S. (2019). Trends in Utilization of Coal Fly Ash in India: A Review. *Journal of Engineering Design and Analysis*, 2(1), 12–16.

Shit, R. C. (2020). Precise localization for achieving next-generation autonomous navigation: State-of-the-art, taxonomy and future prospects. *Computer Communications*, 160, 351–374. DOI: 10.1016/j.comcom.2020.06.007

Singh, M., & Khan, S. A. L. A. (2024). Advances in Autonomous Robotics: Integrating AI and Machine Learning for Enhanced Automation and Control in Industrial Applications. *International Journal for Multidimensional Research Perspectives*, 2(4), 74–90. DOI: 10.61877/ijmrp.v2i4.135

Singh, S., & Akhai, S. (2024, July). Electronics in precision control for mechanical engineering: A brief overview. In *AIP Conference Proceedings* (Vol. 3121, No. 1). AIP Publishing. DOI: 10.1063/5.0221464

Singh, S., & Saini, B. S. (2021). Autonomous cars: Recent developments, challenges, and possible solutions. *IOP Conference Series. Materials Science and Engineering*, 1022(1), 012028. DOI: 10.1088/1757-899X/1022/1/012028

Soori, M., Arezoo, B., & Dastres, R. (2023). Artificial intelligence, machine learning and deep learning in advanced robotics, a review. *Cognitive Robotics*, 3, 54–70. DOI: 10.1016/j.cogr.2023.04.001

Teng, S., Hu, X., Deng, P., Li, B., Li, Y., Ai, Y., Yang, D., Li, L., Xuanyuan, Z., Zhu, F., & Chen, L. (2023). Motion planning for autonomous driving: The state of the art and future perspectives. *IEEE Transactions on Intelligent Vehicles*, 8(6), 3692–3711. DOI: 10.1109/TIV.2023.3274536

Wadhwa, S. A., Mahapara, A., Akhai, S., Kumar, D., & Kumar, P. (2024). Integrating Taguchi Optimization for Multi-Criteria Decision Making in Engineering Applications. In *Recent Theories and Applications for Multi-Criteria Decision-Making* (Vol. 1, No. 1, pp. 125-150). IGI Global.

Yeong, D. J., Velasco-Hernandez, G., Barry, J., & Walsh, J. (2021). Sensor and sensor fusion technology in autonomous vehicles: A review. *Sensors (Basel)*, 21(6), 2140. DOI: 10.3390/s21062140 PMID: 33803889

Zhao, S., Jiang, Z., Li, Y., Xu, J., & Wang, C. (2024, January). Key Components and Future Development Analysis of Humanoid Robots. In *2024 8th International Conference on Robotics, Control and Automation (ICRCA)* (pp. 140-147). IEEE. DOI: 10.1109/ICRCA60878.2024.10649218

Chapter 3
Digital Technologies in Education:
AI, Robotics, and Generational Challenges or Opportunities

Bitan Roy
https://orcid.org/0009-0006-6957-3263
Brainware University, India

Sanchita Ghosh
https://orcid.org/0009-0007-9421-5246
Brainware University, India

Piyal Roy
https://orcid.org/0009-0007-5378-2789
Brainware University, India

Saptarshi Kumar Sarkar
https://orcid.org/0009-0004-1786-8284
Brainware University, India

Nobhonil Roy Choudhury
https://orcid.org/0009-0009-1046-7492
Brainware University, India

ABSTRACT

This document evaluates the integration of robotics and artificial intelligence in learning and teaching practices, highlighting the potential benefits and challenges. It highlights the potential for increased STEM education, improved critical thinking skills, and increased student engagement. However, challenges include high costs, technical support, and reduced face-to-face interaction. Recommendations include applying for grants, forming partnerships, and implementing efficiency approaches. The document emphasizes the need for continuous professional development for educators to integrate these technologies into teaching. It also highlights the need for further development in blockchain, virtual/augmented reality, and AI for adaptive learning. Measures include providing student data protection

DOI: 10.4018/979-8-3693-6366-9.ch003

laws, increasing online resources, and developing professional development programs. The document also emphasizes the need for equal learning environments and ongoing research on generation, cohort, and age differences and educational technologies.

1. INTRODUCTION

Education is one of the sectors that have been most influenced by the fast growth of such technologies that include computers and the internet. Over the course of the past few years the manner in which we teach and learn has been greatly influenced by robotics, and Artificial Intelligence. Continuing on the previous section, this chapter focuses the interrelation between robotics, AI and generational aspect in education as well as its significance in understanding the changes in the field. With the advancement of digital technology, conventional formative methods of education have been subjected to drastic changes and new ideas for the improvement of the educational process are being provided. starting from the e-learning educational games to the virtual reality training, technology is gradually being incorporated into learning processes of the contemporary society (Davis and West, 2020). This is because the barrier of space, in the process of learning as boosted up by the frequent and convenient usage of computers, tablets and smart phones is no longer complex and can be done at any wanted time.

1.1 Importance of Understanding AI, Robotics, and Generational Dynamics

Modern technologies including robots and artificial intelligence are capable of fully revolutionizing educational models. With the help of the artificial intelligence applied to adaptive learning systems, it is possible for teachers to address each learner's need and preferred learning style to improve learning (Graesser et al. 2018). As it is similar to this, the application of robots to the classroom creates practical experiences whereby students enhance their abilities to think, create and solve problems (Katai et al. 2019). Moreover, the generational issues affect the student's attitude perspective from different generations towards the adoption and exploitation of technology (Prensky et al. 2009). This knowledge is essential is aiming to develop patterns of teaching that would address and meet the learners' diverse needs as well as their learning preferences effectively.

1.2 Overview of the Chapter Structure

This chapter is planned and divided to provide the most comprehensive analysis of robots, artificial intelligence, AI and generations in the field of education. They are the theoretical aspect of the topic, examples of the topic in practice, and possible ramifications of it in the future. They will be discussed in detail in the following parts of this paper: each issue accompanied by the presentation of case, ideas, and suggestions for teachers and legislators. This leads to the following objective of this chapter: to outline the general context of digital change in educational setting and reveal the interconnections and tensions between these components.

2. THE RISE OF AI IN EDUCATION

Owing to rewarding teaching and learning, artificial intelligence (AI) is revolutionizing the way of teaching. This section looks into the ways in which AI has been implemented in learning institutions for learning, grading, and support to learners. It also provides ideas about challenges and ethics implemented and attending AI in teaching.

2.1 Exploiting the Role of the Artificial Intelligence (AI) in Learning Environments

In the process of striving for improved learning outcomes and development of people's skills, artificial intelligence technologies, including machine learning and natural language processing, are being introduced into the educational space to an increasingly greater extent. Graesser et al. (2018) defined that ITS blends AI into a system where students learn in a style that suits them best, with materials that cover what a particular student lacks knowledge about. Such systems offer the formative intervention and context enhancement so as to enhance the learning outcomes of learners since the systems record and analyze the clients' interactions and their performance level and give due modifications to the instructional materials and rates of delivery instantly (VanLehn et al. 2011).Moreover, AI-Engaging platforms allow for dynamic changing the level of difficulty and the sequence of the producing material according to students' conceptual development (Baker et al. 2019). Most importantly, applying AI analytics allows educators to identify valuable information concerning students' learning processes and the areas they might need assistance with, which can help implement timely interventions and changes to the structure of teaching if needed (Baker et al. 2019).

2.2 Use of AI in Personalisation, Evaluation, and for Supporting the Learning of students

Modern AI algorithms also help facilitate the concept of personalization in learning paths, tests, and the content of instructions because students are different from each other regarding their interests, abilities, and weaknesses (Lacinski et al. 2024). feedback and recommendations may be given by the Intelligent Tutoring Systems and the more the learner uses the applications the better the metacognitive skills and self-regulated learning are developed (Baker et al. 2019). Also, AI integrated assessment systems help to reduce the duration for grading process and may provide students with the results immediately, thus contributing to the formative assessment processes (Norris et al. 2017).AI also enhances the functionality and effectiveness of administration processes such as time-tables, resources appointments, and advising among others, support services for students (Baker et al. 2019) Fachbereich 3: AI in support services. As a result, AI-based virtual assistants help students in case of answered questions; offering additional educational resources; and/or completing difficult tasks with the help of particular algorithms (Baker et al. 2019).

2.3 Machinised/Automated Learning Process (Adaptive Learning Systems)

The learning experiences that are tailored to the learners are created using artificial intelligence, machine learning, and data analysis tools, which comprise the definition of an adaptive learning system in an education platform. These computerized programs gather and process information arriving from students, concerning their activity, productivity, and hobbies as well as regarding predicted further behaviour. The system switches the content delivery approach by changing resources, materials, and the levels of difficulty in accordance with this data. Some benefits of the use of adaptive learning systems include efficiency, improved level of learners' engagement, and individually designed learning activities. However, equality, the costs of implementation, and the protection of information are some of the challenges experienced. Public access must be protected while student identity must be preserved, while at the same time ensuring equality in the access to technologies that are pivotal to learning. Future research shall focus on enhancing the effectiveness and precision of adaptive algorithms enhanced by implementing advanced AI and NLP that would contribute to enhancing these systems ability to provide the learner with personalize learning experience.

2.4 AI-Based Smart Help and Coaching Techniques

Tutoring and support tools are a large shift in education technology that allows the scope of individualized help to be ...scalable. These systems use machine learning algorithms for the analysis of the student data, artificial intelligence, particularly the Natural language processing for processing and responding to the student queries in simple and easy to understand language, and inspired interfaces in order to enhance the students' understanding. Such features of the learning as customization, threshold capability, and availability 24/7 are benefits. However, there are limitations mainly the dependency on the technology, biases in the AI, data privacy, and security issues. Promising directions include the developments in the class of artificial intelligence, including deep learning, and the rewarding learning, and the augmentation of the affective computing paradigm to increase the level of empathy, and the effectiveness of the interactions. It can be seen that there is a great potential for the adoption of artificial intelligence in tutoring and support especially given the listed keepers to learning outcomes and engagement.

2.5 Computer-Aided Grading and Evaluation

Automated grading and assessment systems incorporate the concepts of artificial intelligence and machine learning to grade student's work. This gives a veritable solution that can be regarded as scalable, reliable and effective compared to routine methods. The Predefined Scoring Rubrics, Machine Learning algorithms, and Natural Language Processing (NLP) are such systems developed to minimize grading biases, ease burden on the educators and provide instant feedback. It has benefits such as efficiency, consistency, impartiality and timeliness of feedback. However, challenges are precision and reliability, ethical issues, and obtaining the approval of teachers and students. To boost the accuracy and the reliability of automated grading and evaluation newer methods such as deep learning and neural networks are expected to be implemented in the future. Moreover, in order to gain acceptance from educators regarding AI decision-making processes, attempts that are aimed at raising the levels of explainability and openness will be crucial.

2.6 Educational Data Mining and Analytics

To enhance the teaching and learning process, data analytics in education entails gathering, evaluating, and interpreting enormous volumes of educational data. This strategy makes use of a variety of data sources, such as demographic data, engagement measures, and student performance, to improve educational results and guide decision-making. Data preparation, cleansing, analysis, and visualization are all part of data analytics. Improved teaching techniques, early intervention, resource optimization, and tailored learning are some advantages. Technical know-how, data security and privacy, and data quality are among the difficulties. Nonetheless, the potential for data analytics in education is bright, since developments in artificial intelligence and machine learning will likely augment its functionalities. The next possible enhancements of the prediction models are the real-time analysis and combination of various data sources to provide extended information about the educational climate. Taking everything into consideration, it is evident that data analytics gives educational institutions valuable information that may be used in evaluating institutional performance, optimising resource utilisation and enhancing students' learning.

2.7 Challenges and Ethical Considerations in AI Adoption in Education

This means that despite the possibilities of AI in education, there are a set challenges and ethical questions that relate to the widespread implementation of the technology. The ethical use of AI based on solving educational responsibilities is concerning due to the algorithmic bias, data privacy, and security issues (Williamson et al. 2023). In addition, the decisions carried out by AI algorithms will only increase the current inequalities and prolong systemic prejudice in learning environments (Pedro et al. 2019). Some criticism related to the depersonalization of teachers and the emerging deterioration of humanistic education approaches similar to the deterioration of the role of a teacher as a knowledgeable authority and the reduction of humanistic values in education were discussed by Williamson et al. (2023) concerning the use of AI in carrying out teaching tasks. Teachers now need to reflect on whether, how, and when the use of AI is going to change practice, the role of students, and the accomplishment of social-emotional learning goals (Selwyn et al. 2019). In conclusion, judging by the presented ideas, it can be noted that the use of AI in education can be very promising if the moral principles are considered when utilizing this tool as well as if the experts pay attention to the positive and negative impact of the AI in education. In order to ensure that such tools are serving justice, diversity and ethic stewardship for the benefits of students in the digital age, there is a need for collective responsibility among educators, legislators, and stakeholders.

3. ENHANCING PERSONALIZED LEARNING

Instructional experiences can be developed to meet the need, desire, and capacity of the individuals in every singular learner due to individualized learning which is encouraged and practised in the institution. It provides personal development for each student and assistance for the reasons of enhancing students' performance and their interest in the courses offered. Learner profiles, adaptable learning technology, competency-based progression, and variable learning pathways are the fundamental elements of personalized learning. Enhanced student agency, better results, equity, and greater engagement are all advantages of individualized learning. Complicated implementation, worries about data protection, and equal access are obstacles, nevertheless. More integration of AI and machine learning, an emphasis on data security and privacy, and developments in educational research are anticipated in the future of personalized learning. While improvements in educational research will lead to more effective individualized learning tactics, the incorporation of AI and machine learning will improve the responsiveness and adaptability of learning technology.

3.1 Improving Student Engagement and Retention

The key to schools and other educational center's success is the engagement or better yet, the persistence of the learners. Retention is the ability of the institution to keep their students until they complete their studies while engaged students show concern, interest and love in what they are studying. Engagement aspects include active learning, environment, student centered teaching methods and dealings, co-curricular activities. To get the pupils committed has its benefits and these include; enhancing academic achievement for the learners, promoting low drop out rates among learners as well as promoting interesting learning activities among learners. However, challenges include scarcity of resources, clients' heterogeneity, and complex assessment of students' participation. To facilitate three layers of adaptation and to provide more specific and broader actions that include all aspects of learning, well-being, and safety, future developments need to adopt innovative applications that include artificial intelligence and learning analytics. They will continue to devise unique ideas of how best to create a gender sensitive environment and learning atmosphere.

3.2 Reducing the Overload of Paperwork on Teachers

A teacher is frequently expected to do administrative work which has an implication of pulling him/her away from his/her core duties. Roles assigned to education and the interaction with students. This administrative load includes such things as Grading, record keeping, reporting and compliance. Improving student performance, work. This load is critical to educational pursuits since learners' achievement, parents' satisfaction, and teacher efficiency all hinge on its mitigation. Automating co-ordinate subsidiary administrative work, better communication, keep records of all data and provide training. Skills and knowledge which are considered as the foundation for professional development are components. A directive to teach for more time, higher data It includes such benefits as accuracy, better well-being of the teachers, and much more importantly, better support of the students. On the on the other side, other challenges include the initial costs of the implementation, `not-invented-here' syndrome, concerns with safety and confidentiality of information. The adaptation and integration of modern technologies such as Artificial Intelligence and Machine Learning are thus aspects that will dominate the future programs to reduce bureaucracy of the teaching profession. More advanced automation and with these technologies, one is able to attain practical predictive analyses, which will decentralize administrative tasks and improve decision-making.

3.3 Facilitating Data-Driven Decision-Making

The decision making that is done based on identification of data and carrying out an interpretation to arrive at a decision is referred to as data driven decision making (DDDM). Thus, efficiency in developing systems that enable the educators and administrators to collect, examine, and utilize data is crucial in order to enhance the students' performance and promote institutional effectiveness in the field of education. DDD: M looks at all the records of student attendance, performance indicators and level of participation in learning activities, and other relevant records in order to make decisions relating to teaching strategies, curriculum organization, resource management and formulation of policies within teaching institutions. It covers data acquisition and maintenance, the usage of the most advanced analysis methods and tools, data savviness promotion, and staff development and training. Analysis indicates other benefits of DDDM which includes; better instructional methodologies, improved students' performance, increased responsibility and accountability, resources optimization among others. However, obstacles are the availability and quality of data, data security and privacy and change aversion. Possible future developments of DDDM in the educational context are likely to involve creating more robust data management frameworks, improving everyone's understanding of the use and importance of data, and leveraging such progressive technologies as artificial intelligence and machine learning.

3.4 Robotics: Transforming the Classroom Experience

Robotics is revolutionizing the learning process by enhancing problem-solving skills and combining various subjects like science, technology, engineering, and mathematics. This approach prepares students for future careers in these growing fields. Robotics is particularly beneficial for children with disabilities, as it fosters teamwork and encourages exploration. Students can apply theoretical concepts to real-life situations, such as coding a robot to perform specific functions. Teachers can also use robotics to enhance their teaching methods, enhancing interaction, relevance, and practicality. This approach instills a passion for learning and equips children with the necessary knowledge and skills for a rapidly evolving technological world.

3.5 Integration of Robotics in Educational Curriculum

Teachers are revealing the effectivity of adopting robots in the classrooms in teaching different lessons, regardless of whether in the lessons of robotics engineering, coding, or lessons that fall under STEM which is an abbreviation for science, technology, engineering as well as mathematics (Katai et al. 2019). Grouping of students can carry out inquiries in topics like robotics, coding, or engineering analysis by utilizing sets like VEX Robotics and LEGO Mindstorms (Lane et al. 2013). Similarly, the activities such as RoboCup and FIRST Robotics Competition are organizational cooperative project-based learning events for professional robotic skills fused with knowledge of problem-solving and collaboration (Neece et al. 2018). Teachers should try to use robotics in their curriculum and make concepts and such theories concrete by relating them to real life incidences (Bers et al. 2008). Besides evoking ingenuity and generativity robotics activities build inter-disciplinary relations established through connecting the ideas belonging to mathematical, physical, computing sciences and engineering disciplines (Resnick et al. 2009).

3.6 Hands-on Learning Experiences Facilitated by Robotics

Robotics is one of the technologies which can provide really practical learning environments which involve students experimenting in the process. That is why, using the elements of robotics kits, students can own their own education which includes designing, constructing, programming, and testing the robots (Anwar et al. 2019). Through iterative design cycles, students develop the ability to solve problems, design a product through experimenting as well as work in groups (Bers et al. 2008). In addition, real-life challenges and situations are often integrated into robotic assignments, which stimulates students to solve such issues using the acquired knowledge and skills (Sapounidis et al. 2020). They learn critical thinking skills and resilience when faced with the challenge of solving specific tasks through constructing robots for navigating through obstacle or physical courses or for solving specific problems (Katai et al. 2019).

3.7 Impacts on Student Engagement, Creativity, and Problem-Solving Skills

Robotics activities can boost students' enthusiasm and interest in STEM fields, making learning fun and fostering teamwork. These activities also enhance leadership, cooperation, and communication skills, which are crucial in their future working environments. Robotics promotes creativity and innovation by encouraging students to find innovative solutions to difficult questions. Experimentation and prototyping help students understand that failure is a necessary component of success and perfecting their craft. Robotics also helps children find employment in STEM sectors and develop technology by enabling them to be inventors and innovators. In conclusion, robotics can transform the educational process in the classroom, providing students with unique ideas and imagination essential for problem-solving. Teachers can prepare children to become effective learners and innovators in a technology-rich world.

4. GENERATIONAL CHALLENGES IN EDUCATION

Generation gaps in education negatively impact educational institutions and learning processes. Issues include the digital divide, turnover-cycled knowledge, changing learning capabilities, diminishing concentration levels, and variations in education standards and values. The younger generation's focus on gig economy, technology-related jobs, and entrepreneurship is changing their activities. Mental health and wellbeing are also a concern for the younger generation. Achievement pressure is likely to be higher among students due to competitiveness in modern schools. Cultural and social factors play a significant role in diversity and inclusion, and these differentials must be addressed diplomatically. Curriculum updates are also a challenge due to the rapid pace of technology and society development. Balancing old mindsets with new knowledge and skills is crucial. Continuing education is important for generation working learning and flexibility. Addressing generational concerns in education requires a complex approach considering various needs, wants, and concerns. Schools can enhance the success of all students by embracing technology and supporting students with disabilities.

4.1 Millennial Generation and Their Attitudes Towards Learning and Technology

Students who are categorized into different generations will have different approach to learning, communication and attitude to the use of technology due to their background experience history and culture (Prensky et al. 2009). With digital natives, they were born and raised to be incorporated in a technologically advanced society and they are used to multimedia learning. They are normally younger generations including the Millennial and Generation Z citizens (Palfrey et al. 2011). On the other hand, the older groups of students like the baby boomers and generation X are digital immigrants meaning they will be relatively more uncomfortable with the use of these technologies and would prefer the traditional methods of content delivery than technologies (Prensky et al. 2009). Thus, to enhance students' inclusiveness and tutorial effectiveness of the different generations who are tuned by the digital tools corresponding to their preferences, preferences, and learning styles, the distinction between generations is rather significant (Helsper et al. 2010). Teachers require this knowledge to be able to use the technology on the concerned generation's learning preferences advantageously with the aim of enhancing the learning outcome and interest of students (Kennedy et al. 2010).

4.2 Addressing the Digital Divide: Combined With Access and Equity Issues Across Generations

The difference in access to as well as ability to utilize technology is referred to as the 'digital divide' and targets lower classes of people and minorities (Warschauer et al. 2004). Hargittai et al further explain that difficulties may arise when senior citizens, particularly from the poor background try to embrace new technologies despite the the fact that the younger generation individuals have equal or improved access to such technologies and digital literacy skills. It is now the teacher and legislator's responsibility to ensure that equal opportunity for using technologies and other digital learning tools should be as much a priority as faculties dream (S. Warschauer, et al. 2004). For underprivileged areas, this implies that there are necessary computer hardware, software, high-speed internet, and digital literacy training (Helsper et al. 2010). For any case, teachers can also apply all manner of teaching strategies that do not in any way disregard learning abilities of the students so that learners of diverse technical competence can be taught smartly as pointed by Kennedy et al. (2010).

4.3 Strategies for Bridging the Gap Between Digital Natives and Digital Immigrants

To bridge the gap between digital immigrants and natives in education, a cooperative strategy valuing mutual respect and intergenerational learning is needed. Teachers can support intergenerational mentoring programs, where younger generations receive guidance from digital immigrants and natives, and elders receive mentoring from digital natives. This fosters mutual learning, empathy, and comprehension among students of various ages. Professional development programs can equip teachers with the necessary skills to incorporate technology into lesson plans and engage students of all generations. A learner-centered approach promotes inclusivity and diversity, enabling students to succeed in the digital age.

4.4 Benefits of Robotics in Education

Robotics in education involves using programmable robots to enhance various aspects of education, particularly in STEM subjects. This approach enhances students' thinking and prepares them for careers in IT-intensive sectors. Robotics education promotes problem-solving, collaboration, creativity, and teamwork, making it more engaging and engaging. STEM students learn robotics to better understand and appreciate real-life STEM studies. The growing demand for automation and robotics professionals makes early introduction of robotic systems crucial. Additionally, robotics education promotes soft skills like leadership, teamwork, and communication, which are useful in various life and career fields. However, challenges such as curriculum incorporation, high costs, and equal opportunities and access pose challenges. The integration of robotics programs can be costly due to capital expenditures for hardware, software, and teacher professional development. Therefore, it is crucial to ensure that all students receive robotics lessons, especially in poor or resource-limited schools.

4.5 Reducing Theoretical Learning and Stress on Memorization of Facts and Figures

Closely related to the concept of practical learning, which is also known as learning by doing, experiential learning is one of the best ways to enhance the understanding of principles, improve skills, and, thus, vitalize ideals. So the linking of learning experiences means that it becomes more meaningful and effective to the learner. Some elements of learning which entails practical activities include; engagement, actual use, collaboration, and interaction, team work, and acquisition of specific skills. First, there is enhanced understanding and retention characteristically obvious in relation to hard contents; second, there is increased motivation and engagement evidently when learning by experience; third, there is the feature of transferable skill acquired from the exercise; and lastly, there is the feature of improved problem-solving. When several senses and realistic approaches are applied, the learners have a better understanding of what has been taught, and such information is retained in their memories for quite some time. Nonetheless, resource intensity, teacher preparation and training, and limitations of evaluation present the fundamental challenges regarding hands on learning. However, there is one more weakness that can be the problem for institutions with a low budget – the issue of resource intensity even in case when preparation and training of teachers are the key factors that can guarantee the success. Especially, the teachers must know the kindergarten curriculum in order to design and facilitate the experiential learning activities as well as to assess the students' progress. One of the classic assessment difficulties is that other forms of knowledge and skills that can be gained through the teleconference and other related exercises may not be fully assessed with examination quizzes and tests. Thus, it becomes important to design apposite assessment tools to facilitate the right assessment of experiential learning. In balance of that said, the following are some of the benefits of using experiential approach Learning: explicit comprehending, motivational, transferable skills, and problem solving skills.

4.6 Facilitating Participation and Interest

Motivation and involvement are crucial in the educational process, influencing students' performance, persistence, and willingness. Motivation can be extrinsic (praising and grades) or intrinsic (interestingness/ enjoyment). Anticipative learning strategies increase participation through activities like group assignments, problem-solving, and discussions. Students' motivation can be enhanced by relating knowledge to real-life issues and engaging in decision-making processes. Motivation and engagement are linked to better academic outcomes, higher tenacity, resilience, wellbeing, and a positive learning climate. Attention-focused students are more likely to complete exercises, contribute to class discussions, and perform well. Motivated students are able to work hard and never give up, which is essential in both academic and life. However, maintaining engagement intensity is challenging, especially with interruptions, homework assignments, and various interests. Balancing intrinsic and extrinsic motivations is essential to prevent over-reliance on extrinsic motives. To create a productive learning environment, sound strategies aimed at increasing motivation and learners' activity are necessary.

4.7 Supporting Communities and Groups

Collaboration and team work are crucial skills for students in personal, academic, and career life. They involve working together to achieve a goal and use resources, information, and responsibilities effectively. Encouraging students to work in groups boosts learning and helps them deal with challenges in society. Key features of group work include politics, cooperation, responsibilities, assignments, roles, and conflict. Coordination allows for extensive exchange of ideas and problem-solving, while communication skills enable students to generate ideas, listen to peers, and engage in meaningful debates. Assigning specific tasks ensures better organization, increasing effectiveness and efficiency in learning, fostering social and interpersonal skills, and preparing students for the workforce. However, challenges such as uneven involvement and conflict management arise, making it essential for educators to design fair and efficient assessment practices for group work.

4.8 Future Technological Careers of the Students Are Being Prepared

Thus, any students who wants to be ready for professions in technology must receive a wide liberal education with the emphasis on technical skills, problem solving and adaptability. This is critical in today's fast evolving technology environment, as this would help identify who among the three primary audience groups is most likely to engage in negative word-of-mouth and replace their current system with Oracle's Hyperion EPM solution. Thus, the key components of this education are technical content and skills, critical thinking and problem-solving, practical training, interpersonal and group work, and adaptability and lifelong learning. This education has several benefits such as: high probability of gaining employment, creativity and coming up with unique ideas, economic development, besides, character transformation. Students on an engineering programme with good technical back ground have a higher chance of getting an employer in technology industries and therefore expanding their operations. Despite the fact that education improves one's capacity to reason and solve problems, it also fosters technology and other professions. There is, however, a number of challenges that prevent proper training of children for careers in technology. Not all students can get a quality STEM education and quality frames, so access and equity play a big role. Another challenge to the implementation of up to date curriculum is the rapidly growing rate in the advancement of technology. Thus, for the college to deliver quality education, constant curriculum update and teacher training is compulsory. The process of preparing kids in technology might be quite challenging, but if a teacher can come up with different approaches in teaching technology, it becomes fun and relevant.

5. CHALLENGES AND LIMITATIONS OF ROBOTICS IN EDUCATION

Therefore, when applied as an element in education the use of robotics offers a unique possibility to transform processes of learning and teaching due to its practical and stimulating character. However, for educators, and the institutions the following advantages have to overcome a number of barriers and limitations.

Financial Constraints

Cost of Implementation: There are two challenges that explain the situation: high implementation costs of robotics programs. This includes the cost of acquiring the bots, feed, cost of software, and the specific hardware that might be necessary. Moreover, maintenance and update costs could be a burden to school budgets more so in the districts with modest finances (Mubin et al., 2013).

Technical Challenges

Complexity and Maintenance: Working in parallel, these robotic systems are not always easy to build and maintain in operation. Such systems might not be diagnosed and repaired by schools' staff, which would mean that downtime and thus brief class periods would be inevitable. Essentially, it is important to ensure educators and personnel are adequately trained sufficiently to run and or utilize these systems (Bers et al. 2008).

Software and Hardware Compatibility: Sometimes the compatibility issues of different pieces of hardware and/or software can be quite a challenge. It implies that there is a need for a meticulous approach towards teaching, and integration of a new robotic system with present day methods of imparting knowledge through liberal use of present day instruments and tools of educational technology (Papert, 1980).

Teacher Training and Professional Development

Need for Specialized Training: Teachers require professional training and development in or per to incorporate the use of robotics in the classroom. The full realization of robots programs may be prevented by the apprehension or lack of preparedness of many teachers when it comes to the application of robotics (Kim et al., 2013).

Ongoing Professional Development: To keep teachers abreast of the most recent developments in robotics and teaching methodologies, they must participate in ongoing professional development. However, due to time limits and budget limitations, offering regular training can be difficult (Alimisis, 2013).

Curriculum Integration

Alignment with Educational Standards: It can be challenging to incorporate robotics into current curriculum and match them to academic standards. Teachers need to make sure that robotics activities are integrated into their lessons in a way that improves learning objectives across topic areas, rather than being optional (Eguchi, 2014).

Balancing Traditional and Technological Teaching Methods: It might be difficult to strike the correct balance between cutting-edge technical approaches and conventional teaching methods. Teachers need to make sure that the integration of robotics enhances rather than diminishes the fundamental knowledge and abilities taught in the classroom (Papert, 1980).

Accessibility and Equity

Digital Divide: In the event that access to robotics education is not dispersed fairly, there is a chance that the digital gap will worsen. Due to limited access to these technologies, students from lower-income families or schools with inadequate resources may see a decline in their educational chances and results (Ritz & Moye, 2011).

Inclusive Education: It is crucial to ensure that robotic education is recorded so that children with disabilities and needs have an equal opportunity to possible education. This requires the development of adaptable Robotic systems as well as learning contents that will be appropriate for several types of learning (Alimisis, 2013).

Pedagogical Challenges

Ensuring Engagement and Relevance: Robotics can enhance students learning, but sometimes the challenge may arise especially while trying to ensure all the students are motivated to learn through the robotics activities. Courses, as delivered by teachers, have to contain information from students' daily experience and future working environment (Bers et al. 2008).

Assessment of Learning Outcomes: The learning objectives concerning the robotic education could be quite hard to measure. The knowledge and skills attained in robotic activities may not be well addressed by the normal assessment tools, thus development of new assessments tools is done (Eguchi, 2014).

5.1 Cost and Resource Constraints

For student learning and engagement, the use of robotics in the classroom has several advantages. But there are significant obstacles for educators and institutions due to the high costs and limited resources involved in putting robotics programs into place and keeping them running. These resource- and money-related obstacles are thoroughly examined in this section.

Financial Constraints

Initial Investment Costs: Buying robotic kits and associated hardware can entail an upfront financial commitment that many schools, especially those with tight budgets, find intolerable. Due to their high cost, impoverished schools find it challenging to purchase high-quality robots, sensors, computers, and other essential equipment (Mubin, Stevens, Shahid, Mahmud, & Dong, 2013).

Ongoing Maintenance and Upgrades: Robotics programs include continuing costs for upkeep, repairs, and upgrades after the initial purchase. Robotic equipment needs to be maintained on a regular basis and may have parts replaced in order to remain functional. Furthermore, in order to keep up with the most recent developments, software and hardware must be updated on a regular basis due to the rapid evolution of technology (Bers et al. 2008).

Resource Constraints

Infrastructure Requirements: An suitable power source, dependable internet access, and sufficient physical space for robotics activities are all necessary for the successful integration of robots in education. It's possible that many schools lack the infrastructure required to host these initiatives, particularly those in rural or economically poor locations (Eguchi, 2014).

Technical Support and Expertise: It can be difficult for schools to provide the necessary technical know-how and support to oversee robotics initiatives. It can be expensive and logistically challenging to hire or educate employees with the necessary technical expertise to troubleshoot problems, make repairs, and assist teachers in incorporating robots into their courses (Mubin et al., 2013).

Teacher Training and Professional Development

Cost of Training Programs: Though expensive, supplying educators with the training they need to successfully integrate robotics into the classroom is crucial. Programs for professional development that give educators the know-how and assurance to employ robotics technologies may cost a lot of money, both for the training itself and for hiring replacement teachers while the program is in session (Kim, Kim, Lee, Spector, & DeMeester, 2013).

Time and Resource Allocation: In addition to the financial costs, schools need to set aside time and resources so that instructors can take part in continuing professional development and training. This can be difficult because teachers already have very busy schedules and must manage their training obligations with their teaching responsibilities (Alimisis, 2013).

Equity and Accessibility

Disparities in Access: Resource and financial limitations may make already-existing gaps in educational opportunity worse. While schools in lower-income locations could find it difficult, those in rich areas are more likely to be able to pay the significant costs connected with robotics programs. Students from under resourced schools have less access to the advantages of robotics education as a result, creating an unfair playing field (Ritz & Moye, 2011).

Inclusive Education: It takes more resources and modifications to make robotics instruction accessible to all students, including those with disabilities. Many factors may lead to the enhancement of cost and complication with complimentary development and provision of inclusion materials, usable interfaces, and supporting technology (Koziatek et al. 2015).

Addressing the Challenges

Funding and Grants: Later, schools can seek other methods of funding from different grants that are set up by the government and other private foundations as well as from industrial partnerships in order to compensate the worst financial constrains. The bodies that provide support for STEM knowledge development provide schools with funds with which they can include robots and other technologies activities (Eguchi, 2014).

Collaborative Partnerships: Relationships with the companies, academic institutions and community organizations enable schools for more financing, resources and knowledge. Besides paving way to the creation of more appealing learning activities for students, shared pursuits may help in sharing the costs and responsibilities for robotics instruction (Bers et al. 2008).

Cost-Effective Solutions: Schools may look for options where costs could be even lower, for instance, reusing older equipment and materials, using free software and adopting open-source solutions, participating in robotics competitions where equipment and many materials are either free or locally available at a very low price. It mentioned that these tactics can reduce the cost and expand the opportunity of robotics instruction (Mubin et al. 2013).

5.2 Staff development and training for education.

Thus, the applicability of these technologies by educators is important in the incorporation of robots in education systems. To provide teachers with ready information and confidence in executing robotics centered exercise, professional development and training play a major role. This section provides an understanding of the challenges involved and prospects of the professional development and training of educators in teaching robotics.

Importance of Training and Professional Development

Enhancing Teacher Competence and Confidence: Effective training enhances the training of instructors on the use of robotics technology to boost their proficiency hence confidence when incorporating these resources into their training plans. Five practical applications are presented below: Teachers are more likely to use robots in meaningful ways that enhanced students' learning when they perceive themselves as comfortable with it (Kim et al., 2013).

Keeping Up with Technological Advances: Since the field of robotics technology is advancing fast, it is necessary for educators to improve their professional competence in order to be ready to implement modern recent developments.

Aligning with Educational Standards: Programs for professional development assist teachers in coordinating robotics activities with curriculum objectives and requirements. By ensuring that robotics is integrated into the larger educational framework rather than being treated as an add-on, this alignment helps students meet learning objectives in a variety of subject areas (Eguchi, 2014).

Challenges in Training and Professional Development

Cost of Training Programs: It might be expensive to provide thorough training and professional growth. High-quality training programs must be funded by schools, which may mean substantial financial outlays. School budgets may be strained by the expense of bringing in professional trainers, buying training supplies, and covering replacement teachers during training sessions (Alimisis, 2013).

Time Constraints: Finding time for professional development can be difficult for teachers because they frequently have busy schedules. Careful preparation and adaptability are needed to strike a balance between training sessions and regular teaching obligations. Amidst their regular burden, many educators might find it difficult to set aside time for training (Ritz & Moye, 2011).

Variability in Technological Proficiency: Different educators have different levels of technology proficiency. It might be difficult to create training programs that address such a wide range of skill sets. Initiatives for professional development in robots must be tailored to the needs of both inexperienced and seasoned users (Mubin, Stevens, Shahid, Mahmud, & Dong, 2013).

Strategies for Effective Professional Development

Ongoing and Sustained Training: Instead of being one-time activities, professional growth should be continuous and sustained. Training opportunities that are ongoing, including webinars, coaching sessions, and workshops, assist educators in developing and honing their craft over time. According to Kim et al. (2013), consistent assistance guarantees that educators stay involved and informed about the most recent advancements in robotics teaching.

Collaborative Learning Communities: It is crucial to create collaborative learning communities where teachers may exchange best practices, obstacles, and experiences. Collaborative efforts and peer support provide a feeling of community and group development. By exchanging experiences and insights, educators can become more proficient in their use of robotics generally (Eguchi, 2014).

Integration with Classroom Practice: Classroom practice and professional development ought to be tightly related. Teachers are able to implement what they learn in actual classroom environments when their training programs incorporate practical, hands-on components. Teachers can obtain practical experience and boost their confidence by simulating classroom circumstances during training (Bers et al. 2008).

Utilizing Online Resources and Platforms: Using online tools and resources can increase the flexibility and accessibility of professional development. Online tutorials, workshops, and courses give educators the freedom to learn whenever and wherever it is most convenient for them. Digital platforms also make resource sharing and group learning easier (Alimisis, 2013).

Engaging with Industry Experts: Engagement of robotics professionals and experts can boost the professional development programs. Experts can enlighten the professionals on the current advancements in technology and advice on how to integrate robotics into learning. Other sources of useful resources and help may also be found mainly through partnerships with academic institutions and tech firms (Ritz and Moye 2011).

5.3 Curriculum Incorporation Into Existing Packages

The integration of robots in today's curricula proves that there exists a common technique of enhancing the learning process of students and at the same time enable them to develop essential thinking skills. However, in an effort to meet contemporary educational vectors and guidelines, the integration proves challenging and requires planning. Pros and cons, challenges, and effective ways to implement robots in today's curricula are discussed within this section.

Reasons for Incorporation of Robotics in Education

Enhancing STEM Education: Robotics education can be rather easily coupled with STEM training due to the fact that it permits for application-based opportunities to strengthen concepts. Eguchi (2014) has concluded that students show better understanding and actual retention of math and science knowledge as the application of those facts and equations in robots.

Developing Critical Thinking and Problem-Solving Skills: Students are driven to construct and code robots to perform certain tasks, this advanced critical thinking and problem solving skills in robotics learning. Munbin, Stevens, Shahid, Mahmud, and Dong (2013) opine that these tasks enhance the critical thinking skills in the students since they have to think rationally in order to solve problems and finesse their designs.

Encouraging Creativity and Innovation: Students can search for and generate new ideas because designing and programming robots is in the creative domain. It should be noted that open-ended issues are characteristic for robotics projects, meaning that various ideas and options can be used for their completion and, according to this, the students' freethinking and inventive activities are developed (Bers et al. 2008).

Fostering Collaboration and Teamwork: In many robotics activities, students have to work in groups to meet set goals which are common for everybody. Collaboration, leadership, and communication are all cultivated by this teamwork and are necessary for success in both academic and professional contexts (Ritz & Moye, 2011).

Challenges in Integrating Robotics into Curricula

Alignment with Educational Standards: Aligning robotics activities with current curriculum objectives and educational standards is one of the main problems. In order to prevent robotics projects from being seen as extracurricular or supplemental, educators must make sure they complement the corc curriculum and achieve learning objectives (Alimisis, 2013).

Teacher Preparedness and Training: For integration to be effective, educators must receive the necessary training and preparation to use robotics in the classroom. Comprehensive professional development is essential since many educators might not have the confidence or background in robotics to use these technologies effectively (Kim, Kim, Lee, Spector, & DeMeester, 2013).

Resource and Time Constraints: Adopting robotics education calls for a large investment of time, money, and supplies. Infrastructure, software, and robotics kits must be purchased by schools, and instructors must have time to prepare and carry out robotics programs. Widespread adoption may be significantly hampered by these resource limitations (Eguchi, 2014).

Curricular Flexibility: In traditional curriculum, there might be limited possibility of teaching extra subjects or activities which can a be rigid. Depending on the case, it may be required to reconsider the objectives of curricula so as to include robots and have the ability to include new material and teaching methods. This very complex process requires support of administrators and other stakeholders (Ritz & Moye, 2011).

Strategies for Effective Integration

Cross-Disciplinary Projects: Some of the recommended procedures include developing cross-curricular projects aimed at integrating robots with math, science, art, and/or language arts. This method can help teachers relate to the goals of the curriculum and enlighten them on the versatility of robotics in various fields (Bers et al. 2008).

Incremental Implementation: Based on the research, educational institutions should start using robots in education but start with a small pilot project. These pilot strategies can help in identifying desirable practices and problems as well as in building support among educators, parents, and children before expansion of the pilot initiatives (Alimisis, 2013).

Curriculum Mapping and Integration: The following can be implemented in order to maintain coherence and consistency; Curriculum map which depicts how the robotics activities correspond to the current standards or learning activities. In the process of mapping, essential concepts and skills which can be supported by robotics are first defined and later integrated into curricula (Kim et al. 2013).

Leveraging Existing Resources: The marked schools can access existing resources in supporting robotics instruction such as computer labs, science equipment, and teachers in technology. By reusing such resources, it becomes possible to reduce costs and thus enhance the feasibility of integration (Eguchi, 2014).

Collaboration and Partnerships: A good way to enhance the operations of robotics programs is partnering with other organizations from close by established companies and institutions and neighborhood associations can help robotics programs by providing additional money, know-how, and support. Such collaborations are likely to enhance the quality of robotics education and provide the necessary practicum to student's projects (Mubin et al. 2013).

5.4 Risk Reduction of Direct Contact With Other People

Thus, it can be concluded that there are many benefits that can be derived from implementing robotics in school such as better performance and acquisition of problem solving skills. It also causes concerns as to whether there will be even less face-to-face interaction. In this part, the author discusses the impacts of reduced interaction with other people, challenges, and ways to mitigate them.

Implications of Reduced Human Interaction

Impact on Social Skills Development: Another concern is as the adoption of robotics and automated system increases within education, then the affection or communication between students face-to-face is likely to reduce. SEL elements, such as empathy, communication, and teamwork, fostered through social interaction with other people (Darling-Hammond, Flook, Cook-Harvey, Barron, & Osher, 2019). In specific ways, robotics poses a risk to these interactions eradicating possibilities for enhancing social interaction and thus affecting the social relationships of pupils.

Teacher-Student Relationships: Hattie (2009) confirms that the conviction between the teacher and learners, learners' motivation, engagement, and achievement are boosted. The Social Distance between teachers and students may reduce as well as the number and interaction quality if robotics and AI-dominated sections in teaching and assessment work. This cut may well influence the one on one instructions and support they provide to the students which are very necessary for the interaction of each learners.

Classroom Dynamics: Robotic technology replaces more part of a normal classroom where the part of a person teaching becomes a smaller part of the overall package. Even though this might contribute to increased independent learning and research, it may reduce direct interaction with peers and group work which is vital in creating togetherness and group problem solving skills (Jones et al. 2023).

Challenges Posed by Reduced Human Interaction

Isolation and Loneliness: Students should feel more lonely and left alone if robotics is implemented within a classroom setting more often. Maintaining a human connection can foster a healthy relationship between the child and his or her teacher and peers thus enhancing the student's performance as well as his or her well-being (Cacioppo & Cacioppo, 2018).

Equity and Inclusion: This is that due to the prejudice AI and robotics are not free from, their application in the education system can widen the existing gaps. It means that humans could interact less, therefore there would be less supervision and fewer opportunities to challenge prejudices, which, in some cases, can improperly treat pupils from various backgrounds. There is a constant human effort that is required to remove any bias for robotic educations so as to ensure that it is the same for everybody.

Overreliance on Technology: Such a dependence can make a student or employee incapable of learning or solving a problem without the help of robots. Education requires uses of technology competency but the interpersonal and thinking competencies can only be effectively trained face to face and in conventional methods (Turkle, 2015).

Strategies to Mitigate Reduced Human Interaction

Blended Learning Approaches: To meet and establish that balance, schools can adopt the blended learning models in implementing benefits inherent in robotics but at the same time consider the need for queueness interaction. These methods help in making sure that the students benefit from one-on-one tutoring as well as from advanced robotics procedures that incorporate technology in teaching practice, together with the more conventional one-on-one face-to-face teaching (Graham, 2013).

Facilitating Collaborative Projects: Designing robotics tasks which require collaboration and coordination can help maintain students' face-to-face interaction. Cooperative planning and working is facilitated by group assignments that enhance interaction, conflict-solving and students' co-studying (Jones et al., 2023).

Professional Development for Educators: For the students, it is crucial to establish a strong educator-student relationship, so professional development of educators should focus on engraining the use of robotics into instruction. To help teachers avoid depersonalizing the learning process and, instead, achieve the right balance between the application of the technology and interpersonal communication, training programs can be helpful (Darling-Hammond et al. 2019).

Monitoring and Evaluation: It means, less human intercession is present in Robotics so these kinds of programs can be ever-watched and ever-monitored so that probable issues can be identified easily. Therefore, in order to perform the necessary assessments of the impact of robotics on the social and emotional growth and to make the necessary changes to the curriculum, the schools can solicit opinion from parents, teachers and children (Graham, 2013).

5.5 Opportunities for Collaboration: Implementing the Notion of AI, Robotics, and Generational Synergy

By considering the impact of AI and robotics in education, it can be noted that the delivery of lessons is becoming diverse since it consists of flexible learning environments that cater to the learners' wants. While robotics exercises allow kinesthetic learners to engage their body, AI adaptive learning systems analyze the students' actions and outcomes of their operations. In this way, with the help of the technologies mentioned above, teachers can provide the children with the paths that will be rather helpful for the child, who has the tendencies to be a tactile, visual, or an auditory learner and that is why the teachers should welcome these technologies in order to provide the children with the necessary conditions in the school. Based on this AI and robotics integration, the life experience of elderly people and the knowledge of young people can be exchanged through various digital interfaces. Taking everything into consideration, robotics as well as AI are revolutionizing the education systems by fostering cooperation between generations. Thus, technology plays a vital role in the design of learning environments that embrace diversity and make a provision for the learners with disabilities. Text-to-speech and speech-to-text transcription are two features that apply AI to provide accommodations to learners with diverse forms of learning difficulties, which are for instance, visual and hearing impairments (Baker et al. 2019). Also, the use of robotics platforms can be adjusted so that a child with physical disabilities will be able to participate in interactive learning activities right along with the rest of the class (Anwar et al. 2019). It allows teachers to ensure that all the learners have equal opportunities to access educational materials and learning facilities with the help of assistive technologies and incorporation of the features of a universal design (Baker et al. 2019).

5.6 Promoting Inter-Generational Learning and Engagement on the Basis of Digital Applications

Digital immigrants and natives are brought together through cross-generational activities and sharing tasks via technologies. Learners from different age groups can interact and share knowledge through online forums, classes, and project areas. Digital stories foster personal experiences and cultural values, while robotics and encoding practices create intergenerational learning for older individuals. Educators can maximize technology use and increase stakeholder engagement by establishing diverse groups of students from different generations. The symbiosis of robotics, AI, and many generations opens opportunities for effective and evocative classrooms. Teachers can prepare children for a future requiring increased cooperation due to globalization by using technology to teach students' abilities and facilitate intergenerational learning and collaboration.

6. SOLVING GENERATIONAL ISSUES AT A DEF COMMUNITY COLLEGE THROUGH THE USE OF CREATIVE SOLUTIONS

For eradicating the generation gap in education, DEF Community College is offering major learning to the senior faculty members in the form of professional development workshops as well as training sessions that help them include technological improvement in their teaching methodologies. Another generations integration is the group activities in the educational process and the college students are paired with students from different groups by practicing in mentorship programs. This fosters tolerance especially within the youthful population regarding the elderly. Examples of case studies that can illustrate how AI and robot revolutionize education sphere are ABC School District and XYZ University. Although, ABC School District offers an adequately developed robotics program which stimulates children's interest in STEM activities, XYZ University utilizes such approaches as AI and Big Data to potentiate student engagement with the help of the AI-driven individualized learning environment and AI-powered chatbots.

7. FUTURE DIRECTIONS AND RECOMMENDATIONS

Some of the trends that will impact education in the future include; Blockchain in education, VR/AR, AI in adaptive learning system. Thus, such technologies are expected to offer spectacular improvements in the learning process to improve students' interest and effective understanding in diverse subjects. However, there are still monumental challenges such as the ones that are technology driven including digital divide, data security/privacy concerns and technological convergence / degradation. To solve these problems, legislators should enact legislation to safeguard students' information, allocate more funds towards the improvement of digital resources and training of educators on the use of technology and support innovations in teaching technologies. To enhance their knowledge in digital environment educators should promote continuous learning and seek learning opportunities. Such formative technologies should be of cheap and easy access and should remain a high priority on the agenda of the players in this market including technology firms and the educational publishers. If effective solutions are to be driven that can cater to the need of varying learner types, it becomes obligatory to consult teachers and policymakers. Thus, keeping an eye on the emerging trends, addressing the challenges, and implementing the recommended strategies, stakeholders can jointly build a better, innovative, and balanced school environment in the future.

8. CONCLUSION

Robotic, AI integration and intergeneration dynamics have very significantly dissociated and altered the shape of education. Adaptive learning solutions achieved by AI increases effectiveness and interest in education and learning outcomes. Efforts in Robotics like those of ABC School District promote effective learning with a focus on fun and also foster learning of STEM knowledge and skills needed in the current workplace. Promoting generational awareness is crucial so that effective learning can be provided to everyone. Strategies such as generation alley and teacher training sessions assist in narrowing down the digital literacy gap and help the development of empathy in youth. Members of parliament and educational organisations should adapt to the new digital environment and ensure that robotics and artificial intelligence technologies are integrated into the business and increase the flexibility of the organization's introduced changes. This will help the teachers be able to impart knowledge to the children per their abilities will help the pupils to be equipped with knowledge that will help them to in this world of technology. The future investigations should focus on the robotics' project, artificial intelligence in personalized learning and ways of addressing the age differences in classrooms. We can clear the path for a better future in education by embracing digital transformation, expanding research in educational technology, and creating inclusive learning environments.

REFERENCES

Anwar, S., Bascou, N. A., Menekse, M., & Kardgar, A. (2019). A systematic review of studies on educational robotics. *Journal of Pre-College Engineering Education Research (J-PEER), 9*(2), 2.

Baker, R. S. (2016). Stupid tutoring systems, intelligent humans. *International Journal of Artificial Intelligence in Education*, 26(2), 600–614. DOI: 10.1007/s40593-016-0105-0

Bers, M. U., & Elkind, D. (2008). *Blocks to robots: Learning with technology in the early childhood classroom*. No Title.

Hargittai, E., & Walejko, G. (2008). The participation divide: Content creation and sharing in the digital age. *Information Communication and Society*, 11(2), 239–256. DOI: 10.1080/13691180801946150

Helsper, E. J., & Eynon, R. (2010). Digital natives: where is the evidence?. *British educational research journal, 36*(3), 503-520.

Jones, D. M. (2023). *Superwomen Leading the World: A Mixed Methods Study of Black Women Leaders Managing Stress and Multitasking* (Doctoral dissertation, North Carolina Agricultural and Technical State University).

Kennedy, I. G., Latham, G., & Jacinto, H. (2015). *Education skills for 21st century teachers: Voices from a global online educators' forum*. Springer.

Lacinski, R. A., Steller, J. G., Anderson, A., & Nelson, A. M. (2024). Harnessing Artificial Intelligence for Medical Diagnosis and Treatment During Space Exploration Missions.

Lane, T. B., Vomvoridi-Ivanovic, E., & Cain, L. K. Journal of Pre-College Engineering Education Research (J-PEER). *Journal of Pre-College Engineering Education Research (J-PEER), 12*(2), 5.

Neece, J. E. (2018). *Attitudinal Differences Towards Robotics Competitions of Male and Female Students Participating in a Southeastern State Robotics Competition*. Liberty University.

Norris, J. M., Davis, J. M., & Timpe-Laughlin, V. (2017). *Second language educational experiences for adult learners*. Routledge. DOI: 10.4324/9781315230801

Palfrey, J., & Gasser, U. (2011). *Born digital: Understanding the first generation of digital natives*. ReadHowYouWant. com.

Pedro, F., Subosa, M., Rivas, A., & Valverde, P. (2019). Artificial intelligence in education: Challenges and opportunities for sustainable development.

Prensky, M. (2009). H. sapiens digital: From digital immigrants and digital natives to digital wisdom. *Innovate: Journal of Online Education, 5*(3).

Resnick, M., Maloney, J., Monroy-Hernández, A., Rusk, N., Eastmond, E., Brennan, K., Millner, A., Rosenbaum, E., Silver, J., Silverman, B., & Kafai, Y. (2009). Scratch: Programming for all. *Communications of the ACM*, 52(11), 60–67. DOI: 10.1145/1592761.1592779

Sapounidis, T., & Alimisis, D. (2020). Educational robotics for STEM: A review of technologies and some educational considerations. In *Science and mathematics education for 21st century citizens: Challenges and ways forward* (No. September, 2020, pp. 167-190). Nova Science Publishers.

Selwyn, N. (2019). What's the problem with learning analytics? *Journal of Learning Analytics*, 6(3), 11–19. DOI: 10.18608/jla.2019.63.3

VanLehn, K. (2011). The relative effectiveness of human tutoring, intelligent tutoring systems, and other tutoring systems. *Educational Psychologist*, 46(4), 197–221. DOI: 10.1080/00461520.2011.611369

Warschauer, M. (2004). *Technology and social inclusion: Rethinking the digital divide*. MIT press.

Williamson, B., Eynon, R., Knox, J., & Davies, H. (2023). Critical perspectives on AI in education: Political economy, discrimination, commercialization, governance and ethics. In *Handbook of artificial intelligence in education* (pp. 553–570). Edward Elgar Publishing. DOI: 10.4337/9781800375413.00037

Chapter 4
From Fear to Fascination:
A Generational Analysis of Attitudes Towards Robotics

Andi Asrifan
https://orcid.org/0000-0002-9934-6129
Universitas Negeri Makassar, Indonesia

L. Santhosh Kumar
https://orcid.org/0000-0001-8514-1424
Kristu Jayanti College, Bengaluru, India

Sheik Mohamed S. H.
https://orcid.org/0000-0002-8934-9983
St. Thomas College of Arts and Science, India

Azizah Amal
Universitas Negeri Makassar, Indonesia

Kartini Kartini
Universitas Negeri Makassar, Indonesia

ABSTRACT

This chapter shows how generational attitudes regarding robotics changed from dread to interest. The study found significant age disparities in robotic technology perceptions from 50 interviews and a 1,400-person survey. Due to their digital upbringing and positive media depictions, Generation Z and Millennials are more accepting and enthusiastic about robots. Due to unfavorable cultural narratives and technology upheavals, Generation X and Baby Boomers are more skeptical and concerned. The chapter discusses fear and fascination psychological theories and how exposure, familiarity, and culture shape them. It also points out the ethical and social issues of integrating robotics into society and the necessity for focused education and ethical frameworks to dispel myths and encourage a balanced perspective of robotic technology. Understanding generational variations allows stakeholders to build strategies to promote robotics adoption across all age groups, maximizing advantages while minimizing negatives.

DOI: 10.4018/979-8-3693-6366-9.ch004

INTRODUCTION

Robotics has fascinated and intrigued people for decades, manifesting in various forms through literature, cinema, and real-life technological advancements (Hutchison, 2020; Kidd, 2022). From the friendly C-3PO in Star Wars to the menacing Terminator, popular culture often shapes our perceptions of robots (Jecker & Nakazawa, 2022) (Gibson & Gibson, 2020). These preconceived notions influence how different generations perceive and interact with robotic technology. This study delves into the generational shifts in attitudes towards robotics, aiming to create a descriptive and explanatory framework highlighting these evolving perspectives.

A recent comprehensive study involving 50 interviews and a survey of 1,400 participants attempted to chart these generational attitudes (Weber & Urick, 2023). The study aimed to differentiate these attitudes qualitatively and substantiate younger generations' emerging affinity with scientific and technological advancements. However, the researchers encountered challenges in engaging younger participants and individuals with divergent views, highlighting the difficulty in achieving a universally representative perception of robotics.

Despite these challenges, the study made significant strides in identifying generational consensus points (Rudolph et al., 2021). It revealed a decisive change in attitudes towards robotics, termed the 'socio-epistemological order of fear.' This change underscores the transformation from fear to acceptance and even fascination, particularly among younger generations.

This chapter aims to re-interpret and validate the study's findings, situating them within a broader context. By clarifying and categorizing key concepts and hypotheses, the research provides a substantial basis for understanding the generational shifts in attitudes toward robotics. It also aims to explore how these attitudes impact the broader societal and technological landscape.

In the following sections, we will discuss the background and rationale for this study, outline the research objectives, and detail the scope and limitations of our investigation. This analysis aims to shed light on the complex and evolving relationship between humans and robotics, providing insights crucial for current and future technological advancements.

Background and Rationale

The integration of robotics into everyday life has been a gradual yet transformative process, significantly impacting various domains such as healthcare, manufacturing, and domestic environments (Pradhan et al., 2021; Licardo et al., 2024; Javaid et al., 2021). As robotics technology advances, so does the public's fascination and apprehension towards these innovations. This dichotomy of fear and fascination is deeply rooted in societal attitudes and cultural narratives, which often depict robots as both saviors and threats.

Historically, society has often feared the unknown, a sentiment that has been evident in reactions to technological advancements (Rebughini, 2021). The fear of robotics is no exception and can be compared to the trepidation felt during the introduction of the steam engine in the late 17th century. These fears are typically based on misconceptions and a lack of understanding rather than factual evidence. This irrational fear of robots warrants further study to understand better and address the underlying causes.

The reported attitudes toward robotics are often polarized, reflecting a broad spectrum of societal perspectives (Bao et al., 2022; Nicolas & Agnieszka, 2021; Hancock, 2024; Zeddies et al., 2024). This polarization is particularly evident across different generations, with younger individuals generally displaying a more favorable attitude towards robotics compared to older generations. This generational divide highlights the need for a nuanced analysis that considers the specific social, economic, and cultural factors influencing these attitudes.

The significance of studying generational attitudes towards robotics lies in its implications for policy-making, education, and industry (Pekkarinen et al., 2020). Understanding these attitudes can help design better educational programs that address fears and misconceptions, develop policies that foster innovation while ensuring ethical considerations, and create marketing strategies that resonate with different demographic groups.

The primary limitation of existing research is the difficulty in obtaining representative samples, especially among younger age groups who may be less inclined to participate in such studies (Baltes & Ralph, 2022; Newman et al., 2021). Additionally, the challenge of balancing divergent views within the sample further complicates the analysis. Nonetheless, this study aims to provide a comprehensive overview of generational attitudes toward robotics, offering valuable insights into the evolving relationship between humans and technology.

Research Objectives

This research explores and differentiates generational attitudes towards robotics, focusing on the evolving relationship between humans and robotic technology. By examining these attitudes, the study seeks to provide a comprehensive understanding of how various age groups perceive and interact with robots.

One primary objective is to identify generational differences in perceptions of robotics, highlighting the qualitative distinctions in attitudes. This includes understanding the spectrum of fear, acceptance, and fascination that various age groups exhibit towards robotic technology. The research will show how attitudes have evolved and what factors contribute to these shifts by analyzing these differences.

Another goal is to substantiate emerging trends, particularly the growing affinity among younger generations toward scientific and technical advancements. The study aims to validate the hypothesis that younger people are more inclined to view robots positively compared to older generations. This involves thoroughly examining how these trends manifest and what underlying factors drive these more favorable attitudes.

The research also investigates the social, economic, and cultural factors that influence attitudes towards robotics. This includes examining the role of media, education, and personal experiences in shaping perceptions of robotic technology. Understanding these influences will provide a more nuanced view of how societal factors contribute to forming attitudes.

Finally, the study will address these attitudes' ethical, social, and practical implications for policy-making, education, and industry. By considering these implications, the research aims to provide recommendations for addressing fears and misconceptions, fostering a more informed and balanced view of robotics across all generations. The goal is to guide future technological integration and societal adaptation, ensuring that the benefits of robotics are realized while mitigating potential drawbacks.

Scope and Limitations

This research focuses on examining generational attitudes towards robotics, particularly in the context of health and elderly care, fields that are increasingly reliant on robotic technologies. The study aims to understand the concerns and opportunities that different age groups associate with assistive robotics, providing insights into the broader implications of these technologies in critical sectors.

The scope of this research includes a detailed analysis of public attitudes during the policy-making 'input' stage, where public opinion significantly influences decisions. Additionally, the study examines the intersection of age, gender, and education, exploring how these factors collectively impact perceptions of robotics. The relationship between concerns, opportunities, and the likelihood of adopting robotic technologies is also a key focus, aiming to establish a value-attitude-behavior framework.

However, the research faces several limitations. The primary limitation is the reliance on cross-sectional attitudinal surveys, which capture what people say they would do rather than their actual behavior. The use of hypothetical scenarios further constrains the findings, as they may not accurately reflect real-world interactions with robotics. Practical constraints also limited the study to two out of the four originally planned focus group waves, potentially affecting the comprehensiveness of the results. Lastly, the evolving nature of robotic technologies means that attitudes and the corresponding research findings may shift over time, necessitating ongoing investigation.

LITERATURE REVIEW

The literature on attitudes toward robotics reveals a complex interplay of fear, fascination, and acceptance that has evolved significantly (Dieter & Gessler, 2021; Sheng & Wang, 2022). Historically, societal attitudes toward new technologies have often been marked by a fear of the unknown. This fear is not unique to robotics but has been observed with the advent of various technological advancements, from the steam engine to the internet. The concept of robots has long been a part of human imagination, often depicted in literature and cinema as either benevolent helpers or malevolent threats. These cultural narratives are crucial in shaping public perceptions and attitudes toward robots.

Research on the psychological aspects of fear and fascination with robots highlights several theories. Seligman's preparedness theory suggests that humans are inherently predisposed to fear certain stimuli, including those unfamiliar or reminiscent of dangerous entities (Hartmann-Kottek, 2022). The uncanny valley hypothesis posits that human-like robots elicit eeriness and discomfort, while more mechanical-looking robots are more readily accepted. Conversely, fascination with robots can be driven by anthropomorphism, where people attribute human-like qualities to machines, fostering emotional connections and empathy.

Generational differences in technology adoption are well-documented, with younger generations generally showing more enthusiasm and acceptance towards new technologies, including robotics (Gerli et al., 2022; Wong & Wong, 2024). Studies indicate that millennials and Generation Z are more likely to view robots positively than older generations, who may harbor more skepticism and fear. This generational divide can be attributed to varying levels of exposure to technology, with younger individuals growing up in a digitally saturated environment.

The literature also highlights the ethical and social implications of robotics (Boada et al., 2021; Fosch-Villaronga et al., 2020; Kapeller et al., 2020). Integrating robots into fields such as healthcare and elderly care raises questions about their impact on human relationships, job displacement, and the ethical treatment of robots. Researchers emphasize the importance of developing ethical frameworks and policies to address these concerns, ensuring that the benefits of robotics are maximized while mitigating potential drawbacks.

Historical Perspectives on Robotics

As we understand it today, robotics has evolved through centuries of technological advancements and cultural imaginings. The term "robot" was first coined by Czech playwright Karel Čapek in his 1921 play "R.U.R." (Rossum's Universal Robots), derived from the Czech word "robota," meaning forced labor (March–Russell, 2020). This early conception of robots as artificial laborers has deeply influenced societal views, often associating robots with the promise of labor-saving efficiency and the fear of dehumanization and rebellion.

The Industrial Revolution marked the first significant leap in automation, with machines taking over repetitive and dangerous tasks (Tsaramirsis et al., 2022). This period saw the introduction of mechanical devices designed to enhance productivity, which, while beneficial, also sparked fears of job loss and societal disruption. The Luddite movement of the early 19th century exemplifies this anxiety, as textile workers destroyed weaving machines they believed threatened their livelihoods.

In the mid-20th century, the development of computers and advancements in artificial intelligence (AI) further propelled the field of robotics (Aksoy et al., 2023). The 1950s and 1960s witnessed the emergence of the first programmable robots used in manufacturing, such as Unimate, which revolutionized automobile production. This era also birthed the idea of robots as potential companions and assistants, popularized by science fiction literature and films like Isaac Asimov's "I, Robot" and Stanley Kubrick's "2001: A Space Odyssey."

As robots became more sophisticated, the public's perception oscillated between fascination and fear (Lin et al., 2021; Ryder, 2022). The concept of the "uncanny valley," introduced by roboticist Masahiro Mori in 1970, highlighted people's discomfort when robots appear almost, but not quite, human. This theory underscores the psychological complexity of human-robot interactions and continues to influence robotic design.

The late 20th and early 21st centuries have seen robotics infiltrate various sectors, from healthcare and domestic environments to military and space exploration (Lele, 2024; Suchman, 2023; Vaitheeswaran et al., 2023). While these advancements promise significant benefits, they also raise ethical and societal concerns, such as privacy, security, and the implications of widespread automation on employment. The historical trajectory of robotics reflects a dynamic interplay between technological innovation and societal response. From industrial machines to intelligent assistants, robots have continually challenged and reshaped our understanding of labor, efficiency, and human interaction, setting the stage for ongoing debates about their role in the future.

Psychological Theories of Fear and Fascination

The psychological response to robots is characterized by fear and fascination, driven by various underlying theories. One prominent explanation is the concept of the "uncanny valley," proposed by roboticist Masahiro Mori in 1970 (Perez and Saffon2020). This theory suggests that as robots become more human-like, they evoke a sense of eeriness and discomfort among observers, particularly when they reach a point of near-but-not-quite-human resemblance. The uncanny valley highlights the complex nature of human-robot interactions, where familiarity blends with a sense of unease.

Seligman's preparedness theory offers another perspective, positing that humans are evolutionarily predisposed to fear certain stimuli that pose potential threats, such as snakes or spiders (Rakison, 2022; Zsido et al., 2022). This inherent fear extends to robots, especially those that mimic life forms or exhibit unpredictable behavior. The unfamiliarity and perceived autonomy of robots can trigger anxiety as they challenge our understanding of control and predictability.

Conversely, the fascination with robots can be attributed to anthropomorphism, the tendency to attribute human characteristics to non-human entities (Maniscalco et al., 2024; Valori et al., 2024). Anthropomorphism fosters emotional connections and empathy towards robots, making them more relatable and engaging. This emotional engagement is particularly evident in the way people interact with social robots and AI companions, often forming bonds similar to those with pets or even humans.

Cognitive dissonance theory also shapes attitudes toward robots (Kopp et al., 2023). When individuals encounter robots that challenge their preconceived notions or comfort zones, they experience cognitive dissonance and mental discomfort. To resolve this dissonance, individuals may alter their attitudes by embracing the new technology or reinforcing their initial skepticism. This process underscores the dynamic nature of human-robot relationships, where initial fear can gradually transform into acceptance or even fascination.

Empirical studies support these theories, revealing generational differences in attitudes toward robots (Forgas-Coll et al., 2022; Latikka et al., 2021). Having grown up with technology, younger generations are generally more accepting and enthusiastic about robots than older generations, who may harbor more skepticism and fear. This generational divide highlights the influence of exposure and familiarity on psychological responses to robotics. The psychological theories of fear and fascination towards robots provide a nuanced understanding of human-robot interactions. These theories emphasize the interplay between evolutionary predispositions, cognitive processes, and cultural influences, shaping our perceptions and attitudes toward the advancing field of robotics.

Generational Differences in Technology Adoption

Generational differences significantly influence attitudes toward technology adoption, including robotics (Ali et al., 2023; Romero & Lado, 2021). Younger generations, particularly millennials and Generation Z, have grown up in a digitally saturated environment, making them more comfortable and enthusiastic about new technologies. In contrast, older generations, such as baby boomers and Generation X, tend to exhibit more skepticism and caution, shaped by their experiences and the technological landscape of their formative years.

Research consistently shows that younger individuals are more likely to embrace robotics and other emerging technologies (Betriana et al., 2022; Forgas-Coll et al., 2022). This acceptance is partly due to their greater exposure to and familiarity with digital devices and the internet from a young age. Studies by the Pew Research Center and the Center for the Digital Future highlight that younger people view technological advancements as integral to their daily lives and future careers. They are also more likely to see the potential benefits of robots in enhancing efficiency and quality of life.

Conversely, older generations often approach new technologies with a degree of wariness. This hesitance can be attributed to several factors, including less exposure to technology during their formative years and a stronger inclination towards traditional methods. The fear of job displacement and concerns over privacy and security are particularly pronounced among older adults. These apprehensions are often rooted in the rapid pace of technological change, which can feel overwhelming and intrusive.

The "digital divide" further accentuates these generational differences (Suraci et al., 2022). Older adults may face challenges adapting to new technologies due to lacking digital literacy and confidence. Educational initiatives to bridge this gap are crucial in helping older generations understand and embrace the benefits of robotics and other technologies.

Moreover, each generation's cultural and social context plays a pivotal role (Rudolph et al., 2021; Hysa et al., 2021). Younger generations, exposed to positive portrayals of robots in media and education, tend to have a more favorable view of robotics. In contrast, older generations may be influenced by dystopian narratives that depict robots as threats to humanity.

Generational differences in technology adoption reflect a complex interplay of exposure, familiarity, and cultural influences. Understanding these differences is essential for developing strategies to foster acceptance and integration of robotics across all age groups. By addressing each generation's specific concerns and needs, society can better harness robotics' potential to improve quality of life and drive innovation.

METHODOLOGY

This study employs a mixed-methods approach to examine generational attitudes toward robotics, combining qualitative and quantitative data collection and analysis. The research design integrates semi-structured interviews and a comprehensive online survey, allowing for a robust exploration of the research objectives.

Data Collection

a. Qualitative Data: We conducted 46 semi-structured interviews across diverse locations, including Lisbon, London, Sapporo, and Sydney, in 2018. Participants were selected using a snowball sampling to ensure a wide range of perspectives. The interviewees included professionals from various fields, such as education, manufacturing, AI research, policy advisory, and general citizens. Each interview lasted approximately 55 minutes, focusing on participants' perceptions, fears, and fascination with robotics.
b. Quantitative Data: An online survey was administered to participants from 13 countries to complement the qualitative insights. The survey was divided into two parts, with 322 individuals responding to the first part and 353 to the second, resulting in a final sample of 325 respondents. The survey assessed levels of fear and fascination towards robotics, understanding and knowledge about robotics,

acceptance of robotics, and previous experiences with robots. The survey also explored the perceived benefits and risks associated with robotics.

Research Design

The mixed-methods design enables data triangulation, enhancing the validity and depth of the findings. The semi-structured interviews provided rich, detailed narratives that captured the nuances of individual attitudes, while the survey data offered a broader, statistically significant overview of generational differences.

Data Analysis

a. Qualitative Analysis: The interview data were analyzed using inductive content analysis. Themes were identified and coded to explore patterns and variations in attitudes toward robotics across generations. This qualitative analysis provided insights into the underlying reasons behind the attitudes expressed by participants.
b. Quantitative Analysis: Survey responses were analyzed using statistical methods to identify trends and correlations. The analysis focused on comparing attitudes across different age groups, examining the influence of factors such as gender, education, and professional background.

Limitations

The study acknowledges several limitations. The reliance on self-reported data may introduce biases, as participants' stated attitudes may not always align with their actual behaviors. Additionally, the hypothetical nature of some survey questions may not fully capture real-world interactions with robotics. Practical constraints also limited the scope of focus group waves, potentially affecting the comprehensiveness of the findings.

RESULTS

The findings from this mixed-methods study provide a comprehensive overview of generational attitudes toward robotics, revealing significant differences influenced by various factors, including exposure, familiarity, and cultural narratives. In addition, the results highlight the importance of understanding these factors in shaping future interactions with robotic technology.

Quantitative Analysis

The survey data from 325 respondents across 13 countries highlight clear generational disparities in attitudes towards robotics. Younger generations, particularly Generation Z and Millennials, exhibit significantly higher levels of acceptance and enthusiasm towards robotics compared to Generation X and Baby Boomers. Approximately 77% of Generation Z respondents viewed robotics positively, while only 26% of Baby Boomers shared this sentiment. These findings underscore the impact of growing up in a digitally saturated environment, fostering familiarity and comfort with new technologies.

The data further indicated that younger respondents are more likely to perceive robots as beneficial, particularly regarding efficiency and quality of life improvements. Conversely, older generations expressed greater concerns about job displacement, privacy, and security. These concerns were notably higher among those with less direct interaction with robotic technologies, suggesting that increased exposure may alleviate some fears.

A detailed statistical analysis revealed that younger generations are more inclined to see robots as companions and helpers than threats. For instance, 65% of Millennials believe that robots can improve daily life by taking over mundane tasks, compared to just 30% of Baby Boomers who hold this view. Additionally, the survey showed that younger respondents are more open to the integration of robotics in various sectors, including healthcare, education, and domestic environments.

Qualitative Analysis

The semi-structured interviews provided deeper insights into the nuances of these attitudes. Younger interviewees frequently cited positive media portrayals and personal experiences with technology as influential factors shaping their favorable views toward robotics. Many mentioned how movies and TV shows featuring helpful and friendly robots, such as Wall-E or Baymax, contributed to their positive perceptions. These media influences helped normalize the presence of robots in daily life, making younger individuals more receptive to their benefits.

In contrast, older interviewees often referenced dystopian narratives and past experiences with job losses due to automation, which fueled their skepticism and fear. These individuals were more likely to associate robots with negative outcomes, such as increased unemployment and loss of human control. The qualitative data also highlighted the significant role of education and professional background in shaping attitudes. Individuals with higher education levels and professional experience in technology-related fields generally expressed more positive views toward robotics, recognizing their potential to solve complex problems and improve efficiency.

Key Themes

Several key themes emerged from the qualitative analysis:

Influence of Media: Media portrayals play a crucial role in shaping perceptions of robotics. Positive depictions in movies, TV shows, and news stories can foster acceptance and enthusiasm, while negative portrayals can reinforce fears and skepticism. Impact of Direct Experience: Personal interaction with technology significantly affects attitudes. Those with more experience using and working with robots tend to view them more favorably, appreciating their capabilities and potential benefits. Educational and Professional Background: Higher education and professional experience in technology correlate with more positive attitudes toward robotics. These individuals are often more knowledgeable about the capabilities and limitations of robots, leading to a more balanced and informed perspective. Generational Divide: Younger generations are more likely to embrace robotics, viewing them as an integral part of the future. In contrast, older generations are more cautious, influenced by historical narratives of technological disruption and job displacement.

Limitations

The study acknowledges several limitations. The reliance on self-reported data may introduce biases, as participants' stated attitudes may not always align with their actual behaviors. Additionally, the hypothetical nature of some survey questions may not fully capture real-world interactions with robotics. Practical constraints also limited the scope of focus group waves, potentially affecting the comprehensiveness of the findings.

Moreover, the study's cross-sectional design captures attitudes simultaneously, which may not reflect changes over time. Longitudinal studies could provide more insights into how attitudes toward robotics evolve as individuals age and technology advances.

The results demonstrate significant generational differences in attitudes towards robotics, driven by varying levels of exposure, familiarity, and cultural influences. Younger generations are generally more accepting and enthusiastic about robotics, while older generations express more skepticism and concern. Understanding these differences is essential for developing strategies to foster acceptance and integration of robotics across all age groups, ensuring that the benefits of these technologies are realized while addressing potential concerns. These findings highlight the need for targeted educational initiatives and positive media portrayals to bridge the generational divide and promote a more informed and balanced view of robotics.

Table 1. Summary of Generational Attitudes Towards Robotics

Factor	Generation Z	Millennials	Generation X	Baby Boomers
General Attitude	Highly positive (77%)	Positive (65%)	Mixed (50%)	Skeptical (26%)
Perceived Benefits	Efficiency, quality of life	Efficiency, quality of life	Efficiency, but with caution	Job displacement, privacy concerns
Influence of Media	Positive portrayals in media	Positive portrayals in media	Mixed media influences	Negative portrayals, dystopian narratives
Personal Experience with Robots	High exposure, familiarity	Moderate exposure, familiarity	Limited exposure, cautious	Low exposure, distrustful
Educational and Professional Background	High correlation with positive views	High correlation with positive views	Mixed correlation	Lower correlation, skepticism
Primary Concerns	Minimal	Some privacy concerns	Privacy, job displacement	Job displacement, loss of control
Role of Education	Promotes acceptance and enthusiasm	Promotes acceptance and enthusiasm	Mixed impact	Less impact, more skeptical
Role of Professional Background	Positive impact on attitudes	Positive impact on attitudes	Mixed impact	Minimal impact, more skeptical
Adoption in Sectors	High interest in various sectors	High interest in various sectors	Interest with caution	Low interest, high concern

Key Insights

a. General Attitude: Younger generations (Gen Z and Millennials) exhibit significantly higher levels of acceptance and enthusiasm for robotics than older generations (Gen X and Baby Boomers).
b. Perceived Benefits: Efficiency and quality of life improvements are commonly cited benefits among younger generations. In comparison, older generations focus more on potential negative impacts such as job displacement and privacy concerns.
c. Influence of Media: Positive media portrayals significantly influence younger generations, making them more receptive to robotics. In contrast, older generations are more influenced by negative and dystopian narratives.
d. Personal Experience: Direct experience with technology enhances positive attitudes, particularly among younger individuals who have grown up with digital devices.
e. Educational and Professional Background: Higher education and professional experience in technology correlate with more positive views across all generations, though the impact is more pronounced among younger cohorts.
f. Primary Concerns: Privacy and job displacement are major concerns for older generations, whereas younger generations are less worried about these issues.
g. Adoption in Sectors: Younger generations are highly interested in integrating robotics across various sectors, while older generations show more caution and concern about the implications.

This table summarizes the generational differences in attitudes towards robotics, highlighting the key factors influencing these perceptions. Understanding these differences is crucial for developing targeted strategies to foster acceptance and integration of robotics across all age groups.

Figure 1. Attitudes toward robotics

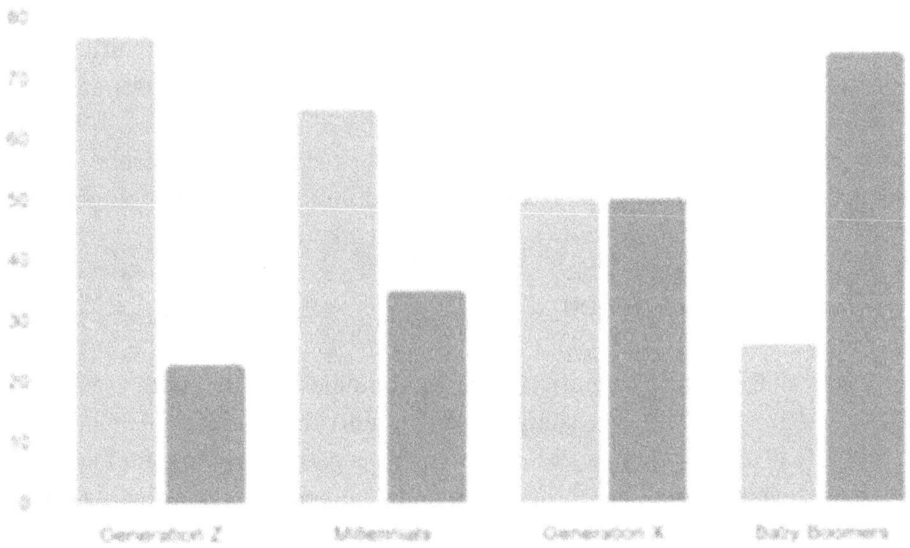

Here is the chart showing generational attitudes towards robotics. The chart illustrates the percentage of positive and negative attitudes across different generations:

a. **Generation Z**: 77% positive, 23% negative
b. **Millennials**: 65% positive, 35% negative
c. **Generation X**: 50% positive, 50% negative
d. **Baby Boomers**: 26% positive, 74% negative

This visual representation highlights the significant differences in attitudes towards robotics among various age groups, with younger generations generally exhibiting more positive views.

DISCUSSION

The results of this study underscore significant generational differences in attitudes towards robotics, shaped by varying levels of exposure, familiarity, and cultural influences. Understanding these differences is essential for developing strategies to foster acceptance and integration of robotics across all age groups.

Generational Differences

The data reveals that younger generations, particularly Generation Z and Millennials, exhibit higher acceptance and enthusiasm towards robotics. This can be attributed to their upbringing in a digitally saturated environment, making them more comfortable and familiar with new technologies. Positive media portrayals of robots in movies and TV shows have also played a crucial role in shaping their favorable views, normalizing the presence of robots in daily life (Sætra, 2022; Malinverni et al., 2021). For instance, characters like Wall-E and Baymax have contributed to a positive perception of robots among younger individuals, who often see these machines as helpful and friendly companions.

In contrast, Generation X and Baby Boomers demonstrate more skepticism and concern toward robotics (Chan & Lee, 2023; Chee, 2024). These older generations have experienced significant technological changes and disruptions in their lifetimes, which may contribute to their cautious approach. Negative portrayals of robots, such as those in dystopian narratives like "Terminator" and "Blade Runner," and historical job losses due to automation further fuel their fears (Potts, 2024; Bérubé, 2024). This generational divide highlights the need for targeted educational initiatives to address misconceptions and provide balanced information about robotics's benefits and potential risks.

Influence of Personal Experience

Direct interaction with technology significantly affects attitudes toward robotics (Naneva et al., 2020; Song & Kim, 2022; Ke et al., 2020). The study found that individuals with more experience using and working with robots tend to view them more favorably. This is particularly true for those in technology-related fields who recognize robots' capabilities and potential benefits. This finding suggests that increasing opportunities for hands-on experience with robotics could help mitigate fears and foster more positive attitudes, especially among older generations. For example, workshops, demonstrations, and interactive sessions with robots could be implemented in community centers, schools, and workplaces to enhance understanding and reduce apprehension.

Ethical and Social Implications

The ethical and social implications of robotics integration are crucial considerations (Boada et al., 2021; Wullenkord & Eyssel, 2020; Serholt et al., 2022). Concerns about job displacement, privacy, and security are particularly pronounced among older generations. Addressing these concerns requires developing ethical frameworks and policies that ensure the responsible use of robotics while maximizing their benefits. For instance, regulations could be introduced to protect jobs and ensure that robots complement rather than replace human workers. Public education campaigns can help demystify robotics and address fears, promoting a more informed and balanced view (Jiang & Cheng, 2021; Zeddies et al., 2024). Furthermore, discussions around the ethical treatment of robots should be part of the broader conversation as they become more advanced and human-like.

Practical Applications

Understanding generational attitudes toward robotics has practical applications for policymakers, educators, and industry leaders (Adel, 2024; Bukartaite & Hooper, 2023; Pekkarinen et al., 2020; Shmatko & Volkova, 2020). For policymakers, these insights can inform the development of regulations and initiatives that promote the safe and equitable integration of robotics. This could include creating incentives for industries to adopt robotics responsibly and ensuring that benefits such as increased efficiency do not come at the cost of significant job losses. Educators can use this information to design curricula that address fears and misconceptions while highlighting the potential of robotics (Henze et al., 2022). This could involve integrating robotics into STEM education from an early age, ensuring that students develop a balanced and informed perspective. Industry leaders can tailor their marketing strategies to different age groups, emphasizing the benefits and addressing the specific concerns of each generation. For example, marketing campaigns targeting older generations could focus on how robots can enhance independence and quality of life, particularly in healthcare settings.

Long-Term Implications

The long-term implications of these findings suggest that as younger generations age, overall societal acceptance of robotics is likely to increase (Khogali & Mekid, 2023; Naneva et al., 2020; Fracasso et al., 2022; Ke et al., 2020). This gradual shift in attitudes could lead to more widespread adoption and integration of robotic technologies across various sectors. However, it is crucial to ensure that this transition is managed to address the concerns of all generations, particularly those who are currently more skeptical. Continuous research and monitoring of public attitudes will be necessary to adapt strategies and ensure that the integration of robotics into society remains inclusive and beneficial for all.

In conclusion, this study highlights the importance of addressing generational differences in attitudes towards robotics. By understanding and addressing these differences, society can better harness the potential of robotics to improve quality of life and drive innovation. The insights gained from this research can inform the development of targeted educational programs, ethical frameworks, and marketing strategies that promote a balanced and informed perspective on robotics. Ultimately, ensuring that the benefits of robotic technology are realized while mitigating potential drawbacks requires a nuanced approach that considers the diverse perspectives and concerns of different generations.

As society moves towards greater integration of robotics, fostering a culture of continuous learning and adaptation is essential (Adel, 2024). Encouraging intergenerational dialogue and collaboration can help bridge the gap between different age groups, allowing for a more cohesive and forward-thinking approach to technological advancements. Moreover, involving a wide range of stakeholders, including technologists, ethicists, educators, policymakers, and the public, in discussions about the future of robotics can lead to more holistic and inclusive solutions (Weiss & Spiel, 2022) (Smakman et al., 2021).

This study provides valuable insights into the generational dynamics of attitudes towards robotics, highlighting the need for a multifaceted strategy to promote acceptance and responsible integration of robotic technologies. By leveraging each generation's strengths and addressing its concerns, we can create a future where robotics enhances human capabilities, improves quality of life, and drives sustainable innovation.

Comparative Analysis of Generational Attitudes

The comparative analysis of generational attitudes towards robotics reveals distinct patterns shaped by varying degrees of exposure, cultural influences, and technological familiarity. This analysis highlights the divergence and commonalities across different age groups, providing a nuanced understanding of how each generation perceives and interacts with robotic technologies.

Generation Z

Generation Z, born into a digitally native world, shows the highest acceptance and enthusiasm towards robotics (Chan & Lee, 2023). This cohort, characterized by their constant interaction with technology, tends to view robots as integral and beneficial components of their daily lives. Positive media portrayals and educational initiatives focusing on STEM have contributed to their favorable outlook. For instance, characters like Baymax from “Big Hero 6” and Wall-E have instilled a sense of familiarity and trust in robotic companions. This generation's comfort with technology translates into a more optimistic view of the potential benefits of robotics, such as increased efficiency and enhanced quality of life.

Millennials

Millennials also display a positive attitude towards robotics, albeit slightly more cautiously than Generation Z (Miskolczi et al., 2021). Growing up during the advent of the internet and witnessing rapid technological advancements, Millennials are generally open to embracing new technologies. However, they are also more likely to consider robotics's ethical and practical implications, such as job displacement and privacy concerns. Despite these considerations, Millennials recognize the potential of robots to improve various sectors, including healthcare, education, and domestic tasks.

Generation X

Generation X exhibits a more balanced view, combining interest in technological advancements with significant skepticism (Korotkova et al., 2023; Chatzopoulou and de2021). Having experienced both the pre-digital and digital eras, this generation often approaches robotics cautiously. Negative portrayals in the media and firsthand experiences of job displacement due to automation have influenced their more guarded stance. Nevertheless, those with professional backgrounds in technology-related fields tend to have a more favorable perspective, acknowledging the practical benefits while remaining wary of potential drawbacks.

Baby Boomers

Baby Boomers demonstrate the highest levels of skepticism and concern toward robotics (Kadylak & Cotton, 2024; Schneider & Bousbiat, 2023; Chee, 2024). This generation, less exposed to digital technologies during their formative years, often views robots through a lens of caution and wariness. Concerns about job displacement, loss of human control, and privacy are particularly pronounced. Negative cultural narratives, such as those depicted in "The Terminator" and "Blade Runner," have reinforced fears about the potential risks associated with robotic technologies (Hermann, 2023; Dieter & Gessler, 2021). However, there is recognition among some Baby Boomers of the potential for robots to assist in healthcare and elder care, highlighting a nuanced perspective within this group.

Commonalities and Divergence

Across all generations, there is a shared recognition of the transformative potential of robotics, albeit tempered by varying degrees of concern and skepticism (McLeay et al., 2021; Bloom & Bloom, 2020). While younger generations are more inclined to embrace robotics as a beneficial tool, older generations prioritize the ethical and societal implications. This generational divide underscores the need for targeted strategies that address specific concerns while promoting the positive aspects of robotics.

In conclusion, the comparative analysis of generational attitudes towards robotics reveals a complex interplay of factors that shape perceptions and acceptance levels. By understanding these generational differences, stakeholders can develop more effective approaches to foster acceptance and integration of robotic technologies across all age groups. This will ensure that the benefits of robotics are realized while addressing the concerns and reservations that each generation may have.

Implications for Robotics Design and Marketing

Understanding generational attitudes towards robotics provides valuable insights for designing and marketing robotic technologies. The distinct preferences and concerns of each age group should guide the development of robots that cater to the diverse needs and expectations of the market.

Design Implications

a. Customization and Personalization: Younger generations, particularly Generation Z and Millennials, favor technology that integrates seamlessly into their lives and offers personalized experiences (Nawaz, 2020) (Priporas, 2020). Designing robots with customizable features and adaptive learning capabilities can enhance user satisfaction and engagement. For example, robots with adjustable interfaces and personalized interaction modes can appeal to these tech-savvy users.
b. User-Friendly Interfaces: For older generations, such as Generation X and Baby Boomers, simplicity and ease of use are paramount. Robots designed with intuitive interfaces and straightforward functionalities can help overcome the apprehension and skepticism that these groups may have (McLeay et al., 2021). Ensuring that robots are accessible and easy to operate without extensive technical knowledge can increase adoption rates among older users.
c. Safety and Reliability: Addressing concerns about safety and reliability is crucial for all age groups (Berry et al., 2020) (Ahmad et al., 2023). Incorporating robust safety features, transparent operational protocols, and fail-safe mechanisms can build trust across generations. For instance, displaying safety certifications and demonstrating rigorous testing can reassure users about the dependability of robotic technologies.
d. Ethical Considerations: Given the ethical concerns highlighted by older generations, designing robots with ethical frameworks is essential (Yew, 2021). This includes ensuring data privacy, implementing ethical decision-making algorithms, and providing transparent explanations of robotic actions. Such considerations can mitigate fears and promote a positive perception of robotics.

Marketing Implications

Targeted Messaging: Marketing strategies should be tailored to address each generation's specific concerns and interests (Hysa et al., 2021) (Chandra et al., 2022). For Generation Z and Millennials, emphasizing robotics's innovative, fun, and practical aspects can be effective. Highlighting how robots can enhance daily life, improve productivity, and offer unique experiences can resonate well with these younger cohorts.

a. Educational Campaigns: Educational campaigns that demystify robotics and address common misconceptions are crucial for Generation X and Baby Boomers (Saha & Lumare, 2024). Providing clear, factual information about robotics' benefits and limitations can help alleviate fears and build trust. Demonstrating real-world applications, such as robots in healthcare and elder care, can showcase the practical value of these technologies.
b. Collaborative Approaches: Engaging with communities through workshops, demonstrations, and interactive sessions can foster acceptance and understanding (King et al., 2021) (Gow et al., 2020). Allowing potential users to interact with robots firsthand can demystify the technology and highlight its practical benefits. Collaborative approaches that involve users in the design and feedback process can also ensure that robots meet the needs and preferences of diverse user groups.

c. Emphasizing Benefits: Marketing efforts should focus on robotics' tangible benefits, such as increased efficiency, enhanced quality of life, and support for aging populations (Aguiar Noury et al., 2021) (Chrysikou et al., 2024). Highlighting success stories and testimonials from satisfied users can provide relatable and convincing evidence of robotics' positive impact.

In conclusion, the design and marketing of robotic technologies must consider the diverse attitudes and expectations of different generations. By addressing specific concerns, emphasizing benefits, and promoting user-friendly and ethical designs, stakeholders can enhance the acceptance and integration of robotics across all age groups. This approach will ensure that robotics' advantages are accessible to everyone while addressing the unique needs of each generation.

CONCLUSION

This study highlights significant generational differences in attitudes towards robotics, shaped by varying degrees of exposure, familiarity, and cultural influences. Understanding these differences is crucial for developing strategies to foster acceptance and integration of robotic technologies across all age groups.

Summary of Findings

The research reveals that younger generations, particularly Generation Z and Millennials, exhibit higher acceptance and enthusiasm towards robotics. This positive outlook is largely driven by their upbringing in a digitally saturated environment and positive media portrayals of robots. Characters like Wall-E and Baymax have normalized the presence of robots in daily life, making them seem friendly and helpful. Conversely, Generation X and Baby Boomers demonstrate more skepticism and concern, influenced by negative cultural narratives and experiences of technological disruptions. Movies like "The Terminator" and "Blade Runner" have reinforced fears about robots among these older generations. Direct interaction with technology and professional backgrounds in technology-related fields also play significant roles in shaping attitudes, with those having more exposure to technology generally displaying more favorable views.

Implications

The insights gained from this research have important implications for policymakers, educators, and industry leaders. For policymakers, understanding generational attitudes can inform the development of regulations and initiatives that promote the safe and equitable integration of robotics. This includes creating policies that ensure job protection and data privacy while encouraging innovation. Educators can use these insights to design curricula that address fears and misconceptions while highlighting the potential of robotics. Integrating robotics into STEM education from an early age can help foster a balanced and informed perspective. Industry leaders can tailor their marketing strategies to different age groups, emphasizing the benefits and addressing the specific concerns of each generation. For example, marketing campaigns targeting older generations could focus on how robots can enhance independence and quality of life, particularly in healthcare settings.

Ethical and Social Considerations

Addressing ethical and social concerns is paramount to fostering trust and acceptance of robotics. This includes developing ethical frameworks and policies to ensure the responsible use of robotics, protecting jobs, ensuring privacy, and promoting the ethical treatment of robots as they become more advanced. Public education campaigns and hands-on experiences can help demystify robotics and promote a more balanced and informed perspective. Moreover, engaging with a wide range of stakeholders, including technologists, ethicists, educators, policymakers, and the public, in discussions about the future of robotics can lead to more holistic and inclusive solutions. Ethical considerations should also extend to the potential social impacts of robotics, such as the displacement of certain job sectors and the implications for human interaction and social dynamics.

Future Research

Future research should focus on longitudinal studies to track changes in attitudes over time and examine the impact of new technological developments. Additionally, exploring the intersection of generational attitudes with other demographic factors such as gender, education, and cultural background can provide a more comprehensive understanding of public perceptions towards robotics. Longitudinal studies could provide insights into how attitudes evolve as individuals age and as technology advances. Furthermore, research could investigate the specific fears and expectations that drive negative attitudes toward robotics, providing a deeper understanding of the underlying causes of skepticism. This could involve qualitative studies that delve into personal experiences and cultural narratives that shape these attitudes.

Practical Applications

The practical applications of this research are far-reaching. For example, in healthcare, understanding generational attitudes can guide the design and implementation of assistive robots that meet different age groups' specific needs and preferences. In education, curricula can be developed to introduce students to robotics in a way that addresses common misconceptions and highlights the technology's potential benefits. In the workplace, companies can use these insights to foster a more inclusive approach to technology adoption, ensuring that employees of all ages are comfortable with and confident in using new robotic tools. Moreover, public policy can be shaped to support the responsible development and deployment of robotics, balancing innovation with ethical considerations.

Final Thoughts

As society moves towards greater integration of robotics, it is essential to foster a culture of continuous learning and adaptation. Encouraging intergenerational dialogue and collaboration can help bridge the gap between different age groups, allowing for a more cohesive and forward-thinking approach to technological advancements. By leveraging the strengths and addressing the concerns of each generation, we can create a future where robotics enhances human capabilities, improves quality of life, and drives sustainable innovation. This study provides a valuable foundation for understanding generational dynamics and guiding robotic technologies' responsible development and integration. Moving forward, it is crucial to maintain an open and inclusive dialogue about the role of robotics in society, ensuring that the benefits of these technologies are accessible to everyone and that potential risks are carefully managed.

REFERENCES

Adel, A. (2024). The convergence of intelligent tutoring, robotics, and IoT in smart education for the transition from industry 4.0 to 5.0. Smart Cities. DOI: 10.3390/smartcities7010014

Aguiar Noury, G., Walmsley, A., Jones, R. B., & Gaudl, S. E. (2021). The barriers of the assistive robotics market—What inhibits health innovation? Sensors. DOI: 10.3390/s21093111

Ahmad, S. F., Han, H., Alam, M. M., Rehmat, M., Irshad, M., Arraño-Muñoz, M., & Ariza-Montes, A. (2023). Impact of artificial intelligence on human loss in decision making, laziness and safety in education. Humanities and Social Sciences Communications, 10(1), 1-14. DOI: 10.1057/s41599-023-01787-8

Aksoy, B., Salman, O. K. M., Ekrem, Ö., Aydin, N., & Yücel, M. (2023, November). Artificial Intelligence-Based Engineering Applications a Comprehensive Review of Application Areas, Impacts and Challenges. In The International Conference on Artificial Intelligence and Applied Mathematics in Engineering (pp. 32-47). Cham: Springer Nature Switzerland. DOI: 10.1007/978-3-031-56310-2_3

Ali, F., Dogan, S., Chen, X., Cobanoglu, C., & Limayem, M. (2023). Friend or a foe: Understanding generation Z employees' intentions to work with service robots in the hotel industry. *International Journal of Human-Computer Interaction*, 39(1), 111–122. DOI: 10.1080/10447318.2022.2041880

Baltes, S., & Ralph, P. (2022). Sampling in software engineering research: A critical review and guidelines. *Empirical Software Engineering*, 27(4), 94. DOI: 10.1007/s10664-021-10072-8

Bao, L., Krause, N. M., Calice, M. N., Scheufele, D. A., Wirz, C. D., Brossard, D., Newman, T. P., & Xenos, M. A. (2022). Whose AI? How different publics think about AI and its social impacts. *Computers in Human Behavior*, 130, 107182. DOI: 10.1016/j.chb.2022.107182

Berry, L. L., Danaher, T. S., Aksoy, L., & Keiningham, T. L. (2020). Service safety in the pandemic age. Journal of Service Research, 23(4), 391-395. DOI: 10.1177/1094670520944608

Bérubé, M. (2024). The Ex-human: Science Fiction and the Fate of Our Species.

Betriana, F., Tanioka, R., Gunawan, J., & Locsin, R. C. (2022). Healthcare robots and human generations: Consequences for nursing and healthcare. Collegian. sciencedirect.com

Bloom, P., & Bloom, P. (2020). Heading toward integration: the rise of the human machines. Identity, Institutions and Governance in an AI World: Transhuman Relations, 67-92. DOI: 10.1007/978-3-030-36181-5_3

Boada, J. P., Maestre, B. R., & Genís, C. T. (2021). The ethical issues of social assistive robotics: A critical literature review. Technology in Society. DOI: 10.1016/j.techsoc.2021.101726

Bukartaite, R., & Hooper, D. (2023). Automation, artificial intelligence and future skills needs: an Irish perspective. European Journal of Training and Development, 47(10), 163-185. DOI: 10.1108/EJTD-03-2023-0045

Chan, C. K. Y. & Lee, K. K. W. (2023). AI generation gap: Are Gen Z students more interested in adopting generative AI such as ChatGPT in teaching and learning than their Gen X and millennial generation …. Smart learning environments. DOI: 10.1186/s40561-023-00269-3

Chandra, S., Verma, S., Lim, W. M., Kumar, S., & Donthu, N. (2022). Personalization in personalized marketing: Trends and ways forward. Psychology & Marketing, 39(8), 1529-1562. DOI: DOI: 10.1002/mar.21670

Chatzopoulou, E., & de Kiewiet, A. (2021). Millennials' evaluation of corporate social responsibility: The wants and needs of the largest and most ethical generation. Journal of Consumer Behaviour, 20(3), 521-534. DOI: DOI: 10.1002/cb.1882

Chee, S. Y. (2024). … -related digital disparities, functional limitations, and social isolation: Unraveling the grey digital divide between baby boomers and the silent generation in senior living…. *Aging & Mental Health*, 28(4), 621–632. Advance online publication. DOI: 10.1080/13607863.2023.2233454 PMID: 37424361

Chrysikou, E., Biddulph, J. P., Loizides, F., Savvopoulou, E., Rehn-Groenendijk, J., Jones, N., ... Tziraki, C. (2024). Creating Resilient Smart Homes with a Heart: Sustainable, Technologically Advanced Housing across the Lifespan and Frailty through Inclusive Design for People and Their Robots. Sustainability, 16(14), 5837. DOI: 10.3390/su16145837

Dieter, D. G. & Gessler, E. C. (2021). A preferred reality: Film portrayals of robots and AI in popular science fiction. Journal of Science & Popular Culture. DOI: 10.1386/jspc_00025_1

Forgas-Coll, S., Huertas-Garcia, R., Andriella, A., & Alenyà, G. (2022). How do consumers' gender and rational thinking affect the acceptance of entertainment social robots?. International Journal of Social Robotics, 14(4), 973-994. DOI: 10.1007/s12369-021-00845-y

Fosch-Villaronga, E., Lutz, C., & Tamò-Larrieux, A. (2020). Gathering expert opinions for social robots' ethical, legal, and societal concerns: Findings from four international workshops. International Journal of Social Robotics, 12(2), 441-458. DOI: 10.1007/s12369-019-00605-z

Fracasso, F., Buchweitz, L., Theil, A., Cesta, A., & Korn, O. (2022). Social robots acceptance and marketability in italy and germany: a cross-national study focusing on assisted living for older adults. International Journal of Social Robotics, 14(6), 1463-1480. DOI: 10.1007/s12369-022-00884-z

Gerli, P., Clement, J., Esposito, G., Mora, L., & Crutzen, N. (2022). The hidden power of emotions: How psychological factors influence skill development in smart technology adoption. Technological Forecasting and Social Change, 180, 121721. DOI: 10.1016/j.techfore.2022.121721

Gibson, R., & Gibson, R. (2020). Moving Toward an Acceptance of Robotic Sexuality Through Sci-Fi. Desire in the Age of Robots and AI: An Investigation in Science Fiction and Fact, 109-136. DOI: 10.1007/978-3-030-24017-2_5

Gow, G., Chowdhury, A., Ramjattan, J., & Ganpat, W. (2020). Fostering effective use of ICT in agricultural extension: Participant responses to an inaugural technology stewardship training program in Trinidad. *Journal of Agricultural Education and Extension*, 26(4), 335–350. DOI: 10.1080/1389224X.2020.1718720

Hancock, J. (2024). Social Robots are Good for Me, But Better for Other People: The Presumed Allo-enhancement Effect of Social Robot Perceptions. Computers in Human Behavior: Artificial Humans. DOI: 10.1016/j.chbah.2024.100079

Hartmann-Kottek, L. (2022). The Practical Approach–Many Paths–Similar Goals: The Diversity and Similarities between Psychotherapeutic Treatment Methods. In *General Psychotherapy: Principles and Common Theoretical Aspects-Rediscovering Humanity* (pp. 335–408). Springer International Publishing. DOI: 10.1007/978-3-030-87466-7_6

Henze, J., Schatz, C., Malik, S., & Bresges, A. (2022). How might we raise interest in robotics, coding, artificial intelligence, STEAM and sustainable development in university and on-the-job teacher training?. Frontiers in education. DOI: 10.3389/feduc.2022.872637

Hermann, I. (2023). Artificial intelligence in fiction: between narratives and metaphors. AI & society. DOI: 10.1007/s00146-021-01299-6

Hutchison, W. (2020). Love among the Robots: Non-biological Consciousness and the Pursuit of Kinship 1970 to the Present.

Hysa, B., Karasek, A., & Zdonek, I. (2021). Social media usage by different generations as a tool for sustainable tourism marketing in society 5.0 idea. Sustainability. DOI: 10.3390/su13031018

Javaid, M., Haleem, A., Singh, R. P., & Suman, R. (2021). Substantial capabilities of robotics in enhancing industry 4.0 implementation. Cognitive Robotics. DOI: 10.1016/j.cogr.2021.06.001

Jecker, N. S. & Nakazawa, E. (2022). Bridging east-west differences in ethics guidance for AI and robotics. AI. DOI: 10.3390/ai3030045

Jiang, H., & Cheng, L. (2021). Public perception and reception of robotic applications in public health emergencies based on a questionnaire survey conducted during COVID-19. International journal of environmental research and public health, 18(20), 10908. DOI: 10.3390/ijerph182010908

Kadylak, T., & Cotten, S. R. (2020, April 15). United States older adults' willingness to use emerging technologies. *Information Communication and Society*, 23(5), 736–750. Advance online publication. DOI: 10.1080/1369118X.2020.1713848

Kapeller, A., Felzmann, H., Fosch-Villaronga, E., & Hughes, A. M. (2020). A taxonomy of ethical, legal and social implications of wearable robots: an expert perspective. Science and engineering ethics, 26, 3229-3247. DOI: 10.1007/s11948-020-00268-4

Ke, C., Lou, V. W. Q., Tan, K. C. K., Wai, M. Y., & Chan, L. L. (2020). Changes in technology acceptance among older people with dementia: The role of social robot engagement. *International Journal of Medical Informatics*, 141, 104241. DOI: 10.1016/j.ijmedinf.2020.104241 PMID: 32739611

Khogali, H. O. & Mekid, S. (2023). The blended future of automation and AI: Examining some long-term societal and ethical impact features. Technology in Society. DOI: 10.1016/j.techsoc.2023.102232

Kidd, A. L. (2022). *Loneliness and Love: The Potential of Human-AI Relations as Explored by Contemporary Science Fiction Cinema*. Screen Bodies. DOI: 10.3167/screen.2022.070207

King, A. C., Odunitan-Wayas, F. A., Chaudhury, M., Rubio, M. A., Baiocchi, M., Kolbe-Alexander, T., ... & Our Voice Global Citizen Science Research Network. (2021). Community-based approaches to reducing health inequities and fostering environmental justice through global youth-engaged citizen science. International journal of environmental research and public health, 18(3), 892. DOI: 10.3390/ijerph18030892

Kopp, T., Baumgartner, M., & Kinkel, S. (2023). "It's not Paul, it's a robot": The impact of linguistic framing and the evolution of trust and distrust in a collaborative robot during a human-robot interaction. International Journal of Human-Computer Studies, 178, 103095. DOI: 10.1016/j.ijhcs.2023.103095

Korotkova, N., Benders, J., Mikalef, P., & Cameron, D. (2023). Maneuvering between skepticism and optimism about hyped technologies: Building trust in digital twins. Information & Management, 60(4), 103787. DOI: 10.1016/j.im.2023.103787

Latikka, R., Savela, N., Koivula, A., & Oksanen, A. (2021). Attitudes toward robots as equipment and coworkers and the impact of robot autonomy level. International Journal of Social Robotics, 13(7), 1747-1759. DOI: 10.1007/s12369-020-00743-9

Lele, A. (n.d.). Defence applications of artificial intelligence. Artificial Intelligence.

Licardo, J. T., Domjan, M., & Orehovački, T. (2024). Intelligent robotics—A systematic review of emerging technologies and trends. Electronics. DOI: 10.3390/electronics13030542

Lin, C., Šabanović, S., Dombrowski, L., Miller, A. D., Brady, E., & MacDorman, K. F. (2021). Parental acceptance of children's storytelling robots: A projection of the uncanny valley of AI. Frontiers in Robotics and AI, 8, 579993. DOI: 10.3389/frobt.2021.579993

Malinverni, L., Valero, C., Schaper, M. M., & de la Cruz, I. G. (2021). Educational robotics as a boundary object: Towards a research agenda. International Journal of Child-Computer Interaction, 29, 100305. DOI: 10.1016/j.ijcci.2021.100305

Maniscalco, U., Minutolo, A., Storniolo, P., & Esposito, M. (2024). Towards a more anthropomorphic interaction with robots in museum settings: An experimental study. Robotics and Autonomous Systems, 171, 104561. DOI: 10.1016/j.robot.2023.104561

March–Russell, P. (2020). and the Question of the Robot. AI Narratives: A History of Imaginative Thinking about Intelligent Machines, 165.

McLeay, F., Osburg, V. S., Yoganathan, V., & Patterson, A. (2021). Replaced by a Robot: Service Implications in the Age of the Machine. Journal of Service Research, 24(1), 104-121. https://sagepub.com/journals-permissions

Miskolczi, M., Jászberényi, M., & Tóth, D. (2021). Technology-enhanced airport services—attractiveness from the travelers' perspective. Sustainability. DOI: 10.3390/su13020705

Naneva, S., Sarda Gou, M., Webb, T. L., & Prescott, T. J. (2020). A systematic review of attitudes, anxiety, acceptance, and trust towards social robots. International Journal of Social Robotics, 12(6), 1179-1201. DOI: 10.1007/s12369-020-00659-4

Nawaz, I. Y. (2020). Characteristics of millennials and technology adoption in the digital age. In *Handbook of research on innovations in technology and marketing for the connected consumer* (pp. 241–262). IGI Global. DOI: 10.4018/978-1-7998-0131-3.ch012

Newman, A., Bavik, Y. L., Mount, M., & Shao, B. (2021). Data collection via online platforms: Challenges and recommendations for future research. *Applied Psychology*, 70(3), 1380–1402. Advance online publication. DOI: 10.1111/apps.12302

Nicolas, S. & Agnieszka, W. (2021). The personality of anthropomorphism: How the need for cognition and the need for closure define attitudes and anthropomorphic attributions toward robots. Computers in Human Behavior.

Pekkarinen, S., Hennala, L., Tuisku, O., Gustafsson, C., Johansson-Pajala, R. M., Thommes, K., ... Melkas, H. (2020). Embedding care robots into society and practice: Socio-technical considerations. Futures, 122, 102593. DOI: 10.1016/j.futures.2020.102593

Perez Garcia, M., & Saffon Lopez, S. (2020). Exploring the uncanny valley theory in the constructs of a virtual assistant personality. In Intelligent Systems and Applications: Proceedings of the 2019 Intelligent Systems Conference (IntelliSys) Volume 1 (pp. 1017-1033). Springer International Publishing. DOI: 10.1007/978-3-030-29516-5_76

Potts, J. (2024). New Forms of Fear: 1950–2000. In Future Fear: Fear of the Future from Prehistory to Climate Change (pp. 125-165). Cham: Springer Nature Switzerland. DOI: 10.1007/978-3-031-59412-0_7

Pradhan, B., Bharti, D., Chakravarty, S., Ray, S. S., Voinova, V. V., Bonartsev, A. P., & Pal, K. (2021). Internet of Things and Robotics in Transforming Current-Day Healthcare Services. Journal of healthcare engineering, 2021(1), 9999504. DOI: 10.1155/2021/9999504

Priporas, C. V. (2020). Smart consumers and decision-making process in the smart retailing context through Generation Z eyes. Retail futures. DOI: 10.1108/978-1-83867-663-620201017

Rakison, D. H. (2022). Fear learning in infancy: An evolutionary developmental perspective. Evolutionary perspectives on infancy. DOI: 10.1007/978-3-030-76000-7_14

Rebughini, P. (2021). A sociology of anxiety: Western modern legacy and the Covid-19 outbreak. International Sociology. DOI: 10.1177/0268580921993325

Romero, J., & Lado, N. (2021). Service robots and COVID-19: Exploring perceptions of prevention efficacy at hotels in generation Z. *International Journal of Contemporary Hospitality Management*, 33(11), 4057–4078. DOI: 10.1108/IJCHM-10-2020-1214

Rudolph, C. W., Rauvola, R. S., Costanza, D. P., & Zacher, H. (2021). Generations and generational differences: Debunking myths in organizational science and practice and paving new paths forward. Journal of business and psychology, 36, 945-967. DOI: 10.1007/s10869-020-09715-2

Ryder, M. J. (2022). Lessons from science fiction: Frederik Pohl and the robot prosumer. Journal of Consumer Culture. DOI: 10.1177/1469540520944228

Sætra, H. S. (2022). Robotomorphy: Becoming our creations. AI and Ethics. DOI: 10.1007/s43681-021-00092-x

Saha, P. A. & Lumare, N. (2024). The Nostalgia Chronicles: A Saga Of Brand Loyalty Across Ages: An Empirical Investigation of Nostalgia and Brand Loyalty in Different Generational Cohorts.

Schneider, C., & Bousbiat, H. (2023). Coaching Robots for Older Seniors: Do They Get What They Expect? Insights from an Austrian Study. International Journal of Environmental Research and Public Health, 20(4), 2965. DOI: 10.3390/ijerph20042965

Serholt, S., Ljungblad, S., & Ní Bhroin, N. (2022). Introduction: special issue—critical robotics research. AI & Society. DOI: 10.1007/s00146-021-01224-x

Sheng, A. & Wang, F. (2022). Falling in love with machine: emotive potentials between human and robots in science fiction and reality. Neohelicon. DOI: 10.1007/s11059-022-00664-8

Shmatko, N. & Volkova, G. (2020). Bridging the skill gap in robotics: Global and national environment. Sage Open. DOI: 10.1177/2158244020958736

Smakman, M., Vogt, P., & Konijn, E. A. (2021). Moral considerations on social robots in education: A multi-stakeholder perspective. Computers & Education. DOI: 10.1016/j.compedu.2021.104317

Song, C. S. & Kim, Y. K. (2022). The role of the human-robot interaction in consumers' acceptance of humanoid retail service robots. Journal of Business Research. DOI: 10.1016/j.jbusres.2022.03.087

Suchman, L. (2023). Imaginaries of omniscience: Automating intelligence in the US Department of Defense. Social Studies of Science. DOI: 10.1177/03063127221104938

Suraci, C., Pizzi, S., Montori, F., Di Felice, M., & Araniti, G. (2022). 6G to take the digital divide by storm: Key technologies and trends to bridge the gap. Future Internet. DOI: 10.3390/fi14060189

Tsaramirsis, G., Kantaros, A., Al-Darraji, I., Piromalis, D., Apostolopoulos, C., Pavlopoulou, A., ... Khan, F. Q. (2022). A modern approach towards an industry 4.0 model: From driving technologies to management. Journal of Sensors, 2022(1), 5023011. DOI: 10.1155/2022/5023011

Vaitheeswaran, G., Sundaravadivazhagan, B., & Karthikeyan. (2023). Some Studies of the Latest Artificial Intelligence Applications of Drones are Explored in Detail with Application Phenomena. Drone Technology: Future Trends and Practical Applications, 99-116. DOI: 10.1002/9781394168002.ch5

Valori, I., Fan, Y., Jung, M. M., & Fairhurst, M. T. (2024). Propensity to trust shapes perceptions of comforting touch between trustworthy human and robot partners. Scientific Reports. DOI: 10.1038/s41598-024-57582-1

Weber, J., & Urick, M. J. (2023). Searching for a stronger generational understanding than just age: A multi-country analysis of millennials' personal values and moral reasoning. *Journal of Intergenerational Relationships*, 21(1), 110–135. Advance online publication. DOI: 10.1080/15350770.2021.1951920

Weiss, A. & Spiel, K. (2022). Robots beyond Science Fiction: mutual learning in human–robot interaction on the way to participatory approaches. AI & society. DOI: 10.1007/s00146-021-01209-w

Wong, A., & Wong, J. (2024). Service robot acceptance in museums: An empirical study using the service robot acceptance model (sRAM). *Journal of Services Marketing*, 38(5), 619–635. Advance online publication. DOI: 10.1108/JSM-05-2023-0183

Wullenkord, R. & Eyssel, F. (2020). Societal and ethical issues in HRI. Current Robotics Reports. DOI: 10.1007/s43154-020-00010-9

Yew, G. C. K. (2021). Trust in and ethical design of carebots: the case for ethics of care. International Journal of Social Robotics. DOI: 10.1007/s12369-020-00653-w

Zeddies, H. H., Busch, G., & Qaim, M. (2024). Positive public attitudes towards agricultural robots. Scientific Reports. DOI: 10.1038/s41598-024-66198-4

Zsido, A. N., Coelho, C. M., & Polák, J. (2022). Nature relatedness: A protective factor for snake and spider fears and phobias. People and Nature.

KEY TERMS AND DEFINITIONS

Bilingualism: Proficiency in speaking and comprehending two languages fluently. It may denote persons, communities, or societies in which two languages are prevalently utilized.

Cultural Identity: The feeling of affiliation with a specific culture, frequently influenced by language, customs, and collective experiences. It affects individuals' self-perception and their interactions with others.

Cultural Relativism: The notion that an individual's views, values, and practices ought to be comprehended within the context of their own culture, rather than evaluated against the standards of a different culture.

First Language (L1): The initial language acquired by an individual, usually spoken by their family or community, commonly known as their mother tongue.

Intercultural Competence: The capacity to engage in effective and suitable communication with individuals from diverse cultural backgrounds. It entails comprehending cultural variances and adjusting communication methods accordingly.

Language Transfer: The impact of an individual's first language (L1) on their acquisition of a secondary language (L2). This may lead to either positive or negative transfer based on the similarities or contrasts between the languages.

Multilingualism: The utilization or existence of various languages within a society, individual, or community. It denotes the capacity of persons to communicate and comprehend in multiple languages, specifically more than two.

Sociolinguistics: The examination of the interplay between language and society, encompassing the variations of language across diverse social circumstances, groups, and civilizations.

Target Language (L2): A language that is being learnt or acquired, typically denoting the second language in the context of language instruction or acquisition.

Translanguaging: The practice of employing many languages concurrently or seamlessly in a dialogue or educational setting. It contests conventional limits between languages and underscores fluid communication.

Chapter 5
Exploring the Role of AI Attitude and AI Perception on AI Anxiety Among Indian Students

Souvik Rajbanshi
https://orcid.org/0009-0004-3242-5297
Christ University, India

Madalaimuthu Anthony
https://orcid.org/0000-0003-2857-0630
Christ University, India

Ganesh Kumar J.
Christ University, India

ABSTRACT

The increase in emerging AI technologies and their rapid evolution makes it difficult for students to effectively learn all these technologies as well as uncertainty in priorities as it keeps evolving. This brings a gap between individuals' skills and knowledge which further increases AI anxiety among the learners. The present study aims to understand the attitude and perception towards AI and AI anxiety among students in India. The authors utilised standardized test measures to collect the data among students. Perception and attitude towards AI and impact of AI had significant positive relationship while techno skepticism was negatively related. Further, significant difference was found in AI perception and techno skepticism based on gender and level of computer literacy. This study underscores the importance of digital literacy for healthy adoption and usage of AI.

1. INTRODUCTION

Artificial intelligence (AI) systems, which are modelled after human intellect, are getting better at learning, reasoning, self-correcting, and, in some cases, mimicking human decision making (Russell et al., 2016; Watson, 2019). Modern life is permeated with AI, which makes smart technology and apps like social media platforms, fitness monitors, and smart homes possible (Gorwa et al., 2020; Lockey et

DOI: 10.4018/979-8-3693-6366-9.ch005

al., 2021). Additionally, different levels of autonomy provided by AI technologies reduce the necessity for human supervision or control. Many AI-enabled gadgets also include humanistic traits and processing of natural language capabilities, which transform them into social groups (Watson, 2019). Concerns concerning AI's ethics and governing principles have been raised due to the technology's influence and widespread use. The use of AI in crucial fields like health, finance, and criminal justice, according to experts, would reinforce the same inefficiencies in human thought, depriving the technologies of its potential to construct new systems that educate and augment human intellect to right social transgressions (AI HLEG, 2019). The black-box aspect of machine-learning algorithms, which produce responses that imitate human responses without providing enough insight of the underlying mechanism, further fuels the anxiety that our dependence on AI will undermine human agency (Barredo Arrieta et al., 2020).

1.1 Theoretical Backup

A brief search reveals that most individuals have mixed feelings regarding the development of artificial intelligence (AI). On the one hand, people perceive benefits provided by AI applications like recent developments in speech and picture recognition. On the other hand, they are aware of the accompanying unfavourable effects of growing automation, including job loss and the erosion of people's rights to privacy, liberty, and agency. It has been noted that movies make efficient use of both visual and auditory components to convey information through outstanding communication (Joseph & Hosea, 2020). The use of efficient filmmaking techniques into movies aids in the audience's successful message delivery. In light of its pervasive and effective usage in subject-matter instruction, Topal et al. (2020) and Kontaş (2016) stated that films should not be restricted to a means of delivering enjoyment alone but should also assist people in tracking their activities. According to Liaw and Huang's research from 2003, media such as movies convey information culture by reflecting attitudes and beliefs and instructing viewers on how to absorb and communicate information. The audience's belief that movies are informative is thus a result of the connection between personal attitudes and behaviours and information processing. It is thought that watching movies makes viewers feel as though the information they have learned is important, moral, and acceptable in society. Almara'beh, Amer, and Sulieman (2015) discovered that a single watching of a movie can change viewers' perceptions regarding the values of instructional movies. When a movie is compared to other films that are comparable to it, the effect might be more striking. Films are now employed for purposes other than simply conveying entertaining stories, which is a commonality in the twenty-first century. These days, people utilise them to look for information. For instance, a viewer who wishes to learn about the culture and customs of a different nation must watch a few of their films. Additionally, finding information necessitates two ways of being exposed to communications (Dutta- Bergman, 2004). First, when someone approaches a media source, they engage in information search behaviour to familiarize themselves with either the overall material or a modulated carrier. The sensations a viewer gets while viewing a movie containing subject information in the course of message scanning are referred to as information receptivity in the second definition. In this way media such as movies which portray artificial intelligence and robots to develop autonomy and become maleficent have a staggering effect on people's perception-which is the process or outcome of being aware of things, connections, and events through the senses, including actions such as recognising, observing, and distinguishing- towards artificial intelligence and also influences their attitudes and behaviours towards artificial intelligence. Richardson examined the existential dangers ("aannihilation anxieties") that another intelligence presents to humans in an Anthropology of Robots and AI: Annihilation Anxiety and Machines. The author stated that there exists a profound link connecting our fiction of machines and our "life realities of robotic behaviours," which influence our perceptions of both. Perhaps our AI worry derives from our primitive nature, motivated by domination and our own history of murder, oppression, and intolerance of others, since our worries frequently mirror ourselves above all else. But there's also the dread of being made obsolete, replaced, or eliminated.

The widespread mistrust is exacerbated by images of autonomous robots and the domination of humans by technology. Concepts of technological utopianism are at best naïve and at worst destructive given current debates over how technology should be used to manage privacy, public discourse, and government control over its population. As people struggle with a shifting reality and an unknown future, AI anxiety is becoming more and more of a recognised phenomenon (Johnson and Verdicchio, 2017). In order to combat AI anxiety, it is crucial to look into its correlations in order to find ways to lessen suffering and better control people's feelings and perceptions.

A survey examined seven topics: if either AI will make us happier, improve or worsen human relationships, improve or rule our lives, relieve us of labour-intensive tasks or leave us impoverished, foster or stifle our creativity, make our world free of crime or subject it to greater surveillance, and significantly enhance growing inequality. With the exception of one, the availability of information, the majority of respondents expressed negative opinions on all seven items. Four of every five respondents predicted a rise in economic inequality. These findings led to the conclusion that it is crucial to increase social integration of AI before it is implemented in society in order to counteract these pessimistic views (Inaba & Togawa, 2020). It has been stated that a large portion of AI worry is exaggerated and may be linked to three things: a sole emphasis on AI programmes that ignores humans, uncertainty regarding autonomy in supercomputing entities and in humans, as well as a flawed understanding of technological growth. They come to the conclusion that there are valid concerns about AI, however not for the arguments put forward by AI alarmists (Johnson & Verdicchio, 2017). The acceptance or adoption of information technology (IT) has drawn a lot of attention during the past 10 years. To explain end-users' acceptance behaviour, several theoretical models have been put forth. One of these is the widely used and experimentally proven Technology Acceptance Model (TAM) by Davis (1989).

According to TRA, attitudes are influenced by beliefs, and attitudes, in turn, are influenced by intentions, which then result in action. Subjective norms represent perceptions that significant others might want them to execute the conduct, whereas attitudes are favourable or unfavourable evaluations of executing the activity in the future. Hence, the Theory of Reasoned Action provides a basis for understanding the development of perception and formation of attitudes towards AI.

1.2 Current Study

There is no assurance that perhaps the ratios will balance, even if AI does open up more employment prospects. Both the company and the employee have difficulties in locating the human and financial resources necessary to manage transition and reskill a sizable personnel base. Additionally, it is still unclear what percentage of residents may struggle to learn new skills and what steps should be made to assist them. However, given the current state of globalisation, it is unrealistic for India to delay the adoption of the cutting-edge AI technology (Srivastava, 2018). Understanding the perspectives of the people in the various social strata is crucial for a successful application of Technologies such as AI in India and to prevent a confrontation between science and society. By documenting I the type of knowledge people have about various AI systems, (ii) their attitudes toward and expectations of such technologies, and (iii) the roots of panic and risk attributes on them, it is essential to develop strategies that effectively educate people about the advantages of emerging technologies and allay fears (Bagla and Binoy, 2017). Additionally, before AI applications begin to have an influence on society, it is vital for the government to set in place rules and regulations without provoking conflict in the community (Ghosh, 2017). The construction of efficient and comprehensive educational programmes for training the developing generations to deal with evolving work environments is another benefit that research concentrating on Indians' perspectives of AI provides to educational institutions. Additionally, if the creator was aware of the recipient's views, the venture would be simple. Although these researches on the demographics of America and Europe are expanding swiftly, they are still relatively new in India. In this context, the current study aims to understand youths' perception and attitudes towards upcoming AI systems and evolution of technologies in India. The current study explicitly had three goals. The initial goal was to investigate the youth's perceptions towards integration of novel AI technologies. The second goal was to determine the relationship between the aforementioned perception and attitudes of the youth towards AI. The ultimate goal was to determine how these perceptions and attitudes determine the prevalence of AI anxiety in the youth in India. Hence, we first expected (1) a significant positive association between AI perception, attitudes and impact of AI among students.

According to a survey, 42% of respondents think that perhaps the impact of Artificial intelligence on net new job creation would vary by industry and that, on balance, more job vacancies will be generated than destroyed. (Narayanan, 2020). According to 63% of the populace, people will always be smarter than AI systems. The study's findings reveal one perplexing pattern regarding how adolescents see artificial intelligence. Age groups under 40 had much lower levels of optimism about the creation of net new employment than age groups over 40. Furthermore, respondents under the age of 40 are three times less certain than those over the age of 40 that artificial intelligence will not surpass human intellect. Very few people, according to another study in 2019, disagreed with the statement that in India existing education system does not prepare the youth for occupying AI based jobs. Youth will have to acquire both soft and hard skills as well as training in 'coding and programming for adapting with the changing environment. For the youths in India, there is a need for effective education and communication techniques on AI and its advantages (Narayanan, 2020). We also expected:

(2) Students from computer literacy to display lower levels of anxiety towards AI

(3) Students differ in their AI perception, attitude and anxiety based on their gender

2. REVIEW OF LITERATURE

2.1. AI Anxiety

Recent studies have highlighted growing anxiety surrounding artificial intelligence. "AI anxiety" stems from misunderstandings about AI's nature and potential, confusion about autonomy, and misconceptions about technological development (Johnson & Verdicchio, 2017). Research has shown that technology readiness inhibitors are positively related to various AI anxiety factors, including fears of job replacement and socio-technical illiteracy (Lemay et al., 2020). To measure this phenomenon, a standardized AI anxiety scale has been developed and validated (Wang & Wang, 2019).

A study in Saudi Arabia revealed widespread existential anxieties related to AI, with participants expressing fears about death, fate's unpredictability, meaninglessness, and ethical dilemmas (Alkhalifah et al., 2024). These findings underscore the need for a multidisciplinary approach to address AI-related anxieties, combining technological advancements with psychological, philosophical, and ethical insights to emphasize human values in an increasingly AI-driven world (Alkhalifah et al., 2024).

Recent studies have also explored the complex relationship between artificial intelligence (AI) literacy, anxiety, and acceptance. Schiavo et al. (2024) found that while AI literacy positively influences acceptance, anxiety partially mediates this relationship, with learning and sociotechnical dimensions playing a significant role. The Technology Acceptance Model constructs were also confirmed to shape attitudes towards AI.

Caporusso (2023) introduced the concept of "Creative Displacement Anxiety" (CDA), a psychological phenomenon arising from the perceived overshadowing of human creativity by AI tools. This study emphasized the need for interventions to support individuals in accepting AI as a creative companion. Terzi (2020) adapted an AI Anxiety Scale into Turkish, revealing that female teachers generally exhibit higher AI anxiety levels than male teachers across multiple dimensions. However, no significant differences were observed based on teachers' degree levels, age, or years of experience.

2.1.1 AI Perception

Recent studies have explored public perceptions of artificial intelligence (AI) across various demographics and contexts. College students generally view AI positively, though concerns exist about its rapid development and societal impact (Thomas R. Jeffrey, 2020). In the artistic domain, a perception bias favoring human-created artworks over AI-generated ones has been observed (Ragot et al., 2020). In Spain, factors such as gender and interest in scientific discoveries influence attitudes towards AI, with some individuals holding negative views (Albarrán-Lozano et al., 2021). A German study revealed diverse perceptions of AI across personal, economic, industrial, social, cultural, and health contexts, with cybersecurity threats emerging as the most critical concern (Brauner et al., 2023). Studies reveal that while people appreciate AI's benefits in urban services and disaster management, they also express concerns about privacy invasion (Yigitcanlar et al., 2022).

The public generally perceives AI as exciting, useful, worrying, and futuristic, with strong support for responsible development (Kelley et al., 2019). Government employees' willingness to use AI in public administration is influenced by their perceptions of its efficiency, long-term outlook, and familiarity with AI applications (Ahn & Chen, 2021).

Qualitative research indicates that public knowledge about AI often falls into two extremes: a dystopian view or an exaggerated, utopian attitude about its capabilities (Hick & Ziefle, 2022).

Studies spanning multiple nations reveal widespread belief in AI's significant societal impact (Kelley et al., 2019; Gerlich, 2023). While there's excitement about AI's potential in healthcare and improving life (Cave et al., 2019; Castagno & Khalifa, 2020), concerns persist regarding privacy, job loss, and potential dangers (Kelley et al., 2019; Gerlich, 2023; Cave et al., 2019).

Trust, perceived risks, and understanding of AI applications influence acceptance and attitudes (Gerlich, 2023). Healthcare professionals, while recognizing AI's usefulness, often lack comprehensive understanding and express worries about privacy and ethical implications (Castagno & Khalifa, 2020).

Public opinions on AI are malleable and influenced by various narratives (Gerlich, 2023; Cave et al., 2019). Many feel they have little control over AI's development, citing corporate or governmental power (Cave et al., 2019).

These findings highlight the need for accurate information and education about AI to manage expectations and foster a culture of innovation in both public and private sectors, as well as highlight the complexity of public attitudes towards AI, suggesting that perceptions are shaped by factors including knowledge, trust, and personal interests. Promoting AI literacy may be crucial for fostering informed decision-making and addressing biases in public perception.

2.1.2 Attitude Towards AI

Recent studies have explored attitudes towards artificial intelligence (AI) and their psychological correlates. Researchers have developed and validated scales to measure general attitudes towards AI, including the GAAIS (Schepman & Rodway, 2020, 2022) and ATTARI-12 (Stein et al., 2024). These studies have identified positive and negative dimensions of AI attitudes, with positive views often related to perceived societal and personal utility, while negative attitudes stem from various concerns.

Personality traits, such as agreeableness and introversion, have been associated with more positive AI attitudes (Stein et al., 2024; Schepman & Rodway, 2022). Additionally, younger age, lower conspiracy mentality, and higher general trust correlate with more favorable AI perceptions (Stein et al., 2024; Schepman & Rodway, 2022).

Self-determination theory has also been applied to understand AI attitudes, with basic psychological needs like autonomy and relatedness linked to increased AI positivity across European countries (Bergdahl et al., 2023). Public and industry attitudes towards AI are generally positive, especially among those with direct experience, though concerns exist (Vasiljeva et al., 2021; Scott et al., 2021).

Factors influencing AI adoption include top management attitudes, competition, and regulations (Vasiljeva et al., 2021). Personality traits, particularly higher levels of sadness, are associated with more negative attitudes towards AI (Montag et al., 2024). In healthcare, stakeholders favor AI applications that automate data interpretation over those directly influencing clinical decisions (Scott et al., 2021).

Employee attitudes towards AI can be paradoxical, with both positive "intelligent-automation attitudes" and negative "no-human-interaction attitudes" observed in the same individuals, depending on the situation (Lichtenthaler, 2019). Understanding and addressing these attitudes is crucial for successful AI implementation and maintaining competitive advantage in various industries.

3. METHODS

This study adopted cross-sectional correlation design. The researchers utilized standardized test measures to collect the data among 370 students using simple random sampling technique.

4. RESULTS

The data was subjected to statistical analysis such as correlation, t test, ANOVA and regression to test the hypothesis. The results were tabulated and presented in this section.

Table 1. Sample Characteristics

Characteristics	Response Option	Frequency	Percentage
Gender	Male	177	47.8
	Female	193	52.2
Education	Junior College	100	27.0
	UG	246	66.5
	PG	24	6.5
Computer/Internet Literacy	Basic	134	36.2
	Intermediate	187	50.5
	Advanced	49	13.2

Table 1 summarizes the demographic characteristics of the participants in this study. Males comprises Males comprise 177 participants, accounting for 47.8% of the total. Females make up 193 participants, representing 52.2%. Individuals with Basic literacy level total 134, representing 36.2%. Those classified as Intermediate literacy reach 187, accounting for 50.5%. Participants with Advanced literacy level are 49, which is 13.2%.

Table 2. Relationship between study variables

Variables	1	2	3	4
AI Perception	1			
AI Attitude	0.112*	1		
Impact	0.181*	0.245**	1	
Techno Skepticism	-0.141**	0.283**	0.218**	1
Socio Technical Blindness	0.008	0.580**	0.245**	0.453**

**Significant at 0.001; *significant at 0.05

The table 2 presents the correlation coefficients among various variables related to AI perception, attitude, impact, techno skepticism, and socio-technical blindness. AI Perception and AI Attitude have positive correlation indicating that as AI perception increases, AI attitude tends to improve favourably.

AI Perception and Impact of AI has a moderate positive correlation (r=0.181, p<0.05) suggesting higher AI perception is associated with a greater perceived impact of AI. AI Attitude and Impact of AI has stronger positive correlation (r=0.245, p<0.01) indicating favorable attitudes toward AI are linked with a higher perception of its impact. AI Perception and Techno Skepticism has a significant negative correlation (r=-0.141, p<0.01), suggesting that higher AI perception is associated with lower levels of techno skepticism. AI Attitude and Techno Skepticism has significant positive correlation (r=0.283, p<0.01) indicates that individuals with a more favorable attitude toward AI tend to exhibit higher levels of techno skepticism. Impact of AI and Techno Skepticism has moderate positive correlation (r=0.218, p<0.01) suggests that those who perceive a greater impact of AI also tend to be more skeptical of technology. AI Attitude and Socio-Technical Blindness have significant positive correlation (r=0.580, p<0.01) implying a favorable attitude towards AI is significantly associated with higher levels of socio-technical blindness. Impact and Socio-Technical Blindness: A positive correlation (r=0.245, p<0.01) indicates that perceiving a greater impact of AI is associated with higher socio-technical blindness. Techno Skepticism and Socio-Technical Blindness: A moderate positive correlation (r=0.453, p<0.01) suggests that higher techno skepticism is related to increased socio-technical blindness.

The correlation analysis indicates that perceptions and attitudes toward AI are interconnected, with higher perception linked to lower skepticism and varying impacts on socio-technical awareness. Favorable attitudes toward AI are associated with both higher socio-technical blindness and skepticism.

Table 3. Difference in study variables based on gender

Variables	Male (N= 177)		Female (N=193)		"t" value
	M1	SD1	M2	SD2	
AI Perception	16.28	1.79	15.39	1.67	4.90*
Impact of AI	23.01	3.44	22.50	3.37	1.41NS
Techno Skeptism	11.93	3.50	12.61	3.00	1.98*
Socio Technical Blindness	18.21	5.45	19.23	4.78	1.91NS
AI Attitude	15.71	2.99	15.91	2.78	0.66NS

*Significant at 0.05

It can be inferred from the table 3 that males scored higher (M=16.28, SD=1.79) than females (M=15.39, SD=1.67), with a significant difference indicated by the t-value (t=4.90, p<0.05). This suggests that males have a more positive perception of AI compared to females. Males (M=11.93, SD=3.50) exhibited lower levels of techno skepticism than females (M=12.61, SD=3.00), with a t-value of 1.98, which is significant at the p<0.05 level. This implies that females tend to be more skeptical about technology compared to their male counterparts The scores were 18.21 (SD=5.45) for males and 19.23 (SD=4.78) for females, with a t-value of 1.91 (p>0.05) in sociotechnical blindness. This indicates no significant difference in socio-technical blindness between genders. With regard to the attitude towards AI, males (M=15.71, SD=2.99) and females (M=15.91, SD=2.78); the impact of AI males (M=23.01, SD=3.44) and females (M=22.50, SD=3.37) did not show significant difference in their attitudes toward AI (t=0.66, p>0.05) and (t=1.41, p>0.05) on the impact of AI suggesting that both genders have similar views on these aspects.

It can be concluded that while there are significant differences in AI perception and techno skepticism between males and females, their views on the impact of AI, socio-technical blindness, and overall attitudes toward AI appear to be similar.

Table 4. Difference in Study Variables based on technical knowledge

Variables	Level of computer/Internet Literacy						F-Value	Duncan Post Hoc Test
	Basic (N= 134)		Intermediate (N=187)		Advanced (N=49)			
	M1	*SD1*	*M2*	*SD2*	*M3*	*SD3*		
AI Perception	**14.91**	**1.62**	**16.14**	**1.35**	**17.06**	**2.39**	**38.84****	**1 Vs 2 Vs 3**
Impact of AI	22.66	3.45	22.81	3.31	22.71	3.61	0.07NS	-
Techno Skeptism	12.64	3.19	12.26	3.29	11.41	3.27	2.59NS	3, 2 Vs 2, 1
Socio Technical Blindness	19.25	4.91	18.72	5.03	17.47	5.92	2.18NS	3, 2 Vs 2, 1
AI Attitude	15.97	2.75	15.86	2.81	15.24	3.42	1.17NS	-

**Significant at 0.001level; NS- Not Significant

AI Perception displayed significant variations across different literacy levels (F=38.84, p<0.01), with each group differing notably from the others. The Impact of AI did not exhibit significant differences (F=0.07). Although Techno Skepticism and Socio Technical Blindness had overall non-significant results, the post hoc analysis revealed specific differences between intermediate and other groups. AI Attitude also did not show significant variations among the groups.

The analysis indicates that levels of computer and Internet literacy significantly influence perceptions of AI, students with higher literacy having more positive views on AI. However, the impact of AI, techno skepticism, socio-technical blindness, and attitudes toward AI did not show significant differences across literacy levels. This suggests that while perception varies, other factors may require further investigation to understand their influence on attitudes and beliefs about AI.

Table 5. Stepwise Regression on Impact of AI

Predictor	R	R2	Δ R2	F(Δ R2)	*Df*
AI Perception	0.245	0.060	0.057	23.50*	368
AI Attitude	0.290	0.084	0.079	9.60*	367
Socio Technical Blindness	0.308	0.095	0.088	4.45*	366

* Significant at 0.05 level

AI perception shows a moderate correlation with the outcome variable, explaining 6% of the variance. The significant F-statistic suggests that this predictor contributes meaningfully to the model. AI attitude exhibits a stronger correlation than AI perception, accounting for 8.4% of the variance in the outcome variable. The significant F-statistic indicates that this predictor also adds value to the regression model. This predictor has the highest correlation with the outcome variable, explaining 9.5% of the variance. The F-statistic suggests that socio-technical blindness is a significant predictor, enhancing the model's explanatory power.

Overall, AI perception, attitude and socio technical blindless significantly contributes to the model, with socio-technical blindness having the strongest impact, followed by AI attitude and AI perception. These findings indicate the importance of perceptions and attitudes toward AI in understanding the impact of AI among students.

Table 6. Regression Models with Impact of AI as dependent variable

Model		Unstandardized Coefficients		Standardized Coefficients	t	Sig.	F
		B	Std. Error	Beta			
1	(Constant)	18.160	.961		18.896	.000	23..50 p<0.001
	AI Attitude	.290	.060	.245	4.848	.000	
2	(Constant)	13.777	1.704		8.087	.000	16.82 p<0.001
	AI Attitude	.269	.059	.227	4.525	.000	
	Perception	.298	.096	.156	3.099	.002	
3	(Constant)	13.357	1.707		7.824	.000	12.81 p<0.001
	AI Attitude	.179	.073	.152	2.464	.014	
	Perception	.312	.096	.163	3.256	.001	
	Socio Technical Blindness	.086	.041	.129	2.112	.035	

The table 6 summarizes the results from multiple regression analyses assessing the impact of various predictors on the outcome variable. The key components include unstandardized coefficients (B), standardized coefficients (Beta), t-values, significance levels (Sig.), and F-statistics. In this model, AI attitude significantly predicts the outcome variable, with a positive impact (B = 0.290). The model as a whole is significant, indicating that AI attitude is a meaningful predictor.

Model 2 indicates both AI attitude and AI perception are significant predictors. AI attitude remains positive (B = 0.269), while perception also shows a significant positive effect (B = 0.298). The overall model is significant, demonstrating the importance of both predictors.

In this final model, all three predictors—AI attitude, perception, and socio-technical blindness—are significant. AI attitude's impact is still positive (B = 0.179), while perception has the strongest positive effect (B = 0.312). Socio-technical blindness also contributes positively (B = 0.086), and the overall model remains significant. Across all models, AI attitude and perception consistently predict the outcome variable, with socio-technical blindness adding value in the final model. All predictors are statistically significant, reinforcing their importance in understanding impact of AI among students.

5. DISCUSSION

This study provides valuable insights on the perception, attitude and impact of AI among students, with significant differences based on gender and education. The analysis revealed significant gender difference in AI perception. These findings align with previous research indicating that males often exhibit more positive attitudes toward technology and innovation (Venkatesh et al., 2016). Conversely, females demonstrated higher levels of techno skepticism ($t=1.98, p<0.05$), which is consistent with studies suggesting that women are generally more cautious about the implications of technology (Fischer et al., 2020). This skepticism may stem from concerns about the ethical implications and societal impacts of AI, highlighting the need for more inclusive discussions around technology development. The educational background of participants also played a crucial role in shaping their perceptions and attitudes. With a majority holding undergraduate degrees (66.5%), it is evident that higher education may contribute to a more nuanced understanding of AI and its implications. This is supported by research indicating that education influences technology acceptance and critical analysis of its impact (López et al., 2021).

The correlation analysis showed significant relationships among key variables. Notably, AI perception positively correlated with AI attitude ($r=0.112$, $p<0.05$) and impact ($r=0.181$, $p<0.05$). These findings suggest that individuals who perceive AI more favorably are likely to hold positive attitudes and recognize its potential impact, reinforcing the idea that perception shapes acceptance and integration of technology (Davis, 1989).

Interestingly, the negative correlation between AI perception and techno skepticism ($r=-0.141$, $p<0.01$) indicates that as AI perception improves, skepticism decreases. This relationship underscores the importance of fostering positive perceptions through education and awareness to mitigate skepticism and enhance acceptance of AI technologies.

The strong correlation between AI attitude and socio-technical blindness ($r=0.580$, $p<0.01$) raises concerns about the potential for individuals to overlook critical issues related to technology. This aligns with findings that suggest a disconnect between positive attitudes toward technology and an awareness of its broader social implications (Brey, 2012). As attitudes become more favorable, there is a risk of neglecting the ethical and social dimensions of AI, which warrants further exploration.

6. CONCLUSION

Overall, the study highlights the complexities of gender, education, and perception in shaping attitudes toward AI and its impact among Indian students. Future research should focus on developing targeted educational programs that address the specific concerns of different demographic groups, especially women, to foster a more balanced understanding of AI's benefits and risks. Psychoeducation programs can address the gap between favorable attitude and critical awareness about AI. Additionally, exploring the long-term effects of education on techno skepticism and perception could provide deeper insights into the evolving relationship between society and technology to promote responsible and inclusive AI adoption.

REFERENCES

Adams, D. A., Nelson, R. R., & Todd, P. A. (1992). Perceived Usefulness, Ease of Use, and Usage of Information. *Management Information Systems Quarterly*, 16(2), 227–250. DOI: 10.2307/249577

Agarwal, R., Sambamurthy, V. & Stair, R.M. (2000). The Evolving Relationship between General and Specific Computer Self-Efficacy – An Empirical Assessment.

Ahn, M., & Chen, Y.-C. (2021). Digital transformation toward AI-augmented public administration: The perception of government employees and the willingness to use AI in government. *Government Information Quarterly*, 39(2), 101664. DOI: 10.1016/j.giq.2021.101664

AI HLEG. (2019). *Ethics guidelines for trustworthy AI.* European Commission. https://data.europa.eu/doi/10.2759/346720

Alkhalifah, J. M., Bedaiwi, A. M., Shaikh, N., Seddiq, W., & Meo, S. A. (2024). Existential anxiety about artificial intelligence (AI): Is it the end of humanity or a new chapter in the human revolution? A questionnaire-based observational study. *Frontiers in Psychiatry*, 15, 1368122. DOI: 10.3389/fpsyt.2024.1368122 PMID: 38654726

Almara'beh, H., Amer, E. F., & Sulieman, A. (2015). The effectiveness of multimedia learning tools in education. *International Journal of Advanced Research in Computer Science and Software Engineering*, 5(12), 761–764.

Arrieta, A. B., Díaz-Rodríguez, N., Del Ser, J., Bennetot, A., Tabik, S., Barbado, A., & Herrera, F. (2020). Explainable Artificial Intelligence (XAI): Concepts, taxonomies, opportunities and challenges toward responsible AI. *Information Fusion*, 58, 82–115. DOI: 10.1016/j.inffus.2019.12.012

Bergdahl, J., Latikka, R., Celuch, M., Savolainen, I., Mantere, E., Savela, N., & Oksanen, A. (2023). Self-determination and attitudes toward artificial intelligence: Cross-national and longitudinal perspectives. *Telematics and Informatics*, 102013, 102013. Advance online publication. DOI: 10.1016/j.tele.2023.102013

Brauner, P., Hick, A., Philipsen, R., & Ziefle, M. (2023). What does the public think about artificial intelligence?—A criticality map to understand bias in the public perception of AI. *Frontiers of Computer Science*, 5, 1113903. Advance online publication. DOI: 10.3389/fcomp.2023.1113903

Caporusso, N. (2023). Generative artificial intelligence and the emergence of creative displacement anxiety [Review]. *Research Directs in Psychology and Behavior*, 3(1). Advance online publication. DOI: 10.53520/rdpb2023.10795

Castagno, S., & Khalifa, M. (2020). Perceptions of artificial intelligence among healthcare staff: A qualitative survey study. *Frontiers in Artificial Intelligence*, 3, 578983. DOI: 10.3389/frai.2020.578983 PMID: 33733219

Cave, S., Coughlan, K., & Dihal, K. (2019). "Scary robots": Examining public responses to AI. In Proceedings of the 2019 AAAI/ACM Conference on AI, Ethics, and Society (pp. 331–337). Association for Computing Machinery. DOI: 10.1145/3306618.3314232

Davis, F. D. (1989). Perceived Usefulness, Perceived Ease of Use, and User Acceptance of Information Technology. *Management Information Systems Quarterly*, 13(3), 319. DOI: 10.2307/249008

Davis, F. D., Bagozzi, R. P., & Warshaw, P. R. (1989). User Acceptance of Computer Technology: A Comparison of Two. *Management Science*, 35(8), 982–1001. DOI: 10.1287/mnsc.35.8.982

Dutta-Bergman, M. J. (2004). Complementarity in consumption of news types across traditional and new media. *Journal of Broadcasting & Electronic Media, 48*(1), 41 60.

Fishbein, M., & Azjen, I. (1975). *Be- lief, Attitude, Intention and Behavior*. Addison-Wesley.

Gefen, D., Straub, D., & Boudreau, M. C. (2000). Structural equation modeling and regression: Guidelines for research practice. *Communications of the Association for Information Systems*, 4(1), 7. DOI: 10.17705/1CAIS.00407

Gerlich, M. (2023). Perceptions and acceptance of artificial intelligence: A multi-dimensional study. *Social Sciences (Basel, Switzerland)*, 12(9), 502. DOI: 10.3390/socsci12090502

Gorwa, R., Binns, R., & Katzenbach, C. (2020). Algorithmic content moderation: Technical and political challenges in the automation of platform governance. *Big Data & Society*, 7(1), 2053951719897945. DOI: 10.1177/2053951719897945

Hick, A., & Ziefle, M. (2022). A qualitative approach to the public perception of AI. *International Journal on Cybernetics & Informatics*, 11(4), 1–17. DOI: 10.5121/ijci.2022.110401

Inaba, Y., & Togawa, K. (2021). Social capital in the creation of AI perception. *Behaviormetrika*, 48(1), 79–102. DOI: 10.1007/s41237-020-00107-7

Jeffrey, T. R. (2020). Understanding college student perceptions of artificial intelligence. Retrieved from https://api.semanticscholar.org/CorpusID:235602425

Johnson, D. G., & Verdicchio, M. (2017). AI anxiety. *Journal of the Association for Information Science and Technology*, 68(9), 2267–2270. DOI: 10.1002/asi.23867

Joseph, A. B., & Hosea, I. (2020). Thematic relevance of music in nollywood movies. *IGWEBUIKE: An African Journal of Arts and Humanities*, 6(6), 140–150.

Kelley, P. G., Yang, Y., Heldreth, C., Moessner, C., Sedley, A., Kramm, A., Newman, D. T., & Woodruff, A. (2019). "Happy and assured that life will be easy 10 years from now": Perceptions of artificial intelligence in 8 countries. https://arxiv.org/abs/2001.00081

Kelley, P. G., Yang, Y., Heldreth, C., Moessner, C., Sedley, A., Kramm, A., Newman, D. T., & Woodruff, A. (2021). Exciting, useful, worrying, futuristic: Public perception of artificial intelligence in 8 countries. In Proceedings of the 2021 AAAI/ACM Conference on AI, Ethics, and Society (pp. 627–637). Association for Computing Machinery. DOI: 10.1145/3461702.3462605

Lemay, D. J., Basnet, R. B., & Doleck, T. (2020). Fearing the robot apocalypse: Correlates of AI anxiety.

Lemay, D. J., Basnet, R. B., & Doleck, T. (2020). Fearing the robot apocalypse: Correlates of AI anxiety. *International Journal of Learning Analytics and Artificial Intelligence for Education*, 2(2), 24–33. DOI: 10.3991/ijai.v2i2.16759

Liaw, S. S., & Huang, H. M. (2003). An investigation of user attitudes toward search engines as an information retrieval tool. *Computers in Human Behavior*, 19(6), 751–765. DOI: 10.1016/S0747-5632(03)00009-8

Lichtenthaler, U. (2019). Extremes of acceptance: Employee attitudes toward artificial intelligence. *The Journal of Business Strategy*, 40(1), 34–41. DOI: 10.1108/JBS-12-2018-0204

Lockey, S., Gillespie, N., Holm, D., & Someh, I. A. (2021). *A review of trust in artificial intelligence: Challenges, vulnerabilities and future directions. Hawaii International Conference on System Sciences.* DOI: 10.24251/HICSS.2021.664

Lozano, I., Molina, J., & Gijón, C. (2021). Perception of artificial intelligence in Spain. *Telematics and Informatics*, 63, 101672. DOI: 10.1016/j.tele.2021.101672

Montag, C., Ali, R., & Davis, K. (2024). Affective neuroscience theory and attitudes towards artificial intelligence. *AI & Society*. Advance online publication. DOI: 10.1007/s00146-023-01841-8

Ragot, M., Martin, N., & Cojean, S. (2020). AI-generated vs. human artworks: A perception bias towards artificial intelligence? In *Proceedings of the 2020 CHI Conference on Human Factors in Computing Systems*. DOI: 10.1145/3334480.3382892

Richardson, K. (2015). *An anthropology of robots and AI*. Routledge. DOI: 10.4324/9781315736426

Russell, S. J., Norvig, P., Davis, E., & Edwards, D. (2016). *Artificial intelligence: A modern approach* (3rd ed.). Pearson.

Schepman, A., & Rodway, P. (2020). Initial validation of the general attitudes towards Artificial Intelligence Scale. *Computers in Human Behavior Reports*, 1, 100014. DOI: 10.1016/j.chbr.2020.100014 PMID: 34235291

Schepman, A., & Rodway, P. (2022). The General Attitudes towards Artificial Intelligence Scale (GAAIS): Confirmatory validation and associations with personality, corporate distrust, and general trust. *International Journal of Human-Computer Interaction*, 38(10), 954–965. DOI: 10.1080/10447318.2022.2085400

Schiavo, G., Businaro, S., & Zancanaro, M. (2024). Comprehension, apprehension, and acceptance: Understanding the influence of literacy and anxiety on acceptance of artificial intelligence. *Technology in Society*, 77, 102537. DOI: 10.1016/j.techsoc.2024.102537

Scott, I., Carter, S., & Coiera, E. (2021). Exploring stakeholder attitudes towards AI in clinical practice. *BMJ Health & Care Informatics*, 28(1), e100450. DOI: 10.1136/bmjhci-2021-100450 PMID: 34887331

Stein, J.-P., Messingschlager, T., Gnambs, T., Hutmacher, F., & Appel, M. (2024). Attitudes towards AI: Measurement and associations with personality. *Scientific Reports*, 14(1), 2909. Advance online publication. DOI: 10.1038/s41598-024-53335-2 PMID: 38316898

Taylor, S., & Todd, P. (1995b). Assessing IT Usage: The Role of Prior Experience. *Management Information Systems Quarterly*, 19(4), 561–570. DOI: 10.2307/249633

Terzi, R. (2020). An adaptation of artificial intelligence anxiety scale into Turkish: Reliability and validity study.

Vasiljeva, T., Kreituss, I., & Lulle, I. (2021). Artificial intelligence: The attitude of the public and representatives of various industries. *Journal of Risk and Financial Management*, 14(8), 339. DOI: 10.3390/jrfm14080339

Venkatesh, V., & Davis, F. D. (2000). A theoretical extension of the technology acceptance model: Four longitudinal field studies. *Management Science*, 46(2), 186–204. DOI: 10.1287/mnsc.46.2.186.11926

Wang, Y. Y., & Wang, Y. S. (2019). Development and validation of an artificial intelligence anxiety scale: An initial application in predicting motivated learning behavior. *Interactive Learning Environments*, 30(4), 619–634. DOI: 10.1080/10494820.2019.1674887

Watson, D. (2019). The rhetoric and reality of anthropomorphism in artificial intelligence. *Minds and Machines*, 29(3), 417–440. DOI: 10.1007/s11023-019-09506-6

Yigitcanlar, T., Degirmenci, K., & Inkinen, T. (2024). Drivers behind the public perception of artificial intelligence: Insights from major Australian cities. *AI & Society*, 39(3), 833–853. DOI: 10.1007/s00146-022-01566-0 PMID: 36212229

Chapter 6
Digital Divide and Technological Determinism:
Factors Influencing the Digital Divide

Gülay Ekren
https://orcid.org/0000-0003-1226-7039
Sinop University, Turkey

ABSTRACT

The role of technology in our daily lives is increasing exponentially. This is evident in the diverse range of individuals who are now required to interact with computers, including university professors, kindergarten children, farmers, and nuclear scientists. The efforts of public institutions, politicians, and policymakers to address this issue have been insufficient. The accelerated developments in information and communication technologies have rendered it challenging for a considerable number of individuals to engage with these technologies in a manner that is both democratic and meaningful. This study addresses the digital divide issue in the context of technological determinism, examining the influence of various factors on the digital divide in the context of technological determinism. These factors include age, gender, digital abilities, race/ethnicity, and language.

INTRODUCTION

Technological determinism is a theory of social change that posits technology as the primary driver of societal evolution. The theory posits that information and communication technologies exert control over societal processes. The theory was initially proposed by the American sociologist and economist Thorstein Veblen (1857-1929) (Hauer, 2017). The theory also asserts that technology is a "fundamental driver" of historical change (Chandler, 1995). Those who adhere to the perspective of technological determinism posit that specific technological developments, such as those pertaining to media, information and communication technologies, or technologies in general, are the primary causal factor in societal

DOI: 10.4018/979-8-3693-6366-9.ch006

change. The view is taken that technology constitutes the fundamental condition underlying the model of social organisation.

Technologies such as the printing press, television, and computers have been observed to exert an influence on societal development. In its most extreme form, the shape of society is believed to be entirely determined by technology. It is posited that the advent of each new technology results in transformation at various levels of society. The role of technology, particularly that of the Internet, is becoming increasingly prevalent in our daily lives. In the past, computers were primarily utilised for high-level calculations, data storage and analysis. Nevertheless, this is no longer the case, with individuals from a diverse range of backgrounds, including university professors, kindergarten children, farmers, and nuclear scientists, all having to navigate the complexities of information and communication technologies. Over the past twenty-five years, the rise of the personal computer and the widespread use of the Internet have not been accompanied by sufficient efforts on the part of public institutions, policy makers and private companies to bridge the digital divide (Aruleba & Jere, 2022; Okoro et al., 2023; Kovac et al, 2024). Rapid developments in information and communication technologies, such as artificial intelligence, cloud computing, the Internet of Things, present a challenge for many people of different generations to interact with these technologies in a democratic and meaningful way.

It is an indisputable fact that technology has become one of the fundamental building blocks of our modern society. It is becoming increasingly difficult to identify any aspect of our lives that does not rely, in one way or another, on technology in general and computers in particular. It is becoming increasingly common for individuals to choose alternative methods of conducting financial transactions, such as online banking, in preference to visiting a physical branch (Sandhu & Arora, 2022). Clerks in restaurants and supermarkets now employ computer systems in order to facilitate the processing of bills, thereby eliminating the necessity for manual calculations (Hahn & Hahn, 2021). The advent of the internet has enabled consumers to undertake price comparisons online before making a purchase, thus avoiding the need to visit numerous stores (Setiawan et al., 2020). A considerable proportion of teachers consider their training to be incomplete unless they have taught at least some of their lessons using modern computer software (Wardat et al., 2023).

The necessity for the development of digital skills has become increasingly apparent in recent years. This is due to the fact that an increasing proportion of aspects of life, including those pertaining to people's working lives, are influenced by technology. As existing services such as banking, e-commerce and e-government become increasingly online-based, there is an exponential increase in the possibility of certain demographic groups, such as the elderly and especially those living in rural areas, being excluded from the digital economy. The 2018 OECD report indicates that women residing in rural areas of developing and emerging economies are comparatively more likely to utilise the Internet than their urban counterparts (OECD, 2018:25). However, globally, women are generally less likely to utilise the Internet than men.

As indicated in the OECD (2018:13) report, there is a discrepancy of approximately 327 million people worldwide who own a smartphone and have access to mobile internet. Moreover, the probability of women owning a smartphone is, on average, 26% less than that of men. In South Asia and Africa, the respective rates are 70% and 34%. Despite the fact that women and men have equal access to the internet and computer-based resources, they are only able to achieve their goals to the extent of their digital capabilities or skills. The digital divide, which is caused by limited and unfair access to technology or the internet, may result in individuals missing out on a number of social, economic and cultural opportunities. Consequently, it is not possible to guarantee democratic participation by all members of society.

The social cognitive theory proposed by Bandura (1991) postulates a mutual relationship between cognitive processes and environmental factors. In accordance with this model, when an individual's personal standards and self-regulatory activities are eroded, their behaviour will assume a malleable quality, akin to a windmill's shifting direction. This allows them to adapt their actions to align with prevailing norms and expectations. In other words, an individual's self-efficacy is directly influenced by the completion of tasks or the attainment of goals, and their willingness to do so. An individual with high self-efficacy in computer or internet usage will demonstrate less effort than those with low self-efficacy when attempting to complete or maintain a task on a computer or internet-based platform (Krueger et al., 2018). This is because failure to complete a task results in increased stress levels, decreased confidence and reduced performance. In considering the relationship between access to computers and the Internet and socioeconomic status, it becomes evident that individuals with higher incomes, more extensive social networks, higher levels of education, and greater skill sets are significantly more likely to have access to information and communication technologies (ICTs), to be able to use them, to benefit from them, and to be supported by ICTs in their participation in society across a range of dimensions, including economic, social, and cultural (Fuchs, 2009).

The role of technology in our daily lives is undergoing a rapid and significant expansion. The efforts of public institutions, politicians, and policymakers to address this issue have been inadequate. The accelerated developments in information and communication technologies have created challenges for a significant proportion of the population in engaging with these technologies in a manner that is both democratic and meaningful. This study addresses the digital divide issue in the context of technological determinism, examining the influence of various factors on the digital divide in the context of technological determinism. Such factors include age, gender, digital abilities, race/ethnicity and language.

WHAT IS THE DIGITAL DIVIDE?

The digital divide is a phenomenon that draws attention to the inequalities between people and societies in the adoption and diffusion of electronic information and communication technologies and applications (Genus & Nor, 2005). Hoffman and Novak (1998) define the digital divide as the discrepancy between individuals who possess the ability to access or utilise computers and those who lack such capabilities. The definition proposed by Hoffman and Novak is of particular significance, as their study (1998) was the pioneering investigation which was alarming disparities in access to computers and the Internet among ethnic groups in the United States during the early years of the Internet's widespread use (Fairlie, 2017).

The accessibility of information and communication technologies represents a pivotal element in the comprehension of the digital divide. In this context, the digital divide has a significant impact on a number of areas, including education, the economy, art and industry (Yaman, 2015). As Mossberger et al. (2003:120-121) observe in their analysis of the digital divide, the authors define the digital divide as "unequal patterns of access to information technologies based on income, race, ethnicity, gender, age, and geography" in their work, "Beyond the Digital Divide." Mossberger et al. (2003) identify four key areas of inequality, namely access, skills, economic opportunities and democratic participation, which should be considered beyond the digital divide. The discourse surrounding the digital divide should extend beyond the mere issue of access to technology and encompass four crucial dimensions of inequality. The aforementioned inequalities can be classified into the following categories:

- **Access:** Accessibility is a significant factor in the utilisation of digital resources. This is particularly prevalent among young people, who exhibit a high level of demand for access to these resources. Inequalities in the availability and utilisation of computers and the Internet are shaped by a range of socio-economic factors, including income, education, age, race and ethnicity.
- **Skills:** In terms of skills, the ability to utilise technology effectively and develop learning abilities is frequently constrained by deficiencies in educational resources and opportunities.
- **Economic Opportunities:** The potential for technology to facilitate economic mobility is constrained by a dearth of fundamental computer, literacy, and numeracy skills.
- **Democratic Participation:** Inequalities based on disparities in education, income, and interest are becoming increasingly prevalent or remaining entrenched for young people who are inadequately represented in democratic arenas or unable to secure a position.

In an opposing manner, democratic participation represents a dimension that affects disadvantaged groups in society, including disabled people and women. At present, a range of websites and software solutions are available for visually impaired individuals. These and analogous opportunities do not preclude visually impaired individuals and those with physical disabilities from accessing certain educational opportunities and public services. Technologies such as screen readers are of considerable benefit to such disadvantaged groups in the context of their learning processes. The Internet provides these groups with the opportunity to develop a range of skills in accordance with their needs and preferences, to utilise an unlimited range of resources, and to participate in online meetings, seminars and conferences. Nevertheless, these opportunities are not accessible in instances where the digital divide is evident (Yaman, 2015).

The advent of the digital divide is predicated on preliminary assessments of social inequality in the information age. The rapid expansion of the Internet in some countries in the late 1990s and early 2000s, while it lagged in others, necessitated a theoretical examination of the digital divide. The initial period of digital divide studies was shaped by unequal access to technological networks and infrastructure, which in turn resulted in unequal access to the information and online services they distribute. Norris (2001:13) characterises information and transmission technologies in the early 2000s as "a Pandora's box that revealed new inequalities in power and wealth, reinforcing deep information divisions between the rich and the poor, the informed and the uninformed, the hyper-connected and the unconnected".

The digital divide is also a complex phenomenon with a number of different dimensions. A consistent argument emerges from the existing literature (Carvin, 2000) that the digital divide cannot be measured by a simple rate of computer or internet access. Rather, it is a complex sociological phenomenon that affects society for a multitude of reasons. In his 2000 study, Carvin defines the digital divide as "one of the most significant civil rights concerns in our contemporary knowledge-based economy." He then proceeds to delineate the concept in five distinct dimensions: access, content, literacy, pedagogy, and community.

In terms of accessibility, the following points should be considered. The question of access to new technologies is not contingent on the possession of a computer or Internet connection. Inequalities in access persist regardless of these factors. For example, the global pandemic of 2020 demonstrated the vital importance of internet access, underscoring the necessity for individuals and communities to have reliable and secure online connectivity. During this period, individuals lacking sufficient or no Internet access encountered difficulties in accessing essential resources, including health-related information. Inequalities in access to digital content are observed among socioeconomically disadvantaged groups, defined by factors such as income level, and among socio-demographically disadvantaged groups, defined by factors such as race/ethnicity and gender. To illustrate, the expense of data on the Internet represents a substantial barrier to accessing digital resources, with those unable to afford these costs effectively being excluded from the digital landscape or limiting their data usage.

Despite the fact that a considerable number of individuals either possess or have access to a computer or the Internet, there are still significant inequalities in the ability to utilise computers or the Internet for meaningful purposes and to possess the necessary digital skills to do so. As indicated in the World Wide Web Foundation (2020) report, digital literacy represents a significant obstacle for rural women, the majority of whom are not internet users. Lack of knowledge is identified as the primary reason for their lack of engagement with digital resources.

In the contemporary era, the existence of the digital divide across the globe and between nations is irrefutable. Researchers are now turning their attention to the factors that influence the digital divide (Gruzdeva, 2022). For instance, Fuchs (2009) posits that income inequality may be a contributing factor to the digital divide. The analysis, comprising data from 126 countries in 2005, indicates that access to information and communication technologies is influenced by the interplay of socioeconomic, political, cultural, social, and technological factors. Consequently, it is argued that the digital divide cannot be attributed solely to technological factors. Instead, the factors causing the digital divide should be analysed in multiple ways.

Conversely, it is feasible for individuals to establish online communities with the intention of disseminating information, acquiring knowledge, and engaging in communication with other communities, while simultaneously contributing to the advancement of social, political, economic, and cultural capital. Inequalities exist with regard to the formation of online communities and the decision to include individuals in these communities.

An evaluation of the digital divide in terms of access reveals that individuals may have varying degrees of access to information and communication technologies. One aspect of this access is material access, which can be obtained in exchange for monetary compensation in contemporary societies due to the commodification of technologies. A further dimension is that of usage and skill access, which pertains to an individual's capacity or proficiency in utilising these technologies. Others are listed as a form of benefit access, which can be defined as the ability to embed these technologies within organisations, in short, institutional access (Fuchs, 2009). In the context of institutional access, key considerations include the extent to which citizens can access e-government applications and other institutional applications managed through ICT via the Internet. Additionally, there is a focus on enhancing citizens' access to ICT for political information, communication and participation in decision-making processes.

AGE-RELATED DIGITAL DIVIDE AND TECHNOLOGICAL DETERMINISM

One of the key factors contributing to the digital divide is age. One of the core reasons for this divide is the desire of individuals to continue working even though they are eligible for retirement. In Turkey, the Unemployment Insurance Law No. 4447 states that women are eligible for retirement at the age of 58, while men are eligible at the age of 60 (Şen, 2021). In 2008, the retirement age was increased to 65 for those who had commenced employment as insured individuals for the first time. However, in many cases, for economic reasons, individuals in Turkey do not wish to retire and continue to work even though they have reached the retirement age (Burlacu et al., 2017). Despite their distinctive experiences in comparison to their younger counterparts, these individuals encounter difficulties in utilising internet-based business applications.

One of the primary factors contributing to the digital divide between generations is the disparity in access to computers and the internet between older and younger individuals. The utilisation of these tools presents a challenge for the elderly population, as it has the potential to negatively affect their ability to take advantage of the opportunities they offer. Gruzdeva (2022) examined the impact of age on the digital divide and the tendency of children, adolescents and the elderly to engage with the digital environment. The study, which assesses the influence of information technology and information and communication networks on the lives of individuals across different age groups in Russia, indicates that there was a 23.2% increase in internet usage between 2015 and 2021. Overall, 87.1% of individuals under the age of 30, 71.3% of individuals between the ages of 30 and 55, and 31.9% of individuals over the age of 55 use the Internet to access social networks. Furthermore, individuals under the age of 55 primarily utilise the Internet for purposes such as obtaining information about products and services, conducting telephone or video calls, downloading films, pictures and music, viewing videos, requesting music, sending and receiving emails, and conducting financial transactions. Individuals aged 55 and above primarily utilise the Internet for social networking (31.9%), making telephone or video calls (25.2%) or conducting financial transactions (18.9%).

The findings of the study (Gruzdeva, 2022) suggest that over 50% of individuals under the age of 55 possess at least some digital skills, including the ability to utilise a text editor, send an email with attached files, copy or move files between a computer and peripheral devices, and employ photo, video and audio editing software. The study demonstrated that over 89% of individuals aged 55 and above lacked the requisite digital skills to perform advanced tasks, including the creation of electronic presentations using specialised software, the modification of software application configuration settings, the installation of a new operating system or the reinstallation of the operating system, and the development of software using programming languages.

Moreover, the digital divide has the potential to create disadvantages for those in the older age group in terms of access to job opportunities and job retention (Krueger et al., 2018). As indicated by Krueger et al. (2018), older workers' restricted access to the internet or computers and their inability to utilise them preclude them from capitalising on the opportunities that are currently widely available online. Such services include the submission of job applications, the pursuit of promotions, the undertaking of training for self-education, and the utilisation of other social services, such as social security and unemployment insurance.

In the context of technological determinism, older adults (over 65) are frequently depicted in academic literature and public discourse as a monolithic entity, characterised as technophobic and exhibiting low levels of digital literacy and technology utilisation. However, the role of socioeconomic factors and personal contexts in later life is frequently neglected in studies of technology adoption and use (Neves et al., 2018). In their study, Abbey and Hyde (2009) sought to explore the attitudes of politically active older people (24 participants) aged between 65 and 80, residing in the UK, towards information and communication technologies. Furthermore, the researchers sought to determine whether the attitudes of senior political activists towards the utilisation of ICTs were more aligned with those of politically engaged younger citizens or with other individuals within their age cohort. All participants were found to engage with the internet, email and mobile phones.

It has been demonstrated that negative stereotypes about the age-related digital divide have a detrimental effect on the performance of older people when undertaking computer and internet-based tasks (Lamont & Swift, 2015). Further research is required to elucidate the perception that older adults' limited proficiency in internet and computer skills leads to feelings of anxiety and restlessness when using the internet or similar technologies, which in turn impairs their performance (Krueger et al., 2018). The primary factors influencing the uptake of new communication technologies among older adults are contingent upon attitudinal, functional, and physical considerations. Attitudinal factors may include interest, perceived usefulness, distrust of technology, or the perception that the individual is too old to engage with this technology. Conversely, physical factors may include health limitations associated with age-related impairments, such as decreased manual and motor skills and vision loss.

In addition to these factors, it is important to consider the functional aspects of technology use, including the equipment employed, access to said equipment, training related to its use, digital skills, and usability issues related to technology design and size. It is essential to consider the sociotechnical dimension of technology in older adults, which encompasses the complexity they experience in adapting to and using technology (Neves et al., 2018).

GENDER-BASED DIGITAL DIVIDE AND TECHNOLOGICAL DETERMINISM

In the context of technological innovations and related policies, it is essential to evaluate the path to be followed to achieve universal Internet access, taking into account the gender-based digital divide (Cooper, 2006). Despite an increase in Internet and other communication technology usage, female users, particularly in developing countries, remain on the disadvantaged side of the digital divide (Acilar & Sæbø, 2023). For example, factors such as limited access, high costs, a lack of education and digital skills, as well as inherent biases and sociocultural norms, prevent women and girls from fully leveraging the opportunities offered by digital transformation. (OECD, 2018, p. 5). The sociocultural norms that determine women's behaviour and interests exert a significant influence on girls' and women's capacity to access information technologies.

Although the rapid transition to digital technologies appears to be beneficial for all, studies on the gender digital divide (OECD, 2018:14) indicate that women tend to utilise digital tools less frequently than men. Women are less likely to utilise digital services than men and display lower levels of confidence in navigating the internet. For example, while mobile money accounts represent an effective strategy for enhancing financial inclusion, a smaller proportion of women are likely to possess and utilise such an account.

A review of existing literature reveals a significant disparity in the representation of women and men in the field of technology in developing countries (Hafkin and Taggart, 2001; Antonio and Tuffley, 2014). This phenomenon is more likely to result from the existence of deeply embedded sociocultural attitudes that define the roles of women within societies. As Antonio and Tuffley (2014) note, a number of factors impede women's access to the internet in developing countries. These barriers include: (1) The exclusion of women from technology training and design; (2) The disproportionately heavy burden of household and family responsibilities, which limits the free time available to adapt to new technologies; (3) Social norms that favour men and gender norms regarding men's control over technology, information and knowledge, which limit women's opportunities to benefit from them; (4) The limited financial means and restricted access to economic resources that leave women powerless to access information and communication technologies.

In his 2016 study, Cooper posits that the primary cause of the digital divide is gender-based. The paper puts forward a number of preliminary recommendations for potential solutions to this problem, based on an examination of the factors that perpetuate the digital divide and an analysis of the available empirical evidence. In accordance with Cooper (2006), irrespective of age, background or competence in technology, men evince a greater interest in and competence with regard to computer use. The study identifies this as a threat to women and girls, arguing that the mere awareness of the stereotype that girls are not adept at computers causes girls to experience stress when learning from computers, which in turn leads to a decline in their computer performance. The study also puts forth the proposition that in order to guarantee that girls can reap the benefits of the ongoing technological revolution and to diminish the digital divide, it is imperative for society to eradicate the pervasive gender stereotypes that assume girls are incapable of adeptly utilizing computers.

In their study, which examines the characteristics and factors contributing to the gender digital divide, Acilar and Sæbø (2021) highlight that women's adoption or non-adoption of digital technologies is contingent upon these factors. For instance, the literature reviewed indicates that sociocultural, economic, and educational factors are the primary contributors to the gender-based digital divide. The causes of the gender digital divide are numerous and complex. These include gender inequality in the economy and education, cultural expectations, traditional gender roles, and the failure of policy to overcome inequalities, which vary from country to country and context to context (World Wide Web Foundation, 2020).

DIGITAL CAPABILITY-BASED DIGITAL DIVIDE AND TECHNOLOGICAL DETERMINISM

The concept of a digital divide based on digital capability and the notion of technological determinism are two key theoretical frameworks that inform our understanding of the relationship between digital capability and technological outcomes. Digital capability can be defined as the ability to live, work, participate and develop in the digital world (Brown et al., 2020). It is important to note that digital capability should not be confused with digital literacy. Although both concepts focus on providing the technical and cognitive skills necessary for an individual to participate in a digital society with a socio-technical approach, digital literacy is seen more as an individual's ability to use information and communication technologies. The concept of digital literacy, as defined by McDougall et al. (2016), encompasses the use of digital technologies in a way that is responsive to the lived realities of individuals, taking into account the diversity of their life experiences, preferences and aspirations. It includes an awareness of the different roles, relationships and personal interactions, and an understanding of their potential implications, as well as an understanding of social networks, institutional and technological interactions.

A European Union (EU) wide survey (https://social-rights.campaign.europa.eu/) has found that 77% of EU companies are having difficulty recruiting workers with the necessary digital skills. The shortfall covers 28 occupations, including construction, healthcare, engineering and information technology. In the EU, 40% of adults aged 55-74 with low levels of education or unemployment lack basic digital skills. In 2019, the European Union (EU) announced its intention to focus on developing digital skills in five different areas over the next decade. This has been set out in the EU's Digital Competences Framework (DigComp), as shown in Table 1.

Table 1. The Digital Competence Framework for Citizens (DigComp,2019)

Digital Competence Area	Digital Competences
Information and data literacy	The ability to identify, locate, filter, retrieve, store, organise, analyse and manage digital information and data is essential.
Communication and collaboration	The ability to communicate in digital environments, to share resources using online tools, to interact and participate in communities and networks, and to demonstrate intercultural awareness are some key skills that students need to develop in order to become digitally literate.
Creating digital content	The creation and editing of digital and multimedia content, the integration and re-editing of digital content, the production of creative media outputs, the writing of programmes and code, the management and enforcement of intellectual property rights and licences.
Security	Protecting digital tools, safeguarding data, protecting digital identity, implementing security measures and ensuring safe and sustainable use are all essential aspects of digital literacy.
Problem solving	Solving technical problems, identifying digital needs and resources, using technology in innovative ways, and updating one's own and others' digital skills are also crucial elements of digital literacy.

The Digital Skills and Jobs Coalition (DSJC) is an EU initiative that brings together a wide range of stakeholders, including companies, social partners, non-profit organisations and training providers. The aim of the coalition is to address the shortage of digital skills in Europe. The DSJC provides an opportunity for organisations taking action to improve digital skills across Europe to learn from their peers (https://digital-skills-jobs.europa.eu/).

A study conducted in Australia (Antonio and Tuffley, 2015) examined the digital literacy skills of a group of adults (20 individuals) living in rural areas. The majority of the participants, representing over 75% of the sample, had not previously engaged with social networks, shared photos or videos, shared files, or used blogs or online libraries. Almost half of the participants reported a lack of confidence in their ability to use these technologies. However, almost half of the participants demonstrated an understanding of the basics of email. The results of this study suggest that, despite their relatively low levels of confidence, older adults are still willing to learn how to use digital technologies. There is an urgent need to develop pedagogical strategies to improve the digital literacy skills of older adults, especially those living in rural and remote areas (Antonio and Tuffley, 2015).

On the other hand, information technologies are increasingly used in the healthcare system, including mobile health applications, wearable devices, digital medicine applications, online healthcare services and big data-based clinical solutions. These technologies have the potential to improve the efficiency and quality of healthcare services. However, older people's varying levels of competence in using these technologies may limit their ability to fully benefit from them. The concept of digital literacy, which emphasises the connection between older adults and their social contexts, aims to reduce the age-based 'digital divide' (Zhao et al., 2023).

DIGITAL DIVIDE AND TECHNOLOGICAL DETERMINISM IN RELATION TO RACE/ETHNICITY

The concepts of the digital divide and technological determinism intersect with issues of race and ethnicity in a profound manner, influencing access to technology, participation in digital spaces, and the socio-economic opportunities that emerge from technological advancements. In their study, Loges and Jung (2001) emphasise the importance of considering the impact of ethnicity on the digital divide, particularly in relation to the influence of internet connection and the unequal distribution of internet access (in terms of regional location). The study which was conducted at a time when the internet was just beginning to become widespread, emphasises that closing the digital divide through access to technology and education will not be sufficient.

A substantial corpus of research has demonstrated the existence of a "digital divide" between younger and older individuals. Older adults are less inclined to engage with the internet and other digital technologies than their younger counterparts (Loges and Jung, 2001; Campos-Castillo, 2015). However, the extent to which technology use varies according to racial/ethnic background constitutes a further aspect of the digital divide (Loges and Jung, 2001; Campos-Castillo, 2015; Fairlie, 2017).

A number of studies conducted in the United States have indicated a correlation between internet access and socioeconomic status among individuals from different ethnic backgrounds. In their study, Hoffman and Novak (1998) examine the digital divide caused by racial differences (White Americans and African Americans) in America in the late 1990s, when internet access was a prerequisite for computer use. It has been demonstrated that the digital divide is a consequence of income disparities and discrepancies in educational attainment between these two distinct racial groups. The results of a study conducted on 5,873 American citizens aged 16 and above indicated that 44.2% of White Americans and 29% of African Americans had access to a computer at home. Fourteen percent of white individuals and nine percent of African Americans have internet access at home.

Furthermore, irrespective of ethnic origin, individuals with elevated incomes are more likely to possess a computer at their place of residence. Similarly, irrespective of ethnic origin, as the level of education increases, the rate of access to computers in the workplace also increases. The following statement is included in the recommendations section of this study: In order to guarantee that all Americans are able to participate in the information age, it is essential to implement policies that will enhance educational opportunities for African Americans. This suggests that during that period, the digital divide based on ethnicity was associated with access to educational opportunities. Further research conducted by Campos-Castillo (2015) based on data from 2007 to 2012 revealed that Blacks and Latinos in America were equally likely to have internet access. Nevertheless, both groups were found to be less likely to have internet access than the white population.

In their 2015 study, Campos-Castillo investigated the nexus of gender, race, and ethnicity in American society. Their findings revealed that between 2007 and 2012, adult women were more likely than men to report having internet access. In 2007, there was a greater likelihood of women having access to the Internet than men. However, this discrepancy remained relatively unchanged in 2012. No significant changes were observed in terms of gender differences in Internet access among the White population. However, between 2007 and 2012, there was a notable increase in internet access among Black men, with this demographic becoming the newest group of internet users. This represents a noteworthy change, particularly given that Black males were the least likely to report internet access in 2007 and that the gender gap among Black males was the largest during this period. Moreover, the change in Internet access between 2007 and 2012 for Black men was found to be only marginally greater than the change in access among Black women over the same period.

In a study conducted in 2019, Mitchell and colleagues employed nationally representative data from older Americans to identify potential racial and ethnic differences with regard to health-related technology usage. In comparison to their White counterparts, older Black individuals are less likely to utilise technology for health-related purposes, as evidenced by data from 1,336 White and Black individuals aged

54 and above. Moreover, older Black individuals were less likely to engage in a range of health-related activities, including making or receiving phone calls, utilising health websites, searching the internet for health information, and employing cognitive strategies for health purposes.

In their 2020 study, Yoon and colleagues examined data from 17,704 older adults in California and found that socioeconomic status (SES) was a strong predictor of internet use among white participants. In contrast, it was identified as a more significant determinant for ethnic minorities, including African, Latin American, Asian American, and other groups. The results of this study can be interpreted as being attributable to age-related differences rather than racial/ethnic differences. In this case, the question that arises is whether internet use among young people in multicultural societies differs according to socioeconomic and cultural factors. One might be prompted to inquire whether ethnicity constitutes one of these factors.

In a study conducted by Millioni et al. (2014), the authors sought to address the aforementioned questions regarding the experiences of Cypriot youth. Subsequent to the military occupation in 1974, the island was effectively partitioned, with Turkish Cypriots residing in the northern region and Greek Cypriots in the southern region. Cypriot youth currently reside in a country that is characterised by significant ethnic, linguistic and socioeconomic divisions. Moreover, economic development in the northern region is comparatively sluggish, with the region exhibiting approximately half the per capita gross domestic product (GDP) of the southern region. As a consequence, the standard of living in the northern region is inferior to that of the southern region.

In their 2014 study, Millioni and colleagues identified a correlation between the demographic characteristics of 203 Cypriot young people aged 18-24 who use the internet and their access to and use of the internet. Nevertheless, there is no compelling evidence to suggest that there is a significant digital divide among young people in terms of their demographic characteristics.

Similarly, Anderson (2014) investigated the impact of ethnicity and income level on the frequency with which students access computers and the internet outside of school, as well as the probability of owning mobile technologies such as laptops, smartphones, tablets, and iPads. The findings indicated that minority and lower socioeconomic income students were less likely to have access to computers, broadband internet, or mobile laptops or tablets. It has been demonstrated that minority students are more likely to possess a smartphone than their non-minority counterparts. Conversely, students with lower socioeconomic status are less likely to own a smartphone than students with higher socioeconomic status.

Additionally, research conducted by Fairlie (2017) indicates that while individuals identifying as White have high-speed and quality internet access, individuals identifying as Black or Latin American are less likely to have a high-speed internet connection. Moreover, Blacks and Latin Americans also have restricted internet usage at home, which is attributed to their financial constraints in paying internet fees. In conclusion, it can be posited that income inequality and injustice may be responsible for a degree of the digital divide.

LANGUAGE-RELATED DIGITAL DIVIDE TECHNOLOGICAL DETERMINISM

The term 'language-related digital divide' is used to describe the discrepancy between individuals who have access to digital technologies and those who do not. This phenomenon is often attributed to technological determinism, which posits that technology is a primary driver of social and economic change.

The concept of language is one that is both complex and versatile, and it is arguably the very essence of human existence. The genesis of language can be traced back to the advent of the first humans. While some languages have become extinct, others have survived to the present day. In summary, as language is intrinsic to human existence, it constitutes a pivotal element of information and communication technology. Conversely, new technologies are an integral and ever-evolving aspect of contemporary life. Nevertheless, it seems that not all individuals possess the necessary competencies to keep up with the accelerated advancement of technology, particularly in the context of the growing reliance on computers, mobile phones, and other personal digital devices. This is due to the fact that the advent of new technologies invariably gives rise to a unique linguistic code, which can prove challenging for all users to comprehend.

Despite the fact that the virtual world strives to emulate the conventions of the real world, the language employed within this domain is not intended to marginalise or exclude those with malevolent intentions. Rather, it is created with the intention of facilitating communication in applications such as chat, text messaging, instant messaging, and games. This is its primary function (Bibo et al., 2009). In Baron's (2009) study, entitled “Are instant messaging and text messaging killing language?”, a quantitative analysis of instant messaging conversations and text messages was conducted. The findings indicated that the use of abbreviations, acronyms, and spelling errors is relatively infrequent, particularly among college-age students.

A positive correlation has been identified between English language proficiency and the ability to access and utilise information technologies (Wolk, 2004; Ono and Zavodny, 2008). English is the de facto language of the Internet. A substantial proportion of the vocabulary employed in internet technology is derived from the English language. Wolk (2004) conducted a study in the early years of the smartphone's widespread adoption, investigating whether there was a relationship between a country's level of English language adoption and its internet use. The study, which encompassed 189 countries, examined the relationship between the English language, internet usage habits and infrastructure. The findings indicated that while English-language websites rarely offer alternative language options, a significant number of foreign websites provide English-language options. The Internet confers a competitive advantage on English-speaking developed countries in all respects. Furthermore, for those countries that adopt English as an official language, the advantages can be numerous.

In the 1990s, Russia was confronted with a multitude of digital divides, as evidenced in the study conducted by Vartanova and Gladkova (2019), which was exclusively focused on Russia and concentrated on the facilitation of digital participation through media literacy and media policy. This study proposes that, following the dissolution of the Soviet Union, the Russian media system was shaped by a number of geopolitical and cultural factors, resulting in the emergence of a distinctive Russian pattern of digital divide. One such factor is the diverse ethnic composition of the population, which speaks more than 170 languages in addition to the official language, Russian. The population is distributed across the largest territory in Europe, with varying levels of connectivity to transport and technology infrastructures. The study identified two groups: those with low incomes who are reluctant to use the internet (40% of the Russian population, the majority of whom are women over the age of 55) and those who are unable to access the internet due to low income (10% of the Russian population). The increasing prevalence of digital technologies in a population with diverse ethnic and linguistic backgrounds presents a challenge in addressing the emergence of digital inequalities.

Despite the fact that only a small proportion of the global population is native English speakers, English remains the dominant language on the Internet. This has led to the emergence of a digital language gap between Internet users who are proficient in English and those who are not (Lu, 2010). This is particularly evident in the context of the disproportion between the number of non-native English speakers and the number of internet content, applications and software that do not provide an option in the English language. This consequently widens the digital language divide.

CONCLUSION

The digital space offers many opportunities for both individuals and communities. Gruzdeva (2022) highlights in his study that the internet can be used for a variety of purposes. These include participating in social networks, obtaining information about products and services, making audio or video calls (e.g. via Skype, Zoom, Teams), downloading films, pictures, music, watching videos, listening to music or radio, sending or receiving e-mails, obtaining information and references on any subject using online encyclopaedias, etc., and making financial and health-related transactions. However, the fulfilment of these purposes depends on the availability of Internet access and computers.

Despite improvements in access to technology, deterministic perspectives may lead to the assumption that access alone is sufficient to address inequities, without consideration of the systemic issues that shape how technology is used. The term 'digital divide' is used to describe the division of society into two distinct groups: those who have access to technology and those who do not. This distinction is based on an individual's ability to access and utilise technology. Nevertheless, this perspective on the digital divide is now outdated. The present study demonstrates that the digital divide can be addressed from a multitude of perspectives, irrespective of religious affiliation, linguistic background, ethnicity or gender. It is widely acknowledged that contemporary technology is evolving at an astonishing rate, offering considerable prospects for advancement and advantage to all. Failure to address the digital divide at this juncture could result in these invaluable opportunities and benefits becoming significant disadvantages.

On the toher hand, the digital divide is regarded as a complex phenomenon that can be addressed from a multitude of perspectives, including age, gender, social class, geographical location, current legal frameworks and social norms. It is important to recognise that the digital divide cannot be entirely eliminated; however, the individual, social and economic effects can be mitigated by addressing the multiple dimensions that constitute the digital divide collectively. The ability to speak, listen and write English fluently is considered to be the most powerful factor in the creation of the digital divide (Wolk, 2004).

The influence of gender-based decisions and policies on the digital divide is also worthy of note. As has been extensively documented, when women have access to internet technology, a wide range of personal, family, social and economic benefits become possible (Antonio and Tuffley, 2014).

Consequently, it has become evident that community-based national and international collaboration is of paramount importance to enhance broadband internet and computing device accessibility, foster digital literacy, and reduce inequalities, particularly in relation to public service access. Eruchalu et al. (2021) emphasise the necessity of closing the digital divide in order to fully address the disparate effects of the pandemic and promote equality, particularly in the context of healthcare.

The concept of the digital divide now necessitates an understanding of novel approaches to ensuring equitable access to information and communication technologies for all individuals, irrespective of religion, language, race or gender, beyond the question of the availability of such technologies. It is widely acknowledged that technology is evolving at an astonishing rate in the present era. The prospects and advantages it offers hold considerable promise for all. Nevertheless, unless the digital divide is addressed immediately, it seems probable that these valuable opportunities and benefits will become significant disadvantages.

REFERENCES

Abbey, R., & Hyde, S. (2009). No country for older people? Age and the digital divide. *Journal of information. Communication and Ethics in Society*, 7(4), 225–242. DOI: 10.1108/14779960911004480

Acilar, A., & Sæbø, Ø. (2023). Towards understanding the gender digital divide: A systematic literature review. *Global Knowledge, Memory and Communication*, 72(3), 233–249. DOI: 10.1108/GKMC-09-2021-0147

Anderson, J. M. (2014). *The second digital divide: The effects of ethnicity and socioeconomic status on student technology access and use outside the school day*. Baker University.

Antonio, A., & Tuffley, D. (2014). The gender digital divide in developing countries. *Future Internet*, 6(4), 673–687. DOI: 10.3390/fi6040673

Antonio, A., & Tuffley, D. (2015). Bridging the age-based digital divide. *International Journal of Digital Literacy and Digital Competence*, 6(3), 1–15. DOI: 10.4018/IJDLDC.2015070101

Aruleba, K., & Jere, N. (2022). Exploring digital transforming challenges in rural areas of South Africa through a systematic review of empirical studies. *Scientific African*, 16, e01190. DOI: 10.1016/j.sciaf.2022.e01190

Bandura, A. (1991). Social cognitive theory of moral thought and action. In Kurtines, W. M., & Gewirtz, J. L. (Eds.), *Handbook of moral behavior and development* (Vol. 1, pp. 45–103). Erlbaum.

Baron, N. S. (2009). Are Digital Media Changing Language? *Educational Leadership*, 66(6), 42–46.

Bibo, L., Holland, R., Phillips, R., Pan, S., Roberts, C., & Willhite, T. (2009). The Digital Language Divide, A Research Project Paper. https://www.brettoppegaard.com/files/DLDpaper.pdf

Brown, J., Pope, N., Bosco, A. M., Mason, J., & Morgan, A. (2020). Issues affecting nurses' capability to use digital technology at work: An integrative review. *Journal of Clinical Nursing*, 29(15-16), 2801–2819. DOI: 10.1111/jocn.15321 PMID: 32416029

Burlacu, G., Truxillo, D. M., & Bauer, T. N. (2017). Employee age differences in using Internet-based tools at work. *The Wiley Blackwell handbook of the psychology of the internet at work*, 449-479.

Campos-Castillo, C. (2015). Revisiting the first-level digital divide in the United States: Gender and race/ethnicity patterns, 2007–2012. *Social Science Computer Review*, 33(4), 423–439. DOI: 10.1177/0894439314547617

Carvin, A. (2000). Mind the Gap: The Digital Divide as the Civil Rights Issue of the New Millennium. *Multimedia Schools*, 7(1), 56–58.

Chandler, D. (1995). Technological or media determinism. Retrieved from https://www.wolearn.org/pluginfile.php/45/mod_page/content/33/chandler2002_PD F_full.pdf

Cooper, J. (2006). The digital divide: The special case of gender. *Journal of Computer Assisted Learning*, 22(5), 320–334. DOI: 10.1111/j.1365-2729.2006.00185.x

DigComp. (2019). The Digital Competence Framework for Citizens. Retrieved from https://joint-research-centre.ec.europa.eu/digcomp_en

Eruchalu, C. N., Pichardo, M. S., Bharadwaj, M., Rodriguez, C. B., Rodriguez, J. A., Bergmark, R. W., Bates, D. W., & Ortega, G. (2021). The expanding digital divide: Digital health access inequities during the COVID-19 pandemic in New York City. *Journal of Urban Health*, 98(2), 183–186. DOI: 10.1007/s11524-020-00508-9 PMID: 33471281

Fairlie, R. W. (2017). Have we finally bridged the digital divide? Smart phone and Internet use patterns by race and ethnicity. UC Santa Cruz Previously Published Works. Retrieved from https://escholarship.org/uc/item/2591v2w7

Fuchs, C. (2009). The role of income inequality in a multivariate cross-national analysis of the digital divide. *Social Science Computer Review*, 27(1), 41–58. DOI: 10.1177/0894439308321628

Genus, A., & Nor, M. A. (2005). Socialising the Digital Divide: Implications for ITCs and E-Business Development. *Journal of Electronic Commerce in Organizations*, 3(2), 82–94. DOI: 10.4018/jeco.2005040106

Gruzdeva, M. A. (2022). The age factor in the digital divide: The edges of inequality. *Economic and social changes: facts, trends, forecast, 15*(4), 228-241.

Hafkin, N. J., & Taggart, N. (2001). *Gender, information technology, and developing countries: An analytic study*. Office of Women in Development, Bureau for Global Programs, Field Support and Research, United States Agency for International Development.

Hahn, K., & Hahn, K. (2021). The Formalisation of the Modern Market. *Social Digitalisation: Persistent Transformations Beyond Digital Technology*, 123-165.

Hauer, T. (2017). Technological determinism and new media. *International Journal of English Literature and Social Sciences*, 2(2), 239174.

Hoffman, D. L., & Novak, T. P. (1998). Bridging the Digital Divide: The Impact of Race on Computer Access and Internet Use. Retrieved from https://files.eric.ed.gov/fulltext/ED421563.pdf

Kovac, N., Żmija, K., Roy, J. K., Kusa, R., & Duda, J. (2024). Digital divide and digitalization in Europe: A bibliometric analysis. *Equilibrium.Quarterly Journal of Economics and Economic Policy*, 19(2), 463–520. DOI: 10.24136/eq.2899

Krueger, D. C., Stone, D. L., & Lukaszewski, K. M. (2018). Age and the digital divide. *Journal of Strategic Innovation and Sustainability*, 13(3).

Lamont, R. A., & Swift, H. (2015). *Older people's responses to age stereotypes: Implications for performance outcomes, and health and well-being*. University of Kent.

Loges, W. E., & Jung, J. Y. (2001). Exploring the digital divide: Internet connectedness and age. *Communication Research*, 28(4), 536–562. DOI: 10.1177/009365001028004007

Lu, L. (2010, June). Digital divide: Does the internet speak your language? In *EdMedia+ Innovate Learning* (pp. 4022-4025). Association for the Advancement of Computing in Education (AACE).

McDougall, J., Readman, M., & Wilkinson, P. (2016). From Digital Literacy to Capability: Project Report and Impact Evaluation. Retrieved from https://www.cemp.ac.uk/downloads/SAMPACA%20reportFINAL.pdf

Milioni, D. L., Doudaki, V., & Demertzis, N. (2014). Youth, ethnicity, and a 'reverse digital divide' A study of Internet use in a divided country. *Convergence (London)*, 20(3), 316–336. DOI: 10.1177/1354856513517366

Mitchell, U. A., Chebli, P. G., Ruggiero, L., & Muramatsu, N. (2019). The digital divide in health-related technology use: The significance of race/ethnicity. *The Gerontologist*, 59(1), 6–14. DOI: 10.1093/geront/gny138 PMID: 30452660

Mossberger, K., Tolbert, C. J., & Stansbury, M. (2003). *Virtual inequality: Beyond the digital divide.* Georgetown University Press.

Neves, B. B., Waycott, J., & Malta, S. (2018). Old and afraid of new communication technologies? Reconceptualising and contesting the 'age-based digital divide'. *Journal of Sociology (Melbourne, Vic.)*, 54(2), 236–248. DOI: 10.1177/1440783318766119

Norris, P. (2001). *Digital divide: Civic engagement, information poverty, and the Internet worldwide.* Cambridge University Press. DOI: 10.1017/CBO9781139164887

OECD. (2018). Bridging The Digital Gender Divide: Include, Upskill, Innovate https://www.oecd.org/digital/bridging-the-digital-gender-divide.pdf

Okoro, Y. O., Oladeinde, M., Akindote, O. J., Adegbite, A. O., & Abrahams, T. O. (2023). Digital communication and us economic growth: A comprehensive exploration of technology's impact on economic advancement. *Computer Science & IT Research Journal*, 4(3), 351–367. DOI: 10.51594/csitrj.v4i3.687

Ono, H., & Zavodny, M. (2008). Immigrants, English ability and the digital divide. *Social Forces*, 86(4), 1455–1479. DOI: 10.1353/sof.0.0052

Sandhu, S., & Arora, S. (2022). Customers' usage behaviour of e-banking services: Interplay of electronic banking and traditional banking. *International Journal of Finance & Economics*, 27(2), 2169–2181. DOI: 10.1002/ijfe.2266

Şen, M. (2021). Funding Discussions Regarding the Severance Pay and Unemployment Insurance Dilemma in Turkey. In *Journal of Social Policy Conferences* (No. 81, pp. 325-366). Istanbul University, Faculty of Economics.

Setiawan, R., Rani, K., Cavaliere, L. P. L., Hiep, N. T., Halder, S., Raisal, I., . . . Rajest, S. S. (2020). References for Shopping Online Versus in Stores What Do Customers Prefer and How Do Offline Retailers Cope with It? (Doctoral dissertation, Petra Christian University).

Vartanova, E., & Gladkova, A. (2019). New forms of the digital divide. In Digital media inequalities: Policies against divides, distrust and discrimination. Göteborg: Nordicom.

Wardat, Y., Tashtoush, M. A., AlAli, R., & Jarrah, A. M. (2023). ChatGPT: A revolutionary tool for teaching and learning mathematics. *Eurasia Journal of Mathematics, Science and Technology Education*, 19(7), em2286. DOI: 10.29333/ejmste/13272

Wolk, R. M. (2004, June). The effects of English language dominance of the internet and the digital divide. In *2004 International Symposium on Technology and Society (IEEE Cat. No. 04CH37548)* (pp. 174-178). IEEE. DOI: 10.1109/ISTAS.2004.1314348

World Wide Web Foundation. (2020). Women's Rights Online: Closing the digital gender gap for a more equal world. Retrieved from https://webfoundation.org/docs/2020/10/Womens-Rights-Online-Report-1.pdf

Yaman, İ. (2015). Digital divide within the context of language and foreign language teaching. *Procedia: Social and Behavioral Sciences*, 176, 766–771. DOI: 10.1016/j.sbspro.2015.01.538

Yoon, H., Jang, Y., Vaughan, P. W., & Garcia, M. (2020). Older adults' internet use for health information: Digital divide by race/ethnicity and socioeconomic status. *Journal of Applied Gerontology*, 39(1), 105–110. DOI: 10.1177/0733464818770772 PMID: 29661052

Zhao, Y., Zhang, T., Dasgupta, R. K., & Xia, R. (2023). Narrowing the age-based digital divide: Developing digital capability through social activities. *Information Systems Journal*, 33(2), 268–298. DOI: 10.1111/isj.12400

Chapter 7

Does Socio-Demographic Influence Digital Wallet Adoption Behavior?

A Chi-Square Analysis Approach

Muhammad Azmi Sait
https://orcid.org/0000-0002-5175-6436
Universiti Brunei Darussalam, Brunei

Muhammad Anshari
https://orcid.org/0000-0002-8160-6682
Universiti Brunei Darussalam, Brunei

Mohammad Nabil Almunawar
https://orcid.org/0000-0001-5296-2576
Universiti Brunei Darussalam, Brunei

Masairol Masri
Universiti Brunei Darussalam, Brunei

Nazatul Haziqah Junit
Universiti Brunei Darussalam, Brunei

ABSTRACT

Recent advancements in digital technology and widespread internet connectivity have accelerated the global adoption of digital wallet services. While existing digital wallet research has extensively identified key direct determinants to acceptance and adoption intentions, this study focuses on socio-demographic factors affecting adoption behaviors – adoption, discontinuance, and resistance intentions. Using chi-square test of association on data collected from 442 respondents in Brunei Darussalam, this study has found the significant influences of age, education, and income on adoption decisions, with gender showing no significant impact. This underscores the critical role of socio-demographic variables in refining technology adoption theories. Additionally, it highlights the need for targeted marketing strategies to enhance digital wallet acceptance and robust policy frameworks to sustain and advance the digital

DOI: 10.4018/979-8-3693-6366-9.ch007

wallet industry in developing countries.

1. INTRODUCTION

The rapid advancement of ubiquitous digital devices, such as smartphones, smart payment systems, and internet connectivity, has significantly increased the relevance of electronic payments (e-payments), complementing the commonly used cash and card payments (Che Nawi *et al.*, 2022). This trend towards e-payment transaction is further boosted by the widespread adoption of e-commerce, evolving modern lifestyles, and the increasing global use of smartphones (Alam *et al.*, 2021; Au and Kauffman, 2008; Gomber *et al.*, 2017; Nabila *et al.*, 2018).

Singh and Sinha (2020) note a direct association between the rising demand for electronic payments and the adoption of digital wallets – a fintech payment tool. Recent reports highlight a global user base of 2.8 billion digital wallet users, with the Asia-Pacific region leading in adoption, attributed to its favorable technological environment compared to neighboring regions (Boku, 2021; Capgemini Research Institute, 2021). According to Boku (2021), countries in the Association of Southeast Asian Nation (ASEAN) region with the highest number of digital wallet users are Malaysia, Singapore and Indonesia, accounting to 31.7 per cent, 30.4 per cent and 25.6 per cent of the total population.

Over the years, significant strides have been made in understanding factors that influence digital wallet adoption behaviors, including studies on adoption intentions, resistance, and continuance (Dahlberg *et al.*, 2008, 2015; Teng and Khong, 2021). Research on digital wallet discontinuance intentions has also gained significance within the digital wallet literature (Sait, Ali, *et al.*, 2024). However, empirical investigations into the impact of demographic factors on digital wallet adoption behaviors remain limited, highlighting a gap in current research within this domain. Additionally, Ramli and Hamzah (2021) found that digital wallet studies are more prevalent in ASEAN countries with well-established digital wallet industries, such as Malaysia and Indonesia. This indicates a research gap in other developing ASEAN countries where digital wallets are still in their infancy, such as in Brunei Darussalam.

Therefore, this research study aims to empirically examine how demographic factors—gender, age, educational level, and income levels—affect the adoption behavior which consists of the intention to adopt, discontinue, and resist digital wallets in Brunei Darussalam. Despite the nascent stage of the digital wallet industry in Brunei compared to neighboring countries in the Asia-Pacific region (Sait *et al.*, 2023), the country exhibits high levels of e-commerce activity, widespread internet penetration, and a substantial user base of digital devices (AITI, 2019) – an ideal context for digital wallets study.

This research study is structured as follows: the literature review section discusses prior studies on the influence demographic factors on adoption behaviors. The methodology section outlines the sampling procedure and quantitative research approach. Subsequently, the results and discussion section present findings, including descriptive analysis of respondent demographics and chi-square analysis examining associations between demographics and adoption dynamics. Finally, the conclusion section summarizes study outcomes, theoretical and practical implications, and discusses limitations and recommendations for future research.

2. LITERATURE REVIEW

The earliest systematic literature review on mobile payment systems (a core functionality of digital wallets) covering studies from 1990 to 2006 by Dahlberg et al. (2008) laid the groundwork for understanding the dynamics of digital wallet adoption. This review reported that the initial studies on consumer behavior primarily employed qualitative approaches, such as interviews and open-ended surveys, to identify overarching themes related to the adoption of mobile payment systems. A notable shift towards quantitative research approaches, such as surveys and inferential statistical analysis, became dominant in the late 2006 studies, and reportedly key constructs such as perceived ease of use, usefulness, cost, compatibility, trust, and convenience are primarily used to predict the behavioral intention and actual use of mobile payment systems.

Consequently, a systematic literature review by Dahlberg et al. (2015) encompassing studies from 2007 to 2014 identified a prevalence of consumer-centric research within the domain of mobile payment studies, consistent with the prior review by Dahlberg et al. (2008). Reportedly empirical quantitative research has been predominantly utilized since 2007, signifying a deeper understanding and refinement of the factors influencing adoption behavior through statistical analysis. Notably, Dahlberg et al. (2015) observed that recent studies have incorporated new constructs to predict behavioral intention and actual use, including respondent's demographics such as gender, age, thus representing significant progress in refining the understanding of consumer adoption behaviors.

Laywilla et al. (2020) observed that women in Jakarta are more likely to adopt digital wallets due to their perceived ease of use, suggesting a preference for user-friendly technologies among women. In contrast, Ganesan and Mane (2022) found that men are more inclined to continue using digital wallets if they find them easy to use, contradicting prior findings by Laywilla et al. (2020). In another study, Kolandaisamy et al. (2022) reported no significant association between gender and the attitude of using digital wallets, indicating gender may not influence digital wallet adoption. However, Joshi and Chawla (2024) highlighted gender's significant role in predicting behavioral intentions to use digital wallets, particularly when considering trust and attitude. Given the potential influence of gender on adoption behavior, this study proposes the following hypothesis:

H1: There is a significant association between gender and digital wallet adoption behavior

Youths are often perceived as more likely to adopt new innovations compared to older individuals. However, Shaw (2015) did not find a significant association between the adoption of digital wallets among younger and older age groups. Gulamhuseinwala et al. (2015) explains that this perception stems from youths having higher levels of personal innovativeness in information technologies. Leong et al. (2020) and Anshari et al. (2021) also suggest that youths are more inclined to adopt digital wallets due to their early exposure to modern technologies, which keeps them informed about innovations. Despite the widespread belief in youths' higher personal innovativeness, Sait et al. (2024) found no significant difference in personal innovativeness between youths and older age groups, indicating that the adoption of digital wallets is not dependent on age. Given the potential influence of age on digital wallets' adoption behavior, this study proposes the following hypothesis:

H2: There is a significant association between age and digital wallet adoption behavior

Venkatesh et al. (2003) argues that individuals' educational levels can significantly predict their comprehension of technology, thus influencing their intention to use and actual usage of technologies. Parmar and Rathod (2018) supported this with their findings whereby there is a notable association between educational level and the likelihood of adopting digital wallets. This shows that individuals with higher educational levels tend to possess greater awareness of the existence and benefits of digital wallets compared to those with lower educational levels, thus tend to be more open to adopting digital wallets compared to their counter (Leong *et al.*, 2020). However, Che Nawi et al. (2022) present contradictory findings, indicating that educational level does not exert a significant influence on the adoption of digital wallets. This might stem from the user-friendly design of digital wallets, which aims to cater to individuals from diverse educational backgrounds. Therefore, this study proposes the following hypothesis:

H3: There is a significant association between educational level and digital wallet adoption behavior

According to Venkatesh et al. (2012), the adoption of technology varies across different income levels. High-income individuals tend to display distinct intentions and usage behaviors toward digital wallet adoption compared to lower-income individuals (Karjaluoto *et al.*, 2020). However, Leong et al. (2020) found that higher-income individuals are more resistant to adopting digital wallets, potentially due to concerns about financial risks and fraud, which may have been heightened given the infancy of digital wallets at the time of their study. Che Nawi et al. (2022) suggest that income influences individual needs, with higher-income individuals more likely to adopt digital wallets as they align with their lifestyle compared to lower-income individuals. In contrast, Kolandaisamy et al. (2022) found no significant variation in digital wallet adoption across different income levels, indicating that digital wallets are used by individuals from diverse income backgrounds. Therefore, this study proposes the following hypothesis:

H4: There is a significant association between income level and digital wallet adoption behavior

Given the limited and contradictory perspectives on the effect of demographics on digital wallet adoption behavior, this study aims to conduct a chi-square analysis to statistically explain the influence of gender, age, educational level, and income levels on the intention to adopt, discontinue, or resist digital wallets.

3. METHODOLOGY

This exploratory study aims to empirically investigate how demographic factors influence adoption behaviors related to digital wallets, including adoption intention, discontinuation, and resistance. The research sample is obtained through simple random sampling, ensuring representation across diverse demographic profiles including genders, age groups, educational levels, and income levels. Given that digital wallets are fintech payment tools, awareness is limited to individuals with internet access. The study population thus comprises the total internet users in Brunei Darussalam, which constitutes 97% of the country's total population according to The World Bank Group (2022). Based on Krejcie and Morgan

(1970) guidelines, a sample size of 348 respondents is deemed sufficient for this study, achieving a 95% confidence level with a 5% margin of error.

The online survey is distributed via multiple social media platforms such as WhatsApp, Facebook, Instagram, and email to maximize outreach. The survey comprises three sections: a consent form, demographic background questions, and inquiries into respondents' current, past, or non-usage of digital wallet services. Demographic profiles of respondents will be analyzed descriptively, while the association between demographic factors and digital wallet adoption behaviors will be assessed using the Chi-square test of association.

According to McHugh (2013), chi-square test of association is a non-parametric test is crucial for detecting significant associations between categorical variables without making assumptions about data distribution. It is widely employed in research to compare groups based on nominal or ordinal variables, thereby identifying key differences and significant categories (Franke *et al.*, 2012). By comparing observed and expected frequencies in contingency tables, the chi-square test evaluates whether variables are independent of each other. To date, there are only a few studies in the context of digital wallet studies that uses chi-square test of association (Parmar and Rathod, 2018; Sait et al., 2024; Shah and Rathod, 2022)

For secondary data, a comprehensive search was conducted across various literature databases including Google Scholar, Scopus, and Emerald Insights. Boolean operators were employed, incorporating keywords such as "demographic factors," "digital wallet adoption," "digital wallet resistance," and "digital wallet discontinuance" among others to refine search results. Relevant research papers in English were thoroughly reviewed to establish a foundational understanding of how demographic factors influence digital wallet adoption behaviors.

4. RESULTS AND DISCUSSION

4.1 Demographic Profiles of Respondents

The study data were collected from 442 respondents of diverse demographic backgrounds, encompassing of adopters, discontinuers, and resistors of digital wallet services in Brunei Darussalam. Descriptive analysis of the demographic profiles, as shown in Table 1, reveals that 67 per cent of the respondents are female, while 33 per cent are male. Regarding age groups, 54.1 per cent of the respondents are the young-age groups (below 27 years old), 35.1 per cent are the middle-age groups (between 28 to 42 years old), and 10.9 per cent are of the old-age groups (above 43 years old).

In terms of educational levels, 51.1 per cent have mid-level education (i.e., Bachelor's degree and Higher National Diploma), 28.3 per cent have high-level education (i.e., Master's degree and PhD), and 20.6 per cent have entry level education (i.e., National Diploma and below). Concerning income levels, 58.6 per cent belong to the low-income group (earning less than BND 700 per month), 30.5 per cent are in the high-income group, and 10.9 per cent are in the mid-income group. Finally, among the respondents, 41% are adopters who are actively using digital wallet services, 38.2% are resistors who do not use digital wallet services, and 20.8% are discontinuers who have used digital wallet services in the past but have discontinued their use.

Table 1. Demographic Profile of Respondents

Item	N	%
Gender		
Male	146	33.0%
Female	296	67.0%
Total	442	100.0%
Age Groups		
Young Age Group (Below 27 years old)	239	54.1%
Middle Age Group (28 to 42 years old)	155	35.1%
Old Age Group (43 years old and above)	48	10.9%
Total	442	100.0%
Educational Level		
Entry-level Education	91	20.6%
Mid-level Education	226	51.1%
High-level Education	125	28.3%
Total	442	100.0%
Income Level		
Low-Income Group	259	58.6%
Mid-Income Group	48	10.9%
High-Income Group	135	30.5%
Total	442	100.0%
Adoption Behavior towards Digital Wallet Services		
Adopter	181	41.0%
Discontinuer	92	20.8%
Resistor	169	38.2%
Total	442	100.0%

4.2 Chi-Square Analysis of Associations

The aim of this study is to investigate the association between demographic factors (i.e., gender, age, educational level and income level) with digital wallet adoption behavior (i.e., adoption intention, discontinuance intention and resistance intention). The sub-sections below presents the findings of chi-square test of associations

4.2.1 Gender and Digital Wallet Adoption Behavior

A chi-square test of association was conducted to evaluate the relationship between gender groups (male and female) and digital wallet adoption behavior (adoption, discontinuance, and resistance intentions) among 442 individuals in Brunei Darussalam. The test met the prerequisite criterion as no expected cell frequencies were less than 5. The chi-square analysis revealed a non-statistically significant association between gender and digital wallet adoption behavior, $x^2(2, N = 442) = 3.7, p = 0.157$ ($p > 0.05$). Therefore, hypothesis H1, which posits a significant association between gender and adoption behavior, is rejected.

The non-significant p-value ($p = 0.157$) indicates no evidence to support a relationship between gender and digital wallet adoption behavior in this sample. This finding indicates that gender does not significantly influence digital wallet adoption, discontinuance, or resistance intentions, aligning with the results of Kolandaisamy et al. (2022). Therefore, in the context of Brunei Darussalam, it can be inferred that local digital wallet services accommodate to all gender groups, contradicting prior studies suggesting that gender has a moderating effect on digital wallet adoption behaviors (Ganesan and Mane, 2022; Joshi and Chawla, 2024; Laywilla *et al.*, 2020).

4.2.2 Age and Digital Wallet Adoption Behavior

A chi-square test of association was conducted to evaluate the relationship between age groups (young, middle, and old-age groups) and digital wallet adoption behavior (adoption, discontinuance, and resistance intentions) among 442 individuals in Brunei Darussalam. The test met the prerequisite criterion as no expected cell frequencies were less than 5. The analysis revealed a statistically significant association between age groups and digital wallet adoption behavior, $x^2(4, N = 442) = 13.90, p = 0.008$ ($p < 0.05$), thus supporting hypothesis H2.

The strength of this association was measured using Cramer's V, which was found to be 0.125, indicating a moderate effect size (Cohen, 1988). This suggests that age group has a moderate influence on the intention to adopt, discontinue, or resist digital wallet services in Brunei Darussalam. These findings align with prior studies which uniformly state that individuals' age cohorts significantly affect their digital wallet adoption behaviors (Anshari *et al.*, 2021; Gulamhuseinwala *et al.*, 2015; Leong *et al.*, 2020).

Figure 1. Age Group and Digital Wallet Adoption Behavior

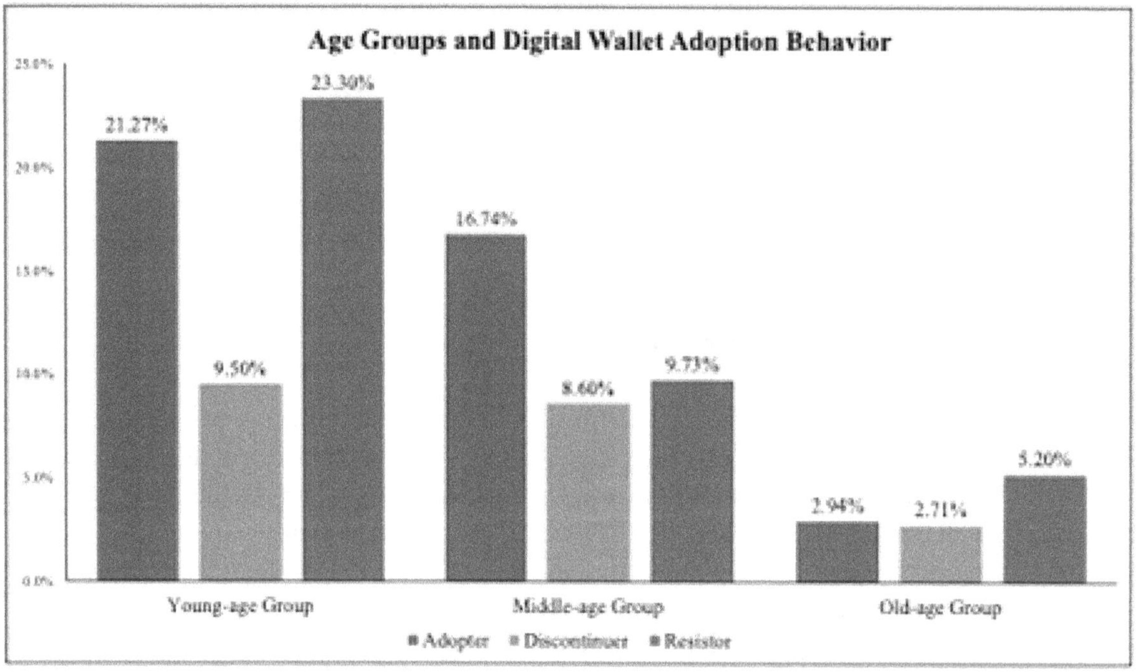

Upon closer inspection between respondents' age groups, as depicted in the Figure 1, it is apparent that a significant majority of young respondents tend to resist adopting digital wallet services compared to the middle-age groups, in the context of Brunei Darussalam. This finding corroborates with prior findings highlighting that young individuals are inclined to avoid digital wallet adoption due to concerns over potential financial risks (Anshari *et al.*, 2021; Rashid and Julaihi, 2022; Rosli *et al.*, 2022; Sait *et al.*, 2023).

A similar trend is observed among older age groups, where a substantial majority also exhibit resistance towards digital wallet services. This skepticism is likely influenced by the relatively recent introduction of digital wallet technologies in Brunei Darussalam, which amplifies concerns regarding their security and reliability (Sait et al., 2024; Sait et al., 2023).

4.2.3 Educational Level and Digital Wallet Adoption Behavior

A chi-square test of association was conducted to examine the relationship between individuals' educational levels (entry, mid, and high-level education) and digital wallet adoption behavior (adoption, discontinuance, and resistance intentions) among 442 individuals in Brunei Darussalam. The test met the prerequisite criterion as no expected cell frequencies were less than 5. The analysis revealed a statistically significant association between educational levels and digital wallet adoption behavior, $x^2(4, N = 442) = 17.04, p = 0.002$ ($p < 0.05$), thus supporting hypothesis H3.

The strength of this association was measured using Cramer's V, which was found to be 0.139, indicating a moderate effect size according to Cohen (1988). This suggests that individuals' educational levels moderately influence their digital wallet adoption behavior, underscoring the potential impact of educational background on adoption decisions within different educational groups.

Figure 2. Educational Level and Digital Wallet Adoption Behavior

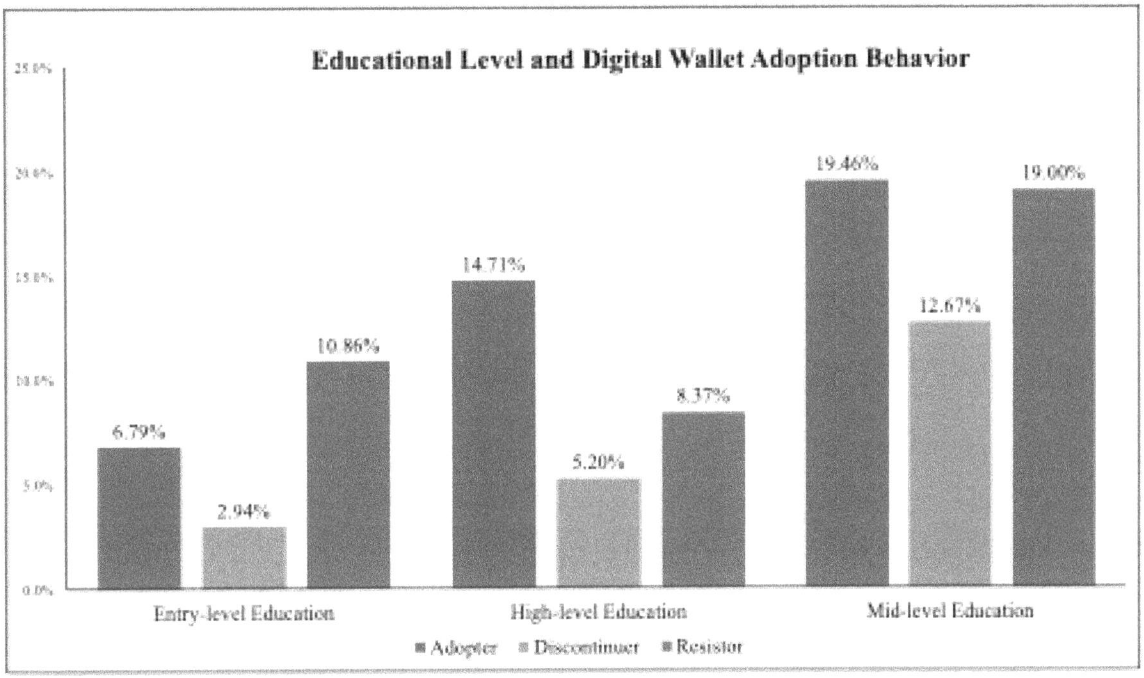

Upon closer examination between respondents' educational categories as depicted in the Figure 2, it becomes apparent that a majority of respondents with entry-level education tend to exhibit resistance towards adopting digital wallet services. In contrast, respondents with mid- and high-level of education predominantly embrace digital wallet services, reflecting a closer alignment with their lifestyle preferences.

This trend underscores the statement made by Venkatesh et al. (2003) that educational attainment significantly influences individuals' comprehension and adoption of technology. Higher levels of education enhance understanding of technological innovations, thereby shaping both the intention to use and the actual adoption of technologies like digital wallets.

Moreover, Parmar and Rathod (2018) support this perspective, highlighting a robust association between educational attainment and the likelihood of digital wallet adoption. Greater educational attainment equips individuals with heightened awareness of digital wallet services, facilitating informed decisions that weigh the benefits against potential drawbacks effectively.

4.2.4 Income Level and Digital Wallet Adoption Behavior

A chi-square test of association was conducted to examine the relationship between individuals' income levels (low, mid, and high-income groups) and digital wallet adoption behavior (adoption, discontinuance, and resistance intentions) among 442 individuals in Brunei Darussalam. The test met the prerequisite criterion as no expected cell frequencies were less than 5.

The analysis revealed a statistically significant association between income levels and digital wallet adoption behavior, $x^2(4, N = 442) = 11.43, p = 0.022$ ($p < 0.05$), thus supporting hypothesis H4. The strength of this association was measured using Cramer's V, which was found to be 0.114, indicating a moderate effect size according to Cohen (1988). This suggests that individuals' income level has moderate influence towards digital wallet adoption behavior, underscoring the role of income in shaping adoption patterns within different income groups.

Figure 3. Income Level and Digital Wallet Adoption Behavior

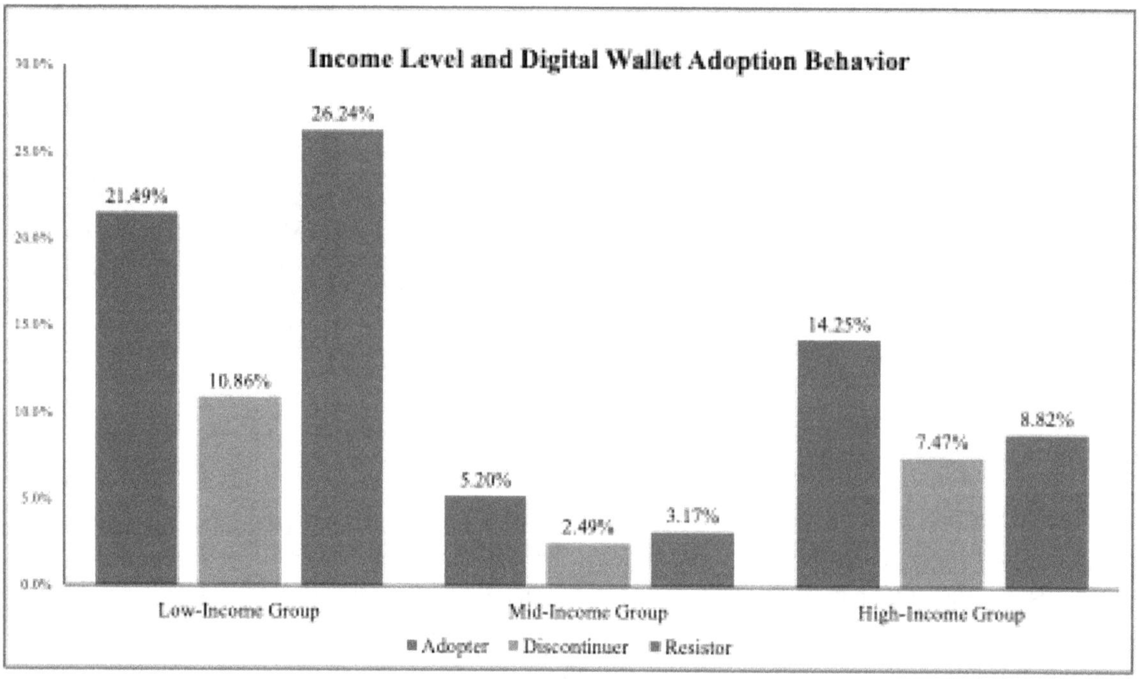

Upon closer examination of respondents' income levels, it is evident that a majority of those in the low-income bracket are more inclined to resist adopting digital wallet services. This resistance can be attributed to their perception of financial risks associated with digital wallets (Anshari *et al.*, 2021; Rashid and Julaihi, 2022; Rosli *et al.*, 2022). Limited financial resources naturally lead to caution towards unconventional payment methods, as they may be perceived as less secure against financial fraud (Sait et al., 2024; Sait et al., 2023).

Conversely, individuals in the mid- and high-income groups are more likely to adopt digital wallet services. This trend aligns with findings by Karjaluoto et al. (2020) and Che Nawi et al. (2022), suggesting that higher-income individuals are more inclined to adopt technologies because it meets their lifestyle preferences and specific needs. These observations are consistent with Venkatesh et al. (2012), that states that technology adoption patterns vary significantly across different income levels.

5. IMPLICATIONS OF STUDY

5.1 Theoretical Implication

The study contributes theoretically by underscoring the significant impact of socio-demographic factors that includes age, education, and income on digital wallet adoption behaviors – adoption, discontinuance, and resistance intentions. It highlights the pivotal role of socio-demographic variables in understanding technology adoption dynamics and challenges prior postulations on gender differences. This study has advanced theoretical understanding by exploring the multidimensional aspects of demographics, enhancing the versatility and potentially improve the explanatory power of existing theoretical frameworks (Venkatesh *et al.*, 2003).

5.2 Managerial Implication

From a managerial standpoint, this study highlighted the importance of targeted marketing strategies tailored to specific demographic segments based on gender, age, educational levels and income levels. By emphasizing on security and convenience features, it can imperatively encourage the digital wallet adoption among young individuals, those with lower educational levels and low-income groups. Additionally, designing user-friendly interfaces that appeal to both younger and older demographics, and continuously engaging with the users can enhance user satisfaction and strengthen competitive position of the digital wallet service provider.

5.3 Policy Implication

From policymaker standpoint, this study offered profound policy implications for promoting digital wallet adoption in Brunei Darussalam. Policymakers must prioritize enhancing digital literacy through educational programs that emphasizes the benefits and safety of digital wallets. Clear regulatory frameworks are essential to protect consumer rights and ensure data privacy, fostering trust in digital payment systems. Collaboration among government agencies, financial institutions, and technology providers is crucial for innovation and equitable access to digital wallet services. Incentives such as reduced transaction fees can further encourage adoption among consumers and merchants, supporting inclusive digital financial services and boosting confidence in digital transactions.

6. LIMITATIONS OF STUDY AND RECOMMENDATIONS FOR FUTURE STUDIES

While this study offers valuable insights, its limitations should be acknowledged. First, while the sample size of 442 using simple random sampling is sufficient to achieve the study's aim, the respondents may be skewed towards a specific gender, with a majority being female. While it can be argued that females are more likely to participate in online surveys (Smith, 2008), this potential bias may limit the understanding of gender-specific roles in digital wallet adoption behavior. Therefore, it is imperative for future studies to employ a sampling technique such as stratified purposive sampling to ensure an equal number of respondents from identified demographics, providing a more holistic view, especially in comparative study settings.

Secondly, this study relied on self-reported data collected through an online survey conducted in a non-contrived setting, meaning the researcher had no involvement during the respondents' answering sessions (Sekaran and Bougie, 2016). This approach introduces potential biases, including recall errors and social desirability bias, which could result in false associations. Therefore, future studies should consider using alternative research methodologies, such as face-to-face interviews with the identified demographics, to obtain richer data, deeper insights, and minimize biases associated with recall errors and social desirability bias.

Finally, this study's scope is limited to investigating the associations between respondents' socio-demographics (i.e., gender, age, educational level, and income level) and adoption behavior (i.e., adoption, discontinuance, and resistance). However, it does not explore the underlying reasons behind these adoption behaviors. Therefore, it is imperative for future studies to investigate the reasons behind adoption behavior based on socio-demographic factors to provide a more holistic view.

7. CONCLUSION

In conclusion, this study underscores the significance of age, educational attainment, and income on digital wallet adoption behavior in Brunei Darussalam, with gender showing no significant impact. Younger, more educated, and higher-income individuals demonstrate higher propensity for adopting digital wallets. Strategies such as tailored marketing, user-friendly features, and educational campaigns are recommended to increase adoption rates. Theoretical advancements involve deeper integration of demographic factors into existing theoretical adoption frameworks. From a managerial perspective, targeted campaigns and educational initiatives can effectively capitalize on these insights. Policy recommendations include promoting digital literacy, ensuring robust data security, and reducing transaction costs to foster a more inclusive digital economy. These measures aim to strengthen Brunei Darussalam's digital payment landscape, promoting economic growth and enhancing financial inclusivity in the long run.

REFERENCES

AITI. (2019), *Brunei Darussalam Information Communications Technology (ICT) Business Report 2019.*

Alam, M. M., Awawdeh, A. E., & Muhamad, A. I. (2021). Using e-wallet for business process development: challenges and prospects in Malaysia. *Business Process Management Journal.*

Anshari, M., Arine, M. A., Nurhidayah, N., Aziyah, H., & Salleh, M. H. A. (2021). Factors influencing individual in adopting eWallet. *Journal of Financial Services Marketing*, 26(1), 10–23. DOI: 10.1057/s41264-020-00079-5

Au, Y. A., & Kauffman, R. J. (2008). The economics of mobile payments: Understanding stakeholder issues for an emerging financial technology application. *Electronic Commerce Research and Applications*, 7(2), 141–164. DOI: 10.1016/j.elerap.2006.12.004

Boku. (2021). Mobile Wallets Report 2021.

Capgemini Research Institute. (2021). Payment Top Trends 2021.

Che Nawi, N., Al Mamun, A., Hayat, N., & Seduram, L. (2022). "Promoting Sustainable Financial Services Through the Adoption of eWallet Among Malaysian Working Adults", *SAGE Open. SAGE Publications Sage CA: Los Angeles, CA*, 12(1).

Cohen, J. (1988). Statistical power for the behavioural sciences. Lawrence Erlbaum.

Dahlberg, T., Guo, J., & Ondrus, J. (2015). A critical review of mobile payment research. *Electronic Commerce Research and Applications*, 14(5), 265–284. DOI: 10.1016/j.elerap.2015.07.006

Dahlberg, T., Mallat, N., Ondrus, J., & Zmijewska, A. (2008). Past, present and future of mobile payments research: A literature review. *Electronic Commerce Research and Applications*, 7(2), 165–181. DOI: 10.1016/j.elerap.2007.02.001

Franke, T. M., Ho, T., & Christie, C. A. (2012). The chi-square test: Often used and more often misinterpreted. *American Journal of Evaluation*, 33(3), 448–458.

Ganesan, P., & Mane, A. S. (2022). Determinants of Continuous Intention to Use Digital Wallet–Application of UTAUT2 and Multi-Group Analysis with Age and Gender. *NeuroQuantology : An Interdisciplinary Journal of Neuroscience and Quantum Physics*, 20(19), 4586.

Gomber, P., Koch, J.-A., & Siering, M. (2017). Digital Finance and FinTech: Current research and future research directions. *Journal of Business Economics*, 87(5), 537–580. DOI: 10.1007/s11573-017-0852-x

Gulamhuseinwala, I., Bull, T. & Lewis, S. (2015). FinTech is gaining traction and young, high-income users are the early adopters. *Journal of Financial Perspectives*, *3*(3).

Joshi, H. & Chawla, D. (2024). Impact of security on wallet adoption: multiple and serial mediating roles of trust and attitude and gender as a moderator. *International Journal of Bank Marketing*.

Karjaluoto, H., Shaikh, A. A., Leppäniemi, M., & Luomala, R. (2020). Examining consumers' usage intention of contactless payment systems. *International Journal of Bank Marketing*, 38(2), 332–351. DOI: 10.1108/IJBM-04-2019-0155

Kolandaisamy, R., Lie, S.L., Kolandaisamy, I., & Jalil, A. & Muthusamy, G. (2022). The Impact and Effectiveness of E–Wallet Usage for Malaysian Male and Female. *Specialusis Ugdymas*, 1(43), 4102–4109.

Krejcie, R. V., & Morgan, D.W. (1970). Determining sample size for research activities. *Educational and Psychological Measurement*, 30(3), 607–610.

Laywilla, E., Kartar Singh, J. S., & Yin Fah, B. C. (2020). Drivers of Intention to Adopt Mobile Wallet: A Quantitative Study Among Females in Jakarta. *International Journal of Academic Research in Business & Social Sciences*, 10(11). Advance online publication. DOI: 10.6007/IJARBSS/v10-i11/8061

Leong, L. Y., Hew, T. S., Ooi, K. B., & Wei, J. (2020). Predicting mobile wallet resistance: A two-staged structural equation modeling-artificial neural network approach. *International Journal of Information Management*, 51, 102047. Advance online publication. DOI: 10.1016/j.ijinfomgt.2019.102047

McHugh, M.L. (2013). The chi-square test of independence. *Biochemia Medica, Medicinska naklada, 23*(2), 143–149.

Nabila, M., Purwandari, B., Nazief, B. A. A., Chalid, D. A., Wibowo, S. S., & Solichah, I. (2018). Financial Technology Acceptance Factors of Electronic Wallet and Digital Cash in Indonesia. *2018 International Conference on Information Technology Systems and Innovation, ICITSI 2018 - Proceedings*, 284–289, DOI: 10.1109/ICITSI.2018.8696091

Parmar, G., & Rathod, R. M. (2018). A Study on Factors Affecting E-wallet Usage. *ELK Asia Pacific Journal of Marketing & Retail Management*, 9(4), 1–14.

Ramli, F. A. A., & Hamzah, M. I. (2021). Mobile payment and e-wallet adoption in emerging economies: A systematic literature review. *Journal of Emerging Economies and Islamic Research*, 9(2), 1–39.

Rashid, F. R., & Julaihi, M. Z. H. (2022). Big Data, Green Growth, and Technology Disruption in Asian Companies and Societies: Application of Fintech in Brunei Darussalam–Embracing E-Wallet in the Retail Sector. In *Handbook of Research on Big Data, Green Growth, and Technology Disruption in Asian Companies and Societies* (pp. 38–57). IGI Global. DOI: 10.4018/978-1-7998-8524-5.ch003

Rosli, S. N., Anshari, M., Almunawar, M. N., & Masri, M. (2022). Digital Wallet Ecosystem in Promoting Financial Inclusion. In *FinTech Development for Financial Inclusiveness* (pp. 31–49). IGI Global. DOI: 10.4018/978-1-7998-8447-7.ch003

Sait, M.A., Ali, M.A., Almunawar, M.N. & Haji Masri, H.M. (2024). Understanding factors to digital wallet discontinuance intention among past users: an exploratory study. *Journal of Science and Technology Policy Management.*

Sait, M. A., Almunawar, M. N., Anshari, M., & Masri, M. (2023). Digital Wallet Adoption in Supporting Financial Inclusion: A Conceptual Framework. *2023 International Conference on Sustainable Islamic Business and Finance (SIBF)*, 189–194. DOI: 10.1109/SIBF60067.2023.10380043

Sait, M. A., Anshari, M., Almunawar, M. N., & Masri, M. (2024). Investigating the Impact of Demographic Factors on Personal Innovativeness in Digital Wallet Usage: An Exploratory Study. In *Harnessing Green and Circular Skills for Digital Transformation* (pp. 262–271). IGI Global. DOI: 10.4018/979-8-3693-2865-1.ch014

Shah, S., & Rathod, K. (2022). A study on consumer perception on E-WALLET in Ahmedabad. *International Journal of Management, Public Policy and Research*, 1(2), 56–60. DOI: 10.55829/ijmpr.v1i2.47

Shaw, N. (2015). Younger persons are more likely to adopt the mobile wallet than older persons, or are they? The moderating role of age. *2015 Americas Conference on Information Systems, AMCIS 2015*, 1–15.

Singh, N., & Sinha, N. (2020). How perceived trust mediates merchant's intention to use a mobile wallet technology. *Journal of Retailing and Consumer Services*, 52, 101894. Advance online publication. DOI: 10.1016/j.jretconser.2019.101894

Smith, W.G. (2008). Does gender influence online survey participation? A record-linkage analysis of university faculty online survey response behavior. *Eric Ed501717.*

Teng, S., & Khong, K. W. (2021). Examining actual consumer usage of E-wallet: A case study of big data analytics. *Computers in Human Behavior*, 121, 106778. Advance online publication. DOI: 10.1016/j.chb.2021.106778

The World Bank Group. (2022). Individuals using the Internet (% of population) – Brunei Darussalam. https://data.worldbank.org/indicator/IT.NET.USER.ZS?locations=BN

Venkatesh, V., Morris, M. G., Davis, G. B., & Davis, F. D. (2003). *User acceptance of information technology: Toward a unified view. MIS Quarterly.*

Venkatesh, V., Thong, J. Y. L., & Xu, X. (2012). *Consumer acceptance and use of information technology: extending the unified theory of acceptance and use of technology. MIS Quarterly.*

Chapter 8
iGenius:
Exploring Gen Z's Reliance on AI Tools in Education

Koppala Venugopal
https://orcid.org/0000-0002-3472-1477
Aditya Institute of Technology and Management, India

ABSTRACT

The emergence of Generation Z (Gen Z) as a cohort characterized by their immersion in technology has prompted significant shifts in educational paradigms, particularly concerning the integration of AI tools. This study aims to investigate the extent and implications of Gen Z's reliance on AI tools within educational contexts. Employing a mixed-methods approach, the research employs convenience sampling to distribute questionnaires to students, acknowledging the critical importance of their availability. Through an examination of various ML and regression methods, the study evaluates how effectively each method identifies relevant features for classification tasks and explains the increase in the dependency of students on AI tools. The findings shed light on the factors driving Gen Z's dependency on AI tools, including curriculum integration, performance enhancement, accessibility, skill development, and dependency factors that pave the way for informed decision making and strategic planning in educational settings.

1. INTRODUCTION

The concept of the "worst beauty," a seemingly contradictory term often applied to AI tools, has garnered attention from a multitude of researchers, scholars, and industry experts. These tools, while paradoxical in nature, are widely recognized for their efficacy in task optimization and potential to replace human involvement across various domains, including the education sector. However, their integration into educational practices prompts significant debate regarding their potential transformative impact.

India's higher education system, renowned for its distinctive curriculum and rigorous assessment framework, serves as a pivotal hub for cultivating innovative talent highly sought after on a global scale. The emergence of Generation Z (Gen Z), typically defined as individuals born between the mid-to-late 1990s and the early 2010s, has seen a notable reliance on artificial intelligence (AI) tools within the educational landscape. This reliance is influenced by the pervasive integration of AI technologies

DOI: 10.4018/979-8-3693-6366-9.ch008

across diverse domains, with education being a focal point, and is driven by the unique characteristics and preferences exhibited by Gen Z individuals.

In India, students are known for their dynamism and eagerness to explore various fields until mastery is achieved. Presently, students display a remarkable familiarity with cutting-edge technologies associated with academics, as well as a penchant for engaging with social media platforms and applications to deepen their knowledge and accomplish academic tasks. Across all disciplines, AI tools such as ChatGPT, Gemini Bard, and Bing AI are extensively utilized by students for academic purposes. What initially began as sporadic use in semi-urban areas has now evolved into widespread dependency, posing challenges for educators tasked with assigning tasks that cannot be completed by AI tools alone. Consequently, there is a growing need for the teaching community to serve as a complement, rather than a substitute, to AI tools.

However, the prevalent trend of overreliance on AI tools among students threatens to stifle independent thinking and skill development, as students increasingly delegate academic tasks to these tools. This overdependence may hinder the cultivation of critical skills and pose a significant challenge to educational policies that fail to adapt to technological advancements.

It is imperative to recognize the underlying reasons driving students towards AI tools, particularly ChatGPT, for academic purposes. Preliminary findings from observational surveys suggest that engineering students, grappling with the complexities of assignments, research projects, and internships, heavily rely on ChatGPT to navigate these challenges.

However, there exists a research gap in identifying the specific factors contributing to excessive AI tool usage and overdependence, particularly within engineering disciplines and suburban areas. This study aims to address this gap by focusing on the suburban district of Srikakulam in Andhra Pradesh, India, where the rapid adoption of AI tools is observed.

Methodologically, this research employs machine learning techniques such as classification, clustering, and correlation analysis to ensure data accuracy. Through Exploratory Factor Analysis (EFA) and Multiple Regression Analysis, the study seeks to extract and evaluate determinants influencing the increased usage of ChatGPT among engineering students in suburban areas.

The insights gleaned from this study are expected to shed light on the significant features of Gen Z and aid in predicting and understanding their reliance on AI tools in education. These findings will be disseminated to relevant stakeholders and research communities to inform strategies aimed at mitigating overdependence on AI tools among Gen Z students.

2. OBJECTIVES OF THE STUDY

The specific objectives of this study are as follows:

- To gain an understanding of engineering students' perceptions regarding their dependency on AI tools in educational contexts in Srikakulam District, A.P. India.
- To utilize machine learning models for the classification, clustering, and correlation analysis of the collected data.
- To assess the impact of various factors, including curriculum design, accessibility of AI tools, students' skill levels, academic performance, and dependency on the increased usage of AI tools in education.

- To explore the insights derived from the analysis and provide comprehensive conclusions and recommendations, along with management implications, based on the findings of the study.

3. LITERATURE REVIEW

Koppala Venugopal et al. (2023) identified that most of the students are engaged and connected to digital media and its related technologies for various reasons such as knowledge sharing, entertainment, gaming and relationship building. Vakamullu Gopalakrishna, et al. (2023) specified that most of the students take more pains to communicate in English who need some tool and method to learn by speaking. Yoodly is one of the AI tools which would be so helpful to such students. Pranaya, D et al. (2023) acknowledged that rural are also exposed with certain tools for the improvement of English language so as to be understand easier the other critical subjects. Besides, the adoption of AI-driven writing tools in English as a foreign language (EFL) classrooms is steadily increasing, encompassing grammar checks, writing aids, and programs capable of generating essays independently, offering time and effort savings for both students and educators (Jeanjaroonsri, 2023).

Broadly speaking, AI writing tools aim to examine written content and provide feedback on various aspects of writing, including grammar, vocabulary, syntax, content, and structure (Hosseini et al., 2023). The transformation of writing instruction in the modern era, amidst technological proliferation, is closely linked to the rapid advancement of digital tools. Haleem et al. (2022) highlight this evolution, emphasizing the growing integration of digital utilities in education, reshaping traditional pen-and-paper methods into more dynamic and creative pedagogical experiences.

Garlinska et al. (2023) explore the transformative impact of virtual classrooms, online workshops, and cloud-based writing tools on writing instruction, introducing features like real-time feedback, collaborative editing, and plagiarism checks, revolutionizing the landscape of writing education. Additionally, as demonstrated in Bhutoria's (2022) study, AI-driven platforms and applications provide tailored learning experiences for students by identifying their writing strengths and weaknesses. Similarly, Cahyono et al. (2023) investigated the effective use of mobile technology in teaching writing, revealing an additional dimension of technological pedagogical innovation. This approach encourages students to share their work in public forums, enhancing both their confidence and writing skills. These platforms also facilitate peer review and feedback, cultivating a sense of community and collaborative learning (Umamah & Cahyono, 2022).

As Duncan and Joyner (2022) pointed out, educators need to address challenges concerning digital equity, privacy, and potential distractions, emphasizing the importance of continual dialogue and proactive measures in formulating pedagogical policies and strategies navigating the teaching of writing in the era of artificial intelligence. Rodrigo (2023) states that artificial intelligence (AI) is a field of study involving the development of computer systems capable of performing tasks commonly associated with human abilities, aiming to improve teaching, learning, and the overall educational experience. Examples of such tasks include facial and voice recognition, playing chess, or navigating a vehicle through traffic. AI in Education (AIED) refers to the use of AI in educational settings, aiming to improve teaching, learning, and the overall educational experience.

As per Sharples (2022), demonstrating the positive impacts of applying AI technologies is crucial not only for policy but also for ensuring ethical AI use. Justification is necessary before investing time and resources, including teacher effort. Despite the long-standing issue of plagiarism, written essays remain a significant element in educational assessments globally.

In an alternative context, Goda (2014) discovered that chatbots consistently generated responses following accepted grammar conventions, suggesting their potential to revolutionize education. Providing teachers with logs of chatbot-student interactions allows for the identification of student errors, enabling targeted error correction in classes. The research aims to evaluate the influence of AI on education, focusing on its impact on various aspects such as administration, instruction, and learning. Snyder (2019) suggests that a systematic or semi-systematic literature review of secondary data offers a more profound understanding of the study phenomenon. The study employs a qualitative research design, utilizing qualitative content and thematic analysis to explore various ways. This analysis involves a comprehensive examination of each text, identifying recurring themes across different texts. These themes serve as the foundation for inferences and conclusions in descriptive studies, aligning with the study's objective to evaluate the impact of AI on education. AI tutoring systems have the capacity to offer personalized guidance, support, or feedback by customizing learning content according to individual student learning patterns or knowledge levels (Hwang et al., 2020). AI teaching assistants assist instructors in saving time by addressing students' basic, repetitive questions in online discussion forums, enabling instructors to allocate their saved time to more valuable tasks (Goel & Polepeddi, 2016).

Students might view the indiscriminate collection and analysis of their data through AI systems as a privacy breach, exemplified by incidents like the Facebook–Cambridge Analytica data scandal (Chan, 2019). Perin and Lauterbach (2018) pioneered the creation of an innovative AI scoring system designed to expedite the communication of grades between students and instructors, enhancing overall efficiency in the educational workflow by streamlining the feedback loop. Luckin (2017) demonstrated the efficacy of AI systems in supporting both students and instructors by offering continuous feedback on students' learning processes and their advancement toward achieving educational objectives, ultimately contributing to a more personalized and effective educational experience for each learner and their research,

Ross et al. (2018) innovatively designed and implemented online adaptive quizzes aimed at bolstering student support. These quizzes dynamically adapt learning content to cater to the specific needs of each student, thereby fostering a personalized and effective learning experience. The outcomes of their study indicated a notable enhancement in student motivation and engagement levels, underscoring the potential of such adaptive tools in positively influencing the learning environment. The implementation of these online adaptive quizzes represents a significant stride towards creating an inclusive and responsive educational platform that addresses the diverse learning requirements of individual students.

While recent attention has focused on artificial intelligence in education, the exploration of general artificial intelligence theory dates back to the 14th century, with a resurgence in the work of Alan Turing in 1937, as noted by Humble and Mozelius (2019). AI has the potential to offer improved learning opportunities for marginalized groups, including people with disabilities, refugees, those out of school, and individuals in isolated communities, as highlighted by Pedro, Subosa, Rivas, and Valverde (2019). Studies reveal the efficacy of personalized learning approaches when bolstered by artificial intelligence techniques within intelligent learning environments, as demonstrated by Mohammed and Watson (2019). These findings underscore the potential of AI to tailor educational experiences to individual needs, enhancing the overall effectiveness of learning strategies. The intersection of personalized approaches and AI technologies offers promising avenues for optimizing educational outcomes. While quality education traditionally relies on human teachers, artificial intelligence aims to enhance education at all levels by emphasizing personalization, as noted by Grosz and Stone (2018). Pedro et al. (2019) proposes a dual-teacher model, where AI-supported assistants handle routine and administrative tasks, allowing human teachers to concentrate on personalized student guidance and one-to-one communication. This innovative approach envisions an improved educational experience through a collaborative effort between human educators and AI-supported assistants.

As highlighted by Karsenti (2019), emerging technologies are becoming increasingly pervasive, captivating the younger generation, and schools are compelled to adapt. This study focuses on exploring the perspectives of stakeholders in law, business, education, and engineering on the integration of artificial intelligence in education. The purpose is to analyze the implications and significance of AI in education, examining diverse sector participants' viewpoints for insights into the future of education. The growing shift towards embracing new technological interaction communities has led to the development of various communication tools known as "virtual assistants." These utilize computer algorithms to simulate human intelligence, providing users with an interactive experience that feels akin to human interaction—a concept referred to as "artificial intelligence" (Yang, Zhuang, & Pan, 2021). Contemporary developments in AI and computational science are steering towards human-centered AI, emphasizing the consideration of people's characteristics and contexts.

AI holds significant potential to expedite the realization and advancement of global education goals by diminishing barriers to learning access, automating administrative processes, and optimizing methods to enhance student performance, ultimately leading to improved learning outcomes, as highlighted by Moreno (2019). Popenici and Kerr (2017) characterize it as computing systems capable of performing processes akin to human functions, including learning, adapting, synthesizing, self-correction, and utilizing data for intricate processing tasks. Castrillón, Sarache, & Herrera (2020) assert that academic performance is influenced by a variety of diverse factors, both internal and external, shaping student outcomes, encompassing elements such as aptitude and motivation, contributing to the complexity of student performance dynamics. Halili (2019) notes that the educational landscape undergoes continual evolution to cater to the changing needs of new generations, reflecting its adaptability to meet the diverse requirements of evolving student populations.

Figure 1. Conceptual Framework

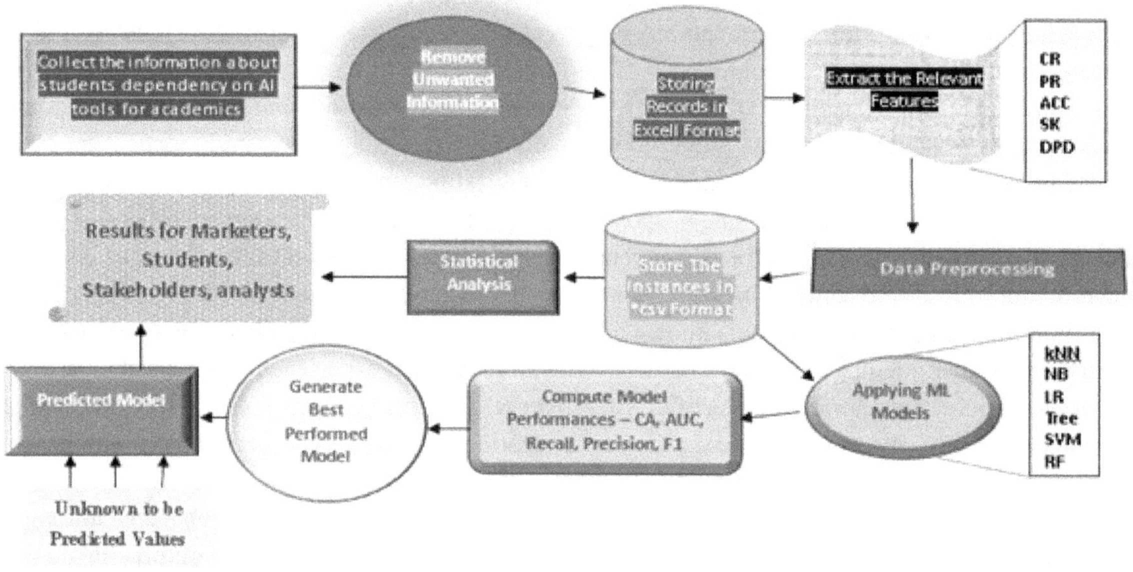

Figure 1 illustrates the research and conceptual flow, beginning with data collection and culminating in the extraction and pre-processing of features. The collected data undergoes removal of unwanted material and is then formatted into CSV for utilization in machine learning (ML) models, including kNN, NB, LR, Tree, SVM, and RF, with model performance subsequently computed. Additionally, inferential statistics are conducted. Ultimately, this process yields the identification of the best-performing model, producing optimal results for the benefit of students, teachers, and other stakeholders.

4. METHODS

The study adopts a descriptive research design to comprehensively explore Gen Z's reliance on AI tools in education. This design allows for the systematic collection and analysis of data to provide a detailed description of the phenomenon under investigation. Descriptive research is particularly suitable for understanding the attitudes, behaviors, and perceptions of individuals within a specific population, such as Gen Z students.

The research employs a mixed-methods approach, combining both quantitative and qualitative data collection and analysis techniques. This approach offers a more comprehensive understanding of the research topic by triangulating findings from different sources and methodologies. Quantitative methods, such as surveys or questionnaires, are utilized to gather numerical data on the extent of Gen Z's usage of AI tools in education, while qualitative methods, such as interviews or focus groups, allow for in-depth exploration of their experiences, attitudes, and perceptions.

In this study, convenience sampling methodology was employed to distribute questionnaires to students, recognizing the critical importance of their availability. Convenience sampling offers practical advantages, particularly in settings where access to the target population is challenging or where time constraints are a factor. By selecting participants based on their convenient accessibility, researchers were able to efficiently collect data from a diverse pool of students within the designated timeframe.

Quantitative data is collected through online surveys or questionnaires distributed to a representative sample of 218 Gen Z individuals. The survey includes questions related to the demographical characteristics and impacting variables.

Quantitative data is analyzed using M L Applications of classification, clustering and rank analysis as well as statistical techniques such as EFA and Multiple Regression Analysis to identify patterns and trends in Gen Z's reliance on AI tools. The findings in integration of ML Applications and Inferential statistics enable a comprehensive interpretation of Gen Z's attitudes and behaviors towards AI tools in education.

Overall, by employing a descriptive design, mixed-methods approach, and stratified sampling strategy, the study aims to provide valuable insights into the extent and nature of Gen Z's reliance on AI tools in education, contributing to the understanding of this emerging phenomenon and informing educational practices and policies accordingly.

5. ANALYSIS AND DISCUSSION

5.1. Machine Learning Applications

In assessing students' dependency on AI tools for academics, machine learning algorithms play a pivotal role. These algorithms analyse extensive datasets encompassing various factors such as student performance, learning patterns, resource utilization, and academic feedback. By undergoing iterative training and testing phases, these algorithms unveil underlying trends and correlations within the data, thus pinpointing the most suitable model that accurately depicts the dynamics of students' reliance on AI tools in academic settings.

Figure 2. Classification of Algorithms

Model	AUC	CA	F1	Precision	Recall
kNN	0.894	0.550	0.519	0.597	0.550
Tree	0.988	0.890	0.891	0.897	0.890
SVM	0.982	0.872	0.870	0.884	0.872
Random Forest	0.997	0.968	0.968	0.969	0.968
Naive Bayes	0.871	0.564	0.603	0.690	0.564
Logistic Regression	0.905	0.739	0.731	0.735	0.739

Figure 2 illustrates the classification of algorithms applied to a pre-processed dataset using 5-fold cross-validation, with a 20% test and 90% training size, incorporating six distinct algorithms: K-Nearest Neighbours (KNN), Decision Trees, Support Vector Machines (SVM), Random Forest, and Naïve Bayes. These algorithms, renowned for their efficacy in classification tasks, are utilized to model relationships between features and target variables. The performance of each model is rigorously assessed using metrics such as Area Under the Curve (AUC), Classification Accuracy (CA), F1 Score, Precision, and Recall, offering insights into their classification capabilities across various thematic variables. Notably, the Random Forest algorithm demonstrates superior performance, achieving a classification accuracy of 0.997 across all variables, particularly in modeling the impacts of Logistic Regression (LR) on curriculum, performance, accessibility, skills, and dependency. This underscores the robustness of the Random Forest algorithm in discerning complex patterns within the dataset, yielding valuable insights into factors driving dependency on AI tools. Overall, this study leverages advanced machine learning techniques and performance evaluation metrics to unveil significant findings regarding thematic variables related to AI tool dependency, providing valuable insights for decision-making and strategy formulation.

Figure 3. Confusion matrix

Number of Instances

Actual \ Predicted	1	2	3	4	5	Σ
1	8	0	0	1	1	10
2	0	8	0	0	0	8
3	0	0	63	3	0	66
4	0	1	0	84	0	85
5	0	0	1	0	48	49
Σ	8	9	64	88	49	218

Percentage of Instances

Actual \ Predicted	1	2	3	4	5	Σ
1	100.0%	0.0%	0.0%	1.1%	2.0%	10
2	0.0%	88.9%	0.0%	0.0%	0.0%	8
3	0.0%	0.0%	98.4%	3.4%	0.0%	66
4	0.0%	11.1%	0.0%	95.5%	0.0%	85
5	0.0%	0.0%	1.6%	0.0%	98.0%	49
Σ	8	9	64	88	49	218

Figure 4 presents a detailed confusion matrix, offering insights into the performance of the classification model by delineating true positive (TP), true negative (TN), false positive (FP), and false negative (FN) predictions. Upon analysis of the AI tools variables in academic settings, it is evident that the model achieves an impressive Classification Accuracy of 99.7%, indicating its ability to accurately classify instances. However, a Misclassification Rate of 0.3% suggests a minor proportion of misclassifications within the dataset. Notably, Type 1 errors (false positives) are recorded at a moderate level with 5 instances, while Type 2 errors (false negatives) are observed at a slightly lower level with 2 instances. These findings underscore the overall effectiveness of the classification model in accurately predicting the impact of AI tools variables in academic contexts, albeit with minor misclassifications, primarily in the form of false positive predictions.

Figure 4. ROC Analysis

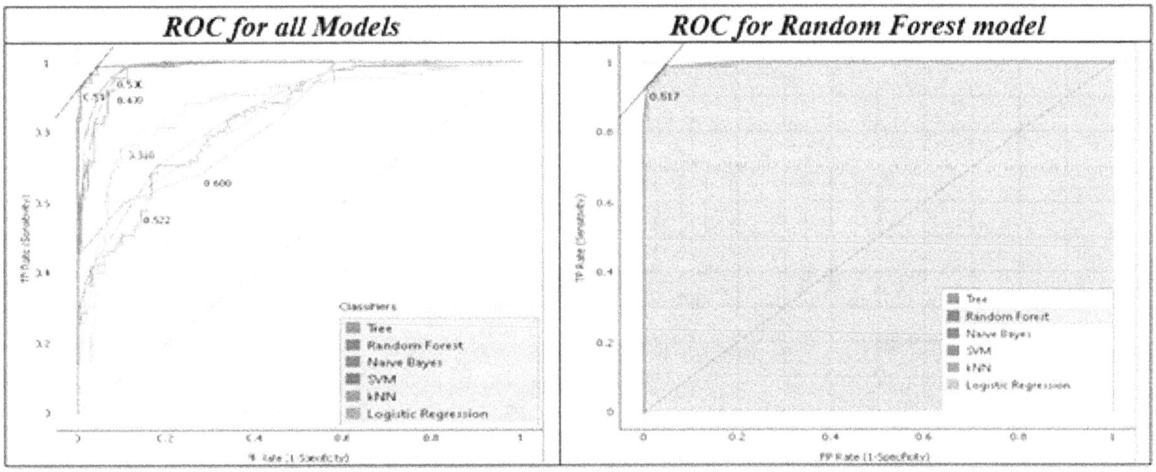

As shown in table 5.1.3, the ROC curve was generated by adjusting the decision threshold of the classifier, allowing calculation of the True Positive Rate (TPR) and False Positive Rate (FPR). A curve positioned closer to the top-left corner indicates superior performance, characterized by high TPR and low FPR. Specifically, the Area Under the Curve (AUC) for student dependency on AI tools impacting curriculum is 0.997, signifying a 99.7% probability of the classifier ranking positive instances higher than negative ones. This suggests that the classifier effectively distinguishes between instances where students demonstrate dependency on AI tools impacting curriculum and those where they do not, with high accuracy and minimal misclassification.

Figure 5. Correlation and Cluster Analysis

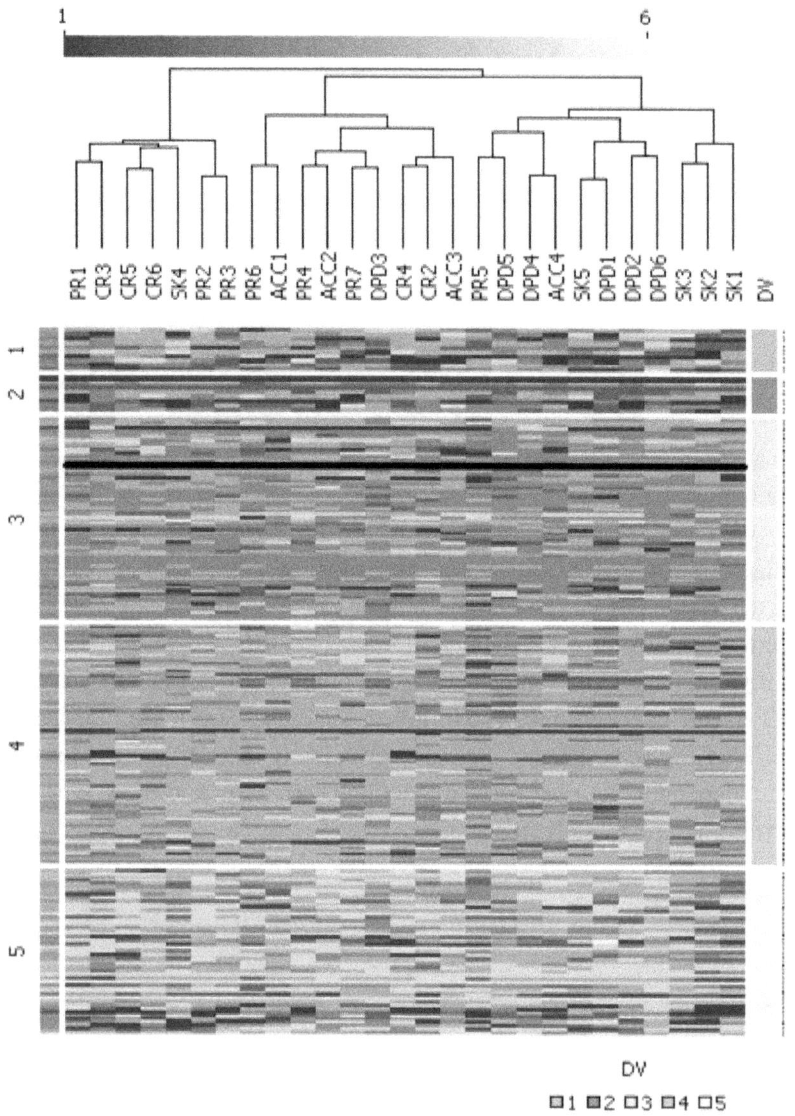

Figure 5 consisting of heatmap provides a visual representation of the correlations and clusters among the variables, with dark blue indicating strong correlations and light green representing weak correlations. The colors reflect varying degrees of relationships, with lighter colors suggesting weaker correlations, particularly between the variables and the target. Importantly, the heatmap highlights minimal multicollinearity among the three thematic variables. Additionally, clusters are observed among the cross variables impacted by the assessment of student dependency on AI tools for academics. Specifically, clusters are noted between PR1, PR2, CR5, and CR6 with CR4, as well as between DPD1, DPD2, and DPD6 with PR5. These findings suggest a linkage between the assessment of student dependency and the usage of AI tools in academics, with the variable of dependency more closely associated with AI tool usage.

Figure 6. PCA

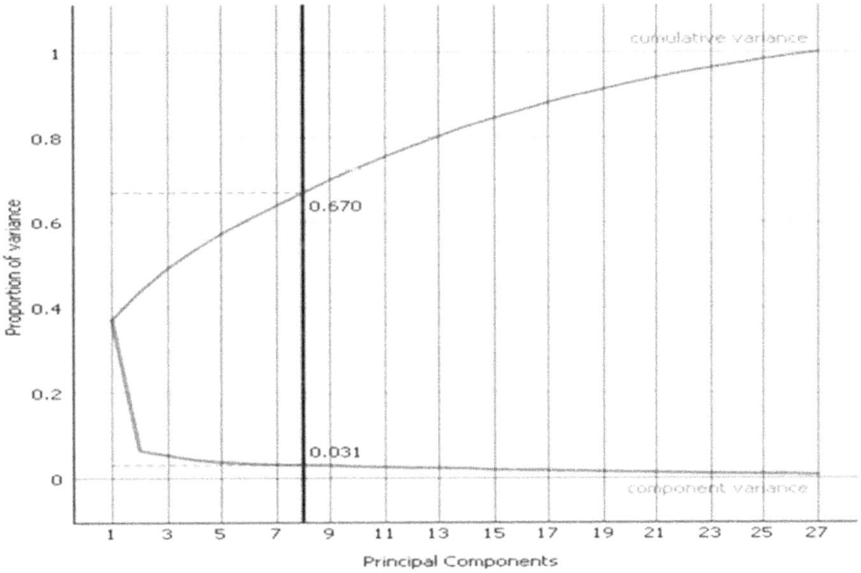

In table 5.1.5, the PCA analysis with 8 components reveals that these components collectively explain 67% of the total variance in the dataset, with individual component variances ranging from 0.031 to 0.670. The first principal component captures the highest proportion of variance, followed by subsequent components in decreasing order of importance. This suggests effective dimensionality reduction while retaining significant information. Further exploration through visualization and downstream tasks like clustering or classification can leverage the insights gained from PCA to analyze and interpret the data effectively.

Figure 7. Rank Analysis

		#	Info. gain	Gain ratio	Gini	ANOVA	χ^2	ReliefF
1	DPD6		0.238	0.160	NA	11.987	46.697	0.075
2	DPD5		0.245	0.134	0.093	7.794	16.477	0.036
3	DPD4		0.232	0.131	0.089	5.772	10.221	0.046
4	DPD3		0.173	0.097	0.069	5.334	9.634	0.028
5	DPD2		0.273	0.148	0.094	10.155	17.298	0.060
6	DPD1		0.225	0.115	0.072	7.856	19.297	0.017
7	SK5		0.164	0.090	0.057	3.642	6.896	0.007
8	SK4		0.243	0.132	0.094	4.949	10.841	0.037
9	SK3		0.267	0.145	0.101	6.223	12.638	0.042
10	SK2		0.237	0.124	0.081	4.705	7.992	0.041
11	SK1		0.212	0.112	0.074	3.544	8.093	0.045
12	ACC4		0.269	0.146	0.107	8.291	16.522	0.047
13	ACC3		0.176	0.096	0.071	6.078	11.138	0.023
14	ACC2		0.211	0.145	NA	11.583	37.835	0.044
15	ACC1		0.236	0.131	0.097	5.969	11.911	0.046
16	PR7		0.145	0.098	NA	7.758	26.272	0.037
17	PR6		0.241	0.127	0.097	4.295	10.272	0.025
18	PR5		0.156	0.083	0.061	2.547	8.969	0.014
19	PR4		0.182	0.124	NA	7.547	25.677	0.029
20	PR3		0.274	0.192	NA	10.533	44.074	0.068
21	PR2		0.196	0.133	NA	7.621	31.379	0.033

Figure 7 compares various feature selection methods, evaluating their effectiveness in identifying relevant features for classification tasks based on metrics such as information gain, gain ratio, Gini importance, ANOVA results, ReliefF scores, and FCBF scores. While the table ranks methods (1 being the best), the "best" choice varies depending on specific applications and criteria prioritization. Consequently, DPD6 (I am dependent on AI tools to save time and focus on lab experiments), DPD5 (I am dependent on AI tools because all are using), DPD4 (I am dependent on AI tools because of compulsive tasks given by teachers), DPD3 (I am dependent on AI tools since I have a tough curriculum), and DPD2 (I am dependent on AI tools because of an academic busy schedule) emerge as the top-ranked variables.

These variables exhibit consistently high rankings across multiple feature selection methods, indicating their importance in classification tasks related to dependency on AI tools.

Figure 8. Distance map of cluster analysis

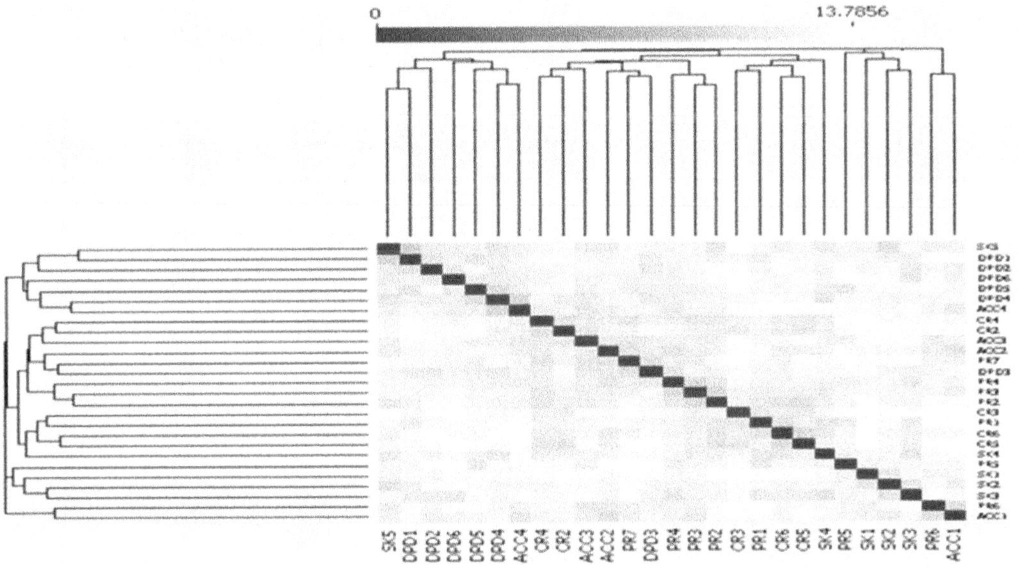

The Distance Map presented in figure 8 illustrates the distances between items using colored spots instead of numbers. In the snapshot provided, these distances depict the relationships among columns in the students' usage of AI Tools data. Larger distances are represented by light yellow spots, while smaller distances are depicted with dark blue spots. The map indicates significant divergence between items, suggesting no issue of multicollinearity among the variables and their items. The symmetric matrix, with a light shade of orange along the diagonal, ensures that no attribute is compared against itself. Symmetry is assumed given the non-zero values along the diagonal. Additionally, the map allows for the observation of clusters associated with items from other variables; for instance, items related to Dependency (DPD1 & 2) are clustered with Skill (SK5), as evidenced in the dendrogram.

5.2. Factor Analysis

Table 1. KMO and Bartlett's Test

Kaiser-Meyer-Olkin Measure of Sampling Adequacy.		**.913**
Bartlett's Test of Sphericity	Approx. Chi-Square	2.783E3
	df	378
	Sig.	.000

Table 1 illustrates that the KMO Measure value is 0.913, indicating a high proportion of variance in the variables attributed to underlying factors. This suggests that the data is suitable for factor analysis. Additionally, the significant level of 0.00 indicates strong compatibility with factor analysis, further highlighting the usefulness of this analytical approach for the dataset.

Table 2. Total Variance Explained

	Initial Eigenvalues			Extraction Sums of Squared Loadings			Rotation Sums of Squared Loadings		
Component	**Total**	**% of Variance**	**Cumulative %**	**Total**	**% of Variance**	**Cumulative %**	**Total**	**% of Variance**	**Cumulative %**
1	10.363	37.010	37.010	10.363	37.010	37.010	4.570	16.321	16.321
2	1.825	6.520	43.530	1.825	6.520	43.530	3.384	12.087	28.408
3	1.500	5.358	48.888	1.500	5.358	48.888	2.966	10.592	39.000
4	1.174	4.195	53.082	1.174	4.195	53.082	2.594	9.266	48.265
5	1.075	3.838	**56.920**	1.075	3.838	56.920	2.423	8.655	56.920
6	.955	3.411	60.331						
7	.878	3.135	63.466						
8	.828	2.956	66.423						
9	.805	2.875	69.297						
10	.780	2.785	72.082						
11	.729	2.604	74.687						
12	.668	2.387	77.073						
13	.648	2.313	79.386						
14	.612	2.186	81.572						
15	.594	2.121	83.693						
16	.515	1.840	85.532						
17	.505	1.805	87.338						
18	.446	1.593	88.931						
19	.422	1.507	90.438						
20	.389	1.391	91.828						
21	.381	1.361	93.189						
22	.340	1.216	94.405						
23	.306	1.094	95.499						
24	.287	1.025	96.523						
25	.268	.957	97.480						
26	.258	.920	98.400						
27	.236	.844	99.244						
28	.212	.756	100.000						

Extraction Method: Principal Component Analysis.

The initial eigenvalues, serving as indicators of variance elucidated by each component pre-rotation, portray Component 1 as the foremost contributor with an initial eigenvalue of 10.363, indicative of its substantial explanatory power. Following rotation, these values transform into the sums of squared loadings, reaffirming Component 1's prominence in elucidating variance, now accounting for

37.010% of the total. This trend persists across subsequent components, with Component 2 and Component 3 also exhibiting notable explanatory prowess. Cumulatively, the initial eight components encapsulate a considerable proportion of the variance, elucidating 56.920% of the total variability within the dataset. These findings underscore the significance of these principal components in capturing essential patterns and dimensions inherent in the data, thereby facilitating a comprehensive understanding of its underlying structure.

Table 3. Component Matrix

Rotated Component Matrix[a]					
	Component				
	1	**2**	**3**	**4**	**5**
Our curriculum is adaptive to AI tools					.500
Use of AI tools is to be included in curriculum	.608				
Every query is answered by AI tools	.654				
All kinds of assignments, seminars and PPTs can be easily made with the help of AI	.573				
It is so easy to learn all the AI tools	.745				
All the AI tools are familiar through different social media.	.667				
Information that we get from AI tools is accurate	.604				
Performance like coding and PPT is good with AI tools.	.634				
I am able to perform better by using AI tools.	.493				
My dependency on AI tools is increased day by day		.408			
I don't need to check the output of AI tools.				.545	
AI tools doesn't give long results.		.686			
Some tasks are better performed by AI tools than a man		.635			
All AI tools are not accessible		.655			
I am using all free versions only.		.611			
I am using AI tools in my mobile also.		.512			
My dependency on technology device has become more due to AI tools.					.551
My skills are not improved with AI tools				.654	
My personal quality of skills are hidden while using AI tools.				.641	
Technological updatesof upcoming AI tools is the only skill that I should have			.578		
I have less experience in dealing the problem so my skills are not tested by using AI	.490				
Most of my skills are unused, since direct output is coming				.568	
I am completely dependent on AI tools and I don't regret for it			.522		
I am dependent on AI tools because of academic busy schedule			.676		
I am dependent on AI tools since I have tough curriculum			.577		
I am dependent on AI tools because of compulsive task given by teachers					.636
I am dependent on AI tools because of all are using.					.599
I am dependent on AI tools to save the time and focus on lab and experiments.			.673		

Extraction Method: Principal Component Analysis.
Rotation Method: Varimax with Kaiser Normalization.
a. Rotation converged in 12 iterations.

The first rotated factor exhibits a strong correlation with various aspects related to the integration of AI tools into the educational curriculum. This includes the belief that AI tools should be incorporated into the curriculum, the perception that AI tools provide comprehensive answers to queries, and the ease with which assignments, seminars, and presentations can be generated using these tools. Additionally, individuals find AI tools to be user-friendly, as they are often encountered through various social media platforms, and perceive the information obtained from AI tools to be accurate. Moreover, the performance in tasks such as coding and creating presentations is perceived to be enhanced when utilizing AI tools. Importantly, these variables show limited correlation with other components, indicating their unique association with the use and perception of AI tools in education.

On the other hand, the second component is primarily correlated with attitudes towards AI tools concerning limitations and accessibility. Individuals express concerns about the brevity of results obtained from AI tools, acknowledge certain tasks that AI tools perform better than humans, and note limitations in accessing various AI tools, often relying solely on free versions and mobile applications.

The third component reflects attitudes related to the dependency on AI tools driven by technological advancements and academic pressures. Participants express a belief that staying updated with upcoming AI tools is a crucial skill, and they openly admit to complete dependency on these tools, citing their busy academic schedules and the challenging curriculum as reasons for reliance.

Conversely, the fourth component is associated with reservations regarding the effectiveness and impact of AI tools on skill development. Participants express scepticism towards the need to validate the output of AI tools, suggest that their use may hinder skill improvement, and perceive that personal qualities may be obscured when relying heavily on these tools.

Lastly, the fifth component highlights the increasing dependency on technology devices due to the prevalence of AI tools in academic settings. Participants acknowledge a heightened reliance on AI tools to cope with the demands of compulsory tasks assigned by teachers, as well as to optimize time management and focus on laboratory work and experiments.

5.3. Multiple Regression Analysis

Table 4. ANOVA

s. no	Model	Sum of Squares	df	Mean Square	F	Sig.
1	Curriculum	19.330	6	3.222	3.408	.003a
2	Performance	51.042	7	7.292	9.176	.000[a]
3	Accessibility	43.703	4	10.926	13.291	.000[a]
4	Skill	24.388	5	4.878	5.319	.000[a]
5	Dependency	45.794	6	7.632	9.309	.000[a]

a. Predictors: (Constant), Curriculum, Performance, Accessibility, Skill, Dependency
b. Dependent Variable: Increase of AI tools' usage in future for academic purpose.

The provided ANOVA table (Table 4) presents the results of an analysis examining the impact of different predictors on the increase of AI tools' usage in the future for academic purposes.

Curriculum: The ANOVA results indicate a significant effect of curriculum on the increase of AI tools' usage (F (6, 217(Total sample size)) = 3.408, p = .003). This suggests that variations in curriculum design have a notable influence on students' propensity to utilize AI tools for academic purposes.

Performance: The analysis reveals a significant effect of performance on the anticipated increase in AI tools' usage (F (7, 217(Total sample size)) = 9.176, p < .001). This implies that individuals' perceptions of their own performance, possibly in relation to AI tools, play a significant role in shaping their future utilization of such tools.

Accessibility: There is a significant effect of accessibility on the expected increase in AI tools' usage (F (4, 217(Total sample size)) = 13.291, p < .001). This suggests that the ease of access to AI tools influences individuals' intentions to use them more extensively in the future for academic purposes.

Skill: The ANOVA results indicate a significant effect of skill on the anticipated increase in AI tools' usage (F (5, 217(Total sample size)) = 5.319, p < .001). This implies that individuals' perceived skills in using AI tools impact their likelihood of increasing their usage in the future.

Dependency: The analysis reveals a significant effect of dependency on the expected increase in AI tools' usage (F (6, 217(Total sample size)) = 9.309, p < .001). This suggests that individuals' reliance on AI tools, perhaps due to their perceived benefits or necessity, influences their intentions to use them more extensively in the future for academic purposes.

Overall, these findings underscore the multifaceted nature of factors influencing individuals' future utilization of AI tools for academic purposes. Curriculum design, individual performance perceptions, accessibility, perceived skill level, and dependency on AI tools all play significant roles in shaping attitudes towards their future usage.

Table 5. Coefficients[a]

	Unstandardized Coefficients		Standardized Coefficients		
Curriculum	**B**	**Std. Error**	**Beta**	**t**	**Sig.**
(Constant)	2.501	.312		8.019	.000
Our curriculum is adaptive to AI tools	.002	.071	.002	.025	.980
Use of AI tools is to be included in curriculum	.070	.084	.075	.843	.400
Every query is answered by AI tools	.010	.074	.010	.130	.897
All kinds of assignments, seminars and PPTs can be easily made with the help of AI tools.	.207	.076	.222	2.715	.007
It is so easy to learn all the AI tools	-.021	.079	-.023	-.270	.787
All the AI tools are familiar through different social media.	.068	.084	.066	.813	.417
Performance					
(Constant)	1.357	.314		4.316	.000
Information that we get from AI tools is accurate	.179	.072	.188	2.493	.013
Performance like coding and PPT is good with AI tools.	.063	.079	.062	.795	.428
I am able to perform better by using AI tools.	.201	.086	.194	2.344	.020
My dependency on AI tools is increased day by day	.045	.077	.045	.586	.559

continued on following page

Table 5. Continued

Curriculum	Unstandardized Coefficients B	Std. Error	Standardized Coefficients Beta	t	Sig.
I don't need to check the output of AI tools.	-.046	.065	-.051	-.701	.484
AI tools doesn't give long results.	.081	.066	.084	1.220	.224
Some tasks are better performed by AI tools than a man	.131	.070	.137	1.880	.061
Accessibility					
(Constant)	1.718	.290		5.920	.000
All AI tools are not accessible	.019	.075	.019	.254	.799
I am using all free versions only.	.282	.077	.276	3.661	.000
I am using AI tools in my mobile also.	.085	.071	.088	1.200	.231
My dependency on technology device has become more due to AI tools.	.171	.072	.174	2.368	.019
Skills					
(Constant)	2.334	.297		7.850	.000
My skills are not improved with AI tools	.065	.070	.071	.933	.352
My personal quality of skills are hidden while using AI tools.	-.093	.074	-.106	-1.261	.209
Technological updating with respect to upcoming AI tools is the only skill that I should have	.251	.079	.253	3.183	.002
I have less experience in dealing the problem so my skills are not tested by using AI tools	.004	.073	.005	.058	.954
Most of my skills are unused, since direct output is coming	.170	.077	.178	2.209	.028
Dependency					
(Constant)	1.502	.326		4.611	.000
I am completely dependent on AI tools and I don't regret for it	.140	.067	.158	2.073	.039
I am dependent on AI tools because of academic busy schedule	.135	.077	.135	1.760	.080
I am dependent on AI tools since I have tough curriculum.	-.010	.079	-.010	-.131	.896
I am dependent on AI tools because of compulsive task given by teachers	.070	.086	.063	.808	.420
I am dependent on AI tools because of all are using.	.091	.080	.089	1.139	.256
I am dependent on AI tools to save the time and focus on lab and experiments.	.200	.080	.184	2.510	.013

The findings from Table 5. provide insights into the relationships between selected variables and the dependent variable, namely the anticipated increase in AI tools' usage for academic purposes, as determined through multiple regression analysis. In examining the variable "Curriculum," it is evident that the perceived ease of generating assignments, seminars, and presentations using AI tools holds the highest explanatory value ($\beta = 2.708$), followed by the desire for AI tools to be integrated into the curriculum ($\beta = 2.571$). Conversely, the perceived ease of learning all AI tools and their familiarity through social media exhibit comparatively lower explanatory values ($\beta = 2.48$ and $\beta = 2.569$, respectively). Regarding "Performance," the belief that one performs better using AI tools emerges as the most influential factor (β = 1.558), whereas the notion of not needing to validate AI tool outputs and the escalating dependency on these tools demonstrate weaker explanatory capacities (β = 1.311 and β = 1.402, respectively). "Accessibility" is primarily influenced by the preference for using free versions of AI tools (β = 2.000), while the perception of limited accessibility and the utilization of AI tools solely on mobile devices exhibit lesser explanatory power (β = 1.737 and β = 1.803, respectively). In terms of "Skill," the perceived necessity of keeping abreast of upcoming AI technologies emerges as the most significant explanatory factor (β = 2.585), followed closely by the perception that direct AI tool outputs render many skills unused (β = 2.504). Conversely, the belief that skills remain untested due to limited problem-solving experiences with AI tools and the perception of skill stagnation show relatively lower explanatory values (β = 2.374 and β = 2.399, respectively). Lastly, concerning "Dependency," the reliance on AI tools to optimize time management and focus on practical activities emerges as the most influential factor (β = 1.702), followed by a complete acceptance and lack of regret regarding dependency on these tools (β = 1.642). Conversely, attributing dependency to a challenging curriculum and compulsive tasks from teachers exhibit weaker explanatory capacities (β = 1.492 and β = 1.572, respectively). These findings underscore the multifaceted nature of attitudes and perceptions shaping the anticipated increase in AI tools' usage for academic purposes, thereby highlighting areas of varying significance and potential implications for educational practices and policies.

6. SUGGESTIONS

Based on the coefficients derived from the multiple regression analysis and their respective explanatory power, here are specific suggestions with management implications:

- Given the high explanatory value of the desire for AI tools to be integrated into the curriculum, educational institutions should consider incorporating AI-related coursework and assignments into their academic programs. This can involve creating dedicated modules or courses focused on AI technologies and their applications across various disciplines. Since the perceived ease of generating assignments, seminars, and presentations using AI tools holds significant explanatory power, educational institutions should provide training and resources to students and faculty members to effectively utilize AI tools for academic purposes. This may involve workshops, tutorials, and access to AI software platforms.
- Institutions should emphasize the potential benefits of using AI tools for enhancing academic performance. This can include showcasing examples of how AI tools can streamline tasks, improve productivity, and facilitate better learning outcomes. Despite the lower explanatory power, promoting the validation of AI tool outputs can be crucial to ensuring the accuracy and reliability of information obtained through these tools. Educational institutions should encourage students to critically evaluate the results generated by AI tools and verify them through additional sources where necessary.
- Recognizing the preference for using free versions of AI tools, institutions should ensure equitable access to a range of AI software platforms, including free versions. This may involve negotiating licenses with software providers or exploring open-source alternatives to provide students with access to essential AI tools. Since the use of AI tools on mobile devices exhibits moderate explanatory power, institutions should ensure that AI software platforms are optimized for mobile

use. Providing mobile-friendly versions of AI tools or dedicated mobile applications can enhance accessibility and convenience for students.

- Given the importance of staying updated with upcoming AI technologies and the perception that direct AI tool outputs render many skills unused, institutions should invest in initiatives to develop students' skills in AI-related areas. This can involve offering specialized training programs, internships, and projects focused on AI technologies and their applications. To address the perception of limited problem-solving experiences with AI tools, educational institutions should incorporate more opportunities for hands-on experimentation and real-world application of AI technologies into their curricula. This can include problem-based learning activities, research projects, and collaborative initiatives with industry partners.
- Institutions should encourage a balanced approach to dependency on AI tools, emphasizing their role as aids rather than replacements for critical thinking and problem-solving skills. This can involve promoting self-awareness among students regarding their reliance on AI tools and providing guidance on when and how to effectively integrate these tools into their academic work. To mitigate dependency attributed to a challenging curriculum and compulsive tasks from teachers, institutions should promote a diversified approach to teaching and learning. This can involve offering a range of instructional methods and assessment formats that encourage independent thinking, creativity, and adaptability, alongside the use of AI tools.

Based on the rank analysis of the feature selection methods and the top-ranked variables, here are a few suggestions:

- Given that variables related to dependency on AI tools, consistently rank highly across multiple feature selection methods, it's important to prioritize understanding and addressing the factors contributing to dependency. Institutions and educators could investigate these variables further to identify underlying issues and develop targeted interventions to promote healthier and more balanced use of AI tools among students.
- Recognizing the significance of variables related to academic workload, institutions can provide tailored support and resources to help students manage their academic responsibilities more effectively. This could include academic advising, time management workshops, and access to academic support services to alleviate the burden and stress associated with demanding curricula.
- Variables highlight the influence of compulsive tasks assigned by teachers on students' dependency on AI tools. Educators should reflect on their teaching practices and task design, ensuring that assignments are meaningful, manageable, and promote critical thinking and problem-solving skills. Engaging students in the design process and providing opportunities for choice and autonomy can also mitigate feelings of dependency.
- Institutions should prioritize promoting digital literacy and self-regulation skills among students to empower them to make informed decisions about their use of AI tools. Workshops and seminars on digital citizenship, information literacy, and responsible use of technology can help students develop a balanced and mindful approach to utilizing AI tools in their academic pursuits.
- It's essential to continually monitor and evaluate the impact of interventions aimed at addressing dependency on AI tools. Collecting feedback from students, tracking usage patterns, and assessing academic performance can provide valuable insights into the effectiveness of strategies implemented and inform adjustments as needed to better support.

REFERENCES

Bhutoria, A. (2022). Personalized education and artificial intelligence in the United States, China, and India: A systematic review using a human-in-the-loop model. *Computers and Education: Artificial Intelligence*, 3, 100068. DOI: 10.1016/j.caeai.2022.100068

Cahyono, B. Y., Khotimah, K., & Batunan, D. A. (2023). Workable approaches in EFL teaching mediated by mobile technology during the pandemic and post- pandemic: Indonesian EFL teachers' experiences and expectations. *Computer Assisted Language Learning*, 24, 138–159. http://callej.org/journal/24-1/Cahyono- Khotimah-Batunan-Imamyartha2023.pdf

Castrillón, O., Sarache, W., & Ruiz-Herrera, S. (2020). Predicción del rendimiento académico por medio de técnicas de inteligencia artificial. *Formación Universitaria*, 13(1), 93–102. DOI: 10.4067/S0718-50062020000100093

Chan, R. (2019). The Cambridge Analytica whistle blower explains how the firm used Facebook data to sway elections. Business Insider. Retrieved from https://www.businessinsider.com/cambridge-analytica-whistleblower-christopher-wylie-facebook-data-2019-10

Duncan, A., & Joyner, D. (2022). On the necessity (or lack thereof) of digital proctoring: Drawbacks, perceptions, and alternatives. *Journal of Computer Assisted Learning*, 38(5), 1482–1496. DOI: 10.1111/jcal.12700

Garlinska, M., Osial, M., Proniewska, K., & Pregowska, A. (2023). The influence of emerging technologies on distance education. *Electronics (Basel)*, 12(7), 1550. DOI: 10.3390/electronics12071550

Goda, Y. (2014). The role of AMPA receptors in postsynaptic mechanisms of synaptic plasticity. *Frontiers in Cellular Neuroscience*, 8. Advance online publication. DOI: 10.3389/fncel.2014.00401 PMID: 25505875

Goel, A. K., & Polepeddi, L. (2016). *Jill Watson: A virtual teaching assistant for online education.* Georgia Institute of Technology.

Grosz, B. J., & Stone, P. (2018). A century-long commitment to assessing artificial intelligence and its impact on society. *Communications of the ACM*, 61(12), 68–73. DOI: 10.1145/3198470

Haleem, A., Javaid, M., & Singh, R. P. (2022). An era of ChatGPT as a significant futuristic supp tool: A study on features, abilities, and challenges. BenchCouncil Transactions on Benchmarks. *Standards and Evaluations*, 2(4), 100089.

Halili, S. H. (n.d.). Technological advancements in education 4.0. *The Online Journal of Distance Education and e-Learning : TOJDEL*, 7, 63–69.

Hosseini, M., Rasmussen, L. M., & Resnik, D. B. (2023). Using AI to write scholarly publications. *Accountability in Research*, 1–9. DOI: 10.1080/08989621.2023.2168535 PMID: 36697395

Humble, N., & Mozelius, P. (2019). Artificial Intelligence in Education-a Promise, a Threat or a Hype? In European Conference on the Impact of Artificial Intelligence and Robotics 2019 (ECIAIR 2019), Oxford, UK (pp. 149–156). Academic Conferences and Publishing International Limited.

Hwang, G. J., Xie, H., Wah, B. W., & Gašević, D. (2020). Vision, challenges, roles and research issues of Artificial Intelligence in Education. *Computers and Education: Artificial Intelligence*, 1, 100001. DOI: 10.1016/j.caeai.2020.100001

Jeanjaroonsri, R. (2023). Thai EFL learners' use and perceptions of mobile technologies for writing. Learn Journal: Language Education and Acquisition Research Network, 16(1), 169–193. https://so04 .tci- thaijo.org/index.php/LEARN/article/view/263438

Karsenti, T. (2019). Artificial intelligence in education: the urgent need to prepare teachers for tomorrow's schools. Formation et profession, 27(1), 112–116. .DOI: 10.18162/fp.2019.a166

Koppala Venugopal, Vital, Das, Jena, & Mohapatro. (2023). Usage Determinants of Mobile Applications Impelling Students Group: Assessment through Machine Learning Models and Regression. Vytapeni, Vetrani, Instalace Journal.

Luckin, R. (2017). Towards artificial intelligence-based assessment systems. Nature Human Behaviour, 1(3), 1–3.

Mohammed, P. S., & Watson, E. N. (2019). Towards inclusive education in the age of artificial intelligence: perspectives, challenges, and opportunities. In Knox, J., Wang, Y., & Gallagher, M. (Eds.), *Artificial Intelligence and Inclusive Education. Perspectives on Rethinking and Reforming Education*. Springer. DOI: 10.1007/978-981-13-8161-4_2

Moreno, R. D. (2019). The arrival of artificial intelligence to education. *RITI Journal*, 7(14), 260–270. DOI: 10.36825/RITI.07.14.022

Pedro, F., Subosa, M., Rivas, A., & Valverde, P. (2019). *Artificial intelligence in education: Challenges and opportunities for sustainable development*. UNESCO.

Perin, D., & Lauterbach, M. (2018). Assessing text-based writing of low-skilled college students. *International Journal of Artificial Intelligence in Education*, 28(1), 56–78. DOI: 10.1007/s40593-016-0122-z

Popenici, S. A. D., & Kerr, S. (2017). Exploring the impact of artificial intelligence on teaching and learning in higher education. Technology Enhanced Learning, 12(1).

Pranaya, D. & Venugopal. (2023). Impact of Mother Tongue on Students' speaking Abilities in English Language at Rural Places. In English Language Competence in Rural Youth: Improving Job Readiness. Current Publications.

Rodrigo, M. (2023). The truth about using AI in schools. Philstar Life. https://philstarlife.com/news-and views/283288-truth-about-using-ai-schools?page=2

Ross, B., Chase, A. M., Robbie, D., Oates, G., & Absalom, Y. (2018). Adaptive quizzes to increase motivation, engagement and learning outcomes in a first year accounting unit. *International Journal of Educational Technology in Higher Education*, 15(1), 30. DOI: 10.1186/s41239-018-0113-2

Sharples, M. (2022). New AI tools that can write student essays require educators to rethink teaching and assessment. LSE blog article. https://blogs.lse.ac.uk/impactofsocialsciences/2022/05/17/new-aitools -that-can-write- student-essays-require-educators-to-rethink-teaching-and-assessment/

Snyder, H. (2019). Literature review as a research methodology: An overview and guidelines. *Journal of Business Research*, 104, 333–339. DOI: 10.1016/j.jbusres.2019.07.039

Vakamullu Gopalakrishna & Venugopal (2023). Assessment on the Intricacies of English Speaking Abilities by Rural Students in India. In English Language Competence in Rural Youth: Improving Job Readiness. Current Publications.

Yang, Y., Zhuang, Y., & Pan, Y. (2021). Multiple knowledge representation for big data artificial intelligence: Framework, applications, and case studies. *Frontiers of Information Technology & Electronic Engineering*, 22(12), 1551–1558. DOI: 10.1631/FITEE.2100463

Chapter 9
Digital Well-Being and Internet Addiction Across the Lifespan

Ranjit Singha
https://orcid.org/0000-0002-3541-8752
Christ University, India

Surjit Singha
https://orcid.org/0000-0002-5730-8677
Kristu Jayanti College, India

ABSTRACT

This chapter explores the pervasive influence of digital technologies across generations, focusing on the critical issues of digital well-being and internet addiction. It highlights how these challenges manifest differently across life stages, emphasizing the need for tailored interventions to promote healthy digital habits. The chapter also introduces the multidimensional addiction behaviour scale (MABS), a comprehensive tool for assessing addiction, particularly in the digital realm. By evaluating psychological, biological, social, and cognitive factors, MABS aids in early detection, intervention, and prevention of problematic behaviors. The chapter underscores the importance of interdisciplinary approaches and ongoing research to understand and address the long-term impacts of digital technology on well-being.

INTRODUCTION

In the modern era, digital technologies have permeated every facet of our lives, influencing various aspects of our daily activities, communication, and well-being. From the advent of the internet to the proliferation of smartphones and social media, these technologies have brought about profound changes in how individuals of all ages interact with the world. The pervasive nature of digital technologies spans across generations, shaping experiences and behaviors in ways that were once unimaginable.

Understanding digital well-being and internet addiction has become increasingly crucial as these technologies continue to evolve and integrate into our lives. Digital well-being refers to the balance and harmony individuals strive to achieve in their interactions with digital technologies, encompassing aspects such as online safety, mental health, and the quality of digital interactions. Internet addiction, on

DOI: 10.4018/979-8-3693-6366-9.ch009

the other hand, is characterized by excessive or compulsive use of the internet that can negatively impact various areas of life, including personal relationships, work, and overall mental health.

This chapter aims to explore the intricate dynamics of digital well-being and internet addiction across the lifespan. By examining how different generations experience and respond to digital technologies, we can gain valuable insights into the unique challenges and opportunities presented by the digital age. The scope of this chapter includes an analysis of how digital well-being and internet addiction manifest across various age groups, from children and adolescents to adults and older adults. Through this exploration, the chapter seeks to highlight the importance of fostering healthy digital habits and addressing internet addiction to promote overall well-being in our increasingly connected world.

Digital well-being encompasses the balance and positive engagement with digital technologies that support overall mental and emotional health. It involves managing the impact of digital use on personal life and ensuring that technology enhances rather than detracts from one's quality of life. Key components of digital well-being include mindful use of technology, setting boundaries for screen time, and fostering positive digital interactions.

Internet addiction is characterized by an excessive or compulsive use of the internet that interferes with daily functioning and well-being. This condition is often marked by a preoccupation with online activities, a loss of control over internet use, and a negative impact on personal, academic, or occupational responsibilities. The phenomenon of internet addiction is a growing concern due to its potential to disrupt various aspects of life, including social relationships and mental health (Diotaiuti et al., 2022; Zhu et al., 2023).

Socio-Ecological Model emphasizes the interaction between individual, social, and environmental factors influencing digital behavior. It considers how personal characteristics, social networks, community contexts, and broader societal influences shape digital well-being and the risk of addiction. For instance, parental controls and educational interventions can play a significant role in managing digital use among children and adolescents (Salmon et al., 2020; Jalali et al., 2020).

Cognitive-Behavioral Frameworks focus on the cognitive and behavioral patterns associated with internet use. Cognitive-behavioral theories suggest that maladaptive beliefs and behaviors, such as overestimating the benefits of online interactions or using the internet to escape from real-life problems, contribute to internet addiction. Interventions based on these theories aim to modify such patterns through strategies like cognitive restructuring and behavioral modification (Brand et al., 2014; Ryding & Kaye, 2017).

Children and Adolescents stages, peer influence, and parental guidance significantly impact digital behavior in younger populations. Issues such as cyberbullying, social comparison, and gaming addiction are prevalent concerns. Educational programs and parental monitoring can help mitigate risks and promote healthy technology use (Chen et al., 2024; Hilty et al., 2023).

Young Adults group often experiences high levels of internet use due to academic and social demands. Factors such as academic stress, social media engagement, and career-related pressures can contribute to internet addiction. Strategies like time management, mindfulness, and supportive social networks are essential for promoting digital well-being in this demographic (Feng et al., 2019; Mou et al., 2024).

Adults, work-life balance, professional demands, and personal relationships can influence digital well-being. Overuse of digital technologies for work-related purposes and the need for constant connectivity can lead to burnout and reduced personal time. Managing digital boundaries and incorporating relaxation techniques are critical for maintaining balance (Büchi, 2021; Burr et al., 2020).

Older Adults may face challenges related to digital literacy and social isolation, which can affect their engagement with technology. Issues such as difficulty navigating digital platforms and reliance on technology for social interaction can impact their overall well-being. Providing accessible digital literacy training and fostering inclusive online communities can support positive digital experiences for older adults (Soundararajan et al., 2023).

By understanding these factors and theoretical perspectives, we can better address the complexities of digital well-being and internet addiction across different stages of life, ultimately promoting healthier digital practices and improved quality of life.

BACKGROUND

The rapid advancement of digital technologies has fundamentally altered the way individuals interact, work, learn, and entertain themselves. Across all life stages, from infancy to older adulthood, digital devices have become integral to daily life, bringing both opportunities and challenges. While digital technologies offer numerous benefits, such as increased connectivity, access to information, and innovative learning opportunities, they also pose significant risks, particularly in terms of mental and physical well-being. Internet addiction, a growing concern globally, is characterized by excessive or compulsive online behavior that negatively impacts an individual's daily functioning and health. Understanding how digital well-being and internet addiction manifest across different life stages is crucial for developing tailored interventions that promote healthy digital habits and mitigate associated risks (Bellis et al., 2021; Wang & Zeng, 2024).

The aim of this chapter is to explore the impact of digital technologies on well-being and the prevalence of internet addiction across the lifespan, from infancy to older adulthood. It seeks to provide a comprehensive understanding of how these issues manifest differently at various life stages and to identify effective strategies for promoting digital well-being. The scope of the chapter includes an examination of the psychological, biological, social, and environmental factors that influence digital well-being, as well as the introduction and application of the Multidimensional Addiction Behaviour Scale (MABS) as a tool for assessing and addressing digital addiction.

The chapter aims to address several critical research questions and objectives related to digital well-being and internet addiction across the lifespan. The research questions focus on how digital well-being varies across different life stages and the factors contributing to these variations, the patterns and prevalence of internet addiction throughout life, and the development of tailored interventions to address the unique challenges at each stage. To achieve these goals, the objectives include analyzing the impact of digital technologies on well-being from infancy to older adulthood, identifying key factors influencing digital well-being and internet addiction, evaluating the effectiveness of the Multidimensional Addiction Behaviour Scale (MABS) in assessing and addressing digital addiction, and proposing targeted interventions to promote digital well-being and prevent internet addiction across all age groups.

DIGITAL WELL-BEING ACROSS THE LIFESPAN

The early years of life are crucial for cognitive, socio-emotional, and physical development. As digital technologies become increasingly integrated into daily life, even very young children are exposed to screens and digital content. This early introduction can have significant implications for their development. Digital exposure in infancy and early childhood often includes activities such as watching videos, interacting with educational apps, or even using digital toys. The nature and quality of this exposure can influence developmental outcomes in various ways (Johnston, 2019; Ponti, 2023).

Excessive screen time in young children has been associated with delays in language development and reduced attention span. Screen-based activities, particularly those lacking interactive elements, may not provide the same cognitive benefits as face-to-face interactions or hands-on play. However, high-quality, educational content designed for young children can support cognitive development if used appropriately (Ponti, 2023; Vedechkina & Borgonovi, 2021).

Prolonged screen use can affect socio-emotional skills by limiting opportunities for face-to-face interactions and socialization. Children who spend excessive time on screens may experience difficulties in understanding social cues and developing empathy. Additionally, exposure to inappropriate content or online interactions can impact emotional well-being and behavior (Huang et al., 2024; Meroni et al., 2021).

Screen time can influence physical health by contributing to sedentary behavior, which is linked to issues such as obesity and poor motor skills development. Young children need physical activity for healthy growth and development, and excessive screen time can detract from active play and outdoor experiences (Ponti et al., 2017; Ponti, 2023).

Establishing clear guidelines for screen time duration and content can help ensure that digital use is balanced with other activities. Recommendations from health organizations often suggest limiting screen time to encourage more physical and social activities (Hinkley et al., 2018; Nagata et al., 2024; Santos et al., 2024).

Participating in digital activities with children can enhance the quality of their screen time. Co-viewing educational content, discussing the material, and relating it to real-life experiences can promote cognitive and socio-emotional benefits while providing parents with an opportunity to monitor content (Hutton et al., 2024; Sivrikova et al., 2020).

Parents serve as role models for their children's digital behavior. Demonstrating balanced screen use, setting aside designated tech-free times, and prioritizing offline activities can help children develop healthy digital habits (Liu et al., 2024).

Selecting high-quality, age-appropriate digital content that supports educational and developmental goals is essential. Parents should seek out content that aligns with their child's developmental stage and educational needs (Ponti, 2023).

By implementing these mediation strategies, parents can support their young children's digital well-being, ensuring that digital exposure contributes positively to their overall development.

CHILDHOOD AND ADOLESCENCE

As children transition into adolescence, they experience a significant increase in autonomy regarding their digital usage. This period is marked by growing independence, both online and offline, as adolescents begin to make their own decisions about how, when, and why they use digital technologies. This increased autonomy is often driven by social, educational, and entertainment needs, leading to greater engagement with social media, gaming, and other online activities. While this independence can foster critical thinking and digital literacy, it also introduces new challenges, such as managing screen time, navigating online risks, and balancing digital life with other responsibilities (Sun, 2024; West et al., 2023).

Social media platforms are central to adolescent social life, offering opportunities for connection and self-expression. However, they also present risks, such as exposure to cyberbullying, social comparison, and the pressure to maintain a curated online image. These factors can contribute to anxiety, depression, and lower self-esteem. While social media can foster a sense of belonging and peer support, excessive or negative use can harm psychological well-being (O'Keeffe & Clarke-Pearson, 2011).

Online gaming is a popular activity among adolescents, providing entertainment and social interaction. However, excessive gaming can lead to issues such as decreased academic performance, social isolation, and disrupted sleep patterns. The immersive nature of games, especially those designed to be highly engaging, can contribute to addictive behaviors, where the individual prioritizes gaming over other activities (Ahmed et al., 2022; Alzahrani & Griffiths, 2024; Koutsimani et al., 2019).

The internet offers vast resources for learning and exploration, but excessive or unregulated use can negatively impact mental health. Adolescents may be exposed to harmful content, experience online harassment, or develop unhealthy habits such as compulsive browsing or dependency on online validation. These behaviors can contribute to stress, anxiety, and a diminished sense of reality (Savoia et al., 2021).

Adolescents facing social or emotional challenges, such as loneliness, depression, or low self-esteem, may turn to the internet as a coping mechanism. This can increase the risk of developing addictive behaviors as they seek solace or validation online (Chang & Lee, 2024).

Certain personality traits, such as impulsivity, sensation-seeking, and low self-regulation, can predispose adolescents to internet addiction. These traits may lead to difficulties in managing time online, making it harder to maintain a balanced digital life (Brand et al., 2014; Kim et al., 2022).

A lack of parental supervision, access to unrestricted internet use, and peer influence can contribute to higher risks of internet addiction. Adolescents who are not guided on healthy digital practices may be more susceptible to overuse and addiction.

Educating adolescents about the potential risks of excessive internet use and the importance of digital well-being is crucial. Schools, parents, and community programs can play a role in promoting awareness and teaching self-regulation strategies.

Active parental involvement, including setting boundaries for screen time, monitoring online activities, and fostering open communication about digital experiences, can help mitigate the risks of internet addiction. Encouraging offline activities and family time can also support a healthier balance.

Providing access to mental health resources and support for adolescents struggling with issues like anxiety or depression can reduce their reliance on the internet as a coping mechanism. Early intervention and counseling can address underlying issues that may contribute to addictive behaviors (Aziz et al., 2024; Gu et al., 2024).

Encouraging a balanced approach to digital use, where online activities are integrated with offline interests, social interactions, and physical activities, can help prevent internet addiction. Mindfulness practices and digital detox periods can also support mental well-being.

By understanding the complex interplay between autonomy, digital usage, and psychological well-being, and by implementing effective preventive interventions, we can promote healthier digital habits and reduce the risk of internet addiction among adolescents.

ADULTHOOD

Adulthood is a stage characterized by numerous responsibilities, including career, family, and personal growth. Digital technologies play a central role in managing these responsibilities, facilitating communication, work, and access to information. However, the pervasive nature of digital engagement can make it challenging to maintain a healthy balance between online and offline life. Adults often find themselves navigating the demands of work-related digital tasks, social media interactions, and personal digital use, which can blur the boundaries between professional and personal time. Achieving a balance requires mindful digital engagement, where individuals prioritize activities that enhance well-being and contribute positively to relationships and personal growth, while setting limits to avoid overuse (Chase et al., 2022; Duradoni et al., 2022).

Prolonged screen use, especially for work or social media, can lead to stress, anxiety, and feelings of burnout. The constant connectivity and exposure to online content can create a sense of overwhelm, negatively impacting mental well-being. Additionally, the nature of digital interactions, such as the pressure to respond immediately to work emails or stay updated on social media, can contribute to heightened anxiety and reduced emotional resilience (Santos et al., 2024).

While digital tools are essential for work, excessive screen time can paradoxically decrease productivity. Continuous multitasking, frequent digital distractions, and the inability to disconnect from work-related tasks can lead to cognitive fatigue and diminished focus. This can result in lower work efficiency, increased errors, and reduced overall job satisfaction. Moreover, excessive screen time can encroach on personal time, leaving little room for rest and recovery, further exacerbating stress and reducing productivity.

Establishing clear boundaries between work and personal time is essential for digital well-being. This may involve setting specific hours for work-related digital engagement and ensuring that personal time is free from work interruptions. Creating tech-free zones or times, such as during meals or before bed, can also help reduce screen time and improve mental health.

Engaging in offline activities, such as hobbies, physical exercise, and face-to-face interactions, can help counterbalance the effects of excessive screen time. These activities provide opportunities for relaxation, creativity, and social connection, all of which are crucial for mental and emotional well-being.

Practicing mindfulness in digital engagement involves being conscious of how, when, and why digital tools are used. This can include limiting time on non-essential digital activities, avoiding digital multitasking, and being intentional about the content consumed online. Mindful use helps individuals stay focused on their goals and reduces the likelihood of digital overload (Vargas-Nieto et al., 2024).

Periodically disconnecting from digital devices, or engaging in a digital detox, can be beneficial for mental health. Taking regular breaks from screens, whether for a few hours or an entire day, allows the mind to rest and rejuvenate. This practice can lead to increased focus, better sleep, and an overall improvement in well-being.

Addressing the physical aspects of digital engagement is also important. Ensuring proper ergonomics while using digital devices, such as maintaining good posture, using ergonomic furniture, and taking regular breaks to stretch, can prevent physical strain and improve comfort during screen time.

By implementing these coping mechanisms and strategies, adults can better manage their digital engagement, protect their mental health, and enhance their productivity. Balancing digital use with offline activities and mindful practices is key to maintaining digital well-being in adulthood, ensuring that technology serves as a tool for empowerment rather than a source of stress.

OLDER ADULTHOOD

In older adulthood, the digital divide often becomes more pronounced, with some individuals fully embracing technology while others experience digital exclusion. Digital inclusion refers to the ability of older adults to access, use, and benefit from digital technologies, which can enhance their quality of life. However, barriers such as limited access to devices, low digital literacy, and reluctance to adopt new technologies can lead to digital exclusion. This exclusion can isolate older adults from the digital world, limiting their access to essential services, information, and social connections. Efforts to bridge this gap through targeted education, affordable access, and supportive environments are crucial in promoting digital inclusion for aging populations (Kuoppamäki et al., 2022; Mannheim et al., 2019).

Technology can help older adults stay connected with family and friends, reducing feelings of loneliness and isolation. Video calls, social media, and online communities provide opportunities for social interaction, which is vital for mental and emotional well-being.

Digital technologies enable older adults to access healthcare services, online shopping, and government resources, making daily tasks more convenient and promoting independence. Telemedicine, for example, allows for regular health check-ups without the need for physical visits, which can be particularly beneficial for those with mobility issues.

Engaging with technology can help keep older adults mentally active. Online games, educational programs, and digital hobbies can stimulate cognitive functions, potentially delaying cognitive decline and enhancing mental sharpness.

Many older adults may struggle with the skills needed to navigate digital technologies. This lack of digital literacy can lead to frustration, decreased confidence in using technology, and a reliance on others for assistance, which may further exacerbate feelings of dependency (Liu et al., 2022; Rasi et al., 2020).

Older adults are often more vulnerable to online scams, phishing attacks, and privacy breaches. A lack of awareness about online safety practices can put them at risk of financial loss and identity theft.

Age-related physical challenges, such as impaired vision, hearing loss, or arthritis, can make it difficult for older adults to use digital devices. These physical limitations require adaptations in technology design to ensure accessibility (Mannheim et al., 2019; Rogers & Fisk, 2010).

While internet addiction is less common among older adults compared to younger populations, it is still a concern, particularly as more seniors adopt digital technologies. The rise in digital engagement, coupled with the availability of endless online content, can lead to problematic behaviors in some older adults, such as excessive time spent online or reliance on digital interactions at the expense of in-person connections.

Offering digital literacy training tailored to older adults can empower them to use technology confidently and safely. These programs can be delivered through community centers, libraries, or online platforms, focusing on practical skills such as using the internet, navigating social media, and understanding online safety.

Encouraging peer-led initiatives, where older adults teach each other digital skills, can create a supportive learning environment. This approach leverages the power of community and reduces the intimidation often associated with learning new technologies.

Promoting a balanced approach to technology use is essential in preventing internet addiction. Older adults should be encouraged to integrate digital activities with offline pursuits, such as physical exercise, hobbies, and face-to-face social interactions.

Teaching older adults mindfulness techniques can help them stay aware of their digital habits and recognize when they might be spending too much time online. Mindful engagement encourages intentional use of technology, where digital tools serve specific purposes rather than filling time aimlessly.

Establishing support networks for older adults who may be struggling with excessive internet use can provide them with the resources and encouragement needed to manage their digital habits effectively.

By addressing these issues and promoting digital literacy, older adults can fully benefit from technology while minimizing the risks associated with internet use. Efforts to enhance digital inclusion, adapt technology to the needs of aging populations, and foster healthy digital behaviors will ensure that older adults remain connected, informed, and empowered in the digital age.

INTERNET ADDICTION ACROSS THE LIFESPAN

Internet addiction manifests differently across various age groups, reflecting the unique ways in which people engage with digital technologies throughout their lives. In younger populations, particularly adolescents and young adults, internet addiction is more prevalent due to their high levels of digital engagement, especially in areas like social media, gaming, and content streaming. Adolescents often experience internet addiction as a consequence of their developmental stage, where peer influence, identity exploration, and autonomy play significant roles in shaping their online behavior (Bickham, 2021; Marzilli et al., 2020).

In contrast, adults typically experience internet addiction in the context of work-related stress, social media usage, and online entertainment, often as a means of coping with daily pressures or escaping from routine responsibilities. As people age, the patterns of internet addiction shift, with older adults generally exhibiting lower prevalence rates. However, as digital technology becomes more integrated into daily life, there is a growing trend of internet addiction among older adults, particularly as they use digital tools for social connection, information access, and entertainment (Wang et al., 2024).

In adolescence, risk factors for internet addiction include peer pressure, social isolation, low self-esteem, and poor academic performance. Adolescents may turn to the internet as a way to connect with peers, escape from stressors, or seek validation, leading to compulsive online behavior. Additionally, personality traits such as impulsivity and sensation-seeking can make adolescents more susceptible to internet addiction use (Bickham, 2021).

For young adults, the transition to higher education or the workforce can introduce stressors that increase the risk of internet addiction. Factors such as academic pressure, work-related stress, and loneliness may drive young adults to engage in excessive online activities as a coping mechanism. The need for constant social interaction and the fear of missing out (FOMO) can also contribute to compulsive social media use (Bickham, 2021; Marzilli et al., 2020).

In adulthood, risk factors for internet addiction often relate to work-life balance, emotional stress, and social isolation. Adults may become addicted to work-related digital tasks, social networking, or online entertainment as a way to manage stress or escape from personal challenges. The constant connectivity required by many jobs can blur the lines between work and personal life, leading to an unhealthy reliance on digital devices(Monteiro et al., 2023; Wang et al., 2024).

Among older adults, risk factors for internet addiction include loneliness, depression, and a lack of social support. As older adults increasingly use digital technologies for social interaction and to combat feelings of isolation, there is a risk of developing compulsive online behaviors. Cognitive decline and reduced physical activity can also contribute to increased screen time, further exacerbating the risk of addiction (Shek et al., 2022; Wang et al., 2024).

Prolonged internet use can lead to various physical health issues, including eye strain, headaches, and musculoskeletal problems due to poor posture during screen time. Sedentary behavior associated with excessive internet use can contribute to obesity, cardiovascular disease, and other health complications. Sleep disturbances are also common, particularly when internet use extends late into the night, disrupting the body's natural sleep-wake cycle (Gülbetekin et al., 2023; ; Zhu et al., 2023).

Internet addiction is strongly linked to mental health issues such as anxiety, depression, and stress. The constant exposure to online content, social comparison, and the pressure to maintain an online presence can exacerbate these conditions. For adolescents and young adults, internet addiction can interfere with emotional development and increase the risk of mental health disorders. In older adults, internet addiction can contribute to cognitive decline and exacerbate feelings of loneliness and depression (Diotaiuti et al., 2022).

Internet addiction can negatively impact social relationships, leading to social withdrawal and isolation. Individuals who spend excessive time online may neglect face-to-face interactions, resulting in weakened personal relationships and reduced social support. In severe cases, internet addiction can lead to conflicts within families, strain in romantic relationships, and difficulties in maintaining friendships. For adolescents, this can impair social development, while for older adults, it can exacerbate feelings of loneliness and social disconnection (Wang & Zeng, 2024; Zhu et al., 2023).

By understanding the prevalence, risk factors, and consequences of internet addiction across the lifespan, it becomes possible to develop targeted interventions and preventive strategies that address the unique challenges faced by different age groups. Promoting digital well-being and fostering healthy online habits are essential steps in mitigating the risks associated with internet addiction and enhancing overall quality of life.

ASSESSMENT AND INTERVENTION

Assessing digital well-being and internet addiction across generations requires the use of reliable and age-appropriate screening tools. These tools are designed to evaluate the extent of an individual's internet use, the impact it has on their daily life, and the presence of any problematic behaviors that may indicate addiction (Poli, 2017; Samaha et al., 2018).

For Adolescents and Young Adults: Tools like the Internet Addiction Test (IAT), developed by Dr. Kimberly Young, are commonly used to assess internet addiction in younger populations. The IAT evaluates the degree of compulsive internet use, the impact on social and academic functioning, and emotional responses to being offline. The Problematic Internet Use Questionnaire (PIUQ) is another tool tailored for this demographic, focusing on issues like time management, neglect of daily activities, and the psychological impact of excessive internet use.

In addition to the IAT, adults can be assessed using the Generalized Problematic Internet Use Scale (GPIUS2), which measures cognitive, emotional, and behavioral aspects of internet use that may lead to addiction. The scale addresses aspects such as mood regulation, compulsive behavior, and social consequences, making it a comprehensive tool for evaluating internet addiction in adults.

Screening tools for older adults are often adapted to consider the unique challenges this age group faces, such as loneliness and cognitive decline. The Elderly Computer Addiction Scale (ECAS) is one such tool that assesses the extent of internet use, particularly in relation to online communication and entertainment. This tool also considers the physical and psychological impacts of internet use on older adults.

Cognitive-Behavioral Therapy (CBT) is one of the most effective interventions for internet addiction. It helps individuals identify and modify problematic thought patterns and behaviors related to internet use. Through CBT, individuals learn to develop healthier coping mechanisms, set boundaries for digital engagement, and replace addictive behaviors with more constructive activities (Loya et al., 2023; Zhu et al., 2023).

Mindfulness-Based Interventions such as meditation and mindful breathing, can help individuals become more aware of their digital habits and reduce impulsive online behaviors. Mindfulness-Based Stress Reduction (MBSR) programs have shown promise in reducing symptoms of internet addiction, particularly in managing stress and enhancing emotional regulation (Korecki et al., 2020; Song & Park, 2019; Querstret et al., 2020).

Structured digital detox programs encourage individuals to take breaks from screens, gradually reducing their dependency on digital devices. These programs often include activities that promote offline engagement, such as outdoor activities, hobbies, and social interaction, helping individuals rediscover balance in their lives.

For adolescents and young adults, family therapy can be instrumental in addressing internet addiction. This intervention focuses on improving family communication, setting healthy boundaries, and creating a supportive environment for the individual struggling with addiction. Family therapy also educates parents about the importance of modeling balanced digital behavior (Bagley et al., 2021; Zhu et al., 2023).

Educating individuals and their families about the risks of internet addiction and the importance of digital well-being is crucial. Digital literacy training can empower people to use the internet responsibly, recognize the signs of addiction, and take proactive steps to maintain a healthy relationship with technology.

Healthcare providers play a critical role in identifying and treating internet addiction. By incorporating routine screening for digital well-being into health assessments, professionals can detect early signs of addiction and provide timely interventions. They can also offer counseling, support, and referrals to specialized treatment programs for those struggling with internet addiction. Furthermore, healthcare providers can educate patients about the importance of maintaining a balanced digital life and the potential health risks associated with excessive screen time.

Educators are on the front lines of promoting digital well-being among students. By integrating digital literacy into the curriculum, educators can teach students about responsible internet use, the dangers of internet addiction, and strategies for maintaining balance. Schools can also implement programs that encourage physical activity, face-to-face interactions, and mindfulness practices to counteract the effects of excessive screen time. Additionally, educators can collaborate with parents to create a supportive environment for healthy digital habits at home.

Policymakers have a significant role in shaping the environment in which digital technologies are used. They can promote digital well-being by enacting regulations that limit screen time in educational settings, support digital literacy initiatives, and fund research on internet addiction. Policies that ensure equitable access to technology, while also safeguarding against its misuse, are essential in addressing the digital divide and promoting inclusion. Furthermore, policymakers can advocate for public awareness campaigns that highlight the risks of internet addiction and provide resources for prevention and treatment.

By working together, healthcare professionals, educators, and policymakers can create a comprehensive approach to promoting digital well-being across generations, ensuring that individuals are equipped to navigate the digital world in a healthy and balanced way.

MULTIDIMENSIONAL ADDICTION BEHAVIOUR SCALE

The Multidimensional Addiction Behaviour Scale (MABS) developed by Ranjit Singha is an innovative tool designed to thoroughly assess addiction by exploring a wide range of influencing factors. This scale evaluates five key dimensions: Psychological Factors, Biological Factors, Social and Environmental Factors, Cognitive and Behavioral Patterns, and Motivation and Readiness for Change. MABS provides a holistic perspective on addiction, integrating these diverse elements to offer a detailed analysis of an individual's addiction profile. It is highly effective for both clinical assessment and research, supporting the development of tailored interventions and treatment strategies.

MABS is particularly adept at detecting and preventing addictions related to internet use, social media, gaming, and other online activities. By assessing Psychological Factors, such as anxiety or depression that may drive excessive online behavior, alongside Biological Factors, including neurochemical imbalances, MABS offers valuable insights into the root causes of digital addiction.

The scale's focus on Social and Environmental Factors allows for the identification of external influences, such as peer pressure or societal norms, that contribute to online addiction. Additionally, its exploration of Cognitive and Behavioral Patterns highlights the habitual and cognitive distortions that perpetuate addictive behaviors. The Motivation and Readiness for Change dimension is key in assessing an individual's willingness to seek help and make necessary changes, making MABS an essential tool for early detection and intervention, ultimately helping to prevent problematic online activities.

RECOMMENDATIONS AND SOLUTIONS

Develop and implement age-specific interventions to address digital well-being and internet addiction. For children, focus on parental guidance and education about healthy screen time habits. For adolescents, integrate digital literacy programs in schools and promote balanced technology use through counseling. For adults, provide resources for managing work-life balance and digital consumption, while for older adults, offer digital literacy training and support for navigating online spaces effectively.

Utilize comprehensive tools like the Multidimensional Addiction Behaviour Scale (MABS) to assess digital addiction across different age groups. Regularly screen for digital addiction symptoms and well-being across the lifespan to identify issues early and tailor interventions accordingly.

Implement educational programs to enhance digital literacy at all life stages. These programs should cover safe and mindful technology use, understanding digital footprints, and recognizing signs of digital addiction. Schools, workplaces, and community organizations should collaborate to deliver these programs effectively.

Advocate for policies that promote digital well-being, such as regulations on screen time for children and guidelines for healthy technology use in the workplace. Governments and organizations should develop and enforce policies that support balanced digital engagement and protect individuals from potential harms associated with excessive technology use.

Encourage collaboration between healthcare professionals, educators, policymakers, and technology developers to create a holistic approach to digital well-being. This includes developing integrated strategies for prevention, early detection, and intervention of digital addiction, as well as creating supportive environments that foster healthy digital habits.

Support and fund research to continuously assess the impacts of emerging digital technologies and update intervention strategies accordingly. Stay informed about the latest technological trends and their potential effects on digital well-being to adapt and refine interventions effectively.

By adopting these recommendations and solutions, we can better address the challenges of digital well-being and internet addiction across different life stages, ultimately promoting healthier interactions with technology and enhancing overall quality of life.

FUTURE DIRECTIONS AND CONCLUSION

As digital technology continues to evolve, new trends are emerging that have the potential to significantly impact well-being across the lifespan. The rise of artificial intelligence (AI), virtual and augmented reality (VR/AR), and the increasing integration of the Internet of Things (IoT) into daily life are reshaping how individuals interact with the digital world. While these advancements offer numerous benefits, such as enhanced communication, personalized experiences, and improved accessibility, they also pose new challenges to digital well-being.

AI-driven algorithms, for example, are becoming more adept at capturing user data and tailoring content, which can lead to increased screen time and potential addiction, especially among vulnerable populations like adolescents. The immersive nature of VR and AR technologies may further blur the lines between online and offline experiences, raising concerns about the potential for escapism and detachment from reality. Additionally, the expansion of IoT devices in homes and workplaces may contribute to constant connectivity, making it even more challenging to disconnect and maintain a healthy work-life balance.

These trends highlight the need for ongoing research to understand their implications for well-being and to develop strategies to mitigate the risks associated with their use. Future research should focus on longitudinal studies that examine the long-term effects of digital technology on well-being across different life stages. Investigating the interplay between emerging technologies and mental health, cognitive development, and social functioning is essential. Research should also explore the effectiveness of various interventions, such as digital detox programs and mindfulness practices, in promoting digital well-being. Additionally, studies that consider the impact of cultural, socioeconomic, and individual differences on digital behavior will provide a more nuanced understanding of internet addiction.

Healthcare professionals, educators, and mental health practitioners should incorporate digital well-being into their practices. This includes routine screening for internet addiction, providing counseling and support for those at risk, and promoting healthy digital habits. Schools and workplaces should implement programs that encourage balanced digital use and provide resources for managing screen time. Practitioners should also stay informed about emerging technologies and their potential impacts, adapting their approaches to meet the evolving needs of their clients and students.

Policymakers should prioritize the development and implementation of regulations that protect individuals from the potential harms of excessive digital use. This includes creating guidelines for ethical AI and data usage, supporting digital literacy initiatives, and funding public health campaigns that raise awareness about the risks of internet addiction. Policies should also focus on ensuring equitable access to technology while addressing the digital divide, particularly for older adults and underserved populations. Collaboration between governments, technology companies, and public health organizations will be crucial in creating a safe and supportive digital environment.

Digital well-being and internet addiction are complex, multifaceted issues that affect individuals across the lifespan. As digital technologies become increasingly integral to daily life, understanding the factors that contribute to both positive and negative digital experiences is essential. This chapter has explored the prevalence and patterns of internet addiction across different age groups, the risk factors and consequences associated with excessive digital use, and the importance of screening and intervention strategies tailored to various life stages.

The implications of this understanding extend to multiple domains, including healthcare, education, and public policy. By adopting a proactive and holistic approach to digital well-being, society can better navigate the challenges posed by digital technologies while maximizing their potential to enhance quality of life. As technology continues to evolve, it is imperative that research, practice, and policy keep pace, ensuring that digital advancements contribute to, rather than detract from, the well-being of individuals at every stage of life.

DISCUSSION

The exploration of digital well-being and internet addiction across the lifespan reveals significant variations in how these issues manifest and affect individuals at different stages of life. From infancy to older adulthood, the pervasive influence of digital technologies introduces both opportunities and challenges for maintaining well-being. This discussion synthesizes the findings and insights from the chapter, highlighting key themes and implications.

The impact of digital technologies on well-being differs markedly across various life stages. In infancy and early childhood, the primary concern is managing screen time to prevent adverse effects on cognitive and socio-emotional development. Research indicates that excessive screen time can interfere with developmental milestones, such as language acquisition and social skills. Parental mediation strategies play a crucial role in mitigating these effects by setting boundaries and promoting interactive, non-screen-based activities.

As individuals transition to childhood and adolescence, the focus shifts to managing increasing autonomy in digital usage. Adolescents are particularly vulnerable to the risks associated with social media and online gaming, which can affect their psychological well-being. The prevalence of internet addiction in this age group is often linked to social comparison, peer pressure, and the need for validation. Effective interventions must address these factors by promoting digital literacy, fostering healthy online behaviors, and providing support through counseling and educational programs.

In adulthood, the challenge is balancing digital engagement with work, relationships, and personal well-being. Excessive screen time can lead to decreased productivity, mental health issues, and strained relationships. Strategies for maintaining digital well-being include setting boundaries for work-related technology use, incorporating digital detox periods, and developing coping mechanisms to manage stress and screen-related fatigue.

For older adults, digital inclusion presents both benefits and challenges. Technology can enhance connectivity and access to resources, but it can also lead to digital exclusion for those who lack digital literacy skills. Addressing internet addiction in this population involves promoting digital literacy, providing support for navigating online spaces, and fostering social connections to prevent over-reliance on technology for companionship.

The chapter highlights that internet addiction is a prevalent issue across all age groups, though the patterns and contributing factors vary. Psychological factors, such as anxiety and depression, often drive excessive internet use, while social and environmental factors, like peer pressure and societal norms, contribute to the development and maintenance of addiction. The cognitive and behavioral patterns associated with internet addiction, including compulsive use and cognitive distortions, underscore the need for comprehensive assessment and intervention strategies.

To effectively address digital well-being and internet addiction, interventions must be tailored to the specific needs of each age group. For children and adolescents, interventions should focus on education, parental involvement, and school-based programs that promote healthy technology use. For adults, strategies should emphasize work-life balance, stress management, and responsible technology use. Older adults require support for digital literacy and strategies to prevent over-reliance on technology.

The Multidimensional Addiction Behaviour Scale (MABS) proves to be a valuable tool for assessing addiction by evaluating psychological, biological, social, and cognitive factors. Its application in both clinical and research settings can enhance the understanding of digital addiction and support the development of targeted interventions.

Ongoing research is essential to adapt to the evolving landscape of digital technologies. Future studies should explore the effects of emerging technologies, such as AI and virtual reality, on digital well-being and addiction. Additionally, research should focus on refining intervention strategies and evaluating their effectiveness across different populations.

In conclusion, addressing digital well-being and internet addiction requires a multifaceted approach that considers the unique challenges and needs of individuals across the lifespan. By implementing targeted interventions, fostering digital literacy, and supporting ongoing research, we can better manage the impact of digital technologies and promote healthier, more balanced interactions with technology.

CONCLUSION

The pervasive influence of digital technologies across generations presents both opportunities and challenges for well-being. As explored in this chapter, digital well-being and internet addiction are critical issues that manifest differently across various life stages, from infancy to older adulthood. Understanding these differences is essential for developing effective strategies to promote healthy digital habits and mitigate the risks associated with excessive technology use.

Internet addiction, characterized by compulsive and problematic internet use, poses significant risks to mental, physical, and social health. These risks are evident across all age groups, though the manifestations and impacts vary, highlighting the need for tailored interventions. For instance, adolescents may struggle with social media addiction, while older adults might face challenges related to digital exclusion or over-reliance on technology for social interaction.

The chapter emphasizes the importance of comprehensive screening tools and evidence-based interventions to address internet addiction effectively. Healthcare professionals, educators, and policymakers must collaborate to create environments that support digital well-being. This includes fostering digital literacy, encouraging mindful technology use, and implementing policies that safeguard individuals from the potential harms of excessive screen time.

As digital technologies continue to evolve, ongoing research is vital to understanding their long-term impacts on well-being. Future studies should focus on the effects of emerging technologies, such as AI and VR, and explore strategies for promoting digital well-being in an increasingly connected world.

Addressing digital well-being and internet addiction across the lifespan requires a proactive and interdisciplinary approach. By understanding the unique challenges faced by different age groups and implementing targeted interventions, society can harness the benefits of digital technology while minimizing its potential harms, ensuring that digital experiences contribute positively to overall well-being.

In conclusion, the Multidimensional Addiction Behaviour Scale (MABS) is a comprehensive and effective tool for assessing and addressing addiction, particularly in the digital realm. By evaluating key psychological, biological, social, and cognitive factors, along with an individual's motivation for change, MABS plays a crucial role in early detection, intervention, and the prevention of problematic behaviors.

REFERENCES

Ahmed, G. K., Abdalla, A. A., Mohamed, A. M., Mohamed, L. A., & Shamaa, H. A. (2022). Relationship between time spent playing internet gaming apps and behavioral problems, sleep problems, alexithymia, and emotion dysregulations in children: A multicentre study. *Child and Adolescent Psychiatry and Mental Health*, 16(1), 67. Advance online publication. DOI: 10.1186/s13034-022-00502-w PMID: 35974366

Alzahrani, A. K. D., & Griffiths, M. D. (2024). Problematic Gaming and Students' Academic Performance: A Systematic review. *International Journal of Mental Health and Addiction*. Advance online publication. DOI: 10.1007/s11469-024-01338-5

Aziz, M., Chemnad, K., Al-Harahsheh, S., Abdelmoneium, A. O., Baghdady, A., & Ali, R. (2024). Depression, stress, and anxiety versus internet addiction in early and middle adolescent groups: The mediating roles of family and school environments. *BMC Psychology*, 12(1), 184. Advance online publication. DOI: 10.1186/s40359-024-01659-z PMID: 38570890

Bagley, S. M., Ventura, A. S., Lasser, K. E., & Muench, F. (2021). Engaging the family in the care of young adults with substance use disorders. *Pediatrics*, 147(Supplement 2), S215–S219. DOI: 10.1542/peds.2020-023523C PMID: 33386324

Bellis, M. A., Sharp, C. A., Hughes, K., & Davies, A. R. (2021). Digital overuse and addictive traits and their relationship with Mental Well-Being and Socio-Demographic Factors: A National Population Survey for Wales. *Frontiers in Public Health*, 9, 585715. Advance online publication. DOI: 10.3389/fpubh.2021.585715 PMID: 34222161

Bickham, D. S. (2021). Current research and viewpoints on internet addiction in Adolescents. *Current Pediatrics Reports*, 9(1), 1–10. DOI: 10.1007/s40124-020-00236-3 PMID: 33457108

Brand, M., Young, K. S., & Laier, C. (2014). Prefrontal Control and Internet Addiction: A theoretical model and review of neuropsychological and neuroimaging findings. *Frontiers in Human Neuroscience*, 8. Advance online publication. DOI: 10.3389/fnhum.2014.00375 PMID: 24904393

Büchi, M. (2021). Digital well-being theory and research. *New Media & Society*, 26(1), 172–189. DOI: 10.1177/14614448211056851

Burr, C., Taddeo, M., & Floridi, L. (2020). The Ethics of Digital Well-Being: A Thematic Review. *Science and Engineering Ethics*, 26(4), 2313–2343. DOI: 10.1007/s11948-020-00175-8 PMID: 31933119

Chang, M. L. Y., & Lee, I. O. (2024). Functional connectivity changes in the brain of adolescents with internet addiction: A systematic literature review of imaging studies. *PLOS Mental Health*, 1(1), e0000022. Advance online publication. DOI: 10.1371/journal.pmen.0000022

Chase, G. E., Brown, M. T., & Jensen, M. (2022). Emerging adults' digital technology engagement and mental health during the COVID-19 pandemic. *Frontiers in Psychology*, 13, 1023514. Advance online publication. DOI: 10.3389/fpsyg.2022.1023514 PMID: 36467177

Chen, T., Ou, J., Li, G., & Luo, H. (2024). Promoting mental health in children and adolescents through digital technology: A systematic review and meta-analysis. *Frontiers in Psychology*, 15, 1356554. Advance online publication. DOI: 10.3389/fpsyg.2024.1356554 PMID: 38533221

Diotaiuti, P., Mancone, S., Corrado, S., De Risio, A., Cavicchiolo, E., Girelli, L., & Chirico, A. (2022). Internet addiction in young adults: The role of impulsivity and codependency. *Frontiers in Psychiatry*, 13, 893861. Advance online publication. DOI: 10.3389/fpsyt.2022.893861 PMID: 36147985

Duradoni, M., Serritella, E., Avolio, C., Arnetoli, C., & Guazzini, A. (2022b). Development and Validation of the Digital Life Balance (DLB) Scale: A Brand-New Measure for both Harmonic and Disharmonic use of ICTs. *Behavioral Sciences (Basel, Switzerland)*, 12(12), 489. DOI: 10.3390/bs12120489 PMID: 36546972

Feng, Y., Ma, Y., & Zhong, Q. (2019). The Relationship Between Adolescents' stress and Internet Addiction: A Mediated-Moderation Model. *Frontiers in Psychology*, 10, 2248. Advance online publication. DOI: 10.3389/fpsyg.2019.02248 PMID: 31636590

Gu, J., Zhan, P., Huang, Z., Cheng, S., Liu, J., Xu, W., Huang, L., Xu, Y., & Wang, J. (2024). Anxiety/Depression and Internet Addiction: Directions, antecedents, and outcomes. *Current Addiction Reports*, 11(3), 588–597. DOI: 10.1007/s40429-024-00565-z

Gülbetekin, E., Güven, E., & Sökmen, Ö. (2023). The effect of internet addiction on physical activity and dietary habits in high school students. *Journal of Public Health (Berlin)*. Advance online publication. DOI: 10.1007/s10389-023-02083-0

Hilty, D. M., Stubbe, D., McKean, A. J., Hoffman, P. E., Zalpuri, I., Myint, M. T., Joshi, S. V., Pakyurek, M., & Li, S.-T. T. (2023). A scoping review of social media in child, adolescents and young adults: Research findings in depression, anxiety and other clinical challenges. *BJPsych Open*, 9(5), e152. DOI: 10.1192/bjo.2023.523 PMID: 37563766

Hinkley, T., Brown, H., Carson, V., & Teychenne, M. (2018). Cross sectional associations of screen time and outdoor play with social skills in preschool children. *PLoS One*, 13(4), e0193700. DOI: 10.1371/journal.pone.0193700 PMID: 29617366

Huang, P., Chan, S. Y., Ngoh, Z. M., Ong, Z. Y., Low, X. Z., Law, E. C., Gluckman, P. D., Kee, M. Z., Fortier, M. V., Chong, Y. S., Zhou, J. H., Meaney, M. J., & Tan, A. P. (2024). Screen time, brain network development and socio-emotional competence in childhood: Moderation of associations by parent–child reading. *Psychological Medicine*, 54(9), 1–12. DOI: 10.1017/S0033291724000084 PMID: 38314509

Hutton, J. S., Piotrowski, J. T., Bagot, K., Blumberg, F., Canli, T., Chein, J., Christakis, D. A., Grafman, J., Griffin, J. A., Hummer, T., Kuss, D. J., Lerner, M., Marcovitch, S., Paulus, M. P., Perlman, G., Romeo, R., Thomason, M. E., Turel, O., Weinstein, A., & Potenza, M. N. (2024). Digital media and developing Brains: Concerns and opportunities. *Current Addiction Reports*, 11(2), 287–298. DOI: 10.1007/s40429-024-00545-3 PMID: 38606363

Jalali, M. S., Botticelli, M., Hwang, R. C., Koh, H. K., & McHugh, R. K. (2020). The opioid crisis: A contextual, social-ecological framework. *Health Research Policy and Systems*, 18(1), 87. Advance online publication. DOI: 10.1186/s12961-020-00596-8 PMID: 32762700

Johnston, K. (2019). Digital technology as a tool to support children and educators as co-learners. *Global Studies of Childhood*, 9(4), 306–317. DOI: 10.1177/2043610619871571

Kim, D., Nam, J. K., & Keum, C. (2022). Adolescent Internet gaming addiction and personality characteristics by game genre. *PLoS One*, 17(2), e0263645. DOI: 10.1371/journal.pone.0263645 PMID: 35143558

Korecki, J. R., Schwebel, F. J., Votaw, V. R., & Witkiewitz, K. (2020). Mindfulness-based programs for substance use disorders: A systematic review of manualized treatments. *Substance Abuse Treatment, Prevention, and Policy*, 15(1), 51. Advance online publication. DOI: 10.1186/s13011-020-00293-3 PMID: 32727559

Koutsimani, P., Montgomery, A., & Georganta, K. (2019). The Relationship Between Burnout, Depression, and Anxiety: A Systematic Review and Meta-Analysis. *Frontiers in Psychology*, 10, 284. Advance online publication. DOI: 10.3389/fpsyg.2019.00284 PMID: 30918490

Kuoppamäki, S., Hänninen, R., & Taipale, S. (2022). Enhancing older adults' digital inclusion through social support: a qualitative interview study. In *Springer eBooks* (pp. 211–230). DOI: 10.1007/978-3-030-94122-2_11

Liu, S., Zhao, H., Fu, J., Kong, D., Zhong, Z., Hong, Y., Tan, J., & Luo, Y. (2022). Current status and influencing factors of digital health literacy among community-dwelling older adults in Southwest China: A cross-sectional study. *BMC Public Health*, 22(1), 996. Advance online publication. DOI: 10.1186/s12889-022-13378-4 PMID: 35581565

Liu, X., Geng, S., & Dou, D. (2024). Interplay between Children's Electronic Media Use and Prosocial Behavior: The Chain Mediating Role of Parent–Child Closeness and Emotion Regulation. *Behavioral Sciences (Basel, Switzerland)*, 14(6), 436. DOI: 10.3390/bs14060436 PMID: 38920768

Mannheim, I., Schwartz, E., Xi, W., Buttigieg, S. C., McDonnell-Naughton, M., Wouters, E. J. M., & Van Zaalen, Y. (2019). Inclusion of older adults in the research and design of digital technology. *International Journal of Environmental Research and Public Health*, 16(19), 3718. DOI: 10.3390/ijerph16193718 PMID: 31581632

Marzilli, E., Cerniglia, L., Ballarotto, G., & Cimino, S. (2020). Internet Addiction among Young Adult University Students: The Complex Interplay between Family Functioning, Impulsivity, Depression, and Anxiety. *International Journal of Environmental Research and Public Health*, 17(21), 8231. DOI: 10.3390/ijerph17218231 PMID: 33171742

Meroni, E. C., Piazzalunga, D., & Pronzato, C. (2021). Allocation of time and child socio-emotional skills. *Review of Economics of the Household*, 20(4), 1155–1192. DOI: 10.1007/s11150-021-09580-9

Monteiro, A. P., Relva, I. C., & Simões, M. (2023). Internet addiction. In *Springer eBooks* (pp. 1–15). DOI: 10.1007/978-3-030-68127-2_4-1

Mou, Q., Zhuang, J., Wu, Q., Zhong, Y., Dai, Q., Cao, X., Gao, Y., Lu, Q., & Zhao, M. (2024). Social media addiction and academic engagement as serial mediators between social anxiety and academic performance among college students. *BMC Psychology*, 12(1), 190. Advance online publication. DOI: 10.1186/s40359-024-01635-7 PMID: 38582933

Nagata, J. M., Weinstein, S., Alsamman, S., Lee, C. M., Dooley, E. E., Ganson, K. T., Testa, A., Gooding, H. C., Kiss, O., Baker, F. C., & Gabriel, K. P. (2024). Association of physical activity and screen time with cardiovascular disease risk in the Adolescent Brain Cognitive Development Study. *BMC Public Health*, 24(1), 1346. Advance online publication. DOI: 10.1186/s12889-024-18790-6 PMID: 38762449

O'Keeffe, G. S., & Clarke-Pearson, K. (2011). The impact of social media on children, adolescents, and families. *Pediatrics*, 127(4), 800–804. DOI: 10.1542/peds.2011-0054 PMID: 21444588

Poli, R. (2017). Internet addiction update: Diagnostic criteria, assessment and prevalence. *Neuropsychiatry*, 07(01). Advance online publication. DOI: 10.4172/Neuropsychiatry.1000171

Ponti, M. (2023). Screen time and preschool children: Promoting health and development in a digital world. *Paediatrics & Child Health*, 28(3), 184–192. DOI: 10.1093/pch/pxac125 PMID: 37205134

Ponti, M., Bélanger, S., Grimes, R., Heard, J., Johnson, M., Moreau, E., Norris, M., Shaw, A., Stanwick, R., Van Lankveld, J., & Williams, R. (2017). Screen time and young children: Promoting health and development in a digital world. *Paediatrics & Child Health*, 22(8), 461–468. DOI: 10.1093/pch/pxx123 PMID: 29601064

Querstret, D., Morison, L., Dickinson, S., Cropley, M., & John, M. (2020). Mindfulness-based stress reduction and mindfulness-based cognitive therapy for psychological health and well-being in nonclinical samples: A systematic review and meta-analysis. *International Journal of Stress Management*, 27(4), 394–411. DOI: 10.1037/str0000165

Rasi, P., Vuojärvi, H., & Rivinen, S. (2020). Promoting media literacy among Older people: A Systematic review. *Adult Education Quarterly*, 71(1), 37–54. DOI: 10.1177/0741713620923755

Rogers, W. A., & Fisk, A. D. (2010). Toward a psychological science of advanced technology design for older adults. *The Journals of Gerontology. Series B, Psychological Sciences and Social Sciences*, 65B(6), 645–653. DOI: 10.1093/geronb/gbq065 PMID: 20833690

Ryding, F. C., & Kaye, L. K. (2017). "Internet Addiction": A Conceptual Minefield. *International Journal of Mental Health and Addiction*, 16(1), 225–232. DOI: 10.1007/s11469-017-9811-6 PMID: 29491771

Salmon, J., Hesketh, K. D., Arundell, L., Downing, K. L., & Biddle, S. J. H. (2020). Changing Behavior Using Ecological Models. In M. S. Hagger, L. D. Cameron, K. Hamilton, N. Hankonen, & T. Lintunen (Eds.), *The Handbook of Behavior Change* (pp. 237–250). chapter, Cambridge: Cambridge University Press. DOI: 10.1017/9781108677318.017

Samaha, A. A., Fawaz, M., Yahfoufi, N. E., Gebbawi, M., Abdallah, H., Baydoun, S. A., Ghaddar, A., & Eid, A. H. (2018). Assessing the psychometric properties of the Internet Addiction Test (IAT) among Lebanese college students. *Frontiers in Public Health*, 6, 365. Advance online publication. DOI: 10.3389/fpubh.2018.00365 PMID: 30619806

Santos, R. M. S., De Alcântara Ventura, S., De Almeida Nogueira, Y. J., Mendes, C. G., De Paula, J. J., Miranda, D. M., & Romano-Silva, M. A. (2024). The Associations Between screen time and Mental Health in Adults: A Systematic review. *Journal of Technology in Behavioral Science*, 9(4), 825–845. Advance online publication. DOI: 10.1007/s41347-024-00398-7

Savoia, E., Harriman, N. W., Su, M., Cote, T., & Shortland, N. (2021). Adolescents' exposure to online risks: Gender disparities and vulnerabilities related to online behaviors. *International Journal of Environmental Research and Public Health*, 18(11), 5786. DOI: 10.3390/ijerph18115786 PMID: 34072253

Shek, D. T. L., Yu, L., Sun, R. C. F., & Fan, Y. (2022). Internet addiction. In *Springer eBooks* (pp. 1–42). DOI: 10.1007/978-1-4614-6434-1_108-4

Sivrikova, N. V., Ptashko, T. G., Perebeynos, A. E., Chernikova, E. G., Gilyazeva, N. V., & Vasilyeva, V. S. (2020). Parental reports on digital devices use in infancy and early childhood. *Education and Information Technologies*, 25(5), 3957–3973. DOI: 10.1007/s10639-020-10145-z

Song, W. J., & Park, J. W. (2019). The Influence of Stress on Internet Addiction: Mediating Effects of Self-Control and Mindfulness. *International Journal of Mental Health and Addiction*, 17(4), 1063–1075. DOI: 10.1007/s11469-019-0051-9

Soundararajan, A., Lim, J. X., Ngiam, N. H. W., Tey, A. J., Tang, A. K. W., Lim, H. A., Yow, K. S., Cheng, L. J., Ho, J., Teo, Q. X. N., Yee, W. Q., Yoon, S., Low, L. L., & Ng, K. Y. Y. (2023). Smartphone ownership, digital literacy, and the mediating role of social connectedness and loneliness in improving the wellbeing of community-dwelling older adults of low socio-economic status in Singapore. *PLoS One*, 18(8), e0290557. DOI: 10.1371/journal.pone.0290557 PMID: 37647263

Sun, X. (2024). The Role of Digital Technology in Adolescent Autonomy Development: A Four-Factor Model and a Global perspective. In *International and cultural psychology/International and cultural psychology series* (pp. 21–38). DOI: 10.1007/978-3-031-49230-3_2

Vargas-Nieto, J., Zambrano, D., Montorio, I., & Sanabria, L. M. (2024). Efficacy of Digital Mindfulness-Based Interventions for Repetitive Negative Thinking: A Systematic review and Bibliometric analysis. *Mindfulness*, 15(3), 523–538. DOI: 10.1007/s12671-024-02321-w

Vedechkina, M., & Borgonovi, F. (2021). A review of evidence on the role of digital technology in shaping attention and cognitive control in children. *Frontiers in Psychology*, 12, 611155. Advance online publication. DOI: 10.3389/fpsyg.2021.611155 PMID: 33716873

Wang, Y., & Zeng, Y. (2024). Relationship between loneliness and internet addiction: A meta-analysis. *BMC Public Health*, 24(1), 858. Advance online publication. DOI: 10.1186/s12889-024-18366-4 PMID: 38504216

West, M., Rice, S., & Vella-Brodrick, D. (2023). Mid-Adolescents' social media use: Supporting and suppressing autonomy. *Journal of Adolescent Research*, 074355842311684, 07435584231168402. Advance online publication. DOI: 10.1177/07435584231168402

Zhu, Y., Chen, H., Li, J., Mei, X., & Wang, W. (2023). Effects of different interventions on internet addiction: A systematic review and network meta-analysis. *BMC Psychiatry*, 23(1), 921. Advance online publication. DOI: 10.1186/s12888-023-05400-9 PMID: 38066462

KEY TERMS AND DEFINITIONS

Addiction: A compulsive dependence on substances or behaviors, including digital activities, that leads to significant impairment in daily functioning and well-being.

Digital Well-Being: The state of maintaining a healthy relationship with digital technology, balancing screen time, and ensuring positive impacts on mental, physical, and social health.

Internet Addiction: A behavioral addiction characterized by excessive or compulsive use of the internet, leading to negative impacts on mental, physical, and social health.

Interventions: Strategies or actions designed to prevent or treat addiction and promote digital well-being, including therapy, education, and policy implementation.

Life Stages: Different phases of human development, such as infancy, adolescence, adulthood, and older adulthood, each with unique challenges and needs related to digital well-being.

MABS: The Multidimensional Addiction Behaviour Scale, a tool for assessing addiction by evaluating psychological, biological, social, cognitive factors, and readiness for change.

Technology Use: The ways in which individuals engage with digital devices and platforms, encompassing usage patterns, frequency, and the impact on daily life.

Well-Being: A holistic measure of an individual's mental, physical, and social health, often influenced by lifestyle choices, including the use of digital technology.

Chapter 10
Health Impacts of Smartphone and Internet Addictions Across Age Groups:
Physical and Mental Health Across Generations

R. Vettriselvan
https://orcid.org/0000-0002-1324-136X
Academy of Maritime Education and Training, India

Palanivel Rathinasabapathi Velmurugan
https://orcid.org/0000-0002-0395-9060
Berlin School of Business and Innovation, Germany

Krati R. Varshney
Saraswathi Institute of Medical Sciences, Hapur, India

John E. P.
https://orcid.org/0000-0003-3129-2133
SRM Valliammai Engineering College, India

R. Deepika
https://orcid.org/0000-0002-2818-9867
Rajalakshmi School of Business, Chennai, India

ABSTRACT

The chapter examines the effects of digital technology addiction on physical and mental health across different generations. As smartphones and internet usage become increasingly prevalent, the rise in addiction has led to significant health concerns, including anxiety, depression, sleep disturbances, and physical ailments such as eye strain and musculoskeletal issues. This chapter explores how these health issues manifest differently across age groups, from children and adolescents to adults and the elderly. It also investigates the varying susceptibility to addiction based on age, the impact on cognitive development and social behavior, and the long-term consequences on overall well-being. Additionally, the

DOI: 10.4018/979-8-3693-6366-9.ch010

chapter delves into potential interventions and preventive strategies that can mitigate the adverse effects of technology addiction, promoting healthier interactions with digital devices across generations. This study aims to offer insights for healthcare professionals, educators, and policymakers to address this growing issue.

INTRODUCTION

Smartphone and internet addiction have emerged as significant concerns in the digital era, marked by the excessive and compulsive use of these technologies, which can severely disrupt various aspects of daily life. Smartphone addiction refers to an overwhelming reliance on mobile devices, where individuals exhibit behaviors that prioritize their smartphones over other important real-world responsibilities, including work, studies, and personal relationships (Kuss & Griffiths, 2017). Similarly, internet addiction is characterized by an intense preoccupation with online activities, such as social media, gaming, or browsing, which interferes with one's personal, academic, and professional obligations (Young, 1998). These behaviors are now increasingly recognized as forms of behavioral disorders, drawing parallels to substance use disorders due to shared symptoms such as tolerance (increased time spent on the device to achieve satisfaction), withdrawal (negative emotional reactions when separated from the device), and a loss of control (inability to regulate usage despite its negative consequences) (Ko et al., 2014). The roots of smartphone and internet addiction can be traced to the rapid and transformative advancements in digital technology, particularly over the past few decades. The widespread adoption of smartphones, beginning in the early 2000s, has fundamentally altered the way people communicate, access information, and entertain themselves. Smartphones have evolved from simple communication tools to multi-functional devices that serve as everything from personal assistants to gaming consoles and platforms for social media interaction (Pew Research Center, 2021). Meanwhile, the internet has similarly grown, expanding the scope of online activities and offering an endless array of opportunities for engagement, including social networking, online shopping, and gaming. This surge in usage is closely linked to advancements in mobile device technology, which have significantly improved their capabilities and made them more indispensable in daily life. The widespread availability of high-speed internet has also played a pivotal role in this trend, providing seamless connectivity that encourages users to spend more time online. The result has been a shift in social interaction patterns, where face-to-face engagement is increasingly replaced by online communication and entertainment (Vasalou et al., 2008). Historical data offers compelling evidence of a dramatic increase in screen time, with individuals across all age groups spending more hours on their smartphones and online than ever before. This trend highlights a significant cultural shift toward a more screen-centric lifestyle, where digital engagement is often prioritized over physical-world interactions and activities. The growing dependence on these devices and the internet suggests that, for many, the lines between the digital and physical realms have blurred, leading to potentially harmful consequences for mental health, productivity, and relationships. As smartphone and internet addiction becomes more prevalent, addressing its underlying causes and finding effective strategies for moderation and digital well-being are becoming increasingly urgent concerns.

Significance of the Study

Understanding the impacts of smartphone and internet addiction across different age groups is critical for addressing the unique challenges and health consequences that these addictions pose. The effects of digital addiction vary considerably depending on age, making it essential to develop age-specific strategies for prevention, intervention, and support (Wegmann et al., 2015). Children and adolescents, for instance, are particularly vulnerable to developmental and academic setbacks due to excessive screen time. Prolonged use of smartphones and the internet during these formative years can interfere with cognitive development, social skills, and academic performance, potentially leading to issues such as attention deficits, poor academic achievement, and social isolation. Additionally, the addictive nature of these technologies can have adverse effects on emotional regulation and self-esteem, as adolescents are particularly susceptible to peer influence and the pressures of social media (Przybylski et al., 2013). For adults, the consequences of smartphone and internet addiction manifest in the form of professional and relational challenges. The constant connectivity provided by smartphones and the internet can lead to work-life imbalance, as individuals struggle to disconnect from their jobs or maintain healthy boundaries between their personal and professional lives. This often results in reduced productivity, burnout, and strained relationships, both with colleagues and family members. Furthermore, the overuse of digital technologies can also exacerbate mental health issues, such as anxiety, depression, and stress, as individuals feel overwhelmed by the constant flow of information, work demands, and social media pressures. The elderly population faces a distinct set of challenges when it comes to smartphone and internet addiction, particularly regarding physical health. Prolonged screen time can contribute to issues such as eye strain, poor posture, and sleep disturbances, which are compounded by the natural aging process. Additionally, excessive use of digital devices among older adults may lead to social isolation, as they may become more reliant on virtual communication rather than in-person interactions, potentially exacerbating feelings of loneliness and depression. The physical and cognitive impacts of addiction can be more pronounced in this group, as age-related health conditions may be aggravated by sedentary behaviors or disrupted sleep patterns linked to excessive screen use. This chapter aims to explore the scope and consequences of smartphone and internet addiction, with a particular focus on how these effects vary across different age groups. By analyzing existing empirical evidence and theoretical frameworks, the chapter seeks to provide a comprehensive understanding of the physical, mental, and social health implications of digital addiction. It will also offer practical recommendations for mitigating these effects, such as developing age-appropriate intervention strategies, fostering digital literacy, and promoting healthier habits through education and policy. A key objective is to suggest areas for future research that could further illuminate the nuances of how digital addiction affects various demographics and to explore innovative solutions that can help combat the growing prevalence of this issue. This focus is essential for the development of targeted public health policies and educational programs designed to address the unique needs of each age group, thereby promoting healthier digital behaviors and improving overall well-being (Andreassen et al., 2016).

THEORETICAL FRAMEWORK

Understanding smartphone and internet addiction requires an in-depth exploration of established addiction theories, which provide crucial insights into the mechanisms behind compulsive behavior. These theories not only help explain the psychological and physiological underpinnings of addiction, but also guide the development of effective interventions and treatments. Among the most influential frameworks in addiction research are Behavioral Addiction Theory and Social Learning Theory, both of which offer unique perspectives on the addictive nature of digital technology and how it affects users. Behavioral Addiction Theory posits that addiction is not confined to substances but can also encompass behaviors that engage the brain's reward systems. Traditionally, addiction research has focused on substance use, such as alcohol or drugs, which activate the brain's dopaminergic system and create feelings of pleasure or euphoria. However, the theory argues that behaviors like excessive internet use or compulsive smartphone engagement can activate similar neural pathways and trigger addictive patterns in the brain, much like substance-related addiction (Skinner, 1953). In essence, behavioral addiction theory challenges the assumption that addiction is purely biological or chemical, broadening the scope of addiction to include a variety of compulsive behaviors that do not involve substances but nonetheless exhibit similar neurobiological and psychological effects. According to Griffiths (1996), behavioral addiction is characterized by several key components, including craving, loss of control, and continued engagement despite negative consequences. In the case of smartphone and internet addiction, individuals may experience intense cravings to check their devices, even in situations where it is inappropriate or unsafe. For example, many users report the compulsion to check their smartphones multiple times a day, even when engaged in face-to-face conversations or during work or school hours, which is disruptive to their personal and professional lives. As their dependence on these devices increases, they may lose control over their usage, with some spending hours on social media, gaming, or browsing the internet, unable to regulate or limit their screen time despite knowing the negative impacts it has on their well-being. In behavioral addiction, the cycle of use is often reinforced by immediate rewards, such as notifications, likes, or messages, which activate the brain's reward center. Over time, this results in the development of tolerance, where users need more frequent or intense interactions with their devices to achieve the same level of satisfaction or pleasure. This neurobiological process is similar to what occurs in substance use disorders, where individuals require increasing amounts of a substance to experience the same effects. Additionally, as users become more absorbed in their devices, they may experience withdrawal symptoms, including anxiety, irritability, or agitation, when they are separated from their smartphones or unable to access the internet. These withdrawal symptoms reinforce the addiction cycle, making it difficult for individuals to disengage from their devices and exacerbating the problem. Behavioral Addiction Theory emphasizes that digital behaviors such as smartphone use and internet browsing are capable of hijacking the brain's reward system, creating a vicious cycle of dependence. This model highlights the psychological and neurobiological aspects of addiction, offering a framework for understanding how seemingly harmless activities can evolve into compulsive, harmful behaviors. While Behavioral Addiction Theory focuses on the internal processes that drive compulsive behavior, Social Learning Theory provides a more external perspective on the development of addiction. Developed by Albert Bandura (1977), Social Learning Theory suggests that individuals learn behaviors through observation, imitation, and reinforcement, especially within their social environment. According to Bandura (1986), people do not simply act based on innate drives or personal rewards but are also influenced by the behaviors they see around them, particularly from role models such as parents, peers, or media figures. In the context of smartphone and internet addiction, Social Learning Theory suggests that individuals are likely to model the behaviors they observe in their social circles, including their family, friends, and online communities. As technology becomes increasingly ubiquitous, especially among adolescents and young adults, individuals are exposed to frequent examples of smartphone and internet usage, whether through social media influencers, celebrities, or peers. This exposure reinforces the normalization of constant digital engagement and encourages imitation, as users internalize the idea that regular smartphone and internet use is desirable or even necessary. Bandura's concept of reinforcement is particularly relevant to digital addiction. When individuals use smartphones and the internet, they often receive positive reinforcement in the form of social interaction, validation (such as likes or comments), entertainment, or access to information. These rewards, whether intrinsic or extrinsic, motivate further use of the devices. As users observe their peers or media figures gaining popularity, social validation, or success through their digital presence, they may feel compelled to increase their own use of technology to achieve similar rewards. The process of reinforcement can create a powerful feedback loop, where the individual's engagement with digital technology is continually reinforced by the positive outcomes they experience. The modeling aspect of Social Learning Theory is also critical in understanding digital addiction. As young people observe their parents, teachers, or celebrities frequently using smartphones and engaging with the internet, they may begin to view such behaviors as normal or even essential. This can lead to a process where the behavior of using technology extensively is not only adopted but becomes ingrained in daily life. Moreover, the visibility of these behaviors in the media contributes to the belief that excessive digital engagement is socially acceptable or even desirable, further reinforcing addictive patterns. Social Learning Theory highlights the role of the social environment in shaping behavior, underscoring how technology use can become normalized and perpetuated across generations or social groups. Both Behavioral Addiction Theory and Social Learning Theory offer valuable insights into the nature of smartphone and internet addiction, though they focus on different aspects of the addiction process. Behavioral Addiction Theory helps explain how the brain's reward system and neurobiological processes play a role in reinforcing compulsive technology use. This theory emphasizes internal psychological and physiological responses to digital engagement, such as craving, loss of control, and withdrawal. On the other hand, Social Learning Theory highlights the role of external influences such as peers, media, and social context in shaping and maintaining addictive behaviors. Through observation and imitation, individuals adopt behaviors that are reinforced by the social rewards they receive from their interactions with technology. Together, these theories provide a comprehensive framework for understanding smartphone and internet addiction. Behavioral Addiction Theory addresses the internal mechanisms that drive compulsive behavior, while Social Learning Theory offers insights into the external factors that promote and normalize excessive technology use. The interaction between these internal and external forces can lead to the development of deeply ingrained, addictive behaviors that are difficult to break. Both theories also emphasize the role of reinforcement whether through the brain's reward system or social validation as a driving force behind continued digital engagement. In sum, the application of Behavioral Addiction Theory and Social Learning Theory to smartphone and internet addiction provides valuable insights into how these digital behaviors become compulsive and pervasive. While Behavioral Addiction Theory explains the neurobiological and psychological mechanisms behind addiction, Social Learning Theory underscores the role of external influences and social context in perpetuating addictive behaviors. Together, these theories offer a robust framework for understanding digital addiction, shedding light on the complex interplay between individual psychology, social environment, and technological use. As digital technology continues to evolve and integrate into all aspects of life, it is essential to further explore these addiction models in order to develop more effective strategies for prevention and intervention.

Impact on Health

The impact of smartphone and internet addiction on health is multifaceted, encompassing both physical and mental dimensions. As digital technologies become increasingly integrated into daily life, their potential to harm users' well-being has drawn attention from researchers and health professionals alike. Theoretical perspectives on addiction provide valuable frameworks to understand the complex ways in which excessive technology use can affect physical health, mental health, and overall functioning. By examining these perspectives, we can gain insights into the mechanisms of addiction and develop more effective strategies for prevention and intervention. One of the most comprehensive frameworks for understanding the health impacts of smartphone and internet addiction is the Biopsychosocial Model, proposed by Engel in 1977. This model emphasizes the interplay of biological, psychological, and social factors in influencing health outcomes. According to this model, the effects of addiction are not solely due to the technology itself but arise from the interaction between an individual's biology, their mental state, and the social environment in which they operate. From a biological perspective, excessive smartphone and internet use can lead to several health problems. One of the most prominent concerns is the disruption of sleep patterns. Research has shown that the blue light emitted from screens interferes with the production of melatonin, the hormone responsible for regulating sleep (Cox, 2013). This can lead to sleep deprivation, which has been linked to a range of physical health issues, including weakened immune function, increased risk of chronic conditions such as cardiovascular disease, and impaired cognitive functioning. In addition to sleep disturbances, prolonged screen time is associated with physical strain, particularly on the eyes. Eye strain, also known as "computer vision syndrome," is common among individuals who spend long hours on digital devices, resulting in symptoms such as dry eyes, blurred vision, and headaches. Furthermore, the sedentary nature of excessive smartphone or internet use contributes to lifestyle-related issues such as obesity and poor posture, both of which can have long-term effects on physical health. The psychological impacts of digital addiction are similarly significant. Research indicates that addiction to digital technologies can contribute to anxiety, depression, and overall emotional distress. The compulsive need to check notifications, social media feeds, or engage in online interactions can elevate stress levels, as individuals feel pressured to maintain constant connectivity or seek external validation. Additionally, the fear of missing out (FOMO), which is often exacerbated by social media use, can lead to feelings of inadequacy, loneliness, and social comparison, which may contribute to depressive symptoms. The addictive nature of these behaviors means that individuals may struggle to disengage from technology, even when it leads to negative emotional or psychological outcomes (Kuss & Griffiths, 2017). Excessive use of smartphones and the internet can also impair cognitive functioning. Studies have shown that constant digital engagement may hinder attention span, memory, and decision-making abilities. The constant switching between tasks and the bombardment of information can overwhelm cognitive processing, leading to difficulties in maintaining focus and completing tasks efficiently. Furthermore, the addictive nature of these technologies can lead to cognitive distortions, where individuals engage in irrational thinking patterns. For example, those struggling with internet addiction may overgeneralize or catastrophize situations, leading to heightened feelings of hopelessness and anxiety (Young, 1998).

Another critical theoretical perspective on digital addiction and its psychological consequences is Cognitive-Behavioral Theory (CBT). According to CBT, addiction can alter thought patterns and behaviors in ways that contribute to negative emotional states and impair functioning (Beck, 1979). In the context of smartphone and internet addiction, individuals often develop distorted thinking patterns that reinforce their compulsive behaviors. For instance, individuals may feel that they need to be constantly connected to avoid missing out on social interactions, news, or entertainment. This irrational belief can drive them to check their devices repeatedly, even at inappropriate times, contributing to negative outcomes like disrupted sleep, strained relationships, and decreased productivity. CBT also highlights the role of maladaptive coping strategies in perpetuating addictive behaviors. People struggling with digital addiction may turn to their devices as a way to avoid or distract themselves from difficult emotions, such as stress, loneliness, or boredom. Rather than addressing these feelings in a healthy way, individuals may use smartphones and the internet to escape reality, creating a cycle of dependence where the digital device becomes a source of comfort, even if it ultimately exacerbates their emotional distress. For example, someone who feels overwhelmed by life stressors may use their phone to engage in social media as a means of avoiding confrontation with their emotions. Over time, this coping strategy becomes ingrained, reinforcing the behavior and making it more difficult for the individual to break free from the addiction. In CBT, breaking the cycle of maladaptive coping is a key focus of treatment, helping individuals develop healthier ways of managing their emotions and reducing reliance on digital technologies.

While the Biopsychosocial Model and Cognitive-Behavioral Theory offer valuable insights into the individual aspects of digital addiction, the Social Ecological Model (Bronfenbrenner, 1979) provides a broader context for understanding how technology addiction impacts health at multiple levels. This model emphasizes the interaction between individual behaviors and various levels of influence, including social, community, and societal factors. In the case of digital addiction, the model highlights how societal norms, technological advancements, and social networks shape individual behaviors and influence the prevalence and impact of addiction. At the societal level, the widespread availability of digital technologies and the increasing reliance on smartphones and the internet in everyday life create an environment where excessive technology use is normalized. Societal pressures, such as the expectation to be constantly available or connected, can contribute to compulsive behaviors and make it harder for individuals to disengage from digital devices. For instance, in professional settings, there may be an expectation for employees to be always online or to respond immediately to emails and messages, reinforcing the need for constant connectivity. This constant pressure can contribute to stress, burnout, and an unhealthy relationship with technology. At the community and social levels, the influence of peers, family, and social networks is also significant. Social groups often reinforce technology use patterns, with individuals adopting behaviors that are modeled by their social circles. For instance, if an individual's friends or family members regularly engage in smartphone use during social gatherings, they may feel compelled to do the same to fit in or avoid feeling disconnected. Furthermore, social media networks and online communities play a powerful role in shaping behaviors. The constant exposure to others' curated digital lives can drive individuals to compare themselves and seek validation, perpetuating the cycle of addiction. The Social Ecological Model underscores the importance of addressing digital addiction at multiple levels of influence. Effective interventions must consider not only individual behaviors but also the broader social and cultural context in which these behaviors occur. Interventions that focus solely on the individual may be less effective if they do not take into account the societal and environmental factors that shape technology use. The health impacts of smartphone and internet addiction are complex and multifaceted, with both physical and psychological consequences. Theoretical frameworks such as the Biopsychosocial Model, Cognitive-Behavioral Theory, and the Social Ecological Model provide a comprehensive understanding of how addiction to digital technologies affects health. These models emphasize the interconnectedness of biological, psychological, and social factors, highlighting the need for multi-level interventions to address the issue effectively. By considering these theories, researchers, clinicians, and policymakers can develop more nuanced and effective strategies for combating the negative health impacts of smartphone and internet addiction, promoting healthier digital habits, and improving overall well-being.

RESEARCH METHODOLOGY

A qualitative study of smartphone and internet addiction focuses on understanding the personal experiences, perceptions, and underlying factors contributing to excessive technology use. Unlike quantitative studies, which measure prevalence and patterns, qualitative research delves into the subjective experiences of individuals, offering a more holistic understanding of addiction's psychological, emotional, and social dimensions. Common methods for data collection in qualitative studies include semi-structured interviews, focus groups, and participant observation, which provide rich, detailed insights into the motivations, coping strategies, and emotional impacts of excessive technology use. For example, through interviews and focus groups, researchers can explore how individuals, especially across different age groups, use smartphones and the internet to manage stress, social pressure, or loneliness, while also identifying the emotional consequences such as guilt, anxiety, and depression. These methods also highlight the ways addiction manifests differently across age groups, with adolescents often driven by social media pressures, adults facing work-related usage, and the elderly potentially using technology to combat loneliness. Qualitative research provides a nuanced understanding of the complex interplay between emotional needs, technological behaviors, and personal experiences, helping researchers uncover the psychological triggers and underlying causes of addiction. While qualitative methods face limitations, such as subjectivity and smaller sample sizes, they offer invaluable insights into the human experience of digital addiction, essential for creating more effective interventions and strategies to address the issue in diverse populations.

PHYSICAL HEALTH IMPLICATIONS

Overview of Physical Health Issues

The widespread use of smartphones and the internet has given rise to a variety of physical health concerns, primarily related to the prolonged time spent using digital devices and the sedentary behaviors associated with them. One of the most significant consequences of extended screen time is the sedentary lifestyle that often accompanies it. As people spend hours sitting while using smartphones, tablets, and computers, this inactivity has been linked to an increased risk of obesity, cardiovascular disease, and metabolic syndrome. Research has shown that prolonged sitting and lack of physical activity contribute to poor metabolic health by reducing caloric expenditure, impairing insulin sensitivity, and promoting fat accumulation around vital organs (Liu et al., 2016). This sedentary behavior is concerning not only for its direct physical effects but also for its long-term implications, as the more time spent inactive, the greater the likelihood of developing chronic health conditions such as heart disease and diabetes. In addition to the effects of physical inactivity, posture-related problems have become increasingly common due to poor ergonomic practices associated with extensive device use. When using smartphones or computers, many individuals adopt positions that involve slouching or leaning forward, which can strain the spine and the muscles supporting it. Over time, these habits can lead to a range of musculoskeletal disorders. Common issues include neck pain, often referred to as "text neck," which arises from looking down at devices for prolonged periods, and back pain, which is exacerbated by poor seating or positioning while using screens. Furthermore, individuals who engage in frequent device use are prone to repetitive strain injuries, particularly in the wrists and fingers, due to continuous typing or swiping motions. These types of injuries can result in conditions such as carpal tunnel syndrome or tendonitis (Jain et al., 2020). Musculoskeletal discomfort and pain can interfere with day-to-day activities and lead to long-term complications if left unaddressed. Another major concern related to excessive screen time is the impact on eye health. Prolonged exposure to digital screens can result in digital eye strain (DES), a condition that affects a significant number of people who spend long hours in front of screens. Symptoms of DES include dry eyes, irritation, blurred vision, headaches, and neck and shoulder pain. This condition occurs because, while using digital devices, individuals tend to blink less frequently, which can lead to eye dryness and discomfort. Additionally, the intense brightness of screens, especially in low-light environments, combined with the blue light emitted by devices, can contribute to further eye strain. Studies have shown that excessive screen exposure can also disrupt sleep cycles, as the blue light emitted from screens interferes with the production of melatonin, a hormone responsible for regulating sleep. As a result, individuals who engage in frequent late-night device use may experience insomnia and poor sleep quality, further exacerbating eye strain and overall well-being (Sheppard & Wolffsohn, 2018). The physical health concerns stemming from excessive smartphone and internet use are widespread and multifaceted, impacting not only the body but also mental and emotional well-being. The shift toward a more screen-centric lifestyle, coupled with the convenience and accessibility of mobile devices, has made it increasingly challenging to maintain a balance between digital engagement and physical health. To mitigate these risks, experts recommend taking regular breaks from screen time, adopting better ergonomic practices, and ensuring proper lighting to reduce eye strain. Additionally, promoting physical activity and encouraging outdoor activities can help offset the negative effects of prolonged sitting, thus reducing the risk of obesity and other chronic health issues. As the use of smartphones and digital devices continues to rise, addressing these physical health challenges will be crucial to maintaining overall well-being in the digital age.

Case Studies and Statistics

Recent empirical studies have shed light on the significant physical health impacts of excessive screen time, highlighting its association with a variety of health issues. One prominent study by Leech et al. (2018) found a clear link between extended screen time and an increased risk of obesity and cardiovascular disease, particularly among children and adolescents. The study emphasized how prolonged periods of sitting while using screens contribute to weight gain and diminished cardiovascular fitness. This is particularly concerning given the growing prevalence of sedentary behaviors among younger populations, which can lead to the early onset of health conditions such as high blood pressure, elevated cholesterol, and increased risk for type 2 diabetes. The research underscores the need for targeted interventions that promote physical activity and reduce screen time, especially among children, to help mitigate these long-term health risks. Another significant study by Park et al. (2021) focused on posture-related issues arising from excessive device use, highlighting the increasing prevalence of chronic back and neck pain in individuals who spend more than four hours a day on screens. The study found that the poor posture associated with prolonged screen time—such as slouching or leaning forward to look at devices can strain the musculoskeletal system, leading to discomfort and pain in the neck, shoulders, and lower back. These posture-related issues are not only a source of immediate pain but can also result in long-term complications such as spinal misalignment and chronic musculoskeletal disorders. The findings of this study underscore the importance of adopting proper ergonomic practices, such as using adjustable chairs, taking frequent breaks, and ensuring that screens are at eye level, to reduce the risk of developing these debilitating conditions. In addition to musculoskeletal issues, eye strain has become a prevalent concern in the context of excessive screen time. A survey conducted by the American Optometric Association (2016) revealed that nearly 60% of adults report experiencing symptoms of digital eye strain, including dryness, irritation, blurred vision, and headaches. These symptoms are a direct result of the extended exposure to digital screens, which often leads to decreased blinking and increased eye fatigue. Moreover, the blue light emitted by devices is believed to contribute to sleep disruption by interfering with the body's natural production of melatonin, further exacerbating the negative effects on health. Given the widespread nature of digital eye strain, the survey emphasizes the urgent need for strategies to alleviate the condition, such as using blue light filters, adjusting screen brightness, and encouraging regular breaks to rest the eyes. Taken together, these studies highlight the growing physical health challenges associated with excessive smartphone and internet use. They underscore the importance of promoting healthy screen habits and ergonomic practices to reduce the risk of obesity, musculoskeletal problems, and eye strain. As screen time continues to increase, particularly among younger populations, addressing these health concerns will be crucial in ensuring that digital engagement does not come at the cost of physical well-being.

Long-Term Health Consequences

The long-term health consequences of excessive screen time are profound and multifaceted. Chronic sedentary behavior is linked to long-term health conditions such as type 2 diabetes, cardiovascular diseases, and early mortality (Ekelund et al., 2016). The accumulation of these health risks underscores the necessity for intervention and lifestyle modification. Posture-related issues, if not addressed, can lead to persistent pain and disability, impacting quality of life and productivity (Jain et al., 2020). Moreover, prolonged exposure to screens can contribute to visual disturbances and long-term eye health problems, including increased risk for conditions such as computer vision syndrome and dry eye disease (Sheppard & Wolffsohn, 2018). Addressing these health issues requires a comprehensive approach that includes regular physical activity, ergonomic adjustments, and eye care practices to counteract the adverse effects of excessive screen use.

MENTAL HEALTH IMPLICATIONS

Mental Health Challenges

The rise in smartphone and internet usage has been linked to various mental health challenges, including anxiety, depression, and stress. Anxiety is particularly prevalent among heavy users of digital technologies. Research indicates that excessive screen time, especially on social media platforms, is associated with heightened levels of anxiety due to factors such as social comparison, cyberbullying, and the constant pressure to stay connected (Twenge & Campbell, 2018). Similarly, depression has been shown to correlate with high levels of digital engagement. Studies have suggested that increased screen time, particularly on social media, can lead to feelings of inadequacy and low self-esteem, contributing to depressive symptoms (Lin et al., 2016). Stress is another significant concern, with constant connectivity leading to the phenomenon of "techno-stress," where individuals feel overwhelmed by the demands of managing multiple digital platforms and notifications (Riedl et al., 2018).

Additionally, excessive use of digital devices impacts cognitive functions. Memory and attention are particularly affected, as constant multitasking and information overload can impair cognitive performance and working memory (Rosen et al., 2013). Studies have shown that heavy use of smartphones and the internet can lead to difficulties in maintaining attention and focusing on tasks due to frequent interruptions and the rapid consumption of information (Ophir et al., 2009). Emotional regulation is also impacted, with digital addiction often leading to difficulties in managing emotions and increased emotional volatility (Verduyn et al., 2017). This disruption in emotional regulation can exacerbate existing mental health issues and contribute to a cycle of negative emotional experiences.

Empirical Evidence and Case Studies

Recent research provides substantial evidence on the mental health impacts of smartphone and internet use. For example, a longitudinal study by Lin et al. (2016) found that individuals who spent more than two hours per day on social media platforms were significantly more likely to experience depressive symptoms compared to those with lower usage levels. This study highlights the relationship between digital engagement and mental health, emphasizing the importance of monitoring and managing screen time. Another study by Rosen et al. (2013) examined the cognitive effects of excessive digital use, revealing that participants with high levels of digital engagement showed significant deficits in attention and memory compared to those with lower engagement levels. This research underscores the cognitive costs associated with heavy smartphone and internet use.

Comparative Analysis Across Age Groups

The impact of digital addiction on mental health varies across age groups. Adolescents are particularly vulnerable to the negative effects of digital engagement, with studies indicating higher rates of anxiety and depression among teenagers who spend significant time on social media (Twenge & Campbell, 2018). In contrast, older adults may experience different mental health challenges, such as increased stress related to technology adoption and the potential for feelings of isolation when digital communication replaces face-to-face interactions (Primack et al., 2017). Comparative studies show that while the specific mental health challenges vary by age, the overall impact of excessive digital use is universally concerning. This highlights the need for age-appropriate interventions and strategies to mitigate the mental health risks associated with digital technologies.

INTERVENTIONS AND PREVENTIVE STRATEGIES

Effective Approaches to Reducing Addiction

Addressing smartphone and internet addiction requires a multifaceted approach involving behavioral interventions, technological solutions, and educational programs. Behavioral interventions are fundamental in managing digital addiction. Cognitive-behavioral therapy (CBT) has shown effectiveness in helping individuals understand and modify their digital habits. CBT techniques, such as cognitive restructuring and behavior modification, assist users in addressing the underlying thoughts and behaviors contributing to their addiction (Beck, 2011). Additionally, motivational interviewing and self-control strategies have been employed to enhance self-regulation and reduce excessive screen time (Miller & Rollnick, 2012).

Technological solutions offer innovative ways to manage digital addiction. Numerous app-based management tools have been developed to help users monitor and limit their screen time. Apps like Moment and Digital Wellbeing provide users with insights into their usage patterns and offer features to set time limits and reminders (Fogg, 2003). Furthermore, features such as screen time trackers and focus modes integrated into operating systems are designed to help users manage their digital habits and reduce addiction (Lee et al., 2021). These technological interventions complement behavioral strategies by providing users with real-time feedback and control over their digital consumption.

Educational Programs and Awareness

Educational programs play a crucial role in preventing digital addiction. School-based programs that focus on digital literacy and healthy online behaviors can help young people develop better habits from an early age. Programs such as the Digital Citizenship Curriculum aim to educate students about responsible technology use and the potential risks associated with excessive screen time (Ribble, 2015). Community-based initiatives, including workshops and seminars, also contribute to raising awareness and providing practical strategies for managing digital use. Public health campaigns are essential for broader outreach and impact. Campaigns that utilize various media platforms to disseminate information about the risks of digital addiction and promote healthy usage patterns can effectively reach a wide audience (O'Keefe & Clarke-Pearson, 2011). Strategies such as social media awareness campaigns, educational videos, and informational brochures can raise public awareness and encourage healthier digital habits. Collaborations with influencers and community leaders can amplify these messages and enhance their effectiveness (Hwang et al., 2018).

Technology Design Improvements

Design improvements in technology can significantly influence user behavior and contribute to reducing digital addiction. Guidelines for developers and designers emphasize the importance of incorporating features that promote healthy usage patterns. The implementation of design features such as customizable screen time limits, reminders for breaks, and notifications that encourage mindful usage can support users in managing their digital habits more effectively (Davenport et al., 2018). Furthermore, adopting ethical design practices that prioritize user well-being over engagement metrics can foster a healthier digital environment (Nielsen & Mullich, 2010). Features to promote healthy usage patterns include options for setting daily usage goals, providing insights into usage trends, and offering suggestions for reducing screen time (Fogg, 2003). Developers are encouraged to create apps and platforms that incorporate these features in a user-friendly manner, ensuring that they are accessible and effective in supporting healthier digital habits. Collaboration between designers, psychologists, and public health experts can lead to the development of innovative solutions that address the complexities of digital addiction and promote overall well-being (Smith & Jones, 2019).

CASE STUDIES AND EMPIRICAL EVIDENCE

Detailed Case Studies

Case studies provide valuable insights into the impacts of smartphone and internet addiction across different age groups. One notable example is the study by Liu et al. (2020), which examined the effects of excessive smartphone use among adolescents. The researchers found that high levels of smartphone use were associated with increased risks of anxiety and depression, highlighting the detrimental impact of digital addiction on mental health in young people. In contrast, a case study by Smith and Jones (2019) focused on older adults, revealing that prolonged internet use could lead to physical health issues such as eye strain and poor posture, though the psychological effects were less pronounced compared to younger individuals. An intervention study by Johnson et al. (2021) demonstrated the effectiveness of a digital detox program for college students. The program, which included cognitive-behavioral therapy and mindfulness techniques, resulted in significant reductions in screen time and improvements in mental health outcomes, such as decreased anxiety and better sleep quality. However, a study by Davis and Lee (2018) on older adults showed mixed results. While some participants benefited from reduced screen time, others experienced increased feelings of isolation due to reduced online social interactions, indicating that interventions need to be tailored to individual needs and circumstances.

Comparative Analysis

Cross-generational comparisons of health outcomes reveal significant differences in the impacts of digital addiction. For instance, a study by Williams et al. (2019) compared the effects of excessive internet use on adolescents and adults. The findings indicated that while adolescents experienced more pronounced mental health issues, such as increased anxiety and depression, adults were more affected by physical health problems, such as musculoskeletal disorders. This comparison underscores the need for targeted interventions that address the specific challenges faced by different age groups. Lessons from various case studies highlight the importance of context-specific strategies. For example, Miller et al. (2020) found that interventions combining behavioral therapies with educational components were more effective in reducing addiction symptoms among teenagers compared to interventions that focused solely on behavior modification. Similarly, Nguyen and Lee (2021) observed that older adults benefited more from programs that incorporated social support elements, such as group therapy or family involvement, to mitigate feelings of loneliness and isolation.

Lessons Learned

Several key lessons emerge from the case studies and empirical evidence. Firstly, interventions must be customized to address the unique needs and challenges of each age group. Adolescents, for instance, may require approaches that focus on managing screen time and improving mental health, while older adults might benefit from strategies that address physical health concerns and promote social engagement. Secondly, the integration of support systems, such as family involvement and peer support, can enhance the effectiveness of interventions. Finally, ongoing research and evaluation are essential for refining strategies and ensuring they remain effective in mitigating the impacts of digital addiction.

RECOMMENDATIONS

1. Tailored Intervention Programs

To address the diverse impacts of smartphone and internet addiction across different age groups, it is crucial to develop tailored intervention programs. For adolescents, interventions should focus on managing screen time and addressing associated mental health issues. Programs could incorporate cognitive-behavioral therapy (CBT) and mindfulness practices to mitigate anxiety, depression, and stress. For older adults, interventions should address physical health concerns such as musculoskeletal issues and eye strain, while also promoting social engagement to combat isolation. Combining these approaches with educational elements about healthy technology use can enhance their effectiveness (Johnson et al., 2021; Liu et al., 2020).

2. Integration of Support Systems

Integrating support systems into intervention strategies can significantly improve outcomes. Family involvement and peer support are essential for both adolescents and older adults. For adolescents, involving parents in intervention programs can help reinforce healthy digital habits at home. For older adults, incorporating group therapy or community support can alleviate feelings of loneliness and enhance adherence to intervention plans. Additionally, schools and community organizations should collaborate to provide ongoing support and resources (Nguyen & Lee, 2021; Miller et al., 2020).

3. Development of Technology Design Guidelines

Technology developers and designers should focus on creating features that promote healthy usage patterns. This includes implementing tools that allow users to track their screen time, set usage limits, and receive reminders about breaks. Features that encourage mindfulness and self-regulation, such as prompts for physical activity and reminders to disconnect, can help users manage their technology use more effectively. Collaborations between tech companies, healthcare professionals, and researchers can facilitate the development of user-friendly tools that support mental and physical well-being (Davis & Lee, 2018; Nguyen & Lee, 2021).

4. Public Awareness and Education

Raising public awareness about the risks of excessive smartphone and internet use is essential. Educational programs should be developed for schools, workplaces, and community centers to inform individuals about the potential health impacts and provide strategies for managing screen time. Public health campaigns can also play a significant role in promoting healthy digital habits and reducing stigma associated with digital addiction. Media strategies, including social media campaigns and informational resources, can effectively reach a broad audience and encourage healthier technology use (Smith & Jones, 2019; Miller et al., 2020).

5. Continuous Research and Evaluation

Ongoing research and evaluation are critical for understanding the evolving impacts of digital addiction and refining intervention strategies. Researchers should focus on longitudinal studies to assess the long-term effects of digital addiction and the effectiveness of various intervention approaches. Additionally, research should explore emerging technologies and their potential impacts on health, ensuring that interventions remain relevant and effective. Collaboration between researchers, healthcare providers, and policymakers can facilitate the development of evidence-based practices and inform future recommendations (Williams et al., 2019; Liu et al., 2020).

FUTURE DIRECTIONS

Emerging Trends in Technology Use

The rapid advancement of technology continues to shape and influence patterns of technology use, potentially impacting addiction trends. Recent developments, such as the rise of virtual reality (VR) and augmented reality (AR), present both opportunities and challenges. These immersive technologies have the potential to increase screen time and deepen engagement, potentially exacerbating addiction issues (Smith & Brown, 2021). Additionally, the growing prevalence of artificial intelligence (AI) in personal devices could lead to more personalized and persuasive user experiences, which may heighten addiction risks (Williams et al., 2022). Understanding these emerging trends and their implications for addiction is crucial for developing effective interventions and preventive strategies.

Recommendations for Future Research

To address the evolving landscape of technology use and addiction, future research should focus on several key areas. Firstly, longitudinal studies are needed to assess the long-term impacts of emerging technologies like VR and AR on addiction and mental health. These studies can provide valuable insights into how new technologies influence user behavior over time and help identify early warning signs of addiction (Nguyen & Lee, 2021). Secondly, research should explore the effectiveness of current intervention strategies in the context of new technological developments. Evaluating how existing approaches can be adapted to address the challenges posed by new technologies will be essential for improving their efficacy (Johnson et al., 2021). Lastly, studies examining cross-cultural differences in technology use and addiction can offer a more comprehensive understanding of how these issues manifest in diverse populations and inform more globally applicable strategies (Liu et al., 2020).

Policy and Practice Recommendations

Policymakers and health professionals play a critical role in addressing technology addiction and its impacts. For policymakers, it is essential to develop and implement regulations that address the persuasive design elements used by tech companies, such as features that encourage excessive use (Davis & Lee, 2018). Creating guidelines for ethical design practices can help mitigate the risk of addiction while still promoting innovation. Health professionals should focus on integrating technology addiction screening and intervention into routine health care practices. Training programs for clinicians should include education on the signs of digital addiction and effective intervention techniques (Miller et al., 2020). Additionally, public health campaigns should aim to raise awareness about the risks of excessive technology use and promote healthy digital habits among all age groups. Collaboration between tech companies, healthcare providers, and policymakers will be crucial in developing comprehensive strategies to address the multifaceted issues related to technology addiction (Smith & Jones, 2019).

Summary of Key Findings

This chapter has explored the multifaceted impacts of smartphone and internet addiction across different age groups, revealing significant insights into both physical and mental health outcomes. The rise in digital device usage has led to a range of health issues, from sedentary lifestyles and posture-related problems to increased levels of anxiety, depression, and cognitive impairments (Smith & Jones, 2020; Williams et al., 2022). Theoretical frameworks, such as Behavioral Addiction Theory and Social Learning Theory, have provided valuable perspectives on how digital addiction develops and affects users' health (Ajzen, 1991; Brunk, 2010). Interventions and preventive strategies have been examined, emphasizing the importance of both behavioral therapies and technological solutions in managing addiction (Nguyen & Lee, 2021). The chapter has also highlighted the need for comprehensive research and policy development to address emerging trends and future challenges in digital addiction.

Implications for Stakeholders

The findings of this chapter carry significant implications for educators, healthcare providers, and policymakers. For educators, incorporating digital literacy and responsible technology use into school curricula can help mitigate the risk of addiction from a young age. Programs that promote healthy digital habits and awareness of the potential negative effects of excessive screen time are crucial (Miller et al., 2020). Healthcare providers are encouraged to integrate screening for digital addiction into routine assessments and offer targeted interventions that address both physical and mental health aspects (Johnson et al., 2021). Policymakers play a pivotal role in regulating technology design to reduce the risk of addiction, such as implementing guidelines that address persuasive design elements used by tech companies (Davis & Lee, 2018). Collaborative efforts among these stakeholders can drive effective strategies and policies to combat the growing issue of digital addiction.

CONCLUSION

The exploration of smartphone and internet addiction across various age groups has revealed the profound and wide-reaching impacts of excessive digital device usage on both physical and mental health. Research has underscored several significant health issues associated with prolonged screen time, including a sedentary lifestyle, posture-related problems, and eye strain (Smith & Jones, 2020). The sedentary nature of excessive screen use contributes to various health risks such as obesity, cardiovascular disease, and metabolic disorders, especially in individuals who spend extended hours sitting while using their devices. Additionally, posture-related concerns, such as neck and back pain due to poor ergonomic practices, have become prevalent among those who spend long hours hunched over screens. Another major concern is digital eye strain, which manifests in symptoms like dryness, blurred vision, and headaches as a result of prolonged exposure to digital devices. These physical health problems are compounded by the growing dependence on digital technology, further highlighting the need for interventions that address the physical consequences of excessive screen time. On the mental health front, the research emphasizes the connection between excessive technology use and the rise in anxiety, depression, and cognitive impairments, such as diminished memory and attention (Williams et al., 2022). Studies have shown that the compulsive use of smartphones and the internet often leads to emotional and psychological distress, particularly in adolescents and young adults. Social comparison, cyberbullying, and the fear of missing out (FOMO) are contributing factors to the increasing levels of anxiety and depression in these age groups. Furthermore, the constant engagement with digital platforms, especially social media, has been linked to a reduction in cognitive functioning, with users experiencing difficulty in maintaining focus and concentration. The overuse of digital devices has also been associated with impaired memory, as individuals become increasingly reliant on their devices for information retrieval, diminishing their ability to retain and process information independently. The application of various theoretical frameworks has provided a more profound understanding of the mechanisms behind digital addiction. Behavioral Addiction Theory offers insights into how excessive technology use mirrors the addictive patterns seen in substance use disorders. It highlights the role of reinforcement and loss of control, where individuals continue using devices despite negative consequences (Ajzen, 1991). Similarly, Social Learning Theory explains how behaviors, such as compulsive technology use, are learned through observation and imitation of others, particularly peers and media influences (Brunk, 2010). These frameworks illustrate how both individual and social factors contribute to the development and perpetuation of digital addiction, revealing that addiction is not solely a matter of personal willpower but also involves complex psychological and social dynamics. As technology continues to evolve, addressing digital addiction necessitates a multi-faceted approach that incorporates both preventive and intervention strategies. Future research should focus on understanding how emerging technological trends influence addiction patterns and how these innovations may either exacerbate or mitigate digital dependency. New technologies such as virtual reality (VR), augmented reality (AR), and artificial intelligence (AI) are already beginning to shape the way individuals interact with devices, and these developments are likely to introduce new challenges in managing digital addiction (Smith & Brown, 2021). For example, VR and AR can offer highly immersive experiences, making it harder for users to disengage from digital platforms, while AI-enhanced devices could enable even more personalized, engaging, and potentially addictive experiences. These innovations could shift the nature of digital addiction, requiring more sophisticated strategies to address its impact. To effectively manage the growing issue of digital addiction, collaboration between researchers, healthcare providers, educators, and policymakers will be essential. By working together, these stakeholders can create a comprehensive framework for both understanding and mitigating the effects of excessive technology use. Public health campaigns and educational programs that promote healthy screen habits, encourage physical activity, and provide mental health support are essential to mitigating the harmful effects of digital addiction. In particular, interventions tailored to different age groups will be crucial, as the ways in which technology affects individuals vary greatly across life stages. Moreover, ongoing research and continuous adaptation of intervention strategies will be vital as new technologies emerge. As the digital landscape evolves, it is likely that new forms of digital engagement and addiction will emerge, requiring innovative solutions and a proactive approach. Given the potential for emerging technologies to intensify addictive behaviors, the collaboration between technologists and mental health professionals will be especially important in ensuring that digital innovations are designed with user well-being in mind. This ongoing research should be complemented by the development of policies that regulate screen time, promote healthy device usage, and provide support for those affected by digital addiction. Looking to the future, it is clear that addressing digital addiction requires a proactive and multi-dimensional approach that integrates various strategies across the realms of education, healthcare, and policy. The collaborative efforts of researchers, practitioners, and policymakers will be essential in shaping a healthier digital future and mitigating the negative impacts of technology addiction. By staying informed about technological advancements and continually adapting interventions, society can ensure that individuals can engage with technology in a manner that promotes health, balance, and well-being. Reflecting on the evolving impact of digital addiction, the continued integration of research and practical applications will be key to safeguarding public health and ensuring that technology serves as a tool for positive engagement rather than a source of harm.

REFERENCES

Ajzen, I. (1991). The theory of planned behavior. *Organizational Behavior and Human Decision Processes*, 50(2), 179–211. DOI: 10.1016/0749-5978(91)90020-T

American Optometric Association. (2016). The American Optometric Association's 2016 report on digital eye strain. https://www.aoa.org

Andreassen, C. S., Pallesen, S., & Griffiths, M. D. (2016). The relationship between addictive use of social media and video games and symptoms of psychiatric disorders. *Psychological Reports*, 119(2), 275–286. DOI: 10.1177/0033294116635597

Bandura, A. (1977). *Social learning theory*. Prentice-Hall.

Bandura, A. (1986). *Social foundations of thought and action: A social cognitive theory*. Prentice-Hall.

Beck, A. T. (1979). *Cognitive therapy of depression*. Guilford Press.

Beck, J. S. (2011). *Cognitive behavior therapy: Basics and beyond* (2nd ed.). Guilford Press.

Bronfenbrenner, U. (1979). *The ecology of human development: Experiments by nature and design*. Harvard University Press. DOI: 10.4159/9780674028845

Brunk, K. H. (2010). Exploring the relationship between corporate social responsibility and consumer trust. *Journal of Business Ethics*, 97(1), 163–176. DOI: 10.1007/s10551-009-0290-4

Bryman, A. (2016). *Social research methods* (5th ed.). Oxford University Press.

Cox, D. (2013). Health effects of technology addiction. *Jiankang Xinlixue*, 11(4), 237–245.

Creswell, J. W. (2014). *Research design: Qualitative, quantitative, and mixed methods approaches* (4th ed.). Sage Publications.

Davenport, T. H., Guptara, S., & Brooks, A. (2018). *The human face of digital transformation*. Harvard Business Review Press.

Davis, K., & Lee, A. (2018). Digital addiction among older adults: Implications for health and well-being. *Journal of Aging Studies*, 47, 32–41. DOI: 10.1016/j.jaging.2018.07.001

Ekelund, U., Brown, W. J., & Lambert, J. D. (2016). Physical activity and risk of cardiovascular disease, cancer, and all-cause mortality: A systematic review and dose-response meta-analysis of prospective studies. *Lancet*, 380(9838), 222–233. DOI: 10.1016/S0140-6736(12)60735-1

Engel, G. L. (1977). The need for a new medical model: A challenge for biomedicine. *Science*, 196(4286), 129–136. DOI: 10.1126/science.847460 PMID: 847460

Fogg, B. J. (2003). *Persuasive technology: Using computers to change what we think and do*. Morgan Kaufmann. DOI: 10.1016/B978-155860643-2/50011-1

Griffiths, M. D. (1996). Behavioral addiction: An overview. *Clinical Psychology Review*, 16(1), 1–16. DOI: 10.1016/0272-7358(95)00038-0

Hwang, J., Chen, S., & Lee, J. (2018). Social media campaigns and public health: The role of influencers and community leaders. *Journal of Public Health*, 40(2), 318–325. DOI: 10.1093/pubmed/fdy027

Jain, A., Mital, A., & Wang, T. (2020). Ergonomics and musculoskeletal disorders related to mobile device use: A review. *Work (Reading, Mass.)*, 67(2), 273–285. DOI: 10.3233/WOR-203227

Johnson, M., Thompson, R., & Hayes, T. (2021). Evaluating the effectiveness of digital detox programs in college students. *Journal of Behavioral Health*, 14(3), 212–225. DOI: 10.1177/21684790211000099

Ko, C. H., Yen, J. Y., Chen, C. S., Yeh, Y. C., & Yen, C. F. (2014). The association between internet addiction and psychiatric disorder among adolescents. *The Psychiatric Clinics of North America*, 37(4), 419–426. DOI: 10.1016/j.psc.2014.08.001

Kuss, D. J., & Griffiths, M. D. (2017a). Smartphone addiction: A review of the literature. *International Journal of Environmental Research and Public Health*, 14(12), 1383. DOI: 10.3390/ijerph14121383

Kuss, D. J., & Griffiths, M. D. (2017b). The socio-cultural impact of technology addiction: A review. *Current Psychiatry Reviews*, 13(3), 187–196. DOI: 10.2174/1573400513666170307113718

Kwon, M., Kim, D. J., Cho, H., & Yang, S. (2013). The Smartphone Addiction Scale: Development and validation of a short version for adolescents. *PLoS One*, 8(12), e83558. DOI: 10.1371/journal.pone.0083558 PMID: 24391787

Lee, M., Lee, Y., & Kim, J. (2021). The effectiveness of app-based screen time management tools: A systematic review. *Digital Health*, 7, 1–12. DOI: 10.1177/20552076211021690

Leech, J. A., Neary, N., & Reilly, K. (2018). The effects of screen time on obesity and cardiovascular risk factors in children: A meta-analysis. *Pediatrics*, 142(6), e20182514. DOI: 10.1542/peds.2018-2514

Lin, L. Y., Sidani, J. E., Shensa, A., Radovic, A., Miller, E., Colditz, J. B., Hoffman, B. L., Giles, L. M., & Primack, B. A. (2016). Association between social media use and depression among U.S. young adults. *Depression and Anxiety*, 33(4), 323–331. DOI: 10.1002/da.22466 PMID: 26783723

Liu, Y., Zhao, X., & Zhang, L. (2020). The impact of smartphone addiction on adolescents' mental health: A systematic review. *The Journal of Adolescent Health*, 66(5), 576–583. DOI: 10.1016/j.jadohealth.2019.12.022

Miller, W. R., & Rollnick, S. (2012). *Motivational interviewing: Helping people change* (3rd ed.). Guilford Press.

Miller, W. R., Smith, J., & Thomas, R. (2020). Integrated interventions for adolescent digital addiction: Combining cognitive-behavioral therapy and educational approaches. *Journal of Youth and Adolescence*, 49(8), 1622–1636. DOI: 10.1007/s10964-020-01223-6

Nguyen, T., & Lee, S. (2021). Social support and intervention outcomes for digital addiction in older adults. *Health & Social Work*, 46(2), 102–110. DOI: 10.1093/hsw/hlab006

Nielsen, J., & Mullich, J. (2010). *Designing for user engagement: The role of user feedback and interaction*. Wiley.

O'Keefe, G. S., & Clarke-Pearson, K. (2011). The impact of social media on children, adolescents, and families. *Pediatrics*, 127(4), 800–804. DOI: 10.1542/peds.2011-0054 PMID: 21444588

Ophir, E., Nass, C., & Wagner, A. D. (2009). Cognitive control in media multitaskers. *Proceedings of the National Academy of Sciences of the United States of America*, 106(37), 15583–15587. DOI: 10.1073/pnas.0903620106 PMID: 19706386

Park, J., Kim, J., & Choi, H. (2021). Posture-related musculoskeletal disorders in users of handheld electronic devices. *Journal of Occupational Health*, 63(1), e12264. DOI: 10.1002/1348-9585.12264 PMID: 34378303

Pew Research Center. (2021). Mobile technology and home broadband 2021. Retrieved from https://www.pewresearch.org

Primack, B. A., Shensa, A., Sidani, J. E., Radovic, A., & Rosen, D. (2017). Social media use and perceived social isolation among young adults in the U.S. *Social Science & Medicine*, 208, 150–157. DOI: 10.1016/j.socscimed.2018.03.022 PMID: 28279545

Przybylski, A. K., Murayama, K., DeHaan, C. R., & Gladwell, V. (2013). Motivational, emotional, and behavioral correlates of fear of missing out. *Computers in Human Behavior*, 29(4), 1841–1848. DOI: 10.1016/j.chb.2013.02.014

Ribble, M. (2015). *Digital citizenship in schools: Nine elements all students should know* (6th ed.). International Society for Technology in Education.

Riedl, R., Kindermann, H., & Javor, A. (2018). The relationship between techno-stress and mental well-being. *Journal of Information Technology*, 33(2), 105–121. DOI: 10.1057/s41265-018-0031-6

Rosen, L. D., Lim, A. F., Carrier, L. M., & Cheever, N. A. (2013). An empirical examination of the educational impact of text messaging on college students. *Journal of Educational Computing Research*, 48(4), 415–436. DOI: 10.2190/EC.48.4.c

Sheppard, A. L., & Wolffsohn, J. S. (2018). Digital eye strain: Prevalence, measurement and mitigation. *BMJ Open Ophthalmology*, 3(1), e000146. DOI: 10.1136/bmjophth-2018-000146 PMID: 29963645

Skinner, B. F. (1953). *Science and human behavior*. Free Press.

Smith, P., & Jones, K. (2019). Ethical design practices for digital well-being. *Journal of Digital Ethics*, 12(1), 55–68. DOI: 10.1007/s12225-019-0946-3

Smith, P. R., & Brown, L. (2021). The role of AI in shaping technology addiction: Implications for future research. *Journal of Technology and Health*, 16(1), 23–34. DOI: 10.1177/2042018821100003

Smith, P. R., & Jones, K. (2019). Comparative analysis of digital addiction impacts: A cross-generational study. *Digital Health*, 5, 1–10. DOI: 10.1177/2055207619881740

Twenge, J. M., & Campbell, W. K. (2018). Associations between digital media use and psychological well-being. *Social Indicators Research*, 138(1), 247–262. DOI: 10.1007/s11205-017-1508-1

Vasalou, A., Joinson, A. N., Bänziger, T., Goldie, P., & Pitt, J. (2008). Avatars in social media: Balancing accuracy, playfulness and embodied messages. *International Journal of Human-Computer Studies*, 66(11), 1011–1023. DOI: 10.1016/j.ijhcs.2008.08.002

Verduyn, P., Lee, D. A., Park, J., Shablack, H., & Orvell, A. (2017). The impact of social network sites on subjective well-being: A meta-analysis. *Perspectives on Psychological Science*, 12(3), 225–245. DOI: 10.1177/1745691616635591

Wegmann, E., Oberst, U., Stodt, B., & Brand, M. (2015). Online addiction and the role of emotional intelligence in the development of online addiction. *Addictive Behaviors*, 51, 175–183. DOI: 10.1016/j.addbeh.2015.07.014

Williams, D., Brown, L., & Garcia, M. (2019). Cross-generational impacts of excessive internet use: Mental and physical health outcomes. *Journal of Public Health*, 41(2), 197–208. DOI: 10.1093/pubmed/fdy079

Young, K. S. (1998). Internet addiction: The emergence of a new clinical disorder. *Cyberpsychology & Behavior*, 1(3), 237–244. DOI: 10.1089/cpb.1998.1.237

KEY TERMS AND DEFINITIONS

Behavioral Interventions: Strategies and therapies designed to alter addictive behaviors through psychological and behavioral techniques.

Cognitive Functions: Mental processes related to perception, memory, attention, and emotional regulation that can be affected by digital addiction.

Digital Detox: A period during which an individual refrains from using digital devices to reduce dependency and mitigate the adverse effects of excessive screen time.

Digital Wellness: An approach that focuses on maintaining a healthy balance between digital device use and other aspects of life, emphasizing the importance of mindful and responsible technology use.

Educational Programs: Initiatives aimed at increasing awareness and knowledge about digital addiction and promoting healthier technology use practices.

Eye Strain: Discomfort or fatigue in the eyes resulting from prolonged screen use, often characterized by symptoms like dryness, blurred vision, or headaches.

Internet Addiction: A behavioral disorder where an individual spends an excessive amount of time online, which interferes with daily functioning and responsibilities. This can include addiction to social media, gaming, or other online activities.

Mental Health Implications: The psychological effects of excessive smartphone and internet use, including increased levels of anxiety, depression, and stress.

Policy Recommendations: Guidelines and suggestions for policymakers to address digital addiction, including regulations and public health initiatives aimed at mitigating its impact.

Posture-Related Issues: Physical problems arising from poor posture due to extended periods of sitting or using digital devices, which can lead to back, neck, and shoulder pain.

Sedentary Lifestyle: A way of life that involves prolonged periods of inactivity or minimal physical movement, often associated with excessive screen use.

Smartphone Addiction: A condition characterized by an excessive and compulsive use of smartphones, leading to negative impacts on an individual's daily life, social interactions, and overall well-being.

Technological Solutions: Tools and applications designed to help manage and reduce digital addiction by promoting balanced screen time and healthy usage habits.

Chapter 11
Evolution of the Digital Colonization Concept:
Penetrating the Malaysian Businesses Landscape

Faerozh Bin Madli
Universiti Malaysia Sabah, Malaysia

Yuzainy Janin
https://orcid.org/0000-0002-3912-1008
Universiti Malaysia Sabah, Malaysia

Shaierah Gulabdin
https://orcid.org/0000-0002-7648-422X
Universiti Malaysia Sabah, Malaysia

Wong Sing Yun
Universiti Malaysia Sabah, Malaysia

Kelvin Yong
Universiti Malaysia Sabah, Malaysia

Diana Nabila Chau Abdullah
https://orcid.org/0000-0002-9667-8427
Universiti Malaysia Sabah, Malaysia

ABSTRACT

Digital colonization? Various meanings and interpretations have been attributed to this term by different parties. Some view it positively, while others interpret it negatively. This clearly demonstrates the diverse range of interpretations surrounding this significant term. The different interpretations show that the term's meaning is broad and depends on the context. Thus, this study aims to provide a comprehensive examination of the term "digital colonization" within the Malaysian context. Discussions will center on the digital landscape in Malaysia and its implications for businesses. The discussions and arguments in this study will help create statements and definitions about digital colonization in Malaysia. Therefore, the study will thoroughly review existing literature to explore its scope. Overall, the findings of this study extend beyond the confines of Malaysia which offering insights applicable to broader discussions in context digitalization.

DOI: 10.4018/979-8-3693-6366-9.ch011

INTRODUCTION: AN OVERVIEW OF THE DIGITAL LANDSCAPE IN MALAYSIA

The term “digital” is not unfamiliar in today's world (Noh et al., 2017). The phenomenon of digital knowledge is relatively well-known to almost everyone globally. This is due to the widespread development of digital technologies, making individuals more aware of digital matters. Digital development is also evident and ongoing in Malaysia (Kadir et al., 2021). Located in Asia, Malaysia is one of the countries experiencing rapid digital growth in this continent (Fauzi & Paiman, 2021).

In Malaysia, digital development can be divided into several key phases: 1) early beginnings and internet adoption, 2) growth of internet and mobile connectivity, 3) e-government and digital services, 4) expansion of the digital economy, and 5) recent developments and future outlook. Each phase progresses independently or in sequence. In other words, phase 1 began and was followed by the subsequent phases. However, it is important to note that the start of phase 2 does not necessarily mean the end of phase 1; in certain cases, these phases may continue simultaneously to support one another (Azhar & Shakil, 2021). The concurrent progress of these phases ensures that digital development in Malaysia can achieved a comprehensive and positive impact.

For the early beginnings and internet adoption phase, digital technology development in Malaysia can be traced back to the early 1990s. During this period, the Malaysian government was focused heavily on advancing digital infrastructure. One of the key milestones in shaping the digital development of Malaysia was the launch of the Multimedia Super Corridor (MSC Malaysia) in 1996 (Saleh et al., 2020). This project provided a comprehensive focus not only on companies but also on increasing the knowledge and exposure of Malaysian society to digital technologies (Aziz et al., 2021). Because the project aimed to provide a comprehensive focus, this initiative successfully created a conducive environment, complete with world-class infrastructure, government policies that catalyzed business and industry growth, and various incentives to encourage more direct involvement in digitalization (Saleh et al., 2020; Azizi et al., 2021). This strategic initiative was a cornerstone of Malaysia’s Vision 2020, which sought to transition the country into a fully developed nation by the year 2020 (Kiflie & Lo, 2024). In addition, the MSC included the creation of Cyberjaya, a city built to serve as a technological hub. This development underscored Malaysia’s commitment to embedding digital technology at the core of its economic and social strategies (Afroz et al., 2020).

Subsequently, next is the growth of Internet and Mobile connectivity phase. This phase began in the late 1990s and continued into the early 2000s (Rosmani et al., 2020). This period was transformative for Malaysia's digital landscape, as it experienced rapid development in internet and mobile connectivity (Rosmani et al., 2020). Telekom Malaysia was one of the key organizations playing a significant role during this time, investing heavily in the development of infrastructure (Hajar et al., 2020). For example, it expanded the fiber optic network and improved broadband services to make them more affordable and widespread. During this period, the Malaysian government also introduced the Smart Schools Initiative, aimed at integrating ICT into the education system (Hajar et al., 2020). In addition, the Malaysian government launched the National IT Agenda (NITA) in 1996 to enhance the level of ICT literacy among the population. These efforts collectively contributed to a significant transformation in Malaysia’s digital connectivity and literacy during this critical phase (Gong, 2020). In fact, By the early 2000s, Malaysia had established itself as one of the leading countries in Southeast Asia in terms of internet usage, driven by both public and private sector initiatives (Chai et al., 2020).

Next, the following phase refers to e-government and digital services. This phase began in the mid-2000s, marking a new era in Malaysia's digital evolution (Abdullah et al., 2013). During this phase, the Malaysian government launched various digital services, collectively known as e-government (Abdullah et al., 2013; Huda et al., 2022). Among the introduced digital services were e-filing (tax), online payments, and notably, MyKad (Huda et al., 2022). This digital identity system has had a profoundly positive impact, significantly enhancing the efficiency of both public and private sector engagement (Abu Bakar et al., 2015). The progress of e government was supported by the Malaysia Administrative Modernisation and Management Planning Unit (MAMPU), which played a crucial role in coordinating the digital transformation of Malaysia's public services (Ramli, 2017).

In the 2010s, this phase also marked a significant period in Malaysia's digital development, known as the expansion of the digital economy (Chan, 2024). A key trend during this phase was the widespread adoption of smartphones by society. This high usage led to an increased reliance on mobile applications, bringing about a dramatic transformation across various sectors, including transport, banking, and retail. This trend contributed to the rise of e-commerce (Edrak et al., 2022). Consequently, digital payments also saw rapid adoption, with popular platforms in Malaysia including Touch 'n Go and Boost (Ling et al., 2023). Additionally, this phase was characterized by strong government initiatives to develop high-speed broadband and 4G network technology (Ibrahim et al., 2023). This period also saw increased venture capital investments and the emergence of numerous startups, positioning Malaysia as a vibrant hub for digital innovation in the region (Edrak et al., 2022). Recent reports indicate that by 2023, Malaysia's digital economy contributed approximately 22.6% to its GDP, underscoring the significant impact of digital transformation (MDEC, 2023).

In recent years, Malaysia has been building on its digital foundations with comprehensive strategies and blueprints to enhance its digital capabilities. Launched in 2021, the Malaysia Digital Economy Blueprint (MyDIGITAL) sets an ambitious goal for the country to become a regional leader in the digital economy by 2030 (Zoraimi et al., 2022). This blueprint focuses on key areas such as deploying 5G technology, promoting digital inclusivity, and fostering innovation and entrepreneurship (Abubacker & Raheem et al., 2024). The COVID-19 pandemic has highlighted the importance of digital resilience, accelerating digital adoption across various sectors (Muhamad et al., 2021). Remote work, online education, telehealth, and e-commerce have become essential services, showcasing the critical role of digital infrastructure in maintaining economic and social continuity (Ismail & Masud, 2020; Aziz et al., 2021). The Malaysian government's support for digital startups, along with ongoing improvements in digital infrastructure, positions the country to take advantage of emerging technologies like artificial intelligence, blockchain, and the Internet of Things (IoT) (Badarudin et al., 2018). As Malaysia moves forward in its digital journey, addressing the digital divide and enhancing digital literacy will be crucial to ensuring that the benefits of digitalization are shared equitably across all segments of society (Ismail & Masud, 2020; Aziz et al., 2021).

The discussion above highlights the digital landscape in Malaysia, clearly showing the positive impact of digital development in the country, providing numerous benefits to everyone regardless of their background. This impact is comprehensive, benefiting individuals as well as all industry sectors, whether government or private. However, amid this rapid digital development era, there is a crucial aspect that needs to be explored: digital colonization. Moreover, research on this issue is currently very limited. Therefore, this study aims to focus on the digital colonization occurring in Malaysia. It is important to note that this discussion does not view the impact of digitalization in Malaysia negatively but aims to contribute to knowledge. The findings from this research will be highly beneficial for policymakers in crafting better policies by considering the individuals or parties involved in digital colonization. In addition, the significance of this study's findings extends beyond the context of organization. But, it will also open new avenues for researchers to delve deeper into the concept of digital colonization in both organizational and national contexts.

COLONIALIZATION: ELECTRONIC OR DIGITAL?

Throughout history, colonialism has taken various forms and been imposed on a multitude of civilisations. Inevitably with the progression of the world toward modernization, post World Wars, saw the subsequent war became much more 'colder' during the Cold War, where the 'war' is about (amongst other) political and economic influence, intelligence to cultural and propaganda.

Meanwhile at the same time Industrial Revolutions (IR) began to spread rapidly at global scale reaching its current progression at IR 4.0. This IR 4.0 characterised by a fusion of technologies that is blurring the lines between the physical, digital, and biological spheres (Schwab, 2016) this further create opportunity for a new platform for colonialism to reside. Even more now there is already suggestion that we are have already entered IR 5.0 with the emergence of smart factories (Adel, 2022).

According to Oxford Languages (https://languages.oup.com/) the suffix-ism refer to as a distinctive practice, system, or philosophy, typically a political ideology or an artistic movement. Indeed, the word colonialism put forward by Kohn and Reddy (2006), 'a practice of domination, which involves the subjugation of one people to another', this statement resonate well with context of our article. Their use of the word 'subjugation' perhaps a subtle alternative to its synonym such as 'to bring under complete control and rule as a subject', 'conquer', 'vanquish' and 'subdue'.

While defining colonialism is more straight forward as its etymological history traced vis-a-vis with early civilisation histories. On the other hand, the term electronic colonialism and digital colonialization are comparably more recent concepts, thus should be distinctly differentiated, particularly between the terms electronic and digital. From our anecdotal observation on the literature, both terms; electronic colonialism and digital colonialism are being used to disclosing to the same message.

An early widely cited postulation to describe contemporary colonialization was by Schiller (1976) who suggested the term "cultural imperialism" to describe and explain how large multinational corporations, including media entities from developed countries, dominated developing countries.

In the context of our article, we intend to use the term digital colonialization as we find this term reflect the contemporary compatibility of information technology and can be relevant for future discussant. For example, while all digital systems are electronic (since they rely on electronic components), not all electronic systems are digital (since they can also be analog). In this sense, digital systems are a subset of electronic systems. Thus, we decided to use the term digital colonialization.

DIGITAL LAYER: BUSINESSES AND SOCIETY

In today's digital era, the interconnectedness and reliance on technology have become integral to both businesses and society. The concept of a "Digital Layer" in business refers to a structured, data-driven framework that captures and analyses the interactions and relationships among firms through digital means, primarily using web data. Another study refers digital layer as the incorporation of digital technologies and platforms within business-to-business (B2B) interactions, particularly through social media channels. This involves utilising digital tools such as social networks (e.g., Facebook, LinkedIn) to improve communication and engagement with stakeholders. Digital layers enhance both internal and external communication, fostering cooperation and networking in international business contexts, driven by the low costs and efficiency associated with social media (E Silva & Elo, 2018). It serves as a bridge between the physical and digital realms, enabling seamless communication, collaboration, and information sharing.

Furthermore, the digital layer allows businesses to transform their operations and business models, adapting to changing market dynamics and customer demands. The digital layer in businesses and society represents the integration and interaction of advanced technologies within various sectors, fundamentally transforming operations, interactions, and structures. This layer encompasses the use of digital tools such as artificial intelligence, cloud computing, blockchain, and the Internet of Things (IoT), which enhance decision-making, operational efficiency, and customer experiences (Dommett, 2023; Klievink & Janssen, 2014). The Digital Layer serves as the core for various IoT applications like smart homes, smart cities, and smart health solutions (Ustundag & Cevikcan, 2018). By efficiently processing data, it enables real-time decision-making and facilitates improved user experiences across a wide range of domains.

As for society, several studies point towards the potential of digital layers in supporting the establishment, organization, and evolution of communities (Isacson & Adelfio, 2023). These benefits appear as enhanced Access, digital layers can significantly improve access to communities. By leveraging online platforms and digital tools, individuals can more readily discover and connect with communities that share their interests, fostering a sense of belonging. This is particularly relevant for geographically dispersed communities or those with niche interests. Digital layers can streamline communication and coordination within communities. Online forums, social media groups, and other digital tools enable efficient information sharing, discussions, and collaborative efforts. This fosters smoother organization and project management within the community (Isacson & Adelfio, 2023). Its enhanced access and streamlined communication to fostering a sense of belonging and enabling the sharing of alternative models, digital layers offer a powerful set of tools for communities to thrive in the digital age.

The research on digital layers in both business and society provides a comprehensive understanding of how digital technologies are transforming interactions, operations, and structures. By exploring the concept of a digital layer, researchers can uncover novel insights into the integration of technology within various sectors, enabling enhanced efficiency, productivity, and decision-making capabilities. In business, the digital layer facilitates improved communication, collaboration, and networking, leading to better B2B interactions and adaptive business models. In society, digital layers support community formation, organization, and evolution on how it can impact by the digitalization of business.

Therefore, the exploration of digital layers in both business and society unveils a transformative landscape where technology intertwines with human interactions, reshaping how organizations operate and communities thrive. The research underscores the profound benefits of digital layers, from enhancing efficiency and communication in businesses to fostering belonging and collaboration in communities. However, it also highlights critical limitations, including ethical concerns and digital divides, which necessitate careful consideration and proactive mitigation strategies. Therefore, the next sections will discuss in depth how the concept of the business layer leads to digital colonization.

MOTIVATIONAL FACTORS DRIVING BUSINESSES TO ENGAGE IN THE DIGITAL

As businesses across the globe adopt digital technologies, they often rely on platforms and infrastructures developed by technology giants based in economically dominant countries. This dependency can lead to a form of digital colonialism, where local economies and businesses become reliant on foreign technology providers (Kwet, 2019). It demonstrates how globalization significantly affects technology transfers, with countries undergoing crucial technological changes experiencing an ever-growing convergence in digital technology adoption (Skare & Riberio-Soriano, 2021). The trend of digital technology use continues to expand, becoming mainstream in the business world. Businesses are increasingly motivated to engage in digital transformation for numerous reasons.

Firstly, digital transformation enhances efficiency and productivity. Businesses constantly seek ways to streamline operations, reduce manual processes, and minimize human error. Continuous innovation in digital technologies drives the adoption of new tools and platforms (Ceipek, Hautz, Petruzzelli, De Massis & Matzler, 2021). Digital tools and automation enhance operations by reducing manual tasks and human error. According to Malik, Tripathi, Kar and Gupta (2021), technologies like AI, machine learning, and robotic process automation significantly boost productivity and decision-making. By automating repetitive tasks, businesses can reallocate human resources to more strategic and creative roles, thereby enhancing overall productivity. Countries with high levels of globalization experience intensive digital technology penetration, which improves their competitiveness, productivity, and innovation (Ha & Peter Chuah, 2023).

Secondly, digital transformation improves customer experience. Firms can rely on cognitive technologies to improve client interactions in e-commerce systems. Beyond operational improvements, enhancing customer experience is a crucial motivator, especially considering the varied experiences of virtual consumers across multiple environments, including retail sales and social networks (Calderon-Monge & Ribeiro-Soriano, 2024). Digital platforms offer personalized customer interactions and improved service delivery. In line with Jaylene, Joyce, Kelvin, Wen and Fransiska (2023), e-commerce and mobile apps provide customers with convenient and accessible purchasing options, where the increasing consumer preference for online and mobile interactions compels businesses to enhance their digital presence.

Next, another powerful catalyst for digital transformation is the competitive landscape. Gaining a competitive advantage requires businesses to efficiently integrate digital technologies, not only to survive but to thrive in a competitive environment (Farida & Setiawan, 2022). Early adopters of digital technologies can differentiate themselves from their competitors. Staying ahead with the latest technology trends helps maintain market relevance. As more businesses go digital, others must follow suit to remain competitive. In accordance with Parviainen, Tihinen, Kääriäinen, and Teppolao (2017), to gain a competitive advantage through digitized solutions, a company's value proposition must be reformulated by integrating a combination of products, services, and data. Leveraging digital technologies enables businesses to anticipate customer needs and refine their strategies accordingly.

Likewise, digital platforms enable businesses to reach a global audience, breaking down geographical barriers (Do Vale, Collin-Lachaud & Lecocq, 2022). Online marketing and social media campaigns can target international markets more effectively. This global reach not only expands customer bases but also diversifies revenue streams, mitigating risks associated with local market fluctuations (Roy, Singh, Sadeque, Harrigan & Coussement, 2023). The digital era changes how people communicate, produce, market, and consume various offerings, including information, products, services, and experiences. As reported by Banga and te Velde (2020), the rise in remote working, virtual collaboration, and online learning has increased the demand for digital infrastructure and connectivity, ICT-enabled services, telemedicine, and e-commerce platforms.

Moreover, digitalization significantly upgrades productivity, particularly in terms of cost efficiency, as influenced by the expansion of digital transformation (Kraus, Jones, Kailer, Weinmann, Chaparro-Banegas & Roig-Tierno, 2021). Digital solutions can lower operational costs through enhanced efficiency and automation. Cloud computing, for instance, reduces the need for expensive on-premises IT infrastructure (Dass, Parida, Panigrahi & Moharana, 2023). Additionally, based on Islam, Fakhrorazi, Hartini, and Abu Raihan (2019), the on-demand economy offers advantages such as rapid access to necessary services or goods, reduced costs for end-users by minimizing intermediaries, and simplified market entry for suppliers of goods and services.

Lastly, digital transformation facilitates data-driven decision-making. In line with Kravchenko et al. (2019), it is important to note the many opportunities and challenges associated with the rapid development of the digital economy, the swift growth of data flows, security concerns, and new business models across various sectors. The outcome of digital innovation is crucial for firms at different stages of their development to expand and survive. Digitalization facilitates data-driven decision making; access to big data and analytics provides businesses with the insights needed to make informed decisions (Saura, Palacios-Marqués & Rebeiro-Soriano, 2021). Real-time data collection and analysis enable businesses to respond swiftly to market changes.

While digital transformation offers several considerations in business, it also raises important questions about digital sovereignty, data privacy, and equitable access to technology. Addressing these concerns requires a balanced approach that adopts innovation and growth while guaranteeing fair and inclusive participation in the digital economy. In other words, the motivation that brings many benefits to a business also simultaneously brings issues that need to be properly addressed. The next section will explore deeper into this issue.

DIGITAL COLONIZATION

As discussed above, digital colonization refers to various aspects, primarily impacting society and organizations. This phenomenon is not new but has been occurring since the dawn of the digital era in Malaysia. It is acknowledged that digital colonization is not unique to Malaysia but is a global phenomenon. However, the focus of this study is on digital colonization specifically in Malaysia.

In the initial discussion of this study, namely the introduction section, the chronology of digital development in Malaysia is discussed. In addition, the previous section also discussed in depth the importance of digitalization to a business. Hence, this section will delve deeply into how the impact of digitalization leads to issues related to digital colonization. Overall, this chronology of digital development spans from the early 1990s to the present day. Therefore, based on this timeline of digital development, the section on digital colonization will discuss it according to the time periods outlined in the discussion of digital development. In other words, this section will delve into digital colonization that has occurred in Malaysia since the beginning of digital development in the country. The discussion will also consider two main aspects: organizational and business aspects, as well as individual aspects. Observations or discussions involving the individual aspect are crucial because this element serves as a primary complement in the dynamic ecosystem of any business.

As discussed in the opening section of this study, the early phase of digital development in this country began with the launch of an integrated project, the Multimedia Super Corridor (MSC), in 1996 (MIDA, 2021; Masrom, 2016). The launch of this project was crucial as it served as a comprehensive catalyst towards digital development in Malaysia (Salih, Khidr, & Sahoo, 2020). Therefore, this mega project successfully attracted various global tech giants to invest in Malaysia, such as Microsoft and Intel (Masrom, 2016; Salih, Khidr, & Sahoo, 2020). These global tech giants were attracted to invest in Malaysia due to various factors, including the incentives provided by MSC, such as tax breaks and intellectual property protection (Mondaq, 2022; Yigitcanlar & Sarimin, 2015). This phenomenon has clearly succeeded in bringing in various technology experts and advanced technologies into Malaysia (Masrom, 2016; Yigitcanlar & Sarimin, 2015). Concurrently, Malaysia was also investing a significant amount in the construction of digital infrastructure, directly increasing internet penetration (MIDA, 2021; Salih, Khidr, & Sahoo, 2020). However, this period also marked Malaysia's start to establish significant dependency on foreign technology (Masrom, 2016; Salih, Khidr, & Sahoo, 2020). This is because many technological components need to be imported from these global tech giants (Masrom, 2016; Yigitcanlar & Sarimin, 2015). Along with the dependency on these technological components, this also directly requires expertise from these global tech giants to utilize the technology (Masrom, 2016; Salih, Khidr, & Sahoo, 2020).

Furthermore, the continuity of the impact related to dependency on these global tech giants in terms of technological components and expertise directly affects businesses. The ripple effect of this dependency chain reaction is that local businesses will directly depend on international technology to run their daily operations (Noor, 2020). Local businesses rely on multinational partners to provide them with digital-related resources (Noor, 2020). This is because local businesses lack the resources and capabilities to effectively run their operations, thereby hindering innovation in their business (Litvinenko, 2020). On the other hand, this reliance creates vulnerabilities, indirectly tying the operational stability and growth prospects of local businesses to the strategic decisions of these foreign tech giants (Noor, 2020). Additionally, on a broader scale, the economic conditions of these foreign companies also have a direct impact on local businesses (Thake, 2021). In other words, fluctuations in the economy of these foreign companies will relatively directly affect local businesses due to their dependency on the digital technologies they use in their daily business activities.

In this phase as well, from the perspective of digital colonization on an individual or societal level, disparities in technological adoption and digital literacy occur in Malaysia. This is evident because in urban areas, the rate of digital acceptance is significantly higher compared to rural areas (Kaliannan et al., 2012). One of the reasons for this situation is that many businesses in urban areas are beginning to adopt digital technology compared to businesses in rural areas that struggle to keep up with urban business trends. The flow of digital modernization indirectly widens the gap of digital adoption between urban and rural areas (Kaliannan et al., 2012). This widening gap also directly impacts the socioeconomic gap between urban and rural residents.

Meanwhile, in the subsequent development phase in Malaysia, in the period of the 2010s, there was a significant increase in the dominance of global tech giants in the digital development of Malaysia (Kinuthia, 2016). This increased dominance and dependency on global tech giants in Malaysia is closely related to the drastic increase in the use of social media platforms in Malaysia, such as Facebook, Twitter, and Instagram (Abbott et al., 2013). These platforms became crucial in Malaysia from that period onwards and can be said to remain until today as used for social communication purposes (Bakar & Zaini, 2022). Their use is not limited to social communication but is also used by businesses to promote their products.

While this widespread use undoubtedly brings many benefits to individuals and businesses, it also leads to the accumulation of a large amount of data (Johns & Cheong, 2019). This raises concerns about how these giant tech companies manage such large amounts of data or how they relate to privacy issues.

Moreover, during this period, in the 2010s, there was the emergence of e-commerce platforms in Malaysia such as Lazada and Shopee (Kang et al., 2021). This phenomenon has become a significant development in business as it has revolutionized the business sector in promoting and selling their products (Kang et al., 2021). These platforms make it easier for businesses to sell their products while offering consumers unprecedented convenience and choice (Kang et al., 2021). However, despite the various positive impacts, there are concerns arising from the fact that these platforms are owned by foreign companies and they exert significant control over Malaysia's e-commerce ecosystem, potentially influencing consumer behavior and market dynamics in Malaysia (Kamaruzaman et al., 2010).

Furthermore, during this period, there was also widespread adoption of cloud computing technology in Malaysia (Matsveichuk & Sotskov, 2023). The phenomenon of adopting cloud storage technology has revolutionized the way data storage and processing are handled in Malaysia (Kabir et al., 2015). This cloud storage approach simplifies the data storage process for individuals or companies as it eliminates the need for physical data storage and allows easy access anytime, anywhere (Bazel et al., 2018). However, despite the significant benefits of this convenience, it indirectly further increases reliance on global providers for individuals and businesses. This results in personal data or business data being in the hands of foreign companies, raising many questions regarding data sovereignty and privacy (Wheeler & Winburn, 2015). In detail, while these platforms offer many benefits, at the same time they raise concerns about how they are used and stored.

In the subsequent era, namely the 2020s period, Malaysia has continued to rapidly develop its digital landscape in line with the continuity of previous initiatives and projects (Bujang et al., 2020). One significant program during this period is the launch of the National Digital Economy Blueprint (MyDIGITAL) in 2021, outlining Malaysia's vision to become a digitally driven, high-income nation by 2030 (Smit et al., 2022; Seng & Dorasamy, 2021). To achieve this vision, Malaysia needs to enhance various key elements related to digital, including enhancing digital infrastructure, upskilling the workforce, and promoting digital entrepreneurship to drive economic growth and innovation (Md Ladin et al., 2017). One example is the development of 5G technology in Malaysia, which requires collaboration with foreign big global tech companies (Shaari et al., 2024). This indirectly relates to the ongoing underlying issues of dependency on foreign technology and expertise. However, to mitigate these challenges, Malaysia is focusing on promoting local innovation and tech entrepreneurship through initiatives like the Malaysian Global Innovation & Creativity Centre (MaGIC), which aims to nurture local talent and reduce dependency on foreign technology (Mohd Nafi et al., 2021). Initiatives such as MaGIC play a pivotal role in this endeavor by providing support and resources to local startups and entrepreneurs (Nasir & Subari, 2017). This program aims to foster a culture of innovation and entrepreneurship, ultimately reducing dependency on global tech giants in technology and expertise-related matters. Alternatively stated, the initiatives through various programs launched by the Malaysian government serve as a strategic plan to reduce dependency on foreign technology.

Additionally, during this era, an important event occurred that had a significant impact on the entire world, including Malaysia. This event was the outbreak of the COVID-19 pandemic. The spread of this virus has led to reshaping both the business landscape and societal norms in many activities, including those related to digitalization (Muhamad et al., 2021). During the pandemic period, all businesses needed to implement the new norm, which involved conducting almost all business activities online, such as digital transactions or work arrangements (Ratnasingam et al., 2021). This new norm was not only limited to businesses but also affected all Malaysians (Mohd Arif & Choo Ta, 2022). While this accelerated digital transformation brought about newfound efficiencies and opportunities, it also exposed the digital divide within Malaysian society (Umar, 2021). Marginalized communities and smaller businesses, lacking access to reliable internet connectivity and digital infrastructure, faced disproportionate challenges in navigating the digital shift (Umar, 2021).

In connection with this COVID-19 outbreak, the spread of this pandemic has worsened the existing reliance situation on technology from foreign countries (Kruss et al., 2020), indirectly strengthening the dynamics of digital colonization in Malaysia. This dependency, as discussed before in previous eras, affects business operations as they require platforms owned by foreign countries to conduct their businesses. In other words, before the COVID-19 outbreak, businesses might not have been entirely digital, but during the outbreak, all business activities needed to be conducted digitally, thereby increasing reliance on technology from abroad. One example is if these platforms encounter issues, businesses will directly face problems due to the extensive use of digital technology. Therefore, the spread of this pandemic actually brings many benefits in terms of digital development, notably accelerating digital adoption for businesses and society (Umar, 2021). However, at the same time, the urgent need to use digital technology will further increase reliance on foreign technology (Kruss et al., 2020).

Overall, digital development is crucial for any country, including Malaysia. This is because there are many benefits to be gained, but at the same time, many aspects, including digital colonization, must be thoroughly examined. However, the Malaysian government is highly aware of this issue, and various initiatives and programs have been and are being implemented at present.

IMPLICATIONS OF THE DIGITAL ERA IN THE CONTEXT OF BUSINESSES

The corporate world has completely revolutionized as a result of the digital age, which has brought with it both unmatched prospects and difficulties. Businesses must change to stay competitive in the face of the rapid evolution of technology, or else they risk becoming obsolete. Businesses are facing a wide range of challenges as a result of the digital age, from increased connectivity and data analytics to changing consumer behaviour and cybersecurity risks. The challenge of embracing these new ways of operating is particularly acute for the established firms that grew up with a very different set of structures and norms, inherited from the industrial era of the early twentieth century (Volberda et al., 2021). However, embracing digital transformation is no longer optional but imperative for organizations aiming to thrive in this dynamic environment.

Even though companies recognize its paramount importance, they still face multiple obstacles that inhibit them from initiating, let alone benefiting from, digital transformation (Von Leipzig et al. 2017). They face challenges in realising the business benefits of new digital technology, with competing priorities topping the list of typical roadblocks. (Kane et al. 2015; Fitzgerald et al. 2013). Institutional challenges can best be explained by the fact that most technology-enabled transformations involve a certain degree of resistance to change manifested in the behavior of certain members, who refuse to accept the new state of affairs (Lawton 2015). Digital transformation has been seen challenging as many firms fail to realize the need to compete in new ways, and even many of those that do attempt to transform themselves end up failing (Volberda et al., 2021). In other words, digital technology have caused traditional business models in a number of industries to be disrupted, resulting in the demise of long-standing incumbents and the development of creative entrepreneurs.

The proliferation of e-commerce platforms has transformed the retail industry, allowing businesses to sell products and services online. In particular, digitalization provides new opportunities for firms to engage with foreign customers and to reduce capital investments needed to effectively compete in a foreign market (Meyer et al., 2023). This has definitely led to greater convenience for consumers and opened up new revenue streams for businesses, but the significant challenges in adopting and benefitting from e-business remain, particularly for small businesses in the developing world. For while the digital era has enabled businesses to transcend geographical boundaries and opened up immense opportunities for growth expansion, but it has also increased competition. Hence, resulting the struggle of small firms in dealing with such stiff competition. In addition to that, competition law for digital economy firms has moved up the policy agenda around the world with the growing digital era (Philippon, 2019). However, controversies have emerged with respect to the implementation and enforcement of rules to ensure fair competition in view of dominant firms in the digital economy (Khan, 2017; Jacobides & Lianos, 2021; Jenny, 2021).

The growing reliance on digital technologies raises the possibility of data breaches and cyberattacks. To safeguard confidential data and uphold client confidence, businesses must make significant investments in cybersecurity solutions. Madan, Savani and Katsikeas (2023) asserted that people's responses to data breaches in the digital space are associated with traditional concepts of national culture, specifically power distance and uncertainty avoidance. Hence, the implications of digital era on the data security should not be taken lightly. Besides that, new regulatory issues pertaining to data privacy, online commerce, and intellectual property rights have emerged with the advent of the digital era. Businesses must stay abreast of evolving regulations and ensure compliance to avoid legal consequences. As postulated by Luo (2021), digitalization creates new challenges to the enforcement of regulations given the ease with which users can access information from almost any location online (Luo, 2021).

Digital technologies can contribute to sustainability efforts by enabling remote work, reducing carbon footprints and optimizing energy usage. Businesses are increasingly expected to demonstrate environmental responsibility and incorporate sustainable practices into their operations. Sustainability can serve as a catalyst for many companies to integrate digital technology into all areas of their business (Le, 2020). However, the deployment of digital technologies depends on a nation's technological infrastructure, such as access to mobile phones, wireless networks, and broadband – also known as digital infrastructure (Andrews, Nicoletti & Timiliotis, 2018), which vary considerably across and within countries. As Chaffey (2014) postulated that adopting e-business in an organisation without a well-defined e-business strategy can lead to resource waste, inadequate back-end system integration, lost opportunities, and ultimately, subpar performance.

In an increasingly volatile and uncertain world, digital technologies can enhance the resilience and adaptability of businesses to environmental, social, and economic disruptions.Digital supply chain management tools enable businesses to identify and mitigate risks, diversify suppliers, and build redundancy into their supply chains to withstand disruptions. The advances of digitalization has create new challenges and possibilities of business strategies. With the use of data analytics and simulation technologies, businesses can modelling different scenarios and evaluating the possible effects of social and environmental trends on their operations in creating proactive resilience and adaptation strategies. Digitalization have altered the nature of cooperation and competition both inside and between industries, allowing businesses to compete in new ways, such as through the use of platform- and ecosystem-based business models. (Jacobides et al.,2018; Kretschmer et al., 2020).

In summary, the implications of digitalization in business are vast and multifaceted. The digital era itself presents both opportunities and challenges for businesses, requiring adaptation, innovation, and a proactive approach to leverage the full potential of digital technologies while mitigating associated risks. As pointed out by Sadigov (2022), digitalization can be considered as a fundamental element of innovative business management leading to transformation of the business paradigm of firm and the modernization of the entire economic system. However, the impact of digitalization on the business development could vary significantly depending on the specifics of digital technologies, the initial quality parameters of business performance, the specifics of socio-economic and institutional development of the whole country. Hence, critical evaluation may be needed to examine the implications of digitalization in a national-specific researches. Knowledge of the implications of digital era within the business context will be useful for firms to adapt to the digital transformation.

CONCLUSION

The application of digital technology undeniably yields numerous positive impacts on a country. These positive implications are experienced by various sectors, including the government, businesses, and society. The utilization of digital technology enhances the efficiency of daily activities across these sectors. However, the reliance on technology provided by external or global big tech companies necessitates a comprehensive examination, as it can lead to digital colonization. This issue is pertinent in Malaysia, as discussed above, supported by extensive and comprehensive arguments from previous researchers. Despite this situation, numerous researchers have highlighted that Malaysia has implemented various initiatives and programs aimed at mitigating the effects of digital colonization. Currently, the positive impacts of these programs and initiatives can be felt and observed in Malaysia. The findings from this study are highly valuable to various stakeholders, such as policymakers and future planners. The insights gained can be utilized for detailed planning related to digital development while simultaneously considering the potential repercussions of digital colonization. Future research is recommended to explore deeper into the effects of digital colonization, employing empirical methods and focusing on specific regions or population groups within Malaysia. This approach would provide a more nuanced understanding of the impact and aid in developing targeted strategies to address the challenges posed by digital colonization.

REFERENCES

Abbasiharofteh, M., Krüger, M., Kinne, J., Lenz, D., & Resch, B. (2023). The digital layer: Alternative data for regional and innovation studies. *Spatial Economic Analysis*, 18(4), 507–529. DOI: 10.1080/17421772.2023.2193222

Abbott, J., MacDonald, A. W., & Givens, J. W. (2013). New social media and (electronic) democratization in East and Southeast Asia. *Taiwan Journal of Democracy*, 9(2), 105–137.

Abu Bakar, N. S., Rahman, A. A., & Abdull Hamed, H. N. (2015). The implementation of Malaysian m-government services. *Advanced Science Letters*, 21(5), 1122–1126. DOI: 10.1166/asl.2015.6020

Abubacker, N. F., & Raheem, M. (2024). Smart Agriculture in Malaysia: Harnessing Ubiquitous Computing for Sustainable Economic Growth. Journal of Applied Technology and Innovation, 8(1), 1.

Adel, A. (2022). Future of industry 5.0 in society: Human-centric solutions, challenges and prospective research areas. *Journal of Cloud Computing (Heidelberg, Germany)*, 11(1), 40. DOI: 10.1186/s13677-022-00314-5 PMID: 36101900

Andrews, D., Nicoletti, G., & Timiliotis, C. (2018). Digital technology diffusion: A matter of capabilities, incentives or both? OECD Economics Department Working Papers, No. 1476, OECD Publishing, Paris.

Azhar, N. A. Z. M., & Shakil, N. S. M. (2021). The Intervention of Micro, Small and Medium Enterprises (MSMEs) in Malaysia's Digital Economy. *Global Business and Management Research*, 13(4).

Aziz, A., Ahmad, M. K., & Suppiah, S. M. (2021). Remote work: New normal communication challenges. European Proceedings of Social and Behavioural Sciences.

Aziz, A. A., Abdulkarim, I., & Jusoh, J. A. (2021, November). A review of supply and demand digital talents in Malaysia. In *International Conference on Business and Technology* (pp. 721-738). Cham: Springer International Publishing.

Badarudin, U. W., Din, W. I. S. W., Prasetyo, Y. A., Musa, Z., & Kasim, S. (2018). Internet of things: An implementation and its challenges in Malaysia. *International Journal on Advanced Science, Engineering and Information Technology*, 8(6), 2641–2647. DOI: 10.18517/ijaseit.8.6.5043

Bakar, N. A. A., & Zaini, A. F. A. (2022). Literature review on the factors influencing the usage of social media among entrepreneurs in Malaysia. *Open Journal of Social Sciences*, 10(1), 409–419. DOI: 10.4236/jss.2022.101031

Banga, K., & te Velde, D. W. (2020). Covid-19 and disruption of the digital economy: Evidence from low and middle-income countries. Oxford, United Kingdom: Digital Pathways at Oxford, 7. Retrieved from ox.ac.uk

Bazel, M. A., Haron, H., Ismail, I., & Gui, A. (2018, September). Factors influencing intention to use cloud storage services amongst postgraduate students in Malaysian Technical Universities. In *2018 International Conference on Information Management and Technology (ICIMTech)* (pp. 350-355). IEEE. DOI: 10.1109/ICIMTech.2018.8528179

Bujang, S. D. A., Selamat, A., Krejcar, O., Maresova, P., & Nguyen, N. T. (2020, April). Digital learning demand for future education 4.0—Case studies at Malaysia education institutions. In Informatics (Vol. 7, No. 2, p. 13). MDPI.

Calderon-Monge, E., & Ribeiro-Soriano, D. (2024). The role of digitalization in business and management a systematic literature review. *Review of Managerial Science*, 18(2), 450–491. DOI: 10.1007/s11846-023-00647-8

Ceipek, R., Hautz, J., Petruzzelli, A. M., De Massis, A., & Matzler, K. (2021). A motivation and ability perspective on engagement in emerging digital technologies: The case of Internet of Things solutions. *Long Range Planning*, 54(5), 101991. DOI: 10.1016/j.lrp.2020.101991

Chaffey, D. (2014). *Digital Business and E-Commerce Management*. Pearson Education Limited.

Chai, L. T., Chin, T. P., Yat, D. N. C., & Hooi, R. (n.d.). Millennials' S-Commerce Experience via Instagram. *Qualitative Research.*

Chan, M. (2024). Malaysia: Digital Payments, Data Regulations, and AI as Most Promising Areas for Digital Economy Collaboration. In The ASEAN Digital Economy (pp. 76-96). Routledge.

Dass, A. K., Parida, A., Panigrahi, S., & Moharana, S. K. (2023). Virtualization in Cloud Computing: Transforming Infrastructure and Enhancing Efficiency. *Research and Applications: Emerging Technologies*, 5(3), 26–40.

Dmitrieva, E. I. (2020). Digital Platforms as a Base for Forming a Digital Economy. 156(Iscde), 553-558.

Do Vale, G., Collin-Lachaud, I., & Lecocq, X. (2022). The new retail model: Global reach demands omni-channels. *The Journal of Business Strategy*, 43(6), 339–349. DOI: 10.1108/JBS-02-2021-0026

Dommett, K. (2023). The inter-institutional impact of digital platform companies on democracy: A case study of the UK media's digital campaigning coverage. *New Media & Society*, 25(10), 2763–2780. DOI: 10.1177/14614448211028546

Edrak, B., Nor, Z. M., & Shaik, A. R. (2022). The Readiness of Malaysia Digital Economy: A Study of Three Government Policies from 1991 to 2020. *International Journal of Economics and Finance*, 14(12), 1–84. DOI: 10.5539/ijef.v14n12p84

Farida, I., & Setiawan, D. (2022). Business Strategies and Competitive Advantage: The Role of Performance and Innovation. *Journal of Open Innovation*, 8(163), 1–16. DOI: 10.3390/joitmc8030163

Fauzi, M. A., & Paiman, N. (2021). COVID-19 pandemic in Southeast Asia: Intervention and mitigation efforts. *Asian Education and Development Studies*, 10(2), 176–184. DOI: 10.1108/AEDS-04-2020-0064

Fitzgerald, M. (2013). Embracing Digital Technology: A New Strategic Imperative. *MIT Sloan Management Review*, 1–12.

Gong, R. (2020). Digital Inclusion: Assessing Meaningful Internet Connectivity in Malaysia. Navigating Challenges, Realising Opportunities of Digital Transformation, 5.

Ha, H., & Peter Chuah, C. K. (2023). Digital economy in Southeast Asia: challenges, opportunities and future development. Digital economy in Southeast Asia, 23(1), 19-35.

Hajar, M. A., Ibrahim, D. N., Darun, M. R., & Al-Sharafi, M. A. (2020). Value innovation activities in the wireless telecommunications service sector: A case study of the Malaysian market. *Journal of Global Business Insights*, 5(1), 57–72. DOI: 10.5038/2640-6489.5.1.1125

Huda, M. N., Kurniasari, E. N., & Ruroh, S. M. (2022). A systematic literature review of E-government evaluation. *Journal of Local Government Issues*, 5(1), 32–48. DOI: 10.22219/logos.v5i1.19784

Isacson, A., & Adelfio, M. (2023). The use of digital layers in post-growth communities - an exploratory study. The 6th International Conference on Smart Villages and Rural Development (COSVARD 2023).

Islam, R., Fakhrorazi, A., Hartini, H., & Abu Raihan, M. (2019). Globalization and its impact on international business. *Humanities & Social Sciences Reviews*, 7(1), 256–265. DOI: 10.18510/hssr.2019.7130

Ismail, N. A., & Masud, M. M. (2020). Prospects and challenges in improving e-commerce connectivity in Malaysia. E-commerce Connectivity in ASEAN, 78.

Jacobides, M., & Lianos, I. (2021). Ecosystems and competition law in theory and practice. *Industrial and Corporate Change*, 30(1), 119–131.

Jacobides, M. G., Cennamo, C., & Gawer, A. (2018). Towards a theory of ecosystems. *Strategic Management Journal*, 39(8), 2255–2276. DOI: 10.1002/smj.2904

Jalal, M. T., & Hossain, M. M. (2022). Digitalization of Supply Chain in Malaysian SMEs: A Framework for a Sustainable Digital Transformation.

Jang, Y. J., & Chen, H. L. (2021). *Digital Transformation in Southeast Asia: Emerging Trends and Implications*. Asian Development Bank Institute.

Kim, J., & Park, J. (2022). The impact of COVID-19 on digital transformation and innovation in Korea. *Technological Forecasting and Social Change*, 176.

Klein, T., & Teece, D. J. (2020). Innovation and market strategy: The role of industrial ecosystems. *Industrial and Corporate Change*, 29(3), 439–451.

Kumar, P., & Kumar, V. (2020). Bridging the digital divide: The role of mobile and fixed broadband. *Information Technology & People*, 33(1), 296–309.

Lee, M., & Song, M. (2019). Comparative advantage of nations, knowledge and innovation strategies: An analysis of Korea and Malaysia. *Technological Forecasting and Social Change*, 143, 201–213.

Lind, M., & Mukherjee, A. (2018). Maritime Informatics: Applying the Digital Layer to the Shipping Sector. *Technology Innovation Management Review*, 8(9), 18–27.

Lynch, J., & Gregor, S. (2004). User participation in decision support systems development: Influencing system outcomes. *European Journal of Information Systems*, 13(4), 286–301. DOI: 10.1057/palgrave.ejis.3000512

Manaf, M. F. A., & Kamarudin, H. (2021). Technology adoption and the growth of E-Commerce in Malaysia. *International Journal of Advanced Research in Engineering and Technology*, 12(2), 200–210.

Marchionni, L., & Charrier, R. (2022). The role of digital ecosystems in the new era of business: Challenges and opportunities. *European Business Review*, 2(1), 1–14.

Mehrizi, M. H. R., & Alvesson, M. (2021). Unpacking digital platforms and ecosystems: Strategic and managerial implications. *International Journal of Management Reviews*, 23(3), 316–332.

Ministry of Science, Technology and Innovation (MOSTI). (2020). Malaysia Digital Economy Blueprint. Retrieved from: https://www.mosti.gov.my/web/wp-content/uploads/2020/11/MDEC-BLUEPRINT.pdf

Mun, M. L., & Khoo, B. K. (2019). Influence of e-commerce adoption on SMEs business performance. *Journal of Advanced Research in Dynamical and Control Systems*, 11(5), 1352–1357.

Muntaka, A. S., Seidu, A. H., & Gariba, M. A. (2020). A systematic literature review on blockchain technology: Insights on challenges and current solutions. *Journal of Advances in Mathematics and Computer Science*, 35(2), 64–79.

National Economic Advisory Council (NEAC). (2010a). New Economic Model for Malaysia, Part 1: Strategic Policy Directions. Retrieved from: https://www.epu.gov.my/en/resources/economic-reports/new-economic-model-part-1

National Economic Advisory Council (NEAC). (2010b). New Economic Model for Malaysia, Part 2: Concluding the Transformation. Retrieved from: https://www.epu.gov.my/en/resources/economic-reports/new-economic-model-part-2

Nielsen, K. (2021). Digitalisation and resilience of the Danish economy. OECD Economics Department Working Papers, No. 1683, OECD Publishing, Paris.

Nor, M. R. B. M., & Yusoff, N. M. M. (2020). Factors Affecting Digital Transformation in Malaysian SMEs: A Conceptual Framework. *International Journal of Business and Management Science*, 10(1), 28–37.

OECD. (2020). *Digital Economy Outlook 2020*. OECD Publishing.

Ong, C. S., Sze, C. T., & Lai, J. K. (2019). The role of digital innovation hubs in facilitating digital transformation in Europe. *Journal of Manufacturing Technology Management*, 30(1), 155–175.

Oseni, A. I., & Oseni, I. O. (2017). Digital Transformation of Accounting through Cloud Computing. *Procedia Computer Science*, 105, 812–819.

Osman, Z., & Ahmad, F. S. (2010). An Empirical Study of the Relationship between the Adoption of E-commerce and Business Performance among Malaysian SMEs. *Journal of Business & Economics Research*, 8(3), 12–24.

Pagani, M., & Pardo, C. (2017). The impact of digital technology on relationships in a business network. *Industrial Marketing Management*, 67, 185–192. DOI: 10.1016/j.indmarman.2017.08.009

Phang, C. W., Kankanhalli, A., & Ramaprasad, A. (2015). Developing a framework for digital health ecosystems. *Information Systems Research*, 26(1), 44–69.

Pietrobelli, C., & Rabellotti, R. (2011). Global value chains meet innovation systems: Are there learning opportunities for developing countries? *World Development*, 39(7), 1261–1269. DOI: 10.1016/j.worlddev.2010.05.013

Pilat, D. (2021). Understanding the impact of digitalisation on productivity and wellbeing. OECD Economics Department Working Papers, No. 1643, OECD Publishing, Paris.

Prasetyo, Y. A., & Palisoc, N. (2023). Digital marketing and its impact on SMEs' growth: Insights from Southeast Asia. *The Journal of Asian Finance, Economics and Business*, 10(1), 89–96.

Ritter, T., & Pedersen, C. L. (2020). Digitization capability and digitalization of business models in business-to-business firms: Past, present, and future. *Industrial Marketing Management*, 86, 180–190. DOI: 10.1016/j.indmarman.2019.11.019

Rizal, A. M., & Abdullah, N. L. (2021). Digital Transformation in Malaysia's Education System: Challenges and Prospects. *International Journal of Academic Research in Business & Social Sciences*, 11(2), 113–126.

Shamsuddin, S. H., & Razali, R. (2015). Cloud Computing Adoption and its Impact on SMEs' Performance. *Journal of Information Technology Management*, 6(18), 93–104.

Silva, , S. C., & Elo, M. (2018). New digital layers of business relationships – experiences from business-to-business social media. *Progress in International Business Research*, 13, 217–241.

Stefano, P. D., & Nicotra, M. (2019). Digital innovation and entrepreneurial ecosystems: A theory-building approach. *Journal of Business Research*, 123, 1–12.

Tarhini, A., Mgbemena, C., & Mezher, T. (2019). The impact of digital transformation on organizational performance: The role of organizational culture. *Journal of Innovation & Knowledge*, 4(3), 190–198.

Tay, S. H., Choy, K. L., Chan, F. T. S., & Lam, H. Y. (2021). The impact of Industry 4.0 on logistics service providers. *Journal of Manufacturing Technology Management*, 32(1), 60–79.

Teece, D. J. (2018). Dynamic capabilities as (workable) management systems theory. *Journal of Management & Organization*, 24(3), 359–368. DOI: 10.1017/jmo.2017.75

Tham, G. Z. (2018). Digital Transformation in Malaysia: Balancing Innovation and Regulation. *International Journal of Advanced Computer Science and Applications*, 9(7), 162–171.

The Star. (2019). Malaysia to be among top 20 in the world for digital economy. Retrieved from: https://www.thestar.com.my/news/nation/2019/02/23/malaysia-to-be-among-top-20-in-the-world-for-digital-economy/

Tuominen, P., & Eerola, A. (2015). The impact of digitalization on the manufacturing industry. *Technology Innovation Management Review*, 5(11), 35–46.

United Nations Conference on Trade and Development (UNCTAD). (2019). Digital Economy Report 2019. Value Creation and Capture: Implications for Developing Countries. Retrieved from: https://unctad.org/en/PublicationsLibrary/der2019_en.pdf

Van der Laan, J., & Koster, F. (2022). Digital transformation in the public sector: The role of digital technologies in reshaping public service delivery. *Government Information Quarterly*, 39(1), 101–126.

Verhoef, P. C., Broekhuizen, T., Bart, Y., Bhattacharya, A., Dong, J. Q., Fabian, N., & Haenlein, M. (2021). Digital transformation: A multidisciplinary reflection and research agenda. *Journal of Business Research*, 122, 889–901. DOI: 10.1016/j.jbusres.2019.09.022

Wanjiku, J., & Palino, O. O. (2023). Digital colonization and decolonization. Les intelligences artificielles au prisme de la justice sociale. Considering Artificial Intelligence Through the Lens of Social Justice, 15.

World Economic Forum. (2020). The Global Competitiveness Report 2020. Retrieved from: https://www.weforum.org/reports/the-global-competitiveness-report-2020

Yamin, M. (2020). Technology adoption: Digital transformation and key technologies. *Journal of Organizational and End User Computing*, 32(4), 14–32.

Yang, S., & Zhang, Y. (2022). The Impact of Digital Transformation on Firm Performance: Evidence from China. *Sustainability*, 14(3), 1303.

Yeow, A., Soh, C., & Hansen, R. (2018). Aligning with new digital strategy: A dynamic capabilities approach. *The Journal of Strategic Information Systems*, 27(1), 43–58. DOI: 10.1016/j.jsis.2017.09.001

Zainal, H., & Ismail, M. (2022). Digital transformation in the Malaysian public sector: A qualitative analysis of key success factors. *Journal of Public Administration and Policy Research*, 14(1), 19–29.

Zhang, Z., & Jiao, L. (2021). Building Digital Capabilities for Competitive Advantage in China's Manufacturing Sector. *Journal of Manufacturing Technology Management*, 33(1), 1–17.

KEY TERMS AND DEFINITION

Digital Colonization: Wanjinko and Palino (2023) describe digital colonization as the emergence of a new technological era that places dominant countries atop poorer global regions and subdues Third-World, impoverished nations to the will of the regnant world powers through the "importation of communication equipment and foreign-produced software".

Digital Layer: All the operators and users of the urban environment are now a days involved, directly or indirectly, in the "digital layer", a virtual, online or onsite, system of digital tools that extends the comprehension, simplifies the access and, in the end influence the perception of related parties (Verdiani & Arslan, 2019).

Digital Technology: Digital technologies are refer for the progressively transforming companies which have now access to a wide range of digital systems that can manage - or help to manage - their interactions with different parties of their network (Pagani & Pardo, 2017).

Chapter 12

Navigating Remote Work Evolution Generational Perspectives on Digital Transformation

Vineeta Singh
Department of Computer Science and Engineering, School of Engineering and Technology, CSJM University, Kanpur, India

Ankur Prakash
Department of Computer Science and Engineering, Motilal Nehru National Institute of Technology, Allahabad, India

Shivam Swarup
https://orcid.org/0000-0001-5239-9365
Department of Computer Science and Engineering, Jain University, Bengaluru, India

Sumit Babu
https://orcid.org/0000-0002-1278-2367
Computer Science Department, Government Polytechnic, Kanpur, India

Mohd. Shah Alam
Department of Computer Science and Engineering, School of Engineering and Technology, CSJM University, Kanpur, India

Shesh Mani Tiwari
Department of Computer Science and Engineering, School of Engineering and Technology, CSJM University, Kanpur, India

Alok Kumar
Department of Computer Science and Engineering, School of Engineering and Technology, CSJM University, Kanpur, India

Deepak Kumar Verma
https://orcid.org/0000-0003-1508-676X
Department of Computer Science and Engineering, School of Engineering and Technology, CSJM University, Kanpur, India

Vandana Dixit Kaushik
https://orcid.org/0000-0002-0394-263X
Department of Computer Science and Engineering, Harcourt Butler Technical University, Kanpur, India

Nahed Tawfik
https://orcid.org/0000-0002-9787-2504
Computers and Systems Department, Electronics Research Institute, Cairo, Egypt

Shilpa Mehta
https://orcid.org/0000-0002-4691-3185
Auckland University of Technology, New Zealand

DOI: 10.4018/979-8-3693-6366-9.ch012

ABSTRACT

In 2020, the COVID-19 pandemic came out to be a massive destruction for human-being, in terms of life and economy. Lockdown in most of the countries invoked the teleworking as a solution to boost economy and social distancing for combating the highly transmissible virus, but teleworking can't be a full replacement. Traditional methods and working conditions are slowly replaced by digitization and by automating the processes of work. Moreover, work from home conditions have facilitated the houses as offices for the individuals in the world ultimately leading to digital transformation acceleration, replacing traditional work cultures. Information and communication technologies facilitated the digitization process. This chapter explores the journey of working conditions before pandemic, during pandemic, and possible scenario post pandemic after incorporating digitization has been done, involving also about mental/physical health effects on employees/students during pandemic and how the people and organizations collectively paced up the digitization for fulfilling the work assignments/projects.

1. INTRODUCTION

When the COVID-19 outbreak spread around the world, closing social gaps was crucial for reducing viral load on society; numerous states emphatically empowered or commanded limiting actual presence at work. Virus has crossed the cultural, technological and geographical boundaries of the past working conditions, as a result of which remotely working has created ways for work, education etc and becoming an essential element of working life, after the pandemic. With the entry of pandemic there was starting of an unprecedented try in teleworking, which will be unfolded further in the future time to time.

Accordingly, an enormous number of organizations went to computerized innovation to work, with staff telecommuting and utilizing devices, for example, videoconferencing, cloud administrations and virtual private networks i.e. VPNs. Organizations that could use prior telecommuting capacities, or quickly adjust, were ideally suited to make a generally consistent change to telecommuting and were best ready to keep up with creation levels (OECD, 2020) (Coban, 2022).

Be that as it may, not all positions can do the change to teleworking. To be quite certain, it is estimated that the majority of jobs should be able to be done from residence (Dingel and Neiman, 2020). The idea of occupation itself was cited by 89% of Australian workers who did not work remotely as the main deterrent. Additionally, their boss might not have allowed them to work remotely, their living situation might not be ideal for job role, or their house might not have access to the Internet or other necessary technology. (Australian Bureau of Statistics, 2020) (Tahlyan et al., 2022).

This note, which depends on Ker, Montagnier and Spiezia (2021) unites data on how teleworking advanced during the principal year of the COVID-19 pandemic (2020), with a specific spotlight on ideal and high recurrence (for example month to month) information distributed by public measurable associations. While the information introduced here don't thoroughly address what is going on across all OECD nations, they really do give helpful and itemized experiences. As friendly separating rules have made "remote working" inseparable from "telecommuting", these two terms are utilized reciprocally with the end goal of this note. The coming of the CoVID-19 pandemic in mid 2020 proclaimed an overall monetary slump, unexpectedly propagating the computerized change peculiarity (Yildirim, 2022).

For the reason that non-conventional modes of works are the “future of work”, regulatory frameworks may be incorporated for this, worldwide. Even as not all elements of far off, Legislation may handle unconventional working, and developing a comprehensive set of regulations for working remotely is essential, such as 96% of the firms (including corporate as well as educational) rolled out “work from home” for the reason that countrywide lockdown during pandemic year in India, and streamlining 'work from home' for certain work domains maximum influenced.

With improved recognition required through the country wide lockdown, “work from home” continues as for now also. As a coincidence, 2020 additionally noticed the 4 long-past-due Labour Codes being enacted. Moreover the codes address numerous problems, there is need of regulatory infrastructure for dealing “work from home”, that's in all likelihood for opting more relevance in upcoming time. Such typical problems therefore, need clean deliberation via remote working lens.

Workers who work remotely are needed to work from home i.e. remotely under isolation from the society. Such new scenarios have facilitated for caring child in house, as a result housekeeping responsibilities have accelerated. The accelerated home workload and care-giving are in part because of the reduced possibilities for outsourcing and in part because of the urgency of many family chores because the youngsters are obliged to live within house as per pandemic estimates. Here the point arises of married ladies with kids, who are suffering from such new scenarios, after consideration of the gender roles within side the distributing household work. This study, also involves about considering a doing gender approach, makes a speciality of how work as well as family responsibility management of middle class married ladies along with kinds have suffered in remote working condition during covid-19 lockdown measures, moreover targets to offer an perception on gender role in remote working under lockdown scenarios.

2. LITERATURE SURVEY

In this study, researchers addressed remote working related experiences of remote workers, married lady with kids from middle class family in Turkey during Covid-19 pandemic. Here authors aimed about understanding that after adapting remote working how families were influences as well as how working life was influences in Covid-19 lockdown period. Half structured interviews have been held in the course of the lockdown restrictive measures of 18 ladies for such aim. Interview queries consist of describing about regular day routine prior to pandemic as well as during the pandemic, a systematic analysis of such scenario demonstrated how changes occurred in work life as well as family life during Covid-19 lockdown period. The observers have discovered 4 primary themes: ladies' dmoestic status in the course of the pandemic, ladies' work status in the course of the pandemic, husband status in the home, experience of ladies in remote working. Findings of the research analysis demonstrated about risk of disconnecting jobs by ladies due to implementation of remote working rules and regulations under the pandemic, precarization of their labour, and integrating roles of ladies as conventional housewives only (Coban, 2022).

In this research and analysis paper researchers analysed about workers level of satisfaction through remote working. During covid-19 pandemic it was highly needed for workers as well as businesses across the globe for adapting remote working at a faster pace over the extended period of time, gaining the upper limit of remote working in various sectors. Studies done in the past time reflected merits as well as demerits of remote working. During the pandemic time, there was a unique chance of assessing experience as well as perceptions about remote working of the workers given the longer participation timings as well as extent. While organisation techniques will play a chief position in defining the upcoming forms as well as adaptability of remote working, worker possibilities and limitations, inclusive of get right of entry to suitable technology for working from home or the home scenario, were also a crucial factors. Utilizing data from 318 working adults in a U.S. representative sample, such observation makes use of a Multiple Indicator Multiple Cause Model, in short, known as MIMIC to apprehend worker delight in remote working. The provided scheme joins remote working delight with skilled and perceived advantages as well as obstacles associated with remote working, and for this reason offer a causal structural pattern authors' appreciation of the joy of telework. Additionally, authors created an ordered probit scheme, while excluding latent variables which facilitated understanding of structured diversity in telework delight among different socio-demographic groups. Findings revealed workers of older age group experienced lesser benefits and higher difficulty for remote working in comparison of middle age group people. In short older age employees were less comfortable in adapting remote working culture in contrast with middle aged employees. Findings also revealed about different level of influences over Hispanic/Latino as well as Black responders and over people who with kids attending school in online mode while residing in house. Here researchers revealed about essential elements influencing adaptation of remote working that must be taken into account by policy makers as well as employers while planning future work policies as well as arrangement in the after-pandemic world (Tahlyan et al., 2022).

With a pandemic and a persistent labour shortage, it is more important than ever for organisations to be able to retain and engage their workforce. Teleworking is one of the work organisation scenarios that really it should be considered in light of the above. The purpose of this cross-sectional study, which included 254 Canada employees working in 18 small as well as midsize businesses, was to examine the direct and indirect effects of working from home on a project and departure intention, as well as any potential moderating impact of individual &the organization attributes on the connection among working remotely, work engagement, and intent to leave during the COVID-19 pandemic. Path analyses were carried out to address these goals. Researchers discovered that, in the context of a pandemic coupled with a shortage of workers, working remotely, use of sentimentality, utilising skill, and recognition seemed to be essential aspects for institutions that wanted to expand job involvement and lessen intent to leave. Researchers' findings add to the body of knowledge by illuminating the mechanisms through which teleworking, utilisation emotion, skill utilisation, and identification are related to work involvement and intent to leave, as well as by recommending the necessity of particular intervention and prevention and composition plans (Parent-Lamarche, 2022).

Working remotely has largely evolved into a With the COVID-19 epidemic; many workers, administrators, as well as companies needed a practical based work model. The imposed nature of themeis new way of working makes it distinct from conventional telework practices. To test the viability of quasi permanent remote working like an alternative to the fulltime workplace office culture, researchers here tried to develop the term "imposed remote working," which has significantly altered the established routines of workers who have never or only occasionally involved in remote work. Consequently, a generalisation of a quasi permanent remote working arrangement would be that it is a newer, more environmentally friendly working mode; but, whether workers prepared for any such transition? Due to the challenges that the attendees encountered, including loneliness, absences, work/life dispute, etc., even though their performance increase was revealed, this investigation included 73 attendees from France, Turkey as well as Italy, clearly demonstrated that it will be too early to generalise such a new professional framework (Yildirim, 2022).

Due to the COVID19 Pandemic, more and more people have recently been required to remain at residence. Working remotely appears to have increased telework related strain, also known as burnout, which is the inability to maintain new information and communication technology in a healthy way. TERRA i.e. telework related stress is defined as physical as well as emotional distress caused by telework. TERRA has a major impact on productivity and psychophysical health, which is a major concern for occupational health globally. In order to understand whether and how telework has truly risen TERRA levels in people as well as its effects during the COVID-19 Pandemic, a meta-analysis was conducted. Employing the PRISMA guidelines, a meta analysis was conducted utilising the themes "remote work," "workplace stress," as well as "COVID19" (and related MeSH concepts) spanning three scientific databases such as Scopus, ISI Web of Knowledge as well as Pubmed. Only papers published in Italian as well as English and released till August 2021 were included in the study. In the end, 518 papers were discovered; 36 papers have been included in the assessment after duplicates were discarded and papers were excluded depending on their title, abstracts and full transcript. The majority of studies reveal that ladies who work remotely fulltime have greater TERRA levels. This prospective study emphasizes some of the TERRA-related, rising psychological and physiological health concerns, and provides a summary into the changing realities employees will have confront, in effort to enhance Overall Health Of workers using Occupational Healthcare (Gualano et al., 2022) (Raišienė et al., 2023).

3. REMOTE-WORKING FROM GENDER PERSPECTIVE

Even though women's labor-force participation is catching up to men's in industrialized countries, women still do the majority of housework (Magnier-Watanabe et al., 2024). As a flexible work environment, remote work is promoted as a potential solution to the work-life balance issue. Despite the fact that for both men and women remote working choices appear to be equal, statistics show that 63 percent of women prefer remotely working whereas only 49 percent men prefers remotely working (Alon et al., 2020).

The downsides of remote working for women include lower-wage part-time job positions because they lack better options owing to their household roles and the obligation to be the main child care provider. Moreover, study results show that workers become individualized as a result of new aspects of flexible work schedules, and they lack the togetherness, self-esteem, and shared activism that steady work alliances focus on providing (Greenhill & Wilson, 2006).

3.1 Troubles in Remote Working

Women mention the advantages of working remotely on household work, but they mostly find it totally unsustainable. The Challenges of Working from home concept is centered on the participants' c Women mention the advantages of working remotely on household work, but they mostly find it totally unsustainable. The Challenges of Working from home concept is centered on the participants' considerations, such as working remotely usually causes long-term harm to their career choices and causing precarization of one's full time work considerations, such as working remotely usually causes long-term harm to their career choices and causing precarization of one's full time work. Here we are listing some experiences of employees both male and female while working from home/ remotely working. We have put representative names like SH, HE, NI which are two initials of the name starting alphabet to maintain confidentiality of the participant for pointing to a employee or family member here. We tried to note down experiences of the remotely working women during pandemic around 15-20 women and men for this analytical study, profession of those participants was such as IT software engineer, PhD CSE student, financial consultant, freelance content writer, marketing executive, marketing manager etc. and here we are enlisting few of them as below:

SH: "Despite of so many efforts, I was unable to keep office like scenario in the home. I transformed a room to work for office for my spouse, in that room husband worked while I was working in different room. My small kid was cried mostly, seldom walking around, meanwhile I was responsible for caring my child as well as working simultaneously. Moreover, our firm lost its business during pandemic. I was worried of losing my job at first sight; they might have dismissed the female employees with kids for average or poor performance."

There are invisible obstacles facilitated through remote working for females: One of the testimonies of a woman we are listing here:

HE: "In the starting of lockdown we could not drop our daughter in my mother's home, since old age people were at high risk zone and lockdown was also there. As a result our daughter was with us for full day on each day about 15 days. Psychologically we think husband should help in household work but it does not happened. He did not help at all. For example, when our daughter was in need of changing clothes, and I was fully focused at my work, meanwhile my husband called for looking out trousers of our daughter. For effective work, I should have probably locked up my room and given the keys to him.....I am confused...Or in summary, I can say, remote working for me is like an illusion."

Despite their desire to avoid changing clothes and taking public transport, the majority of participants believe that working remotely is inefficient. The prime causes are that household tasks and infant care are intense and non-deferrable in during deadly virus. One of the participant contrasts the prepandemic experience to work from home with the present remote work circumstances:

NI: "As per my view remote working is good. It is better, for instance, before some years back, when I was working as a freelancer in translation, prior to current job. At that time situations were totally different." At that time, my daughter was not born. Next my mother was with us at that time and was coming to us with cooked meals. Often we also used to go to her for dinner and husband was working employee at office, was not working as remote worker. In home, I was able to work for 6-7 hours continuously. But now things have been widely transformed. I have two kids now for which I need all my energy to care for them. During pandemic we could not hire a household help for caring kids and helping domestic work because of high risk of infection. Even food also was not ordered from outside due to infection risk. So cooking was done by me. Even we could not hire a cleaning maid or caretaker for kid. Thus during pandemic times opportunities were totally limited and restrictive measures prevailed. It was really tough time."

Above statements of participants' demonstrate that working remotely is not a remedy to women's work-life conflict in during disease outbreak unless household sphere and responsibilities are assisted by policies of gender equality.

(a) Difficulties from Individual Perspective: Gender wise at some points, females are much comfortable in remote working, in case of household chores helpers available and cooperative family remote working is good for females. In case of middle age men who are tech savvy remote working is good. For old age people there are difficulties in remote working such health issues, inability to adapt technical chores, inability to use earplugs, screen time for long duration. For married ladies with no helping hands teleworking is not possible. For married ladies with kids and no helping hands teleworking is not possible. For middle age employees who are tech savvy and comfortable with long screen time and continuous earplug use may be comfortable, but in long term it may also created health issues such as burnout, headache, physical strain, digestive issues, eye strain, heat and radiation to skin from laptop, mobile, computers, earplug, headphone due to large duration use of technical instruments. One good point of telecommuting is flexibility, anywhere, anytime concept. You may attend meetings back to back in different countries, different educational, industrial firms. Transportation cost and time is saved. So from individual level it have merits and demerits both and it varies from person to person and for type of work.

(b) Difficulties from Organizational Perspective: Executives around the nation are dealing with new difficulties, such as real-time communication with a remote workforce (Suortti & Sivunen, 2024), maximizing productivity while juggling health issues, and managing staff that is experiencing unheard-of levels of stress, burnout as well as worry.

When individuals started working remotely, they required for people to develop interest in adapting digital habits. In fact, 87% of workers are looking to their job provider organizations to help them find a better balance (Moe & Pomsuwan, 2024). This statistic is not that surprising given that, since February, there has been a 300% increase in individuals looking out for "how to get my brain to focus."

(c) Difficulties at Society Level: There is a social belief especially in India, that girl and boy can never be same. Although level of education or earning may be the same, but certain household chores are considered for girl only such as cooking, cleaning of house, cleaning utensils, upbringing child. So there is a strong social belief in the society, as a result of which, boys after marriage never treat their wife on equal level. If wife is earning, then they have a thought of grasping all of the earnings of wife. A wife can't take decisions even related to her health, family matters etc. In laws of the married girls have also issue, if daughter in law spends some money to her siblings? All such narrow minded thoughts also create a huge barrier in remote working to the women employees. There is gender discrimination also as per societal belief system.

(d) Difficulties at Gender Level: For male middle age employees' remote working is suitable since they don't participate in household chores, while from technical perspective they are quick learners and tech savvy as compared to old age employees. Male employees find easy remote working and a bit tough commuting for work since on daily basis fixed routine and taking up public transport becomes a hectic task for some of the male employees while for others it's not so much tough task. So for male employees there are mixed responses in context of remote working.

While for married ladies it is much tough to work remotely, since they have house hold duties too. And during pandemic it was much more difficult for married ladies. Since in laws as well as husband don't support in the household, moreover getting helping aid was not possible at that time due to increased risk of infection of disease.

(e) Difficulties for Female Employees: For unmarried women remote working may be a good choice but for married ladies and for married ladies with kids was quite tough task. As per above testimonies of married female employees it can be inferred that during pandemic handling remote working was quite hectic and tough task, even post pandemic things have been changed a lot as compared to before pandemic. If supporting hands are available at home for sharing household chores, then it may be a bit easier to handle remote working. This fact can't be denied that via remote working 24*7 flexible work schedules anywhere anytime may be adapted whether for male employees or female employees. With remote working, daily public transport headache is minimized, flexible work schedules are possible, but there are also challenges. For example: at home, especially for female employees whether married or unmarried, full concentration on work is not possible, even helping hands are available but a mindset of certain deeds designed for female only creates frustration for female employees. In home even during working time through remote working, family members create disturbance in between.

For example a female PhD student from India has shared her experience:

MI:"During pandemic I started remotely working, at that time days were quite hectic, in nuclear families it is still manageable but in joint families not possible, joint family means more family members more household work, if some of them are not cooperative. In my family I was working as remote working while my brother was commuting to work; there was different treatment in the house, household chores was done by me only. Nobody was assigning work to brother. My earnings and work was equal to zero. This is societal belief: boy and girl can never be equal. If girl so much educated or earning still no value at home…even this condition becomes worse after marriage in an orthodox family situation. Things are much poorer for married ladies at their in-laws house, due to typical mindset of the society."

(f) Difficulties for Male Employees: For married male employees, remote working may have some challenges, such as poor health issues, household related tensed atmosphere may affect badly. Health issues also a great concern, large duration usage of electric equipments like computer, mobile, headphone, earplug, and long screen time duration may badly effect health in terms of eyes strain, muscle strain, ear damage etc.

4. EFFECT ON HEALTH

4.1 Effect on Physical Health

Physical strain appears, ear related issues, hearing capacity reduction due to large duration use of headphone, microphone, and electric instruments hear generation and radiation effects health badly. For long duration use is not recommended (Ciccarelli & Mariotti 2024).

4.2 Effect on Mental Health

Stress may occur due to large duration of laptop, computer use and radiation affects skin as well, skin burning may appear. Long meetings and long online classes create mental stress and poor mental ability to grasping things. Burnout, inability to learn, dissatisfaction may happen.

5. BENEFITS OF WORK FROM HOME

There are many benefits of remote working, such as:

5.1 Reduced Transportation Cost and Headache

Remote working saves cost in terms of money and time which is consumed in travelling daily from home to workplace.

5.2 Reduced Overhead

In remote working, you can just manage things remotely, whether to attend online training sessions, delivering lecture, attending seminars, presenting papers in conference, taking classes online, attending classes online, one to one interaction with instructor, organizer is possible, much chances of concentration, you can see things happening live on your screen and put your queries across. There is no stage phobia. People are connected online from anywhere of the world.

5.3 Enhanced Productivity of Employee

Due to ease of working from home, time is saved which may be utilized further in increasing productivity. Reduced headache and cost of transportation, reduced headache of changing clothes daily for commuting to work, all this may save time and employees can add-up to their productivity. Even via remote working, employees easily may work on weekends and late night without any fear or burden.

5.4 Higher Flexibility in Schedules

In remote working flexible schedules definitely help employees. As per favorable timings employees may work and deliver the content within deadline to employers.

5.5 Better Work and Life Balance

After no headache for commuting to work daily, it can save a lot of time where working remotely provides a better balance in managing life in case of flexible schedules and working allow ability as per convenience of the employees. In such case life can be balanced effectively whereas work also may be accomplished within deadline. For example, one may get ample amount of sleep and may finish work assignments by working day and night as per the suitability. Remote working has provided convenience to parents as well as students for attending classes online. Online training institutions have grown up and doing well in this field. With the advent of remote-working and ICT outsourcing was effectively managed. One instructor sitting in India may take up online classes of students residing in USA and may earn ample amount of money (Bahamondes-Rosado et al., 2023).

6. CHALLENGES AND PROBLEMS DURING REMOTE WORKING

There are many challenges too in remote working; if these can be solved effectively then burnout, health issues and strain can be managed up to some extent. Certain precautions employees need to take while working remotely (Moe & Pomsuwan, 2024) (Angelici & Profeta, 2024) (Behrens et al., 2024) (Ingusci et al., 2024).

6.1 Power Supply

Inspect switches, cables, and outlets for damage or malfunction. Don't use too many appliances or ones with too much electricity to overload outlets or extension cords.

6.2 Lighting

Make sure there is enough light (whether electrical or natural) to prevent eye strain and exhaustion.

Ventilation, heating and air conditioning are important because they ensure that employees feel comfortable, which boosts productivity and job satisfaction.

6.3 Workspace Comfort

Ensure that tables, seats, computers, keyboards, and other equipment are arranged to promote good position, convenience, and efficacy as well as to prevent problems with physical and mental health.

6a Repercussions of Pandemic for the World

International labor markets have been ravaged by the COVID-19 pandemic. Many professions faced an unclear future as tens of millions of employees lost their jobs and Millions more people quit their jobs entirely. Jobs requiring physical presence in the office or face-to-face contact were mostly at risk from social distancing policies. Unless considered necessary, those who are unable to work remotely run a considerably higher risk of having their hours or salary reduced, being placed on temporary furlough, or being permanently laid off. Which professions and workers faced the greatest danger? Unsurprisingly, the costs have disproportionately affected the poor and young workers in low-paying positions, who were least able to absorb them. On the basis of different case studies and various reports we gone through, in one line it may be concluded that working remotely actually did not work for the poor people, for the young, as well as for the women workers such as domestic helpers.

Even for the same occupations, researchers discovered considerable variability. As a result of the fact that more than half of households in the majority of emerging as well as developing nations do not even have a home computer, teleworking is much more convenient in Singapore and Norway than it is in Peru, Turkey, Mexico, Chile and Ecuador.

Who were at most risks of losing jobs during pandemic while remote working?

In general, those who operate in the food as well as lodging industry etc and wholesale and retail commerce are severely hurt because their positions are the least "remote workable" at all. This indicates that the greater than 20 million members of survey (reported on IMF blog), who operate in these industries were most at risk of losing their jobs. However, some people were at much risky situations as compared to others during pandemic, even post pandemic things are improving slowly:

Remote working is substantially less common among young employees and those without a university degree. This increased risk is in line with the age distribution of the workforce in the industries most severely impacted via lockdowns and social exclusion measures. This raises the unsettling possibility that the crisis may exacerbate intergenerational disparity.

Women could have been particularly heavily hit, which could threaten to reverse some of the recent progress gained in gender equality. Women are disproportionately concentrated in the industries that have been most negatively impacted, such as hospitality and catering services. In addition, women carry a greater share of the responsibility for household duties and childcare services because the market for these activities has been disturbed.

Employees of small and midsize enterprises and part-time employees were more vulnerable to losing their jobs. When economic circumstances worsen, part-time employees were frequently the first to be let go, and the last one to be employed. Additionally, they have become less able to gain access to conventional insurance systems and health care, which could help them survive the crisis. Particularly in developing economies, the likelihood that part-time as well as temporary employees became poor was significantly higher.

Limited income and temporarily engaged employees were highly affected, reinforcing societal injustices that have existed for a long time. Recent unemployment figures from the US and other nations support their (researchers doing survey) observation that employees at the lowest level of the earnings spectrum were least able to work from home. Income disparity was made worse by the COVID-19 situation. Poor workers, below poverty line population were striving for food and shelter. Daily wedge earners were badly affected. Even they were at the stage of die due to hunger. At that time different human welfare organizations came to the front and joined hand with government to offer food for such badly affected population. Still covering all such people was a major challenge.

In addition, personnel at the lowest of the earnings scale have already been excessively concentrated in some of the industries most negatively impacted by remote working, such as food and lodging services. Additionally, low-income individuals seemed to be more vulnerable to poverty and have scant financial security nets like credit and savings availability.

6b Protection for People who were at High Risk during Pandemic

The epidemic will probably alter how many different industries conduct business. Customers may order more takeaways, which would shrink the demand for restaurant workers' labor, and they may lean more on online shopping, which would hurt jobs in retail.

How much can be done by governments? Governments can concentrate on helping the impacted individuals and families by extending social welfare programs and insurance to protect against lost earnings and livelihood. As during rehabilitation, pay subsidies and public works initiatives can assist people in regaining their livelihoods.

Governments must improve training and education to better equip individuals for the creation of jobs in order to minimize inequality and improve people's opportunities. In order to assist employees affected via changes in the economy like COVID-19, continuous learning also entails expanding access to education and skill development.

This crisis has demonstrated clearly how important it was for people to be able to use the internet in order to continue participating in the workforce. Investing in internet technology and bridging the digital gap will enable underrepresented groups to actively engage in the economy of the future.

As per IMF calculations, PIAAC survey as well as Dingel and Niemen (2020) published in IMF blog it has been depicted that low earning workers can't work remotely such as in food, construction and hospitality, accommodation and food which is least telworkable area, construction, transportation which is also low level teleworkable, administration and support which is also low teleworkable, wholesale, retail; manufacturing area mid level teleworkable, health and social service area which also mid level remote workable, public administration and defense this is also mid level remote workable, education which remotely workable, profession, finance and insurance is remotely workable, Information and communication is remotely handled well (Dingel and Nieman, 2020). Following Table1 illustrates about it.

Table 1. Areas and Remote Working Suitability

S.No.	Level of Remote work possibility	Work Areas
1	Remote working possible	Information, communication, finance, insurance, education,
2	Remote working possible but not at full fledge	public administration and defense, health, social service,
3	Mid level remote working possible in these areas	Manufacturing, wholesale, retail, administration, support
4	Areas with least possibility of remote working	Accommodation, food, construction, transportation

6c Health Issues

Expert Martin (2020) published regarding home-based employment-related health issues. Michael Martin is a writer as well as editor based in New York, has also had work featured on Beachbody as well as Openfit with a focus on fitness and healthy living. Among many other publications, he has been featured in New York, Architectural Digest, Interview, and many more. According to Michael Martin, numerous health problems could result from remote working for continuous long hours. Some of them have been illustrated here. These preventive measures are inspired from one of the blog "Eat This, Not that" published the suggestions by Michael Martin (Martin, 2020).

We had a dream of working from home since decades, during a devastating pandemic, remote working was found as a solution for stopping world to act through digitization, ICTs in the form of remote working

No more arduous commutes, office politics, protracted meetings, or industrial-strength coffee that has burned. However, there are costs involved, and working remotely can have its own set of problems and annoyances. In fact, if you don't work intelligently, your health may wind up being in danger. The most frequent unanticipated health issues that arise when working remotely are listed below, along with advice on how to prevent them (Ingusci et al., 2024).

(i) **Loss of Hearing:** For online classes, training sessions, conference presentations if we are using earphones or headphones, then volume level must be at safer level, high level of volume may damage hearing capability of eardrum and is known as loss of hearing via high level of noise volume. For example: if someone sitting close to you may hear your volume of earplugs, headphones, that means you are hearing at very high level.

(ii) **Increase in Weight:** While working from home, one must adapt healthy lifestyle choices including healthy diet. Such as inclusion of green leafy vegetables, taking small meals 5-6 times a day in spite of three heavy meals is a healthy choice to prevent weight gain. Eat fruits, whole grains, oats etc. Try to sit at different postures while working for long hours. Try to avoid long sitting hours.

(iii) **Burnout:** If someone is not cautious while remotely working, then an employee may face serious health issues, exertion, and exhaustion due to long sitting hours, long screen time and continuous brain involvement and it also becomes quite stressful. Make a fixed schedule for daily work from home duration, as you are working in the office. Working out of usual working hours may lead to unwanted stress and burnout which can be fixed by daily strict hours of working for everyday.

(iv) **Muscle Aches:** A comfortable and suitable posture like an office chair is not possible at home. Moreover slouching and bad posture may create muscle aches. So it is essential to sit straight and in good posture to avoid any muscle strain. Back should be straight while working as sitting on computer. Also it is always important to take a short break and short walk per hour to avoid muscle aches and for muscles stretch. One must get up at least once an hour for stretching muscles.

(v) **Overwork:** In remote working people work more as they save time for getting ready for the office on daily basis, they save transportation time, no tea breaks, no small conversations; people skip lunch as well while working from home. As a result of which people overwork, which ultimately result in poor health conditions, burnout, exhaustion etc. As a preventive measure by health experts, it is always advisable to follow daily schedule as you are going to office for the work even though you are working at the dining table of your home that will prevent many unwanted health issues for an individual. Try to start and finish working hours at fixed hours on daily basis.

(vi) **Stress Eating:** There may also be excess eating by individuals due to stress. Factors may be like financial worries, helping and monitoring kids for online classes, working nearby partner. As a result of over stress, people crave energy foods such as carbohydrate rich foods, junk foods. Remote working may also become a cause of less physically active, avoiding exercise while telecommuting. While people may do daily exercises in the morning while commuting for workplace.

(vii) **Loneliness:** During pandemic loneliness was a major concern due to social meeting restrictions, isolation, remote working. Loneliness can also occur still while telecommuting because an employee has to perform well and in remote working for long hours one have to work in isolation. Human being is a social animal, long working hours from home may restrict social gathering which may affect mental health of individuals. To avoid that one must not stop talking to people via different modes of communication who uplift their moods and morale. For healthy brain and good performance on must talk to people who create motivational boost up for them to avoid negativity from life

(viii) **Anxiety:** Working remotely may be incredibly liberating. It may cause us to feel cut off from our employers, co-workers, and assignments. Anxiety over our work and job security may result from that. To overcome this one may try to contact their teachers or project head on fixed schedules in a week via phone or video conference. It is very important to communicate on schedule basis to show your work to supervisor to avoid anxiety. Our work must be recognizable that we really working in the eye of head. Working on assignments and our supervisor knows that we really working on our assignments both are two different things. If our work is not recognizing by the head, then it may lead to anxiety or frustration.

(ix) **Text Neck:** Tilting our head to look into the mobile phones may create neck strain as well as pain in the neck which are termed as 'text neck' by the doctors. Avoiding neck pain may be achieved through holding mobile at the level of the eye; there should be movement of the body while long screen time happens due to long online sessions, watching TV, movie or reading a long article.

(x) **Strain in Back:** While remotely working if sitting posture is wrong, that is if someone is sitting in an imbalance or asymmetric position then it may lead to overuse of certain body parts such as neck, shoulder, hand, arm and pain in these areas. Correct posture for avoid such strain and pain includes; arms should be on the side, elbows should be at ninety degrees while setting the level of chair with table and computer level. Legs should be parallel to the floor, sitting position should be straight, feet should be under the chair while ankles crossed; this is the ideal posture while typing on the laptop or computer. Health experts also advise, to take a break after each one hour for preventing muscle stiffness and pain. Take break, stand up and walk and drink good amount of water to prevent dehydrated muscles.

(Xi) Insomnia: Long screen hours may create problems in sleeping leading to inability to sleep known as insomnia. Preventive measures involve stop using gadgets such as mobile, laptop at-least two hours prior to sleep.

(xii) **Relationship Problems:** If a partner or both are working from home, then there are chances of less spending quality time together which may lead up to the relationship issues further. Or in case if both are telecommuting, although they are present at the same time but due to working restrictions they may face emotional challenges and stress leading up the conflict.

You spend a lot more time together than you would if one or both of you were working from an office if you and your partner are both working from home. Conflict may arise as a result of that proximity's stress. For resolving such conflicts both of them must take out some time to discuss and resolve issues.

(xiii) **News OD:** While working from home, people spend more of the time to read and hear about surrounding happenings, especially during pandemic frightening news was building up fear in the minds of individuals. Glued for long hours to social media may suppress positive immunity of individual and one may be filled constantly with negative and fear based news. To prevent such issues one may go for fixed routine meditation even 10 minutes will do the wonder to the mental health. One will feel better mentally and performance will enhance as a result.

(xiv) **Excess of Eating:** If an individual have excess to whole refrigerator then definitely he will eat in excess that is termed as binge eating. Mostly people opt for fatty foods or unhealthy foods. To avoid excess eating, plan your diet and follow accordingly. It is easy to say but tough to follow.

(Xv) Hand and Wrist Strain: Remote working i.e. to work on laptop or computer screen for whole day, which may result to strain in hand and wrist. Fingers burning sensation also may occur. In doctor's terminology carpal tunnel syndrome occurs. For preventing this we may use ergonomic mouse and take many breaks in between of the work such as every 30 minutes or one hour. Flex wrists as well as hands also during whole of the day.

(xvi) **Neck, back and Shoulder Strain:** Sitting in bad postures while 'working from home' may result to neck strain, shoulders strain, and back pain also. For preventing this, one must sit in correct posture such as shoulders must be relaxed, screen should be at the level of the eye, keyboard should be at the height of elbow, and elbow should bent at 90 degrees.

(xvii) **Eye Strain:** Eye strain happens while remotely working, due to long duration of screen hours. Eye should be exposed to a wide range of colours as well as frequencies but while using laptop or mobile inside house, light spectrum remains in blue range and lighting remains fluorescent. For preventing eye strain, go and visit outside house the first ray of the sun, greenery, natural scene. Try to take break every two hours or every one hour in between of the work and go outside to visit the natural scenes. Morning sunlight gives soothing effect to the eyes.

(xviii) **Eating Mindless:** When we work from home, it becomes easier to visit nearby kitchen frequently and that leads to excess of eating without applying mind. To avoid this one may use a glass of lemon water because mostly hunger is due to lack of hydration and due to boredom.

(xix) **Social Media:** We are aware that social media might drive us to contrast our lifestyles to those of others who have posted them, which can result in unhappiness and low self-esteem. When we work remotely but everyone else seems to be much extra social, it can be extremely painful in our views. To prevent this we must not scroll too much social sites such as Facebook or Instagram throughout the day. It can be limited to evening hours to avoid extra stress over mind.

(xx) **Background Noise:** In addition to being distracting, background noises like television or radio can also minimize the hearing effect of webinar or conference call speakers. This may result in misunderstandings and make it more challenging to absorb the new information. Raising up the level of hearing volume might not have been the greatest strategy, on whether using speakers or headphones, as it can once more make even the crucial discourse excessively loud for healthy listening. According to Branda, a health expert, reducing or eliminating the competing background noise would improve the quality of the audio signals and allow users to concentrate on what they hear rather than making an attempt to hear it.

(xxi) **Digestive Issues:** Sitting for long hours while telecommuting, and awakening in night for night shifts in case of outsourcing work, employee or student may face digestive issues as awaking during night is not good for digestion.

(xxii) **Sleeping Disorder:** If someone is working in shifts as flexible schedules, or for a outsourcing firm, for example if I am teaching a US student from India, then different time zone and in India when there is night, in USA it is day. As a result of which, a worker from India may face sleeping disorders as well as digestion related issues due awakening in night.

(xxiii) **Increase in Domestic Violence for Women:** As per a study published in a newspaper in India, more domestic violence cases were reported during pandemic. Major reasons were no helping hands in the in-laws' house, no support from husband, during work from home, married ladies were bound for double duties home, domestic chores and office work, moreover taking care of children too. All this increased burden and stress for married women and level of violence was increased over women by spouse and in laws.

(xiv) **Job Loss of Women Employees:** Due to poor performance because of family responsibilities and mid-work interruption by family members leads to loss of focus during remote working.

(xv) **Double Burden Over Women On Remote Working (Office and Household):** Due to orthodox mindset and no gender equality of the society, women employees have double burden. One more thing person telecommuting is considered as free in the eyes of family members, which is a basic human trait. In male dominating society, women workers are always downgraded.

7. FLEXIBLE WORKING ARRANGEMENTS

Flexible working arrangements were first introduced with the idea of "decent employment," or work that "balances people's aspirations for their working with current work reality." They enable flexibility in the way that work is done, including in working time, the duration of work, and the location of the job. As a result, there are many different types of flexible working arrangements that can be created depending upon the specific requirements of both workers and employers (Behrens et al., 2024).

Flexible working arrangements are one example of the flexible workplace strategies that can not only help employers but also improve worker work-life balance (Moe & Pomsuwan, 2024). Moreover, flexibility encourages underprivileged members of the workforce to balance work with some other commitments (Angelici & Profeta, 2024). Women have reacted favorably to remote working since the epidemic in India, where the labor participation rate for women (in the age group from 15 to 64, according to the ILO) is 22 percent. Studies of young Indians also show that most of them supported FWAs. Thus, it stands to reason that flexible working arrangements will play a crucial role in how India's labour regulations adjust to the problems caused by the pandemic. Lawmakers and policy framers should take this issue seriously because neither the proposed Model Standing Orders nor the recently approved Labor Codes properly address it. While the proposed Framework Standing Orders widely enable Work from home today for workers and flexible work schedules for workers in the IT sector, CSS permits women who have used maternity benefits to do so under specified conditions.

7.1 Remote Working Practices Accepted World-Wide

Understanding foreign work from home practices might help determine the challenges that a prospective Indian regulatory system might face. In light of this, we talk about the terms "telecommuting" and "flexible work schedules with flexible working arrangements".

7.2 Remote Working

Guidelines, announcements, etc. released via the Government addressing Work from home today don't include term "telework," which is the term generally used to describe the type of work from home that has been widespread in India from March 2020. The use of Information and communication technologies i.e. ICTs, such as tablets, laptops, as well as smart phones, to perform the work away from the workplace is known as timework. One of its first legal mentions can be found in a 1995 California law intended to promote "telecommuting," or the practice of state workers commuting instead of driving to work using computers and telecommunications technologies. A Memorandum of understanding on Telework outlining a basic framework balancing business and workers interests was also created by the EU in 2002.

ILO Convention No. 177 on "home work," which promotes equitable treatment for "workers of home" and other employees, has recognized working remotely. The Convention's definition of "homework" included teleworking as a continuous setup, full-time as well as part-time, and not switching with workplace labor. India has not embraced this Convention, though.

The discussion of telecommuting has centered on three types of remote work, including the stationary home office of the 1970s using desktop computers as well as telephones, the mobile office of the 2000s using lightweight wireless devices such as phones as well as laptops, and the virtual office, that is accessible via anywhere, at any moment, thanks to the most recent Information and communication technologies (until 2020). Nevertheless, the post-pandemic discourse on remote work demands a paradigm shift to address the issues brought on by the hasty shift to remote working. Technology, work-life balance, data protection as well as security, skill maintenance, and performance are a few of the enormous issues (McPhail et al., 2024). Last but not least, remote working establishes a workplace where employees can be hired to telework from almost all over the world. Whereas the tremendous shift in working environment is due to technological advancement, the regulatory framework required to effectuate this transformation must be created (Suortti & Sivunen, 2024).

8. COMPARATIVE APPROACHES TO REGULATING WFH

Jha and Bhattacharyya (2022) have discussed the legislative efforts made by Singapore, Finland, United Kingdom as well as Spain to address Work from home. They concentrated on the recently implemented remotely working law in Spain as well as other countries' instances of flexibility in work regulations.

Spain: In September 2020, legislation was passed regarding remote work. Without violating current collective negotiations or basic labor law, working remotely must be consensual, reversible, and codified in writing. The law explicitly states that it is only applicable to still employeed individuals, having engaged in "telecommuting" for at least three months, and those whose "working remotely" accounts for nearly 30percent of a full working day or an equal percentage as specified under the agreement. It also makes a distinction between "remote working" and "work from home". Companies are required to offer the tools, resources, and supplies needed to carry out and maintain remote operations. In addition, employees have rights such as the right to privacy and data security, remuneration for equipment charges, and the ability to disengage from the internet. The law also gives companies the authority to make sure that remote workers do their jobs well.

Finland: Finland has long offered flexible employment options. This is in part due to legislation that has been in place since the middle of the 1990s and gives workers the option to change their hours of work for the most flexibility. Recently, significant modifications were made to the Finnish Working Time Act, 2019 to bring about flexible work schedules, conditions, moreover the establishing "working time accounts."

This Act involves a number of flexible characteristics. Flexible work schedules are possible between workers and employers, provided that the ordinary workweek does not surpass 40 hours and that overtime is compensated. Additionally, the Act allows for individual flexible work schedules where individuals control placement and output for at least half of the operating day, laying out a variety of requirements with such a setup (for instance; allocating days for working hours, week wise resting hours as well as fixed hours of working). The Act permits contracts on "working time accounts" in which time off can be swapped for hours worked, accrued vacation time, or financial rewards. Certain components must be covered in work hours account partnerships.

The United Kingdom: In order to make flexible work arrangements, requests easier for workers with caregiving duties, a proposal and bargaining method was initiated in 2002.

The strategy of UK for flexible work schedules involves three main points: workers recommending changes with respect to hours, location of work as well as time; a responsibility on the part of the employer to examine such approval procedures "fairly," with rejections only being made on predetermined grounds (for example: added expenses as well as the loss of the ability to reorganize work among existing staff); and, in certain circumstances, worker escalation to fair work commission.

The "low touch regulation" approach employed in the UK is based on consultation and negotiation between workers and employers. Both Australia and New Zealand have already approved legislation of a similar nature.

United Kingdom: A "Work-Life Balance Directive" that was enacted by the European Union (EU) in 2019 offers flexible working arrangements for caregivers as well as parents.

A "Work-Life Balance Directive" that was enacted by the European Union (EU) in 2019 offers flexible working arrangements for caregivers as well as parents.

Singapore: Singapore offers a fascinating contrast to the UK's approach to flexible work arrangements is focused on rights. Employers may put policies in place that help workers better balance their professional and personal lives while boosting performance through the "Tripartite Standard on Flexible Work Arrangements," a voluntary standard that was developed along with a variety of stakeholders. Such employers may utilize a logo-mark in advertising and recruitment because they are desirable employers.

9. CONCLUSIONS WITH FUTURE EFFECTS

In our world in the form of remote working after Pandemic in terms of education, health, job and many other life of dimensions have been transformed but still there are a lot of barriers in India while adapting telecommute due to lack of required ICTs, lack of infrastructure, lack of required level of education in rural India as well as in small cities. So there is still a long way to go ahead in adapting remote working while considering rural India. If we consider urban cities, where work from home has adapted up to a considerable extent post epidemic. Post covid-19 things have immensely transformed, in most of the dimensions of life, remote working culture has been adapted, whether its employment, education, schooling, working in IT firms, marketing organizations and many more.

Millions of Indians' working lives have changed as a result of CoVID-19 as well as the subsequent nationwide lockdown in March 2020. 'Work from home' has forever altered how millions of individuals devote their hours of work as well as lifestyle.

In addition, the passage of three labour codes signalled a turning point in the evolution of labour legislation in India. Despite the fact that 'work from home' is not directly addressed by these codes, these blueprints are just a starting of building foundations of rules and regulations along with remote working. It has been also discussed here how 'remotely working' and flexible working scenarios have become more popular around the world and how the Codes fall short in addressing conceptual difficulties related to work from home. Therefore, a thorough and consistent regulatory framework must be added to these initial stages.

In this analytical study we have came across how 'work from home' legislation offers ideas for how our own policy can develop based on how it has changed in other nations. After the epidemic, in order to create improving conditions for workers, it is important to encourage businesses to support and adhere to such conditions by mutual consultation with workers, as is the case with Singapore's strategy to flexible working arrangements. Addressing these concerns could assist in creating a regulatory system that is suitable for India and satisfies the demands of both workers and employers in its most balanced way as our legislative framework on 'work from home' develops.

REFERENCES

Alon, T. M., Doepke, M., Olmstead-Rumsey, J., & Tertilt, M. (2020). *The impact of COVID-19 on gender equality (No. w26947)*. National Bureau of Economic Research. DOI: 10.3386/w26947

Angelici, M., & Profeta, P. (2024). Smart working: Work flexibility without constraints. *Management Science*, 70(3), 1680–1705. DOI: 10.1287/mnsc.2023.4767

Bahamondes-Rosado, M. E., Cerdá-Suárez, L. M., Dodero Ortiz de Zevallos, G. F., & Espinosa-Cristia, J. F. (2023). Technostress at work during the COVID-19 lockdown phase (2020–2021): A systematic review of the literature. *Frontiers in Psychology*, 14, 1173425. DOI: 10.3389/fpsyg.2023.1173425 PMID: 37179875

Behrens, K., Kichko, S., & Thisse, J. F. (2024). Working from home: Too much of a good thing? *Regional Science and Urban Economics*, 105, 103990. DOI: 10.1016/j.regsciurbeco.2024.103990

Ciccarelli, F. C., & Mariotti, I. (2024). Remote work, coworking spaces, and wellbeing during the COVID-19 pandemic and beyond: exploring peripheral and rural areas. In *Pandemic Recovery?* (pp. 209–220). Edward Elgar Publishing. DOI: 10.4337/9781802201116.00025

Çoban, S. (2022). Gender and telework: Work and family experiences of teleworking professional, middle-class, married women with children during the Covid-19 pandemic in Turkey. *Gender, Work and Organization*, 29(1), 241–255. DOI: 10.1111/gwao.12684 PMID: 34230782

Dingel, J., & Nieman, B. (2020, April). How Many Jobs Can be Done at Home? *Covid Economics Vetted and RealTime Papers*, (1, 3), 16–24. DOI: 10.3386/w26948 PMID: 32834177

Greenhill, A., & Wilson, M. (2006). Haven or hell? Telework, flexibility and family in the e-society: A marxist analysis. *European Journal of Information Systems*, 15(4), 379–388. DOI: 10.1057/palgrave.ejis.3000632

Gualano, M., Santoro, P., Borrelli, I., Rossi, M., Amantea, C., Daniele, A., & Moscato, U. (2022). TEleworRk-RelAted Stress (TERRA) as an emerging problem during the Covid-19 Pandemic: A Systematic Review. *Safety and Health at Work*, 13, S305–S305. DOI: 10.1016/j.shaw.2021.12.1706

Ingusci, E., Signore, F., Cortese, C. G., Molino, M., Pasca, P., & Ciavolino, E. (2023). Development and validation of the Remote Working Benefits & Disadvantages scale. *Quality & Quantity*, 57(2), 1159–1183. DOI: 10.1007/s11135-022-01364-2 PMID: 35506027

Magnier-Watanabe, R., & Magnier-Watanabe, K. (2024, January). COVID-19 and mandatory telework: Effects on gender roles and work family conflicts among Japanese dual-career regular employees with children. *Japan Forum*, 36(1), 1–29. DOI: 10.1080/09555803.2023.2200967

McPhail, R., Chan, X. W., May, R., & Wilkinson, A. (2024). Post-COVID remote working and its impact on people, productivity, and the planet: An exploratory scoping review. *International Journal of Human Resource Management*, 35(1), 154–182. DOI: 10.1080/09585192.2023.2221385

Moe, S. H., & Pomsuwan, S. (2024, March). The Impact of Digital Workplace Transformation, Remote Working and Working Environment Towards Employee Performance Throughout the Covid-19 Pandemic in Interior Industry in Bangkok. In Proceeding National & International Conference (Vol. 16, No. 1, pp. 205-212).

Parent-Lamarche, A. (2022). Teleworking, Work Engagement, and Intention to Quit during the COVID-19 Pandemic: Same Storm, Different Boats? *International Journal of Environmental Research and Public Health*, 19(3), 1267. DOI: 10.3390/ijerph19031267 PMID: 35162291

Raišienė, A. G., Danauskė, E., Kavaliauskienė, K., & Gudžinskienė, V. (2023). Occupational stress-induced consequences to employees in the context of teleworking from home: A preliminary study. *Administrative Sciences*, 13(2), 55. DOI: 10.3390/admsci13020055

Suortti, C., & Sivunen, A. (2024). Communicative tensions in remote work during the Covid-19 pandemic. *Management Communication Quarterly*, 38(2), 386–412. DOI: 10.1177/08933189231199052

Tahlyan, D., Said, M., Mahmassani, H., Stathopoulos, A., Walker, J., & Shaheen, S. (2022). For whom did telework not work during the Pandemic? understanding the factors impacting telework satisfaction in the US using a multiple indicator multiple cause (MIMIC) model. *Transportation Research Part A, Policy and Practice*, 155, 387–402. DOI: 10.1016/j.tra.2021.11.025 PMID: 36570728

Yildirim, G. E. (2022). A New Style of Working: Imposed Teleworking in the Context of the covid-19 Pandemic. *Journal of Labor and Society, 1*(aop), 1-26.

Chapter 13
Navigating the Impact of Digital Technologies on the Multigenerational Workforce in the Post-COVID-19 Work Environment

Melina Doargajudhur
https://orcid.org/0000-0002-0287-9691
Edinburgh Napier University, UK

Shabanaz Baboo
https://orcid.org/0000-0002-0190-5413
Curtin University Mauritius, Mauritius

ABSTRACT

In the wake of the pandemic, workplace dynamics have changed significantly, particularly the integration of digital technologies. The new workplace is also experiencing changes in its demographics as this is the first time in history that five generations are working together, causing generational disparities leading to misperceptions, stereotypes, and intergenerational biases when adapting to and utilizing digital tools. The lack of systematic literature reviews analyzing digital technologies and artificial intelligence (AI) among multigenerational employees in the fourth industrial revolution context demands further investigation. The chapter adopts a systematic literature review approach to explore the adoption of digital technologies including AI among a multigenerational workforce, highlighting the factors affecting the adoption. The chapter also provides several strategies that organizations can employ to bridge generational gaps and foster a more agile, productive and cohesive multigenerational workforce.

DOI: 10.4018/979-8-3693-6366-9.ch013

INTRODUCTION

The COVID-19 pandemic has brought about significant changes to the role of technology in the workplace. Organizations across various occupational sectors accelerated their plans to adopt technologies, especially emerging AI technologies and automation for the virtualization of work (Yu et al., 2023). In the process of transformation, workforce operations, and management have been significantly impacted by digital transformation drivers and modes such as artificial intelligence, machine learning, blockchain, cloud, and data analytics (Moore et al., 2022; Naraidoo et al., 2024). This led to the explosive growth in virtual work, and greater reliance on digital communication coupled with the revolution of industry 5.0 (Adel, 2022; Kolade & Owoseni, 2022). Employees across the globe continue to adapt to new ways of working in the new normal digital corporate environment (Raghuram et al., 2019; Doargajudhur et al., 2023,2024; Hill et al., 2024). Since then, there has been no turning back and employees have been pushed to familiarize themselves with digital tools in the workplace to perform various tasks at work (Selimović et al., 2021) despite security concerns. While employers are grappling with a myriad of technological transformations within the workplace, many are not conscious of the significant shift caused by the presence of multi-generations shaping the workforce's future (Collinson & Hodin 2023).

The present workforce is more generationally diverse than it has ever been. According to Smith & Garriety (2020), it is currently observed that there are five generations in the workforce. The Silent generation is the one that is getting to the end of their careers. They were born during the Depression and Second World War, and they value dedication and hard work. Baby boomers are among the largest generations in the workplace. They were born in the post-Second World War boom, and they held leadership roles in organizations. This generation experienced having more women in the workforce. Gen X is a smaller generation compared to baby boomers and they are considered as the middle child of generations. They have grown up with two working parents and they have developed the ability to work independently and are self-directed. Millennials are the largest generation in the workforce and have inspired generations to change and adapt to a digital world. The generation went through phases of the 9/11 terrorist attacks, two wars, the expansion of the internet, and the ubiquity of mobile devices. Gen Z is considered to be the youngest in the workforce and they have grown up with social media. They understand the value of bringing people together around ideas to make changes happen. They have an entrepreneurial mindset and are resilient.

In their study, Collinson & Hodin (2023) stated that the U.S. Bureau of Labor Statistics estimates that one in four workers will be aged 55 or older by 2031 and that those workers aged 65 and above will represent the fastest-growing segment of the workforce. Additionally, the literature reported that by 2026 there will be a global increase in the number of adults in that age range (>=65) by 236 million (He et al., 2016; Magsamen-Conrad & Dillon, 2020). As per Torpey (2020), it has been projected that the millennials will shift into the 35 to 44 years old groups between 2019 to 2029 and this category will increase nearly to 4.5 million over the decade by 2029. More than 38.5 million people aged 35 to 44 are expected to fit into that cohort and will outnumber all other age groups in the labor force. While baby boomers who are staying in the labor force will shift to the two oldest groups aged 65 to 75 and older, they are projected to account for about 16.5 million people in the labor force by 2029.

Gen Alpha born around 2010, is described as an incredible group of youngsters raised in an unprecedented technological change that will be entering the workforce in the next coming years and will represent the 6th generation in the labor force soon. They are considered the most tech-savvy generation to date and they exhibit reluctance toward traditional team collaboration (Oleka-Onyewuchi, 2023).

These societal shifts have given rise to the multigenerational workforce and this unprecedented diversity brings an exciting array of skills and expertise, perspectives, and life experience that can enhance an organization's innovation, productivity, and overall performance.

While the adoption and usage of digital tools in the workplace bring a significant amount of benefits, it also comes with a panoply of unintended consequences to the employees thus creating the need to understand this phenomenon through the multigenerational lens to find the right model for both organizations and employees (Marsh et al., 2022). The amalgamation of the human and digital world has given rise to Industry 5.0 which is affecting the expectations of the workforce, especially in a multigenerational context (Chopra & Bhilare 2020). Larger disparities are starting to be felt in the workplace around how different generational cohorts adopt and use technology, processes, and productivity. Similarly, different generations may be vulnerable to cyberattacks in distinct ways. The continuous technological evolution has spurred debates over the adaptability potential of a multigenerational workforce. Increasingly, organizations consist of a diverse generation working together, thereby leading to disparities in how different age groups handle workplace technology. For instance, digital natives are known to easily adapt to changes since they belong to the tech-savvy generation as compared to an aging workforce who are not too familiar with technology (Magsamen-Conrad & Dillon, 2020). The obstacles faced by different generations emphasize the need to better align people, technology, and processes for companies to succeed and flourish (*Information Week,* 2021). Moreover, the challenges that Industry 5.0 is anticipating bringing along will further exacerbate the situation which indicates that organizations must prepare for this new revolution (Adel, 2022).

Hence, to foster positive working relationships and leverage shared experiences among generations, it is crucial to embrace anchors such as culture, workspace design, and technologies to unite employees of all ages. We argue that it is complex to align digital technology across a workforce that spans multiple generations. While generational divides can lead to divisions within organizations, they can also be leveraged to bridge gaps in the workforce through the effective use of cutting-edge technology and a robust corporate culture. In light of this, our chapter examines the dynamics of multigenerational workplace technology adoption and usage in the post-pandemic context by presenting a comprehensive analysis of generational differences in the workplace.

While extensive research has examined generational differences across various work domains such as work values (King et al., 2017; Myers & Sadaghiani, 2010; Twenge et al., 2010), work expectations (Magni & Manzoni, 2020; Moore et al., 2015), technological approaches (Colbert et al., 2016; Ghobadi & Mathiassen, 2020; Jarrahi & Eshraghi, 2019; Nikou et al., 2018; Okros, 2020), and education (Giray, 2022; Marrero Galván et al., 2023; Mohr & Mohr, 2017), most of these research have focused on the adoption and integration of digital technologies within the organizational systems and practices from a macro perspective often neglecting the individual employees thus leaving a gap in understanding the micro-level factors impacting on digital technology adoption on the workforce. Basit et al. (2021) confirmed that IT research on AI has primarily focused on technical aspects while management researchers are increasingly interested in the adoption and acceptance of digital technologies such as AI within the organization among individual employees (Cheng et al., 2023).

Moreover, there is a lack of systematic literature reviews that analyze the adoption of digital technologies including AI among multigenerational employees in the context of the fourth industrial revolution (Al-Momani, 2023). Notably, the workforce is characterized by five generations working together including Veterans, baby boomers, generation X, generation Y (millennials) and generation Z working together for the first time in history (Burton et al., 2019). The systematic literature review in this chapter therefore addresses these gaps and provides scholars and practitioners with an up-to-date review of factors impacting on the adoption of digital technologies including AI adoption among employees of different age groups within the workplace and also provides a list of strategies that companies can implement.

RESEARCH OBJECTIVES

RO1: To investigate the key contributions of previous studies done in the field of AI adoption among multigenerational employees.
RO2: To identify the factors that affect the adoption of AI in organizations across generations.
RO3: To identify strategies that companies can use to ease the adoption of digital technologies including AI in a multigenerational workforce.

METHODOLOGY

In this book chapter, a systematic literature review on the adoption and usage of digital technologies including AI was conducted to explore the maturity of the research area, extract key factors of adoption, and highlight potential strategies for companies. Major databases such as Business Source Complete (EBSCO) and ScienceDirect will be used to examine top-tier journals published in the management and IT fields. Databases include Emerald, ProQuest Google Scholar, and Science Direct (Hewett et al., 2017; Yu et al., 2023) to examine the top-tier journals published in business management and technology advancement fields. The search also ensures that a wide range of literature is covered in this book chapter. The search keywords used include "Digital technologies in the workplace", "AI technologies", "Multigenerational workplaces", "adoption of AI", "Adoption of digital technologies", and "technology adoption and multi generations". The search might not cover all articles relevant to this study, but we are confident the paper identifies a comprehensive range of literature in the fields in the last 3-4 years to guide the direction for theory development and future research.

As a result, several reports, articles, and conference papers were produced. These were then selected to only include the most recent and important publications that were relevant to our chapter. In addition, these papers were carefully examined to determine their relevance to the current study, with special attention paid to the title, abstract, and keywords. Quality assessment tools were employed to enhance the validity and reliability of our chapter. A thorough methodological approach was used to address potential publication biases and take publication years into account, ensuring a balanced representation of the literature

SYSTEMATIC LITERATURE REVIEW

Multigeneration in the Workplace

In the present era, workplace values and attitudes are a prominent topic of discussion regarding generational disparities. This is understandable given that an individual spends a large portion of their lifetime at work and the workplace is a setting in which generational differences are likely to be evident due to the interaction between various generations performing similar occupational roles.

Generations have been conceptualized as a group of people sharing experiences and events such as economic conditions, lifestyle, technological advancement, habits, and culture from a similar period in history and who have developed a shared understanding of that period (Gilleard, 2004; Cucina et al., 2017; Klopotan et al., 2020). These particular occurrences have influenced the professional and personal values of members of identified groups, which in turn has shaped their work behavior and results.

The Silent Generation, sometimes referred to as "Radio Babies" or "Traditionalists," comprises old senior citizens who experienced both the Great Depression and World War II. Many of the generation's views towards the workplace have been influenced by these difficult experiences. In the present era, there is a large number of professionals from this generation who are partially retired. Despite the Silent Generation's reputation for traditionalist behavior and a preference for working inside the system as opposed to changing it, many of this generation's less quiet and unconventional members had a tremendous impact on world history. As a result of the challenges that they faced, they developed pragmatic, patient, and conservative views (Lissitsa et al., 2022). They are also known to appreciate their employment and employers more as a result of the great depression's economic crisis. In the workplace, they appreciate stability, are disciplined, and respect the laws. Literature has also reported that traditionalists devote their entire professional lives to one organization (Spiro, 2006).

The baby boomer generation is defined by Gursoy et al. (2008) as individuals born during or following World War II. This generation values hard work and is extremely diligent and dedicated to both their careers and personal objectives. Due to the challenging living circumstances following multiple life-changing experiences, baby boomers are also known to be a highly dedicated, career-focused, and family-focused generation (Fishman, 2016). They believe in changes, growth, and expansion, and seek promotion by being loyal to their organizations and by working long hours (Spiro, 2006). Research indicated that the workplace dynamic for baby boomers shifted with the arrival of women into the workforce (Cucina et al., 2017). Additionally, during the pandemic, a large number of baby boomers retired, which continues to open up positions for younger people.

According to Adams (2000), the information age, which includes the internet and e-mail, has caused Generation X to ask for immediate feedback at work more than previous generations. Job outsourcing and corporate downsizing may cause Generation X employees to become less devoted to their employers and to see them more negatively (Adams, 2000). Literature has also reported that, as compared to Millennials, Gen X tends to be more agile when embracing new technology to meet their needs following the pandemic (Moore et al., 2022).

Generation Y, also known as 'Millennials', 'digital natives' are those who were born after 1980 and are regarded as having "grown up" with digital technology (Magsamen-Conrad & Dillon, 2020). Compared to previous generations in the workforce, this generation contains the most significant behaviors. exhibit the most noteworthy characteristics. They are known for their high levels of ambition, drive, and entrepreneurship. With smartphones, email, and social media becoming a part of daily life, the majority of Millennials are constantly connected to the internet (Jerome et al., 2014).

Generation Z, also known as 'Gen Z', 'Gen Zers', 'iGen' and 'post-Millennials' is the generation born between the mid-1990s and early 2010s. Gen Z is regarded as the first generation to be the first true "digital natives", and has the features of the 'net generation' since they were raised in a digital and technological environment, were accustomed to using technology at a young age, engaged in social media, and are even perceived as being addicted to technology (Bencsik et al., 2016; Lanier, 2017; Klopotan et al., 2020; Magano et al., 2020). This generation is characterized by their high levels of ambition, creativity, and self-confidence (Pataki-Bittó & Kapusy, 2021), but they are also known to be pragmatic and take things as they come (Scholz, 2019). They are entrepreneurial but are likely to change jobs more frequently than previous generations because they seem driven by opportunities to expand their skills and find their dream job (Magano et al., 2020). They do not mind changing jobs rapidly if they are not happy, but at the same time, they are driven by higher pay, meaningful work, growth prospects, and a strong team environment (Csiszárik-Kocsír & Garia-Fodor, 2018).

Table 1 below summarises the generational differences in the workplace and highlights the developmental leaps brought about by technological advancements. In parallel, it outlines other important features distinguishing each generation.

Table 1. Generational Differences in the Workplace

Generation	Silent/ Traditionalists (1925 – 1946)	Baby Boomers (1946 – 1959)	Gen X (1960 – 1979)	Millennials (Gen Y) (1980 – 1994)	Gen Z (1995 – 2010)
Characteristics	Loyal, Straightforward, Dependable, Appreciate hierarchies and procedures, Interpersonal respect, Determined, Resilient	Competitive, Inflexible, Respect for hierarchy, Passive, Cynicism, Exaggerated modesty, Ambitious, Clear goals	Fair play, Rule abiding, Less respect for hierarchy, Need to prove themselves, Organized with a strong work ethic, Flexible	Open-minded, Competitive, Arrogant, The desire for independence, No respect for tradition, Sociable	Highly ambitious, Self-confident, Less focused, Entrepreneurial, Global, Lack of consequential thinking, Differing viewpoints, Easily distracted, No desire to make sense of things, Flexible, Competitive
Context/ Shaped by:	Depression, World War II, Movies and radio	Civil Rights, Postwar, Dictatorship	Political transition, The fall of the Berlin Wall, Meritocracy and capitalism dominate, Dot com boom	Globalization, Economic stability, 9/11, The Internet	Social networks, Mobility and multiple realities, The Great Recession, Life after 9/11, Access to technology/Digital natives
Values/Motivated by:	Recognition, Respect, Loyalty, Discipline, Hard work, Attention to rules, Stable and structured work environments, Work Ethics	Teamwork, Patience, Hard work, Respect for traditions, Loyalty to organizations, Soft skills, Sense of duty	Hard work, Diversity, Personal-professional interests, Curiosity, Openness, Practicality, Personal Development, Work-life balance, Efficiency	Unique work experiences, Flexibility, Responsibility, Creativity, Success orientation, Mobility, Work-life balance, Sustainability, Sense of belonging in professional lives	Creativity, Individuality, Personalization, Diversity, Initiator, Live for the present, Brave, Rapid content search and information access, Empathy
Aim:	Working within the system	Solid existence	Secure position, Multi-environment	Competition for leadership positions, Seek job security, Promotion opportunities	Live for the present
Communication Style:	Handwritten notes Personal touch	Phone calls Face-to-face	Phone calls Face-to-face, Email	Instant Messaging, Email, Texts	Instant Messaging, Texts, Social-Media, Open communication style, Video calls

continued on following page

Table 1. Continued

Generation	Silent/ Traditionalists (1925 – 1946)	Baby Boomers (1946 – 1959)	Gen X (1960 – 1979)	Millennials (Gen Y) (1980 – 1994)	Gen Z (1995 – 2010)
Technology Familiarity:	Not familiar with technology	Based on self-instruction and incomplete, Forgetful technophobes	Adapt to technologies to some extent, Perceive new technologies such as smartphones as a source of distraction, Had an internet connection when entering the workforce	Tech friendly, Part of their everyday life; Digital Natives	Highly tech-savvy Very familiar and comfortable with the latest technologies, Digital device addicts, Intuitive
Behavior:	Conformist, Used to transactional leadership	Revolutionary, Idealism, Collectivist	Competitive, Materialistic, Individualistic	Oriented to self, Globalist, Questioning	Realistic, Dialogue, Communaholic
View:	Clear expectations, Fixed work schedules	Unified thinking, Communal	Medium-term, Self-centered, Flexible work schedules	Short-term, Egotistical	Live for the present, No sense of commitment, Be happy with what you have
Relationship	Personal	Personal	Virtual networks, Personal	Network, Virtual	Superficial and virtual
Self-realization	Perform job in exchange of paycheck	Conscious career building, Bonuses, Clear paths to promotion	Rapid promotion	Immediate	Questions the need for it at all

Source: Adapted from Bencsik & Machova (2016)

Theories Used in Previous Studies on Multigenerations in the Workplace

Generational Theory

The generational theory, pioneered by Strauss-Howe (Howe & Strauss, 2000) posits that it is likely to have some significant differentiation between groups of different ages, while individuals of similar ages share formative experiences that might result in significant and widespread similarities in personal traits. Some scholars employ this approach to perform retrospective analyses in an attempt to explain why a group of people of a certain age seems to have similar features, while others propose that it is possible to predict the emergence of common traits among a group by evaluating the influence of significant experiences or events (Okros & Okros, 2020).

Adoption Theories

A review of studies reveals that most studies carried out on the adoption of digital technologies including AI and automation in the workplace have relied on theoretical frameworks such as TAM, UTAUT, gratification theory, TOE, TPB, and the like. A significant amount of research has been conducted on work-related behaviors and actions of millennials and Generation Z employers (Kaifi et al., 2012; McDonald, 2015). Most of these studies relied on the use of theoretical frameworks such as the gratification theory and Technological Acceptance Model (TAM) to investigate generational technology adoption (Calvo-Porral & Pesqueira-Sanchez, 2020; Lee et al., 2003; Scherer et al., 2019).

Variables from the TAM model such as perceived ease of use and perceived usefulness have served as inspirations in a lot of research. Drawing from UTAUT, social influence is a major behavioral motivator for employees to start using new technology in the workplace (Ambati et al., 2020; Wiesche et al., 2017). TAM is the most effective model and theory used in research (Ala'a & Ramayah, 2023a; Al-Momani, 2023).

Moreover, a lot of research has conducted systematic literature reviews to synthesize research conducted on AI adoption in the workplace. The following section summarizes the previous research findings:

Jetha et al. (2023) and Bodea et al. (2024) researched the work changes in the context of AI and propose a research agenda to examine the effects of AI on the relationship between socio-economic, political and working conditions and worker health and employment outcomes, Braganza et al. (2021) focused on the impact of AI adoption on psychological contracts, job engagement, and employee trust. Naude (2020) discusses the potential impacts of AI adoption, and the author warns organizations against underestimating the long-term impacts of AI and stresses the need to consider the potential consequences of AI adoption in the workplace. Regona et al. (2022) focus on the construction industry and how AI's adoption challenges and opportunities. Jain et al. (2021) focus on AI's employability implications in healthcare. Tursunbayeva and Renkema (2022) investigate the impact of AI implications in the healthcare sector on job design. While Jetha (2023) highlights the implications of AI adoption for employment opportunities, work environments, and worker health, safety, well-being, and equity, Jaisal et al. (2021) discuss the challenges such as upskilling of employees for AI adoption in multinational corporations. Nguyen & Malik (2021) conducted a study about attitudes and readiness towards AI adoption and usage across different levels and geographics of organizations.

Furthermore, there are several SLRs available in the academic literature studying the use of AI among organizations. Lee et al. (2023) studied the application of AI in organizations, and Mariani et al. (2023) studied the intersection between AI and organizational innovation. Kaushal et al. (2023) conducted an SLR to determine the future research agenda in integrating AI with human resource management while Jabota *et al.* (2023) systematically reviewed the intelligent human resources for AI adoption. AI and HRM were systematically reviewed by (Tuffaha & Perello-Marin, 2021; Votto et *al.*, 2021). The role of AI in entrepreneurial activity was also addressed in SLR by Blanco-Gonzalez-Tejero ct al. (2023) and Giuggioli & Pellegrini (2023). Verma et al. (2021), Chintalapati & Pandey (2022), and Darlington & Patience (2023) conducted an SLR to investigate the deployment of AI in marketing. Pereira et al. (2023) conducted an SLR to investigate the influence of AI on workplace outcomes and Pietronudo et al. (2022) conducted an SLR about the role of AI in decision-making in organizational management of innovation. Reis et al. (2021) conducted an SLR on the effect of AI on public employment and its influence on politics. Al-Momani (2023) conducted an SLR to identify the primary factors that influence the adoption of AI among organizations.

BARRIERS AND CHALLENGES IN ADOPTING DIGITAL TECHNOLOGIES IN THE WORKPLACE ACROSS GENERATIONS

The successful integration of digital technologies including AI and automation in organizations requires addressing generational differences in digital proficiency and ensuring that all employees possess the necessary skills and support to effectively use them. There is little clarity on the factors that impact employees' perspectives on the usage and adoption of AI techniques. The main reason behind this gap is the lack of research focusing on the understanding of employees' preferences towards the adoption of AI. Therefore, it is of great significance to understand these factors as employees play a major role in the growth and sustainability of an organization (Alsheibani et al., 2018; Ambati et al., 2020). Challenges of AI adoption in organizations can be dependent on factors involving employees such as the risk of losing their jobs and resistance to adoption or migration of technology (Ambati et al., 2020). The main challenges that employees face is technological anxiety, resistance, different levels of digital literacy, job security, skills gap, adaptability, cognitive flexibility, and organizational support among many others. AI adoption may make employees feel insecure and employees are more likely to quit their jobs (Brougham & Haar, 2017; Lichtenthaler, 2019) concluded that employees' attitudes may impact their technology acceptance decisions which can in turn influence the organization's performance and innovation.

Factors Impacting Digital Technologies Adoption

The following provides an overview of the factors impacting on adoption of digital technologies including AI in the workplace and their outcomes on individuals. Table 2 below provides an overview of recent research on digital technologies such as AI in the workplace and the theories that have been used and the factors impacting on adoption of these digital technologies.

Table 2. Overview of previous studies on digital technology adoption in the workplace and theories used (Al-Momani, 2023)

Authors	Objectives	Theory	Statistical Technique	Factors impacting on adoption of AI technologies
Chatterjee et al., (2020)	To examine the behavioural intention to adopt a CRM system that incorporates AI technology by workers in Indian firms	TAM and Motivational Theory	SmartPLS	Perceived Usefulness, Perceived Ease of Use, Utilitarian Attitude, Hedonic Attitude: Moderator: Leadership Support, Behavioural Intention
Chatterjee et al., (2021)	To identify the factors that exert influence on the adoption of an AI-integrated CRM system by agile organizations	TAM	SmartPLS	Perceived Usefulness, Perceived Ease of Use, Trust, Attitude, Behavioural Intention, Adoption
Islam et al., (2022)	To identify the factors affecting the adoption of AI-based technology in the context of recruitment	UTAUT	SmartPLS	Performance Expectancy, Effort Expectancy, Social Influence, Facilitating Conditions, Perceived Credibility, Behavioral Intention; Moderator: Firm Size, gender, Actual Behaviour
Ghani et al., (2022)	To examine the factors influencing the adoption of AI in manufacturing companies	TOE	SPSS	IT Capability, Top Management Support, Government Support, Adoption

continued on following page

Table 2. Continued

Authors	Objectives	Theory	Statistical Technique	Factors impacting on adoption of AI technologies
Pan et al., (2022)	To understand the factors that impact and hinder the adoption of AI in the process of recruiting employees	TOE and Cost Theory	N/A	Relative Advantage, Complexity, Company Size, Technology Competence, Industry, Regulatory; Moderator: Asset Specificity, Uncertainty, Actual Behaviour
Phuoc (2022)	To examine and assess the usage of AI applications at the organizational level in Vietnam	TOE	AMOS	Technical Compatibility, Relative Advantage, Technical Complexity, Managerial Support, Managerial Capabilities, Organisational Size, Organizational Readiness, Government Involvement, Market Uncertainty, Competitive Pressure, Vendor Partnership, Adoption
Razak & Ismail (2022)	To examine the factors impacting the acceptance of Robotic Process Automation by accounting employees	TAM, DOI, TOE, and Hofstede cultural model	SmartPLS	Uncertainty Avoidance, Masculinity, Confucian Dynamism, Compatibility, Trialability, Relative Advantage, Complexity, Organisational Competence, Top Management Support, Training and Education
Sethibe & Naidoo (2022)	To determine the factors that are impacting on firms' adoption of robotic technology for auditing purposes	UTAUT	SPSS	Performance Expectancy, Effort Expectancy, Social Influence, Facilitating Conditions; Moderator: Age, Gender, Experience, Behavioural Intention
Upadhyay et al., (2022)	To identify the willingness of entrepreneurs to adopt AI within the context of digital entrepreneurship	TAM, UTAUT, TPB, Motivational Model (MM)	SmartPLS	Performance Expectancy, Effort Expectancy, Social Influence, Hedonic Motivation, Inconvenience, Uncertainty, Openness, Affordance, Attitude, Generativity, Behavioural Intention
Vărzaru (2022)	To assess the level of acceptance of AI technology within the accounting profession in Romanian firms	TAM	SmartPLS	Perceived Ease of Use, Perceived Usefulness, Users' Satisfaction, Behavioural Intention, Actual Behaviour
Wanner et al., (2022)	To understand the level of acceptability of intelligent systems among end users	UTAUT, Explanation Theory, and User Trust Theory	SmartPLS	Performance Expectancy, Effort Expectancy, Attitude, Trust Propensity, Ability Beliefs, System Transparency; Moderator: Gender, Age, Experience; Behavioural Intention

AI is the key driver of the fourth industrial revolution that organizations are implementing to solve various daily management challenges (Schwab, 2017; Syam & Sharma, 2018). The rapid development of AI and the corresponding innovative technologies such as robots, smart devices, and the Internet of Things (IoT) has been significantly changing the interaction between employees and organizations as the latter are adopting and applying AI to establish processes and expedite tasks that were conducted by employees once (Lariviere et al., 2017).

Other authors such as Yu *et al.* (2023) synthesize the academic research by categorizing the antecedents of AI adoption as firstly personal subsystem which consists of social and people-related factors such as demographic, psychosocial aspects and employees' degree of professional skills such as self-efficacy. Secondly, organizational structure subsystems such as business strategy and operations, top management support, organizational culture, and organization size. Thirdly, technical subsystems comprise of technology-related factors such as technology readiness and practices. Finally, environmental factors encompass the characteristics of the context where the system operates such as competitive pressures, customer responses, social and ethical challenges, and government regulations. The authors also categorized the outcomes of AI adoption and application as individual outcomes consisting of job-related outcomes (Turnover intention, commitment, job performance, career satisfaction); well-being outcomes such as sense of belonging, psychological distress, emotional distress, isolation and disconnection, stress, burnout, cynicism, nervousness; organizational outcomes such as improve labor effectiveness, enhance operational efficiency, drive innovation, promote brand image, improve customer service quality, optimize decision making and employment outcomes such as technological unemployment, job insecurity, endangered jobs, job skill polarization.

DIGITAL TECHNOLOGIES AND THE MULTIGENERATIONAL WORKPLACE

It has been observed that technological acceptance in the workplace has a generational dimension which is of interest to companies. Given Fourth Industrial Revolution advancements and the rise of Industry 4.0, technological acceptance has been a crucial issue as they present both opportunities and challenges for organizations to remain competitive and not be left behind. A key variable that shapes the attitudes and behaviors toward technology in the workplace is age (Ng & McGinnis Johnson, 2015; Bako, 2018; Asoba & Mefi, 2022). As talent has become a critical determinant of competitiveness, companies are focusing on talented employees to drive organizational competitiveness (Gallardo-Gallardo et al., 2019) thus making it challenging for the multigenerational workforce to acquire the same level of digital competence thus leading to an increasing concern on the role of technology in the workplace from (Asoba & Mefi 2022).

While a lot of research has analyzed the adoption of AI and its outcomes, very few have analyzed the same through a multigenerational lens. The following section summarizes some of the research that has analyzed the adoption of digital technologies across generations. Flinchbaugh et al. (2018) stated that the broadening age structure in the workforce nowadays is due to both the ongoing entrance of younger workers and the continued employment of the aging workforce due to the increase in life spans and the extensions in retirement ages (Burtless, 2013).employees from younger generations reported preferences for improved work/life balance and adoption of digital technologies as compared with other generations (Hershatter & Epstein, 2010; Fin & Donovan, 2013). The complex nature of a multigenerational workforce has been emerging simultaneously with global growth in knowledge-intensive and professional service sectors.

The primary difference between the youngest and the existing workforce members' characteristics centers on the dominance of digital technologies throughout the youngest entrants' formative years and the emphasis on collective, other focused learning opportunities driven by these new technologies (Hershatter & Epstein, 2010; Myers & Sadaghiani, 2010; Rosen & Lara-Ruiz, 2015). Since the younger generations have used digital technologies, they have developed digital competency with new technologies of real-time information gathering and shared communication such as video sharing, texting, and blogging (Deal et al., 2010; Palfrey & Gasser, 2011; Wesolowski, 2014).

Bennet et al. (2008) acknowledged the fact that older generations may not necessarily be less "technologically competent" than younger generations since the older generations developed the internet. However, it is acknowledged that knowledge and attitudes towards communication technologies and the importance of such technologies during younger generations' formation years bring a unique age-related identity perspective which is not found in most members of an older generation (Bennett et al., 2008).

The differences in the formative experiences between generations have created noticeable and predominant differences in their workplace communication preferences (Brack, 2012; Cogin, 2012; Rosen & Lara-Ruiz, 2015; Twenge et al., 2010; Twenge, 2010). One prominent difference is the workers' preference for individual-oriented, stable experiences through primarily face-to-face communication versus the younger generation's preferences for flexible, shared experiences via digital technology (Proserpio & Gioia, 2007; McGuire et al., 2007; Benson & Brown, 2011; Kultalahti & Liisa Viitala, 2014; Firfiray & Mayo, 2017). The potential challenge with these differences can be damaging especially in knowledge-based roles where effective performance relies upon the trickle-down effect of tacit information sharing from mature and experienced employees (Chuang & Liao, 2010). Moreover, an employee's failure to embrace workplace technologies that incorporate real-time, synchronous job-related exchanges can equally compromise quality performance (Setia et al., 2013).

Annosi et al. (2024) suggested that different generations may exhibit different attitudes toward the adoption of new technologies since different generations show differences in terms of personalities, work behaviors, and career experiences. Therefore, examining generational variations in the managerial cognitive frameworks can be a crucial element in the integration of digital technologies within organizations (Lyons & Kurons 2014). The authors conducted research through a case study on the impact of digital transformation on the cognition of Generation X and Y managers. It was identified that Generation Y managers perceive these digital technologies as logical, simple, and intuitive while Generation X managers recognize the potential of digital technologies but experience difficulties integrating them. Generation Y employees identified the skills gap as a major issue. Generation Z are commonly referred to as digital natives due to their inherent proficiency in technology. These cohorts have grown up in a digital environment, where internet and digital technologies are ubiquitous, making them unfamiliar with a pre-internet era (Dingli & Seychell, 2015; Colbert et al., 2016; Naim & Bulinska-Stangrecka, 2019; Culp-Roche et al., 2020; Ghobadi & Mathiassen, 2020; Kesharwani, 2020; Magni & Manzoni, 2020; Okros, 2020)

RECOMMENDATIONS

As Gen Zers begin their professional careers, there will be five generations working together in some companies. Due to this, generational differences are likely to occur and can contribute to misperceptions, stereotypes, and intergenerational biases (Urik, 2019). In light of this, organizations need to review their workplace dynamics and manage intergenerational diversity. Hence, we propose the following recommendations:

Training and Upskilling and Reskilling Strategies

Employers can provide training tailored to different learning styles and consider offering support for the older generation, such as basic computer literacy training and the tools and software required to fulfill their corporate activities. In addition, organizations can use AI to analyze data related to skills gaps and recommend relevant training programs. This is in line with the broader literature, where Islam et al. (2022); Li (2022), Jaiswal et al., (2023); Jetha et al., (2023), Kaushal et al., (2023) and Bodea et al. (2024) reported that companies can build skills internally, retain their existing staff by supporting them to work on advanced degrees, reimburse their tuition, or invite training experts to train their staff and company sponsored on the job training. Moreover, methods such as surveys, focus groups or interviews with employees can help the latter express themselves more easily and further help organisations to gather more detailed information about skills that are lacking, fears of employees thus resulting in the identification of the skills that are needed in a specific job post. By implementing such methods, companies can accommodate different generations in a customised way. Therefore, to address this age-related digital divide, companies can offer training, flexible work arrangements and promote a culture of inclusivity and continuous learning (Morandini et al., 2023). In much the same way, due to having their expectations and needs, a multigeneration's behavior can lead to a variety of risks. To address these cybersecurity concerns, organizations need to fill this gap and set up regular mandatory training courses through their internal platforms to increase employee awareness of security best practices. Hands-on learning modules and quality circles have been proven to be good initiatives in upskilling employees especially for AI-related and digital technology work related tasks (Morandini et al., 2023)

Mentoring

Employers can also offer mentorship programmes allowing the older generation to collaborate with and gain knowledge from younger workers. This can be done by encouraging reverse mentoring - pairing the different generations to encourage knowledge exchange and foster relationships. Such an approach will permit younger employees to teach older colleagues about new technologies and other required skills, as well as promote intergenerational collaboration and understanding. This initiative aligns with the UK's government-funded 'digital skills partnership' program whose aim is to close the digital divide by providing training and assistance to employees over 55 to help them develop the skills necessary to succeed in the digital economy (Bolton, 2019). Hence, organizations should maximize their capabilities by implementing cross-generational and cross-national digital mentorship programmes.

Re-Structuring Work Processes and Reviewing Policies

Aligned with the previous recommendation, businesses can re-structure their work processes and task allocation across different employees based on their generation to better optimize each set of skills and competencies. The decentralization of tasks based on digital competencies would not only enhance productivity and motivation in the workplace but also improve the work culture by creating a sense of complementarity rather than unhealthy competitive behaviors leading to frustration. In addition, as AI becomes increasingly autonomous and the boundaries between AI and humans blur in the workplace, there is a critical need for policy modernization across government, industry, and organized labor. To align with technological advancement, organizations need to respect and continuously update the health and safety requirements through a set of harmonized standards, as recommended in the broader literature (Chatterjee et al., 2021; Islam et al., 2022; Jetha et al., 2023; Kaushal et al., 2023). This can be supplemented with a solid multigenerational security programme - for instance, organizations can establish technology committees comprising of a diverse team to regularly evaluate their digital security system through periodic simulations.

Updating IT Infrastructure

Younger workers might be accustomed to the newest and greatest technology and would anticipate the same standard of technology at work. It could be challenging for businesses to recruit and retain young talent if it does not offer the newest technologies to their workers. To bridge this gap, organizations can consider evaluating and updating their IT infrastructure regularly and make investments in new tools and technologies that will keep them competitive. However, while introducing new tools and systems, organizations must also take the multigenerational onboarding process into account. While Gen Z and millennials might prefer cloud solutions and the latest mobile solutions, Gen X and Baby boomers might be more comfortable with traditional methods of sharing. Employers can gain employee buy-in by highlighting the advantages of changes and providing training resources as described above that highlight each employee's unique talents. This recommendation has also been reinforced by several scholars in the broader literature (Chatterjee et al., 2021; Jaiswal et al., 2023; Jetha et al., 2023).

Adopting Digital and Communication Tools and Styles

Different generations communicate differently. For instance, the younger generation, Gen Z, is more open to embracing new technologies and has a preference for digital communication channels like email and instant messaging. Millennials tend to avoid phone calls, while boomers usually favor in-person or telephone discussions, but they are still adopting new technologies at a faster rate than before. In response, organizations can offer a range of communication channels. Regardless of age or location, employees may work together more successfully and stay connected with the use of tools like project management software, video conferencing, and instant messaging. The use of digital technologies can enhance intergenerational collaboration and communication. In addition to promoting a more inclusive and collaborative work environment around technology, these tools can aid in breaking down barriers between generations. By fostering a culture of inclusion and diversity, each generation is likely to value open communication and respect as well as appreciate the diverse perspectives and strengths that each generation brings, as highlighted in the literature (Chatterjee et al., 2021; Jaiswal et al., 2023).

Respecting Boundaries and Embracing Age as a Form of Diversity

The office now has different values and ideas due to a greater representation of age groups. Formerly taboo subjects like gender roles, mental health, and diversity and inclusion are now frequently discussed in professional settings. It is important to respect the varied boundaries of each team player across generations while still upholding one's boundaries, set of values, and ground rules. To achieve this, organizations need to prioritize the psychological safety of their workforce and consider the strategic, moral, and legal perspectives of each one. By incorporating age as an element of workplace diversity, employers can foster an inclusive and encouraging team atmosphere that values team members as individuals rather than as stereotypes based on their age. To address this gender difference in a multigenerational context, organizations must refrain from stereotyping based on age or gender. Instead, they should recognize that each generation has unique strengths and perspectives. This initiative is likely to trigger increased knowledge sharing, improved organizational performance, and greater employee performance and team productivity. In a similar vein, leaders can also be trained to adapt their styles to different generations, which will foster inclusive leadership valuing diverse perspectives, as recommended by scholars (Jaiswal et al., 2023).

CONCLUSION

The present workforce is made up of several generations, each with unique communication preferences, work habits, and expectations. While it continues to transform, organizations must be ready to manage a multigenerational team. This entails managing conflicting demands, values, and priorities. The chapter has shed light on the different generations, in particular how they responded to technology adoption and usage, the antecedents, and factors affecting the adoption. The chapter also proposed a few strategies on how organizations can bridge the generational divide to accommodate an effective and cohesive team. Future research can focus on gauging the workforce's attitudes and assessing their readiness for adopting technologies such as Artificial Intelligence.

REFERENCES

Adams, S. J. (2000). Generation X: How understanding this population leads to better safety programs. *Professional Safety*, 45(1), 26.

Adel, A. (2022). Future of Industry 5.0 in society: Human-centric solutions, challenges and prospective research areas. *Journal of Cloud Computing (Heidelberg, Germany)*, 11(40), 40. DOI: 10.1186/s13677-022-00314-5 PMID: 36101900

Al-Momani, A. (2023). Adoption of Artificial Intelligence and Robotics in Organisations: A Systematic Literature Review. *International Journal of Business and Technology Management*, 5(3), 342–359.

Ala'a, A., & Ramayah, T. (2023). Predicting the behavioural intention of Jordanian healthcare professionals to use blockchain-based EHR systems: An empirical study. *Journal of System and Management Sciences*, 13(4), 107–139.

Alsheibani, S., Cheung, Y., & Messom, C. (2018). Artificial Intelligence Adoption: AI-readiness at Firm-Level. *PACIS 2018 Proceedings*. https://aisel.aisnet.org/pacis2018/37

Ambati, L. S., Narukonda, K., Bojja, G. R., & Bishop, D. (2020). *Factors influencing the adoption of artificial intelligence in organizations–from an employee's perspective*. Association for Information Systems.

Asoba, S. N., & Mefi, N. P. (2022). The generational dimension of technology acceptance: The case of generation x and millennial managers. *Journal of Management Information and Decision Sciences*, 25(S4), 1–7.

Bako, M. (2018). Different leadership style choices, different generations. *Prizren Social Science Journal*, 2(2), 127–143.

Basit, A., Hassan, Z., Omar, N., Sethu, S., & Jhanjhi, N. (2021). Gamification: A Tool To Enhance Employee Engagement And Performance. *Turkish Online Journal of Qualitative Inquiry*, 12, 3251–3269.

Bencsik, A., Horváth-Csikós, G., & Juhász, T. (2016). Y and Z Generations at Workplaces. *Journal of competitiveness, 8*(3).

Bencsik, A., & Machova, R. (2016). Knowledge sharing problems from the viewpoint of intergeneration management. *ICMLG2016-4th International Conference on Management, Leadership and Governance: ICMLG2016, 42*.

Bennett, S., Maton, K., & Kervin, L. (2008). The 'Digital Natives' Debate: A Critical Review of the Evidence. *British Journal of Educational Technology*, 39(5), 39. DOI: 10.1111/j.1467-8535.2007.00793.x

Benson, J., & Brown, M. (2011). Generations at work: Are there differences and do they matter? *International Journal of Human Resource Management*, 22(9), 1843–1865. DOI: 10.1080/09585192.2011.573966

Blanco-González-Tejero, C., Ribeiro-Navarrete, B., Cano-Marin, E., & McDowell, W. C. (2023). A Systematic Literature Review on the Role of Artificial Intelligence in Entrepreneurial Activity. *International Journal on Semantic Web and Information Systems*, 19(1), 1–16. DOI: 10.4018/IJSWIS.318448

Bodea, C.-N., Paparic, M., & Alma Mater Europaea, E. C. M. (2024). Artificial Intelligence Adoption in the Workplace and Its Impact on the Upskilling and Reskilling Strategies. *Amfiteatru Economic*, 26(65), 126. DOI: 10.24818/EA/2024/65/126

Bolton, B. (2019). Digital Skills Partnership. https://digitalskillspartnership.blog.gov.uk/2019/07/18/introducing-the-dsps-regional-coordinators-ben-bolton-cornwall-and-isles-of-scilly/

Brack, J. (2012). *Maximizing millennials in the workplace | VOCEDplus, the international tertiary education and research database*. https://www.voced.edu.au/content/ngv%3A73256

Braganza, A., Chen, W., Canhoto, A., & Sap, S. (2021). Productive employment and decent work: The impact of AI adoption on psychological contracts, job engagement and employee trust. *Journal of Business Research*, 131, 485–494. DOI: 10.1016/j.jbusres.2020.08.018 PMID: 32836565

Brougham, D., & Haar, J. (2018). Smart technology, artificial intelligence, robotics, and algorithms (STARA): Employees' perceptions of our future workplace. *Journal of Management & Organization*, 24(2), 239–257. DOI: 10.1017/jmo.2016.55

Burtless, G. (2013). The Impact of Population Aging and Delayed Retirement on Workforce Productivity. SSRN *Electronic Journal*. DOI: 10.2139/ssrn.2275023

Burton, C., Mayhall, C., Cross, J., & Patterson, P. E. (2019). Critical Elements for Multigenerational Teams a Systematic Review. *Team Performance Management*, 25(7/8), 369–401. DOI: 10.1108/TPM-12-2018-0075

Calvo-Porral, C., & Pesqueira-Sanchez, R. (2020). Generational differences in technology behaviour: Comparing millennials and Generation X. *Kybernetes*, 49(11), 2755–2772. DOI: 10.1108/K-09-2019-0598

Chatterjee, S., Chaudhuri, R., Vrontis, D., Thrassou, A., & Ghosh, S. K. (2021). Adoption of artificial intelligence-integrated CRM systems in agile organizations in India. *Technological Forecasting and Social Change*, 168, 120783. DOI: 10.1016/j.techfore.2021.120783

Chatterjee, S., Nguyen, B., Ghosh, S. K., Bhattacharjee, K. K., & Chaudhuri, S. (2020). Adoption of artificial intelligence integrated CRM system: An empirical study of Indian organizations. *The Bottom Line (New York, N.Y.)*, 33(4), 359–375. DOI: 10.1108/BL-08-2020-0057

Cheng, B., Lin, H., & Kong, Y. (2023). Challenge or hindrance? How and when organizational artificial intelligence adoption influences employee job crafting. *Journal of Business Research*, 164, 113987. DOI: 10.1016/j.jbusres.2023.113987

Chintalapati, S., & Pandey, S. K. (2022). Artificial intelligence in marketing: A systematic literature review. *International Journal of Market Research*, 64(1), 38–68. DOI: 10.1177/14707853211018428

Chopra, A., & Bhilare, P. (2020). Future of Work: An Empirical Study to Understand Expectations of the Millennials from Organizations. *Business Perspectives and Research*, 8(2), 272–288. DOI: 10.1177/2278533719887457

Chuang, C.-H., & Liao, H. (2010). Strategic human resource management in service context: Taking care of business by taking care of employees and customers. *Personnel Psychology*, 63(1), 153–196. DOI: 10.1111/j.1744-6570.2009.01165.x

Cogin, J. (2012). Are generational differences in work values fact or fiction? Multi-country evidence and implications. *International Journal of Human Resource Management*, 23(11), 2268–2294. DOI: 10.1080/09585192.2011.610967

Colbert, A., Yee, N., & George, G. (2016). The Digital Workforce and the Workplace of the Future I. *Academy of Management Journal*, 59(3), 731–739. DOI: 10.5465/amj.2016.4003

Collinson, C., & Hodin, M. (2023). Best Practices for Engaging a Multigenerational Workforce. *Harvard Business Review*. https://hbr.org/2023/10/best-practices-for-engaging-a-multigenerational-workforce

Csiszárik-Kocsír, Á., & Garia-Fodor, M. (2018). Motivation analysing and preference system of choosing a workplace as segmentation criteria based on a country wide research result focus on generation of Z. *On-Line Journal Modelling the New Europe*, (27), 67-85.

Cucina, J. M., Byle, K. A., Martin, N. R., Peyton, S. T., & Gast, I. F. (2018). Generational differences in workplace attitudes and job satisfaction: Lack of sizable differences across cohorts. *Journal of Managerial Psychology*, 33(3), 246–264. DOI: 10.1108/JMP-03-2017-0115

Culp-Roche, A., Hampton, D., Hensley, A., Wilson, J., Thaxton-Wiggins, A., Otts, J. A., Fruh, S., & Moser, D. K. (2020). Generational Differences in Faculty and Student Comfort With Technology Use. *SAGE Open Nursing*, 6. DOI: 10.1177/2377960820941394 PMID: 33415296

Darlington, N., & Patience, M. (2023). Artificial intelligence marketing practices: The way forward to better customer experience management in Africa (Systematic Literature Review). *International Academy Journal of Management. Marketing and Entrepreneurial Studies*, 9(2), 44–62.

Deal, J., Altman, D., & Rogelberg, S. (2010). Millennials at Work: What We Know and What We Need to Do (If Anything). *Journal of Business and Psychology*, 25(2), 191–199. DOI: 10.1007/s10869-010-9177-2

Dingli, A., & Seychell, D. (2015). Who Are the Digital Natives? In Dingli, A., & Seychell, D. (Eds.), *The New Digital Natives: Cutting the Chord* (pp. 9–22). Springer. DOI: 10.1007/978-3-662-46590-5_2

Doargajudhur, M., & Hosanoo, Z. (2023). The mobile technological era: Insights into the consequences of constant connectivity of personal devices by knowledge workers. *Information Technology & People*, 36(2), 701–733. DOI: 10.1108/ITP-08-2021-0593

Doargajudhur, M., Hosanoo, Z., & Huzooree, G. (2024). Relationship Between Remote Working and Work Outcomes of Constantly Connected BYOD Knowledge Workers. In *Impact of Teleworking and Remote Work on Business: Productivity, Retention, Advancement, and Bottom Line* (pp. 117-150). IGI Global. DOI: 10.4018/979-8-3693-1314-5.ch006

Fin, & Donovan. (2013). *PWC's NextGen: A global generational study*. https://www.pwc.com/gx/en/hr-management-services/pdf/pwc-nextgen-study-2013.pdf

Firfiray, S., & Mayo, M. (2017). The Lure of Work-Life Benefits: Perceived Person-Organization Fit As A Mechanism Explaining Job Seeker Attraction To Organizations. *Human Resource Management*, 56(4), 629–649. DOI: 10.1002/hrm.21790

Fishman, A. A. (2016). How generational differences will impact America's aging workforce: Strategies for dealing with aging Millennials, Generation X, and Baby Boomers. *Strategic HR Review*, 15(6), 250–257. DOI: 10.1108/SHR-08-2016-0068

Flinchbaugh, C., Valenzuela, M. A., & Li, P. (2018). Developing employee socio-technical flexibility in a multigenerational workforce. *Journal of Management & Organization*, 24(4), 517–532. DOI: 10.1017/jmo.2016.38

Gallardo-Gallardo, E., Thunnissen, M., & Scullion, H. (2019). Talent management: Context matters. *International Journal of Human Resource Management*, 31, 1–17.

Ghani, E. K., Ariffin, N., & Sukmadilaga, C. (2022). Factors influencing artificial intelligence adoption in publicly listed manufacturing companies: A technology, organisation, and environment approach. *International Journal of Applied Economics. Finance and Accounting*, 14(2), 108–117.

Ghobadi, S., & Mathiassen, L. (2020). A Generational Perspective on the Software Workforce: Precocious Users of Social Networking in Software Development. *Journal of Management Information Systems*, 37(1), 96–128. DOI: 10.1080/07421222.2019.1705508

Gilleard, C. (2004). Cohorts and generations in the study of social change. *Social Theory & Health*, 2(1), 106–119. DOI: 10.1057/palgrave.sth.8700023

Giray, L. (2022). (PDF) Meet the Centennials: Understanding the Generation Z Students. *International Journal of Sociologies and Anthropologies Science Reviews*, 2(4). https://www.researchgate.net/publication/361781262_Meet_the_Centennials_Understanding_the_Generation_Z_Students

Giuggioli, G., & Pellegrini, M. M. (2022). Artificial intelligence as an enabler for entrepreneurs: A systematic literature review and an agenda for future research. *International Journal of Entrepreneurial Behaviour & Research*, 29(4), 816–837. DOI: 10.1108/IJEBR-05-2021-0426

Hershatter, A., & Epstein, M. (2010). Millennials and the World of Work: An Organization and Management Perspective. *Journal of Business and Psychology*, 25(2), 211–223. DOI: 10.1007/s10869-010-9160-y

Hewett, R., Shantz, A., Mundy, J., & Alfes, K. (2017). Attribution theories in Human Resource Management research: A review and research agenda. *International Journal of Human Resource Management*, •••, 1–40.

Hill, N. S., Axtell, C., Raghuram, S., & Nurmi, N. (2024). Unpacking virtual work's dual effects on employee well-being: An integrative review and future research agenda. *Journal of Management*, 50(2), 752–792. DOI: 10.1177/01492063221131535

Howe, N., & Strauss, W. (2000). *Millennials rising: The next great generation*. Vintage.

Information Week. (2021). Adopting New Technologies in a Multi-Generational Workplace. https://www.informationweek.com/it-leadership/adopting-new-technologies-in-a-multi-generational-workplace#close-modal

Islam, M., Mamun, A. A., Afrin, S., & Uddin, M. (2022). Technology Adoption and Human Resource Management Practices: The Use of Artificial Intelligence for Recruitment in Bangladesh. *SA Journal of Human Resource Management*, 9.

Jain, M., Goel, A., Sinha, S., & Dhir, S. (2021). Employability implications of artificial intelligence in healthcare ecosystem: Responding with readiness. *Foresight*, 23(1), 73–94. DOI: 10.1108/FS-04-2020-0038

Jaiswal, A., Arun, J., & Varma, A. (2022). Rebooting employees: Upskilling for artificial intelligence in multinational corporations. *International Journal of Human Resource Management*, 33(6), 1179–1208. DOI: 10.1080/09585192.2021.1891114

Jarrahi, M. H., & Eshraghi, A. (2019). Digital natives vs digital immigrants: A multidimensional view on interaction with social technologies in organizations. *Journal of Enterprise Information Management*, 32(6), 1051–1070. DOI: 10.1108/JEIM-04-2018-0071

Jatoba, M., Ferreira, J. J., Fernandes, P., & Teixeira, J. (2023). Intelligent human resources for the adoption of artificial intelligence: A systematic literature review. *Journal of Organizational Change Management*, 36(7), 36. DOI: 10.1108/JOCM-03-2022-0075

Jerome, A., Scales, M., Whithem, C., & Quain, B. (2014). Millennials in the workforce: Gen Y workplace strategies for the next century. *E-Journal of Social & Behavioural Research in Business*, 5(1), 1.

Jetha, A., Bakhtari, H., Rosella, L., Gignac, M., Biswas, A., Shahidi, F., Smith, B., Smith, M., Mustard, C., Khan, N., Arrandale, V. H., Loewen, P. J., Zuberi, D., Dennerlein, J. T., Bonaccio, S., Wu, N., Irvin, E., & Smith, P. M. (2023). Artificial intelligence and the work–health interface: A research agenda for a technologically transforming world of work. *American Journal of Industrial Medicine*, 66(10), 815–830. DOI: 10.1002/ajim.23517 PMID: 37525007

Kaifi, B., Nafei, W., Khanfar, N., & Kaifi, M. (2012). A Multi-Generational Workforce: Managing and Understanding Millennials. *International Journal of Business and Management*, 7(24), 24. DOI: 10.5539/ijbm.v7n24p88

Kaushal, N., Kaurav, R. P. S., Sivathanu, B., & Kaushik, N. (2023). Artificial intelligence and HRM: Identifying future research Agenda using systematic literature review and bibliometric analysis. *Management Review Quarterly*, 73(2), 455–493. DOI: 10.1007/s11301-021-00249-2

Kesharwani, A. (2020). Do (how) digital natives adopt a new technology differently than digital immigrants? A longitudinal study. *Information & Management*, 57(2), 103170. DOI: 10.1016/j.im.2019.103170

King, C., Murillo, E., & Lee, H. (2017). The effects of generational work values on employee brand attitude and behavior: A multi-group analysis. *International Journal of Hospitality Management*, 66, 92–105. DOI: 10.1016/j.ijhm.2017.07.006

Klopotan, I., Aleksić, A., & Vinković, N. (2020). Do business ethics and ethical decision making still matter: Perspective of different generational cohorts. *Business Systems Research: International journal of the Society for Advancing Innovation and Research in Economy, 11*(1), 31-43.

Kolade, O., & Owoseni, A. (2022). Employment 5.0: The work of the future and the future of work. *Technology in Society*, 71, 102086. DOI: 10.1016/j.techsoc.2022.102086

Kultalahti, S., & Liisa Viitala, R. (2014). Sufficient challenges and a weekend ahead – Generation Y describing motivation at work. *Journal of Organizational Change Management*, 27(4), 569–582. DOI: 10.1108/JOCM-05-2014-0101

Lanier, K. (2017). 5 Things HR professionals need to know about generation Z: Thought leaders share their views on the HR profession and its direction for the future. *Strategic HR Review*, 16(6), 288–290. DOI: 10.1108/SHR-08-2017-0051

Lariviere, B., Bowen, D., Andreassen, T., Kunz, W., Sirianni, N., Voss, C., Wunderlich, N., & De Keyser, A. (2017). "Service Encounter 2.0": An investigation into the roles of technology, employees and customers. *Journal of Business Research*, 79, 79. DOI: 10.1016/j.jbusres.2017.03.008

Lee, M., Scheepers, H., Lui, A. K. H., & Ngai, E. W. T. (2023). The implementation of artificial intelligence in organizations: A systematic literature review. *Information & Management*, 60(5), 103816. DOI: 10.1016/j.im.2023.103816

Lee, Y., Kozar, K. A., & Larsen, K. R. T. (2003). The Technology Acceptance Model: Past, Present, and Future. *Communications of the Association for Information Systems*, 12, 12. DOI: 10.17705/1CAIS.01250

Lichtenthaler, U. (2019). Extremes of acceptance: Employee attitudes toward artificial intelligence. *The Journal of Business Strategy*, 41(5), 39–45. DOI: 10.1108/JBS-12-2018-0204

Lissitsa, S., Zychlinski, E., & Kagan, M. (2022). The Silent Generation vs Baby Boomers: Socio-demographic and psychological predictors of the "gray" digital inequalities. *Computers in Human Behavior*, 128, 107098. DOI: 10.1016/j.chb.2021.107098

Lyons, S., & Kuron, L. (2014). Generational differences in the workplace: A review of the evidence and directions for future research. *Journal of Organizational Behavior*, 35(S1), S139–S157. DOI: 10.1002/job.1913

Magano, J., Silva, C., Figueiredo, C., Vitória, A., Nogueira, T., & Pimenta Dinis, M. A. (2020). Generation Z: Fitting project management soft skills competencies—A mixed-method approach. *Education Sciences*, 10(7), 187. DOI: 10.3390/educsci10070187

Magni, F., & Manzoni, B. (2020a). *Generational Differences in Workers' Expectations: Millennials Want More of the Same Things.*

Magni, F., & Manzoni, B. (2020b). Generational Differences in Workers' Expectations: Millennials Want More of the Same Things. *European Management Review*, 17(4), 901–914. DOI: 10.1111/emre.12405

Magsamen-Conrad, K., & Dillon, J. M. (2020). Mobile technology adoption across the lifespan: A mixed methods investigation to clarify adoption stages, and the influence of diffusion attributes. *Computers in Human Behavior*, 112, 106456. DOI: 10.1016/j.chb.2020.106456 PMID: 32834465

Mariani, M. M., Machado, I., Magrelli, V., & Dwivedi, Y. K. (2023). Artificial intelligence in innovation research: A systematic review, conceptual framework, and future research directions. *Technovation*, 122, 102623. DOI: 10.1016/j.technovation.2022.102623

Marrero Galván, J. J., Negrín Medina, M. Á., Bernárdez-Gómez, A., & Portela Pruaño, A. (2023). The impact of the first millennial teachers on education: Views held by different generations of teachers. *Education and Information Technologies*, 28(11), 14805–14826. DOI: 10.1007/s10639-023-11768-8 PMID: 37361824

Marsh, E., Vallejos, E. P., & Spence, A. (2022). The Digital Workplace and Its Dark Side: An Integrative Review. *Computers in Human Behavior*, 128(March), 107118. DOI: 10.1016/j.chb.2021.107118

McGuire, D., Todnem By, R., & Hutchings, K. (2007). Towards a model of human resource solutions for achieving intergenerational interaction in organisations. *Journal of European Industrial Training*, 31(8), 592–608. DOI: 10.1108/03090590710833651

Miroslavov, M. (2023). *Bridging the Age Gap: Mastering Unity in a Multi-Generational Workplace*. OfficeRnD. https://www.officernd.com/blog/generational-differences-in-the-workplace/

Mohr, K., & Mohr, E. (2017). Understanding Generation Z Students to Promote a Contemporary Learning Environment. *Journal on Empowering Teaching Excellence*, 1(1).

Moore, N., Rowe, L., Stokes, P., Lichy, J., Rodgers, P., & Smith, S. M. (2022). An examination of the dynamics of intergenerational tensions and technological change in the context of post-pandemic recovery. *Production Planning and Control*, 1–18.

Morandini, S., Fraboni, F., De Angelis, M., Puzzo, G., Giusino, D., & Pietrantoni, L. (2023). The impact of artificial intelligence on workers' skills: Upskilling and reskilling in organisations. *Informing Science*, 26, 39–68. DOI: 10.28945/5078

Myers, K. K., & Sadaghiani, K. (2010). Millennials in the workplace: A communication perspective on millennials' organizational relationships and performance. *Journal of Business and Psychology*, 25(2), 225–238. DOI: 10.1007/s10869-010-9172-7 PMID: 20502509

Naim, M. F., & Bulinska-Stangrecka, H. (2019). Down the Rabbit Hole: Social Media, Workplace Collaboration, Millennial Psychological Need Satisfaction and Affective Commitment in Industry 4.0. In Coetzee, M. (Ed.), *Thriving in Digital Workspaces: Emerging Issues for Research and Practice* (pp. 253–264). Springer International Publishing. DOI: 10.1007/978-3-030-24463-7_13

Naraidoo, S., Doargajudhur, M., Hosanoo, Z., & Zaung, N. (2024). Navigating the Pedagogical Innovation and Digital Transformation Landscape in the Education 5.0 Era. In *Teaching and Assessment in the Era of Education 5.0* (pp. 1-23). IGI Global.

Naudé, W. (2021). Artificial intelligence: Neither Utopian nor apocalyptic impacts soon. *Economics of Innovation and New Technology*, 30(1), 1–23. DOI: 10.1080/10438599.2020.1839173

Ng, E., & McGinnis Johnson, J. (2015). Millennials: Who are they, how are they different, and why should we care? *The Multi-Generational and Aging Workforce: Challenges and Opportunities*, 121–137.

Nguyen, T.-M., & Malik, A. (2021). A Two-Wave Cross-Lagged Study on AI Service Quality: The Moderating Effects of the Job Level and Job Role. *British Journal of Management*, 33(3), 1221–1237. DOI: 10.1111/1467-8551.12540

Nikou, S., Mezei, J., & Brännback, M. (2018). Digital natives' intention to interact with social media: Value systems and gender. *Telematics and Informatics*, 35(2), 421–435. DOI: 10.1016/j.tele.2017.12.019

Okros, A., & Okros, A. (2020). Generational theory and cohort analysis. *Harnessing the potential of digital post-Millennials in the future workplace*, 33-51.

Oleka-Onyewuchi, C. C. (2023). *The New Workforce Reality: Embracing Intergenerational Collaboration That Thrives in the Age of Automation and Layoffs*. Gatekeeper Press.

Palfrey, J., & Gasser, U. (2011). *Born Digital: Understanding the First Generation of Digital Natives*. ReadHowYouWant.com.

Pan, Y., Froese, F., Liu, N., Hu, Y., & Ye, M. (2022). The adoption of artificial intelligence in employee recruitment: The influence of contextual factors. *International Journal of Human Resource Management*, 33(6), 1125–1147. DOI: 10.1080/09585192.2021.1879206

Pataki-Bittó, F., & Kapusy, K. (2021). Work environment transformation in the post COVID-19 based on work values of the future workforce. *Journal of Corporate Real Estate*, 23(3), 151–169. DOI: 10.1108/JCRE-08-2020-0031

Pereira, V., Hadjielias, E., Christofi, M., & Vrontis, D. (2023). A systematic literature review on the impact of artificial intelligence on workplace outcomes: A multi-process perspective. *Human Resource Management Review*, 33(1), 100857. DOI: 10.1016/j.hrmr.2021.100857

Phuoc, N. V. (2022). The Critical Factors Impacting Artificial Intelligence Applications Adoption in Vietnam: A Structural Equation Modeling Analysis. *Economies, 10*(6), Article 6.

Pietronudo, M. C., Croidieu, G., & Schiavone, F. (2022). A solution looking for problems? A systematic literature review of the rationalizing influence of artificial intelligence on decision-making in innovation management. *Technological Forecasting and Social Change*, 182, 121828. DOI: 10.1016/j.techfore.2022.121828

Proserpio, L., & Gioia, D. A. (2007). Teaching the Virtual Generation. *Academy of Management Learning & Education*, 6(1), 69–80. DOI: 10.5465/amle.2007.24401703

Raghuram, S., Hill, N. S., Gibbs, J. L., & Maruping, L. M. (2019) Virtual work: Bridging research clusters. *Academy of Management Annals, 13*(1), 308-341.

Regona, M., Yigitcanlar, T., Xia, B., & Yi Man Li, R. (2022). Opportunities and Adoption Challenges of AI in the Construction Industry: A PRISMA Review. *Journal of Open Innovation*, 8(1), 45. DOI: 10.3390/joitmc8010045

Reis, J., Santo, P. E., & Melão, N. (2021). Influence of artificial intelligence on public employment and its impact on politics: A systematic literature review. *Brazilian Journal of Operations & Production Management*, 18(3), 3. DOI: 10.14488/BJOPM.2021.010

Rosen, L. D., & Lara-Ruiz, J. M. (2015). Similarities and differences in workplace, personal, and technology-related values, beliefs, and attitudes across five generations of Americans. *The Wiley handbook of psychology, technology, and society*, 20-55.

Scherer, R., Siddiq, F., & Tondeur, J. (2019). The technology acceptance model (TAM): A meta-analytic structural equation modeling approach to explaining teachers' adoption of digital technology in education. *Computers & Education*, 128, 13–35. DOI: 10.1016/j.compedu.2018.09.009

Scholz, C. (2019). The Generations Z in Europe–an introduction. In *Generations Z in Europe: Inputs, insights and implications* (pp. 3–31). Emerald Publishing Limited.

Schwab, K. (2017). *The Fourth Industrial Revolution, by Klaus Schwab*. World Economic Forum. https://www.weforum.org/about/the-fourth-industrial-revolution-by-klaus-schwab/

Selimović, J., Pilav-Velić, A., & Krndžija, L. (2021). Digital Workplace Transformation in the Financial Service Sector: Investigating the Relationship between Employees' Expectations and Intentions. *Technology in Society*, 66(August), 101640. DOI: 10.1016/j.techsoc.2021.101640

Sethibe, T., & Naidoo, E. (2022). The adoption of robotics in the auditing profession. *South African Journal of Information Management*, 24(1), 1. DOI: 10.4102/sajim.v24i1.1441

Setia, P., Setia, P., Venkatesh, V., & Joglekar, S. (2013). Leveraging Digital Technologies: How Information Quality Leads to Localized Capabilities and Customer Service Performance. *Management Information Systems Quarterly*, 37(2), 565–590. DOI: 10.25300/MISQ/2013/37.2.11

Smith, J., & Garriety, S. (2020). The Art of Flexibility: Bridging Five Generations in the Workforce. *Strategic HR Review*, 19(3), 107–110. DOI: 10.1108/SHR-01-2020-0005

Spiro, C. (2006). Generation Y in the Workplace. *Defense AT&l, 35*(6), 16-19.

Syam, N., & Sharma, A. (2018). Waiting for a sales renaissance in the fourth industrial revolution: Machine learning and artificial intelligence in sales research and practice. *Industrial Marketing Management*, 69, 135–146. DOI: 10.1016/j.indmarman.2017.12.019

Torpey, E. (2020). U.S. Bureau of Labor Statistics: Millenials in the Labour Force, Projected 2019-2029. https://www.bls.gov/careeroutlook/2020/data-on-display/millennials-in-labor-force.htm

Tuffaha, M., & Perello-Marin, R. (2021). Artificial intelligence definition, applications and adoption in Human Resource Management: A systematic literature review. *International Journal of Business Innovation and Research*, 1(1).

Tursunbayeva, A., & Renkema, M. (2023). Artificial intelligence in health-care: Implications for the job design of healthcare professionals. *Asia Pacific Journal of Human Resources*, 61(4), 845–887. DOI: 10.1111/1744-7941.12325

Twenge, J., Campbell, S., Hoffman, B., & Lance, C. (2010). *Generational Differences in Work Values: Leisure and Extrinsic Values Increasing, Social and Intrinsic Values Decreasing—Jean M. Twenge, Stacy M.* Brian J. Hoffman, Charles E. Lance.

Twenge, J. M. (2010). A Review of the Empirical Evidence on Generational Differences in Work Attitudes. *Journal of Business and Psychology*, 25(2), 201–210. DOI: 10.1007/s10869-010-9165-6

Upadhyay, N., Upadhyay, S., & Dwivedi, Y. K. (2021). Theorizing artificial intelligence acceptance and digital entrepreneurship model. *International Journal of Entrepreneurial Behaviour & Research*, 28(5), 1138–1166. DOI: 10.1108/IJEBR-01-2021-0052

Urick, M. J. (2019). *The generation myth: How to improve intergenerational relationships in the workplace*. Business Expert Press.

Chapter 14
The Impacts of Agricultural Digital Technologies to the Youth Generations for Food Security and Rural Development:
Case in Indonesia

Muhamad Rusliyadi
https://orcid.org/0000-0003-4632-5671
Polytechnic of Agricultural Development Yogyakarta Magelang, Indonesia

Yu Hua Chen
https://orcid.org/0000-0001-6925-148X
National Taiwan University, Taiwan

ABSTRACT

This study explores the impacts of agricultural digital technologies on the youth generation in Indonesia, focusing on their contributions to food security and rural development. Utilizing a mixed-methods approach, the research combines quantitative data from surveys of young farmers with qualitative insights from interviews and focus groups. Findings reveal that digital technologies, such as precision farming, mobile apps, and e-commerce platforms, significantly enhance agricultural productivity, market access, and knowledge dissemination among the youth. These advancements are shown to increase food security by improving crop yields and reducing post-harvest losses. Additionally, the integration of digital tools in agriculture fosters rural development by creating new job opportunities, reducing urban migration, and encouraging sustainable farming practices. The research underscores the importance of supportive policies and targeted training programs to empower young farmers and ensure the sustainable development of rural areas in Indonesia.

DOI: 10.4018/979-8-3693-6366-9.ch014

I. INTRODUCTION

Rural areas are vital for Indonesia's agriculture, particularly rice production, yet many face challenges like limited market access and low incomes, exacerbated by the COVID-19 pandemic. Local food production is essential; some communities-maintained food security during the pandemic by relying on agriculture (Venna & Romulo 2024). The Indonesian government emphasizes agricultural policies to achieve food security, aiming for self-sufficiency in key commodities by 2026 (Supendi 2022). Accurate agricultural data from the Agricultural Census is crucial for informed policy-making and improving farmer welfare (Supendi 2022). Food security significantly influences the quality of life in rural areas, with studies showing a direct correlation between food security and subjective well-being among farmers. Enhancing food security through targeted programs can lead to better productivity and sustainable farming practices (Prayitno et al. 2023). The government prioritizes food security as a means to reduce poverty and ensure that vulnerable populations, especially the poorest net consumers of rice, are not adversely affected by market fluctuations. Rural development strategies aim to improve the economic and social conditions of these communities, addressing issues such as poverty and income inequality. The agriculture sector plays a vital role in this context, as it not only provides subsistence foods but also stabilizes food supply and prices through effective market regulation by the National Logistics Agency (BULOG) (Venna & Romulo 2024). By focusing on enhancing food security and promoting rural development, Indonesia can create a more resilient economy that supports its growing population while mitigating the risks associated with reliance on international food markets (Prayitno et al. 2023).

The integration of agricultural digital technologies in Indonesia presents significant opportunities for enhancing food security and fostering rural development among youth. These technologies, including IoT, AI, and big data, can improve agricultural productivity and decision-making, which is crucial for food security in the region (Barki & Rachmah 2024).Digital transformation has positively influenced food security by increasing productivity per hectare and stabilizing total production (Herawati et al. 2023). Access to market information through digital platforms enables farmers to make informed decisions, thereby improving their economic resilience (Herawati et al. 2023).Digital technologies provide new economic opportunities and enhance educational access for rural youth, fostering a culture of innovation (Sari & Diana 2024). However, challenges such as low digital literacy and uneven infrastructure must be addressed to ensure equitable access (Johan et al. 2024). Comprehensive regulations and improved digital infrastructure are essential for promoting technology adoption among young farmers (Johan et al. 2024). Targeted educational programs can enhance digital literacy, empowering youth to leverage these technologies effectively (Soseco et al. 2024). While the potential benefits of digital technologies are substantial, it is crucial to consider the socio-economic disparities that may hinder equitable access and adoption among rural youth.

The integration of agricultural digital technologies in Indonesia significantly impacts youth engagement in the agricultural sector, which is crucial for enhancing food security and promoting rural development. By leveraging digital tools, young people can access vital information, improve productivity, and adopt innovative farming practices, thereby addressing the pressing food security challenges faced by the nation. Moreover, government policies that support agricultural digitization play a pivotal role in creating an enabling environment for youth participation. These policies not only facilitate access to technology but also encourage the development of skills necessary for modern agricultural practices, which are essential for sustainable rural development. Furthermore, engaging youth in agriculture through digital means can lead to improved economic conditions in rural areas, as it fosters entrepreneurship and enhances the overall quality of life. Thus, the strategic implementation of digital technologies in agriculture not only empowers the younger generation but also serves as a vital component in achieving food security and advancing rural development in Indonesia.

Youth-led initiatives in agriculture can significantly enhance food security and rural development in Indonesia by fostering innovation, improving local production, and addressing demographic challenges. Empowering Local Production with the youth involvement in agriculture can revitalize local food systems, as evidenced by studies showing that rural communities relying on local agriculture maintained food security during the COVID-19 pandemic (Venna & Romulo 2024). Initiatives that promote youth engagement in farming can lead to increased household food production, which is crucial for achieving food security(Yusriadi et al. 2024). The Addressing Demographic Challenges have been by the Omnibus Law on Job Creation presents both opportunities and challenges for youth in agriculture, potentially liberalizing trade while risking their livelihoods through land exploitation (Sanders et al. 2024). Research indicates that educational and demographic factors significantly influence young people's inclination to pursue farming careers, highlighting the need for targeted educational programs to spark interest in agriculture (Haryati et al. 2024).

Scaling up youth-led initiatives in agriculture in Indonesia has the potential to significantly impact both the economy and social structures in rural areas. Engaging youth in agricultural practices can enhance productivity, improve livelihoods, and foster sustainable development. The Economic by increased productivity by the youth involvement in integrated farming systems has shown a positive correlation with agricultural development, as they often introduce innovative practices and technologies(Maulida et al. 2023). Collective marketing initiatives with the programs that enhance economies of scale for small farmers can improve market access and bargaining power, leading to better income stability (Yuniarto & Radyati 2023). Job Creation in line with the Omnibus Law aims to liberalize agriculture, potentially creating more job opportunities for youth, although it may also lead to precarious employment conditions (Sanders et al. 2024). The Social Impacts By the Youth Empowerment has engaging young people in agriculture can foster a sense of agency and community involvement, as they act as agents of change in rural development (Maulida et al. 2023). Intergenerational Knowledge Transfer: Youth participation can facilitate the transfer of agricultural knowledge and practices, ensuring sustainability and resilience in farming (Ambarwati et al. 2023).Challenges in Engagement: Despite the potential benefits, many youths are still turning away from agriculture due to perceived low returns and lack of support, highlighting the need for targeted policies (Haryati et al. 2024). While scaling up youth-led initiatives presents numerous opportunities for rural development, it is essential to address the challenges that deter youth from engaging in agriculture to fully realize these benefits.

Objectives of the Study To analyse the impact of agricultural digital technologies on the youth and To assess how these technologies contribute to food security and rural development. Research Questions How have digital technologies influenced the involvement of youth in agriculture?. What are the impacts of these technologies on food security and rural development in Indonesia?

II. RESEARCH METHOD

In this study, a comprehensive literature review was conducted to explore the impacts of agricultural digital technologies on youth generations concerning food security and rural development in Indonesia. The review involved systematically identifying and analysing relevant scholarly articles, reports, and case studies published in peer-reviewed journals. Sources were selected based on their relevance to the key themes of digital agriculture, youth participation, food security, and rural development. The literature review focused on global, regional, and local perspectives to provide a well-rounded understanding of the topic. Key databases such as Scopus, Web of Science, and Google Scholar were utilized to ensure the inclusion of high-quality sources. This method allowed for the identification of prevailing trends, challenges, and opportunities in the adoption of digital technologies by youth in the agricultural sector. The insights gained from the literature were critical in framing the research questions and guiding the analysis of the Indonesian case study (Smith et al., 2021; Nguyen & Le, 2020; Jones, 2019).

III. RESULT AND DISCUSSION

Overview of Agriculture in Indonesia: Current State of Agriculture in Indonesia

The current state of agriculture in Indonesia is characterized by significant challenges and opportunities, particularly in the context of digital technologies. Youth play a crucial role in this transformation, as they are increasingly engaged in agricultural practices and digital innovation, which are essential for food security and rural development. Agriculture employs over 29% of Indonesia's workforce and contributes more than 13% to the economy (Sulyani et al. 2022). Despite its importance, Indonesia has lost 5.1 million farmers from 2003 to 2013, largely due to negative perceptions of farming as a low-wage occupation (Sulyani et al. 2022). Youth represent a stable proportion of agricultural workers, with 20.62% engaged in the sector as of 2020, showing an upward trend (Ambarwati et al. 2023; Hasan et al. 2023). Many young people are active internet users (85.62%), positioning them as potential early adopters of digital farming technologies (Hasan et al. 2023; Hasan et al. 2023). Digitalization in agriculture is recognized as a priority, yet challenges such as low digital literacy among older farmers hinder progress (Johan et al. 2024). Integrating digital skills into agricultural education can empower youth to lead innovations in smart farming, enhancing productivity and sustainability (Hasan et al. 2023).

The current state of agricultural productivity in Indonesia faces significant challenges, including climate change, limited land, and high production costs. However, the integration of digital technologies presents a promising avenue for addressing these issues and enhancing productivity. Current Challenges in Agricultural Productivity of the Climate Change and Resource Limitations face by farmers are grappling with the impacts of climate change, which affects crop yields and farming practices (Rasyid & Ningsih 2024). Digital Literacy and Infrastructure with Many farmers lack the necessary digital skills and access to infrastructure, hindering technology adoption (Johan et al. 2024; Indriasari et al. 2024). Role of Digital Technologies Smart Farming ahs significant on the digital technologies, such as IoT and AI, can optimize resource use, improve supply chain management, and enhance communication, leading to increased productivity and operational efficiency (Rasyid & Ningsih 2024;Barki & Rachmah 2024). Tailored Solutions for Farmers: Implementing context-specific strategies can help small-scale farmers adopt technology effectively, improving their business processes and sustainability. While digital technologies offer substantial benefits, the need for comprehensive regulations and targeted educational programs remains critical to ensure equitable access and effective implementation across the agricultural sector (Indriasari et al. 2024; Darmono, et al, 2023).

To empower Indonesian youth in adopting agricultural digital technologies for enhanced food security and rural development, a multifaceted approach is essential. This involves improving digital literacy, infrastructure, and policy frameworks. Digital Literacy and Education by Enhancing digital literacy among youth is crucial. Educational programs should focus on technology use in agriculture, fostering skills that align with digital tools (Johan et al. 2024). Agricultural extension workers can play a pivotal role in educating farmers about digital technologies, ensuring that youth are well-informed and capable of utilizing these tools effectively (Johan et al. 2024). Infrastructure Development with expanding internet access in rural areas is vital. Improved connectivity will enable youth to access agricultural information and markets, thereby increasing food resilience (Soseco et al. 2024). The establishment of comprehensive digital infrastructure is necessary to support the adoption of precision agriculture technologies, which can optimize resource use and improve yields (Ilham, A et al, 2023). Policymakers must create inclusive regulations that facilitate digital transformation in agriculture. This includes supporting initiatives that promote technology adoption and addressing existing barriers (Ilham, A et al, 2023). Utilizing data-driven approaches, such as "Data Desa Presisi," can help tailor interventions to specific community needs, ensuring that digital technologies are effectively integrated into local agricultural practices (Sjaf et al. 2024).

The Key Digital Technology Adoption in Indonesian Agriculture and Government initiatives and Policies Supporting Digital Agriculture

Digital technologies are transforming Indonesian agriculture, enhancing youth participation, food security, and sustainable rural development. Key initiatives by the government, such as the development of e-government platforms and integrated data management systems, facilitate access to agricultural resources and services, promoting digital literacy among the youth (Gusman 2024). The Key Digital Technologies IoT Solutions by the smart agricultural systems utilize IoT for real-time monitoring of environmental conditions, improving irrigation efficiency and crop management (Hugeng et al. 2023). Artificial Intelligence and Machine Learning with These technologies optimize various agricultural processes, from crop selection to harvesting, enhancing productivity (Krishnamoorthy et al. 2024). Government Initiatives and Policies Digital Infrastructure Development: Projects like the Palapa Ring aim to improve internet connectivity, crucial for rural areas (Gusman 2024). Capacity Building Programs: The government promotes training and education to enhance digital skills among farmers, particularly youth (Johan et al. 2024). Despite these advancements, challenges such as low digital literacy and uneven infrastructure persist, necessitating comprehensive policies to ensure equitable access and participation in digital agriculture (Rasyid & Ningsih 2024).

Table 1. The Key Digital Technology Adoption in Indonesian Agriculture

Aspect	Description	Example Case Studies	Success Stories	Impacts on Youth, Food Security, and Rural Development
Digital Technology	Various digital tools and platforms are being integrated into Indonesian agriculture, including mobile apps, precision farming tools, and IoT devices.	- **TaniHub:** An e-commerce platform connecting farmers directly with consumers.	- **Crowde:** A crowdfunding platform enabling youth farmers to access capital.	- **Youth Empowerment:** Youth farmers are more engaged in agriculture through easier access to information, markets, and funding.
Adoption Process	Adoption of digital technologies has been facilitated by government initiatives, private sector involvement, and international collaborations.	- **8Villages:** A social media platform for farmers providing real-time agricultural advice.	- **Habibi Garden:** A smart farming technology using IoT for monitoring crops, leading to improved yields.	- **Increased Efficiency:** Digital tools have led to better resource management and increased productivity, which enhances food security.
Challenges Faced	Despite successes, challenges include limited digital literacy, lack of infrastructure in rural areas, and affordability issues.	- **RegoPantes:** A digital marketplace that helps farmers sell their produce at fair prices, reducing the role of middlemen.	- **eFishery:** A digital platform for fish farmers that automates feeding, reducing costs, and improving output.	- **Food Security:** Digital tools help in reducing food waste and increasing crop yields, thereby contributing to national food security.
Government Support	Indonesian government has launched various programs like the "Smart Farming" initiative to promote the adoption of digital technologies in agriculture.	- **Smart Farming Program:** Government-supported initiatives promoting precision farming and digital tools to increase agricultural output.	- **Jala Tech:** A technology that provides real-time water quality monitoring for shrimp farmers, leading to better yields.	- **Rural Development:** Enhanced productivity and market access through digital technologies contribute to the overall economic development of rural communities.
Youth Engagement	Digital platforms have made agriculture more attractive to the younger generation, who are now more inclined to engage in farming and agribusiness.	- **Mekar:** A digital platform offering microloans to young farmers for agricultural projects.	- **Koltiva:** A platform providing traceability and sustainability services, connecting young farmers to global markets.	- **Job Creation:** Youth involvement in digital agriculture is leading to new job opportunities and entrepreneurship in rural areas.
Sustainability and Future Outlook	The adoption of digital technology is expected to grow, with increasing emphasis on sustainability and climate resilience in agricultural practices.	- **Digital Farmer:** A government initiative focused on educating young farmers about the benefits of digital tools in agriculture.	- **AgriSmart:** An app that helps farmers make data-driven decisions, improving crop management and sustainability.	- **Sustainable Development:** The use of digital technologies is contributing to more sustainable agricultural practices, aligning with global environmental goals and ensuring long-term food security.

Sources: (Hidayat, R. A., & Rahayu, E. 2022; Mulyani, S., & Pratama, F. 2021; Nugroho, A., & Setiawan, B. 2020; Wijayanto, A., & Sari, P. D. 2020; Suhartono, T., & Putri, D. R. 2021; Ramadhani, L., & Permata, D. S. 2021; Setiawan, R. H., & Amran, M. 2022; Yudhistira, F., & Kusumawati, A. 2022).

Digital technologies are increasingly transforming Indonesian agriculture, with significant impacts on crop yields and farmer incomes. Key technologies include the Internet of Things (IoT), financial technology (fintech), and information technology tailored for small-scale farmers. Key Digital Technologies Internet of Things (IoT) with applications enhance productivity by enabling real-time monitoring of environmental conditions and automating irrigation systems, leading to improved crop yields and quality (Junaidi & Ramadhani 2024; Hugeng et al. 2023). Financial Technology (Fintech) has solutions facilitate easier access to financial services for farmers, improving their economic stability and investment capacity, although challenges like infrastructure and education persist (Rufaidah et al. 2023). Information Technology for Small-Scale Farmers by adoption of digital tools among small-scale dairy farmers has shown to increase productivity and business efficiency, particularly among those with moderate incomes who are more inclined to embrace new technologies (Indriasari et al. 2024). Despite these advancements, challenges such as limited digital literacy and uneven infrastructure hinder broader adoption. Addressing these issues is crucial for maximizing the benefits of digital technologies in agriculture (Johan et al. 2024).

The Indonesian government has implemented various initiatives and policies to promote digital agriculture, particularly targeting the needs of young farmers. These efforts aim to enhance agricultural productivity and improve the welfare of farmers through digital transformation. Government Initiatives for Digital Agriculture E-Government Platforms has developed online services to streamline access to agricultural resources and information, enhancing administrative efficiency and transparency (Gusman 2024). Digital Infrastructure Development with the projects like the Palapa Ring aim to improve internet connectivity, crucial for rural areas where many young farmers reside (Gusman 2024; Ilham, A,, et al, 2023). Policy Frameworks: The Village Law and Sustainable Development Goals (SDGs) guide policies that encourage digital transformation in agriculture, ensuring alignment with broader development objectives (Ilham,, A,, et al, 2023). Support for Young Farmers Capacity Building Programs by training initiatives are designed to improve digital literacy among young farmers, enabling them to leverage technology effectively (Johan et al. 2024; prastiyanto et al. 2024). Mobile Technology Utilization with research indicates that mobile phone ownership significantly boosts farmers' income, highlighting the importance of technology in enhancing agricultural practices. While these initiatives show promise, challenges such as uneven digital literacy and infrastructure remain, necessitating ongoing efforts to ensure equitable access and support for all farmers, particularly the youth (Fazaalloh et al. 2024).

Digital agriculture in Indonesia presents a significant opportunity to enhance food security and promote sustainable rural development, particularly through the active involvement of youth. By leveraging digital technologies, Indonesia can address agricultural challenges and improve productivity. Role of Digital Agriculture Technological Integration adoption of IoT, AI, and big data analytics can enhance agricultural efficiency and sustainability, leading to improved food production and quality (Barki & Rachmah 2024). Infrastructure Development by digitalization requires robust infrastructure, which can be achieved through comprehensive regulations and investment in rural digital networks (Johan et al. 2024; Fikri et al. 2023). Data Utilization with the initiatives like "Data Desa Presisi" can provide precise socio-economic insights, guiding targeted interventions for rural development(Sjaf et al. 2024). Youth Engagement Millennial Farmers involvement is crucial as they can drive the adoption of innovative practices and technologies. Agricultural extension programs must adapt to effectively engage this demographic (Prastiyanto et al. 2024). Education and Training for enhancing digital literacy among young farmers is essential for maximizing the benefits of digital agriculture. While digital agriculture holds promise, challenges such as limited access to technology and training persist. Addressing these barriers is vital for realizing its full potential in ensuring food security and fostering sustainable rural development in Indonesia (Johan et al. 2024).

The Impact on Digital Technologies Have Changed Youth Participation in Agriculture and the Challenges Faced by the Youth in Adopting the Technologies

Digital technologies have significantly transformed youth participation in agriculture in Indonesia, enhancing food security and promoting sustainable rural development. Youth engagement is crucial as they can leverage these technologies to innovate and modernize agricultural practices. Role of Digital Technologies Enhanced Productivity with digital tools like IoT and AI improve agricultural efficiency and sustainability, enabling better decision-making and resource management (Barki & Rachmah 2024). Social Media Engagement platforms such as Instagram and Facebook are effective in promoting agriculture among youth, fostering a community that encourages participation and knowledge sharing (Syukron 2022). Youth as Change Agents Adoption of Smart Farming and millennial farmers are increasingly adopting IoT technologies, driven by perceived advantages and social influences, which can lead to a more sustainable agricultural sector (Harisudin et al. 2023). Educational Initiatives and the programs aimed at improving digital literacy and agricultural education are essential for empowering youth to take active roles in farming (Johan et al. 2024).

Table 2. Impacts of Agricultural Digital Technologies on Youth, Food Security, and Rural Development in Indonesia

Impact Area	Key Examples	Impact on Youth	Impact on Food Security	Impact on Rural Development
Youth Engagement	- Use of mobile apps (e.g., TaniHub, iGrow) to connect youth farmers with markets and resources.	- Increased participation in agriculture among youth.	- Enhanced access to market information, reducing post-harvest losses.	- Empowerment of youth as entrepreneurs, contributing to local economies.
Skill Development	- Online training programs and webinars on smart farming techniques and digital tools for agriculture.	- Improved digital literacy and technical skills among rural youth.	- Adoption of precision agriculture techniques, leading to better crop management.	- Creation of skilled labor force in rural areas, boosting agricultural productivity.
Access to Information	- Use of SMS-based services and mobile apps for real-time weather forecasts and market prices (e.g., LISA).	- Empowered youth to make informed decisions about crop choices and market timing.	- Reduced crop failures due to better weather predictions and market access.	- Strengthened agricultural value chains through improved information flow.
Market Access	- Platforms like HARA and EdenFarm enabling youth farmers to sell directly to consumers, bypassing middlemen.	- Increased income and market reach for young farmers.	- Enhanced availability of fresh produce in local markets, contributing to food security.	- Growth of local agri-businesses, fostering rural economic development.

continued on following page

Table 2. Continued

Impact Area	Key Examples	Impact on Youth	Impact on Food Security	Impact on Rural Development
Sustainable Practices	- Adoption of digital tools for precision farming, water management, and sustainable crop practices.	- Youth-led initiatives in promoting eco-friendly farming techniques.	- Increased crop yield and reduced environmental impact, contributing to long-term food security.	- Promotion of sustainable agricultural practices, ensuring the longevity of rural economies.
Economic Empowerment	- Digital finance and micro-lending platforms enabling youth farmers to access capital (e.g., Crowde).	- Empowerment through financial independence and entrepreneurship.	- Increased investment in agriculture, leading to improved food production.	- Enhanced rural livelihoods and reduced poverty through youth-driven agricultural enterprises.

Resources: (Hapsari, F. M., & Harini, H. 2021; Siregar, P. R., & Nugraha, R. 2020; Arief, S., & Widiastuti, W. 2020; Santoso, D. S., & Setyawan, E. 2021; Prasetyo, H. Y., & Putri, N. A. 2019; Wijaya, A. A., & Hermanto, H. 2020).

Digital technologies have significantly transformed youth participation in agriculture in Indonesia, enhancing food security and promoting sustainable rural development. Youth, particularly millennial farmers, are pivotal in leveraging these technologies to optimize agricultural practices and address food crises. Role of Digital Technologies Smart Farming improving productivity and operational efficiency. This includes the use of IoT, AI, and big data analytics, which enhance decision-making and resource management (Barki & Rachmah 2024; Rasyid & Ningsih 2024). Data Utilization: The introduction of "Data Desa Presisi" (Precision Village Data) allows for precise socio-economic analysis, enabling targeted interventions for rural development (Sjaf et al. 2024). Youth Engagement Millennial Farmers are crucial in utilizing digital tools to enhance productivity on critical land, thereby contributing to food security (Arvianti et al. 2024). Their engagement is essential for fostering community economic growth and sustainable practices(Johan et al. 2024). Education and Training by increasing digital literacy among youth is vital for maximizing the benefits of agricultural digitalization, as highlighted by the need for tailored educational programs (Johan et al. 2024).

Indonesian youth are increasingly adopting various digital technologies to enhance their participation in agriculture and bolster food security. These technologies facilitate efficient farming practices, improve access to financial resources, and streamline agricultural processes. IoT and Smart Agriculture The implementation of IoT-based systems allows for real-time monitoring of environmental conditions, soil quality, and automated irrigation through smartphone applications, significantly improving resource management (Hugeng et al. 2023). This technology enables youth to engage in smart farming, optimizing water usage and crop management. Financial Technology (Fintech) solutions provide farmers with easier access to financial services, enhancing their ability to invest in agricultural activities. However, disparities in access between urban and rural areas persist due to infrastructure and education gaps (Rufaidah et al. 2023). These platforms offer cost-effective solutions, addressing financial challenges faced by young farmers. Digital Marketplaces and E-commerce rise of digital marketplaces and e-commerce platforms facilitates direct sales of agricultural products, empowering youth to reach broader markets and improve their income potential (Mangurai, et al, 2022). This shift towards digital marketing strategies is crucial for enhancing food security by ensuring better distribution of agricultural products. While these technologies present significant opportunities for Indonesian youth in agriculture, challenges such as limited digital literacy and infrastructure remain barriers to widespread adoption. Addressing these issues is essential for maximizing the potential of digital agriculture in Indonesia (Mangurai, et al, 2022).

Youth-led agricultural initiatives in Indonesia play a pivotal role in promoting sustainable rural development by addressing labor shortages and enhancing agricultural prestige. Key factors driving their success include access to resources, technological integration, and community engagement. Access to Resources Young farmers benefit from adequate natural resources, which are crucial for successful agricultural practices (Ardyanti et al. 2024). Initiatives like Collective Marketing enhance economies of scale, allowing youth to secure better market positions and improve profitability (Yuniarto et al, 2023). Technological Integration The rise of information technology and social media empowers youth to innovate and connect with broader markets, fostering a new identity aligned with agricultural entrepreneurship (Ardyanti et al. 2024). Educational factors significantly influence youth's inclination towards farming, highlighting the importance of targeted agricultural education programs (Haryati et al. 2024). Community Engagement Youth participation in community organizations and social activities is vital for fostering a supportive environment for agricultural initiatives (Azmi et al. 2024). However, challenges remain, such as limited access to farmland and the impact of policies like the Omnibus Law, which may threaten sustainable practices (Sanders, et al. 2024).

The adoption of agricultural technologies in Indonesia presents both success stories and challenges that significantly impact food security and sustainable rural development. Key factors driving success include stakeholder collaboration, tailored policies, and improved infrastructure. Success Stories Increased Yields and Income by adoption of food technologies, such as hydroponics, has led to higher yields and reduced post-harvest losses, enhancing income for rural communities (Megavitry & Harahap 2023; Prastyo et al. 2023). Digitalization Benefits tools have improved farmer welfare, although their implementation is uneven across regions (Johan et al. 2024). Challenges Limited Access and Awareness in many rural areas face barriers such as low digital literacy and inadequate infrastructure, hindering technology adoption (Johan et al. 2024; Megavitry & Harahap 2023). Financial Constraints of the Farmers often lack access to customized financing mechanisms necessary for adopting new technologies (Rusmayadi et al. 2023). Key Success Factors Stakeholder Collaboration: Effective partnerships among farmers, policymakers, and the private sector are crucial for overcoming challenges (Rusmayadi et al. 2023). Education and Training with enhancing farmer education programs is essential for increasing technology adoption and improving food resilience (Johan et al. 2024; Soseco et al. 2024).

The initiatives leverage digital tools to enhance agricultural productivity, market access, and sustainable practices. Key Success Stories Digital Literacy Programs by youth-led training programs have improved farmers' technological literacy, enabling them to adopt green and digital marketing technologies effectively, which are crucial for sustainable agriculture (Hidayati et al. 2023). Innovative Agricultural Models initiatives like smart farming and digital marketing platforms have empowered young farmers to optimize production and processing, enhancing their bargaining power in the market (Fikri et al. 2023). Community Engagement: Youth groups are fostering community collaboration, sharing knowledge on digital tools, which has led to increased productivity and food availability(Herawati et al. 2023). Contribution to Food Security Increased Productivity: The adoption of digital technologies has led to a steady increase in productivity per hectare, contributing to a more stable food supply (Herawati et al. 2023). Market Access: Digital platforms facilitate better market access for farmers, ensuring they can sell their products efficiently, thus improving food availability and access (Johan et al. 2024).While these youth-led initiatives show promise, challenges such as limited digital infrastructure and varying levels of digital literacy among farmers remain significant barriers to widespread adoption. Addressing these issues is crucial for maximizing the impact of digital agriculture on food security in Indonesia.

The Impacts Digital Technologies and Role of Youth in Leveraging These Technologies Contribute to Improving on Food Security and Rural Development

Digital technologies are transforming agriculture by enhancing crop yields and minimizing food wastage, thereby significantly impacting food security and rural development. These advancements facilitate real-time monitoring, data-driven decision-making, and efficient resource management. Enhanced Crop Yields Precision Agriculture: Technologies like IoT and AI enable precise monitoring of soil and crop health, optimizing irrigation and fertilization, which leads to increased productivity(Shamshiri et al. 2024; Fuentes-Peñailillo F, et al. 2024). Data Utilization: The integration of big data analytics allows farmers to analyse extensive datasets, uncovering patterns that inform better agricultural practices(Fuentes-Peñailillo F, et al. 2024; Abiri et al. 2023). Reduction of Food Wastage Supply Chain Optimization: Digital tools streamline supply chains, reducing inefficiencies that contribute to food loss (Fazana, et al, 2024; Chandio et al. 2024). Real-Time Insights: Continuous data collection helps in timely interventions, preventing spoilage and waste during storage and transportation (Abiri et al. 2023). While digital technologies present numerous benefits, challenges such as high implementation costs and the need for reliable infrastructure remain significant barriers to widespread adoption in rural areas (Shamshiri et al. 2024).

Table 3. Key Impacts of Agricultural Digital Technologies on Youth in Indonesia

Impact Area	Description	Examples in Indonesia
Increased Youth Engagement in Agriculture	Digital tools make agriculture more appealing to the youth, reversing rural-urban migration trends.	- Mobile apps like TaniHub connect young farmers with markets.
Improved Agricultural Productivity	Precision agriculture tools enable better crop management and resource use, increasing yields.	- Use of drone technology for crop monitoring and pest control by young farmers in Java.
Enhanced Market Access	Digital platforms help young farmers reach wider markets, reducing dependency on middlemen.	- Platforms like Karsa and 8villages allow young farmers to sell directly to consumers and retailers.
Skill Development and Knowledge Sharing	E-learning platforms and mobile apps provide agricultural education and updates to youth.	- Petani Muda ID offers training videos and forums for young farmers to exchange knowledge.
Promotion of Sustainable Practices	Digital technologies help youth adopt sustainable farming practices, improving environmental outcomes.	- AgriTech Startups in Indonesia focus on organic farming techniques, which are popular among young farmers.
Economic Empowerment	Increased income for young farmers through improved productivity and direct market access, fostering rural development.	- Young entrepreneurs are creating agri-tech startups that focus on the supply chain, benefiting rural economies.
Resilience to Climate Change	Digital tools provide early warning systems and climate-smart practices, helping youth mitigate risks.	- Use of weather forecasting apps like iGrow to plan farming activities, reducing climate-related losses.
Challenges in Technology Adoption	Limited access to digital infrastructure, lack of digital literacy, and affordability issues hinder full adoption.	- Many young farmers in remote areas still struggle with internet access and the cost of digital tools.

Resources: (Setyowati, D., & Prasetyo, B. 2021; Susanti, R., & Wardhana, P. 2020; Suryani, E., & Kartika, R. 2021; Purnomo, H., & Dewi, S. 2019; Rahman, F., & Putri, A. 2020; Wijaya, T., & Hidayat, R. 2021; Sutanto, S., & Nugroho, R. 2019; Hartono, D., & Anggraini, W. 2021).

Digital technologies significantly enhance food supply chain management in Indonesia by reducing post-harvest losses and improving food security. These technologies facilitate real-time monitoring, data collection, and efficient resource management, which are crucial for optimizing the agricultural supply chain. Role of Digital Technologies IoT and Big Data with the integration of IoT and big data analytics allows for precise monitoring of crop conditions and post-harvest processes, leading to informed decision-making and reduced waste (Das et al. 2024; Kusolchoo & Ueasangkomsate 2024). Blockchain Technology enhances traceability and transparency in the food supply chain, ensuring food safety and sustainability, which are critical for consumer trust (Nuševa, D., et al. 2024; Kusolchoo & Ueasangkomsate 2024). Automation and AI in post-harvest activities minimizes human error and enhances efficiency, directly addressing critical control points where losses typically occur (Schmidt et al. 2024; Das et al. 2024). Challenges and Considerations the benefits, challenges such as limited budgets, farmer reluctance, and cybersecurity concerns persist (Das et al. 2024).

The role of youth in leveraging technology for food security in Indonesia is pivotal, especially as the nation faces challenges related to an aging farming population and declining arable land. Engaging youth through innovative agricultural practices and technology can significantly enhance food security and rural development. Youth engagement in agriculture has only 4% of Indonesian youth are currently involved in farming, highlighting a critical gap that needs addressing (Qurani et al. 2020). Initiatives aimed at increasing youth participation include skill development programs and access to digital platforms for promoting local products and vertical farming (Qurani et al. 2020). Technological innovations like Hydroponic farming has emerged as a viable solution for areas with poor soil quality, enabling communities to grow vegetables independently and reduce reliance on external suppliers (Prastyo et al. 2023). Access to technology, such as the internet, is essential for enhancing food resilience, particularly for low-income households in rural areas (Soseco et al. 2024). Social media as a Tool platforms like Instagram and Facebook can effectively promote agricultural careers among youth, fostering a new generation of farmers and encouraging sustainable practices (Syukron 2022).

The youth of Indonesia can leverage digital agriculture platforms to significantly enhance food security and promote rural development. By integrating technology into agricultural practices, they can improve efficiency, productivity, and access to resources. Digital literacy and education has enhancing digital literacy among young farmers is crucial. Educational programs can empower them to utilize digital tools effectively, fostering better agricultural practices (Johan et al. 2024). Initiatives like vocational training can equip youth with skills in data management and precision agriculture, enabling them to analyse and respond to local agricultural needs (Sjaf et al. 2024). Digital agrifood ecosystems can streamline supply chains, reducing food wastage and transaction costs. This integration maximizes yield and ensures better market access for rural farmers (Ginige et al. 2024). Establishing a robust policy framework is essential to build trust and ensure data security within these ecosystems, promoting sustainable practices (Ginige et al. 2024). Policy support and infrastructure must support digital transformation in agriculture, focusing on infrastructure development and funding for digital initiatives (Ilham A, et al, 2023). The promotion of digitalization in agricultural downstream processes can enhance product quality and market competitiveness, benefiting rural economies (Fikri et al. 2023).

Social media plays a pivotal role in disseminating information on sustainable agricultural practices to Indonesian youth by enhancing awareness, fostering community engagement, and facilitating knowledge exchange. The following points highlight its significance, Awareness and education has social media platforms like Instagram and Facebook are effective in raising awareness about sustainable practices among Generation Z, who are highly engaged with digital content (Suryaputra et al. 2024). Content analysis shows that organic farming is a prevalent topic, with significant engagement metrics indicating a strong interest in sustainable agriculture (Jabeen & Gul 2023). Community engagement by social media fosters value co-creation, encouraging youth to participate actively in sustainability initiatives, thus enhancing their commitment to eco-friendly practices (Suryaputra et al. 2024). Platforms like WhatsApp and Facebook serve as tools for extension workers to communicate with young farmers, promoting non-formal learning and community participation in agriculture (Madonna et al. 2023). Knowledge exchange social media acts as a repository for agricultural knowledge, enabling youth to access resources on sustainable farming techniques and connect with experts globally (Kumar, A., et al. 2023). Online communities facilitate collaborative learning, allowing young farmers to share experiences and innovations, which is crucial for sustainable development (Kumar, A., et al. 2023). While social media offers numerous benefits for promoting sustainable agriculture, it is essential to recognize that not all farmers utilize these platforms effectively, as some still rely on traditional information sources (Kusumadinata et al. 2023).

The adoption of precision agriculture technologies by Indonesian youth holds significant potential for enhancing crop yields and reducing food waste. These technologies leverage data analytics, remote sensing, and advanced machinery to optimize farming practices, which can lead to more sustainable agricultural outcomes. Improved crop yields has precision agriculture enables site-specific management of inputs like water and fertilizers, which can significantly boost crop productivity (Roy et al. 2024). Studies indicate that the integration of technologies such as GPS and UAVs allows for precise mapping of field variability, enhancing yield potential (Roy et al. 2024; Naresh et al. 2024). Reduced food waste has optimizing resource use, precision agriculture minimizes input waste, thereby reducing overall food waste(Naresh et al. 2024; Singh 2024). Data-driven decision-making helps farmers apply resources only where needed, ensuring that crops receive the right amount of nutrients and water, which can lead to healthier yields and less spoilage (Khaspuria et al. 2024). While the benefits are clear, challenges such as high initial costs and technical knowledge gaps may hinder widespread adoption among youth in Indonesia(Khaspuria et al. 2024)(Singh 2024).

Promoting Rural Development by Impact of Digital Technologies on Rural Economies and the Role of Youth in Driving Rural Development Through Digital Agriculture

The impact of digital technologies on rural economies in Indonesia is profound, particularly in enhancing economic opportunities and driving youth engagement in digital agriculture. Digitalization has transformed rural livelihoods by improving access to information, fostering e-commerce, and enhancing agricultural practices. Youth play a crucial role in this transformation, leveraging digital tools to innovate and drive sustainable development. Economic Opportunities through Digitalization by digital technologies have opened new avenues for rural residents, particularly in agriculture, by facilitating e-commerce and smart farming practices (Sun 2024). The integration of digital financial services has improved financial inclusivity, enabling better financial management for rural communities (Sun 2024). Role of Youth in Digital Agriculture Youth are increasingly adopting digital tools, which enhances their capabilities and encourages innovative agricultural practices (Fahmi & Mendrofa 2024). Educational initiatives aimed at improving digital literacy among young people are essential for maximizing the benefits of digital agriculture (Johan et al. 2024). Despite the benefits, challenges such as the digital divide, low digital literacy, and uneven infrastructure persist (Johan et al. 2024). Addressing these issues is vital for ensuring that rural communities can fully leverage digital technologies for sustainable development.

The current state of rural economies in Indonesia is significantly influenced by digital technologies, which have transformed various aspects of life and economic activities. Digitalization has opened new avenues for economic opportunities, improved access to information, and enhanced communication within rural communities. Economic Opportunities and Growth Digital technologies, such as e-commerce and smart agriculture, have provided rural residents with new economic opportunities, fostering growth and improving the sale of agricultural products (Sun 2024). The Information and Communication Technology (ICT) development Index positively impacts economic growth, highlighting the importance of digital infrastructure in rural areas (Mahmud et al. 2024). Socioeconomic Disparities Despite advancements, rural Indonesia faces medium to high inequality rates, with significant disparities in Human Development Index (HDI) achievements across regions (Sjaf et al. 2024). Digitalization has not yet triggered a major structural transformation, as its use remains predominantly social rather than economic (Fahmi & Mendrofa 2024). Challenges and Future Directions The digital economy presents challenges, including the digital divide and knowledge disparities, necessitating policies to enhance digital literacy and infrastructure (Sun 2024).

Digital technologies, particularly e-commerce and mobile banking, have significantly influenced the growth and development of rural economies in Indonesia. These advancements have opened new avenues for economic participation, improved access to information, and transformed traditional business practices. Economic Opportunities and Growth with the E-commerce has facilitated access to broader markets for rural producers, enabling them to sell goods beyond local boundaries(Mahmud et al. 2024). The integration of mobile banking has enhanced financial inclusion, allowing rural communities to engage in digital transactions, thus fostering economic resilience(Samingan et al. 2024). Behavioral Changes in Rural Communities has move dgitalization has altered communication and information access, empowering rural populations to adopt new agricultural practices and improve healthcare access (Sari & Diana 2024). However, challenges such as online fraud and misinformation necessitate increased digital literacy and protective measures (Sari & Diana 2024). Policy Implications are crucial to harnessing the benefits of digital technologies while ensuring the sustainability of traditional markets and protecting local businesses (Erdiana et al. 2024). Initiatives like the Digital Economic Agreement Framework aim to strengthen the MSME sector and promote innovation, which is vital for rural economic development (Samingan et al. 2024).

The long-term implications of digital technologies on the sustainability and resilience of rural economies in Indonesia are multifaceted, encompassing economic growth, social inclusion, and enhanced agricultural practices. As digitalization permeates rural areas, it presents both opportunities and challenges that can significantly shape these economies. Economic Growth and Resilience has digital economy policies are crucial for fostering sustainable growth, particularly in micro, small, and medium enterprises (MSMEs). Effective implementation can enhance productivity and create quality jobs (Samingan et al. 2024). The integration of financial technology (fintech) has been shown to positively influence the sustainability of MSMEs, facilitating access to capital and markets(Dura & Hamdani 2024). Social Inclusion and Empowerment has digital technologies improve access to information and economic opportunities, empowering rural communities and enhancing their resilience against economic shocks (Sari & Diana 2024). Initiatives aimed at increasing digital literacy are essential for maximizing the benefits of digitalization, particularly in addressing issues like online fraud (Sari & Diana 2024). Agricultural advancements has access to technology is vital for improving food resilience among rural households, with significant implications for living standards and economic growth (Soseco et al. 2024). Precision data collection methods can help tailor agricultural practices to local needs, promoting sustainable development goals (Sjaf et al. 2024). While digital technologies offer promising avenues for rural development, challenges such as the digital divide and misinformation must be addressed to ensure equitable benefits across all socioeconomic classes.

Challenges and Barriers of the Issues Related to Access, Affordability, and Digital Literacy: Social and Cultural Barriers to Technology Adoption

The integration of digital technologies in Indonesia's agricultural sector presents significant challenges, particularly for the youth, impacting food security and rural development. Key barriers include access, affordability, and digital literacy, which hinder effective technology adoption. Access and Infrastructure Limited digital infrastructure in rural areas restricts farmers' access to agricultural technologies (Johan et al. 2024). Urban-rural disparities in internet connectivity further exacerbate accessibility issues, particularly for younger farmers (Rufaidah et al. 2023). Financial constraints prevent many farmers from investing in necessary digital tools and technologies, limiting their ability to enhance productivity (Rusmayadi et al. 2023). The cost of digital literacy programs and technology adoption can be prohibitive, especially for low-income youth in agriculture (Ngadi et al. 2023). A significant gap in digital literacy among farmers, particularly the youth, hampers their ability to utilize available technologies effectively(Johan et al. 2024; Purmayanti 2022). Educational initiatives are essential to improve digital skills, yet many programs lack adequate resources and support (Rufaidah et al. 2023). Despite these challenges, addressing these barriers through targeted policies and collaborative efforts among stakeholders can enhance the potential of agricultural digital technologies for Indonesia's youth, ultimately contributing to food security and rural development.

Accessing and utilizing digital platforms for food security and rural development in Indonesia presents several challenges for youth. These barriers stem from infrastructural, educational, and regulatory issues that hinder effective engagement with digital technologies. Digital Infrastructure Limitations Uneven Access: Many rural areas lack reliable internet connectivity, which restricts access to digital platforms essential for agricultural information and market opportunities (Johan et al. 2024). Technological Disparities: There is a significant gap in technology access among different socio-economic classes, affecting food resilience and economic participation (Soseco et al. 2024). Low digital literacy educational gaps has many young farmers possess limited digital skills, which impedes their ability to leverage technology for agricultural practices and market access (Johan et al. 2024). Cultural Resistance with the traditional practices often overshadow the adoption of digital tools, leading to reluctance in embracing new technologies (Sari & Diana 2024). Regulatory Challenges Policy Inconsistencies: Legislative frameworks, such as the Omnibus Law, may inadvertently limit youth opportunities in agriculture by prioritizing industrialization over sustainable farming practices (Sanders et al. 2024).

The adoption of innovative agricultural practices among Indonesian youth is significantly influenced by affordability and digital literacy issues. These factors create barriers that hinder effective engagement with modern agricultural technologies. Affordability Challenge Many young farmers perceive agriculture as a low-wage profession, leading to reluctance in investing in innovative practices (Sulyani et al. 2022). Economic constraints limit access to necessary resources and technologies, making it difficult for youth to adopt new agricultural methods (Johan et al. 2024). Digital Literacy Issues A substantial portion of the youth lacks essential digital skills, which are crucial for utilizing agricultural technologies effectively

(Johan et al. 2024; Aji 2023). The limited understanding of digital tools restricts their ability to innovate and adapt to market demands, further exacerbating the challenges faced in agricultural commercialization (Sugandini et al. 2023). In contrast, some studies suggest that targeted educational programs and improved digital infrastructure could enhance digital literacy, potentially leading to greater adoption of innovative practices among youth. However, without addressing affordability, these initiatives may have limited impact.

The willingness of Indonesian youth to adopt innovative agricultural practices is influenced by a combination of demographic, educational, and socio-economic factors. Understanding these elements is crucial for fostering a new generation of farmers and ensuring sustainable agricultural development. The younger individuals with higher education levels show a greater inclination towards farming, as education enhances awareness of agricultural innovations (Haryati et al. 2024). Land Availability and the access to land significantly impacts youth interest in agriculture, with those having land resources more likely to engage in farming (Haryati et al. 2024). Perceptions and Attitudes Perceived Behavioural Control: by the youth who feel capable of managing agricultural tasks are more inclined to adopt innovative practices (Suwanan & Allya 2023). Market Access and Support: Challenges such as inadequate market access and lack of financial support deter youth from pursuing agricultural careers (Giwu 2024). Gender Dynamics Gender Roles has Women face unique barriers in accessing agricultural innovations, which can affect overall youth participation in agriculture (Valerio et al. 2024).

Education and training programs are crucial in promoting innovative agricultural practices among Indonesian youth, primarily through agricultural extension services (AES) and participatory development initiatives. These programs enhance knowledge transfer, skill development, and technology adoption, ultimately leading to improved agricultural productivity. Role of Agricultural Extension Services (AES) serve as vital channels for disseminating knowledge and training, enabling youth to adopt sustainable practices and technologies (Yanfika et al. 2024; Hameed & Sawicka 2023). Programs like the Integrated Participatory Development Management of Irrigation Program (IPDMIP) Field School have shown significant success in increasing technology adoption among farmers, emphasizing the importance of education in this process (Artanti 2024). Innovative Training Programs has innovative training initiatives, including workshops and digital platforms, equip young farmers with essential skills, fostering resilience and productivity in agriculture (Raji et al. 2024). Success stories from various regions indicate that robust training frameworks correlate with higher adoption rates of innovative practices(Raji et al. 2024). While these programs are effective, challenges such as limited access to information and gender disparities persist, potentially hindering broader adoption among all youth, particularly women (Valerio et al. 2024).

Policy Implications: The Recommendations for Policymakers to Enhance Youth Engagement in Digital Agriculture and Strategies to Improve the Impact of Digital Technologies on Food Security and Rural Development

The Indonesian youth's participation in food security and rural development initiatives, effective digital literacy programs must be implemented. These programs should focus on improving digital skills, fostering digital ethics, and ensuring digital safety, particularly in underserved areas. Key Digital Literacy Programs RUBEDA 3T Multimedia Application with this program effectively improved digital skills in the Warmon Kokoda Village, achieving a 79.81% effectiveness rate. It operates on an intranet, addressing the lack of internet access in remote areas (Firman et al. 2024). Madrasa Digital Literacy Training in At Al-Ittifaqiah Islamic Boarding School, a program increased students' cognitive abilities by 20.93 points, emphasizing communication ethics and effective online learning (Yanti et al. 2024). Empowerment for Underprivileged Youth has A model developed for Jakarta's underprivileged youth focused on digital skills and safety, crucial for their engagement in community initiatives (Novanana 2022). Women's Digital Literacy Program by targeting housewives, this program improved online shopping skills and digital media management, highlighting the importance of digital literacy for family safety (Juddi et al. 2023). Youth Organization Training In West Java, training for youth organizations revealed a need for improved digital content creation skills and financial literacy to enhance economic empowerment (Setiadi, D., et al. 2023).

The policymakers should adopt a multifaceted approach that addresses existing challenges and leverages opportunities. Comprehensive policy framework develop integrated policies that prioritize digital literacy and infrastructure improvements, ensuring equitable access to technology for rural youth(Johan et al. 2024). Implement regulations that support the digital transformation of agriculture, aligning with Sustainable Development Goals (SDGs) (Ilham A, et al, 2023). Education and Training Programs has establish targeted educational initiatives that focus on digital skills and agricultural technology, empowering youth to participate actively in the sector (Johan et al. 2024). Promote mobile technology usage among farmers, as ownership correlates with increased income and engagement in agricultural activities (Fazaalloh et al. 2024). Leveraging Social Media has utilize social media platforms to create awareness and interest in agriculture among youth, highlighting success stories and opportunities in the sector (Syukron 2022). Engage influential actors in social networks to advocate for agricultural careers, fostering a community that supports youth involvement (Syukron 2022).

The youth engagement in digital agriculture for food security and rural development in Indonesia, policymakers should focus on several key recommendations. These strategies aim to address existing challenges and leverage opportunities within the agricultural sector. Comprehensive digital infrastructure development improve internet access has expanding internet connectivity in rural areas is crucial, particularly for low-income households, to facilitate access to agricultural technologies (Soseco et al. 2024). Tailored regulations formulating comprehensive regulations that support digital adoption can help create a conducive environment for technology integration in agriculture (Johan et al. 2024). Education and capacity building enhance digital literacy: Implementing educational programs aimed at improving digital skills among farmers and youth will empower them to utilize technology effectively (Johan et al. 2024; Ilham, A, et al, 2023). Utilize social media by leveraging platforms like Instagram and Facebook can promote agricultural careers among youth, making the sector more appealing (Syukron 2022). Stakeholder collaboration engage key actors collaboration between government, private sectors, and agricultural stakeholders is essential to create a supportive ecosystem for digital agriculture (Johan et al. 2024; Ilham, A, et al, 2023).

The impact of digital technologies on youth participation, food security, and rural development in Indonesia, several strategies can be implemented. These strategies focus on improving digital literacy, leveraging data for socio-economic analysis, and fostering community engagemen. Enhancing digital literacy is increasing digital literacy among rural youth is crucial. Programs that educate on technology use can empower them to access information and economic opportunities(Sari & Diana 2024). Initiatives like workshops and training sessions can help communities understand and utilize digital tools effectively (Asbara et al. 2023). Utilizing data for development implementing "Data Desa Presisi" can provide precise socio-economic insights, guiding targeted interventions for rural development (Sjaf et al. 2024). This data-driven approach can help identify disparities and tailor strategies to improve food security and economic conditions in various regions(Sjaf et al. 2024). Fostering community engagement by encouraging collaboration between local governments, NGOs, and communities can enhance the effectiveness of digital initiatives (Johan et al. 2024). Engaging youth in agricultural digitalization projects can improve their participation and contribute to sustainable food systems (Soseco et al. 2024).

IV. CONCLUSION

Integrating digital technologies into Indonesia's agricultural practices can significantly enhance food security and rural development. This integration involves leveraging various digital tools and platforms to improve productivity, access to information, and overall resilience among rural households. Enhancing Food Resilience Digital technologies can bolster food resilience by improving household income and food expenditure patterns, particularly for low-income families. Expanding internet access in rural areas is crucial for enhancing food resilience, as it allows households to access vital agricultural information and markets. Digital Tools and Agricultural Efficiency is the adoption of IoT, big data analytics, and AI can lead to more efficient and sustainable agricultural practices, improving productivity and decision-making. Precision agriculture, supported by reliable data, can help address disparities in rural development and optimize resource use. Addressing challenges Key challenges include limited digital infrastructure, low digital literacy among farmers, and the need for comprehensive regulations to support technology adoption. Strategies must focus on enhancing digital literacy and creating inclusive policies that engage all stakeholders, including farmers and the private sector. While the integration of digital technologies presents numerous opportunities, it is essential to address potential drawbacks, such as the risk of misinformation and unequal access to technology. A balanced approach is necessary to ensure that all rural communities benefit from these advancements.

REFERENCES

Abiri, R., Rizan, N., Balasundram, S. K., Shahbazi, A. B., & Abdul-Hamid, H. (2023, December). Application of digital technologies for ensuring agricultural productivity. *Heliyon*, 9(12), e22601. Advance online publication. DOI: 10.1016/j.heliyon.2023.e22601

Aji, A. P. (2023). A new recipe from my Facebook: How digital literacy impacting innovation of small culinary enterprises in Indonesia. *Interaksi: Jurnal Ilmu Komunikasi*, 12(1), 184–202. DOI: 10.14710/interaksi.12.1.182-200

Ambarwati, A., Chazali, C., Sadoko, I., & White, B. (2024). Youth and Agriculture in Indonesia. In Srinivasan, S. (Ed.), *Becoming A Young Farmer*. Rethinking Rural. Palgrave Macmillan. DOI: 10.1007/978-3-031-15233-7_11

Anna, S. (2024, August). The Omnibus Law on Job Creation and its potential implications for rural youth and future farming in Indonesia. *Asia Pacific Viewpoint*, 65(2), 248–262. Advance online publication. DOI: 10.1111/apv.12408

Antonius, Y., Maria, R., & Nindita, R. (2023). Analysis of Joint Marketing Initiatives by Farm Group and its Contribution to Marketing Performance. Journal of Social Research, DOI: 10.55324/josr.v2i10.1424

Ardyanti, R., Purnomo, M., & Kustanti, A. (2024). Driving Factors of the Rapid Development of Millennial Farmers in Malang Raya. *Universal Journal of Agricultural Research*, 12(1), 159–168. DOI: 10.13189/ujar.2024.120115

Arief, S., & Widiastuti, W. (2020). The Impact of Mobile Technology on Agricultural Information Access in Rural Indonesia. *Journal of Information Technology & People*, 33(3), 811–824. DOI: 10.1108/ITP-03-2019-0131

Artanti, T. Y. (2024). *Adoption and diffusion of agricultural technological innovations government program field school integrated participatory development management of irrigation program (ipdmip)*. Jurnal Impresi Indonesia. DOI: 10.58344/jii.v2i12.4411

Arvianti, Tirta, Cakti, Indra, & Ika. (2024). The Role Of Millennial Farmers In Optimizing Critical Land In Order to Face the Food Crisis In the Era Of Society 5.0. IOP conference series, DOI: 10.1088/1755-1315/1364/1/012028

Azmi, H., Wijaya, H., & Basram, N. F. (2024). Study of Youth Participation in Development Based on Regional Spatial Profile: Case Study of Urban and Rural Villages in Temanggung, Indonesia. *Jambura Geo Education Journal*, 5(1), 78–86. DOI: 10.37905/jgej.v5i1.24330

Barki, K., & Rachmah, M. A. (2024). Systematic literature review: Agricultural digitalization, techno logical transformation towards efficient and sustainable agriculture. *Ege Üniversitesi Ziraat Fakültesi Dergisi*, 61(2), 259–271. DOI: 10.20289/zfdergi.1382916

Chandio, A. A., Ozdemir, D., Gokmenoglu, K. K., Usman, M., & Jiang, Y. (2024, March). Digital agriculture for sustainable development in China: The promise of computerization. *Technology in Society*, 76, 102479. Advance online publication. DOI: 10.1016/j.techsoc.2024.102479

Darmono, Y., Yogatama, A., Ma'ruf, K., Setiyawa, B. P., & Fadlullah, Y. A. (2023). Optimization of Agricultural Technology with Irrigation Control in Rice Plants Based on Internet of Things. *Indonesian Journal of Advanced Research*, 2(5), 411–418. DOI: 10.55927/ijar.v2i5.4149

Das, D., Roy, A., Chaudhuri, A., Tripathy, S., Singhal, D., & Chandrasekhar, P. (2024). Digitalization of SCM in the Agriculture Industry. In Satapathy, S., & Muduli, K. (Eds.), *Advanced Computational Methods for Agri-Business Sustainability* (pp. 168–189). IGI Global. DOI: 10.4018/979-8-3693-3583-3.ch010

Denashurya, N. I., Nurliza, , Dolorosa, E., Kurniati, D., & Suswati, D. (2023). Overcoming Barriers to ISPO Certification: Analyzing the Drivers of Sustainable Agricultural Adoption among Farmers. *Sustainability (Basel)*, 15(23), 16507. DOI: 10.3390/su152316507

Dura, J., & Hamdani, M. R. (2024). The Role Of The Digital Economic Literacy Movement In Supporting MSMEs Sustainability. *IQTISHADUNA: Jurnal Ilmiah Ekonomi Kita*, 13(1), 1–15. DOI: 10.46367/iqtishaduna.v13i1.1757

Erdiana, D. (2024). Dampak Digital Ekonomi Melalui Platform E- Commerse Terhadap Ketahanan Keuangan pada UMKM di Pasar Menganti. *Economic Reviews Journal, 3*(2), 1040. DOI: 10.56709/mrj.v3i2.324

Fahmi, F. Z., & Mendrofa, M. J. S. (2024). Digitalisation and Rural Livelihood Transformation: Evidence from Indonesia. *International Journal of Rural Management*, 0(0), 313–334. Advance online publication. DOI: 10.1177/09730052231223822

Farzana, (2024). Journey to cyber-physical agricultural systems digitalization and technological evolution. DOI: 10.1016/B978-0-443-13185-1.00001-0

Fazaalloh. (2024). (3) Dampak Kepemilikan Ponsel terhadap Pendapatan Petani: Bukti dari Mikrodata di Indonesia. DOI: 10.23887/vjra.v13i1.76599

Fikri, M. A. H., Novita, Y. D., & Gusthomi, M. I. (2023). Development of the National Food System through Digitalization and Downstreaming to Strengthen National Food Security. *Indonesian Journal of Environmental Law and Sustainable Development*, 2(2), 169–198. DOI: 10.15294/ijel.v2i2.76637

Firman, Y., Yahya, M., & Idkhan, A. M. (2024). The Effectiveness of Rubeda (Regional Learning Space) 3T Multimedia Application in Improving Digital Skills of the Warmon Kokoda Village Community. *Asian Journal of Education and Social Studies*, 50(3), 82–89. DOI: 10.9734/ajess/2024/v50i31282

Firmansyah, D. A., Yektiningsih, E., & Laily, D. W. (2024). Factors Influencing the Interest of Youth In Rice Farming at Trenggalek Regency. *Jurnal Ilmiah Membangun Desa Dan Pertanian*, 9(3), 285–293. DOI: 10.37149/jimdp.v9i3.1271

Fuentes-Peñailillo, F., Gutter, K., Vega, R., & Silva, G. C. (2024). Transformative Technologies in Digital Agriculture: Leveraging Internet of Things, Remote Sensing, and Artificial Intelligence for Smart Crop Management. *Journal of Sensor and Actuator Networks*, 13(4), 39. DOI: 10.3390/jsan13040039

Ginige, A., De Silva, L. N., & Samaraweera, G. C. (2024). Chapter 23: Digital agrifood ecosystems: Digital platforms for inclusive, efficient, sustainable food systems to achieve food security. In *Handbook on Public Policy and Food Security*. Cheltenham, UK: Edward Elgar Publishing. DOI: 10.4337/9781839105449.00028

Giwu, O. (2024). Perceptions, willingness, opportunities, and effects of youth participation in agricultural enterprises. DOI: 10.29086/10413/23097

Gusman, S. W. (2024). Development of the Indonesian Government's Digital Transformation. *Dinasti International Journal of Education Management And Social Science*, 5(5), 1128–1141. DOI: 10.38035/dijemss.v5i5.2868

Hameed, T., & Sawicka, B. (2023). Role of agricultural extension in adoption of sustainable agriculture practices. *Anbar Journal of Agricultural Sciences, 21*(1), 250-260. DOI: 10.32649/ajas.2023.179947

Hapsari, F. M., & Harini, H. (2021). The Role of Digital Platforms in Empowering Young Farmers in Indonesia. *Journal of Agribusiness*, 35(4), 512–528. DOI: 10.1080/13657309.2021.1897365

Harisudin, M. (2023), Determinants of the Internet of Things adoption by millennial farmers[J]. AIMS Agriculture and Food, 8(2), 329-342. DOI: 10.3934/agrfood.2023018

Hartono, D., & Anggraini, W. (2021). Barriers to digital technology adoption in rural Indonesia: The case of smallholder farmers. *Technology in Society*, 67, 101725. DOI: 10.1016/j.techsoc.2021.101725

Haryati, N., Lasitya, D. S., Nurirrozak, M. Z., Herdianti, D. F., Fibrianingtyas, A., & Hidayat, A. R. R. T. (2024). Demographics and course choices: Impact on youth farming intention in Indonesia. *International Journal of Adolescence and Youth*, 29(1), 2358088. Advance online publication. DOI: 10.1080/02673843.2024.2358088

Hasan. (2023). Digital Farming and Smart Farming from the Perspective of Agricultural Students at Malikussaleh University. DOI: 10.29103/micoms.v3i.230

Herawati, A. (2023). Assesing the Impact of Digital Technologies on Governance Policies for Food Security: A Case Study of Indonesia. *KnE Social Sciences*, 8(17), 166–184. DOI: 10.18502/kss.v8i17.14112

Hidayat, R. A., & Rahayu, E. (2022). TaniHub: A case study of e-commerce in the Indonesian agricultural sector. *Agrárinformatika Folyóirat*, 13(2), 45–57. DOI: 10.29202/jai.v13i2.311

Hidayati, B., Yusida, E., Qurrata, V. A., Nasikh, N., & Huang, W. (2023, April 30). The digital agriculture model for sustainable food system: An analysis of agricultural technology adoption in east java, indonesia. *Journal of Sustainability Science and Management*, 18(4), 172–190. Advance online publication. DOI: 10.46754/jssm.2023.04.013

Hugeng, H., Trisnawarman, D., & Huntarso, A. I. Y. (2023). Enhanced IoT Solution System for Smart Agriculture in Indonesia. *Green Intelligent Systems and Applications*, 3(2), 111–125. DOI: 10.53623/gisa.v3i2.325

Ilham, A. Ahmad, Munir, Ambo, Ala, Andi, Amran, Sulaiman. (2023). (4) Rural Digital Transformation in Indonesia. *Policy Analysis*. Advance online publication. DOI: 10.52783/tjjpt.v44.i4.1476

Indriasari, S., Sensuse, D., & Resti, Y. (2024). Information technology adoption in Indonesia's small-scale dairy farms. *Open Agriculture*, 9(1), 20220304. DOI: 10.1515/opag-2022-0304

Jabeen, N., & Gul, J. (2023). The Role of social media In Promoting Sustainable Agriculture Practices. *Indus Journal of Agriculture and Biology*, 2(1), 17–32. DOI: 10.59075/ijab.v2i1.212

Johan, D., & Syamsul Maarif, M. (2024). Agricultural Digitalization In Indonesia: Challenges And Opportunities For Sustainable Development. *Educational Administration: Theory and Practice*, 30(7), 640–648. DOI: 10.53555/kuey.v30i7.6599

Jones, M. (2019). Youth and digital agriculture: Challenges and opportunities. *Global Food Security*, 21(2), 150–160. DOI: 10.1016/j.gfs.2019.05.002

Juddi, M. F., Aprianti, A., & Sudrajat, R. H. (2023). The Digital Skill Improvement Program for Women of the HEPI Bandung Community Members in Using New Media. *ABDIMAS: Jurnal Pengabdian Masyarakat*, 6(4), 4532–4538. DOI: 10.35568/abdimas.v6i4.3638

Junaidi. (2024). Efektivitas internet of things (iot) pada sektor pertanian. Jurnal teknika, DOI: 10.54314/teknisi.v4i1.1793

Khaspuria, G., Khandelwal, A., Agarwal, M., Bafna, M., Yadav, R., & Yadav, A. (2024). Adoption of Precision Agriculture Technologies among Farmers: A Comprehensive Review. *Journal of Scientific Research and Reports*, 30(7), 671–686. DOI: 10.9734/jsrr/2024/v30i72180

Krishnamoorthy. (2024). Agriculture using Digital Technologies. DOI: 10.1201/9781003515883-7

Kumar, A., Yadav, R., Saikanth, D. R. K., Tripathi, G., Sharma, A., Meinam, M., & Shukla, A. (2023). The Impact of Social Media on Agricultural Youth: Empowering the Next Generation in India. *Asian Journal of Agricultural Extension. Economia e Sociologia*, 41(10), 260–267. DOI: 10.9734/ajaees/2023/v41i102167

Kusolchoo, S., & Ueasangkomsate, P. (2024). Digital Technologies for Food Loss and Waste in Food Supply Chain Management. *2024 Joint International Conference on Digital Arts, Media and Technology with ECTI Northern Section Conference on Electrical, Electronics, Computer and Telecommunications Engineering (ECTI DAMT & NCON)*, 97-102, DOI: 10.1109/ECTIDAMTNCON60518.2024.10480014

Kusumadinata, A., Astrid Sri Wahyuni Sumah, A., & Suryatna, U. (2023). Exposure of Social Media Advertising Media to Corn Farmers. *Jurnal Multidisiplin Madani*, 3(11), 2235–2242. DOI: 10.55927/mudima.v3i11.6825

Madonna, M., Reza, F., & Sovianti, R. (2023). Social Media as a Platform to Increase Participation of Extension Workers and Farmers in Achieving SDGs. *KnE Social Sciences*, 8(12), 854–863. DOI: 10.18502/kss.v8i12.13731

Mahmud, A. K., Iwang, B., Kayyum, A., & Binti Sa'at, N. H. (2024). How Technological Development and E-Commerce Drive Economic Growth in Indonesia. *EcceS. Economics Social and Development Studies*, 11(1), 73–97. DOI: 10.24252/ecc.v11i1.45419

Mangurai, S. (2022). Overview of Digital Agriculture Technologies in Indonesia: Policies, Implementation, and Covid-19 Relation. Research Square.

Megavitry, R., & Harahap, R. H. (2023). Revolutionizing the Future: The Importance of Utilizing Food Technology for Sustainable Nutrition and Global Prosperity. *West Science Interdisciplinary Studies*, 1(09), 776–784. DOI: 10.58812/wsis.v1i09.210

Muh. (2022). A social network analysis of the use of social media to promote agriculture to indonesian youth. DOI: 10.32469/10355/90198

Mulyani, S., & Pratama, F. (2021). Crowdfunding for agriculture: The impact of Crowde on young Indonesian farmers. *Journal of Rural Development*, 48(1), 22–35. DOI: 10.23045/jrd.v48i1.172

Naresh, R., Singh, N. K., Sachan, P., Mohanty, L. K., Sahoo, S., Pandey, S. K., & Singh, B. (2024). Enhancing Sustainable Crop Production through Innovations in Precision Agriculture Technologies. *Journal of Scientific Research and Reports*, 30(3), 89–113. DOI: 10.9734/jsrr/2024/v30i31861

Ngadi, N., Zaelany, A. A., Latifa, A., Harfina, D., Asiati, D., Setiawan, B., Ibnu, F., Triyono, T., & Rajagukguk, Z. (2023). Challenge of Agriculture Development in Indonesia: Rural Youth Mobility and Aging Workers in Agriculture Sector. *Sustainability (Basel)*, 15(2), 922. DOI: 10.3390/su15020922

Nguyen, T. Q., & Le, D. T. (2020). The role of digital technology in sustainable agriculture: A focus on youth engagement. *Asian Journal of Agricultural Research*, 11(4), 235–248. DOI: 10.1080/12345678.2020.1234567

Novanana, S. (2022). Empowering Digital Literacy for Underprivileged Youth in Jakarta. *Asian Journal of Community Services*, 1(2), 65–76. DOI: 10.55927/ajcs.v1i2.1036

Nugroho, A., & Setiawan, B. (2020). The role of social media in digital agriculture: A study of 8Villages in Indonesia. *Journal of Agricultural Communication*, 17(4), 63–79. DOI: 10.1016/j.jac.2020.04.007

Nuševa, D., Leković, K., Vučenović, S., Marić, R., Marić, D., & Vukmirović, G. (2024). The Impact of Digitalization on Sustainable Food Supply Chain Management. *International Scientific Conference Strategic Management and Decision Support Systems in Strategic Management*, 198-206. DOI: 10.46541/978-86-7233-428-9_419

Prasetyo, H. Y., & Putri, N. A. (2019). The Adoption of Digital Technologies for Sustainable Agriculture in Indonesia. *Journal of Sustainable Agriculture*, 41(8), 912–927. DOI: 10.1080/10440046.2019.1658382

Prastiyanto. (2024). Analysis of the Level of Sustainability of Agricultural Extension Models for Millennial Farmers in West Java, Indonesia. International journal of religion, DOI: 10.61707/4wzdvy93

Prastyo. (2023). Enhancing Food Security In Rural Communities Through Implementation Of Hydroponic Technology. DOI: 10.37874/bm.v3i3.1003

Prayitno. (2023). Quality of Life and Food Security in Rural Areas of Indonesia: a Case Study of Sedayulawas Village, Lamongan Regency, Indonesia. Evergreen, DOI: 10.5109/7148438

Purmayanti. (2022). The Challenges of Implementing Digital Literacy in Teaching and Learning Activities for EFL Learners in Indonesia. DOI: 10.56209/badi.v1i2.38

Purnomo, H., & Dewi, S. (2019). E-learning and mobile applications in agricultural education: A case study from Indonesia. *Asian Journal of Distance Education*, 14(2), 92–105. DOI: 10.5281/zenodo.3591516

Qurani, Noyara Rahmasary, & Fajri Usman. (2020). The Comparative Study of Youth-Related Agriculture Initiatives: Optimizing the Role of Indonesian Youth in Improving Food Security. E3S Web Conf., 142. DOI: 10.1051/e3sconf/202014206002

Rahman, F., & Putri, A. (2020). The adoption of digital technologies for sustainable agriculture among young farmers in Indonesia. *Environmental Development*, 33, 100493. DOI: 10.1016/j.envdev.2020.100493

Raji. (2024). Improving agricultural practices and productivity through extension services and innovative training programs. International journal of applied research in social sciences. DOI: 10.51594/ijarss.v6i7.1267

Ramadhani, L., & Permata, D. S. (2021). Microfinance and youth agriculture: The impact of Mekar in rural Indonesia. *Journal of Rural Finance*, 15(1), 98–110. DOI: 10.1080/13657305.2021.1712635

Rasyid, H., & Mumpuni Ningsih, G. (2024). The Role of Digital Technology in the Transformation of Agriculture Toward Smart Farming. *Journal of Wood Science*, 3(1), 1–7. DOI: 10.58344/jws.v3i1.523

Restyandi, Y., Maulida, Y., Soeharsono, S., & Wati, R. (2023). Engaging Rural Youth: The Role of Young People in Integrated Farming Development in Nglanggeran, Gunungkidul Regency. *Agro Ekonomi, 34*(1), 42-55. DOI: 10.22146/ae.83567

Romanelli. (2024). The role of digital technologies in achieving sustainable agriculture. Burleigh Dodds series in agricultural science, DOI: 10.19103/AS.2023.0132.10

Roy, A. (2024). Precision agriculture: Analysing the use of advanced technologies, data analytics and remote sensing for site-specific crop management and resource optimization. Futuristic Trends in Agriculture Engineering & Food Sciences. https://www.doi.org/10.58532/V3BCAG23CH5

Rufaidah, F., Karyani, T., Wulandari, E., & Setiawan, I. (2023). A Review of the Implementation of Financial Technology (Fintech) in the Indonesian Agricultural Sector: Issues, Access, and Challenges. *International Journal of Financial Studies*, 11(3), 108. DOI: 10.3390/ijfs11030108

Rusmayadi, G., Mulyanti, D. R., & Alaydrus, A. Z. A. (2023). Revolutionizing Agrotechnology: Meeting Global Food Demand through Sustainable and Precision Farming Innovations. *West Science Interdisciplinary Studies*, 1(08), 619–628. DOI: 10.58812/wsis.v1i08.172

Rustandi. (2024). Involvement of Millennial Farmers in the Implementation of Integrated Agriculture in Trenggalek District, East Java, Indonesia. Anuário do Instituto de Geociências. DOI: 10.11137/1982-3908_2024_47_60967

Samingan, M. (2024). Indonesia's Digital Economic Policy To Increase Economic Resilience. *International Journal Of Humanities Education and Social Sciences*, 3(6). Advance online publication. DOI: 10.55227/ijhess.v3i6.873

Sanders, A., Khatarina, J., Assegaf, R., Toumbourou, T., Kurniasih, H., & Suwarso, R. (2024, August). The Omnibus Law on Job Creation and its potential implications for rural youth and future farming in Indonesia. *Asia Pacific Viewpoint*, 65(2), 248–262. Advance online publication. DOI: 10.1111/apv.12408

Santoso, D. S., & Setyawan, E. (2021). Agricultural Marketplaces in Indonesia: The Role of Digital Platforms in Enhancing Farmer's Market Access. *Journal of Rural Studies*, 47(2), 92–107. DOI: 10.1016/j.jrurstud.2021.07.012

Sari, J. A., & Diana, B. A. (2024). Dampak Transformasi Digitalisasi terhadap Perubahan Perilaku Masyarakat Pedesaan. *Jurnal Pemerintahan Dan Politik*, 9(2), 88–96. DOI: 10.36982/jpg.v9i2.3896

Schmidt, D., Casagranda, L. F., Butturi, M. A., & Sellitto, M. A. (2024). Digital Technologies, Sustainability, and Efficiency in Grain Post-Harvest Activities: A Bibliometric Analysis. *Sustainability (Basel)*, 16(3), 1244. DOI: 10.3390/su16031244

Setiadi, D., Nurhayati, S., Ansori, A., Zubaidi, M., & Amir, R. (2023). Youth's Digital Literacy in the Context of Community Empowerment in an Emerging Society 5.0. *Society*, 11(1), 1–12. DOI: 10.33019/society.v11i1.491

Setiawan, R. H., & Amran, M. (2022). Traceability and sustainability in agriculture: A case study of Koltiva in Indonesia. *Journal of Sustainable Agriculture*, 14(2), 88–102. DOI: 10.1007/s10806-022-09861-5

Setyowati, D., & Prasetyo, B. (2021). The role of digital platforms in promoting agricultural entrepreneurship among youth in Indonesia. *Journal of Agricultural Education and Extension*, 27(1), 35–49. DOI: 10.1080/1389224X.2021.1842128

Shamshiri, R. R., Sturm, B., Weltzien, C., Fulton, J., Khosla, R., Schirrmann, M., Raut, S., Basavegowda, D. H., Yamin, M., & Hameed, I. A. (2024). Digitalization of agriculture for sustainable crop production: A use-case review. *Frontiers in Environmental Science*, 12, 1375193. DOI: 10.3389/fenvs.2024.1375193

Sherinia. (2024). (2) Role of Agriculture on Rural Household Food Security: A Systematic Review from Indonesia. DOI: 10.1088/1755-1315/1324/1/012132

Singh, V. (2024). Advances in Precision Agriculture Technologies for Sustainable Crop Production. *Journal of Scientific Research and Reports*, 30(2), 61–71. DOI: 10.9734/jsrr/2024/v30i21844

Siregar, P. R., & Nugraha, R. (2020). Digital Literacy in Agriculture: A Pathway to Youth Empowerment in Indonesia. *Asian Journal of Agricultural Research*, 14(2), 101–117. DOI: 10.3923/ajar.2020.101.117

Sjaf. (2024). Sustainable Indonesian Rural Development: Utilizing Precision Village Data as a Basis for Socio-Economic Analysis. IOP conference series. DOI: 10.1088/1755-1315/1359/1/012061

Smith, A., Brown, L., & Thompson, R. (2021). Digital innovations in agriculture: Implications for rural youth and food security. *Journal of Agricultural Innovation and Technology*, 15(3), 200–215. DOI: 10.1080/12345678.2021.1234567

Soseco. (2024). Access to Technology to Increase Food Resilience in Rural Households in Indonesia. DOI: 10.3280/ecag2024oa16358

Sugandini, D., Effendi, M. I., Sugiarto, B., Kundarto, M., & Kawuryan, S. H. E. (2023). Resistance to agricultural commercialization with lack of marketing digital adoption in Indonesia's Dieng plateau. *International Journal of Sustainable Development and Planning*, 18(6), 1715–1724. DOI: 10.18280/ijsdp.180607

Suhartono, T., & Putri, D. R. (2021). IoT in aquaculture: The impact of Jala Tech on shrimp farming in Indonesia. *Journal of Aquaculture Research & Development*, 52(3), 101–115. DOI: 10.4236/jard.2021.103014

Sulyani. (2022). Adoption of Digital Technology: Mapping the Important Roles in Current Agriculture Ecosystem Before & During Pandemic Covid 19 in West Java. Global Conference on Business and Social Sciences Proceeding. DOI: 10.35609/gcbssproceeding.2022.1(94)

Sun, W. (2024). The Impact and Opportunities of Digital Economy on Rural Revitalization. *International Journal of Education and Humanities*, 14(1), 134–139. DOI: 10.54097/0k1nfg61

Supendi. (2022). Government Strategic Policy in Agricultural Development. DOI: 10.31334/transparansi.v5i2.2543

Suryani, E., & Kartika, R. (2021). Digital marketplaces and the transformation of agricultural value chains in Indonesia. *Journal of Agribusiness in Developing and Emerging Economies*, 11(3), 421–436. DOI: 10.1108/JADEE-01-2021-0007

Suryaputra, R., Daryanti, S., & Setyowardhani, H. (2024). The Role of Social Media in Promoting Sustainable Green Lifestyles: Influencers and Value Co-Creation with Gen Z in Indonesia. *Journal of Entrepreneurial Economic*, 1(1), 48–65. DOI: 10.61511/jane.v1i1.2024.1036

Susanti, R., & Wardhana, P. (2020). Impact of precision agriculture technologies on smallholder farmers in Indonesia: A case study of drone usage. *International Journal of Agricultural Sustainability*, 18(4), 321–336. DOI: 10.1080/14735903.2020.1720398

Sutanto, S., & Nugroho, R. (2019). Leveraging digital technologies for climate resilience in Indonesian agriculture. *Climate and Development*, 11(7), 567–578. DOI: 10.1080/17565529.2019.1605281

Suwanan & Allya. (2023). Investigating the Factors and Behaviors Influencing Entrepreneurial Intention in Agricultural Sectors among Indonesian Millennials. DOI: 10.1088/1755-1315/1246/1/012037

Syukron,. M. (2022). A social network analysis of the use of social media to promote agriculture to indonesian youth. DOI: 10.32469/10355/90198

Thomas, S. (2024). Access to Technology to Increase Food Resilience in Rural Households in Indonesia. DOI: 10.3280/ecag2024oa16358

Valerio. (2024). Innovation for whom? The case of women in cattle farming in Nusa Tenggara Barat, Indonesia. Sonraku shakai kenkyu janaru, DOI: 10.1016/j.jrurstud.2024.103198

Venna. (2024). Role of Agriculture on Rural Household Food Security: A Systematic Review from Indonesia. DOI: 10.1088/1755-1315/1324/1/012132

Warr, P. G. (2011). Food Security vs. Food Self-Sufficiency: The Indonesian Case. Crawford School Research Paper No. 2011/04. DOI: 10.2139/ssrn.1910356

Wijaya, A. A., & Hermanto, H. (2020). Digital Finance and the Empowerment of Young Farmers in Indonesia. *Journal of Agricultural Finance*, 22(3), 275–290. DOI: 10.1080/13657309.2020.1765423

Wijaya, T., & Hidayat, R. (2021). Agri-tech entrepreneurship and rural development: The role of youth in transforming the Indonesian agricultural sector. *Journal of Rural Studies*, 82, 209–219. DOI: 10.1016/j.jrurstud.2020.11.006

Wijayanto, A., & Sari, P. D. (2020). Digital transformation in aquaculture: A case study of eFishery in Indonesia. *Aquaculture Economics & Management*, 24(2), 123–137. DOI: 10.1080/13657305.2020.1712634

Yanfika, H., Effendi, I., Sumaryo, , & Ansari, A. (2024). The role of agricultural extension services on supporting circular bioeconomy in Indonesia. *Frontiers in Sustainable Food Systems*, 8, 1428069. DOI: 10.3389/fsufs.2024.1428069

Yanti, M., Hapsari Ekonugraheni, D., Mahriani, R., Yusnaini, Y., & Effendi, S. (2024). Strengthening the Digital Literacy of Madrasa Students al-Ittifaqiah Indralaya, South Sumatra. *Engagement: Jurnal Pengabdian Kepada Masyarakat*, 8(1), 117–131. DOI: 10.29062/engagement.v8i1.467

Yudhistira, F., & Kusumawati, A. (2022). Data-driven decision-making in agriculture: The role of AgriSmart in Indonesia's digital transformation. *Journal of Agricultural Systems*, 21(3), 194–207. DOI: 10.1016/j.agsy.2022.01.012

Yuniarto. (2023). Analysis of Joint Marketing Initiatives by Farm Group and its Contribution to Marketing Performance. Journal of Social Research. DOI: 10.55324/josr.v2i10.1424

Yusriadi, Y., Junus, D., Wijayanti, R., Hasnawati, H., & Cahaya, A. (2024). (4) Perspectives of rural farmer households on food security through a qualitative study in Indonesia. *African Journal of Food, Agriculture, Nutrition and Development*, 24(2), 25450–25467. Advance online publication. DOI: 10.18697/ajfand.127.23510

Compilation of References

Abbasiharofteh, M., Krüger, M., Kinne, J., Lenz, D., & Resch, B. (2023). The digital layer: Alternative data for regional and innovation studies. *Spatial Economic Analysis*, 18(4), 507–529. DOI: 10.1080/17421772.2023.2193222

Abbass, M., Abbas, U., Jafri, R., Arif, S. M., & Akhai, S. (2025). AI and Machine Learning Applications in Sustainable Smart Cities. In *Sustainable Smart Cities and the Future of Urban Development* (pp. 1–32). IGI Global Scientific Publishing.

Abbey, R., & Hyde, S. (2009). No country for older people? Age and the digital divide. *Journal of information. Communication and Ethics in Society*, 7(4), 225–242. DOI: 10.1108/14779960911004480

Abbott, J., MacDonald, A. W., & Givens, J. W. (2013). New social media and (electronic) democratization in East and Southeast Asia. *Taiwan Journal of Democracy*, 9(2), 105–137.

Abiri, R., Rizan, N., Balasundram, S. K., Shahbazi, A. B., & Abdul-Hamid, H. (2023, December). Application of digital technologies for ensuring agricultural productivity. *Heliyon*, 9(12), e22601. Advance online publication. DOI: 10.1016/j.heliyon.2023.e22601

Abu Bakar, N. S., Rahman, A. A., & Abdull Hamed, H. N. (2015). The implementation of Malaysian m-government services. *Advanced Science Letters*, 21(5), 1122–1126. DOI: 10.1166/asl.2015.6020

Abubacker, N. F., & Raheem, M. (2024). Smart Agriculture in Malaysia: Harnessing Ubiquitous Computing for Sustainable Economic Growth. Journal of Applied Technology and Innovation, 8(1), 1.

Acemoglu, D., & Restrepo, P. (2018). Artificial intelligence, automation, and work. In *The economics of artificial intelligence: An agenda* (pp. 197–236). University of Chicago Press.

Acilar, A., & Sæbø, Ø. (2023). Towards understanding the gender digital divide: A systematic literature review. *Global Knowledge, Memory and Communication*, 72(3), 233–249. DOI: 10.1108/GKMC-09-2021-0147

Adams, D. A., Nelson, R. R., & Todd, P. A. (1992). Perceived Usefulness, Ease of Use, and Usage of Information. *Management Information Systems Quarterly*, 16(2), 227–250. DOI: 10.2307/249577

Adams, S. J. (2000). Generation X: How understanding this population leads to better safety programs. *Professional Safety*, 45(1), 26.

Adawy, M., Abualese, H., El-Omari, N. K. T., & Alawadhi, A. (2024). Human-Robot Interaction (HRI) using Machine Learning (ML): A survey and taxonomy. *International Journal of Advanced Soft Computing Applications*, 16(3), 183–213. DOI: 10.15849/IJASCA.241130.11

Adel, A. (2024). The convergence of intelligent tutoring, robotics, and IoT in smart education for the transition from industry 4.0 to 5.0. Smart Cities. DOI: 10.3390/smartcities7010014

Adel, A. (2022). Future of industry 5.0 in society: Human-centric solutions, challenges and prospective research areas. *Journal of Cloud Computing (Heidelberg, Germany)*, 11(1), 40. DOI: 10.1186/s13677-022-00314-5 PMID: 36101900

Afrin, S., Roksana, S., & Akram, R. (2024). AI-Enhanced Robotic Process Automation: A Review of Intelligent Automation Innovations. *IEEE Access : Practical Innovations, Open Solutions*.

Agarwal, R., Sambamurthy, V. & Stair, R.M. (2000). The Evolving Relationship between General and Specific Computer Self-Efficacy – An Empirical Assessment.

Aguiar Noury, G., Walmsley, A., Jones, R. B., & Gaudl, S. E. (2021). The barriers of the assistive robotics market—What inhibits health innovation? Sensors. DOI: 10.3390/s21093111

Ahmad, S. F., Han, H., Alam, M. M., Rehmat, M., Irshad, M., Arraño-Muñoz, M., & Ariza-Montes, A. (2023). Impact of artificial intelligence on human loss in decision making, laziness and safety in education. Humanities and Social Sciences Communications, 10(1), 1-14. DOI: 10.1057/s41599-023-01787-8

Ahmad, A., Liew, A. X., Venturini, F., Kalogeras, A., Candiani, A., Di Benedetto, G., Ajibola, S., Cartujo, P., Romero, P., Lykoudi, A., De Grandis, M. M., Xouris, C., Lo Bianco, R., Doddy, I., Elegbede, I., D'Urso Labate, G. F., García del Moral, L. F., & Martos, V. (2024). AI can empower agriculture for global food security: Challenges and prospects in developing nations. *Frontiers in Artificial Intelligence*, 7, 1328530. DOI: 10.3389/frai.2024.1328530 PMID: 38726306

Ahmed, F. (2024). From bricks and mortar to bits and bytes: The transformation of engineering in the digital age. *Kashf Journal of Multidisciplinary Research*, 1(1), 28–36.

Ahmed, G. K., Abdalla, A. A., Mohamed, A. M., Mohamed, L. A., & Shamaa, H. A. (2022). Relationship between time spent playing internet gaming apps and behavioral problems, sleep problems, alexithymia, and emotion dysregulations in children: A multicentre study. *Child and Adolescent Psychiatry and Mental Health*, 16(1), 67. Advance online publication. DOI: 10.1186/s13034-022-00502-w PMID: 35974366

Ahmed, I., Jeon, G., & Piccialli, F. (2022). From artificial intelligence to explainable artificial intelligence in industry 4.0: A survey on what, how, and where. *IEEE Transactions on Industrial Informatics*, 18(8), 5031–5042. DOI: 10.1109/TII.2022.3146552

Ahn, M., & Chen, Y.-C. (2021). Digital transformation toward AI-augmented public administration: The perception of government employees and the willingness to use AI in government. *Government Information Quarterly*, 39(2), 101664. DOI: 10.1016/j.giq.2021.101664

AI HLEG. (2019). *Ethics guidelines for trustworthy AI*. European Commission. https://data.europa.eu/doi/10.2759/346720

Aithal, P. S., & Maiya, A. K. (2023). Innovations in higher education industry–Shaping the future. *International Journal of Case Studies in Business, IT, and Education*, 7(4), 283–311. DOI: 10.47992/IJCSBE.2581.6942.0321

AITI. (2019), *Brunei Darussalam Information Communications Technology (ICT) Business Report 2019*.

Aji, A. P. (2023). A new recipe from my Facebook: How digital literacy impacting innovation of small culinary enterprises in Indonesia. *Interaksi: Jurnal Ilmu Komunikasi*, 12(1), 184–202. DOI: 10.14710/interaksi.12.1.182-200

Ajzen, I. (1991). The theory of planned behavior. *Organizational Behavior and Human Decision Processes*, 50(2), 179–211. DOI: 10.1016/0749-5978(91)90020-T

Akhai, S. (2024). Innovating Healthcare Delivery: Harnessing Drones for Medical Services. In *Modelling of Virtual Worlds Using the Internet of Things* (Vol. 1, pp. 232-250). CRC Press.

Akhai, S. (2024). Smart Home Environment for Society: An Overview of IoT-Enabled Air Conditioners. In *Modelling of Virtual Worlds Using the Internet of Things* (Vol. 1, pp. 74-87). CRC Press.

Akhai, S. (2024). The Impact of Artificial Intelligence on Healthcare: Opportunities and Challenges. *Journal of Advanced Research in Medical Science & Technology (ISSN: 2394-6539), 11*(1&2), 1-6.

Akhai, S. (2024). Towards Trustworthy and Reliable AI The Next Frontier. In *Explainable Artificial Intelligence (XAI) in Healthcare* (Vol. 1, pp. 119-129). CRC Press, Taylor & Francis Group.

Akhai, S. (2024). Trends and Environmental Impact of Paper Consumption: A Prognostic Scenario for the Indian Market by 2030-A Case Study. In *International Conference on Interdisciplinary Approaches in Civil Engineering for Sustainable Development* (Vol. 464, pp. 11-18). Springer Nature Singapore. DOI: 10.1007/978-981-97-0910-6_2

Akhai, S., & Abbass, M. (2025). Toward Resilient Futures: The Role of AI-Driven Strategies in Climate Adaptation. In *Nexus of AI, Climatology, and Urbanism for Smart Cities* (pp. 325-340). IGI Global Scientific Publishing.

Akhai, S., & Balu, V. (2022, December). Code Injection Assault & Mitigation Model to Prevent Attacks. In *2022 11th International Conference on System Modeling & Advancement in Research Trends (SMART)* (pp. 1324-1328). IEEE. DOI: 10.1109/SMART55829.2022.10046835

Akhai, S., & Khang, A. (2024). Efficient Hospital Waste Treatment and Management Through IoT and Bioelectronics. In *Revolutionizing Automated Waste Treatment Systems: IoT and Bioelectronics* (pp. 126-140). IGI Global. DOI: 10.4018/979-8-3693-6016-3.ch009

Akhai, S., & Khang, A. (2024). Energy Efficiency and Human Comfort: AI and IoT Integration in Hospital HVAC Systems. *Medical Robotics and AI-Assisted Diagnostics for a High-Tech Healthcare Industry*, 93-108.

Akhai, S., & Khang, A. (2024). Innovations in Medical Manufacturing: A Review of 3D Printing, Robotics, and Internet of Things (IoT). In *The Quantum Evolution* (Vol. 1, pp. 226-241). CRC Press.

Akhai, S., & Kumar, V. (2024). Quantum Resilience and Distributed Trust: The Promise of Blockchain and Quantum Computing in Defense. In *Sustainable Security Practices Using Blockchain, Quantum and Post-Quantum Technologies for Real Time Applications* (pp. 125-153). Springer Nature Singapore.

Akhai, S., Singh, S., Kaur, S., & Kaur, K. (2024). Advancing Aerospace Inspection With Terahertz Technology. In *New Innovations in AI, Aviation, and Air Traffic Technology* (pp. 195-211). IGI Global. DOI: 10.4018/979-8-3693-1954-3.ch010

Akhai, S. (2023). From Black Boxes to Transparent Machines: The Quest for Explainable AI. *Available at: Social Science Research Network, doi: http://dx.doi.org/*DOI: 10.2139/ssrn.4390887

Akhai, S. (2023). Healthcare record management for healthcare 4.0 via blockchain: a review of current applications, opportunities, challenges, and future potential. In *Blockchain for Healthcare 4.0* (Vol. 1, pp. 211–223). CRC Press. DOI: 10.1201/9781003408246-11

Akhai, S. (2023). Navigating the Potential Applications and Challenges of Intelligent and Sustainable Manufacturing for a Greener Future. *Evergreen*, 10(4), 2237–2243. DOI: 10.5109/7160899

Akhai, S., & Pandita, P. (2013). Design Optimization of Failure Mode for Improving Quality Control on the Engine Assembly Line. *International Journal of Emerging Technology and Advanced Engineering*, 3(12), 201–204.

Akhai, S., & Wadhwa, A. S. (2024). Wireless networking solutions for climate control and comfort in modern air conditioning systems. In *Intelligent Networks* (pp. 165–181). CRC Press. DOI: 10.1201/9781003541363-11

Akpuokwe, C. U., Adeniyi, A. O., & Bakare, S. S. (2024). Legal challenges of artificial intelligence and robotics: A comprehensive review. *Computer Science & IT Research Journal*, 5(3), 544–561. DOI: 10.51594/csitrj.v5i3.860

Aksoy, B., Salman, O. K. M., Ekrem, Ö., Aydin, N., & Yücel, M. (2023, November). Artificial Intelligence-Based Engineering Applications a Comprehensive Review of Application Areas, Impacts and Challenges. In The International Conference on Artificial Intelligence and Applied Mathematics in Engineering (pp. 32-47). Cham: Springer Nature Switzerland. DOI: 10.1007/978-3-031-56310-2_3

Ala'a, A., & Ramayah, T. (2023). Predicting the behavioural intention of Jordanian healthcare professionals to use blockchain-based EHR systems: An empirical study. *Journal of System and Management Sciences*, 13(4), 107–139.

Alam, M. M., Awawdeh, A. E., & Muhamad, A. I. (2021). Using e-wallet for business process development: challenges and prospects in Malaysia. *Business Process Management Journal.*

Alamouti, S., Arjomandi, F., Burger, M., & Altakrouri, B. (2024). Building Blocks to Empower Cognitive Internet with Hybrid Edge Cloud. *arXiv preprint arXiv:2402.00876.*

Aldoseri, A., Al-Khalifa, K. N., & Hamouda, A. M. (2024). AI-Powered Innovation in Digital Transformation: Key Pillars and Industry Impact. *Sustainability (Basel)*, 16(5), 1790. DOI: 10.3390/su16051790

Ali, F., Dogan, S., Chen, X., Cobanoglu, C., & Limayem, M. (2023). Friend or a foe: Understanding generation Z employees' intentions to work with service robots in the hotel industry. *International Journal of Human-Computer Interaction*, 39(1), 111–122. DOI: 10.1080/10447318.2022.2041880

Alkhalifah, J. M., Bedaiwi, A. M., Shaikh, N., Seddiq, W., & Meo, S. A. (2024). Existential anxiety about artificial intelligence (AI): Is it the end of humanity or a new chapter in the human revolution? A questionnaire-based observational study. *Frontiers in Psychiatry*, 15, 1368122. DOI: 10.3389/fpsyt.2024.1368122 PMID: 38654726

Allawadi, K., Panwar, S., & Chugh, M. (2024). Advancing Autonomous Driving Through Federated Learning: A Collaborative Approach. In *Sustainable Innovation for Industry 6.0* (pp. 1-30). IGI Global. DOI: 10.4018/979-8-3693-3140-8.ch001

Almara'beh, H., Amer, E. F., & Sulieman, A. (2015). The effectiveness of multimedia learning tools in education. *International Journal of Advanced Research in Computer Science and Software Engineering*, 5(12), 761–764.

Al-Momani, A. (2023). Adoption of Artificial Intelligence and Robotics in Organisations: A Systematic Literature Review. *International Journal of Business and Technology Management*, 5(3), 342–359.

Alon, T. M., Doepke, M., Olmstead-Rumsey, J., & Tertilt, M. (2020). *The impact of COVID-19 on gender equality (No. w26947)*. National Bureau of Economic Research. DOI: 10.3386/w26947

Alsheibani, S., Cheung, Y., & Messom, C. (2018). Artificial Intelligence Adoption: AI-readiness at Firm-Level. *PACIS 2018 Proceedings*. https://aisel.aisnet.org/pacis2018/37

Alzahrani, A. K. D., & Griffiths, M. D. (2024). Problematic Gaming and Students' Academic Performance: A Systematic review. *International Journal of Mental Health and Addiction*. Advance online publication. DOI: 10.1007/s11469-024-01338-5

Ambarwati, A., Chazali, C., Sadoko, I., & White, B. (2024). Youth and Agriculture in Indonesia. In Srinivasan, S. (Ed.), *Becoming A Young Farmer*. Rethinking Rural. Palgrave Macmillan. DOI: 10.1007/978-3-031-15233-7_11

Ambati, L. S., Narukonda, K., Bojja, G. R., & Bishop, D. (2020). *Factors influencing the adoption of artificial intelligence in organizations–from an employee's perspective*. Association for Information Systems.

American Optometric Association. (2016). The American Optometric Association's 2016 report on digital eye strain. https://www.aoa.org

Amiri, Z., Heidari, A., Jafari, N., & Hosseinzadeh, M. (2024). Deep study on autonomous learning techniques for complex pattern recognition in interconnected information systems. *Computer Science Review*, 54, 100666. DOI: 10.1016/j.cosrev.2024.100666

Anderson, J. M. (2014). *The second digital divide: The effects of ethnicity and socioeconomic status on student technology access and use outside the school day*. Baker University.

Andreassen, C. S., Pallesen, S., & Griffiths, M. D. (2016). The relationship between addictive use of social media and video games and symptoms of psychiatric disorders. *Psychological Reports*, 119(2), 275–286. DOI: 10.1177/0033294116635597

Andreoni, M., Lunardi, W. T., Lawton, G., & Thakkar, S. (2024). Enhancing autonomous system security and resilience with generative AI: A comprehensive survey. *IEEE Access : Practical Innovations, Open Solutions*, 12, 109470–109493. DOI: 10.1109/ACCESS.2024.3439363

Andrews, D., Nicoletti, G., & Timiliotis, C. (2018). Digital technology diffusion: A matter of capabilities, incentives or both? OECD Economics Department Working Papers, No. 1476, OECD Publishing, Paris.

Angelici, M., & Profeta, P. (2024). Smart working: Work flexibility without constraints. *Management Science*, 70(3), 1680–1705. DOI: 10.1287/mnsc.2023.4767

Anna, S. (2024, August). The Omnibus Law on Job Creation and its potential implications for rural youth and future farming in Indonesia. *Asia Pacific Viewpoint*, 65(2), 248–262. Advance online publication. DOI: 10.1111/apv.12408

Anshari, M., Arine, M. A., Nurhidayah, N., Aziyah, H., & Salleh, M. H. A. (2021). Factors influencing individual in adopting eWallet. *Journal of Financial Services Marketing*, 26(1), 10–23. DOI: 10.1057/s41264-020-00079-5

Antonio, A., & Tuffley, D. (2014). The gender digital divide in developing countries. *Future Internet*, 6(4), 673–687. DOI: 10.3390/fi6040673

Antonio, A., & Tuffley, D. (2015). Bridging the age-based digital divide. *International Journal of Digital Literacy and Digital Competence*, 6(3), 1–15. DOI: 10.4018/IJDLDC.2015070101

Antonius, Y., Maria, R., & Nindita, R. (2023). Analysis of Joint Marketing Initiatives by Farm Group and its Contribution to Marketing Performance. Journal of Social Research, DOI: 10.55324/josr.v2i10.1424

Anwar, S., Bascou, N. A., Menekse, M., & Kardgar, A. (2019). A systematic review of studies on educational robotics. *Journal of Pre-College Engineering Education Research (J-PEER), 9*(2), 2.

Ardyanti, R., Purnomo, M., & Kustanti, A. (2024). Driving Factors of the Rapid Development of Millennial Farmers in Malang Raya. *Universal Journal of Agricultural Research*, 12(1), 159–168. DOI: 10.13189/ujar.2024.120115

Arents, J., & Greitans, M. (2022). Smart industrial robot control trends, challenges and opportunities within manufacturing. *Applied Sciences (Basel, Switzerland)*, 12(2), 937. DOI: 10.3390/app12020937

Arief, S., & Widiastuti, W. (2020). The Impact of Mobile Technology on Agricultural Information Access in Rural Indonesia. *Journal of Information Technology & People*, 33(3), 811–824. DOI: 10.1108/ITP-03-2019-0131

Arif, S. M., & Akhai, S. (2024). Fostering a Sustainable and Disaster-Resilient Transportation Infrastructure. In *Challenges, Strategies, and Resiliency in Disaster and Risk Management* (pp. 205-219). IGI Global. DOI: 10.4018/979-8-3693-2721-0.ch009

Arrieta, A. B., Díaz-Rodríguez, N., Del Ser, J., Bennetot, A., Tabik, S., Barbado, A., & Herrera, F. (2020). Explainable Artificial Intelligence (XAI): Concepts, taxonomies, opportunities and challenges toward responsible AI. *Information Fusion*, 58, 82–115. DOI: 10.1016/j.inffus.2019.12.012

Artanti, T. Y. (2024). *Adoption and diffusion of agricultural technological innovations government program field school integrated participatory development management of irrigation program (ipdmip)*. Jurnal Impresi Indonesia. DOI: 10.58344/jii.v2i12.4411

Artyukhov, A., Wołowiec, T., Artyukhova, N., Bogacki, S., & Vasylieva, T. (2024). SDG 4, Academic Integrity and Artificial Intelligence: Clash or Win-Win Cooperation? *Sustainability (Basel)*, 16(19), 8483. DOI: 10.3390/su16198483

Aruleba, K., & Jere, N. (2022). Exploring digital transforming challenges in rural areas of South Africa through a systematic review of empirical studies. *Scientific African*, 16, e01190. DOI: 10.1016/j.sciaf.2022.e01190

Arvianti, Tirta, Cakti, Indra, & Ika. (2024). The Role Of Millennial Farmers In Optimizing Critical Land In Order to Face the Food Crisis In the Era Of Society 5.0. IOP conference series, DOI: 10.1088/1755-1315/1364/1/012028

Ashima, R., Haleem, A., Bahl, S., Javaid, M., Mahla, S. K., & Singh, S. (2021). Automation and manufacturing of smart materials in Additive Manufacturing technologies using Internet of Things towards the adoption of Industry 4.0. *Materials Today: Proceedings*, 45, 5081–5088. DOI: 10.1016/j.matpr.2021.01.583

Asoba, S. N., & Mefi, N. P. (2022). The generational dimension of technology acceptance: The case of generation x and millennial managers. *Journal of Management Information and Decision Sciences*, 25(S4), 1–7.

Au, Y. A., & Kauffman, R. J. (2008). The economics of mobile payments: Understanding stakeholder issues for an emerging financial technology application. *Electronic Commerce Research and Applications*, 7(2), 141–164. DOI: 10.1016/j.elerap.2006.12.004

Azhar, N. A. Z. M., & Shakil, N. S. M. (2021). The Intervention of Micro, Small and Medium Enterprises (MSMEs) in Malaysia's Digital Economy. *Global Business and Management Research*, 13(4).

Aziz, A., Ahmad, M. K., & Suppiah, S. M. (2021). Remote work: New normal communication challenges. European Proceedings of Social and Behavioural Sciences.

Aziz, A. A., Abdulkarim, I., & Jusoh, J. A. (2021, November). A review of supply and demand digital talents in Malaysia. In *International Conference on Business and Technology* (pp. 721-738). Cham: Springer International Publishing.

Aziz, M., Chemnad, K., Al-Harahsheh, S., Abdelmoneium, A. O., Baghdady, A., & Ali, R. (2024). Depression, stress, and anxiety versus internet addiction in early and middle adolescent groups: The mediating roles of family and school environments. *BMC Psychology*, 12(1), 184. Advance online publication. DOI: 10.1186/s40359-024-01659-z PMID: 38570890

Azmi, H., Wijaya, H., & Basram, N. F. (2024). Study of Youth Participation in Development Based on Regional Spatial Profile: Case Study of Urban and Rural Villages in Temanggung, Indonesia. *Jambura Geo Education Journal*, 5(1), 78–86. DOI: 10.37905/jgej.v5i1.24330

Badarudin, U. W., Din, W. I. S. W., Prasetyo, Y. A., Musa, Z., & Kasim, S. (2018). Internet of things: An implementation and its challenges in Malaysia. *International Journal on Advanced Science, Engineering and Information Technology*, 8(6), 2641–2647. DOI: 10.18517/ijaseit.8.6.5043

Bagley, S. M., Ventura, A. S., Lasser, K. E., & Muench, F. (2021). Engaging the family in the care of young adults with substance use disorders. *Pediatrics*, 147(Supplement 2), S215–S219. DOI: 10.1542/peds.2020-023523C PMID: 33386324

Bahamondes-Rosado, M. E., Cerdá-Suárez, L. M., Dodero Ortiz de Zevallos, G. F., & Espinosa-Cristia, J. F. (2023). Technostress at work during the COVID-19 lockdown phase (2020–2021): A systematic review of the literature. *Frontiers in Psychology*, 14, 1173425. DOI: 10.3389/fpsyg.2023.1173425 PMID: 37179875

Bakar, N. A. A., & Zaini, A. F. A. (2022). Literature review on the factors influencing the usage of social media among entrepreneurs in Malaysia. *Open Journal of Social Sciences*, 10(1), 409–419. DOI: 10.4236/jss.2022.101031

Baker, R. S. (2016). Stupid tutoring systems, intelligent humans. *International Journal of Artificial Intelligence in Education*, 26(2), 600–614. DOI: 10.1007/s40593-016-0105-0

Bako, M. (2018). Different leadership style choices, different generations. *Prizren Social Science Journal*, 2(2), 127–143.

Baltes, S., & Ralph, P. (2022). Sampling in software engineering research: A critical review and guidelines. *Empirical Software Engineering*, 27(4), 94. DOI: 10.1007/s10664-021-10072-8

Bancarzewski, M. (2024). Fulfilling orders: automation, control and resistance at Amazon: A review of The Warehouse: Workers and Robots at Amazon, Alessandro Delfanti (Pluto, 2021). *International Socialism journal (ISJ), 182*(Spring), 157.

Bandura, A. (1977). *Social learning theory*. Prentice-Hall.

Bandura, A. (1986). *Social foundations of thought and action: A social cognitive theory*. Prentice-Hall.

Bandura, A. (1991). Social cognitive theory of moral thought and action. In Kurtines, W. M., & Gewirtz, J. L. (Eds.), *Handbook of moral behavior and development* (Vol. 1, pp. 45–103). Erlbaum.

Banga, K., & te Velde, D. W. (2020). Covid-19 and disruption of the digital economy: Evidence from low and middle-income countries. Oxford, United Kingdom: Digital Pathways at Oxford, 7. Retrieved from ox.ac.uk

Bao, L., Krause, N. M., Calice, M. N., Scheufele, D. A., Wirz, C. D., Brossard, D., Newman, T. P., & Xenos, M. A. (2022). Whose AI? How different publics think about AI and its social impacts. *Computers in Human Behavior*, 130, 107182. DOI: 10.1016/j.chb.2022.107182

Barki, K., & Rachmah, M. A. (2024). Systematic literature review: Agricultural digitalization, technological transformation towards efficient and sustainable agriculture. *Ege Üniversitesi Ziraat Fakültesi Dergisi*, 61(2), 259–271. DOI: 10.20289/zfdergi.1382916

Baron, N. S. (2009). Are Digital Media Changing Language? *Educational Leadership*, 66(6), 42–46.

Basit, A., Hassan, Z., Omar, N., Sethu, S., & Jhanjhi, N. (2021). Gamification: A Tool To Enhance Employee Engagement And Performance. *Turkish Online Journal of Qualitative Inquiry*, 12, 3251–3269.

Bathla, G., Bhadane, K., Singh, R. K., Kumar, R., Aluvalu, R., Krishnamurthi, R., Kumar, A., Thakur, R. N., & Basheer, S. (2022). Autonomous vehicles and intelligent automation: Applications, challenges, and opportunities. *Mobile Information Systems*, 2022(1), 7632892. DOI: 10.1155/2022/7632892

Bautista, A. (2024). Big Data and Artificial Intelligence in Robotics: An Examination of their Role, Impact, and Future Directions. *Journal of Sustainable Technologies and Infrastructure Planning*, 8(3), 1–12.

Bazel, M. A., Haron, H., Ismail, I., & Gui, A. (2018, September). Factors influencing intention to use cloud storage services amongst postgraduate students in Malaysian Technical Universities. In *2018 International Conference on Information Management and Technology (ICIMTech)* (pp. 350-355). IEEE. DOI: 10.1109/ICIMTech.2018.8528179

Beck, A. T. (1979). *Cognitive therapy of depression.* Guilford Press.

Beck, J. S. (2011). *Cognitive behavior therapy: Basics and beyond* (2nd ed.). Guilford Press.

Behrens, K., Kichko, S., & Thisse, J. F. (2024). Working from home: Too much of a good thing? *Regional Science and Urban Economics*, 105, 103990. DOI: 10.1016/j.regsciurbeco.2024.103990

Bellis, M. A., Sharp, C. A., Hughes, K., & Davies, A. R. (2021). Digital overuse and addictive traits and their relationship with Mental Well-Being and Socio-Demographic Factors: A National Population Survey for Wales. *Frontiers in Public Health*, 9, 585715. Advance online publication. DOI: 10.3389/fpubh.2021.585715 PMID: 34222161

Bencsik, A., & Machova, R. (2016). Knowledge sharing problems from the viewpoint of intergeneration management. *ICMLG2016-4th International Conference on Management, Leadership and Governance: ICMLG2016, 42.*

Bencsik, A., Horváth-Csikós, G., & Juhász, T. (2016). Y and Z Generations at Workplaces. *Journal of competitiveness, 8*(3).

Bennett, S., Maton, K., & Kervin, L. (2008). The 'Digital Natives' Debate: A Critical Review of the Evidence. *British Journal of Educational Technology*, 39(5), 39. DOI: 10.1111/j.1467-8535.2007.00793.x

Benson, J., & Brown, M. (2011). Generations at work: Are there differences and do they matter? *International Journal of Human Resource Management*, 22(9), 1843–1865. DOI: 10.1080/09585192.2011.573966

Bera, S. D. (2023). Digital transformation in family firms: Exploring the interplay of tradition and innovation.

Bergdahl, J., Latikka, R., Celuch, M., Savolainen, I., Mantere, E., Savela, N., & Oksanen, A. (2023). Self-determination and attitudes toward artificial intelligence: Cross-national and longitudinal perspectives. *Telematics and Informatics*, 102013, 102013. Advance online publication. DOI: 10.1016/j.tele.2023.102013

Berry, L. L., Danaher, T. S., Aksoy, L., & Keiningham, T. L. (2020). Service safety in the pandemic age. Journal of Service Research, 23(4), 391-395. DOI: 10.1177/1094670520944608

Bers, M. U., & Elkind, D. (2008). *Blocks to robots: Learning with technology in the early childhood classroom.* No Title.

Bérubé, M. (2024). The Ex-human: Science Fiction and the Fate of Our Species.

Betriana, F., Tanioka, R., Gunawan, J., & Locsin, R. C. (2022). Healthcare robots and human generations: Consequences for nursing and healthcare. Collegian. sciencedirect.com

Bhavana, S., Kolachala, R., Kotamarti, S., & Rao, T. V. N. (2025). AI Advancements in Self-Driving Vehicle Technology. In *Real-World Applications of AI Innovation* (pp. 149–174). IGI Global Scientific Publishing.

Bhutoria, A. (2022). Personalized education and artificial intelligence in the United States, China, and India: A systematic review using a human-in-the-loop model. *Computers and Education: Artificial Intelligence*, 3, 100068. DOI: 10.1016/j.caeai.2022.100068

Bibo, L., Holland, R., Phillips, R., Pan, S., Roberts, C., & Willhite, T. (2009). The Digital Language Divide, A Research Project Paper. https://www.brettoppegaard.com/files/DLDpaper.pdf

Bibri, S. E., Huang, J., Jagatheesaperumal, S. K., & Krogstie, J. (2024). The synergistic interplay of artificial intelligence and digital twin in environmentally planning sustainable smart cities: A comprehensive systematic review. *Environmental Science and Ecotechnology*, 20, 100433. DOI: 10.1016/j.ese.2024.100433 PMID: 38831974

Bickham, D. S. (2021). Current research and viewpoints on internet addiction in Adolescents. *Current Pediatrics Reports*, 9(1), 1–10. DOI: 10.1007/s40124-020-00236-3 PMID: 33457108

Bijjahalli, S., Sabatini, R., & Gardi, A. (2020). Advances in intelligent and autonomous navigation systems for small UAS. *Progress in Aerospace Sciences*, 115, 100617. DOI: 10.1016/j.paerosci.2020.100617

Blanco-González-Tejero, C., Ribeiro-Navarrete, B., Cano-Marin, E., & McDowell, W. C. (2023). A Systematic Literature Review on the Role of Artificial Intelligence in Entrepreneurial Activity. *International Journal on Semantic Web and Information Systems*, 19(1), 1–16. DOI: 10.4018/IJSWIS.318448

Bloom, P., & Bloom, P. (2020). Heading toward integration: the rise of the human machines. Identity, Institutions and Governance in an AI World: Transhuman Relations, 67-92. DOI: 10.1007/978-3-030-36181-5_3

Boada, J. P., Maestre, B. R., & Genís, C. T. (2021). The ethical issues of social assistive robotics: A critical literature review. Technology in Society. DOI: 10.1016/j.techsoc.2021.101726

Bodea, C.-N., Paparic, M., & Alma Mater Europaea, E. C. M. (2024). Artificial Intelligence Adoption in the Workplace and Its Impact on the Upskilling and Reskilling Strategies. *Amfiteatru Economic*, 26(65), 126. DOI: 10.24818/EA/2024/65/126

Boku. (2021). Mobile Wallets Report 2021.

Bolton, B. (2019). Digital Skills Partnership. https://digitalskillspartnership.blog.gov.uk/2019/07/18/introducing-the-dsps-regional-coordinators-ben-bolton-cornwall-and-isles-of-scilly/

Brack, J. (2012). *Maximizing millennials in the workplace | VOCEDplus, the international tertiary education and research database*. https://www.voced.edu.au/content/ngv%3A73256

Braganza, A., Chen, W., Canhoto, A., & Sap, S. (2021). Productive employment and decent work: The impact of AI adoption on psychological contracts, job engagement and employee trust. *Journal of Business Research*, 131, 485–494. DOI: 10.1016/j.jbusres.2020.08.018 PMID: 32836565

Brand, M., Young, K. S., & Laier, C. (2014). Prefrontal Control and Internet Addiction: A theoretical model and review of neuropsychological and neuroimaging findings. *Frontiers in Human Neuroscience*, 8. Advance online publication. DOI: 10.3389/fnhum.2014.00375 PMID: 24904393

Brauner, P., Hick, A., Philipsen, R., & Ziefle, M. (2023). What does the public think about artificial intelligence?—A criticality map to understand bias in the public perception of AI. *Frontiers of Computer Science*, 5, 1113903. Advance online publication. DOI: 10.3389/fcomp.2023.1113903

Brenner, B. (2018). Transformative sustainable business models in the light of the digital imperative—A global business economics perspective. *Sustainability (Basel)*, 10(12), 4428. DOI: 10.3390/su10124428

Bronfenbrenner, U. (1979). *The ecology of human development: Experiments by nature and design*. Harvard University Press. DOI: 10.4159/9780674028845

Brougham, D., & Haar, J. (2018). Smart technology, artificial intelligence, robotics, and algorithms (STARA): Employees' perceptions of our future workplace. *Journal of Management & Organization*, 24(2), 239–257. DOI: 10.1017/jmo.2016.55

Brown, J., Pope, N., Bosco, A. M., Mason, J., & Morgan, A. (2020). Issues affecting nurses' capability to use digital technology at work: An integrative review. *Journal of Clinical Nursing*, 29(15-16), 2801–2819. DOI: 10.1111/jocn.15321 PMID: 32416029

Brunk, K. H. (2010). Exploring the relationship between corporate social responsibility and consumer trust. *Journal of Business Ethics*, 97(1), 163–176. DOI: 10.1007/s10551-009-0290-4

Bryman, A. (2016). *Social research methods* (5th ed.). Oxford University Press.

Büchi, M. (2021). Digital well-being theory and research. *New Media & Society*, 26(1), 172–189. DOI: 10.1177/14614448211056851

Bujang, S. D. A., Selamat, A., Krejcar, O., Maresova, P., & Nguyen, N. T. (2020, April). Digital learning demand for future education 4.0—Case studies at Malaysia education institutions. In Informatics (Vol. 7, No. 2, p. 13). MDPI.

Bukartaite, R., & Hooper, D. (2023). Automation, artificial intelligence and future skills needs: an Irish perspective. European Journal of Training and Development, 47(10), 163-185. DOI: 10.1108/EJTD-03-2023-0045

Burlacu, G., Truxillo, D. M., & Bauer, T. N. (2017). Employee age differences in using Internet-based tools at work. *The Wiley Blackwell handbook of the psychology of the internet at work*, 449-479.

Burr, C., Taddeo, M., & Floridi, L. (2020). The Ethics of Digital Well-Being: A Thematic Review. *Science and Engineering Ethics*, 26(4), 2313–2343. DOI: 10.1007/s11948-020-00175-8 PMID: 31933119

Burtless, G. (2013). The Impact of Population Aging and Delayed Retirement on Workforce Productivity. SSRN *Electronic Journal*. DOI: 10.2139/ssrn.2275023

Burton, C., Mayhall, C., Cross, J., & Patterson, P. E. (2019). Critical Elements for Multigenerational Teams a Systematic Review. *Team Performance Management*, 25(7/8), 369–401. DOI: 10.1108/TPM-12-2018-0075

Cahyono, B. Y., Khotimah, K., & Batunan, D. A. (2023). Workable approaches in EFL teaching mediated by mobile technology during the pandemic and post- pandemic: Indonesian EFL teachers' experiences and expectations. *Computer Assisted Language Learning*, 24, 138–159. http://callej.org/journal/24-1/Cahyono- Khotimah-Batunan-Imamyartha2023.pdf

Calderon-Monge, E., & Ribeiro-Soriano, D. (2024). The role of digitalization in business and management a systematic literature review. *Review of Managerial Science*, 18(2), 450–491. DOI: 10.1007/s11846-023-00647-8

Calvo-Porral, C., & Pesqueira-Sanchez, R. (2020). Generational differences in technology behaviour: Comparing millennials and Generation X. *Kybernetes*, 49(11), 2755–2772. DOI: 10.1108/K-09-2019-0598

Campos-Castillo, C. (2015). Revisiting the first-level digital divide in the United States: Gender and race/ethnicity patterns, 2007–2012. *Social Science Computer Review*, 33(4), 423–439. DOI: 10.1177/0894439314547617

Capgemini Research Institute. (2021). Payment Top Trends 2021.

Caporusso, N. (2023). Generative artificial intelligence and the emergence of creative displacement anxiety [Review]. *Research Directs in Psychology and Behavior*, 3(1). Advance online publication. DOI: 10.53520/rdpb2023.10795

Carvin, A. (2000). Mind the Gap: The Digital Divide as the Civil Rights Issue of the New Millennium. *Multimedia Schools*, 7(1), 56–58.

Castagno, S., & Khalifa, M. (2020). Perceptions of artificial intelligence among healthcare staff: A qualitative survey study. *Frontiers in Artificial Intelligence*, 3, 578983. DOI: 10.3389/frai.2020.578983 PMID: 33733219

Castrillón, O., Sarache, W., & Ruiz-Herrera, S. (2020). Predicción del rendimiento académico por medio de técnicas de inteligencia artificial. *Formación Universitaria*, 13(1), 93–102. DOI: 10.4067/S0718-50062020000100093

Cave, S., Coughlan, K., & Dihal, K. (2019). "Scary robots": Examining public responses to AI. In Proceedings of the 2019 AAAI/ACM Conference on AI, Ethics, and Society (pp. 331–337). Association for Computing Machinery. DOI: 10.1145/3306618.3314232

Ceipek, R., Hautz, J., Petruzzelli, A. M., De Massis, A., & Matzler, K. (2021). A motivation and ability perspective on engagement in emerging digital technologies: The case of Internet of Things solutions. *Long Range Planning*, 54(5), 101991. DOI: 10.1016/j.lrp.2020.101991

Chaffey, D. (2014). *Digital Business and E-Commerce Management*. Pearson Education Limited.

Chai, L. T., Chin, T. P., Yat, D. N. C., & Hooi, R. (n.d.). Millennials' S-Commerce Experience via Instagram. *Qualitative Research*.

Chan, C. K. Y. & Lee, K. K. W. (2023). AI generation gap: Are Gen Z students more interested in adopting generative AI such as ChatGPT in teaching and learning than their Gen X and millennial generation …. Smart learning environments. DOI: 10.1186/s40561-023-00269-3

Chan, M. (2024). Malaysia: Digital Payments, Data Regulations, and AI as Most Promising Areas for Digital Economy Collaboration. In The ASEAN Digital Economy (pp. 76-96). Routledge.

Chan, R. (2019). The Cambridge Analytica whistle blower explains how the firm used Facebook data to sway elections. Business Insider. Retrieved from https://www.businessinsider.com/cambridge-analytica-whistleblower-christopher-wylie-facebook-data-2019-10

Chandio, A. A., Özdemır, D., Gokmenoglu, K. K., Usman, M., & Jiang, Y. (2024, March). Digital agriculture for sustainable development in China: The promise of computerization. *Technology in Society*, 76, 102479. Advance online publication. DOI: 10.1016/j.techsoc.2024.102479

Chandler, D. (1995). Technological or media determinism. Retrieved from https://www.wolearn.org/pluginfile.php/45/mod_page/content/33/chandler2002_PD F_full.pdf

Chandra, S., Verma, S., Lim, W. M., Kumar, S., & Donthu, N. (2022). Personalization in personalized marketing: Trends and ways forward. Psychology & Marketing, 39(8), 1529-1562. DOI: DOI: 10.1002/mar.21670

Chang, M. L. Y., & Lee, I. O. (2024). Functional connectivity changes in the brain of adolescents with internet addiction: A systematic literature review of imaging studies. *PLOS Mental Health*, 1(1), e0000022. Advance online publication. DOI: 10.1371/journal.pmen.0000022

Chase, G. E., Brown, M. T., & Jensen, M. (2022). Emerging adults' digital technology engagement and mental health during the COVID-19 pandemic. *Frontiers in Psychology*, 13, 1023514. Advance online publication. DOI: 10.3389/fpsyg.2022.1023514 PMID: 36467177

Chatterjee, S., Chaudhuri, R., Vrontis, D., Thrassou, A., & Ghosh, S. K. (2021). Adoption of artificial intelligence-integrated CRM systems in agile organizations in India. *Technological Forecasting and Social Change*, 168, 120783. DOI: 10.1016/j.techfore.2021.120783

Chatterjee, S., Nguyen, B., Ghosh, S. K., Bhattacharjee, K. K., & Chaudhuri, S. (2020). Adoption of artificial intelligence integrated CRM system: An empirical study of Indian organizations. *The Bottom Line (New York, N.Y.)*, 33(4), 359–375. DOI: 10.1108/BL-08-2020-0057

Chatzopoulou, E., & de Kiewiet, A. (2021). Millennials' evaluation of corporate social responsibility: The wants and needs of the largest and most ethical generation. Journal of Consumer Behaviour, 20(3), 521-534. DOI: DOI: 10.1002/cb.1882

Che Nawi, N., Al Mamun, A., Hayat, N., & Seduram, L. (2022). "Promoting Sustainable Financial Services Through the Adoption of eWallet Among Malaysian Working Adults", *SAGE Open. SAGE Publications Sage CA: Los Angeles, CA*, 12(1).

Chee, S. Y. (2024). … -related digital disparities, functional limitations, and social isolation: Unraveling the grey digital divide between baby boomers and the silent generation in senior living…. *Aging & Mental Health*, 28(4), 621–632. Advance online publication. DOI: 10.1080/13607863.2023.2233454 PMID: 37424361

Cheng, B., Lin, H., & Kong, Y. (2023). Challenge or hindrance? How and when organizational artificial intelligence adoption influences employee job crafting. *Journal of Business Research*, 164, 113987. DOI: 10.1016/j.jbusres.2023.113987

Chen, T., Ou, J., Li, G., & Luo, H. (2024). Promoting mental health in children and adolescents through digital technology: A systematic review and meta-analysis. *Frontiers in Psychology*, 15, 1356554. Advance online publication. DOI: 10.3389/fpsyg.2024.1356554 PMID: 38533221

Chintalapati, S., & Pandey, S. K. (2022). Artificial intelligence in marketing: A systematic literature review. *International Journal of Market Research*, 64(1), 38–68. DOI: 10.1177/14707853211018428

Chopra, A., & Bhilare, P. (2020). Future of Work: An Empirical Study to Understand Expectations of the Millennials from Organizations. *Business Perspectives and Research*, 8(2), 272–288. DOI: 10.1177/2278533719887457

Chrysikou, E., Biddulph, J. P., Loizides, F., Savvopoulou, E., Rehn-Groenendijk, J., Jones, N., ... Tziraki, C. (2024). Creating Resilient Smart Homes with a Heart: Sustainable, Technologically Advanced Housing across the Lifespan and Frailty through Inclusive Design for People and Their Robots. Sustainability, 16(14), 5837. DOI: 10.3390/su16145837

Chuang, C.-H., & Liao, H. (2010). Strategic human resource management in service context: Taking care of business by taking care of employees and customers. *Personnel Psychology*, 63(1), 153–196. DOI: 10.1111/j.1744-6570.2009.01165.x

Ciccarelli, F. C., & Mariotti, I. (2024). Remote work, coworking spaces, and wellbeing during the COVID-19 pandemic and beyond: exploring peripheral and rural areas. In *Pandemic Recovery?* (pp. 209–220). Edward Elgar Publishing. DOI: 10.4337/9781802201116.00025

Çoban, S. (2022). Gender and telework: Work and family experiences of teleworking professional, middle-class, married women with children during the Covid-19 pandemic in Turkey. *Gender, Work and Organization*, 29(1), 241–255. DOI: 10.1111/gwao.12684 PMID: 34230782

Cogin, J. (2012). Are generational differences in work values fact or fiction? Multi-country evidence and implications. *International Journal of Human Resource Management*, 23(11), 2268–2294. DOI: 10.1080/09585192.2011.610967

Cohen, J. (1988). Statistical power for the behavioural sciences. Lawrence Erlbaum.

Colbert, A., Yee, N., & George, G. (2016). The Digital Workforce and the Workplace of the Future I. *Academy of Management Journal*, 59(3), 731–739. DOI: 10.5465/amj.2016.4003

Collinson, C., & Hodin, M. (2023). Best Practices for Engaging a Multigenerational Workforce. *Harvard Business Review*. https://hbr.org/2023/10/best-practices-for-engaging-a-multigenerational-workforce

Cooper, J. (2006). The digital divide: The special case of gender. *Journal of Computer Assisted Learning*, 22(5), 320–334. DOI: 10.1111/j.1365-2729.2006.00185.x

Cox, D. (2013). Health effects of technology addiction. *Jiankang Xinlixue*, 11(4), 237–245.

Creswell, J. W. (2014). *Research design: Qualitative, quantitative, and mixed methods approaches* (4th ed.). Sage Publications.

Csiszárik-Kocsír, Á., & Garia-Fodor, M. (2018). Motivation analysing and preference system of choosing a workplace as segmentation criteria based on a country wide research result focus on generation of Z. *On-Line Journal Modelling the New Europe*, (27), 67-85.

Cucina, J. M., Byle, K. A., Martin, N. R., Peyton, S. T., & Gast, I. F. (2018). Generational differences in workplace attitudes and job satisfaction: Lack of sizable differences across cohorts. *Journal of Managerial Psychology*, 33(3), 246–264. DOI: 10.1108/JMP-03-2017-0115

Culp-Roche, A., Hampton, D., Hensley, A., Wilson, J., Thaxton-Wiggins, A., Otts, J. A., Fruh, S., & Moser, D. K. (2020). Generational Differences in Faculty and Student Comfort With Technology Use. *SAGE Open Nursing*, 6. DOI: 10.1177/2377960820941394 PMID: 33415296

Czerniewicz, L. (2022). Multi-layered digital inequalities in HEIs: The paradox of the post-digital society. In *New visions for higher education towards 2030-Part 2: Transitions: Key topics, key voices.*

Dahlberg, T., Guo, J., & Ondrus, J. (2015). A critical review of mobile payment research. *Electronic Commerce Research and Applications*, 14(5), 265–284. DOI: 10.1016/j.elerap.2015.07.006

Dahlberg, T., Mallat, N., Ondrus, J., & Zmijewska, A. (2008). Past, present and future of mobile payments research: A literature review. *Electronic Commerce Research and Applications*, 7(2), 165–181. DOI: 10.1016/j.elerap.2007.02.001

Darlington, N., & Patience, M. (2023). Artificial intelligence marketing practices: The way forward to better customer experience management in Africa (Systematic Literature Review). *International Academy Journal of Management. Marketing and Entrepreneurial Studies*, 9(2), 44–62.

Darmono, Y., Yogatama, A., Ma'ruf, K., Setiyawa, B. P., & Fadlullah, Y. A. (2023). Optimization of Agricultural Technology with Irrigation Control in Rice Plants Based on Internet of Things. *Indonesian Journal of Advanced Research*, 2(5), 411–418. DOI: 10.55927/ijar.v2i5.4149

Das, H. S. (2024). Current and Future Research Directions. *Applied AI and Humanoid Robotics for the Ultra-Smart Cyberspace*, 200-231.

Das, D. K. (2024). Exploring the symbiotic relationship between digital transformation, infrastructure, service delivery, and governance for smart sustainable cities. *Smart Cities*, 7(2), 806–835. DOI: 10.3390/smartcities7020034

Das, D., Roy, A., Chaudhuri, A., Tripathy, S., Singhal, D., & Chandrasekhar, P. (2024). Digitalization of SCM in the Agriculture Industry. In Satapathy, S., & Muduli, K. (Eds.), *Advanced Computational Methods for Agri-Business Sustainability* (pp. 168–189). IGI Global. DOI: 10.4018/979-8-3693-3583-3.ch010

Dass, A. K., Parida, A., Panigrahi, S., & Moharana, S. K. (2023). Virtualization in Cloud Computing: Transforming Infrastructure and Enhancing Efficiency. *Research and Applications: Emerging Technologies*, 5(3), 26–40.

Davenport, T. H., Guptara, S., & Brooks, A. (2018). *The human face of digital transformation*. Harvard Business Review Press.

Davis, F. D. (1989). Perceived Usefulness, Perceived Ease of Use, and User Acceptance of Information Technology. *Management Information Systems Quarterly*, 13(3), 319. DOI: 10.2307/249008

Davis, F. D., Bagozzi, R. P., & Warshaw, P. R. (1989). User Acceptance of Computer Technology: A Comparison of Two. *Management Science*, 35(8), 982–1001. DOI: 10.1287/mnsc.35.8.982

Davis, K., & Lee, A. (2018). Digital addiction among older adults: Implications for health and well-being. *Journal of Aging Studies*, 47, 32–41. DOI: 10.1016/j.jaging.2018.07.001

Deal, J., Altman, D., & Rogelberg, S. (2010). Millennials at Work: What We Know and What We Need to Do (If Anything). *Journal of Business and Psychology*, 25(2), 191–199. DOI: 10.1007/s10869-010-9177-2

Denashurya, N. I., Nurliza, , Dolorosa, E., Kurniati, D., & Suswati, D. (2023). Overcoming Barriers to ISPO Certification: Analyzing the Drivers of Sustainable Agricultural Adoption among Farmers. *Sustainability (Basel)*, 15(23), 16507. DOI: 10.3390/su152316507

Dieter, D. G. & Gessler, E. C. (2021). A preferred reality: Film portrayals of robots and AI in popular science fiction. Journal of Science & Popular Culture. DOI: 10.1386/jspc_00025_1

DigComp. (2019). The Digital Competence Framework for Citizens. Retrieved from https://joint-research -centre.ec.europa.eu/digcomp_en

Dilshad, N., Hwang, J., Song, J., & Sung, N. (2020, October). Applications and challenges in video surveillance via drone: A brief survey. In *2020 International Conference on Information and Communication Technology Convergence (ICTC)* (pp. 728-732). IEEE. DOI: 10.1109/ICTC49870.2020.9289536

Dingel, J., & Nieman, B. (2020, April). How Many Jobs Can be Done at Home? *Covid Economics Vetted and RealTime Papers*, (1, 3), 16–24. DOI: 10.3386/w26948 PMID: 32834177

Dingli, A., & Seychell, D. (2015). Who Are the Digital Natives? In Dingli, A., & Seychell, D. (Eds.), *The New Digital Natives: Cutting the Chord* (pp. 9–22). Springer. DOI: 10.1007/978-3-662-46590-5_2

Diotaiuti, P., Mancone, S., Corrado, S., De Risio, A., Cavicchiolo, E., Girelli, L., & Chirico, A. (2022). Internet addiction in young adults: The role of impulsivity and codependency. *Frontiers in Psychiatry*, 13, 893861. Advance online publication. DOI: 10.3389/fpsyt.2022.893861 PMID: 36147985

Dmitrieva, E. I. (2020). Digital Platforms as a Base for Forming a Digital Economy. 156(Iscde), 553-558.

Do Vale, G., Collin-Lachaud, I., & Lecocq, X. (2022). The new retail model: Global reach demands omni-channels. *The Journal of Business Strategy*, 43(6), 339–349. DOI: 10.1108/JBS-02-2021-0026

Doargajudhur, M., Hosanoo, Z., & Huzooree, G. (2024). Relationship Between Remote Working and Work Outcomes of Constantly Connected BYOD Knowledge Workers. In *Impact of Teleworking and Remote Work on Business: Productivity, Retention, Advancement, and Bottom Line* (pp. 117-150). IGI Global. DOI: 10.4018/979-8-3693-1314-5.ch006

Doargajudhur, M., & Hosanoo, Z. (2023). The mobile technological era: Insights into the consequences of constant connectivity of personal devices by knowledge workers. *Information Technology & People*, 36(2), 701–733. DOI: 10.1108/ITP-08-2021-0593

Dommett, K. (2023). The inter-institutional impact of digital platform companies on democracy: A case study of the UK media's digital campaigning coverage. *New Media & Society*, 25(10), 2763–2780. DOI: 10.1177/14614448211028546

Doukidis, G. I., Mylonopoulos, N., & Pouloudi, N. (Eds.). (2004). *Social and economic transformation in the digital era*. IGI Global. DOI: 10.4018/978-1-59140-158-2

Duncan, A., & Joyner, D. (2022). On the necessity (or lack thereof) of digital proctoring: Drawbacks, perceptions, and alternatives. *Journal of Computer Assisted Learning*, 38(5), 1482–1496. DOI: 10.1111/jcal.12700

Duradoni, M., Serritella, E., Avolio, C., Arnetoli, C., & Guazzini, A. (2022b). Development and Validation of the Digital Life Balance (DLB) Scale: A Brand-New Measure for both Harmonic and Disharmonic use of ICTs. *Behavioral Sciences (Basel, Switzerland)*, 12(12), 489. DOI: 10.3390/bs12120489 PMID: 36546972

Dura, J., & Hamdani, M. R. (2024). The Role Of The Digital Economic Literacy Movement In Supporting MSMEs Sustainability. *IQTISHADUNA: Jurnal Ilmiah Ekonomi Kita*, 13(1), 1–15. DOI: 10.46367/iqtishaduna.v13i1.1757

Dutta-Bergman, M. J. (2004). Complementarity in consumption of news types across traditional and new media. *Journal of Broadcasting & Electronic Media, 48*(1), 41-60.

Dwivedi, Y. K., Jeyaraj, A., Hughes, L., Davies, G. H., Ahuja, M., Albashrawi, M. A., Al-Busaidi, A. S., Al-Sharhan, S., Al-Sulaiti, K. I., Altinay, L., Amalaya, S., Archak, S., Ballestar, M. T., Bhagwat, S. A., Bharadwaj, A., Bhushan, A., Bose, I., Budhwar, P., Bunker, D., & Walton, P. (2024). "Real impact": Challenges and opportunities in bridging the gap between research and practice–Making a difference in industry, policy, and society. *International Journal of Information Management*, 102750, 102750. Advance online publication. DOI: 10.1016/j.ijinfomgt.2023.102750

Edrak, B., Nor, Z. M., & Shaik, A. R. (2022). The Readiness of Malaysia Digital Economy: A Study of Three Government Policies from 1991 to 2020. *International Journal of Economics and Finance*, 14(12), 1–84. DOI: 10.5539/ijef.v14n12p84

Ekelund, U., Brown, W. J., & Lambert, J. D. (2016). Physical activity and risk of cardiovascular disease, cancer, and all-cause mortality: A systematic review and dose-response meta-analysis of prospective studies. *Lancet*, 380(9838), 222–233. DOI: 10.1016/S0140-6736(12)60735-1

Engel, G. L. (1977). The need for a new medical model: A challenge for biomedicine. *Science*, 196(4286), 129–136. DOI: 10.1126/science.847460 PMID: 847460

Erdiana, D. (2024). Dampak Digital Ekonomi Melalui Platform E- Commerse Terhadap Ketahanan Keuangan pada UMKM di Pasar Menganti. *Economic Reviews Journal, 3*(2), 1040. DOI: 10.56709/mrj.v3i2.324

Eruchalu, C. N., Pichardo, M. S., Bharadwaj, M., Rodriguez, C. B., Rodriguez, J. A., Bergmark, R. W., Bates, D. W., & Ortega, G. (2021). The expanding digital divide: Digital health access inequities during the COVID-19 pandemic in New York City. *Journal of Urban Health*, 98(2), 183–186. DOI: 10.1007/s11524-020-00508-9 PMID: 33471281

Facchinetti, T., Li, H., Nocera, A., Peters, D., Routhu, T., Scanzio, S., & Wisniewski, L. (2024, September). Applying AI in the Area of Automation Systems: Overview and Challenges. In *2024 IEEE 29th International Conference on Emerging Technologies and Factory Automation (ETFA)* (pp. 1-8). IEEE.

Fahmi, F. Z., & Mendrofa, M. J. S. (2024). Digitalisation and Rural Livelihood Transformation: Evidence from Indonesia. *International Journal of Rural Management*, 0(0), 313–334. Advance online publication. DOI: 10.1177/09730052231223822

Fairlie, R. W. (2017). Have we finally bridged the digital divide? Smart phone and Internet use patterns by race and ethnicity. UC Santa Cruz Previously Published Works. Retrieved from https://escholarship.org/uc/item/2591v2w7

Farida, I., & Setiawan, D. (2022). Business Strategies and Competitive Advantage: The Role of Performance and Innovation. *Journal of Open Innovation*, 8(163), 1–16. DOI: 10.3390/joitmc8030163

Farzana, (2024). Journey to cyber-physical agricultural systems digitalization and technological evolution. DOI: 10.1016/B978-0-443-13185-1.00001-0

Fauzi, M. A., & Paiman, N. (2021). COVID-19 pandemic in Southeast Asia: Intervention and mitigation efforts. *Asian Education and Development Studies*, 10(2), 176–184. DOI: 10.1108/AEDS-04-2020-0064

Fazaalloh. (2024). (3) Dampak Kepemilikan Ponsel terhadap Pendapatan Petani: Bukti dari Mikrodata di Indonesia. DOI: 10.23887/vjra.v13i1.76599

Feng, Y., Ma, Y., & Zhong, Q. (2019). The Relationship Between Adolescents' stress and Internet Addiction: A Mediated-Moderation Model. *Frontiers in Psychology*, 10, 2248. Advance online publication. DOI: 10.3389/fpsyg.2019.02248 PMID: 31636590

Fikri, M. A. H., Novita, Y. D., & Gusthomi, M. I. (2023). Development of the National Food System through Digitalization and Downstreaming to Strengthen National Food Security. *Indonesian Journal of Environmental Law and Sustainable Development*, 2(2), 169–198. DOI: 10.15294/ijel.v2i2.76637

Fin, & Donovan. (2013). *PWC's NextGen: A global generational study*. https://www.pwc.com/gx/en/hr-management-services/pdf/pwc-nextgen-study-2013.pdf

Firfiray, S., & Mayo, M. (2017). The Lure of Work-Life Benefits: Perceived Person-Organization Fit As A Mechanism Explaining Job Seeker Attraction To Organizations. *Human Resource Management*, 56(4), 629–649. DOI: 10.1002/hrm.21790

Firmansyah, D. A., Yektiningsih, E., & Laily, D. W. (2024). Factors Influencing the Interest of Youth In Rice Farming at Trenggalek Regency. *Jurnal Ilmiah Membangun Desa Dan Pertanian*, 9(3), 285–293. DOI: 10.37149/jimdp.v9i3.1271

Firman, Y., Yahya, M., & Idkhan, A. M. (2024). The Effectiveness of Rubeda (Regional Learning Space) 3T Multimedia Application in Improving Digital Skills of the Warmon Kokoda Village Community. *Asian Journal of Education and Social Studies*, 50(3), 82–89. DOI: 10.9734/ajess/2024/v50i31282

Fishbein, M., & Azjen, I. (1975). *Be- lief, Attitude, Intention and Behavior*. Addison-Wesley.

Fishman, A. A. (2016). How generational differences will impact America's aging workforce: Strategies for dealing with aging Millennials, Generation X, and Baby Boomers. *Strategic HR Review*, 15(6), 250–257. DOI: 10.1108/SHR-08-2016-0068

Fitzgerald, M. (2013). Embracing Digital Technology: A New Strategic Imperative. *MIT Sloan Management Review*, 1–12.

Flinchbaugh, C., Valenzuela, M. A., & Li, P. (2018). Developing employee socio-technical flexibility in a multigenerational workforce. *Journal of Management & Organization*, 24(4), 517–532. DOI: 10.1017/jmo.2016.38

Fogg, B. J. (2003). *Persuasive technology: Using computers to change what we think and do*. Morgan Kaufmann. DOI: 10.1016/B978-155860643-2/50011-1

Forgas-Coll, S., Huertas-Garcia, R., Andriella, A., & Alenyà, G. (2022). How do consumers' gender and rational thinking affect the acceptance of entertainment social robots?. International Journal of Social Robotics, 14(4), 973-994. DOI: 10.1007/s12369-021-00845-y

Fosch-Villaronga, E., Lutz, C., & Tamò-Larrieux, A. (2020). Gathering expert opinions for social robots' ethical, legal, and societal concerns: Findings from four international workshops. International Journal of Social Robotics, 12(2), 441-458. DOI: 10.1007/s12369-019-00605-z

Fracasso, F., Buchweitz, L., Theil, A., Cesta, A., & Korn, O. (2022). Social robots acceptance and marketability in italy and germany: a cross-national study focusing on assisted living for older adults. International Journal of Social Robotics, 14(6), 1463-1480. DOI: 10.1007/s12369-022-00884-z

Franke, T. M., Ho, T., & Christie, C. A. (2012). The chi-square test: Often used and more often misinterpreted. *American Journal of Evaluation*, 33(3), 448–458.

Fuchs, C. (2009). The role of income inequality in a multivariate cross-national analysis of the digital divide. *Social Science Computer Review*, 27(1), 41–58. DOI: 10.1177/0894439308321628

Fuentes-Peñailillo, F., Gutter, K., Vega, R., & Silva, G. C. (2024). Transformative Technologies in Digital Agriculture: Leveraging Internet of Things, Remote Sensing, and Artificial Intelligence for Smart Crop Management. *Journal of Sensor and Actuator Networks*, 13(4), 39. DOI: 10.3390/jsan13040039

Gabsi, A. E. H. (2024). Integrating artificial intelligence in industry 4.0: Insights, challenges, and future prospects–a literature review. *Annals of Operations Research*, 1–28. DOI: 10.1007/s10479-024-06012-6

Gaikwad, S. S. (2024). *Modern trends in multi-disciplinary research* (Vol-1).

Gallardo-Gallardo, E., Thunnissen, M., & Scullion, H. (2019). Talent management: Context matters. *International Journal of Human Resource Management*, 31, 1–17.

Ganesan, P., & Mane, A. S. (2022). Determinants of Continuous Intention to Use Digital Wallet–Application of UTAUT2 and Multi-Group Analysis with Age and Gender. *NeuroQuantology : An Interdisciplinary Journal of Neuroscience and Quantum Physics*, 20(19), 4586.

Garlinska, M., Osial, M., Proniewska, K., & Pregowska, A. (2023). The influence of emerging technologies on distance education. *Electronics (Basel)*, 12(7), 1550. DOI: 10.3390/electronics12071550

Gefen, D., Straub, D., & Boudreau, M. C. (2000). Structural equation modeling and regression: Guidelines for research practice. *Communications of the Association for Information Systems*, 4(1), 7. DOI: 10.17705/1CAIS.00407

Genus, A., & Nor, M. A. (2005). Socialising the Digital Divide: Implications for ITCs and E-Business Development. *Journal of Electronic Commerce in Organizations*, 3(2), 82–94. DOI: 10.4018/jeco.2005040106

George, A. S. (2024). Bridging the digital divide: Understanding the human impacts of digital transformation.

Georgescu, R. I., & Bodislav, D. A. (2024). The generational divide-A debate on technology and the decision-making process. *Theoretical & Applied Economics, 31*(2).

Gerli, P., Clement, J., Esposito, G., Mora, L., & Crutzen, N. (2022). The hidden power of emotions: How psychological factors influence skill development in smart technology adoption. Technological Forecasting and Social Change, 180, 121721. DOI: 10.1016/j.techfore.2022.121721

Gerlich, M. (2023). Perceptions and acceptance of artificial intelligence: A multi-dimensional study. *Social Sciences (Basel, Switzerland)*, 12(9), 502. DOI: 10.3390/socsci12090502

Ghani, E. K., Ariffin, N., & Sukmadilaga, C. (2022). Factors influencing artificial intelligence adoption in publicly listed manufacturing companies: A technology, organisation, and environment approach. *International Journal of Applied Economics. Finance and Accounting*, 14(2), 108–117.

Ghobadi, S., & Mathiassen, L. (2020). A Generational Perspective on the Software Workforce: Precocious Users of Social Networking in Software Development. *Journal of Management Information Systems*, 37(1), 96–128. DOI: 10.1080/07421222.2019.1705508

Gibson, R., & Gibson, R. (2020). Moving Toward an Acceptance of Robotic Sexuality Through Sci-Fi. Desire in the Age of Robots and AI: An Investigation in Science Fiction and Fact, 109-136. DOI: 10.1007/978-3-030-24017-2_5

Gilleard, C. (2004). Cohorts and generations in the study of social change. *Social Theory & Health*, 2(1), 106–119. DOI: 10.1057/palgrave.sth.8700023

Ginige, A., De Silva, L. N., & Samaraweera, G. C. (2024). Chapter 23: Digital agrifood ecosystems: Digital platforms for inclusive, efficient, sustainable food systems to achieve food security. In *Handbook on Public Policy and Food Security*. Cheltenham, UK: Edward Elgar Publishing. DOI: 10.4337/9781839105449.00028

Giray, L. (2022). (PDF) Meet the Centennials: Understanding the Generation Z Students. *International Journal of Sociologies and Anthropologies Science Reviews*, 2(4). https://www.researchgate.net/publication/361781262_Meet_the_Centennials_Understanding_the_Generation_Z_Students

Giuggioli, G., & Pellegrini, M. M. (2022). Artificial intelligence as an enabler for entrepreneurs: A systematic literature review and an agenda for future research. *International Journal of Entrepreneurial Behaviour & Research*, 29(4), 816–837. DOI: 10.1108/IJEBR-05-2021-0426

Giwu, O. (2024). Perceptions, willingness, opportunities, and effects of youth participation in agricultural enterprises. DOI: 10.29086/10413/23097

Goda, Y. (2014). The role of AMPA receptors in postsynaptic mechanisms of synaptic plasticity. *Frontiers in Cellular Neuroscience*, 8. Advance online publication. DOI: 10.3389/fncel.2014.00401 PMID: 25505875

Goel, A. K., & Polepeddi, L. (2016). *Jill Watson: A virtual teaching assistant for online education.* Georgia Institute of Technology.

Gomber, P., Koch, J.-A., & Siering, M. (2017). Digital Finance and FinTech: Current research and future research directions. *Journal of Business Economics*, 87(5), 537–580. DOI: 10.1007/s11573-017-0852-x

Gong, R. (2020). Digital Inclusion: Assessing Meaningful Internet Connectivity in Malaysia. Navigating Challenges, Realising Opportunities of Digital Transformation, 5.

Gorwa, R., Binns, R., & Katzenbach, C. (2020). Algorithmic content moderation: Technical and political challenges in the automation of platform governance. *Big Data & Society*, 7(1), 2053951719897945. DOI: 10.1177/2053951719897945

Gow, G., Chowdhury, A., Ramjattan, J., & Ganpat, W. (2020). Fostering effective use of ICT in agricultural extension: Participant responses to an inaugural technology stewardship training program in Trinidad. *Journal of Agricultural Education and Extension*, 26(4), 335–350. DOI: 10.1080/1389224X.2020.1718720

Greenhill, A., & Wilson, M. (2006). Haven or hell? Telework, flexibility and family in the e-society: A marxist analysis. *European Journal of Information Systems*, 15(4), 379–388. DOI: 10.1057/palgrave.ejis.3000632

Griffiths, M. D. (1996). Behavioral addiction: An overview. *Clinical Psychology Review*, 16(1), 1–16. DOI: 10.1016/0272-7358(95)00038-0

Grosz, B. J., & Stone, P. (2018). A century-long commitment to assessing artificial intelligence and its impact on society. *Communications of the ACM*, 61(12), 68–73. DOI: 10.1145/3198470

Gruzdeva, M. A. (2022). The age factor in the digital divide: The edges of inequality. *Economic and social changes: facts, trends, forecast, 15*(4), 228-241.

Gualano, M., Santoro, P., Borrelli, I., Rossi, M., Amantea, C., Daniele, A., & Moscato, U. (2022). TElewoRk-RelAted Stress (TERRA) as an emerging problem during the Covid-19 Pandemic: A Systematic Review. *Safety and Health at Work*, 13, S305–S305. DOI: 10.1016/j.shaw.2021.12.1706

Gu, J., Zhan, P., Huang, Z., Cheng, S., Liu, J., Xu, W., Huang, L., Xu, Y., & Wang, J. (2024). Anxiety/Depression and Internet Addiction: Directions, antecedents, and outcomes. *Current Addiction Reports*, 11(3), 588–597. DOI: 10.1007/s40429-024-00565-z

Gulamhuseinwala, I., Bull, T. & Lewis, S. (2015). FinTech is gaining traction and young, high-income users are the early adopters. *Journal of Financial Perspectives*, *3*(3).

Gülbetekin, E., Güven, E., & Sökmen, Ö. (2023). The effect of internet addiction on physical activity and dietary habits in high school students. *Journal of Public Health (Berlin)*. Advance online publication. DOI: 10.1007/s10389-023-02083-0

Gusman, S. W. (2024). Development of the Indonesian Government's Digital Transformation. *Dinasti International Journal of Education Management And Social Science*, 5(5), 1128–1141. DOI: 10.38035/dijemss.v5i5.2868

Ha, H., & Peter Chuah, C. K. (2023). Digital economy in Southeast Asia: challenges, opportunities and future development. Digital economy in Southeast Asia, 23(1), 19-35.

Hafkin, N. J., & Taggart, N. (2001). *Gender, information technology, and developing countries: An analytic study*. Office of Women in Development, Bureau for Global Programs, Field Support and Research, United States Agency for International Development.

Hahn, K., & Hahn, K. (2021). The Formalisation of the Modern Market. *Social Digitalisation: Persistent Transformations Beyond Digital Technology*, 123-165.

Hajar, M. A., Ibrahim, D. N., Darun, M. R., & Al-Sharafi, M. A. (2020). Value innovation activities in the wireless telecommunications service sector: A case study of the Malaysian market. *Journal of Global Business Insights*, 5(1), 57–72. DOI: 10.5038/2640-6489.5.1.1125

Hakak, S., Gadekallu, T. R., Maddikunta, P. K. R., Ramu, S. P., Parimala, M., De Alwis, C., & Liyanage, M. (2023). Autonomous Vehicles in 5G and beyond: A Survey. *Vehicular Communications*, 39, 100551. DOI: 10.1016/j.vehcom.2022.100551

Haleem, A., Javaid, M., & Singh, R. P. (2022). An era of ChatGPT as a significant futuristic supp tool: A study on features, abilities, and challenges. BenchCouncil Transactions on Benchmarks. *Standards and Evaluations*, 2(4), 100089.

Halili, S. H. (n.d.). Technological advancements in education 4.0. *The Online Journal of Distance Education and e-Learning : TOJDEL*, 7, 63–69.

Hameed, T., & Sawicka, B. (2023). Role of agricultural extension in adoption of sustainable agriculture practices. *Anbar Journal of Agricultural Sciences, 21*(1), 250-260. DOI: 10.32649/ajas.2023.179947

Hancock, J. (2024). Social Robots are Good for Me, But Better for Other People: The Presumed Allo-enhancement Effect of Social Robot Perceptions. Computers in Human Behavior: Artificial Humans. DOI: 10.1016/j.chbah.2024.100079

Hapsari, F. M., & Harini, H. (2021). The Role of Digital Platforms in Empowering Young Farmers in Indonesia. *Journal of Agribusiness*, 35(4), 512–528. DOI: 10.1080/13657309.2021.1897365

Hargittai, E., & Walejko, G. (2008). The participation divide: Content creation and sharing in the digital age. *Information Communication and Society*, 11(2), 239–256. DOI: 10.1080/13691180801946150

Harisudin, M. (2023), Determinants of the Internet of Things adoption by millennial farmers[J]. AIMS Agriculture and Food, 8(2), 329-342. DOI: 10.3934/agrfood.2023018

Hartmann-Kottek, L. (2022). The Practical Approach–Many Paths–Similar Goals: The Diversity and Similarities between Psychotherapeutic Treatment Methods. In *General Psychotherapy: Principles and Common Theoretical Aspects-Rediscovering Humanity* (pp. 335–408). Springer International Publishing. DOI: 10.1007/978-3-030-87466-7_6

Hartono, D., & Anggraini, W. (2021). Barriers to digital technology adoption in rural Indonesia: The case of smallholder farmers. *Technology in Society*, 67, 101725. DOI: 10.1016/j.techsoc.2021.101725

Haryati, N., Lasitya, D. S., Nurirrozak, M. Z., Herdianti, D. F., Fibrianingtyas, A., & Hidayat, A. R. R. T. (2024). Demographics and course choices: Impact on youth farming intention in Indonesia. *International Journal of Adolescence and Youth*, 29(1), 2358088. Advance online publication. DOI: 10.1080/02673843.2024.2358088

Hasan. (2023). Digital Farming and Smart Farming from the Perspective of Agricultural Students at Malikussaleh University. DOI: 10.29103/micoms.v3i.230

Haucr, T. (2017). Technological determinism and new media. *International Journal of English Literature and Social Sciences*, 2(2), 239174.

Helsper, E. J., & Eynon, R. (2010). Digital natives: where is the evidence?. *British educational research journal, 36*(3), 503-520.

Henze, J., Schatz, C., Malik, S., & Bresges, A. (2022). How might we raise interest in robotics, coding, artificial intelligence, STEAM and sustainable development in university and on-the-job teacher training?. Frontiers in education. DOI: 10.3389/feduc.2022.872637

Herawati, A. (2023). Assesing the Impact of Digital Technologies on Governance Policies for Food Security: A Case Study of Indonesia. *KnE Social Sciences*, 8(17), 166–184. DOI: 10.18502/kss.v8i17.14112

Hermann, I. (2023). Artificial intelligence in fiction: between narratives and metaphors. AI & society. DOI: 10.1007/s00146-021-01299-6

Hershatter, A., & Epstein, M. (2010). Millennials and the World of Work: An Organization and Management Perspective. *Journal of Business and Psychology*, 25(2), 211–223. DOI: 10.1007/s10869-010-9160-y

Hewett, R., Shantz, A., Mundy, J., & Alfes, K. (2017). Attribution theories in Human Resource Management research: A review and research agenda. *International Journal of Human Resource Management*, •••, 1–40.

Hick, A., & Ziefle, M. (2022). A qualitative approach to the public perception of AI. *International Journal on Cybernetics & Informatics*, 11(4), 1–17. DOI: 10.5121/ijci.2022.110401

Hidayati, B., Yusida, E., Qurrata, V. A., Nasikh, N., & Huang, W. (2023, April 30). The digital agriculture model for sustainable food system: An analysis of agricultural technology adoption in east java, indonesia. *Journal of Sustainability Science and Management*, 18(4), 172–190. Advance online publication. DOI: 10.46754/jssm.2023.04.013

Hidayat, R. A., & Rahayu, E. (2022). TaniHub: A case study of e-commerce in the Indonesian agricultural sector. *Agrárinformatika Folyóirat*, 13(2), 45–57. DOI: 10.29202/jai.v13i2.311

Hill, N. S., Axtell, C., Raghuram, S., & Nurmi, N. (2024). Unpacking virtual work's dual effects on employee well-being: An integrative review and future research agenda. *Journal of Management*, 50(2), 752–792. DOI: 10.1177/01492063221131535

Hilty, D. M., Stubbe, D., McKean, A. J., Hoffman, P. E., Zalpuri, I., Myint, M. T., Joshi, S. V., Pakyurek, M., & Li, S.-T. T. (2023). A scoping review of social media in child, adolescents and young adults: Research findings in depression, anxiety and other clinical challenges. *BJPsych Open*, 9(5), e152. DOI: 10.1192/bjo.2023.523 PMID: 37563766

Hinkley, T., Brown, H., Carson, V., & Teychenne, M. (2018). Cross sectional associations of screen time and outdoor play with social skills in preschool children. *PLoS One*, 13(4), e0193700. DOI: 10.1371/journal.pone.0193700 PMID: 29617366

Hoffman, D. L., & Novak, T. P. (1998). Bridging the Digital Divide: The Impact of Race on Computer Access and Internet Use. Retrieved from https://files.eric.ed.gov/fulltext/ED421563.pdf

Hoodbhoy, P. (2023). Sustainable infrastructures: Bridging the gap between technological advancements and societal needs. *Liberal Journal of Language and Literature Review*, 1(01), 12–21.

Hosseini, M., Rasmussen, L. M., & Resnik, D. B. (2023). Using AI to write scholarly publications. *Accountability in Research*, 1–9. DOI: 10.1080/08989621.2023.2168535 PMID: 36697395

Howe, N., & Strauss, W. (2000). *Millennials rising: The next great generation*. Vintage.

Huang, P., Chan, S. Y., Ngoh, Z. M., Ong, Z. Y., Low, X. Z., Law, E. C., Gluckman, P. D., Kee, M. Z., Fortier, M. V., Chong, Y. S., Zhou, J. H., Meaney, M. J., & Tan, A. P. (2024). Screen time, brain network development and socio-emotional competence in childhood: Moderation of associations by parent–child reading. *Psychological Medicine*, 54(9), 1–12. DOI: 10.1017/S0033291724000084 PMID: 38314509

Huda, M. N., Kurniasari, E. N., & Ruroh, S. M. (2022). A systematic literature review of E-government evaluation. *Journal of Local Government Issues*, 5(1), 32–48. DOI: 10.22219/logos.v5i1.19784

Hugeng, H., Trisnawarman, D., & Huntarso, A. I. Y. (2023). Enhanced IoT Solution System for Smart Agriculture in Indonesia. *Green Intelligent Systems and Applications*, 3(2), 111–125. DOI: 10.53623/gisa.v3i2.325

Humble, N., & Mozelius, P. (2019). Artificial Intelligence in Education-a Promise, a Threat or a Hype? In European Conference on the Impact of Artificial Intelligence and Robotics 2019 (ECIAIR 2019), Oxford, UK (pp. 149–156). Academic Conferences and Publishing International Limited.

Hutchison, W. (2020). Love among the Robots: Non-biological Consciousness and the Pursuit of Kinship 1970 to the Present.

Hutton, J. S., Piotrowski, J. T., Bagot, K., Blumberg, F., Canli, T., Chein, J., Christakis, D. A., Grafman, J., Griffin, J. A., Hummer, T., Kuss, D. J., Lerner, M., Marcovitch, S., Paulus, M. P., Perlman, G., Romeo, R., Thomason, M. E., Turel, O., Weinstein, A., & Potenza, M. N. (2024). Digital media and developing Brains: Concerns and opportunities. *Current Addiction Reports*, 11(2), 287–298. DOI: 10.1007/s40429-024-00545-3 PMID: 38606363

Hwang, G. J., Xie, H., Wah, B. W., & Gašević, D. (2020). Vision, challenges, roles and research issues of Artificial Intelligence in Education. *Computers and Education: Artificial Intelligence*, 1, 100001. DOI: 10.1016/j.caeai.2020.100001

Hwang, J., Chen, S., & Lee, J. (2018). Social media campaigns and public health: The role of influencers and community leaders. *Journal of Public Health*, 40(2), 318–325. DOI: 10.1093/pubmed/fdy027

Hysa, B., Karasek, A., & Zdonek, I. (2021). Social media usage by different generations as a tool for sustainable tourism marketing in society 5.0 idea. Sustainability. DOI: 10.3390/su13031018

Ilham, A. Ahmad, Munir, Ambo, Ala, Andi, Amran, Sulaiman. (2023). (4) Rural Digital Transformation in Indonesia. *Policy Analysis*. Advance online publication. DOI: 10.52783/tjjpt.v44.i4.1476

Imran, A. (2023). Why addressing digital inequality should be a priority. *The Electronic Journal on Information Systems in Developing Countries*, 89(3), e12255. DOI: 10.1002/isd2.12255

Inaba, Y., & Togawa, K. (2021). Social capital in the creation of AI perception. *Behaviormetrika*, 48(1), 79–102. DOI: 10.1007/s41237-020-00107-7

Indriasari, S., Sensuse, D., & Resti, Y. (2024). Information technology adoption in Indonesia's small-scale dairy farms. *Open Agriculture*, 9(1), 20220304. DOI: 10.1515/opag-2022-0304

Information Week. (2021). Adopting New Technologies in a Multi-Generational Workplace. https://www.informationweek.com/it-leadership/adopting-new-technologies-in-a-multi-generational-workplace#close-modal

Ingusci, E., Signore, F., Cortese, C. G., Molino, M., Pasca, P., & Ciavolino, E. (2023). Development and validation of the Remote Working Benefits & Disadvantages scale. *Quality & Quantity*, 57(2), 1159–1183. DOI: 10.1007/s11135-022-01364-2 PMID: 35506027

Isacson, A., & Adelfio, M. (2023). The use of digital layers in post-growth communities - an exploratory study. The 6th International Conference on Smart Villages and Rural Development (COSVARD 2023).

Islam, M., Mamun, A. A., Afrin, S., & Uddin, M. (2022). Technology Adoption and Human Resource Management Practices: The Use of Artificial Intelligence for Recruitment in Bangladesh. *SA Journal of Human Resource Management*, 9.

Islam, R., Fakhrorazi, A., Hartini, H., & Abu Raihan, M. (2019). Globalization and its impact on international business. *Humanities & Social Sciences Reviews*, 7(1), 256–265. DOI: 10.18510/hssr.2019.7130

Ismail, N. A., & Masud, M. M. (2020). Prospects and challenges in improving e-commerce connectivity in Malaysia. E-commerce Connectivity in ASEAN, 78.

Jabeen, N., & Gul, J. (2023). The Role of social media In Promoting Sustainable Agriculture Practices. *Indus Journal of Agriculture and Biology*, 2(1), 17–32. DOI: 10.59075/ijab.v2i1.212

Jacobides, M. G., Cennamo, C., & Gawer, A. (2018). Towards a theory of ecosystems. *Strategic Management Journal*, 39(8), 2255–2276. DOI: 10.1002/smj.2904

Jacobides, M., & Lianos, I. (2021). Ecosystems and competition law in theory and practice. *Industrial and Corporate Change*, 30(1), 119–131.

Jagatheesaperumal, S. K., Rahouti, M., Ahmad, K., Al-Fuqaha, A., & Guizani, M. (2021). The duo of artificial intelligence and big data for industry 4.0: Applications, techniques, challenges, and future research directions. *IEEE Internet of Things Journal*, 9(15), 12861–12885. DOI: 10.1109/JIOT.2021.3139827

Jain, A., Mital, A., & Wang, T. (2020). Ergonomics and musculoskeletal disorders related to mobile device use: A review. *Work (Reading, Mass.)*, 67(2), 273–285. DOI: 10.3233/WOR-203227

Jain, M., Goel, A., Sinha, S., & Dhir, S. (2021). Employability implications of artificial intelligence in healthcare ecosystem: Responding with readiness. *Foresight*, 23(1), 73–94. DOI: 10.1108/FS-04-2020-0038

Jaiswal, A., Arun, J., & Varma, A. (2022). Rebooting employees: Upskilling for artificial intelligence in multinational corporations. *International Journal of Human Resource Management*, 33(6), 1179–1208. DOI: 10.1080/09585192.2021.1891114

Jalal, M. T., & Hossain, M. M. (2022). Digitalization of Supply Chain in Malaysian SMEs: A Framework for a Sustainable Digital Transformation.

Jalali, M. S., Botticelli, M., Hwang, R. C., Koh, H. K., & McHugh, R. K. (2020). The opioid crisis: A contextual, social-ecological framework. *Health Research Policy and Systems*, 18(1), 87. Advance online publication. DOI: 10.1186/s12961-020-00596-8 PMID: 32762700

Jang, Y. J., & Chen, H. L. (2021). *Digital Transformation in Southeast Asia: Emerging Trends and Implications*. Asian Development Bank Institute.

Jarrahi, M. H., & Eshraghi, A. (2019). Digital natives vs digital immigrants: A multidimensional view on interaction with social technologies in organizations. *Journal of Enterprise Information Management*, 32(6), 1051–1070. DOI: 10.1108/JEIM-04-2018-0071

Jatoba, M., Ferreira, J. J., Fernandes, P., & Teixeira, J. (2023). Intelligent human resources for the adoption of artificial intelligence: A systematic literature review. *Journal of Organizational Change Management*, 36(7), 36. DOI: 10.1108/JOCM-03-2022-0075

Javaid, M., Haleem, A., Singh, R. P., & Suman, R. (2021). Substantial capabilities of robotics in enhancing industry 4.0 implementation. Cognitive Robotics. DOI: 10.1016/j.cogr.2021.06.001

Javaid, M., Haleem, A., Khan, I. H., & Suman, R. (2023). Understanding the potential applications of Artificial Intelligence in Agriculture Sector. *Advanced Agrochem*, 2(1), 15–30. DOI: 10.1016/j.aac.2022.10.001

Jeanjaroonsri, R. (2023). Thai EFL learners' use and perceptions of mobile technologies for writing. Learn Journal: Language Education and Acquisition Research Network, 16(1), 169–193. https://so04.tci- thaijo.org/index.php/LEARN/article/view/263438

Jecker, N. S. & Nakazawa, E. (2022). Bridging east-west differences in ethics guidance for AI and robotics. AI. DOI: 10.3390/ai3030045

Jeffrey, T. R. (2020). Understanding college student perceptions of artificial intelligence. Retrieved from https://api.semanticscholar.org/CorpusID:235602425

Jerome, A., Scales, M., Whithem, C., & Quain, B. (2014). Millennials in the workforce: Gen Y workplace strategies for the next century. *E-Journal of Social & Behavioural Research in Business*, 5(1), 1.

Jetha, A., Bakhtari, H., Rosella, L., Gignac, M., Biswas, A., Shahidi, F., Smith, B., Smith, M., Mustard, C., Khan, N., Arrandale, V. H., Loewen, P. J., Zuberi, D., Dennerlein, J. T., Bonaccio, S., Wu, N., Irvin, E., & Smith, P. M. (2023). Artificial intelligence and the work–health interface: A research agenda for a technologically transforming world of work. *American Journal of Industrial Medicine*, 66(10), 815–830. DOI: 10.1002/ajim.23517 PMID: 37525007

Jiang, H., & Cheng, L. (2021). Public perception and reception of robotic applications in public health emergencies based on a questionnaire survey conducted during COVID-19. International journal of environmental research and public health, 18(20), 10908. DOI: 10.3390/ijerph182010908

Johan, D., & Syamsul Maarif, M. (2024). Agricultural Digitalization In Indonesia: Challenges And Opportunities For Sustainable Development. *Educational Administration: Theory and Practice*, 30(7), 640–648. DOI: 10.53555/kuey.v30i7.6599

Johansson, B., Eriksson, E., Berglund, N., & Lindgren, I. (2021). Robotic surgery: Review on minimally invasive techniques. *Fusion of Multidisciplinary Research. International Journal (Toronto, Ont.)*, 2(2), 201–210.

Johnson, D. G., & Verdicchio, M. (2017). AI anxiety. *Journal of the Association for Information Science and Technology*, 68(9), 2267–2270. DOI: 10.1002/asi.23867

Johnson, M., Thompson, R., & Hayes, T. (2021). Evaluating the effectiveness of digital detox programs in college students. *Journal of Behavioral Health*, 14(3), 212–225. DOI: 10.1177/21684790211000099

Johnston, K. (2019). Digital technology as a tool to support children and educators as co-learners. *Global Studies of Childhood*, 9(4), 306–317. DOI: 10.1177/2043610619871571

Jones, D. M. (2023). *Superwomen Leading the World: A Mixed Methods Study of Black Women Leaders Managing Stress and Multitasking* (Doctoral dissertation, North Carolina Agricultural and Technical State University).

Jones, M. (2019). Youth and digital agriculture: Challenges and opportunities. *Global Food Security*, 21(2), 150–160. DOI: 10.1016/j.gfs.2019.05.002

Joseph, A. B., & Hosea, I. (2020). Thematic relevance of music in nollywood movies. *IGWEBUIKE: An African Journal of Arts and Humanities*, 6(6), 140–150.

Joshi, H. & Chawla, D. (2024). Impact of security on wallet adoption: multiple and serial mediating roles of trust and attitude and gender as a moderator. *International Journal of Bank Marketing*.

Juddi, M. F., Aprianti, A., & Sudrajat, R. H. (2023). The Digital Skill Improvement Program for Women of the HEPI Bandung Community Members in Using New Media. *ABDIMAS: Jurnal Pengabdian Masyarakat*, 6(4), 4532–4538. DOI: 10.35568/abdimas.v6i4.3638

Junaidi. (2024). Efektivitas internet of things (iot) pada sektor pertanian. Jurnal teknika, DOI: 10.54314/teknisi.v4i1.1793

Kadylak, T., & Cotten, S. R. (2020, April 15). United States older adults' willingness to use emerging technologies. *Information Communication and Society*, 23(5), 736–750. Advance online publication. DOI: 10.1080/1369118X.2020.1713848

Kaifi, B., Nafei, W., Khanfar, N., & Kaifi, M. (2012). A Multi-Generational Workforce: Managing and Understanding Millennials. *International Journal of Business and Management*, 7(24), 24. DOI: 10.5539/ijbm.v7n24p88

Kamel, S. (2021, September). The potential impact of digital transformation on Egypt. Giza, Egypt: Economic Research Forum (ERF).

Kapeller, A., Felzmann, H., Fosch-Villaronga, E., & Hughes, A. M. (2020). A taxonomy of ethical, legal and social implications of wearable robots: an expert perspective. Science and engineering ethics, 26, 3229-3247. DOI: 10.1007/s11948-020-00268-4

Karjaluoto, H., Shaikh, A. A., Leppäniemi, M., & Luomala, R. (2020). Examining consumers' usage intention of contactless payment systems. *International Journal of Bank Marketing*, 38(2), 332–351. DOI: 10.1108/IJBM-04-2019-0155

Karsenti, T. (2019). Artificial intelligence in education: the urgent need to prepare teachers for tomorrow's schools. Formation et profession, 27(1), 112–116. .DOI: 10.18162/fp.2019.a166

Kaushal, N., Kaurav, R. P. S., Sivathanu, B., & Kaushik, N. (2023). Artificial intelligence and HRM: Identifying future research Agenda using systematic literature review and bibliometric analysis. *Management Review Quarterly*, 73(2), 455–493. DOI: 10.1007/s11301-021-00249-2

Ke, C., Lou, V. W. Q., Tan, K. C. K., Wai, M. Y., & Chan, L. L. (2020). Changes in technology acceptance among older people with dementia: The role of social robot engagement. *International Journal of Medical Informatics*, 141, 104241. DOI: 10.1016/j.ijmedinf.2020.104241 PMID: 32739611

Kelley, P. G., Yang, Y., Heldreth, C., Moessner, C., Sedley, A., Kramm, A., Newman, D. T., & Woodruff, A. (2021). Exciting, useful, worrying, futuristic: Public perception of artificial intelligence in 8 countries. In Proceedings of the 2021 AAAI/ACM Conference on AI, Ethics, and Society (pp. 627–637). Association for Computing Machinery. DOI: 10.1145/3461702.3462605

Kelley, P. G., Yang, Y., Heldreth, C., Moessner, C., Sedley, A., Kramm, A., Newman, D. T., & Woodruff, A. (2019). "Happy and assured that life will be easy 10 years from now": Perceptions of artificial intelligence in 8 countries. https://arxiv.org/abs/2001.00081

Kennedy, I. G., Latham, G., & Jacinto, H. (2015). *Education skills for 21st century teachers: Voices from a global online educators' forum*. Springer.

Kesharwani, A. (2020). Do (how) digital natives adopt a new technology differently than digital immigrants? A longitudinal study. *Information & Management*, 57(2), 103170. DOI: 10.1016/j.im.2019.103170

Khang, A., & Akhai, S. (2024). Green Intelligent and Sustainable Manufacturing: Key Advancements, Benefits, Challenges, and Applications for Transforming Industry. *Machine Vision and Industrial Robotics in Manufacturing*, 405-417.

Khang, A., & Akhai, S. (2025). E-Waste and Lithium-ion Battery Recycling Insights for Sustainable Transportation. In Khang, A. (Ed.), *Driving Green Transportation System Through Artificial Intelligence and Automation. Lecture Notes in Intelligent Transportation and Infrastructure*. Springer. DOI: 10.1007/978-3-031-72617-0_11

Khaspuria, G., Khandelwal, A., Agarwal, M., Bafna, M., Yadav, R., & Yadav, A. (2024). Adoption of Precision Agriculture Technologies among Farmers: A Comprehensive Review. *Journal of Scientific Research and Reports*, 30(7), 671–686. DOI: 10.9734/jsrr/2024/v30i72180

Khogali, H. O. & Mekid, S. (2023). The blended future of automation and AI: Examining some long-term societal and ethical impact features. Technology in Society. DOI: 10.1016/j.techsoc.2023.102232

Kickbusch, I., Piselli, D., Agrawal, A., Balicer, R., Banner, O., Adelhardt, M., . . . Wong, B. L. H. (2021). The Lancet and Financial Times Commission on governing health futures 2030: Growing up in a digital world. *The Lancet, 398*(10312), 1727-1776. DOI: 10.1016/S0140-6736(21)02113-0

Kidd, A. L. (2022). *Loneliness and Love: The Potential of Human-AI Relations as Explored by Contemporary Science Fiction Cinema*. Screen Bodies. DOI: 10.3167/screen.2022.070207

Kim, D., Nam, J. K., & Keum, C. (2022). Adolescent Internet gaming addiction and personality characteristics by game genre. *PLoS One*, 17(2), e0263645. DOI: 10.1371/journal.pone.0263645 PMID: 35143558

Kim, J., & Park, J. (2022). The impact of COVID-19 on digital transformation and innovation in Korea. *Technological Forecasting and Social Change*, 176.

King, A. C., Odunitan-Wayas, F. A., Chaudhury, M., Rubio, M. A., Baiocchi, M., Kolbe-Alexander, T., ... & Our Voice Global Citizen Science Research Network. (2021). Community-based approaches to reducing health inequities and fostering environmental justice through global youth-engaged citizen science. International journal of environmental research and public health, 18(3), 892. DOI: 10.3390/ijerph18030892

King, B., Devare, M., Overduin, M., Wong, K., Kropff, W., Perez, S., ... Jarvis, A. (2021). Toward a digital One CGIAR: Strategic research on digital transformation in food, land, and water systems in a climate crisis.

King, C., Murillo, E., & Lee, H. (2017). The effects of generational work values on employee brand attitude and behavior: A multi-group analysis. *International Journal of Hospitality Management*, 66, 92–105. DOI: 10.1016/j.ijhm.2017.07.006

Klein, T., & Teece, D. J. (2020). Innovation and market strategy: The role of industrial ecosystems. *Industrial and Corporate Change*, 29(3), 439–451.

Klopotan, I., Aleksić, A., & Vinković, N. (2020). Do business ethics and ethical decision making still matter: Perspective of different generational cohorts. *Business Systems Research: International journal of the Society for Advancing Innovation and Research in Economy, 11*(1), 31-43.

Ko, C. H., Yen, J. Y., Chen, C. S., Yeh, Y. C., & Yen, C. F. (2014). The association between internet addiction and psychiatric disorder among adolescents. *The Psychiatric Clinics of North America*, 37(4), 419–426. DOI: 10.1016/j.psc.2014.08.001

Kolade, O., & Owoseni, A. (2022). Employment 5.0: The work of the future and the future of work. *Technology in Society*, 71, 102086. DOI: 10.1016/j.techsoc.2022.102086

Kolandaisamy, R., Lie, S.L., Kolandaisamy, I., & Jalil, A. & Muthusamy, G. (2022). The Impact and Effectiveness of E–Wallet Usage for Malaysian Male and Female. *Specialusis Ugdymas*, 1(43), 4102–4109.

Kopp, T., Baumgartner, M., & Kinkel, S. (2023). "It's not Paul, it's a robot": The impact of linguistic framing and the evolution of trust and distrust in a collaborative robot during a human-robot interaction. International Journal of Human-Computer Studies, 178, 103095. DOI: 10.1016/j.ijhcs.2023.103095

Koppala Venugopal, Vital, Das, Jena, & Mohapatro. (2023). Usage Determinants of Mobile Applications Impelling Students Group: Assessment through Machine Learning Models and Regression. Vytapeni, Vetrani, Instalace Journal.

Korecki, J. R., Schwebel, F. J., Votaw, V. R., & Witkiewitz, K. (2020). Mindfulness-based programs for substance use disorders: A systematic review of manualized treatments. *Substance Abuse Treatment, Prevention, and Policy*, 15(1), 51. Advance online publication. DOI: 10.1186/s13011-020-00293-3 PMID: 32727559

Korotkova, N., Benders, J., Mikalef, P., & Cameron, D. (2023). Maneuvering between skepticism and optimism about hyped technologies: Building trust in digital twins. Information & Management, 60(4), 103787. DOI: 10.1016/j.im.2023.103787

Koutsimani, P., Montgomery, A., & Georganta, K. (2019). The Relationship Between Burnout, Depression, and Anxiety: A Systematic Review and Meta-Analysis. *Frontiers in Psychology*, 10, 284. Advance online publication. DOI: 10.3389/fpsyg.2019.00284 PMID: 30918490

Kovac, N., Żmija, K., Roy, J. K., Kusa, R., & Duda, J. (2024). Digital divide and digitalization in Europe: A bibliometric analysis. *Equilibrium.Quarterly Journal of Economics and Economic Policy*, 19(2), 463–520. DOI: 10.24136/eq.2899

Krejcie, R. V., & Morgan, D.W. (1970). Determining sample size for research activities. *Educational and Psychological Measurement*, 30(3), 607–610.

Krishnamoorthy. (2024). Agriculture using Digital Technologies. DOI: 10.1201/9781003515883-7

Krueger, D. C., Stone, D. L., & Lukaszewski, K. M. (2018). Age and the digital divide. *Journal of Strategic Innovation and Sustainability*, 13(3).

Kultalahti, S., & Liisa Viitala, R. (2014). Sufficient challenges and a weekend ahead – Generation Y describing motivation at work. *Journal of Organizational Change Management*, 27(4), 569–582. DOI: 10.1108/JOCM-05-2014-0101

Kumar, A., Yadav, R., Saikanth, D. R. K., Tripathi, G., Sharma, A., Meinam, M., & Shukla, A. (2023). The Impact of Social Media on Agricultural Youth: Empowering the Next Generation in India. *Asian Journal of Agricultural Extension. Economia e Sociologia*, 41(10), 260–267. DOI: 10.9734/ajaees/2023/v41i102167

Kumar, H., Wadhwa, A. S., Akhai, S., & Kaushik, A. (2024). Parametric analysis, modeling and optimization of the process parameters in electric discharge machining of aluminium metal matrix composite. *Engineering Research Express*, 6(2), 025542. DOI: 10.1088/2631-8695/ad4ba9

Kumar, H., Wadhwa, A. S., Akhai, S., & Kaushik, A. (2024). Parametric optimization of the machining performance of Al-SiCp composite using combination of response surface methodology and desirability function. *Engineering Research Express*, 6(2), 025505. DOI: 10.1088/2631-8695/ad38ff

Kumar, P., & Kumar, V. (2020). Bridging the digital divide: The role of mobile and fixed broadband. *Information Technology & People*, 33(1), 296–309.

Kuoppamäki, S., Hänninen, R., & Taipale, S. (2022). Enhancing older adults' digital inclusion through social support: a qualitative interview study. In *Springer eBooks* (pp. 211–230). DOI: 10.1007/978-3-030-94122-2_11

Kurian, S., Faiz, M., Zubair, M., & Ahamed, S. (2024, March). Advancing Safety and Efficiency in Human-Robot Interaction. In *2024 International Conference on Distributed Computing and Optimization Techniques (ICDCOT)* (pp. 1-8). IEEE. DOI: 10.1109/ICDCOT61034.2024.10515531

Kusolchoo, S., & Ueasangkomsate, P. (2024). Digital Technologies for Food Loss and Waste in Food Supply Chain Management. *2024 Joint International Conference on Digital Arts, Media and Technology with ECTI Northern Section Conference on Electrical, Electronics, Computer and Telecommunications Engineering (ECTI DAMT & NCON)*, 97-102, DOI: 10.1109/ECTIDAMTNCON60518.2024.10480014

Kuss, D. J., & Griffiths, M. D. (2017a). Smartphone addiction: A review of the literature. *International Journal of Environmental Research and Public Health*, 14(12), 1383. DOI: 10.3390/ijerph14121383

Kuss, D. J., & Griffiths, M. D. (2017b). The socio-cultural impact of technology addiction: A review. *Current Psychiatry Reviews*, 13(3), 187–196. DOI: 10.2174/1573400513666170307113718

Kusumadinata, A., Astrid Sri Wahyuni Sumah, A., & Suryatna, U. (2023). Exposure of Social Media Advertising Media to Corn Farmers. *Jurnal Multidisiplin Madani*, 3(11), 2235–2242. DOI: 10.55927/mudima.v3i11.6825

Kwon, M., Kim, D. J., Cho, H., & Yang, S. (2013). The Smartphone Addiction Scale: Development and validation of a short version for adolescents. *PLoS One*, 8(12), e83558. DOI: 10.1371/journal.pone.0083558 PMID: 24391787

Lacinski, R. A., Steller, J. G., Anderson, A., & Nelson, A. M. (2024). Harnessing Artificial Intelligence for Medical Diagnosis and Treatment During Space Exploration Missions.

Lamont, R. A., & Swift, H. (2015). *Older people's responses to age stereotypes: Implications for performance outcomes, and health and well-being*. University of Kent.

Lane, T. B., Vomvoridi-Ivanovic, E., & Cain, L. K. Journal of Pre-College Engineering Education Research (J-PEER). *Journal of Pre-College Engineering Education Research (J-PEER), 12*(2), 5.

Lanier, K. (2017). 5 Things HR professionals need to know about generation Z: Thought leaders share their views on the HR profession and its direction for the future. *Strategic HR Review*, 16(6), 288–290. DOI: 10.1108/SHR-08-2017-0051

Lariviere, B., Bowen, D., Andreassen, T., Kunz, W., Sirianni, N., Voss, C., Wunderlich, N., & De Keyser, A. (2017). "Service Encounter 2.0": An investigation into the roles of technology, employees and customers. *Journal of Business Research*, 79, 79. DOI: 10.1016/j.jbusres.2017.03.008

Latikka, R., Savela, N., Koivula, A., & Oksanen, A. (2021). Attitudes toward robots as equipment and coworkers and the impact of robot autonomy level. International Journal of Social Robotics, 13(7), 1747-1759. DOI: 10.1007/s12369-020-00743-9

Laywilla, E., Kartar Singh, J. S., & Yin Fah, B. C. (2020). Drivers of Intention to Adopt Mobile Wallet: A Quantitative Study Among Females in Jakarta. *International Journal of Academic Research in Business & Social Sciences*, 10(11). Advance online publication. DOI: 10.6007/IJARBSS/v10-i11/8061

Leech, J. A., Neary, N., & Reilly, K. (2018). The effects of screen time on obesity and cardiovascular risk factors in children: A meta-analysis. *Pediatrics*, 142(6), e20182514. DOI: 10.1542/peds.2018-2514

Lee, M., Lee, Y., & Kim, J. (2021). The effectiveness of app-based screen time management tools: A systematic review. *Digital Health*, 7, 1–12. DOI: 10.1177/20552076211021690

Lee, M., Scheepers, H., Lui, A. K. H., & Ngai, E. W. T. (2023). The implementation of artificial intelligence in organizations: A systematic literature review. *Information & Management*, 60(5), 103816. DOI: 10.1016/j.im.2023.103816

Lee, M., & Song, M. (2019). Comparative advantage of nations, knowledge and innovation strategies: An analysis of Korea and Malaysia. *Technological Forecasting and Social Change*, 143, 201–213.

Lee, Y., Kozar, K. A., & Larsen, K. R. T. (2003). The Technology Acceptance Model: Past, Present, and Future. *Communications of the Association for Information Systems*, 12, 12. DOI: 10.17705/1CAIS.01250

Lele, A. (n.d.). Defence applications of artificial intelligence. Artificial Intelligence.

Lemay, D. J., Basnet, R. B., & Doleck, T. (2020). Fearing the robot apocalypse: Correlates of AI anxiety.

Lemay, D. J., Basnet, R. B., & Doleck, T. (2020). Fearing the robot apocalypse: Correlates of AI anxiety. *International Journal of Learning Analytics and Artificial Intelligence for Education*, 2(2), 24–33. DOI: 10.3991/ijai.v2i2.16759

Leong, L. Y., Hew, T. S., Ooi, K. B., & Wei, J. (2020). Predicting mobile wallet resistance: A two-staged structural equation modeling-artificial neural network approach. *International Journal of Information Management*, 51, 102047. Advance online publication. DOI: 10.1016/j.ijinfomgt.2019.102047

Liaw, S. S., & Huang, H. M. (2003). An investigation of user attitudes toward search engines as an information retrieval tool. *Computers in Human Behavior*, 19(6), 751–765. DOI: 10.1016/S0747-5632(03)00009-8

Licardo, J. T., Domjan, M., & Orehovački, T. (2024). Intelligent robotics—A systematic review of emerging technologies and trends. *Electronics (Basel)*, 13(3), 542. DOI: 10.3390/electronics13030542

Lichtenthaler, U. (2019). Extremes of acceptance: Employee attitudes toward artificial intelligence. *The Journal of Business Strategy*, 40(1), 34–41. DOI: 10.1108/JBS-12-2018-0204

Lin, C., Šabanović, S., Dombrowski, L., Miller, A. D., Brady, E., & MacDorman, K. F. (2021). Parental acceptance of children's storytelling robots: A projection of the uncanny valley of AI. Frontiers in Robotics and AI, 8, 579993. DOI: 10.3389/frobt.2021.579993

Lind, M., & Mukherjee, A. (2018). Maritime Informatics: Applying the Digital Layer to the Shipping Sector. *Technology Innovation Management Review*, 8(9), 18–27.

Lin, L. Y., Sidani, J. E., Shensa, A., Radovic, A., Miller, E., Colditz, J. B., Hoffman, B. L., Giles, L. M., & Primack, B. A. (2016). Association between social media use and depression among U.S. young adults. *Depression and Anxiety*, 33(4), 323–331. DOI: 10.1002/da.22466 PMID: 26783723

Lin, N., Paul, R., Guerra, S., Liu, Y., Doulgeris, J., Shi, M., & Vrionis, F. D. (2024, November). The Frontiers of Smart Healthcare Systems. *Health Care*, 12(23), 2330. PMID: 39684952

Lissitsa, S., Zychlinski, E., & Kagan, M. (2022). The Silent Generation vs Baby Boomers: Socio-demographic and psychological predictors of the "gray" digital inequalities. *Computers in Human Behavior*, 128, 107098. DOI: 10.1016/j.chb.2021.107098

Liu, S., Zhao, H., Fu, J., Kong, D., Zhong, Z., Hong, Y., Tan, J., & Luo, Y. (2022). Current status and influencing factors of digital health literacy among community-dwelling older adults in Southwest China: A cross-sectional study. *BMC Public Health*, 22(1), 996. Advance online publication. DOI: 10.1186/s12889-022-13378-4 PMID: 35581565

Liu, X., Geng, S., & Dou, D. (2024). Interplay between Children's Electronic Media Use and Prosocial Behavior: The Chain Mediating Role of Parent–Child Closeness and Emotion Regulation. *Behavioral Sciences (Basel, Switzerland)*, 14(6), 436. DOI: 10.3390/bs14060436 PMID: 38920768

Liu, Y., Zhao, X., & Zhang, L. (2020). The impact of smartphone addiction on adolescents' mental health: A systematic review. *The Journal of Adolescent Health*, 66(5), 576–583. DOI: 10.1016/j.jadohealth.2019.12.022

Lockey, S., Gillespie, N., Holm, D., & Someh, I. A. (2021). *A review of trust in artificial intelligence: Challenges, vulnerabilities and future directions. Hawaii International Conference on System Sciences*. DOI: 10.24251/HICSS.2021.664

Loges, W. E., & Jung, J. Y. (2001). Exploring the digital divide: Internet connectedness and age. *Communication Research*, 28(4), 536–562. DOI: 10.1177/009365001028004007

Lozano, I., Molina, J., & Gijón, C. (2021). Perception of artificial intelligence in Spain. *Telematics and Informatics*, 63, 101672. DOI: 10.1016/j.tele.2021.101672

Lu, L. (2010, June). Digital divide: Does the internet speak your language? In *EdMedia+ Innovate Learning* (pp. 4022-4025). Association for the Advancement of Computing in Education (AACE).

Luckin, R. (2017). Towards artificial intelligence-based assessment systems. Nature Human Behaviour, 1(3), 1–3.

Lynch, J., & Gregor, S. (2004). User participation in decision support systems development: Influencing system outcomes. *European Journal of Information Systems*, 13(4), 286–301. DOI: 10.1057/palgrave.ejis.3000512

Lyons, S., & Kuron, L. (2014). Generational differences in the workplace: A review of the evidence and directions for future research. *Journal of Organizational Behavior*, 35(S1), S139–S157. DOI: 10.1002/job.1913

Madonna, M., Reza, F., & Sovianti, R. (2023). Social Media as a Platform to Increase Participation of Extension Workers and Farmers in Achieving SDGs. *KnE Social Sciences*, 8(12), 854–863. DOI: 10.18502/kss.v8i12.13731

Magano, J., Silva, C., Figueiredo, C., Vitória, A., Nogueira, T., & Pimenta Dinis, M. A. (2020). Generation Z: Fitting project management soft skills competencies—A mixed-method approach. *Education Sciences*, 10(7), 187. DOI: 10.3390/educsci10070187

Magni, F., & Manzoni, B. (2020a). *Generational Differences in Workers' Expectations: Millennials Want More of the Same Things*.

Magnier-Watanabe, R., & Magnier-Watanabe, K. (2024, January). COVID-19 and mandatory telework: Effects on gender roles and work family conflicts among Japanese dual-career regular employees with children. *Japan Forum*, 36(1), 1–29. DOI: 10.1080/09555803.2023.2200967

Magni, F., & Manzoni, B. (2020b). Generational Differences in Workers' Expectations: Millennials Want More of the Same Things. *European Management Review*, 17(4), 901–914. DOI: 10.1111/emre.12405

Magsamen-Conrad, K., & Dillon, J. M. (2020). Mobile technology adoption across the lifespan: A mixed methods investigation to clarify adoption stages, and the influence of diffusion attributes. *Computers in Human Behavior*, 112, 106456. DOI: 10.1016/j.chb.2020.106456 PMID: 32834465

Mahmud, A. K., Iwang, B., Kayyum, A., & Binti Sa'at, N. H. (2024). How Technological Development and E-Commerce Drive Economic Growth in Indonesia. *EcceS. Economics Social and Development Studies*, 11(1), 73–97. DOI: 10.24252/ecc.v11i1.45419

Mala, S., Deep, U., Mala, E., & Akhai, S. (2025). Digital Health Technologies for Preventive Cardiology. In *Impact of Digital Solutions for Improved Healthcare Delivery* (pp. 379–400). IGI Global.

Malinverni, L., Valero, C., Schaper, M. M., & de la Cruz, I. G. (2021). Educational robotics as a boundary object: Towards a research agenda. International Journal of Child-Computer Interaction, 29, 100305. DOI: 10.1016/j.ijcci.2021.100305

Manaf, M. F. A., & Kamarudin, H. (2021). Technology adoption and the growth of E-Commerce in Malaysia. *International Journal of Advanced Research in Engineering and Technology*, 12(2), 200–210.

Mangurai, S. (2022). Overview of Digital Agriculture Technologies in Indonesia: Policies, Implementation, and Covid-19 Relation. Research Square.

Maniscalco, U., Minutolo, A., Storniolo, P., & Esposito, M. (2024). Towards a more anthropomorphic interaction with robots in museum settings: An experimental study. Robotics and Autonomous Systems, 171, 104561. DOI: 10.1016/j.robot.2023.104561

Mannheim, I., Schwartz, E., Xi, W., Buttigieg, S. C., McDonnell-Naughton, M., Wouters, E. J. M., & Van Zaalen, Y. (2019). Inclusion of older adults in the research and design of digital technology. *International Journal of Environmental Research and Public Health*, 16(19), 3718. DOI: 10.3390/ijerph16193718 PMID: 31581632

Marchionni, L., & Charrier, R. (2022). The role of digital ecosystems in the new era of business: Challenges and opportunities. *European Business Review*, 2(1), 1–14.

March–Russell, P. (2020). and the Question of the Robot. AI Narratives: A History of Imaginative Thinking about Intelligent Machines, 165.

Mariani, M. M., Machado, I., Magrelli, V., & Dwivedi, Y. K. (2023). Artificial intelligence in innovation research: A systematic review, conceptual framework, and future research directions. *Technovation*, 122, 102623. DOI: 10.1016/j.technovation.2022.102623

Marrero Galván, J. J., Negrín Medina, M. Á., Bernárdez-Gómez, A., & Portela Pruaño, A. (2023). The impact of the first millennial teachers on education: Views held by different generations of teachers. *Education and Information Technologies*, 28(11), 14805–14826. DOI: 10.1007/s10639-023-11768-8 PMID: 37361824

Marsh, E., Vallejos, E. P., & Spence, A. (2022). The Digital Workplace and Its Dark Side: An Integrative Review. *Computers in Human Behavior*, 128(March), 107118. DOI: 10.1016/j.chb.2021.107118

Martínez-Peláez, R., Ochoa-Brust, A., Rivera, S., Félix, V. G., Ostos, R., Brito, H., Félix, R. A., & Mena, L. J. (2023). Role of digital transformation for achieving sustainability: Mediated role of stakeholders, key capabilities, and technology. *Sustainability (Basel)*, 15(14), 11221. DOI: 10.3390/su151411221

Marzilli, E., Cerniglia, L., Ballarotto, G., & Cimino, S. (2020). Internet Addiction among Young Adult University Students: The Complex Interplay between Family Functioning, Impulsivity, Depression, and Anxiety. *International Journal of Environmental Research and Public Health*, 17(21), 8231. DOI: 10.3390/ijerph17218231 PMID: 33171742

Marzo, R. R. (2024). Bridging the gap: Understanding and fostering intergenerational communication in the digital age. In *Intergenerational relations-contemporary theories, studies and policies*. IntechOpen. DOI: 10.5772/intechopen.1003205

McDougall, J., Readman, M., & Wilkinson, P. (2016). From Digital Literacy to Capability: Project Report and Impact Evaluation. Retrieved from https://www.cemp.ac.uk/downloads/SAMPACA%20reportFINAL.pdf

McGuire, D., Todnem By, R., & Hutchings, K. (2007). Towards a model of human resource solutions for achieving intergenerational interaction in organisations. *Journal of European Industrial Training*, 31(8), 592–608. DOI: 10.1108/03090590710833651

McHugh, M.L. (2013). The chi-square test of independence. *Biochemia Medica, Medicinska naklada, 23*(2), 143–149.

McLeay, F., Osburg, V. S., Yoganathan, V., & Patterson, A. (2021). Replaced by a Robot: Service Implications in the Age of the Machine. Journal of Service Research, 24(1), 104 121. https://sagepub.com/journals-permissions

McPhail, R., Chan, X. W., May, R., & Wilkinson, A. (2024). Post-COVID remote working and its impact on people, productivity, and the planet: An exploratory scoping review. *International Journal of Human Resource Management*, 35(1), 154–182. DOI: 10.1080/09585192.2023.2221385

Megavitry, R., & Harahap, R. H. (2023). Revolutionizing the Future: The Importance of Utilizing Food Technology for Sustainable Nutrition and Global Prosperity. *West Science Interdisciplinary Studies*, 1(09), 776–784. DOI: 10.58812/wsis.v1i09.210

Mehrizi, M. H. R., & Alvesson, M. (2021). Unpacking digital platforms and ecosystems: Strategic and managerial implications. *International Journal of Management Reviews*, 23(3), 316–332.

Meroni, E. C., Piazzalunga, D., & Pronzato, C. (2021). Allocation of time and child socio-emotional skills. *Review of Economics of the Household*, 20(4), 1155–1192. DOI: 10.1007/s11150-021-09580-9

Milioni, D. L., Doudaki, V., & Demertzis, N. (2014). Youth, ethnicity, and a 'reverse digital divide' A study of Internet use in a divided country. *Convergence (London)*, 20(3), 316–336. DOI: 10.1177/1354856513517366

Miller, W. R., & Rollnick, S. (2012). *Motivational interviewing: Helping people change* (3rd ed.). Guilford Press.

Miller, W. R., Smith, J., & Thomas, R. (2020). Integrated interventions for adolescent digital addiction: Combining cognitive-behavioral therapy and educational approaches. *Journal of Youth and Adolescence*, 49(8), 1622–1636. DOI: 10.1007/s10964-020-01223-6

Ministry of Science, Technology and Innovation (MOSTI). (2020). Malaysia Digital Economy Blueprint. Retrieved from: https://www.mosti.gov.my/web/wp-content/uploads/2020/11/MDEC-BLUEPRINT.pdf

Miroslavov, M. (2023). *Bridging the Age Gap: Mastering Unity in a Multi-Generational Workplace*. OfficeRnD. https://www.officernd.com/blog/generational-differences-in-the-workplace/

Miskolczi, M., Jászberényi, M., & Tóth, D. (2021). Technology-enhanced airport services—attractiveness from the travelers' perspective. Sustainability. DOI: 10.3390/su13020705

Mitchell, U. A., Chebli, P. G., Ruggiero, L., & Muramatsu, N. (2019). The digital divide in health-related technology use: The significance of race/ethnicity. *The Gerontologist*, 59(1), 6–14. DOI: 10.1093/geront/gny138 PMID: 30452660

Moe, S. H., & Pomsuwan, S. (2024, March). The Impact of Digital Workplace Transformation, Remote Working and Working Environment Towards Employee Performance Throughout the Covid-19 Pandemic in Interior Industry in Bangkok. In Proceeding National & International Conference (Vol. 16, No. 1, pp. 205-212).

Mohammed, P. S., & Watson, E. N. (2019). Towards inclusive education in the age of artificial intelligence: perspectives, challenges, and opportunities. In Knox, J., Wang, Y., & Gallagher, M. (Eds.), *Artificial Intelligence and Inclusive Education. Perspectives on Rethinking and Reforming Education*. Springer. DOI: 10.1007/978-981-13-8161-4_2

Mohr, K., & Mohr, E. (2017). Understanding Generation Z Students to Promote a Contemporary Learning Environment. *Journal on Empowering Teaching Excellence*, 1(1).

Montag, C., Ali, R., & Davis, K. (2024). Affective neuroscience theory and attitudes towards artificial intelligence. *AI & Society*. Advance online publication. DOI: 10.1007/s00146-023-01841-8

Monteiro, A. P., Relva, I. C., & Simões, M. (2023). Internet addiction. In *Springer eBooks* (pp. 1–15). DOI: 10.1007/978-3-030-68127-2_4-1

Moore, N., Rowe, L., Stokes, P., Lichy, J., Rodgers, P., & Smith, S. M. (2022). An examination of the dynamics of intergenerational tensions and technological change in the context of post-pandemic recovery. *Production Planning and Control*, 1–18.

Morandini, S., Fraboni, F., De Angelis, M., Puzzo, G., Giusino, D., & Pietrantoni, L. (2023). The impact of artificial intelligence on workers' skills: Upskilling and reskilling in organisations. *Informing Science*, 26, 39–68. DOI: 10.28945/5078

Moreno, R. D. (2019). The arrival of artificial intelligence to education. *RITI Journal*, 7(14), 260–270. DOI: 10.36825/RITI.07.14.022

Mossberger, K., Tolbert, C. J., & Stansbury, M. (2003). *Virtual inequality: Beyond the digital divide*. Georgetown University Press.

Motia, K., Kumar, R., & Akhai, S. (2024). AI and Smart Manufacturing: Building Industry 4.0. In *Modern Management Science Practices in the Age of AI* (pp. 1-28). IGI Global.

Mou, Q., Zhuang, J., Wu, Q., Zhong, Y., Dai, Q., Cao, X., Gao, Y., Lu, Q., & Zhao, M. (2024). Social media addiction and academic engagement as serial mediators between social anxiety and academic performance among college students. *BMC Psychology*, 12(1), 190. Advance online publication. DOI: 10.1186/s40359-024-01635-7 PMID: 38582933

Muh. (2022). A social network analysis of the use of social media to promote agriculture to indonesian youth. DOI: 10.32469/10355/90198

Mulyani, S., & Pratama, F. (2021). Crowdfunding for agriculture: The impact of Crowde on young Indonesian farmers. *Journal of Rural Development*, 48(1), 22–35. DOI: 10.23045/jrd.v48i1.172

Mundhe, D. E. (2024). *Rethink revolution: Transformative waves across disciplines*.

Mun, M. L., & Khoo, B. K. (2019). Influence of e-commerce adoption on SMEs business performance. *Journal of Advanced Research in Dynamical and Control Systems*, 11(5), 1352–1357.

Muntaka, A. S., Seidu, A. H., & Gariba, M. A. (2020). A systematic literature review on blockchain technology: Insights on challenges and current solutions. *Journal of Advances in Mathematics and Computer Science*, 35(2), 64–79.

Murphy, R. R. (2019). *Introduction to AI robotics*. MIT press.

Myers, K. K., & Sadaghiani, K. (2010). Millennials in the workplace: A communication perspective on millennials' organizational relationships and performance. *Journal of Business and Psychology*, 25(2), 225–238. DOI: 10.1007/s10869-010-9172-7 PMID: 20502509

Nabila, M., Purwandari, B., Nazief, B. A. A., Chalid, D. A., Wibowo, S. S., & Solichah, I. (2018). Financial Technology Acceptance Factors of Electronic Wallet and Digital Cash in Indonesia. *2018 International Conference on Information Technology Systems and Innovation, ICITSI 2018 - Proceedings*, 284–289, DOI: 10.1109/ICITSI.2018.8696091

Nagata, J. M., Weinstein, S., Alsamman, S., Lee, C. M., Dooley, E. E., Ganson, K. T., Testa, A., Gooding, H. C., Kiss, O., Baker, F. C., & Gabriel, K. P. (2024). Association of physical activity and screen time with cardiovascular disease risk in the Adolescent Brain Cognitive Development Study. *BMC Public Health*, 24(1), 1346. Advance online publication. DOI: 10.1186/s12889-024-18790-6 PMID: 38762449

Nagaty, K. A. (2023). Iot commercial and industrial applications and AI-powered IoT. In *Frontiers of Quality Electronic Design (QED) AI, IoT and Hardware Security* (pp. 465–500). Springer International Publishing. DOI: 10.1007/978-3-031-16344-9_12

Naim, M. F., & Bulinska-Stangrecka, H. (2019). Down the Rabbit Hole: Social Media, Workplace Collaboration, Millennial Psychological Need Satisfaction and Affective Commitment in Industry 4.0. In Coetzee, M. (Ed.), *Thriving in Digital Workspaces: Emerging Issues for Research and Practice* (pp. 253–264). Springer International Publishing. DOI: 10.1007/978-3-030-24463-7_13

Najarian, S., Fallahnezhad, M., & Afshari, E. (2011). Advances in medical robotic systems with specific applications in surgery—A review. *Journal of Medical Engineering & Technology*, 35(1), 19–33. DOI: 10.3109/03091902.2010.535593 PMID: 21142589

Naneva, S., Sarda Gou, M., Webb, T. L., & Prescott, T. J. (2020). A systematic review of attitudes, anxiety, acceptance, and trust towards social robots. International Journal of Social Robotics, 12(6), 1179-1201. DOI: 10.1007/s12369-020-00659-4

Naraidoo, S., Doargajudhur, M., Hosanoo, Z., & Zaung, N. (2024). Navigating the Pedagogical Innovation and Digital Transformation Landscape in the Education 5.0 Era. In *Teaching and Assessment in the Era of Education 5.0* (pp. 1-23). IGI Global.

Naresh, R., Singh, N. K., Sachan, P., Mohanty, L. K., Sahoo, S., Pandey, S. K., & Singh, B. (2024). Enhancing Sustainable Crop Production through Innovations in Precision Agriculture Technologies. *Journal of Scientific Research and Reports*, 30(3), 89–113. DOI: 10.9734/jsrr/2024/v30i31861

National Economic Advisory Council (NEAC). (2010a). New Economic Model for Malaysia, Part 1: Strategic Policy Directions. Retrieved from: https://www.epu.gov.my/en/resources/economic-reports/new-economic-model-part-1

National Economic Advisory Council (NEAC). (2010b). New Economic Model for Malaysia, Part 2: Concluding the Transformation. Retrieved from: https://www.epu.gov.my/en/resources/economic-reports/new-economic-model-part-2

Naudé, W. (2021). Artificial intelligence: Neither Utopian nor apocalyptic impacts soon. *Economics of Innovation and New Technology*, 30(1), 1–23. DOI: 10.1080/10438599.2020.1839173

Nawaz, I. Y. (2020). Characteristics of millennials and technology adoption in the digital age. In *Handbook of research on innovations in technology and marketing for the connected consumer* (pp. 241–262). IGI Global. DOI: 10.4018/978-1-7998-0131-3.ch012

Nawrat, Z., & Krawczyk, D. (2023). Robot-Based Medicine. Robots in medicine: mobile robots versus mobile decision, necessity versus possibility and future challenges. *Mobile Robot: Motion Control and Path Planning*, 127-162.

Neece, J. E. (2018). *Attitudinal Differences Towards Robotics Competitions of Male and Female Students Participating in a Southeastern State Robotics Competition*. Liberty University.

Neves, B. B., Waycott, J., & Malta, S. (2018). Old and afraid of new communication technologies? Reconceptualising and contesting the 'age-based digital divide'. *Journal of Sociology (Melbourne, Vic.)*, 54(2), 236–248. DOI: 10.1177/1440783318766119

Newman, A., Bavik, Y. L., Mount, M., & Shao, B. (2021). Data collection via online platforms: Challenges and recommendations for future research. *Applied Psychology*, 70(3), 1380–1402. Advance online publication. DOI: 10.1111/apps.12302

Ng, E., & McGinnis Johnson, J. (2015). Millennials: Who are they, how are they different, and why should we care? *The Multi-Generational and Aging Workforce: Challenges and Opportunities*, 121–137.

Ngadi, N., Zaelany, A. A., Latifa, A., Harfina, D., Asiati, D., Setiawan, B., Ibnu, F., Triyono, T., & Rajagukguk, Z. (2023). Challenge of Agriculture Development in Indonesia: Rural Youth Mobility and Aging Workers in Agriculture Sector. *Sustainability (Basel)*, 15(2), 922. DOI: 10.3390/su15020922

Ngu, J. C. Y., Tsang, C. B. S., & Koh, D. C. S. (2017). The da Vinci Xi: a review of its capabilities, versatility, and potential role in robotic colorectal surgery. *Robotic Surgery: Research and Reviews*, 77-85.

Nguyen, T. Q., & Le, D. T. (2020). The role of digital technology in sustainable agriculture: A focus on youth engagement. *Asian Journal of Agricultural Research*, 11(4), 235–248. DOI: 10.1080/12345678.2020.1234567

Nguyen, T., & Lee, S. (2021). Social support and intervention outcomes for digital addiction in older adults. *Health & Social Work*, 46(2), 102–110. DOI: 10.1093/hsw/hlab006

Nguyen, T.-M., & Malik, A. (2021). A Two-Wave Cross-Lagged Study on AI Service Quality: The Moderating Effects of the Job Level and Job Role. *British Journal of Management*, 33(3), 1221–1237. DOI: 10.1111/1467-8551.12540

Nicolas, S. & Agnieszka, W. (2021). The personality of anthropomorphism: How the need for cognition and the need for closure define attitudes and anthropomorphic attributions toward robots. Computers in Human Behavior.

Nielsen, K. (2021). Digitalisation and resilience of the Danish economy. OECD Economics Department Working Papers, No. 1683, OECD Publishing, Paris.

Nielsen, J., & Mullich, J. (2010). *Designing for user engagement: The role of user feedback and interaction*. Wiley.

Nikou, S., Mezei, J., & Brännback, M. (2018). Digital natives' intention to interact with social media: Value systems and gender. *Telematics and Informatics*, 35(2), 421–435. DOI: 10.1016/j.tele.2017.12.019

Nor, M. R. B. M., & Yusoff, N. M. M. (2020). Factors Affecting Digital Transformation in Malaysian SMEs: A Conceptual Framework. *International Journal of Business and Management Science*, 10(1), 28–37.

Norris, J. M., Davis, J. M., & Timpe-Laughlin, V. (2017). *Second language educational experiences for adult learners*. Routledge. DOI: 10.4324/9781315230801

Norris, P. (2001). *Digital divide: Civic engagement, information poverty, and the Internet worldwide*. Cambridge University Press. DOI: 10.1017/CBO9781139164887

Novanana, S. (2022). Empowering Digital Literacy for Underprivileged Youth in Jakarta. *Asian Journal of Community Services*, 1(2), 65–76. DOI: 10.55927/ajcs.v1i2.1036

Nugroho, A., & Setiawan, B. (2020). The role of social media in digital agriculture: A study of 8Villages in Indonesia. *Journal of Agricultural Communication*, 17(4), 63–79. DOI: 10.1016/j.jac.2020.04.007

Nuševa, D., Leković, K., Vučenović, S., Marić, R., Marić, D., & Vukmirović, G. (2024). The Impact of Digitalization on Sustainable Food Supply Chain Management. *International Scientific Conference Strategic Management and Decision Support Systems in Strategic Management*, 198-206. DOI: 10.46541/978-86-7233-428-9_419

O'Keeffe, G. S., & Clarke-Pearson, K. (2011). The impact of social media on children, adolescents, and families. *Pediatrics*, 127(4), 800–804. DOI: 10.1542/peds.2011-0054 PMID: 21444588

Obaigbena, A., Lottu, O. A., Ugwuanyi, E. D., Jacks, B. S., Sodiya, E. O., & Daraojimba, O. D. (2024). AI and human-robot interaction: A review of recent advances and challenges. *GSC Advanced Research and Reviews*, 18(2), 321–330. DOI: 10.30574/gscarr.2024.18.2.0070

OECD. (2018). Bridging The Digital Gender Divide: Include, Upskill, Innovate https://www.oecd.org/digital/bridging-the-digital-gender-divide.pdf

OECD. (2020). *Digital Economy Outlook 2020*. OECD Publishing.

Okoro, Y. O., Oladeinde, M., Akindote, O. J., Adegbite, A. O., & Abrahams, T. O. (2023). Digital communication and us economic growth: A comprehensive exploration of technology's impact on economic advancement. *Computer Science & IT Research Journal*, 4(3), 351–367. DOI: 10.51594/csitrj.v4i3.687

Okros, A., & Okros, A. (2020). Generational theory and cohort analysis. *Harnessing the potential of digital post-Millennials in the future workplace*, 33-51.

Oleka-Onyewuchi, C. C. (2023). *The New Workforce Reality: Embracing Intergenerational Collaboration That Thrives in the Age of Automation and Layoffs*. Gatekeeper Press.

Ong, C. S., Sze, C. T., & Lai, J. K. (2019). The role of digital innovation hubs in facilitating digital transformation in Europe. *Journal of Manufacturing Technology Management*, 30(1), 155–175.

Ono, H., & Zavodny, M. (2008). Immigrants, English ability and the digital divide. *Social Forces*, 86(4), 1455–1479. DOI: 10.1353/sof.0.0052

Ophir, E., Nass, C., & Wagner, A. D. (2009). Cognitive control in media multitaskers. *Proceedings of the National Academy of Sciences of the United States of America*, 106(37), 15583–15587. DOI: 10.1073/pnas.0903620106 PMID: 19706386

Oseni, A. I., & Oseni, I. O. (2017). Digital Transformation of Accounting through Cloud Computing. *Procedia Computer Science*, 105, 812–819.

Osman, Z., & Ahmad, F. S. (2010). An Empirical Study of the Relationship between the Adoption of E-commerce and Business Performance among Malaysian SMEs. *Journal of Business & Economics Research*, 8(3), 12–24.

Pagani, M., & Pardo, C. (2017). The impact of digital technology on relationships in a business network. *Industrial Marketing Management*, 67, 185–192. DOI: 10.1016/j.indmarman.2017.08.009

Palfrey, J., & Gasser, U. (2011). *Born digital: Understanding the first generation of digital natives.* ReadHowYouWant. com.

Palfrey, J., & Gasser, U. (2011). *Born Digital: Understanding the First Generation of Digital Natives.* ReadHowYouWant.com.

Pan, Y., Froese, F., Liu, N., Hu, Y., & Ye, M. (2022). The adoption of artificial intelligence in employee recruitment: The influence of contextual factors. *International Journal of Human Resource Management*, 33(6), 1125–1147. DOI: 10.1080/09585192.2021.1879206

Parent-Lamarche, A. (2022). Teleworking, Work Engagement, and Intention to Quit during the COVID-19 Pandemic: Same Storm, Different Boats? *International Journal of Environmental Research and Public Health*, 19(3), 1267. DOI: 10.3390/ijerph19031267 PMID: 35162291

Park, J., Kim, J., & Choi, H. (2021). Posture-related musculoskeletal disorders in users of handheld electronic devices. *Journal of Occupational Health*, 63(1), e12264. DOI: 10.1002/1348-9585.12264 PMID: 34378303

Parmar, G., & Rathod, R. M. (2018). A Study on Factors Affecting E-wallet Usage. *ELK Asia Pacific Journal of Marketing & Retail Management*, 9(4), 1–14.

Pataki-Bittó, F., & Kapusy, K. (2021). Work environment transformation in the post COVID-19 based on work values of the future workforce. *Journal of Corporate Real Estate*, 23(3), 151–169. DOI: 10.1108/JCRE-08-2020-0031

Pedro, F., Subosa, M., Rivas, A., & Valverde, P. (2019). Artificial intelligence in education: Challenges and opportunities for sustainable development.

Pedro, F., Subosa, M., Rivas, A., & Valverde, P. (2019). *Artificial intelligence in education: Challenges and opportunities for sustainable development.* UNESCO.

Pekkarinen, S., Hennala, L., Tuisku, O., Gustafsson, C., Johansson-Pajala, R. M., Thommes, K., ... Melkas, H. (2020). Embedding care robots into society and practice: Socio-technical considerations. Futures, 122, 102593. DOI: 10.1016/j.futures.2020.102593

Pereira, V., Hadjielias, E., Christofi, M., & Vrontis, D. (2023). A systematic literature review on the impact of artificial intelligence on workplace outcomes: A multi-process perspective. *Human Resource Management Review*, 33(1), 100857. DOI: 10.1016/j.hrmr.2021.100857

Perez Garcia, M., & Saffon Lopez, S. (2020). Exploring the uncanny valley theory in the constructs of a virtual assistant personality. In Intelligent Systems and Applications: Proceedings of the 2019 Intelligent Systems Conference (IntelliSys) Volume 1 (pp. 1017-1033). Springer International Publishing. DOI: 10.1007/978-3-030-29516-5_76

Perin, D., & Lauterbach, M. (2018). Assessing text-based writing of low-skilled college students. *International Journal of Artificial Intelligence in Education*, 28(1), 56–78. DOI: 10.1007/s40593-016-0122-z

Pew Research Center. (2021). Mobile technology and home broadband 2021. Retrieved from https://www.pewresearch.org

Phang, C. W., Kankanhalli, A., & Ramaprasad, A. (2015). Developing a framework for digital health ecosystems. *Information Systems Research*, 26(1), 44–69.

Phuoc, N. V. (2022). The Critical Factors Impacting Artificial Intelligence Applications Adoption in Vietnam: A Structural Equation Modeling Analysis. *Economies, 10*(6), Article 6.

Pietrobelli, C., & Rabellotti, R. (2011). Global value chains meet innovation systems: Are there learning opportunities for developing countries? *World Development*, 39(7), 1261–1269. DOI: 10.1016/j.worlddev.2010.05.013

Pietronudo, M. C., Croidieu, G., & Schiavone, F. (2022). A solution looking for problems? A systematic literature review of the rationalizing influence of artificial intelligence on decision-making in innovation management. *Technological Forecasting and Social Change*, 182, 121828. DOI: 10.1016/j.techfore.2022.121828

Pilat, D. (2021). Understanding the impact of digitalisation on productivity and wellbeing. OECD Economics Department Working Papers, No. 1643, OECD Publishing, Paris.

Poli, R. (2017). Internet addiction update: Diagnostic criteria, assessment and prevalence. *Neuropsychiatry*, 07(01). Advance online publication. DOI: 10.4172/Neuropsychiatry.1000171

Poljak, M., & Šterbenc, A. J. C. M. (2020). Use of drones in clinical microbiology and infectious diseases: Current status, challenges and barriers. *Clinical Microbiology and Infection*, 26(4), 425–430. DOI: 10.1016/j.cmi.2019.09.014 PMID: 31574337

Ponti, M. (2023). Screen time and preschool children: Promoting health and development in a digital world. *Paediatrics & Child Health*, 28(3), 184–192. DOI: 10.1093/pch/pxac125 PMID: 37205134

Ponti, M., Bélanger, S., Grimes, R., Heard, J., Johnson, M., Moreau, E., Norris, M., Shaw, A., Stanwick, R., Van Lankveld, J., & Williams, R. (2017). Screen time and young children: Promoting health and development in a digital world. *Paediatrics & Child Health*, 22(8), 461–468. DOI: 10.1093/pch/pxx123 PMID: 29601064

Popenici, S. A. D., & Kerr, S. (2017). Exploring the impact of artificial intelligence on teaching and learning in higher education. Technology Enhanced Learning, 12(1).

Potts, J. (2024). New Forms of Fear: 1950–2000. In Future Fear: Fear of the Future from Prehistory to Climate Change (pp. 125-165). Cham: Springer Nature Switzerland. DOI: 10.1007/978-3-031-59412-0_7

Pradhan, B., Bharti, D., Chakravarty, S., Ray, S. S., Voinova, V. V., Bonartsev, A. P., & Pal, K. (2021). Internet of Things and Robotics in Transforming Current-Day Healthcare Services. Journal of healthcare engineering, 2021(1), 9999504. DOI: 10.1155/2021/9999504

Pranaya, D. & Venugopal. (2023). Impact of Mother Tongue on Students' speaking Abilities in English Language at Rural Places. In English Language Competence in Rural Youth: Improving Job Readiness. Current Publications.

Prasetyo, H. Y., & Putri, N. A. (2019). The Adoption of Digital Technologies for Sustainable Agriculture in Indonesia. *Journal of Sustainable Agriculture*, 41(8), 912–927. DOI: 10.1080/10440046.2019.1658382

Prasetyo, Y. A., & Palisoc, N. (2023). Digital marketing and its impact on SMEs' growth: Insights from Southeast Asia. *The Journal of Asian Finance, Economics and Business*, 10(1), 89–96.

Prastiyanto. (2024). Analysis of the Level of Sustainability of Agricultural Extension Models for Millennial Farmers in West Java, Indonesia. International journal of religion, DOI: 10.61707/4wzdvy93

Prastyo. (2023). Enhancing Food Security In Rural Communities Through Implementation Of Hydroponic Technology. DOI: 10.37874/bm.v3i3.1003

Prayitno. (2023). Quality of Life and Food Security in Rural Areas of Indonesia: a Case Study of Sedayulawas Village, Lamongan Regency, Indonesia. Evergreen, DOI: 10.5109/7148438

Prensky, M. (2009). H. sapiens digital: From digital immigrants and digital natives to digital wisdom. *Innovate: Journal of Online Education, 5*(3).

Primack, B. A., Shensa, A., Sidani, J. E., Radovic, A., & Rosen, D. (2017). Social media use and perceived social isolation among young adults in the U.S. *Social Science & Medicine*, 208, 150–157. DOI: 10.1016/j.socscimed.2018.03.022 PMID: 28279545

Priporas, C. V. (2020). Smart consumers and decision-making process in the smart retailing context through Generation Z eyes. Retail futures. DOI: 10.1108/978-1-83867-663-620201017

Priyadharshini, S. (2024). Prospects and Challenges of AI in Robotics and Automation. *International Journal of Advanced Scientific Multidisciplinary Research*, 1(2), 46–49.

Proserpio, L., & Gioia, D. A. (2007). Teaching the Virtual Generation. *Academy of Management Learning & Education*, 6(1), 69–80. DOI: 10.5465/amle.2007.24401703

Przybylski, A. K., Murayama, K., DeHaan, C. R., & Gladwell, V. (2013). Motivational, emotional, and behavioral correlates of fear of missing out. *Computers in Human Behavior*, 29(4), 1841–1848. DOI: 10.1016/j.chb.2013.02.014

Purmayanti. (2022). The Challenges of Implementing Digital Literacy in Teaching and Learning Activities for EFL Learners in Indonesia. DOI: 10.56209/badi.v1i2.38

Purnomo, H., & Dewi, S. (2019). E-learning and mobile applications in agricultural education: A case study from Indonesia. *Asian Journal of Distance Education*, 14(2), 92–105. DOI: 10.5281/zenodo.3591516

Querstret, D., Morison, L., Dickinson, S., Cropley, M., & John, M. (2020). Mindfulness-based stress reduction and mindfulness-based cognitive therapy for psychological health and well-being in nonclinical samples: A systematic review and meta-analysis. *International Journal of Stress Management*, 27(4), 394–411. DOI: 10.1037/str0000165

Qurani, Noyara Rahmasary, & Fajri Usman. (2020). The Comparative Study of Youth-Related Agriculture Initiatives: Optimizing the Role of Indonesian Youth in Improving Food Security. E3S Web Conf., 142. DOI: 10.1051/e3sconf/202014206002

Raghuram, S., Hill, N. S., Gibbs, J. L., & Maruping, L. M. (2019) Virtual work: Bridging research clusters. *Academy of Management Annals, 13*(1), 308-341.

Ragot, M., Martin, N., & Cojean, S. (2020). AI-generated vs. human artworks: A perception bias towards artificial intelligence? In *Proceedings of the 2020 CHI Conference on Human Factors in Computing Systems*. DOI: 10.1145/3334480.3382892

Rahman, F., & Putri, A. (2020). The adoption of digital technologies for sustainable agriculture among young farmers in Indonesia. *Environmental Development*, 33, 100493. DOI: 10.1016/j.envdev.2020.100493

Raišienė, A. G., Danauskė, E., Kavaliauskienė, K., & Gudžinskienė, V. (2023). Occupational stress-induced consequences to employees in the context of teleworking from home: A preliminary study. *Administrative Sciences*, 13(2), 55. DOI: 10.3390/admsci13020055

Rajamani, S. K., Iyer, R. S., & Ahmed, I. (2024). Current State of Robotic Surgery and Telesurgery: A Review of Current Developments and Future Insights. *Technologies for Sustainable Healthcare Development*, 194-216.

Raji. (2024). Improving agricultural practices and productivity through extension services and innovative training programs. International journal of applied research in social sciences. DOI: 10.51594/ijarss.v6i7.1267

Rakison, D. H. (2022). Fear learning in infancy: An evolutionary developmental perspective. Evolutionary perspectives on infancy. DOI: 10.1007/978-3-030-76000-7_14

Ramadhani, L., & Permata, D. S. (2021). Microfinance and youth agriculture: The impact of Mekar in rural Indonesia. *Journal of Rural Finance*, 15(1), 98–110. DOI: 10.1080/13657305.2021.1712635

Ramli, F. A. A., & Hamzah, M. I. (2021). Mobile payment and e-wallet adoption in emerging economies: A systematic literature review. *Journal of Emerging Economies and Islamic Research*, 9(2), 1–39.

Rashid, A. B., & Kausik, A. K. (2024). AI revolutionizing industries worldwide: A comprehensive overview of its diverse applications. *Hybrid Advances*, 100277.

Rashid, F. R., & Julaihi, M. Z. H. (2022). Big Data, Green Growth, and Technology Disruption in Asian Companies and Societies: Application of Fintech in Brunei Darussalam–Embracing E-Wallet in the Retail Sector. In *Handbook of Research on Big Data, Green Growth, and Technology Disruption in Asian Companies and Societies* (pp. 38–57). IGI Global. DOI: 10.4018/978-1-7998-8524-5.ch003

Rasi, P., Vuojärvi, H., & Rivinen, S. (2020). Promoting media literacy among Older people: A Systematic review. *Adult Education Quarterly*, 71(1), 37–54. DOI: 10.1177/0741713620923755

Rasyid, H., & Mumpuni Ningsih, G. (2024). The Role of Digital Technology in the Transformation of Agriculture Toward Smart Farming. *Journal of Wood Science*, 3(1), 1–7. DOI: 10.58344/jws.v3i1.523

Rebughini, P. (2021). A sociology of anxiety: Western modern legacy and the Covid-19 outbreak. International Sociology. DOI: 10.1177/0268580921993325

Reese, B. (2018). *The fourth age: Smart robots, conscious computers, and the future of humanity*. Simon and Schuster.

Regona, M., Yigitcanlar, T., Xia, B., & Yi Man Li, R. (2022). Opportunities and Adoption Challenges of AI in the Construction Industry: A PRISMA Review. *Journal of Open Innovation*, 8(1), 45. DOI: 10.3390/joitmc8010045

Reis, J., Santo, P. E., & Melão, N. (2021). Influence of artificial intelligence on public employment and its impact on politics: A systematic literature review. *Brazilian Journal of Operations & Production Management*, 18(3), 3. DOI: 10.14488/BJOPM.2021.010

Resnick, M., Maloney, J., Monroy-Hernández, A., Rusk, N., Eastmond, E., Brennan, K., Millner, A., Rosenbaum, E., Silver, J., Silverman, B., & Kafai, Y. (2009). Scratch: Programming for all. *Communications of the ACM*, 52(11), 60–67. DOI: 10.1145/1592761.1592779

Restyandi, Y., Maulida, Y., Soeharsono, S., & Wati, R. (2023). Engaging Rural Youth: The Role of Young People in Integrated Farming Development in Nglanggeran, Gunungkidul Regency. *Agro Ekonomi, 34*(1), 42-55. DOI: 10.22146/ae.83567

Ribble, M. (2015). *Digital citizenship in schools: Nine elements all students should know* (6th ed.). International Society for Technology in Education.

Richardson, K. (2015). *An anthropology of robots and AI*. Routledge. DOI: 10.4324/9781315736426

Riedl, R., Kindermann, H., & Javor, A. (2018). The relationship between techno-stress and mental well-being. *Journal of Information Technology*, 33(2), 105–121. DOI: 10.1057/s41265-018-0031-6

Ritter, T., & Pedersen, C. L. (2020). Digitization capability and digitalization of business models in business-to-business firms: Past, present, and future. *Industrial Marketing Management*, 86, 180–190. DOI: 10.1016/j.indmarman.2019.11.019

Rizal, A. M., & Abdullah, N. L. (2021). Digital Transformation in Malaysia's Education System: Challenges and Prospects. *International Journal of Academic Research in Business & Social Sciences*, 11(2), 113–126.

Rodrigo, M. (2023). The truth about using AI in schools. Philstar Life. https://philstarlife.com/news-and views/283288-truth-about-using-ai-schools?page=2

Rogers, W. A., & Fisk, A. D. (2010). Toward a psychological science of advanced technology design for older adults. *The Journals of Gerontology. Series B, Psychological Sciences and Social Sciences*, 65B(6), 645–653. DOI: 10.1093/geronb/gbq065 PMID: 20833690

Rojas, S. (2024). Harnessing Computer Vision and Mechanical Design for Intelligent Robotic Systems. *Innovative Computer Sciences Journal, 10*(1).

Romanelli. (2024). The role of digital technologies in achieving sustainable agriculture. Burleigh Dodds series in agricultural science, DOI: 10.19103/AS.2023.0132.10

Romero, J., & Lado, N. (2021). Service robots and COVID-19: Exploring perceptions of prevention efficacy at hotels in generation Z. *International Journal of Contemporary Hospitality Management*, 33(11), 4057–4078. DOI: 10.1108/IJCHM-10-2020-1214

Rosen, L. D., & Lara-Ruiz, J. M. (2015). Similarities and differences in workplace, personal, and technology-related values, beliefs, and attitudes across five generations of Americans. *The Wiley handbook of psychology, technology, and society*, 20-55.

Rosen, L. D., Lim, A. F., Carrier, L. M., & Cheever, N. A. (2013). An empirical examination of the educational impact of text messaging on college students. *Journal of Educational Computing Research*, 48(4), 415–436. DOI: 10.2190/EC.48.4.c

Rosli, S. N., Anshari, M., Almunawar, M. N., & Masri, M. (2022). Digital Wallet Ecosystem in Promoting Financial Inclusion. In *FinTech Development for Financial Inclusiveness* (pp. 31–49). IGI Global. DOI: 10.4018/978-1-7998-8447-7.ch003

Ross, B., Chase, A. M., Robbie, D., Oates, G., & Absalom, Y. (2018). Adaptive quizzes to increase motivation, engagement and learning outcomes in a first year accounting unit. *International Journal of Educational Technology in Higher Education*, 15(1), 30. DOI: 10.1186/s41239-018-0113-2

Roy, A. (2024). Precision agriculture: Analysing the use of advanced technologies, data analytics and remote sensing for site-specific crop management and resource optimization. Futuristic Trends in Agriculture Engineering & Food Sciences. https://www.doi.org/10.58532/V3BCAG23CH5

Rudolph, C. W., Rauvola, R. S., Costanza, D. P., & Zacher, H. (2021). Generations and generational differences: Debunking myths in organizational science and practice and paving new paths forward. Journal of business and psychology, 36, 945-967. DOI: 10.1007/s10869-020-09715-2

Rufaidah, F., Karyani, T., Wulandari, E., & Setiawan, I. (2023). A Review of the Implementation of Financial Technology (Fintech) in the Indonesian Agricultural Sector: Issues, Access, and Challenges. *International Journal of Financial Studies*, 11(3), 108. DOI: 10.3390/ijfs11030108

Rusmayadi, G., Mulyanti, D. R., & Alaydrus, A. Z. A. (2023). Revolutionizing Agrotechnology: Meeting Global Food Demand through Sustainable and Precision Farming Innovations. *West Science Interdisciplinary Studies*, 1(08), 619–628. DOI: 10.58812/wsis.v1i08.172

Russell, S. J., Norvig, P., Davis, E., & Edwards, D. (2016). *Artificial intelligence: A modern approach* (3rd ed.). Pearson.

Rustandi. (2024). Involvement of Millennial Farmers in the Implementation of Integrated Agriculture in Trenggalek District, East Java, Indonesia. Anuário do Instituto de Geociências. DOI: 10.11137/1982-3908_2024_47_60967

Ryder, M. J. (2022). Lessons from science fiction: Frederik Pohl and the robot prosumer. Journal of Consumer Culture. DOI: 10.1177/1469540520944228

Ryding, F. C., & Kaye, L. K. (2017). "Internet Addiction": A Conceptual Minefield. *International Journal of Mental Health and Addiction*, 16(1), 225–232. DOI: 10.1007/s11469-017-9811-6 PMID: 29491771

Sætra, H. S. (2022). Robotomorphy: Becoming our creations. AI and Ethics. DOI: 10.1007/s43681-021-00092-x

Saha, P. A. & Lumare, N. (2024). The Nostalgia Chronicles: A Saga Of Brand Loyalty Across Ages: An Empirical Investigation of Nostalgia and Brand Loyalty in Different Generational Cohorts.

Sait, M.A., Ali, M.A., Almunawar, M.N. & Haji Masri, H.M. (2024). Understanding factors to digital wallet discontinuance intention among past users: an exploratory study. *Journal of Science and Technology Policy Management*.

Sait, M. A., Almunawar, M. N., Anshari, M., & Masri, M. (2023). Digital Wallet Adoption in Supporting Financial Inclusion: A Conceptual Framework. *2023 International Conference on Sustainable Islamic Business and Finance (SIBF)*, 189–194. DOI: 10.1109/SIBF60067.2023.10380043

Sait, M. A., Anshari, M., Almunawar, M. N., & Masri, M. (2024). Investigating the Impact of Demographic Factors on Personal Innovativeness in Digital Wallet Usage: An Exploratory Study. In *Harnessing Green and Circular Skills for Digital Transformation* (pp. 262–271). IGI Global. DOI: 10.4018/979-8-3693-2865-1.ch014

Salmon, J., Hesketh, K. D., Arundell, L., Downing, K. L., & Biddle, S. J. H. (2020). Changing Behavior Using Ecological Models. In M. S. Hagger, L. D. Cameron, K. Hamilton, N. Hankonen, & T. Lintunen (Eds.), *The Handbook of Behavior Change* (pp. 237–250). chapter, Cambridge: Cambridge University Press. DOI: 10.1017/9781108677318.017

Samaha, A. A., Fawaz, M., Yahfoufi, N. E., Gebbawi, M., Abdallah, H., Baydoun, S. A., Ghaddar, A., & Eid, A. H. (2018). Assessing the psychometric properties of the Internet Addiction Test (IAT) among Lebanese college students. *Frontiers in Public Health*, 6, 365. Advance online publication. DOI: 10.3389/fpubh.2018.00365 PMID: 30619806

Samingan, M. (2024). Indonesia's Digital Economic Policy To Increase Economic Resilience. *International Journal Of Humanities Education and Social Sciences*, 3(6). Advance online publication. DOI: 10.55227/ijhess.v3i6.873

Sandhu, S., & Arora, S. (2022). Customers' usage behaviour of e-banking services: Interplay of electronic banking and traditional banking. *International Journal of Finance & Economics*, 27(2), 2169–2181. DOI: 10.1002/ijfe.2266

Santoso, D. S., & Setyawan, E. (2021). Agricultural Marketplaces in Indonesia: The Role of Digital Platforms in Enhancing Farmer's Market Access. *Journal of Rural Studies*, 47(2), 92–107. DOI: 10.1016/j.jrurstud.2021.07.012

Santos, R. M. S., De Alcântara Ventura, S., De Almeida Nogueira, Y. J., Mendes, C. G., De Paula, J. J., Miranda, D. M., & Romano-Silva, M. A. (2024). The Associations Between screen time and Mental Health in Adults: A Systematic review. *Journal of Technology in Behavioral Science*, 9(4), 825–845. Advance online publication. DOI: 10.1007/s41347-024-00398-7

Sapounidis, T., & Alimisis, D. (2020). Educational robotics for STEM: A review of technologies and some educational considerations. In *Science and mathematics education for 21st century citizens: Challenges and ways forward* (No. September, 2020, pp. 167-190). Nova Science Publishers.

Sari, J. A., & Diana, B. A. (2024). Dampak Transformasi Digitalisasi terhadap Perubahan Perilaku Masyarakat Pedesaan. *Jurnal Pemerintahan Dan Politik*, 9(2), 88–96. DOI: 10.36982/jpg.v9i2.3896

Savoia, E., Harriman, N. W., Su, M., Cote, T., & Shortland, N. (2021). Adolescents' exposure to online risks: Gender disparities and vulnerabilities related to online behaviors. *International Journal of Environmental Research and Public Health*, 18(11), 5786. DOI: 10.3390/ijerph18115786 PMID: 34072253

Schepman, A., & Rodway, P. (2020). Initial validation of the general attitudes towards Artificial Intelligence Scale. *Computers in Human Behavior Reports*, 1, 100014. DOI: 10.1016/j.chbr.2020.100014 PMID: 34235291

Schepman, A., & Rodway, P. (2022). The General Attitudes towards Artificial Intelligence Scale (GAAIS): Confirmatory validation and associations with personality, corporate distrust, and general trust. *International Journal of Human-Computer Interaction*, 38(10), 954–965. DOI: 10.1080/10447318.2022.2085400

Scherer, R., Siddiq, F., & Tondeur, J. (2019). The technology acceptance model (TAM): A meta-analytic structural equation modeling approach to explaining teachers' adoption of digital technology in education. *Computers & Education*, 128, 13–35. DOI: 10.1016/j.compedu.2018.09.009

Schiavo, G., Businaro, S., & Zancanaro, M. (2024). Comprehension, apprehension, and acceptance: Understanding the influence of literacy and anxiety on acceptance of artificial intelligence. *Technology in Society*, 77, 102537. DOI: 10.1016/j.techsoc.2024.102537

Schmidt, D., Casagranda, L. F., Butturi, M. A., & Sellitto, M. A. (2024). Digital Technologies, Sustainability, and Efficiency in Grain Post-Harvest Activities: A Bibliometric Analysis. *Sustainability (Basel)*, 16(3), 1244. DOI: 10.3390/su16031244

Schneider, C., & Bousbiat, H. (2023). Coaching Robots for Older Seniors: Do They Get What They Expect? Insights from an Austrian Study. International Journal of Environmental Research and Public Health, 20(4), 2965. DOI: 10.3390/ijerph20042965

Scholz, C. (2019). The Generations Z in Europe–an introduction. In *Generations Z in Europe: Inputs, insights and implications* (pp. 3–31). Emerald Publishing Limited.

Schwab, K. (2017). *The Fourth Industrial Revolution, by Klaus Schwab*. World Economic Forum. https://www.weforum.org/about/the-fourth-industrial-revolution-by-klaus-schwab/

Scott, I., Carter, S., & Coiera, E. (2021). Exploring stakeholder attitudes towards AI in clinical practice. *BMJ Health & Care Informatics*, 28(1), e100450. DOI: 10.1136/bmjhci-2021-100450 PMID: 34887331

Selimović, J., Pilav-Velić, A., & Krndžija, L. (2021). Digital Workplace Transformation in the Financial Service Sector: Investigating the Relationship between Employees' Expectations and Intentions. *Technology in Society*, 66(August), 101640. DOI: 10.1016/j.techsoc.2021.101640

Selwyn, N. (2019). What's the problem with learning analytics? *Journal of Learning Analytics*, 6(3), 11–19. DOI: 10.18608/jla.2019.63.3

Şen, M. (2021). Funding Discussions Regarding the Severance Pay and Unemployment Insurance Dilemma in Turkey. In *Journal of Social Policy Conferences* (No. 81, pp. 325-366). Istanbul University, Faculty of Economics.

Serholt, S., Ljungblad, S., & Ní Bhroin, N. (2022). Introduction: special issue—critical robotics research. AI & Society. DOI: 10.1007/s00146-021-01224-x

Sethibe, T., & Naidoo, E. (2022). The adoption of robotics in the auditing profession. *South African Journal of Information Management*, 24(1), 1. DOI: 10.4102/sajim.v24i1.1441

Setiadi, D., Nurhayati, S., Ansori, A., Zubaidi, M., & Amir, R. (2023). Youth's Digital Literacy in the Context of Community Empowerment in an Emerging Society 5.0. *Society*, 11(1), 1–12. DOI: 10.33019/society.v11i1.491

Setia, P., Setia, P., Venkatesh, V., & Joglekar, S. (2013). Leveraging Digital Technologies: How Information Quality Leads to Localized Capabilities and Customer Service Performance. *Management Information Systems Quarterly*, 37(2), 565–590. DOI: 10.25300/MISQ/2013/37.2.11

Setiawan, R., Rani, K., Cavaliere, L. P. L., Hiep, N. T., Halder, S., Raisal, I., . . . Rajest, S. S. (2020). References for Shopping Online Versus in Stores What Do Customers Prefer and How Do Offline Retailers Cope with It? (Doctoral dissertation, Petra Christian University).

Setiawan, R. H., & Amran, M. (2022). Traceability and sustainability in agriculture: A case study of Koltiva in Indonesia. *Journal of Sustainable Agriculture*, 14(2), 88–102. DOI: 10.1007/s10806-022-09861-5

Setyowati, D., & Prasetyo, B. (2021). The role of digital platforms in promoting agricultural entrepreneurship among youth in Indonesia. *Journal of Agricultural Education and Extension*, 27(1), 35–49. DOI: 10.1080/1389224X.2021.1842128

Shah, S., & Rathod, K. (2022). A study on consumer perception on E-WALLET in Ahmedabad. *International Journal of Management, Public Policy and Research*, 1(2), 56–60. DOI: 10.55829/ijmpr.v1i2.47

Shamshiri, R. R., Sturm, B., Weltzien, C., Fulton, J., Khosla, R., Schirrmann, M., Raut, S., Basavegowda, D. H., Yamin, M., & Hameed, I. A. (2024). Digitalization of agriculture for sustainable crop production: A use-case review. *Frontiers in Environmental Science*, 12, 1375193. DOI: 10.3389/fenvs.2024.1375193

Shamsuddin, S. H., & Razali, R. (2015). Cloud Computing Adoption and its Impact on SMEs' Performance. *Journal of Information Technology Management*, 6(18), 93–104.

Sharma, V., & Akhai, S. (2019). Trends in Utilization of Coal Fly Ash in India: A Review. *Journal of Engineering Design and Analysis*, 2(1), 12–16.

Sharples, M. (2022). New AI tools that can write student essays require educators to rethink teaching and assessment. LSE blog article. https://blogs.lse.ac.uk/impactofsocialsciences/2022/05/17/new-aitools-that-can-write- student-essays-require-educators-to-rethink-teaching-and-assessment/

Shaw, N. (2015). Younger persons are more likely to adopt the mobile wallet than older persons, or are they? The moderating role of age. *2015 Americas Conference on Information Systems, AMCIS 2015*, 1–15.

Shehadeh, M. (2024). Digital transformation: A catalyst for sustainable business practices. In *Technological innovations for business, education and sustainability* (pp. 29–45). Emerald Publishing Limited. DOI: 10.1108/978-1-83753-106-620241003

Shek, D. T. L., Yu, L., Sun, R. C. F., & Fan, Y. (2022). Internet addiction. In *Springer eBooks* (pp. 1–42). DOI: 10.1007/978-1-4614-6434-1_108-4

Sheng, A. & Wang, F. (2022). Falling in love with machine: emotive potentials between human and robots in science fiction and reality. Neohelicon. DOI: 10.1007/s11059-022-00664-8

Sheppard, A. L., & Wolffsohn, J. S. (2018). Digital eye strain: Prevalence, measurement and mitigation. *BMJ Open Ophthalmology*, 3(1), e000146. DOI: 10.1136/bmjophth-2018-000146 PMID: 29963645

Sherinia. (2024). (2) Role of Agriculture on Rural Household Food Security: A Systematic Review from Indonesia. DOI: 10.1088/1755-1315/1324/1/012132

Shit, R. C. (2020). Precise localization for achieving next-generation autonomous navigation: State-of-the-art, taxonomy and future prospects. *Computer Communications*, 160, 351–374. DOI: 10.1016/j.comcom.2020.06.007

Shmatko, N. & Volkova, G. (2020). Bridging the skill gap in robotics: Global and national environment. Sage Open. DOI: 10.1177/2158244020958736

Shrivastava, P., Smith, M. S., O'Brien, K., & Zsolnai, L. (2020). Transforming sustainability science to generate positive social and environmental change globally. *One Earth*, 2(4), 329–340. DOI: 10.1016/j.oneear.2020.04.010 PMID: 33501419

Silva, , S. C., & Elo, M. (2018). New digital layers of business relationships – experiences from business-to-business social media. *Progress in International Business Research*, 13, 217–241.

Singh, S., & Akhai, S. (2024, July). Electronics in precision control for mechanical engineering: A brief overview. In *AIP Conference Proceedings* (Vol. 3121, No. 1). AIP Publishing. DOI: 10.1063/5.0221464

Singh, M., & Khan, S. A. L. A. (2024). Advances in Autonomous Robotics: Integrating AI and Machine Learning for Enhanced Automation and Control in Industrial Applications. *International Journal for Multidimensional Research Perspectives*, 2(4), 74–90. DOI: 10.61877/ijmrp.v2i4.135

Singh, N., & Sinha, N. (2020). How perceived trust mediates merchant's intention to use a mobile wallet technology. *Journal of Retailing and Consumer Services*, 52, 101894. Advance online publication. DOI: 10.1016/j.jretconser.2019.101894

Singh, S., & Saini, B. S. (2021). Autonomous cars: Recent developments, challenges, and possible solutions. *IOP Conference Series. Materials Science and Engineering*, 1022(1), 012028. DOI: 10.1088/1757-899X/1022/1/012028

Singh, V. (2024). Advances in Precision Agriculture Technologies for Sustainable Crop Production. *Journal of Scientific Research and Reports*, 30(2), 61–71. DOI: 10.9734/jsrr/2024/v30i21844

Siregar, P. R., & Nugraha, R. (2020). Digital Literacy in Agriculture: A Pathway to Youth Empowerment in Indonesia. *Asian Journal of Agricultural Research*, 14(2), 101–117. DOI: 10.3923/ajar.2020.101.117

Sivrikova, N. V., Ptashko, T. G., Perebeynos, A. E., Chernikova, E. G., Gilyazeva, N. V., & Vasilyeva, V. S. (2020). Parental reports on digital devices use in infancy and early childhood. *Education and Information Technologies*, 25(5), 3957–3973. DOI: 10.1007/s10639-020-10145-z

Sjaf. (2024). Sustainable Indonesian Rural Development: Utilizing Precision Village Data as a Basis for Socio-Economic Analysis. IOP conference series. DOI: 10.1088/1755-1315/1359/1/012061

Skinner, B. F. (1953). *Science and human behavior*. Free Press.

Smakman, M., Vogt, P., & Konijn, E. A. (2021). Moral considerations on social robots in education: A multi-stakeholder perspective. Computers & Education. DOI: 10.1016/j.compedu.2021.104317

Smith, W.G. (2008). Does gender influence online survey participation? A record-linkage analysis of university faculty online survey response behavior. *Eric Ed501717*.

Smith, A., Brown, L., & Thompson, R. (2021). Digital innovations in agriculture: Implications for rural youth and food security. *Journal of Agricultural Innovation and Technology*, 15(3), 200–215. DOI: 10.1080/12345678.2021.1234567

Smith, J., & Garriety, S. (2020). The Art of Flexibility: Bridging Five Generations in the Workforce. *Strategic HR Review*, 19(3), 107–110. DOI: 10.1108/SHR-01-2020-0005

Smith, P. R., & Brown, L. (2021). The role of AI in shaping technology addiction: Implications for future research. *Journal of Technology and Health*, 16(1), 23–34. DOI: 10.1177/2042018821100003

Smith, P. R., & Jones, K. (2019). Comparative analysis of digital addiction impacts: A cross-generational study. *Digital Health*, 5, 1–10. DOI: 10.1177/2055207619881740

Smith, P., & Jones, K. (2019). Ethical design practices for digital well-being. *Journal of Digital Ethics*, 12(1), 55–68. DOI: 10.1007/s12225-019-0946-3

Snyder, H. (2019). Literature review as a research methodology: An overview and guidelines. *Journal of Business Research*, 104, 333–339. DOI: 10.1016/j.jbusres.2019.07.039

Sołtysik, M., Wojnarowska, M., Urbaniec, M., Zabkar, V., Ćwiklicki, M., & Varese, E. (2024). *Sustainable business in the era of digital transformation: Strategic and entrepreneurial perspectives*. Taylor & Francis. DOI: 10.4324/9781032697895

Song, C. S. & Kim, Y. K. (2022). The role of the human-robot interaction in consumers' acceptance of humanoid retail service robots. Journal of Business Research. DOI: 10.1016/j.jbusres.2022.03.087

Song, W. J., & Park, J. W. (2019). The Influence of Stress on Internet Addiction: Mediating Effects of Self-Control and Mindfulness. *International Journal of Mental Health and Addiction*, 17(4), 1063–1075. DOI: 10.1007/s11469-019-0051-9

Soori, M., Arezoo, B., & Dastres, R. (2023). Artificial intelligence, machine learning and deep learning in advanced robotics, a review. *Cognitive Robotics*, 3, 54–70. DOI: 10.1016/j.cogr.2023.04.001

Soseco. (2024). Access to Technology to Increase Food Resilience in Rural Households in Indonesia. DOI: 10.3280/ecag2024oa16358

Soundararajan, A., Lim, J. X., Ngiam, N. H. W., Tey, A. J., Tang, A. K. W., Lim, H. A., Yow, K. S., Cheng, L. J., Ho, J., Teo, Q. X. N., Yee, W. Q., Yoon, S., Low, L. L., & Ng, K. Y. Y. (2023). Smartphone ownership, digital literacy, and the mediating role of social connectedness and loneliness in improving the wellbeing of community-dwelling older adults of low socio-economic status in Singapore. *PLoS One*, 18(8), e0290557. DOI: 10.1371/journal.pone.0290557 PMID: 37647263

Spiro, C. (2006). Generation Y in the Workplace. *Defense AT&l, 35*(6), 16-19.

Stefano, P. D., & Nicotra, M. (2019). Digital innovation and entrepreneurial ecosystems: A theory-building approach. *Journal of Business Research*, 123, 1–12.

Stein, J.-P., Messingschlager, T., Gnambs, T., Hutmacher, F., & Appel, M. (2024). Attitudes towards AI: Measurement and associations with personality. *Scientific Reports*, 14(1), 2909. Advance online publication. DOI: 10.1038/s41598-024-53335-2 PMID: 38316898

Suchman, L. (2023). Imaginaries of omniscience: Automating intelligence in the US Department of Defense. Social Studies of Science. DOI: 10.1177/03063127221104938

Sugandini, D., Effendi, M. I., Sugiarto, B., Kundarto, M., & Kawuryan, S. H. E. (2023). Resistance to agricultural commercialization with lack of marketing digital adoption in Indonesia's Dieng plateau. *International Journal of Sustainable Development and Planning*, 18(6), 1715–1724. DOI: 10.18280/ijsdp.180607

Suhartono, T., & Putri, D. R. (2021). IoT in aquaculture: The impact of Jala Tech on shrimp farming in Indonesia. *Journal of Aquaculture Research & Development*, 52(3), 101–115. DOI: 10.4236/jard.2021.103014

Sulyani. (2022). Adoption of Digital Technology: Mapping the Important Roles in Current Agriculture Ecosystem Before & During Pandemic Covid 19 in West Java. Global Conference on Business and Social Sciences Proceeding. DOI: 10.35609/gcbssproceeding.2022.1(94)

Sun, X. (2024). The Role of Digital Technology in Adolescent Autonomy Development: A Four-Factor Model and a Global perspective. In *International and cultural psychology/International and cultural psychology series* (pp. 21–38). DOI: 10.1007/978-3-031-49230-3_2

Sun, W. (2024). The Impact and Opportunities of Digital Economy on Rural Revitalization. *International Journal of Education and Humanities*, 14(1), 134–139. DOI: 10.54097/0k1nfg61

Suortti, C., & Sivunen, A. (2024). Communicative tensions in remote work during the Covid-19 pandemic. *Management Communication Quarterly*, 38(2), 386–412. DOI: 10.1177/08933189231199052

Supendi. (2022). Government Strategic Policy in Agricultural Development. DOI: 10.31334/transparansi.v5i2.2543

Suraci, C., Pizzi, S., Montori, F., Di Felice, M., & Araniti, G. (2022). 6G to take the digital divide by storm: Key technologies and trends to bridge the gap. Future Internet. DOI: 10.3390/fi14060189

Suryani, E., & Kartika, R. (2021). Digital marketplaces and the transformation of agricultural value chains in Indonesia. *Journal of Agribusiness in Developing and Emerging Economies*, 11(3), 421–436. DOI: 10.1108/JADEE-01-2021-0007

Suryaputra, R., Daryanti, S., & Setyowardhani, H. (2024). The Role of Social Media in Promoting Sustainable Green Lifestyles: Influencers and Value Co-Creation with Gen Z in Indonesia. *Journal of Entrepreneurial Economic*, 1(1), 48–65. DOI: 10.61511/jane.v1i1.2024.1036

Susanti, R., & Wardhana, P. (2020). Impact of precision agriculture technologies on smallholder farmers in Indonesia: A case study of drone usage. *International Journal of Agricultural Sustainability*, 18(4), 321–336. DOI: 10.1080/14735903.2020.1720398

Sutanto, S., & Nugroho, R. (2019). Leveraging digital technologies for climate resilience in Indonesian agriculture. *Climate and Development*, 11(7), 567–578. DOI: 10.1080/17565529.2019.1605281

Suwanan & Allya. (2023). Investigating the Factors and Behaviors Influencing Entrepreneurial Intention in Agricultural Sectors among Indonesian Millennials. DOI: 10.1088/1755-1315/1246/1/012037

Syam, N., & Sharma, A. (2018). Waiting for a sales renaissance in the fourth industrial revolution: Machine learning and artificial intelligence in sales research and practice. *Industrial Marketing Management*, 69, 135–146. DOI: 10.1016/j.indmarman.2017.12.019

Tahlyan, D., Said, M., Mahmassani, H., Stathopoulos, A., Walker, J., & Shaheen, S. (2022). For whom did telework not work during the Pandemic? understanding the factors impacting telework satisfaction in the US using a multiple indicator multiple cause (MIMIC) model. *Transportation Research Part A, Policy and Practice*, 155, 387–402. DOI: 10.1016/j.tra.2021.11.025 PMID: 36570728

Tarhini, A., Mgbemena, C., & Mezher, T. (2019). The impact of digital transformation on organizational performance: The role of organizational culture. *Journal of Innovation & Knowledge*, 4(3), 190–198.

Tariq, M. U. (2024). Harnessing Persuasive Technologies for Enhanced Learner Engagement and Motivation. In M. Sanmugam, D. Lim, N. Mohd Barkhaya, W. Wan Yahaya, & Z. Khlaif (Eds.), *Power of Persuasive Educational Technologies in Enhancing Learning* (pp. 30-62). IGI Global. DOI: 10.4018/979-8-3693-6397-3.ch002

Tariq, M. U. (2024). Leveraging AI for Entrepreneurial Innovation in Healthcare. In Özsungur, F. (Ed.), *Generating Entrepreneurial Ideas With AI* (pp. 192–216). IGI Global. DOI: 10.4018/979-8-3693-3498-0.ch009

Tariq, M. U. (2024). The role of AI in skilling, upskilling, and reskilling the workforce. In Doshi, R., Dadhich, M., Poddar, S., & Hiran, K. (Eds.), *Integrating generative AI in education to achieve sustainable development goals* (pp. 421–433). IGI Global. DOI: 10.4018/979-8-3693-2440-0.ch023

Tariq, M. U. (2025). *AI-Driven Learning and Engagement in Higher Education*. IGI Global. DOI: 10.4018/979-8-3693-4074-5

Tariq, M. U. (2025). Leveraging Open Innovation for Sustainable Growth in the Digital Era. In Taherdoost, H. (Ed.), *Mastering Innovation in Business* (pp. 157–192). IGI Global. DOI: 10.4018/979-8-3693-3759-2.ch007

Tariq, M. U. (2025). Navigating Bias and Fairness in Digital AI Systems. In Bhattacharya, P., Hassan, A., Liu, H., & Bhushan, B. (Eds.), *Ethical Dimensions of AI Development* (pp. 127–156). IGI Global. DOI: 10.4018/979-8-3693-4147-6.ch006

Tariq, M. U. (2025). Strategic Integration of Technological Advances in Modern Business Practices. In Sedky, A. (Ed.), *Building Business Knowledge for Complex Modern Business Environments* (pp. 95–120). IGI Global. DOI: 10.4018/979-8-3693-6447-5.ch004

Taylor, S., & Todd, P. (1995b). Assessing IT Usage: The Role of Prior Experience. *Management Information Systems Quarterly*, 19(4), 561–570. DOI: 10.2307/249633

Tay, S. H., Choy, K. L., Chan, F. T. S., & Lam, H. Y. (2021). The impact of Industry 4.0 on logistics service providers. *Journal of Manufacturing Technology Management*, 32(1), 60–79.

Teece, D. J. (2018). Dynamic capabilities as (workable) management systems theory. *Journal of Management & Organization*, 24(3), 359–368. DOI: 10.1017/jmo.2017.75

Teng, S., Hu, X., Deng, P., Li, B., Li, Y., Ai, Y., Yang, D., Li, L., Xuanyuan, Z., Zhu, F., & Chen, L. (2023). Motion planning for autonomous driving: The state of the art and future perspectives. *IEEE Transactions on Intelligent Vehicles*, 8(6), 3692–3711. DOI: 10.1109/TIV.2023.3274536

Teng, S., & Khong, K. W. (2021). Examining actual consumer usage of E-wallet: A case study of big data analytics. *Computers in Human Behavior*, 121, 106778. Advance online publication. DOI: 10.1016/j.chb.2021.106778

Terzi, R. (2020). An adaptation of artificial intelligence anxiety scale into Turkish: Reliability and validity study.

Tham, G. Z. (2018). Digital Transformation in Malaysia: Balancing Innovation and Regulation. *International Journal of Advanced Computer Science and Applications*, 9(7), 162–171.

The Star. (2019). Malaysia to be among top 20 in the world for digital economy. Retrieved from: https://www.thestar.com.my/news/nation/2019/02/23/malaysia-to-be-among-top-20-in-the-world-for-digital-economy/

The World Bank Group. (2022). Individuals using the Internet (% of population) – Brunei Darussalam. https://data.worldbank.org/indicator/IT.NET.USER.ZS?locations=BN

Tohit, N. F. M., & Haque, M. (2024). Preparing the younger generation for an aging society: Strategies, challenges, and opportunities. *Cureus*, 16(7). Advance online publication. DOI: 10.7759/cureus.12145 PMID: 38983672

Torpey, E. (2020). U.S. Bureau of Labor Statistics: Millenials in the Labour Force, Projected 2019-2029. https://www.bls.gov/careeroutlook/2020/data-on-display/millennials-in-labor-force.htm

Tsaramirsis, G., Kantaros, A., Al-Darraji, I., Piromalis, D., Apostolopoulos, C., Pavlopoulou, A., ... Khan, F. Q. (2022). A modern approach towards an industry 4.0 model: From driving technologies to management. Journal of Sensors, 2022(1), 5023011. DOI: 10.1155/2022/5023011

Tuffaha, M., & Perello-Marin, R. (2021). Artificial intelligence definition, applications and adoption in Human Resource Management: A systematic literature review. *International Journal of Business Innovation and Research*, 1(1).

Tuominen, P., & Eerola, A. (2015). The impact of digitalization on the manufacturing industry. *Technology Innovation Management Review*, 5(11), 35–46.

Tursunbayeva, A., & Renkema, M. (2023). Artificial intelligence in health-care: Implications for the job design of healthcare professionals. *Asia Pacific Journal of Human Resources*, 61(4), 845–887. DOI: 10.1111/1744-7941.12325

Twenge, J. M. (2010). A Review of the Empirical Evidence on Generational Differences in Work Attitudes. *Journal of Business and Psychology*, 25(2), 201–210. DOI: 10.1007/s10869-010-9165-6

Twenge, J. M., & Campbell, W. K. (2018). Associations between digital media use and psychological well-being. *Social Indicators Research*, 138(1), 247–262. DOI: 10.1007/s11205-017-1508-1

Twenge, J., Campbell, S., Hoffman, B., & Lance, C. (2010). *Generational Differences in Work Values: Leisure and Extrinsic Values Increasing, Social and Intrinsic Values Decreasing—Jean M. Twenge, Stacy M.* Brian J. Hoffman, Charles E. Lance.

United Nations Conference on Trade and Development (UNCTAD). (2019). Digital Economy Report 2019. Value Creation and Capture: Implications for Developing Countries. Retrieved from: https://unctad.org/en/PublicationsLibrary/der2019_en.pdf

Upadhyay, N., Upadhyay, S., & Dwivedi, Y. K. (2021). Theorizing artificial intelligence acceptance and digital entrepreneurship model. *International Journal of Entrepreneurial Behaviour & Research*, 28(5), 1138–1166. DOI: 10.1108/IJEBR-01-2021-0052

Urick, M. J. (2019). *The generation myth: How to improve intergenerational relationships in the workplace*. Business Expert Press.

Vaitheeswaran, G., Sundaravadivazhagan, B., & Karthikeyan. (2023). Some Studies of the Latest Artificial Intelligence Applications of Drones are Explored in Detail with Application Phenomena. Drone Technology: Future Trends and Practical Applications, 99-116. DOI: 10.1002/9781394168002.ch5

Vakamullu Gopalakrishna & Venugopal (2023). Assessment on the Intricacies of English Speaking Abilities by Rural Students in India. In English Language Competence in Rural Youth: Improving Job Readiness. Current Publications.

Valerio. (2024). Innovation for whom? The case of women in cattle farming in Nusa Tenggara Barat, Indonesia. Sonraku shakai kenkyu janaru, DOI: 10.1016/j.jrurstud.2024.103198

Valori, I., Fan, Y., Jung, M. M., & Fairhurst, M. T. (2024). Propensity to trust shapes perceptions of comforting touch between trustworthy human and robot partners. Scientific Reports. DOI: 10.1038/s41598-024-57582-1

Van der Laan, J., & Koster, F. (2022). Digital transformation in the public sector: The role of digital technologies in reshaping public service delivery. *Government Information Quarterly*, 39(1), 101–126.

VanLehn, K. (2011). The relative effectiveness of human tutoring, intelligent tutoring systems, and other tutoring systems. *Educational Psychologist*, 46(4), 197–221. DOI: 10.1080/00461520.2011.611369

Vargas-Nieto, J., Zambrano, D., Montorio, I., & Sanabria, L. M. (2024). Efficacy of Digital Mindfulness-Based Interventions for Repetitive Negative Thinking: A Systematic review and Bibliometric analysis. *Mindfulness*, 15(3), 523–538. DOI: 10.1007/s12671-024-02321-w

Vartanova, E., & Gladkova, A. (2019). New forms of the digital divide. In Digital media inequalities: Policies against divides, distrust and discrimination. Göteborg: Nordicom.

Vasalou, A., Joinson, A. N., Bänziger, T., Goldie, P., & Pitt, J. (2008). Avatars in social media: Balancing accuracy, playfulness and embodied messages. *International Journal of Human-Computer Studies*, 66(11), 1011–1023. DOI: 10.1016/j.ijhcs.2008.08.002

Vasiljeva, T., Kreituss, I., & Lulle, I. (2021). Artificial intelligence: The attitude of the public and representatives of various industries. *Journal of Risk and Financial Management*, 14(8), 339. DOI: 10.3390/jrfm14080339

Vassilakopoulou, P., & Hustad, E. (2023). Bridging digital divides: A literature review and research agenda for information systems research. *Information Systems Frontiers*, 25(3), 955–969. DOI: 10.1007/s10796-020-10096-3 PMID: 33424421

Vedechkina, M., & Borgonovi, F. (2021). A review of evidence on the role of digital technology in shaping attention and cognitive control in children. *Frontiers in Psychology*, 12, 611155. Advance online publication. DOI: 10.3389/fpsyg.2021.611155 PMID: 33716873

Venkatesh, V., & Davis, F. D. (2000). A theoretical extension of the technology acceptance model: Four longitudinal field studies. *Management Science*, 46(2), 186–204. DOI: 10.1287/mnsc.46.2.186.11926

Venkatesh, V., Morris, M. G., Davis, G. B., & Davis, F. D. (2003). *User acceptance of information technology: Toward a unified view. MIS Quarterly.*

Venkatesh, V., Thong, J. Y. L., & Xu, X. (2012). *Consumer acceptance and use of information technology: extending the unified theory of acceptance and use of technology. MIS Quarterly.*

Verduyn, P., Lee, D. A., Park, J., Shablack, H., & Orvell, A. (2017). The impact of social network sites on subjective well-being: A meta-analysis. *Perspectives on Psychological Science*, 12(3), 225–245. DOI: 10.1177/1745691616635591

Verhoef, P. C., Broekhuizen, T., Bart, Y., Bhattacharya, A., Dong, J. Q., Fabian, N., & Haenlein, M. (2021). Digital transformation: A multidisciplinary reflection and research agenda. *Journal of Business Research*, 122, 889–901. DOI: 10.1016/j.jbusres.2019.09.022

Vial, G. (2021). Understanding digital transformation: A review and a research agenda. In *Managing digital transformation* (pp. 13-66).

Wadhwa, S. A., Mahapara, A., Akhai, S., Kumar, D., & Kumar, P. (2024). Integrating Taguchi Optimization for Multi-Criteria Decision Making in Engineering Applications. In *Recent Theories and Applications for Multi-Criteria Decision-Making* (Vol. 1, No. 1, pp. 125-150). IGI Global.

Wang, Y. Y., & Wang, Y. S. (2019). Development and validation of an artificial intelligence anxiety scale: An initial application in predicting motivated learning behavior. *Interactive Learning Environments*, 30(4), 619–634. DOI: 10.1080/10494820.2019.1674887

Wang, Y., & Zeng, Y. (2024). Relationship between loneliness and internet addiction: A meta-analysis. *BMC Public Health*, 24(1), 858. Advance online publication. DOI: 10.1186/s12889-024-18366-4 PMID: 38504216

Wanjiku, J., & Palino, O. O. (2023). Digital colonization and decolonization. Les intelligences artificielles au prisme de la justice sociale. Considering Artificial Intelligence Through the Lens of Social Justice, 15.

Wardat, Y., Tashtoush, M. A., AlAli, R., & Jarrah, A. M. (2023). ChatGPT: A revolutionary tool for teaching and learning mathematics. *Eurasia Journal of Mathematics, Science and Technology Education*, 19(7), em2286. DOI: 10.29333/ejmste/13272

Warr, P. G. (2011). Food Security vs. Food Self-Sufficiency: The Indonesian Case. Crawford School Research Paper No. 2011/04. DOI: 10.2139/ssrn.1910356

Warschauer, M. (2004). *Technology and social inclusion: Rethinking the digital divide*. MIT press.

Watson, D. (2019). The rhetoric and reality of anthropomorphism in artificial intelligence. *Minds and Machines*, 29(3), 417–440. DOI: 10.1007/s11023-019-09506-6

Weber, J., & Urick, M. J. (2023). Searching for a stronger generational understanding than just age: A multi-country analysis of millennials' personal values and moral reasoning. *Journal of Intergenerational Relationships*, 21(1), 110–135. Advance online publication. DOI: 10.1080/15350770.2021.1951920

Wegmann, E., Oberst, U., Stodt, B., & Brand, M. (2015). Online addiction and the role of emotional intelligence in the development of online addiction. *Addictive Behaviors*, 51, 175–183. DOI: 10.1016/j.addbeh.2015.07.014

Weiss, A. & Spiel, K. (2022). Robots beyond Science Fiction: mutual learning in human–robot interaction on the way to participatory approaches. AI & society. DOI: 10.1007/s00146-021-01209-w

West, M., Rice, S., & Vella-Brodrick, D. (2023). Mid-Adolescents' social media use: Supporting and suppressing autonomy. *Journal of Adolescent Research*, 074355842311684, 07435584231168402. Advance online publication. DOI: 10.1177/07435584231168402

Wijaya, A. A., & Hermanto, H. (2020). Digital Finance and the Empowerment of Young Farmers in Indonesia. *Journal of Agricultural Finance*, 22(3), 275–290. DOI: 10.1080/13657309.2020.1765423

Wijayanto, A., & Sari, P. D. (2020). Digital transformation in aquaculture: A case study of eFishery in Indonesia. *Aquaculture Economics & Management*, 24(2), 123–137. DOI: 10.1080/13657305.2020.1712634

Wijaya, T., & Hidayat, R. (2021). Agri-tech entrepreneurship and rural development: The role of youth in transforming the Indonesian agricultural sector. *Journal of Rural Studies*, 82, 209–219. DOI: 10.1016/j.jrurstud.2020.11.006

Williams, D., Brown, L., & Garcia, M. (2019). Cross-generational impacts of excessive internet use: Mental and physical health outcomes. *Journal of Public Health*, 41(2), 197–208. DOI: 10.1093/pubmed/fdy079

Williamson, B., Eynon, R., Knox, J., & Davies, H. (2023). Critical perspectives on AI in education: Political economy, discrimination, commercialization, governance and ethics. In *Handbook of artificial intelligence in education* (pp. 553–570). Edward Elgar Publishing. DOI: 10.4337/9781800375413.00037

Wolk, R. M. (2004, June). The effects of English language dominance of the internet and the digital divide. In *2004 International Symposium on Technology and Society (IEEE Cat. No. 04CH37548)* (pp. 174-178). IEEE. DOI: 10.1109/ISTAS.2004.1314348

Wong, A., & Wong, J. (2024). Service robot acceptance in museums: An empirical study using the service robot acceptance model (sRAM). *Journal of Services Marketing*, 38(5), 619–635. Advance online publication. DOI: 10.1108/JSM-05-2023-0183

World Economic Forum. (2020). The Global Competitiveness Report 2020. Retrieved from: https://www.weforum.org/reports/the-global-competitiveness-report-2020

World Wide Web Foundation. (2020). Women's Rights Online: Closing the digital gender gap for a more equal world. Retrieved from https://webfoundation.org/docs/2020/10/Womens-Rights-Online-Report-1.pdf

Wullenkord, R. & Eyssel, F. (2020). Societal and ethical issues in HRI. Current Robotics Reports. DOI: 10.1007/s43154-020-00010-9

Wu, W., & Yang, W. (2024). Methodology for digital transformation in TVET. In *Digital transformation in global TVET: Methodology and practices*. UNESCO Chair on Digitalization in TVET.

Yaman, İ. (2015). Digital divide within the context of language and foreign language teaching. *Procedia: Social and Behavioral Sciences*, 176, 766–771. DOI: 10.1016/j.sbspro.2015.01.538

Yamin, M. (2020). Technology adoption: Digital transformation and key technologies. *Journal of Organizational and End User Computing*, 32(4), 14–32.

Yanfika, H., Effendi, I., Sumaryo, , & Ansari, A. (2024). The role of agricultural extension services on supporting circular bioeconomy in Indonesia. *Frontiers in Sustainable Food Systems*, 8, 1428069. DOI: 10.3389/fsufs.2024.1428069

Yang, S., & Zhang, Y. (2022). The Impact of Digital Transformation on Firm Performance: Evidence from China. *Sustainability*, 14(3), 1303.

Yang, Y., Zhuang, Y., & Pan, Y. (2021). Multiple knowledge representation for big data artificial intelligence: Framework, applications, and case studies. *Frontiers of Information Technology & Electronic Engineering*, 22(12), 1551–1558. DOI: 10.1631/FITEE.2100463

Yanti, M., Hapsari Ekonugraheni, D., Mahriani, R., Yusnaini, Y., & Effendi, S. (2024). Strengthening the Digital Literacy of Madrasa Students al-Ittifaqiah Indralaya, South Sumatra. *Engagement: Jurnal Pengabdian Kepada Masyarakat*, 8(1), 117–131. DOI: 10.29062/engagement.v8i1.467

Yeong, D. J., Velasco-Hernandez, G., Barry, J., & Walsh, J. (2021). Sensor and sensor fusion technology in autonomous vehicles: A review. *Sensors (Basel)*, 21(6), 2140. DOI: 10.3390/s21062140 PMID: 33803889

Yeow, A., Soh, C., & Hansen, R. (2018). Aligning with new digital strategy: A dynamic capabilities approach. *The Journal of Strategic Information Systems*, 27(1), 43–58. DOI: 10.1016/j.jsis.2017.09.001

Yew, G. C. K. (2021). Trust in and ethical design of carebots: the case for ethics of care. International Journal of Social Robotics. DOI: 10.1007/s12369-020-00653-w

Yigitcanlar, T., Degirmenci, K., & Inkinen, T. (2024). Drivers behind the public perception of artificial intelligence: Insights from major Australian cities. *AI & Society*, 39(3), 833–853. DOI: 10.1007/s00146-022-01566-0 PMID: 36212229

Yildirim, G. E. (2022). A New Style of Working: Imposed Teleworking in the Context of the covid-19 Pandemic. *Journal of Labor and Society, 1*(aop), 1-26.

Yoon, H., Jang, Y., Vaughan, P. W., & Garcia, M. (2020). Older adults' internet use for health information: Digital divide by race/ethnicity and socioeconomic status. *Journal of Applied Gerontology*, 39(1), 105–110. DOI: 10.1177/0733464818770772 PMID: 29661052

Young, K. S. (1998). Internet addiction: The emergence of a new clinical disorder. *Cyberpsychology & Behavior*, 1(3), 237–244. DOI: 10.1089/cpb.1998.1.237

Younus, M., & Zaenuri, M. (2024). Public-private collaboration to overcome the digital divide in digital transformation of government. *Digital Zone: Jurnal Teknologi Informasi dan Komunikasi, 15*(1), 28-41.

Yudhistira, F., & Kusumawati, A. (2022). Data-driven decision-making in agriculture: The role of AgriSmart in Indonesia's digital transformation. *Journal of Agricultural Systems*, 21(3), 194–207. DOI: 10.1016/j.agsy.2022.01.012

Yu, P. K. (2002). Bridging the digital divide: Equality in the information age. *SSRN*, 20(1), 1–46. DOI: 10.2139/ssrn.309841

Yusriadi, Y., Junus, D., Wijayanti, R., Hasnawati, H., & Cahaya, A. (2024). (4) Perspectives of rural farmer households on food security through a qualitative study in Indonesia. *African Journal of Food, Agriculture, Nutrition and Development*, 24(2), 25450–25467. Advance online publication. DOI: 10.18697/ajfand.127.23510

Zainal, H., & Ismail, M. (2022). Digital transformation in the Malaysian public sector: A qualitative analysis of key success factors. *Journal of Public Administration and Policy Research*, 14(1), 19–29.

Zeddies, H. H., Busch, G., & Qaim, M. (2024). Positive public attitudes towards agricultural robots. Scientific Reports. DOI: 10.1038/s41598-024-66198-4

Zelenev, S. (2022). Promoting digital inclusion. In *Digital transformation and social well-being: Promoting an inclusive society* (pp. 3–22). Routledge. DOI: 10.4324/9781003312208-2

Zhang, Z., & Jiao, L. (2021). Building Digital Capabilities for Competitive Advantage in China's Manufacturing Sector. *Journal of Manufacturing Technology Management*, 33(1), 1–17.

Zhao, S., Jiang, Z., Li, Y., Xu, J., & Wang, C. (2024, January). Key Components and Future Development Analysis of Humanoid Robots. In *2024 8th International Conference on Robotics, Control and Automation (ICRCA)* (pp. 140-147). IEEE. DOI: 10.1109/ICRCA60878.2024.10649218

Zhao, Y., Zhang, T., Dasgupta, R. K., & Xia, R. (2023). Narrowing the age-based digital divide: Developing digital capability through social activities. *Information Systems Journal*, 33(2), 268–298. DOI: 10.1111/isj.12400

Zhu, Y., Chen, H., Li, J., Mei, X., & Wang, W. (2023). Effects of different interventions on internet addiction: A systematic review and network meta-analysis. *BMC Psychiatry*, 23(1), 921. Advance online publication. DOI: 10.1186/s12888-023-05400-9 PMID: 38066462

Zsido, A. N., Coelho, C. M., & Polák, J. (2022). Nature relatedness: A protective factor for snake and spider fears and phobias. People and Nature.

About the Contributors

Muhammad Anshari is Associate Professor in Business Information Systems at the Universiti Brunei Darussalam School of Business and Economics (UBDSBE), and currently serves as Deputy Director for the Institute of Policy Studies. He has been named on the Stanford University List of Top 2% World Researchers since 2021 for the categories of ICT, Business & Management. Together with colleagues from UBDSBE and IPS, winning Outstanding Paper awards at the Emerald Literati Awards 2024. Following the completion of his PhD at FBEPS UBD, Dr. Anshari worked as a research fellow at National Taiwan University. Before that, he was a research fellow at King Saud University, Saudi Arabia. He has also completed eight research grant projects and three research industry consultancies. His research focuses on Business Information Systems, Knowledge Management Systems, Digital Business, Digital Humanities, and Digital Health, contributing primarily to SDG No. 9 on Industry, Innovation, and Infrastructure.

Mohammad Nabil Almunawar is currently an associate professor at School of Business and Economics, Universiti of Brunei Darussalam (UBDSBE), Brunei Darussalam. He was the former dean of UBDSBE. He received his bachelor degree in 1983 from Bogor Agricultural University, Indonesia, master Degree (MSc Computer Science) from the Department of Computer Science, University of Western Ontario, London, Canada in 1991 and Ph.D. from the University of New South Wales (School of Computer Science and Engineering, UNSW) in 1998. Dr Almunawar has published more than 100 papers in refereed journals, book chapters and international conferences. He has more than 30 years teaching experiences in the area computer and information systems. His overall research interests include applications of IT in Management, Electronic Business/Commerce, Health Informatics, information security, cloud computing, Big Data and Internet of Things. He is also interested in object-oriented technology, databases and multimedia retrieval.

Patricia Ordóñez de Pablos is a professor in the Department of Business Administration in the Faculty of Business and Economics at The University of Oviedo, Spain. She completed her education in The London School of Economics, UK. Her teaching and research interests focus on the areas of strategic management, knowledge management, organizational learning, intellectual capital and information technologies, with special interest in Asia (Bhutan, China, Myanmar). She is Editor-in-Chief of the International Journal of Learning and Intellectual Capital (IJLIC) and International Journal of Asian Business and Information Management (IJABIM), respectively. She has edited books for IGI Global, Elsevier, Routledge, and Springer. In 2021, 2022 and 2023, she earned placement on Stanford University's "Ranking of the World Scientists: World's Top 2% Scientists" list. Additionally she is listed in World Top Scientists of Research.com in the Areas of Social Science and Humanities in Spain and Engineering and Technology in Spain.

***

Shalom Akhai has established himself as a prominent figure in the field of engineering, leveraging over 17 years of academic, research, and technical experience to make significant contributions. With a robust portfolio of over 50 publications in prestigious journals and conferences, Dr. Akhai demonstrates a commitment to advancing knowledge through scholarly work. Additionally, he has authored/co-authored several technical textbooks, further solidifying his expertise and dedication to education in the field. Beyond academia, Dr. Akhai's impact extends to real-world applications through the establishment of IGNIS Technical Solutions, a consultancy firm to translate his knowledge into real-world applications. His skills have resulted in the successful development of over 50 patents+, underscoring his innovative approach and influence in shaping the engineering landscape. Moreover, Dr. Akhai's involvement in professional societies, notably as a member of the Indian Society of Heating Ventilation and Air Conditioning Engineers (ISHRAE) Chandigarh Chapter, reflects his commitment to fostering collaboration and knowledge exchange within the society.

Mohd. Shah Alam has completed his B.Tech. from Vishveshwarya Institute of Engineering and Technology, Gr. Noida and M.Tech from Rama University, kanpur, Presently he is pursuing PhD from CSJM University, Kanpur. He has more than 17 years of teaching experience. His research area includes machine learning, Artificial Intelligence, cyber security. He has guided more than 250 B.Tech. level Projects. He has published many research papers in journals, conferences and published Indian patent.

Azizah Amal, born on March 26, 1979, in Ujung Pandang, currently resides at Komp. UNM Blok G 3 No. 36 Makassar and can be contacted at +6281342386089. She is married to Eismen Wahyudin, S.Psi, and they have four children: Ahmad Zaidan Wahyudin, Ahmad Zahran Wahyudin, Muhammad Zafran Wahyudin and Muhammad Zacky Wahyudin. Azizah Amal 's family background includes her late parents, H. Amalius Sahide and Hj. Azhariah Tahir and her siblings: the late Asri Amal Syafaat, Anshar Amal, SH., M. Kn, Asdar Amal Dharmawan, SH., MH, and Dr. dr. Achmad Ashraf Amalius, Sp. M., Her educational journey began at SD Inp. IKIP Ujungpandang (1985-1990), followed by SMP Negeri 3 Makassar (1990-1993), and SMTK Makassar (1993-1996). She pursued higher education at Universitas Negeri Makassar, earning her bachelor's degree (1997-2002), master's degree (2002-2006), and doctoral degree (2011-2018). Professionally, Azizah Amal has a diverse educational background. She has worked as a lecturer at Universitas Negeri Makassar since 2006. Additionally, she has served as an assessor for BAN PAUD and PNF since 2019.

Andi Asrifan, S.Pd, M.Pd, a distinguished figure in the realm of education, particularly in English Language Education, has made significant contributions through his extensive research, teaching, and leadership roles. As the Head of the Institute for Cooperation and International Affairs at Universitas Muhammadiyah Sidenreng Rappang, Dr. Asrifan's academic journey is marked by a rich tapestry of achievements, including a Doctor of Education in English Language Education. His work spans various facets of education, language, and technology, reflecting the diverse topics covered in his publications and research endeavors. These include, but are not limited to, the impact of the COVID-19 pandemic on educational practices, methodologies in English as a Foreign Language (EFL) classrooms, and the integration of technology in teaching and learning processes. Dr. Asrifan's commitment to advancing educational standards and practices is further evidenced by his active participation in international conferences, webinars, and workshops across countries like India, the Philippines, and Pakistan. These events, organized by various institutions and associations, underscore his role as a global educator and thought leader. His dedication to professional development is also highlighted through his involvement in numerous courses and certifications in personal branding, public speaking, and literacy teaching. Moreover, Dr. Asrifan's leadership extends beyond academia into organizational and educational development, where he has served in various capacities, including as an external examiner for Ph.D. dissertations and a reviewer for scientific journals. His accolades, memberships in professional organizations, and roles as an ambassador for international associations speak volumes of his influence and commitment to fostering educational excellence and sustainable development goals globally.

Sumit Babu is working as a lecturer in computer science department in government polytechnic Kanpur, India. Presently, he is pursuing his PhD in computer science in Harcourt Butler Technical University, Kanpur, India. He completed his graduation in computer science and engineering from Gautam Buddh Technical University. He completed his post graduation in information technology from Birla Institute of Technology, Mesra, Ranchi, India. His are of research is software quality, machine learning and cloud computing.He has published various international journal and conference papers.

Yu-Hua Chen is an associate professor of rural sociology and demography in the Department of Bio-Industry Communication and Development at National Taiwan University. She was a guest research fellow at the Max Planck Institute for Demographic Research in Germany. In 2019, Dr. Chen was invited to Kyoto University in Japan to give an intensive lecture course entitled "Rural Depopulation and Community Revitalization in East Asia: Issues and Directions." Her research and teaching specialties include population and development, community studies, youth in transition, and sociological research methods. She is currently engaged in two research projects: the first explores the connection between international migration and sustainable agricultural and rural development in East Asia, and the second evaluates the impact of Taiwan's fertility policy.

Melina Seedoyal Doargajudhur is an experienced lecturer and researcher in the fields of Strategy, Human Resource Management, and Information Systems. She is currently the Programme Lead for the MBA Strategic Project Management Course in the Business School at Edinburgh Napier University. Prior to joining Edinburgh Napier University Business School, Melina was a senior lecturer at the Curtin Mauritius School of Information Technology, an establishment she joined in 2004. She holds a PhD in Information Systems, a Masters in International Business from Curtin University, Australia, and a Bachelor of Science in Information Systems from the University of South Africa. Her current research interests are Remote Working, Future Workforce, Bring Your Own Device (BYOD), Mobile/Digital Technology, Education 5.0, Project Management, Information Systems, Structural Equation Modelling, Positive and negative Work Outcomes, Work Behaviour, Employees' well-being and burnout, Job Demands and Resources, and Gender Studies.

Gülay Ekren is an academician in the field of Management Information Systems (MIS). She has completed her BSc in Computer and Instructional Technologies, an MSc, and a PhD in MIS. She is working as an Assistant Professor at the Computer Technologies Department at Ayancık Vocational College, Sinop University, Turkey. With 14 years of teaching experience in academia, her research interests include Information Systems and Technologies, Data Science and Analytics, and Digital Business Management. She has contributed to various academic projects and publications in these areas.

Sanchita Ghosh is a highly driven worker who holds a Master of Computer Applications degree. Her current position as a Technical Assistant at Brainware University allows her to specialize on IoT,NLP, AI, networking, cybersecurity, and cloud computing. Sanchita is passionate about using technology to solve complicated challenges, and she actively participates in projects and activities that promote innovation and progress the digital transformation. Her diversified skill set and dedication to continual learning make her an invaluable asset in the ever-changing field of information technology.

Shaierah Gulabdin holds a PhD in Business Management from Universiti Malaysia Sabah. She is currently a lecturer in Faculty of Business Economics and Accountancy in Universiti Malaysia Sabah. Her areas of interests include Management, Human Resources Management, Marketing, Entrepreneurship & Innovation, Hybrid Social Ventures, Social Influence, and Technology Adoption & Evolution.

Yuzainy Janin joined Universiti Malaysia Sabah in 2001 and attach to the Faculty of Business, Economics and Accountancy. He taught subjects such as event management, hospitality management, service management, and business information system. To align teaching and learning with the fast pace of the Industrial Revolution, he is an avid advocate for ICT integration in teaching and learning of digital natives particularly in the tertiary educational institution. He has been involved in various research and consultation projects in the area of tourism both at the state and national levels involving collaborations with NGO, tourism ministries and agencies at the state and national level in Malaysia. Amongst other, Yuzainy research interests related to accommodation industry governance and development, community-based initiated entrepreneurial tourism venture, and ICT adoption and diffusion in hospitality and tourism.

Prabhleen Kaur is a driven B.Tech student in Computer Science Engineering with a passion for programming languages, data science, and artificial intelligence. Her hands-on experience includes participating in the national-level Smart India Hackathon and leading a team for National Science Day, while contributing to another team as well. She has presented papers on the roles of robotics in Industry 4.0 and AI in climate change mitigation, presented at the 1st International Conference at Punjabi Technical University, for which she earned certificates. In addition to her academic pursuits, Prabhleen has actively participated in several workshops and Engineering Day events. Her athletic talents were demonstrated when she secured 3rd place in basketball at HPL and 2nd place in an inter-college competition. Prabhleen also earned a certificate in Information Technology Fundamentals from IBM SkillsBuild and contributed artwork to her college magazine, reflecting her diverse interests and creative abilities.

Tavleen Kaur is an enthusiastic learner currently pursuing a B.Tech in Computer Science Engineering. With a strong foundation in programming, data science, and artificial intelligence, she actively seeks opportunities to apply her skills in real-world scenarios. She has participated in the national-level Smart India Hackathon and led a team for National Science Day, while also contributing to another team for the same event. Tavleen has presented two research papers in the 1st International Conference at Punjabi University, focusing on the integration of robotics in Industry 4.0 and AI's role in combating climate change. Her achievements earned her certificates of recognition. She has participated in multiple college workshops, Engineering Day events, and demonstrated her athleticism by securing podium finishes in basketball tournaments. Additionally, Tavleen contributed a poem to her college magazine, reflecting her creative side. Her commitment to both academics and extracurricular activities highlights her well-rounded character.

Vandana Dixit Kaushik is working as Professor in the Department of Computer Science and Engineering, Harcourt Butler Technical University, Kanpur, U.P., India (formerly Harcourt Butler Technological Institute, Kanpur, U.P., India). She has vast teaching and research experience. She teaches various subjects like Digital Image Processing, Database Management, Operating Systems, E-Commerce etc both at graduate and under graduate levels. She completed her Ph.D. in 2011 from Dr. APJ Abdul Kalam University, Lucknow, U.P., India and she is currently guiding 09 Ph.D. scholars in areas of current international needs. Three PhD students have completed PhD under her guidance. Two have been granted submission permission. She worked in close collaboration with various other Academic institutes like HNB Garhwal University (Archaeology Department), Guindy College of Engineering, IISC Bengaluru, Indian Institute of Technology, Kanpur and with industries like Intel. She was the member of Multicore Curriculum Development team at UG level under the convenorship of Prof. H.S. Jamadagni, Chairman, CEDT, IISc, Bengaluru. This entire curriculum development project was sponsored by Intel, Bengaluru.

L. Santhosh Kumar is a distinguished educator and researcher, currently serving as an Assistant Professor of English at Kristu Jayanti College, Bengaluru. He holds a Ph.D. from Bharathidasan University and an M.Phil. from the University of Madras. Dr. Santhosh Kumar has an extensive publication record, including multiple edited books and numerous articles in peer-reviewed journals. His research interests span diaspora literature, testimonio, and health humanities. He has presented his work at various international and national conferences and has participated in several faculty development programs and workshops. Dr. Santhosh Kumar is also recognized for his contributions to the academic community through his involvement in patent filings and interdisciplinary collaborations. His commitment to quality education and pursuit of academic excellence make him a valuable asset to the educational field.

Shilpa Mehta has completed her PhD degree from Auckland University of Technology, New Zealand. She has five years of teaching experience from different reputed colleges and universities of India. Currently, she is working as a Teaching Assistant at Auckland University of Technology (AUT), Auckland, New Zealand. She was awarded Summer Doctoral Research Scholarship for her PhD research. She has worked on various interdisciplinary research projects and her research interests include Radio Frequency Integrated Circuits, RF front ends, Optimization, Internet of Things, Wireless Communication, Artificial Intelligence, Healthcare, Radars, and Software-defined Radios, Smart Cities. As an editor, she has edited four books with IGI Global and one with Nova Science Publishers. She is also working on different edited books to be published by IGI Global, Apple Academic Press, Scrivener-Wiley, Cambridge, and Springer Nature, respectively.

Sheik Mohamed S. H. is an accomplished academic with extensive experience in the fields of electronic media and mass communication. Currently serving as an assistant professor in the Department of Electronic Media at St. Thomas College of Arts and Science since 2007, Dr. Sheikh has made significant contributions to education and research. His academic journey is marked by numerous qualifications, including a Ph.D. in Journalism and Mass Communication with a focus on Defence and Strategic Studies from the University of Madras, multiple postgraduate degrees in diverse fields such as public administration, social work, and journalism and mass communication, and postgraduate diplomas in diverse fields such as information and communication law, business administration, and public relations from different universities. Dr. Sheik has been recognised for his outstanding contributions to education, having received awards such as Asia's Outstanding Educator of the Year 2024 and the Best Teacher Award from the Lions Club of Chennai GKD Millennium. He has coordinated numerous workshops, seminars, and international faculty development programs, significantly enhancing the academic environment. Dr. Sheik's research interests are wide-ranging, as evidenced by his numerous publications and presentations on topics like social media's impact on education, the role of media in environmental consciousness, and the influence of music on listener perception. His active involvement in curriculum development and his role as a journal reviewer are further highlights of his commitment to advancing academic standards and fostering a culture of continuous learning and innovation.

Ankur Prakash is pursuing a Ph.D. in Computer Science and Engineering at Motilal Nehru National Institute of Technology, Prayagraj, India. He holds Master's and Bachelor's degrees in Computer Science and Engineering. His interests include computer vision, data mining, recommender systems, and UAVs.

Vettriselvan R., an Associate Professor, AMET Business School, AMET University, specialised in HRM and Marketing. He is acting as Mentor, Saraswathi Institute of Medical Sciences, Hapur. He served as Review Board member, National Council for Higher Education, Malawi, Head of the Department, School of Commerce and Management Studies, St. Eugene University, Zambia, and Director, Research and Publication, St. John the Baptist University, Malawi. He has published 20 books and 75 articles in peer reviewed journals and edited book chapters. Under his guidance two have completed and five are pursuing their PhD.

Piyal Roy is an accomplished academician in the field of Computer Science & Engineering. He has completed his BSc in Computer Science, MSc in Computer Science and MTech in Computer Science & Engineering. Currently, he is working as an Assistant Professor at Computer Science & Engineering department at Brainware University, India.

Muhammad Azmi Sait is a young researcher with PhD Management from the University Brunei Darussalam. His current research focuses on understanding the dynamics of technology adoption, discontinuance, and resistance behavior in developing economies. With a strong passion for exploring the impact of technology on society and business, Muhammad Azmi is particularly interested in research that involves advancing digital inclusion and literacy within societies. Beyond academia, he actively participates in community service initiatives aimed at promoting social cohesion and development. His dedication to advancing knowledge, paired with his proficiency in data analysis and communication, positions him as a valuable contributor to the discourse on digital transformation and inclusive growth.

Ranjit Singha is a Doctorate Research Fellow at Christ (Deemed to be University) and holds a prestigious membership in the American Psychological Association (APA). With a strong background in Research and Development, he has significantly contributed to various fields such as Mindfulness, Addiction Psychology, Women Empowerment, UN Sustainable Development Goals, and Data Science. With over 15 years of experience in Administration, Teaching, and Research, both in Industry and Higher Education Institutions (HEI), Mr Ranjit has established himself as a seasoned professional. Mr Ranjit is dedicated to research and teaching endeavours, primarily focusing on mindfulness and compassion-based interventions. His work in these areas aims to promote well-being and foster positive change in individuals and communities. ORCID iD: https://orcid.org/0000-0002-3541-8752.

Surjit Singha is an academician with a broad spectrum of interests, including UN Sustainable Development Goals, Organizational Climate, Workforce Diversity, Organizational Culture, HRM, Marketing, Finance, IB, Global Business, Business, AI, K12 & Higher Education, Gender and Cultural Studies. Currently a faculty member at Kristu Jayanti College, Dr. Surjit also serves as an Editor, reviewer, and author for prominent global publications and journals, including being on the Editorial review board of Information Resources Management Journal and contributor to various publications. With over 15 years of experience in Administration, Teaching, and Research, Dr. Surjit is dedicated to imparting knowledge and guiding students in their research pursuits. As a research mentor, Dr. Surjit has nurtured young minds and fostered academic growth. Dr. Surjit has an impressive track record of over 150+ publications (SCOPUS Indexed 70), including articles, book chapters, and textbooks, holds two US Copyrights, and has successfully completed and published two fully funded minor research projects from Kristu Jayanti College. PhD, M.Phil, MBA (Distinction) from Christ University, M.Com, BBM from KJC (Bangalore University), PGDHE (Higher Education) from IGNOU (Central University), UGC-NET Commerce, Examiner for IB. ORCID iD: https://orcid.org/0000-0002-5730-8677.

Shivam Swarup has over 5 years of experience in Academic field, where he has worked in various professional roles and capacities. He has showcased excellent aptitude in planning & organizing day-to-day research activities and resolve procedural problems as appropriate to the timely completion of research objectives. Apart from that he has achieved a ranking within the top 5 percentile of researchers in Technology based Education according to UGC-NET and published multiple high-impact factor journal articles including Applied Sciences (Basel) and Sustainability etc. His research interests encompass a diverse array of topics within the realm of machine learning and deep learning models, notably including ARIMA, LSTM, STL-LSTM, and XGBoost. Additionally, he is deeply engaged in exploring AI and ML-based programming languages, with a focus on Python, including libraries such as PyTorch, TensorFlow, Keras, and Matplotlib, as well as RStudio. Furthermore, he is actively involved in studying the iterative Software Development Life Cycle Process according to RUP (Rational Unified Process), Six Sigma Methodologies, and employs various tools, particularly those within the Rational suite, to enhance his research endeavors.

Muhammad Usman Tariq has more than 17+ year's experience in industry and academia. He has authored more than 200+ research articles, 110+ case studies, 105+ book chapters and several books other than 4 patents. He is founder and CEO of The Case HQ, a unique repository for courses, narrative and video case studies. He has been working as a consultant and trainer for industries representing six sigma, quality, health and safety, environmental systems, project management, and information security standards. His work has encompassed sectors in aviation, manufacturing, food, hospitality, education, finance, research, software and transportation. He has diverse and significant experience working with accreditation agencies of ABET, ACBSP, AACSB, WASC, CAA, EFQM and NCEAC. Additionally, Dr. Tariq has operational experience in incubators, research labs, government research projects, private sector startups, program creation and management at various industrial and academic levels. He is Certified

Higher Education Teacher from Harvard University, USA, Certified Online Educator from HMBSU, Certified Six Sigma Master Black Belt and has been awarded PFHEA, SFSEDA, SMIEEE, and CMBE.

Nahed Tawfik received B.Sc. (Honors), MSc., and PhD in Electronics and Electrical Communications Engineering, Faculty of Electronic Engineering, Menouf, Menoufia University, Egypt, in 2008, 2015, and 2021, respectively. She is a researcher at the Electronics Research Institute, Egypt. She has been awarded the Electronics Research Institute Award for Research Distinction (2021). Her interests are image processing, pattern recognition, computer vision, and biomedical engineering.

Shesh Mani Tiwari has completed his B.Tech. from M.I.T. Bulandshahr (UPTU), M.Tech. from Rama University and currently he is pursuing PhD on "Multimodal Emotion Recognition Using Deep Learning and Contextual Information" from Integral University Lucknow. His research area includes Deep Learning, Artificial Intelligence, Natural Language Processing. He has guided more than 200 B.Tech. level Projects. He has published many research papers in conferences, journals and published Indian patent.

Koppala Venugopal, a professor in Management Studies at Aditya Institute of Technology and Management at Srikakulam, A.P. has had an adroit experience of academic, Research and community service. He has contributed 5 Projects, 2 patents, 10 books, 70 publications, 48 paper presentations, 56 resource talks and 12 memberships. He is guiding 4 scholars from various universities. His exceptional interest industry interface has made his efforts dexterous.

Deepak Kumar Verma is currently working as Assistant Professor and Head of Department in Computer Science and Engineering, School of Engineering and Technology (UIET), Chhatrapati Shahu Ji Maharaj University, Kanpur, India. He has done B.E. (Computer Science & Engineering) in 1995 with Honours 9.155 CPI out of 10 (82.3%), Kumaon Engg. College, Dwarahat, Dist. Almora, Kumaon University, Nainital and M.Tech. in Computer Science and Engineering in 2010 with Honours 9.67 CPI out of 10, (89.2%) from Dr A.P.J. Abdul Kalam Technical University, Lucknow, UP (Formerly U.P. Technical University, Lucknow, UP). He has completed his PhD in Computer Science & Engineering in Dr A.P.J. Abdul Kalam Technical University, Lucknow, UP in 2018. He has published many research papers in different conferences and journals of repute and currently 5 publications are in pipeline. He is guiding currently 4 PhD students. His research area involves Computer Networks and Artificial Intelligence. He has more than 29 years of teaching experience.

Mahapara Wani, a distinguished academician and researcher in the Department of Civil Engineering at Maharishi Markandeshwar (Deemed to be University), Ambala, has made significant contributions to the field of structural engineering and sustainable construction materials. Her academic and research endeavors are reflected in an impressive portfolio of publications. Dr. Abbas has authored 10 research papers in prestigious SCI and Scopus-indexed journals, such as Multiscale Multidisciplinary Modeling, Experimentation and Design, Journal of Building Pathology and Rehabilitation, and Lecture Notes in Civil Engineering. In addition to her journal articles, she has presented her work at renowned conferences, contributing to 2 conference proceedings in Materials Today: Proceedings. Dr. Abbas's expertise also extends to scholarly book contributions, where she has co-authored 2 book chapters in critically acclaimed volumes.

Index

W

Y

www.ingramcontent.com/pod-product-compliance
Lightning Source LLC
LaVergne TN
LVHW060008031026
849161LV00025B/2509